BENNETT CERF'S BUMPER CROP

BENNETT CERF'S

VOLUME 1

BUMPER CROP

of Anecdotes and Stories,
Mostly Humorous,
About the Famous and Near Famous

His 5 Biggest Best Sellers—
The Life of the Party, Try and
Stop Me, Good for a Laugh,
Laughter Incorporated, Shake
Well Before Using—Complete
and Unabridged, in Two Volumes

GARDEN CITY BOOKS
Garden City, New York

THE LIFE
OF THE PARTY

A New Collection of Stories and Anecdotes

BENNETT CERF

Drawings by Carl Rose

FOREWORD

A stranger dashed frantically into "Doc" Sherman's Madison Avenue pharmacy this spring, hollering, "Quick, Doc! I've swallowed poison by mistake! I must have an antidote!"

"You've come to the right place," beamed Sherman. "It seems there once were two Irishmen named Pat and Mike . . ."

The good doctor, who had filled thousands of prescriptions, knew that laughter is the "best medicine for weary bones"—that the very sound of it is reassuring and healing. There is nothing like a hearty laugh to clear the atmosphere—or deflate windbags and phonies!

The Life of the Party is my eighth collection of anecdotes and stories, designed, for the most part, just to provoke the laughs I value so highly. Like the contents of its predecessors, every item included is absolutely new—unless, of course, you've heard it before. I culled many of them from my "Cerfboard" column in *This Week*, "Trade Winds" in the *Saturday Review*, and my daily box, "Try and Stop Me" for King Features. The title of this book was suggested by my friend and dentist, the aptly named Dr. Edward Pullman. He has pulled many a good one in his day.

Oliver Gogarty, Irish raconteur and wit, advises, "Tell a funny story on every possible occasion, and tell it as well as you know how, too. People will remember your jokes and forget your speeches. Monuments are built over solemn asses—but people remember in their hearts the men who have made them laugh."

I remember an old legend about a human who told the Sun he had discovered one spot on earth that was eternally dark. "Impossible," scoffed the Sun. He hastened to the spot described and searched high and low, but could not find even the suspicion of a shadow.

The moral is clear. Carry your own sunshine with you, and there will be fewer dark places in your life. In other words, let a smile be your umbrella. You'll get wet from time to time—but you won't give a darn!

BENNETT CERF

Mount Kisco, New York
September 1956

THE LIFE OF THE PARTY

CHAPTER ONE

BABES IN THE HOLLYWOODS

Picture making in Hollywood has one thing in common with serving in the infantry in wartime. For every minute of decisive action and excitement, there are twenty of the infinite boredom of "standing by" waiting for something to happen. It's a caution to watch internationally famous stars twiddling their thumbs— at about two thousand dollars a twiddle—while directors, scriptors, and technicians battle on into the night about a fragment of dialogue or the lighting of a set.

Some stars take to crocheting or knitting during these interminable lulls. Others answer fan mail or agonize over crossword puzzles. A few even read books. Cary Grant, one of the best

actors, as well as most charming personally, in the business, took advantage of a historic studio stalemate to invent a mythical picture company that first enlisted the enthusiastic co-operation of Ingrid Bergman (just before she decamped to Italy), Alfred Hitchcock, and Joe Cotten, and then bloomed prodigiously all over Hollywood.

The object of this intriguing time killer was to people an imaginary studio with characters whose names were most appropriate for their assignments. From a list submitted to me by Cary and his accomplices, I have selected the following outstanding examples:

> *Dolly Shot: the heroine*
> *May Cup: her mother*
> *Lee Dingman: the hero*

Mike Shadow: the villain
Pan Ova: a ballet dancer
Manny Takes: the director
Mimi O'Graph: the script girl
Phil Mer: the cameraman
Herr Dresser: the make-up man
Alec Trician: lights
Bill Board: publicity

Etc., etc., until you're so tired you Fala Sleep.

The insidious feature of Grant's game, of course, is that you've no sooner learned about it than you start applying it to your own business. I, for instance, immediately began dreaming up the perfect cast for a publishing house—fellows like Hy Perbole, the blurb writer; Eddie Tor, the blue-pencil wielder; Reggie Ment, the censor; Mae Hem, the mystery writer; Paul Verize, the shipping clerk; Ty Pograph, the printer; and Mister Market, the writer whose manuscript came in too late.

The death of Will Hays reminded Hy Gardner of the first list of "don'ts" Mr. Hays promulgated when he was appointed custodian of film makers' morals. There were twelve major "thou shalt nots" on the list, prompting the show-business bible, *Variety*, to headline the story, "Hays Two Up on Moses!"

A fat movie producer seized a lovely young starlet in his arms and kissed her violently four times. "What did you think of my performance?" he asked arrogantly after releasing the girl. "Magnificent," she scoffed. "But if I were you, I'd print only takes number one and four."

I was sitting in the patio of a famous film magnate's retreat at Palm Springs, California, while a sudden windstorm was sending swirls of sand high into the air around us. Like every other resident of the Springs, however, my host was convinced that *his* property was completely protected from occasionally violent wind gusts. "Notice how quiet it is right here?" he inquired complacently. "Anywhere else in town, this wind would bowl you over like a duckpin."

He completed his observation in the nick of time. At that moment two of his treasured palm trees were uprooted, and toppled over into the swimming pool.

Norman Reilly Raine recalls a famous Hollywood magnate who decided he wanted to produce an epic on Custer's last stand, but then promptly turned thumbs down on seven scripts. The final veto broke Raine's spirit completely. "I'm ready to give up," he admitted. "I really slaved over this last script. It's the best I can do. Just what is there about it that displeases you?" "I'll tell you," confided the magnate. "I hate Indians."

Here's a story I never heard before about Sam Goldwyn, the inimitable motion-picture pioneer, and it comes from Miriam Howell, who was one of his chief lieutenants some years ago. "Miriam," proposed Sam one morning, "we've got to get some new blood around here. I want to sign up some young writer, talented but completely unknown, who'll bring us fresh ideas and a fresh viewpoint." "Splendid," enthused Miriam, "and I know just the man for you." "What's his name?" asked Goldwyn. "He's a young playwright named John Patrick," said Miss Howell. "Never heard of him," said Mr. Goldwyn. "Who else can you think of?"

Arthur Mayer, author of the amusing Hollywood memoir, *Merely Colossal*, nominates Adolph Zukor, long-time headman at Paramount Pictures, as the politest gent in the world of the cinema. "I have a telegram to prove it," continues Mayer. "It reads, 'You're fired. Best regards.'"

An epic of Napoleonic times was being shot on location near the Twentieth Century-Fox lot when an airplane halted all activities by circling about for a full hour overhead. Finally an ingenious cameraman hollered to the director, "We could go ahead if you'd put in an explanatory line of dialogue. Let's have the hero shake his fist at the sky, and say, 'There goes that pig of a Raoul up there—a full hundred and fifty years before his time!'"

A favorite story of movie exhibitors concerns the beautiful princess in ancient Egypt who found a baby in a wicker basket drifting down the Nile and took it to her father, the Pharaoh. "Isn't this a beautiful baby?" she exclaimed. "Oh, Daddy, I want to adopt him." The Pharaoh snorted, "He doesn't look so beautiful to me. In fact, I'll state definitely I think he's as ugly as any I've ever seen." The princess murmured defensively, "He looked awfully good in the rushes."

Paramount had just finished shooting a scene from one of those biblical pictures in which ten thousand extras, dressed as Egyptians, Romans, and what not, wandered around the place, and everybody made a break for lunch at the same time. The director, pleased with his morning's work, was in an expansive mood when he entered the bar and grill across the avenue from the studio. Noting a tableful of extra girls still in costume near the door, he waved happily to them and told the bartender, "See what the gals in the Old Testament'll have!"

In Hollywood, veteran Mack Sennett, discoverer of Gloria Swanson, Madeline Hurlock, and a score of other callipygian bathing beauties, explained the real reason for all the woes of the movie magnates. "Things began going to pot," recalled Sennett bitterly, "the tragic day when Jean Harlow first stumbled upon a man in the studio who had a book under his arm. She promptly spent a whole week's salary enrolling in a school and getting herself educated. Before we knew what had hit us, every actor and actress in Hollywood started following suit. The fashion for reading spread through the colony like measles in a kindergarten. First thing you knew, they even started reading the scripts of their pictures. From that moment on, there was hell to pay."

Sennett first laid eyes on Marie Dressler when he was a kid in Northampton, Massachusetts. Miss Dressler appeared in a play called *Lady Slavey*. Enraptured, he decided on the spot to seek a career on the stage. His mother's lawyer agreed to give him a note of introduction. The lawyer's name was not yet famous. His note read: "Dear Miss Dressler: This boy wants to go on the stage. Yours truly, Calvin Coolidge."

Mabel Normand was the star Mack Sennett loved best, but he almost lost her services because one of his right-hand men, Chester Conklin, failed in the part of Sir Walter Raleigh. It was raining cats and dogs one morning, and the pavement in front of Keystone was inches deep in mud and water. Conklin spied Mabel on the other side of the street, wondering how to get across, and made a magnificent gesture. He whipped off his

brand-new coat and spread it in the mud. Miss Normand smiled gratefully, stepped daintily—and disappeared into a manhole.

Hollywood weddings differ from the regular formula in only one small detail, reports a returning tourist. Out that way the brides keep the bouquet and throw the groom away.

Mere mention of the name of Howard Hughes, the millionaire toolmaker and movie tycoon, makes Hollywood folk rush to tell you a hundred stories about his unconventional behavior. Hughes is notoriously careless about his attire; seeing him for the first time, visitors often refuse point-blank to believe that the unshaven, sloppily dressed young man with the soiled, scuffed white sneakers can possibly be one of the richest and most powerful figures on the West Coast.

At one time Hughes went on a long-distance telephone kick, tying up the only booth in a Los Angeles drugstore for hours at a time. The indignant druggist, unaware of Hughes's identity, finally ordered him from the premises. Hughes promptly had the phone company install a second booth. "Satisfied now?" he asked. The druggist was not only satisfied, but speechless. He had tried vainly for two years to get that second booth!

Another time, recalls Stewart White, Hughes was working on a deal involving twenty million dollars. He told his assistant, who was conducting the New York end of the negotiations, "Phone me the minute they say 'yes' or 'no.'" Then he added, "Come to think of it, you'd better call after six and get the night rate."

The Waldorf Astoria staff remembers the time Howard Hughes told a room clerk, "Hold onto my suite for me. I'll be back in a few days." Back he was, too, exactly seventy-two hours later. In the meantime he had flown completely around the world.

Neil Morgan tells of the time Hughes flew his giant Constellation air liner to a San Diego powwow, but returned to Hollywood by car with an aide. Weeks later an operations officer from the San Diego airport managed to get Hughes on the phone, demanding angrily, "Whatcha want us to do with that blank blank Constellation of yours?" There was a long pause, then Hughes murmured sheepishly, "So that's where it is! I knew I left it somewhere!"

General Electric threatens to add one more new element to the recent upheaval in the motion-picture field. In a process immediately dubbed "Smell-o-rama" by Schenectady wits, it promises to add odor to the general effect. Selected groups have been treated to secret screenings of a rose garden, in the course of which the lovely scent of rose perfume filled the theater. True, this is just an extension of an old idea introduced by Irving Berlin in one of his Music Box Revues where, while John Steele was warbling "In an Orange Grove in California," ushers sprayed the house with attar of orange blossoms. And in Washington this summer, the page on which an ad for a popular brand of dill pickles appeared had been sprayed with some substance that made every reader feel he was smack in the middle of Reuben's delicatessen.

The General Electric experiment was so successful that one man came out of the theater predicting it would up nationwide receipts by twenty per cent at least. "Think of all the delicious aromas with which we can assail the nostrils of our customers," he enthused—but suddenly he paled. "Good heavens," he whispered. "Don't look now—but isn't that fellow behind us a director of the Hoggenspieler Packing Plant? What can *he* have in mind?"

Hollywood is full of stories about the late Barney Dean, studio dialogue "doctor" and constant companion of Bob Hope, Bing Crosby, Jack Benny, and other great stars.

Barney never used a typewriter. He couldn't even remember people's names. Royalty meant no more to him than the lowest grip on a movie set. One day Bob Hope told him, "If you hurry, Barney, you can meet the King and Queen of Greece. They're

17

just leaving the music department." "What do I need with them now?" scoffed Barney. "Where were they last night when I needed them for a full house?" Later Barney was crossing Hollywood Boulevard at Vine against a traffic light. The policeman at the corner blew his whistle and hollered, "Hey there, you!" Barney, all innocence, asked, "How fast was I going, Officer?"

After Jack Benny had rung in the name of Barney Dean on three consecutive radio programs, his then supporting star, Phil Harris, exploded, "Who *is* this Barney Dean you're always talking about?" Benny retorted, "Just drop a cigar butt and you'll find out." Barney told Benny later, "I could have sued you, but I was afraid you'd prove it on me."

Bing Crosby took Dean with him once when he visited the sumptuous estate of a member of the Rockefeller clan. Barney kept silent while their car threaded through the miles of private roads leading to the manor house, but refused to get out when the butler opened the car door for them. "What's the matter?" asked Crosby. "Overwhelmed by the grandeur?" "It isn't that," explained Barney. "I forgot to bring my library card." After dinner Barney was visibly impressed by the huge indoor swimming pool and tennis court. When a fellow guest inquired, "Have you any idea where Mrs. Stotesbury might be?" Barney replied solemnly, "I think she's upstairs playing polo."

A Hollywood director, famous for his onslaughts on the English language, returned from New York, vastly impressed with the Metropolitan Opera Company's new look. "You've got to give credit," he enthused, "to those fellows, Bing and Bing!" Later he added, "My favorite is still *Madame Butterfield.*"

Another director is married to a girl who is hipped on psychoanalysis. The day after their first son was born, the director appeared at the studio commissary, passed out the customary cigars, and announced cheerfully, "Well, I've deposited five thousand dollars in the bank to take care of the kid's complete analysis. Now, when he learns to talk, if he ever raises his voice to

18

me once, I'll have no compunction whatever in beating the be-jabbers out of him."

It's hard to keep track of family trees out Hollywood way, with divorces and remarriages so prevalent among the movie elite. They say two lads at an executive's estate got into a big fight, with one star's son taunting another, "My father can lick the daylights out of your father." "Don't be silly," answered the other calmly. "Your father *is* my father!"

On every movie lot in Hollywood there's a little red school-house where starlets under eighteen who do not already boast high-school diplomas are required by California law to study at least three hours a day.

Of course these screenland scholars often are earning ten times as much as their teachers. And the three R's that interest them most are Rehearsin', Romancin', and Reducin'. Nor is it easy for a pedagogue to maintain the usual discipline with a roomful of kids answering to names like Judy Garland, Mickey Rooney, Shirley Temple, Betty Grable, and Elizabeth Taylor (all studio students in their day). He's apt to begin by calling the roll and end by collecting autographs!

"To hold the attention of these movie moppets," a teacher at one major studio assured me, "you have only to remember that the problems must be presented properly. Ask them, for instance, to multiply two thousand dollars by fifty-two—with time and a half for overtime. Teach Johnnie to read the tiniest print in a contract. Show a little lady how to write her name in electric lights, instead of on paper.

"These youngsters really want to learn how to face *Life*—not to mention Hopper, Parsons, Skolsky, and the *Hollywood Reporter*."

A Park Avenue psychiatrist was somewhat surprised to find one of Hollywood's most successful, publicized, and effervescent glamor girls waiting anxiously to see him. "Oh, Doctor," she explained piteously, "I need your help so badly! I can't sing; I can't dance; I can't act. It's so frustrating!" The psychiatrist adopted his most soothing manner. "You can quit show business entirely," he reminded her. "Oh no," she contradicted promptly. "I'm a big star!"

Two vacationing businessmen on the beach at Bermuda were having a fine time debating the many charms of movie star Jane Russell. "Don't know what everybody sees in her," deprecated one. "Take away her eyes, her hair, her lips, and her figure, and what have you got?" The other gave a heartfelt sigh and said, "My wife."

A famous film beauty was sun-bathing at her secluded pool, attired in absolutely nothing, when a brash photographer invaded the premises, snapped her picture, and made for the exit on the double. The star was after him in no time flat. "I'll teach you to play a dirty trick like that," she screamed. "You shot the wrong profile!"

A Beverly Hills nouveau riche, boasting about his new estate, topped it off by declaring, "And you ought to see the tennis court! I bet it's the biggest one in California." The reporter who brought in the story added, "This character is at heart just an old-fashioned kid. He drank six of them while I was interviewing him."

Harry Sauber tells about a writer, in search of material, who interviewed a bit player at a major Hollywood studio. How did he become an aspiring movie actor? Well, explained the player, he had been a handler in a Forty-second Street flea circus, and had been bitten by Felix, the star flea of the troupe. While recuperating, he came to the Coast for a visit and drifted into films. "I've heard plenty of people say it," enthused the writer, "but you are positively the first person who actually became an actor because he was bitten by an acting bug."

An alert visitor can pick up several useful hints in the golden sunshine of California, where the flying movie agents play. For instance, one opens every conversation with a client by saying bitterly, "I shouldn't even be talking to you, you so-and-so. I heard exactly what you said about me two days ago." This forestalls many a beef by a dissatisfied client. Chances are excellent he really did vilify his agent somewhere along the line and, if he didn't, he thinks he did. He now definitely has lost the offensive and is off balance for the rest of the meeting.

Leland Hayward, now one of the country's leading producers (*South Pacific, Mr. Roberts,* etc.), made his debut out Hollywood way as an agent—and a mighty shrewd one too. Last year he was bent on acquiring a certain property for a screen play, but objected vigorously to the price tag of seventy-five thousand dollars agent Irving Lazar had put on it. "Irving," implored Hayward, "who taught you to be such a pirate?" Lazar answered quite truthfully, "You did!"

Harry Kurnitz recalls the day a writer invaded the two-by-four office of a struggling Hollywood agent with a small package in his arms. "What's in that package?" demanded the suspicious agent. "An inflatable lifeboat that will hold eight men," said the writer. "One more wisecrack," decreed the agent, "and I no longer represent you. Now what's in that package?" So the writer opened the package, pushed the button on the compressed-air cylinder, and fled. The boat backed the agent so tightly into a corner it took the fire department to hack him out.

At a literary cocktail party a well-known agent made a spectacular exit. He fell down a flight of stairs. As he picked himself up, miraculously unhurt, he called up to the crowd above, "You noticed, I hope, that I hit only every tenth step."

Memorable moments in Hollywood high life:

1. A press agent called a columnist to report the death of a producer client. "I'm sorry," said the columnist firmly, "but I used his name last week."

2. A winsome chick reproved a bold Wilshire wolf with "You know I'm going to be married tomorrow! Call me in about three weeks."

3. Greta Garbo is rumored to have dreamed one night that she sprinkled six boxes of grass seed in her hair. She awakened moaning, "I vant to be a lawn."

4. Groucho Marx proposed this toast to a socialite hostess: "I drink to your charm, your beauty, and your brains—which will give you a rough idea of how hard up I am for a drink."

5. Zsa Zsa Gabor went on a caviar-and-filet-mignon diet and took off $135 in three days.

6. A visitor asked a starlet, "Did you buy that sable wrap out of your earnings?" The starlet gave a chuckle—or was it a Peale of laughter?—and replied, "I owe it all to my Power of Positive Winking."

7. A movie queen's personal maid knocked on the door of her portable dressing room and announced, "There's a bishop out

here who says he married you in 1943." "That's funny," mused the star. "I'm practically certain I never married a bishop." Later she added, "I can't help getting married all the time. I'm a sucker for a rite." She's a remarkable housekeeper, however. Every time she wangles a divorce, she keeps the house.

Marilyn, We Roll Along

Marilyn Monroe Miller is easily the favorite actress of every writer on the Fox lot: when she's around, who bothers listening to the dialogue?

"We sent her up on location to northern Canada," recalls publicist Harry Brand, "and the Royal Mounted Police forgot all about getting their man. They just concentrated on Marilyn—and she was wearing three sweaters and two pairs of pants, too! That girl doesn't believe in frozen assets. On her, the end justifies the jeans."

Between rehearsals, the story has it that Marilyn went trout fishing. She hooked a whopper, but he finally broke loose and swam like all get-out to rejoin the other trout. "Wow, fellows," he gasped. "You should have seen the one I got away from."

A fashion editor was asked to describe the dress Marilyn had worn to an Academy Award dinner. "Well," answered the editor cautiously, "in most places it looked a lot like Marilyn."

At the Fox lot one summer, life was enlivened by weekly baseball pools. Each of sixteen actors or actresses drew out of a hat a pill that represented one of the major-league ball teams, and paid a dollar therefor. At the end of the week, the total sixteen-dollar pot went to the actor whose team had scored the most runs in games played during that period. Marilyn Monroe had been taking aureomycin pills to cure a cold, and as a scene was being rehearsed for *The Seven Year Itch*, she thoughtlessly took one from her purse and gulped it down. Suddenly she realized she had made a slight mistake. "Help," she wailed. "I just swallowed the Baltimore Orioles!"

Mae West, who is reputed to know a thing or two about sex appeal herself, was asked recently by a Las Vegas reporter for *her* critical estimate of Marilyn Monroe. "She's a good kid," conceded Miss West, "and they've handled her publicity well. But I just don't think she has the equipment."

What Miss West needs is a new oculist.

Herb Stein has written an entire Hollywood success story in just three sentences: 1. I haven't got a phone yet, but you can get me through the drugstore at our corner. 2. Give me a ring, old thing. I'm in the book. 3. "The subscriber has requested that we do not give out her new number."

That hardy perennial of movie classics, *Gone with the Wind*, has been reissued for the steenth time. Alan Green suggests it's about time they rename it *Gone with the Second Wind*.

Cecil B. DeMille was asked by Leo Guild why he made so many biblical pictures. DeMille chuckled. "Why let two thousand years of publicity go to waste?"

One of the men who deliver sandwiches and soft drinks to the personnel in the offices of M-G-M has the harmless foible of referring to famous personages by their first names. He's forever dropping pearls like "I bumped into Dore last night," or "Marlon's new part fits him like a glove," or "If I were Grace, I'd make the Prince appear in her next picture."

Recently he was given a pair of seats to a special showing of *Julius Caesar*. Next morning he didn't let his audience down. "Well, folks," he announced cheerfully, "I caught Julius last night."

Visiting Hollywood a few years before his death, French playwright Henri Bernstein was heard to observe, "Genius, geniuses everywhere I turn! If only there was some talent!"

A star came to New York between pictures with a wad of five thousand dollars burning a hole in his pocket. Problem: should he buy a small piece of a pal's new musical revue, or get the little woman the mink coat for which she had been yearning? He compromised by buying into the show but promising his wife *two* coats if it was a hit.

After the tryout, the star sent his wife this wire: "I've got bad news for you. Your coats closed in New Haven last night."

25

CHAPTER TWO

ANIMAL LIFE

Reigning Cats and Dogs

I am a firm believer in the old theory that there is a time and a place for everything—and that goes double for funny stories.

For instance, I told a story to an assemblage of several thousand schoolteachers in Detroit recently that won me about three times as solid a response as I figured it warranted. There was a reason!

The story concerned a prosperous New York merchant who went South on vacation to do a little hunting. He rented a hound-dog for five dollars at the lodge he patronized, and sallied forth. It soon became apparent that this dog was a champion. In one hour the merchant was back with a full bag, his reputation as a huntsman greatly enhanced.

The next year he demanded the same dog. "You mean 'Teacher,'" the lodge owner assured him. "He's so good we've raised the price to ten dollars." The year following, the dog's name had been changed to "Principal," and the price was up to twenty dollars.

The huntsman grumbled but couldn't do a thing about it. He just had to have that dog! So again he arrived at the lodge and put in his claim. But the owner registered despondency and sighed, "You can't have that dog any longer, mister. It's our fault. We've ruined him for hunting. This spring we renamed him 'State Superintendent of Schools,' and from that moment on all he's done is sit on his fanny and bark!"

Now, here's why those teachers laughed so hard. The gentleman who had introduced me, and was the only man sitting on the platform behind me, was the State Superintendent of Schools in Michigan!

Governor and Mrs. Averell Harriman have an oceanside estate in Hobe Sound, Florida, and one sure sign they are in residence is the sight of their prize dachshund frisking about on the beach. The name of this dachshund is Gary Cooper.

Last winter a jokester sent a post card to the dog addressed "Gary Cooper, c/o the Harrimans." An alert real-estate promoter spotted the card at the post office and figured he had a hot prospect to work on. He rushed over to the Harriman place, declaiming, "It's imperative that I see Mr. Cooper immediately."

"He must be around here somewhere," said an obliging maid. "Here, Gary! Here, Gary!"

27

A man boasted day and night about the wonderful dog he owned. Walking on the beach with this beloved pooch, he met a friend and promptly launched forth with, "You've got to see the new trick I just taught Fido." He picked up a stick and hurled it into the water. With one bound, Fido was after it, but not for him so commonplace a feat as swimming in the briny! Fido ran lightly on *top* of the waves, retrieved the stick, and, returning on the water's surface, deposited it at his master's feet.

"I'll show you that was no accident," boasted the dog's owner. A second time he threw the stick, and a second time Fido fetched it via the surface of the sea.

"Well?" exulted the owner. "What do you think of a dog that can do a trick like that?" "Not too much," deprecated the friend. "He can't even swim!"

George Gobel complained that he couldn't teach his prize boxer, Irving, not to chase after automobiles. A noted dog expert assured Gobel, "Every boxer chases cars." "I know," said George, "but Irving catches them."

"A small town," opines A. W. Perrine, "is a place where a fellow has to walk around a dog enjoying a nap on the sidewalk."

One dog woke up when five-year-old Kathy skipped by, barked happily, and followed her home. Kathy did not know that her new friend was a female. She loved the dog so that her parents couldn't find it in their hearts to call the A.S.P.C.A. She had her moment of triumph some weeks later when she came home from school and found her dog being pursued by every male dog in the neighborhood. "How do you like that, Mom?" she inquired proudly. "Our dog is just a natural-born leader."

In Los Angeles, Matt Weinstock tells about a lady who loves cats who was dining with her husband in her apartment one night when she fancied she heard a cat meowing a floor or two away. "I'll bet that pussy is lonely," she remarked to her husband, and playfully meowed back.

To her surprise the cat answered her! She repeated her meow, this time putting extra feeling into her performance, and there then ensued the darnedest cat conversation ever heard in that neighborhood. It continued for a full half hour, while the husband marveled.

The next day her triumph was deflated when a neighbor dropped down to borrow some sugar. "The funniest thing happened last night," said the neighbor. "I meowed at a cat and he meowed back—and we must have kept it up for forty minutes!"

A Cleveland resident, reports Paul Steiner, lost confidence in a cat who snoozed unconcernedly in the sun while dozens of mice scurried happily by, so he bought a mousetrap. Its first victim was the cat.

At the country estate of a distinguished Doubleday editor, a small boy's head appeared over the fence, and a meek voice inquired, "Please, Mr. Beecroft, could I have my arrow back?" "Certainly, my boy," responded the editor with that spontaneous love for the young that has made him famous. "Where is it?" "I think," said the small boy, "that it's stuck in one of your cats."

Animal Spirits

"I had a bit of a hassle," admitted an intrepid horseman, "with my fiery steed in Central Park this morning. He wanted to go in one direction, and I wanted to go in the other." "How did you settle it?" he was asked. "Oh," he answered airily, "the horse tossed me for it."

An Eastern lady, vacationing at a Nevada dude ranch, essayed a ride on a spirited pony and was promptly sent flying head over heels into a pile of—well, dust in a corner of the corral. "This pony bucks," she cried angrily as she struggled to her feet. A cowboy who had watched the performance with keen enjoyment drawled, "Shucks, lady, that wasn't no buck. That pony only coughed!"

Up in Maine a man bought himself a horse and, after he had paid for it, asked, "Now that the deal is closed, tell me honestly: is the horse any good?" The shrewd Yankee who had sold the animal answered, "Depends on what you mean to do with him." "I'm a sea captain," said the buyer, "and I plan to take him aboard ship tonight." "You're lucky," said the Yankee. "On land he's no good at all."

Danny Kaye comes up with a story about a friend named Nussbaum who took it into his head to go to the Malay Peninsula to hunt tigers. When he came back a friend demanded, "What is a nice, well-brought-up fellow like you doing risking his life with tigers, yet?" "You don't understand," said Nussbaum loftily. "This was a safari to end all safaris! There is no thrill like stalking through the jungle, knowing that a great man-eating tiger may leap at you any minute." "Nu," said the friend, "how many tigers did you kill?" "None," admitted Nussbaum. "The safari was a failure then?" persisted the friend. "Of course not," maintained Nussbaum. "It was a glorious success. When you're hunting tigers, none is *plenty*."

A man strolled into a neighborhood tavern with a huge, mangy yellow dog in tow and sat minding his own business until another guest, leading a ferocious-looking bulldog, challenged him.

"Whatcha doing with a mutt like that?" he demanded. "You should get a pedigreed dog like mine." The first man answered quietly, "Five hundred dollars says my yellow 'mutt' can lick the daylights out of that bull of yours."

The bet was made, and sure enough, the yellow dog made mincemeat of the bull in about two minutes flat. The bartender swept up the carnage and asked respectfully, "Where did that yellow dog come from anyhow?"

Its owner explained, "A friend sent him to me from Africa. All I had to do was cut off his mane and tail!"

That reminds me of the time Tallulah Bankhead forswore canine companionship for a time and acquired a playful lion cub as a pet. "Winston Churchill" she called him. Her friends fled when he came around for a romp. Once he almost bit off Noel Coward's hand. When Coward cried bloody murder, Tallulah silenced him with, "Don't be a spoilsport. Winston is just teething."

Arthur Wise, Los Angeles financier, writes about the bank clerk who entered a pet shop and announced he was in the market for a parrot. "I have a dandy here," boasted the proprietor. "He can say Uncle Herbert, Aunt Minnie, Hooray for the Dodgers, and Wait Till Next Year." "Never mind all that," interrupted the bank clerk. *Is he tender?*"

The favorite animal story of the late H. T. Webster, creator of Caspar Milquetoast and "Life's Darkest Moment," concerned the kangaroo who suddenly leaped twelve feet over the barrier at the Bronx Park Zoo and took off in the direction of Yonkers at eighty miles an hour. A keeper dashed up to the baffled lady who had been standing in front of the kangaroo's cage and demanded, "What on earth did you do to that kangaroo to make him run that way?" "Nothing, really," the lady declared. "I just tickled him a little." "You'd better tickle me in the same place," suggested the keeper grimly. "I've got to catch him!"

There was a state fair in the Middle West recently where interest ran high in the award for the champion bull. Two entries were already famous in those parts and feeling—and wagering—ran high on which would win out. When the time came, the judges couldn't decide themselves. The chairman stepped into the center of the arena and announced, "These bulls are so evenly matched, we simply can't make up our minds which one is best. We're going to leave it to the governor's son here to name the champion."

The governor's son was exactly six years old. He gravely inspected the two magnificent bulls and finally piped, "I pick this one."

The crowd cheered, the blue ribbon was pinned on his selection, and then the chairman asked, "Why did you choose the one you did?" The governor's son answered, "Because I think he'll give the most milk."

CHAPTER THREE

ARTISTS AND MODELS

On a sub-zero day in midwinter a lovely young model complained that the studio was too cold for posing in the nude. "You're right," agreed the artist who had hired her. "I don't feel like painting today anyhow. Sit down and have a cup of coffee and a sandwich with me." Some minutes later he heard a determined pounding on the door. "Quick," he commanded the model. "Get your clothes off! It's my wife!"

A Cincinnati camera club, tired of photographing the Ohio River and the local ball players, threw caution to the winds and hired a model for some nude photographic studies. But when the moment for action arrived, it developed that the model had been wearing such tight garters, their imprint on her legs could not be erased.

The members decided she must wait in an anteroom for an hour while they went out for dinner. When they came back, the marks on her legs were gone all right—but alas, she had been sitting the entire hour on a cane-bottomed chair!

One model agency believes in giving its girls unusual names. Three that seemed to carry things a bit far were: Miss September Maughan, Miss Eyeful Tower and Miss Berthe Daye Sutes.

Models of distinction:

1. The cover girl who suddenly turned up at Palm Beach on the arm of an eligible playboy. "Hallelujah!" marveled a friend. "Where did you dig up this one?" "I'm not sure," admitted the playboy. "I opened my wallet and there she was!"

2. The model from Honolulu who taught all the other girls the hula. "It's easy," she maintained. "First you put a crop of grass on one hip. Then you put a crop of grass on the other. Then you rotate the crops."

3. The model who was so ugly that when she walked into a studio three mice jumped up on chairs.

4. The model who refused to pose for one magazine illustrator. Her reason: "He's tall, dark—and hands."

5. The model Peter Lind Hayes discovered in New Rochelle. "She has absolutely everything a man desires," insists Peter, "including muscles and a mustache."

The late H. T. Webster had completed a dozen cartoons in a single day and decided he needed a bit of relaxation. He chose twenty friends at random and sent them a one-word telegram: "Congratulations!"

34

Only two phoned to ask what he was talking about. The other eighteen sent notes of thanks. Each had recently completed some minor achievement he deemed entirely worthy of Webster's congratulatory wire!

Salvador Dali, the famous but eccentric painter, refused to come to America with his wife Gala until Caresse Crosby, Boston socialite and collector, agreed to shepherd them. They sailed aboard the *Champlain*, Dali bundled up in sweaters and mittens in a third-class cabin near the engine room. "I stay next to the engine," he explained, "so that I'll get there quicker." To each of his precious pictures he had affixed a string; the other ends of the strings were tied to his clothing or his fingers. He was packed and ready to leave the ship four days before they steamed past the Statue of Liberty.

When the reporters streamed aboard, Caresse told them about Salvador Dali. None of them had ever heard of the gentleman, but they trooped obediently after her to his cabin. One look at his magnificent mustachio and another at his canvases, and Caresse, alas, was completely forgotten. "A portrait of my wife," announced Dali in French. "What's that on her shoulders?" asked a pop-eyed reporter. "Lamb chops," said Dali. That did it! The next morning, Dali and his lamb chops hit the headlines, and Caresse, for possibly the only time in her life, was relegated to a footnote on page nine.

In his disarming autobiography, *Lying in State*, Stanton Griffis tells about a day he and a Wall Street friend wandered into a Paris gallery to see an exhibition of modern pictures. The friend thought one or two of them would improve the décor of his private office.

"How do you go about buying these things without getting the daylights socked out of you?" he asked. "Put in low bids on all of them," advised the knowing Mr. Griffis. "When the show is over, you'll probably find that a couple have fallen virtually into your lap."

The frock-coated manager indicated that this procedure was highly unusual, but graciously consented to enter the bids. A few mornings later, Mr. Griffis received a frantic phone call from his friend. "My God," wailed the friend. "I've bought forty-six pictures!"

CHAPTER FOUR

'TENSHUN!

"Life's certainly taken a turn for the better at Camp Lee since a beautiful blonde was assigned to our barracks," boasted a GI in a Richmond bar. "What is she—a WAC?" asked an incredulous bystander. "Not at all," said the GI. "She's just one of 'the boys.' Does the regular routine, eats and sleeps like one of us, even takes showers where we do." "For the love of mud," gasped the bystander. "How does she get away with it?" The GI winked and said, "Who's gonna snitch?"

37

A squad of draftees in Oklahoma was engaged in enlarging and painting barracks, being driven like Furies by a tough and uncompromising sergeant. Just behind them, another squad of soldiers was busy tearing down the barracks as soon as they were painted. A roving correspondent watched the operation with some wonderment for a few minutes, then asked the painting sergeant how come. The sergeant replied, "I got my orders and they got theirs, but I'll tell you one thing, boy: I'm having a heck of a time staying ahead of them!"

When asked to furnish his school and college affiliations, a New England job applicant paused briefly, then wrote, "Korea, Clash of 1952."

On sick call one morning, a draftee heard two hardened veterans discussing the doctor in charge. "He doesn't kid around," asserted one. "Fellow came in saying he had ptomaine poisoning, so the doc cut off his big toe." "Yeah," agreed the second, "and remember the guy with erysipelas? The doctor just sliced away his left ear." By this time the draftee had turned a sickly green. "Let me out of here," he begged. "I've got asthma!"

John Straley tells about a lonesome draftee who had frittered away all but a twenty-five-cent piece of the money he had saved on a wild and vaguely disappointing weekend. The last quarter was to be his bus fare back to camp. Slumped at the bar, however, the quarter slipped out of his hand, and, before he could retrieve it, the proprietor's pet monkey had leaped from his perch, grabbed the coin, and swallowed it.

The grouchy proprietor, furthermore, flatly refused to make restitution. "Hang on to yer money better, bud," he growled. "I ain't responsible for dat monkey's actions." The outraged draftee hauled off and socked the grinning monkey right in the solar plexus. "Grab my last quarter, will you?" he began, but then let out a yell of glee. "I'm independently rich," he cried, scooping up coins from the bar, where the monk had coughed up nine dollars and seventy-five cents!

The sergeant glared at an undersized, sharp-eyed rookie and demanded, "You, there, what's the first thing you do when you clean a rifle?" "Look at the serial number," was the immediate reply. "The serial number!" roared the sergeant. "Why?" "To make certain," explained the rookie, "that I'm cleaning my own rifle."

General Al Gruenther reports that an army unit near NATO headquarters is out to get a famous Parisian glamor girl. Seems she's been contributing to the delinquency of a major.

Young Johnny Malone always had wanted to be a sailor, and he enlisted the day after he was eighteen. His first letter home, however, denoted a certain measure of disillusionment. It read: "Dear Mom: I joined the Navy because I loved the way the ships were kept so spick-and-span—but I never knew until this week who keeps them so spick-and-span. Love, Johnny."

A Missouri boy, a plebe at Annapolis, wrote a letter home, explaining, "The first thing I had to learn down here was how to use my sextant." "Well," declared his mother, aghast, "the things they teach in college nowadays!"

The news from Norfolk is that enlisted men are showing a new respect for their officers, regardless of their sex. A sailor was observed retrieving a handkerchief that had been dropped by a trim WAVE lieutenant, and handing it to her with a heartfelt "I think you dropped this, toots, sir."

Bob Sylvester reports that the Navy is working on an atomic submarine which will stay under water for four solid years—coming up just long enough to allow the crew to re-enlist.

39

HORATIO ALGER

CHAPTER FIVE

BUSINESS AS USUAL

A deserving young man went to work one Monday morning in the lowest position in a huge manufacturing plant. His starting salary was only ten dollars a week, but determinedly he began his climb up the ladder.

Inside of a month he was head of the shipping department at a hundred a week. Two months later he was in the front office, earning a thousand a week. And exactly one year after his humble start, the big boss called him in and said, "My boy, you've done well. You are hereby named president of the company, at a hundred thousand a year!"

"Thank you," said the young man.

"Thank you, he tells me," grumbled the big boss. "Haven't you anything else to say for yourself?"

"Yes," said the young man. "Please tell Mama I won't be home for dinner."

In Los Angeles, there dwelt a head accountant who labored for a big furniture house for forty years. Every morning he unlocked his desk at eight-thirty on the nose, peered into the center drawer for a moment, then locked everything up again. What was in that center drawer? Assistants, visiting salesmen, even the owner himself, never came close to solving the mystery. One day the accountant died suddenly, and after a decent interval everybody rushed to pry open the center drawer. It was found to contain just one little slip of paper. Printed in capital letters thereon were the words, THE SIDE TOWARD THE WINDOW IS THE DEBIT SIDE!

The new typist, fresh from college, was so pretty that nobody had the heart to reprimand her for obvious shortcomings. The boss saw her frantically searching through the files one morning, and after pausing to enjoy the rear view said consolingly, "There, there, Mary. If you've lost something again, it isn't serious enough to burst into tears about it." "It certainly is," said Mary, choking back a sob. "This time it's my lunch."

A short time before his death, Thomas A. Edison was asked the secret of his success. "Two things that had nothing to do with my knack for inventing things had a lot to do with it," he replied candidly. "One was good luck. The other was that nobody ever was able to convince me that it was unfair to my fellow workers to put forth my best efforts in my work. I'm glad there was no such thing as the eight-hour day when I was a young man. I won't say it isn't a boon to others—but if my own life had been restricted to eight-hour days, I don't think I would have accomplished a great deal. This country wouldn't be where it is today if the young men of fifty years ago had been afraid they might earn more than they were paid for!"

How many of you have heard of the Horatio Alger Award? Named after the author of rags-to-riches sagas that delighted—and inspired—the younger generation at the turn of the century, it is awarded annually to a group of self-made industrial leaders by the American Schools and Colleges Association. Among the outstanding citizens who snagged Alger awards in recent years were the late Tom Watson, of International Business Machines, whose first job as bookkeeping apprentice netted him exactly two dollars a week; Paul Hoffman, of Studebaker and Ford Foundation fame, who began his business career as a porter in a used-car lot in Chicago; Walter Fuller, who rose through self-education from lowly mill hand to head of the Curtis Publishing Company, and Adolph Zukor, who added forty dollars of borrowed capital to what he had managed to save from a two-dollar-a-week salary in a fur store, and opened a penny arcade. He became the guiding genius of Paramount Pictures.

Speaking of Mr. Watson of IBM, he was famous for his insistence on having signs commanding "THINK" plastered all over his palatial premises. Nobody ever discovered the identity of the miscreant who penciled "OR THWIM" on the bottom of all of them after the staff had gone home one night.

"And now," beamed the business-school teacher, "tell the class what you do when your employer rings for someone to take dictation." "I pick up my notebook," recited perky little Miss Hastings, "sharpen my pencils, and answer the buzzard promptly." Obviously, Miss Hastings was destined for success in the business world. Her first boss regarded her chassis with undisguised approval, but a few hours later was moved to point to the portable on her desk and remark, "There is one thing you must remember, my dear. If my wife bursts in suddenly any time without knocking, please apply yourself to that contraption. It's a typewriter."

Miss Hastings progressed rapidly. The boss learned to give her reports and say, "Make a dozen copies of this—and circulate the one with the fewest mistakes."

It was only a question of time till a subsequent boss (aged seventy) asked Miss Hastings to be his bride. The morning after the nuptials, the seventy-year-old groom was bristling with his usual vigor, but the young bride was listless and bedraggled. "When he told me," she wailed, "he'd been saving for twenty years—I thought he meant *money!*"

The *Town Journal* reports that a slick saleslady, after talking a customer into buying a mink coat at a Fifth Avenue specialty shop, asked gently, "How would your husband prefer being billed, modom? In a series of piddling amounts or in one staggering sum?"

A New York dress-shop owner is thinking seriously of framing a letter of complaint that reached him, by courtesy of the ingenious U. S. Post Office Department, the other morning. It reads: "The Big Store: Dear Mr. B. Store: Please cancel my order for maternity dress, Model 61, which you were supposed to deliver me three weeks ago. My delivery turned out faster than yours. Respectfully, etc., etc."

Zsa Zsa Hornblow, the doughty old maid who had inherited the Hornblow Nut and Bolt Factory from her father, Uriah Hornblow, and ran it with an iron hand, caught sight of a young fellow leaning idly against the wall, whistling and twiddling his thumbs. The outraged Zsa Zsa shrilled, "You there! What's your weekly salary?" "Thirty bucks," vouchsafed the idler. "Hmphh!"

snorted Zsa Zsa. "Here's thirty dollars. Now scram! Vamoose! You're fired." The young man pocketed the thirty and left, exuding good will. Zsa Zsa watched till he was off the premises, then demanded of foreman Al Vidor, "How long was that waster on the payroll of the Hornblow Nut and Bolt Works?" "He never worked for us, ma'am," said Al patiently. "He was just taking orders for Cokes and sandwiches for the drugstore."

A small-town druggist was down but not out. Closed by the sheriff, he posted this notice on the window: "Our doors are locked. The following services, formerly available here, may be had as follows: Ice water at fountain in park. General information from cop at the corner. Change of a dollar at bank. Matches and scratch pads at hotel. Rest rooms at home. Magazine for browsing at doctor's office. Bus information at the terminal. And loafing at any other location of your own choosing."

In Des Moines, Gardner Cowles, publisher of *Look*, goaded his sales force to new deeds of derring-do with the tale of an untried clerk in a clothing store who sold nineteen suits on his first day on the job. "A great start," enthused his boss, "but if you're really the world-beater you appear to be, you'll fob off this overloud, outmoded number with the broad purple stripes we've been stuck with for three years. Get sixty dollars for it, and I'll give you a raise immediately." Three days later the clerk reported that the monstrosity had been sold. "You're wonderful," conceded the boss. "Did you have a tough time persuading the customer to take it?" "The customer was docile as a lamb," admitted the clerk, "but I had one hell of an argument with his seeing-eye dog!"

A pawnbroker loaded his show window with unredeemed saxophones, banjos, tubas—and shotguns. "Very interesting display," commented a friend, "but does it sell merchandise?" "Does it!" enthused the pawnbroker. "One day a fellow buys a sax or a tuba. Two days later his neighbors buy the shotguns."

Walter Lowen tells about a salesgirl in a chain candy store who always had customers lined up waiting for her while other salesgirls stood twiddling their thumbs. The owner of the chain noted her popularity and asked for her secret. "It's easy enough," she replied. "The other girls scoop up more than a pound of candy and then start taking away. I always scoop up less than a pound and then add to it."

The president of a billion-dollar corporation faced his board of directors with an unusually grim look on his face. "I'm going to put it squarely to you, J.D.," he said to the first vice-president. "Have you been taking out my secretary after hours?" "Gosh, chief," blushed J.D. "I didn't think you'd mind." In turn, two lesser vice-presidents, the comptroller, and the chief statistician sheepishly admitted that they, too, had not been immune to the charms of the prexy's secretary. The newest and youngest member of the board, however, was made of sterner stuff. "I'm happy to say," he announced, "that I've had no extracurricular activities whatever with the young lady in question." "You're just the man we're looking for," boomed the president, relief in his voice. "Get right outside and fire her!"

A Stamford, Connecticut, businessman named Thomas Edward Saxe, Jr., has designated one corner of his inner sanctum as official headquarters for the most soothing and undemanding institution in the country today: the Sittin', Starin' 'n' Rockin' Club.

Its close to two thousand members (including a couple of movie stars, TV and sports personalities and ordinary folk like bank presidents and you and me) have neither meetings nor policies to fret about. The only thing they must do to stay in good standing—or sitting—is to propel themselves gently to and fro in a rocking chair a few minutes every day.

Saxe discovered one morning, while vacationing in Sarasota, Florida, that an old rockin' chair had "gotten" him. It relaxed his nerves, soothed his brow, brightened his skies. He resolved

45

then and there to form his club and pass on the good word. The news spread so quickly that he soon was swamped with applications.

"I had to call a halt," he says ruefully. "I was so busy mailing out new membership cards, I had practically no time left for rocking myself."

There's not a thing in the world, of course, to stop you from forming a club all your own. Your sole need is a handy rocking chair.

Just wait calmly every twenty-four hours with your personally selected clubfellows for the end of a perfect sway.

Mr. Huebsch told his secretary at 9:30 A.M. that he needed some documents in a hurry. When she hadn't produced them by eleven, he went after her in a rage. She didn't help matters by looking very aggrieved indeed and telling him, "Hold your horses, Mr. Huebsch! I haven't even found the filing cabinet yet!"

A group of well-heeled young executives were exchanging confidences on how they had overcome early difficulties. "Things were pretty tough for me," admitted Rogers when his turn came, "but I just gritted my teeth, rolled up my sleeves, spat on my hands—and borrowed another hundred thousand dollars from my father."

Anxious to get on in the world, a nice young couple were entertaining the boss and his wife at dinner—doing pretty well, too, until their ten-year-old hopeful burst into view. He cased the boss's wife with obvious interest, then asked his dad, "Does she really wrestle on TV?"

Marshall Field, founder of the great Chicago store, loved to tell this story at the expense of his friend, P. D. Armour, the meat packer. Armour once hired a new office clerk but didn't mention the time to report for work. The new employee showed up the first day at 8:00 A.M., to find P. D. Armour and his staff in shirt sleeves, plunged into the morning accounts. The next day the young man showed up at seven. Armour, hard at work, only glowered. The third day the new clerk managed to get in at six-thirty. Armour glared up from his paper-littered desk. "Young man," he bellowed, "just what is it you do with your forenoons?"

In a nationally known department store in Dallas, where, if you search hard enough, you can pick up a handkerchief for as little as $8.75, they staged a fashion exposition that had the customers hanging from the rafters. So many well-heeled Dallas ladies—and their husbands—turned up, in fact, there was no room left for the models to change their costumes on the exhibition floor. A special elevator whisked them up two flights, where an assembly line, similar to the Ford setup at its Highland Park plant, lay in wait for them.

One attendant yanked away their hats. Another unzipped them and peeled off their dresses. Another pulled off their shoes. At the end of the line, each model stood in her barest essentials waiting for her next costume to be trotted out.

Things were going swimmingly, the crowd cheering, the models changing into ever more dazzling—and expensive—ensembles, when a slight hitch marred the proceedings.

The haughtiest and wealthiest customer of the establishment stepped blithely into the wrong elevator. . . .

Do I have to go on with this story?

In the bridal department of a Fort Wayne emporium, writes Cliff Milnor, a customer stopped the usually quick-witted consultant cold. What she wanted was "a maternity wedding gown"! "Sorry," gasped the consultant, "but I doubt that you'll find a garment like that in the entire state of Indiana." "Time you people snapped up around here," said the customer scornfully. "They've got 'em in Kentucky!"

A famous Brooklyn department store decided to honor its two millionth customer. She was embraced by the store president, interviewed on TV, and loaded down with a dozen fancily wrapped packages of choice merchandise.

She then proceeded to her original destination—the complaint desk.

"I've got to get a present," confided a customer to a department-store clerk, "for a very rich old aunt who can hardly walk. Any suggestions?" The clerk considered a moment, then came up with, "How about some floor wax?"

After pulling out half the stock in an unsuccessful attempt to please a pernickety lady customer, the shoe salesman mopped his brow and inquired, "Mind if I rest a moment, lady? Your feet are killing me!"

An heiress was riding in an elevator in a Midwest department store when something went wrong with the mechanism. The elevator plunged to the basement, and the heiress landed on her posterior. She sued for the hundred thousand dollars she felt this affront to her dignity was worth.

"I take it," the defense attorney remarked caustically, "that when you realized a crash was inevitable, the sins of your entire life passed before your eyes?"

"Certainly not," snapped the heiress. "We only fell eleven floors."

A small boy invaded the lingerie section of a big department store and shyly presented his problem to a lady clerk. "I want to buy my mom a present of a slip," he said, "but I'm darned if I know what size she wears." The clerk said, "It would help to know if your mom is tall or short, fat or skinny." "She's just perfect," beamed the small boy, so the clerk wrapped up a size 34 for him.

Two days later, Mom came to the store herself and changed it to a size 52.

To be serious for a moment, Marihelen Macduff describes a young shopper in a fashionable Dallas emporium whose behavior in the brides' salon was puzzling the personnel. She would pick up one piece of material after another, and pace up and down with it held against her side—but never once did she look into the mirror.

"It's not the looks of my bridal gown that bother me at all," she finally explained. "I want to know what it will *sound* like. My husband-to-be lost his eyesight in Korea. I want him to *hear* me at his side."

Garfinkel was selling lightweight summer suits at such a low figure that one customer, at least, smelled a rat. "They shrink maybe when it rains?" he inquired. "Nonsense," answered Garfinkel heatedly. "Three yards in every hundred maybe at the most." The customer was convinced but, after the first rainstorm, angrily returned with a garment shrunken almost beyond recognition. Garfinkel, however, had a ready explanation. "Can I help

49

it," he demanded, "if you were unlucky enough to get those three yards?"

A continental refugee in London had one big ambition in life: to be able to afford an English suit, made to order by a really first-class English tailor. He scrimped and saved, and finally had enough to order not only the suit, but all the trimmings to match—homburg, shirt, tie, oxfords, stick. The day came for the final fitting, and he was able to study the full ensemble in a full-length mirror. Suddenly he burst into tears. The tailor, dismayed, begged, "Tell me what's wrong, sir. Are you displeased with the fit? Do any of the accessories bother you?" "No, no," the refugee assured him between sobs. "The clothes are perfect. *But why did we have to lose India?*"

Himmel and Bimmel, who shared a floor of a loft building in the garment district, were fierce competitors in the cloak-and-suit industry, but managed to preserve a personal friendship nonetheless. Every day they would lunch together and catalogue their respective trials and tribulations.

"Son-in-laws," moaned Himmel one noon, "you expect to be dumb, but my son-in-law Morris is dumber even than you could imagine. Let me show you, Bimmel, what I got to contend with." Thereupon, he summoned Morris, handed him a five-dollar bill, and said, "Morris, I want you should go down to the corner and buy me a new automobile."

Morris took the bill silently, departed, and Himmel shot a look of triumph at his friend. Bimmel, however, refused to be impressed. "My son, Nathan," he announced, "is ten times dumber than your Morris." He called Nathan in, pressed a shiny half dollar in his palm, and said, "Nathan, run down by the barbershop in the basement and let me know quick if I am there." Nathan scurried off, leaving the two older men moaning and wagging their heads.

In the elevator, Morris and Nathan met and exchanged greetings. "My father-in-law thinks I'm stupid," grumbled Morris.

"But he gives me five dollars to buy him a hotomobile and never once says what make or color it should be." "My papa's worse even," consoled Nathan. "A half dollar he squanders so I should see if he's in the barbershop, when for just a dime he could have telephoned and found out for himself!"

The fixtures and equipment of a big barbershop in a metropolitan hotel are a lot flossier than those of a tonsorial parlor in a small town, but the atmosphere and conversation are remarkably similar and unchanging.

The same cutups perform both in the chairs and behind them; the same badinage, political soothsaying and sporting data are exchanged; the same amorous if doddering patrons furtively squeeze the hands of the same coy manicurists.

The familiar barber pole with the red stripes is a throwback to the time of King Henry VIII of England, when barbers were also allowed to practice minor surgery and dentistry. The red stripe presumably symbolized blood, and was designed as a guidepost for a majority of the citizenry who couldn't read. Later, American barbers added a dash of blue for patriotic reasons.

In one shop a customer demanded a brand-new face lotion. "I have a date with a luscious babe tonight," he explained, "and I want to have the most provocative tang possible." "Here's one guaranteed to knock her cold," enthused the barber. "It has an ether base."

Al, the tony barber at the New Weston, was surprised to get a tip from editor Haas *before* the latter climbed into his chair. "You're the first customer who ever tipped me *before* I gave him any service," commented Al. "That's not a tip," Haas announced brusquely. "That's *hush* money."

The world traveler entered the hotel barbershop, and as luck would have it, chose the chair of the barber who, for some reason, always seemed to average the biggest tips. "I suppose you

51

shave a lot of famous characters in this shop?" essayed the traveler. "Not at all," the barber assured him gravely. "You're the first one this month, sir."

"Can you *prove* this is a good hair tonic?" an oft-fooled baldhead asked his druggist. "I'll tell you how I can prove it," asserted the druggist. "One lady customer took the cork out of the bottle with her teeth and twenty-four hours later she had a mustache!"

Herb Shriner, waiting his turn to have his hair cut, picked up a magazine for expectant fathers and came across this bit of advice: "It will help to place the diaper in the shape of a baseball diamond, with you at bat. Fold second base over home plate. Place baby on the pitcher's mound. Then pin first base and third base to home plate and you're all set." "All set, my eye," commented Shriner. "I tried that very trick on my first-born, but we had to call the game on account of wet grounds."

An overpersistent insurance solicitor followed the late W. C. Fields into a barbershop one afternoon. Fields, spluttering shaving cream, finally exploded, "I've told you 'no' ten times now. Just to shut you up, I'll put the proposition up to my lawyer the next time I see him."

"Will you take the proper step," persisted the solicitor, "if he says it's okay?"

"I certainly will," asserted Fields. "I'll get another lawyer."

The bigger they are, the harder they fall—for life insurance policies. That, at least, is the unqualified announcement by the Provident Mutual of Philadelphia and, when the demon statisticians and actuaries of a company like that get finished with their computations, there's no more margin for error than in time or tide.

The lowest insurance is held by individuals who are exactly five feet high, avers B. F. Blair, president of Provident Mutual.

Their policies average $2,979. The five-foot-six-inch clan averages $3,976. Strapping six-footers average $5,070. And the folks who tower over us at six feet four hold average policies of $6,180. The Provident Mutual people emphasize that they're not pointing out any moral with all this, nor have they any idea of whys and wherefores; they're just giving the facts, ma'am.

By actual count there are now over one hundred and sixty thousand full-time life insurance agents in the United States, and by a curious coincidence it seems that most of them were classmates of mine in college. That's what they tell me over the phone, anyhow. The minute I hear, "Hi, Beans"—a nickname nobody has used since the day I graduated—I know what I'm in for.

Ralph Engelsman, one of the most successful insurance men in the country, once took on a recruit straight out of the Social Register. "If you see enough prospects," this rich but honest neophyte was told, "the law of averages will work for you. Enough commissions eventually will come along to make every sales talk worth fifteen dollars and twenty-two cents."

One of the neophyte's first prospects was his richest uncle. "Sorry," he was told, "but I have enough policies." "That's all right," said the fledgling agent. "I just made fifteen dollars and twenty-two cents!"

When the uncle heard the explanation, he said cheerfully, "Any time you need another fifteen dollars and twenty-two cents, come around and let me turn you down again."

One of the greatest feats of salesmanship in the annals of the insurance business was performed by an irresistible force in Vermont who overcame an immovable body named President Calvin Coolidge. Cal signed for a thousand-dollar policy.

Apparently the inducement that appealed to him most was the free medical check-up, for when he appeared at the doctor's, he had his aged father in tow.

"If it won't cost anything," he said, "I'd like you to look Pa over at the same time."

A big Madison Avenue ad agency is buzzing with the rebuff suffered by a lady operative who was ordered to telephone several hundred big shots and ask what brand of cigarettes they fancied most. She got along fine until she lured Dr. Alfred Kinsey, author of *Sexual Behavior in the Human Female*, to the phone in Indiana.

"We'd like to ask you," said she, "what cigarette you smoke."

Dr. Kinsey, the tireless investigator, snapped, "I never discuss my personal affairs for publication," and hung up.

Two ulcers stopped to exchange greetings on Madison Avenue. Sighed one, "I feel terrible. I must be getting an advertising man!"

Undoubtedly this ulcer had heard about the account executive who worried so much his hair turned charcoal gray.

Average mortals never realize how many things they crave until a cagey advertising expert points out the facts to them.

A thriving little industrial plant in Panama employed twenty local women. One day they just stopped coming, and such inducements as higher pay and shorter hours didn't budge them an inch. They had earned all they needed for months at least, they explained: why work any more? The boss, after much worry, finally hit upon a solution. He sent each of them a thousand-page Chicago mail-order catalogue. They were back at their places—every last one of them—the following Monday.

Peter Lind Hayes tells the tragic story of a lady who bought a large-economy flask of "Poof" and blew her arm off.

A very wise public-relations counsel cautions letter writers to delete the pronoun "I" as much as possible. "A weekend thank-you note which opens 'I had a wonderful time,'" he points out, "is not half so captivating as one beginning, 'You are a wonderful hostess.' Both say 'thank you,' but, ah, my friends, the second is the one that will get you asked back!"

The junior account executive of an ad agency married a glamor puss, bought a suburban villa twice too big for his income, and threw a monster housewarming party. His directions to friends were most explicit: "Get off the Merritt Parkway at Exit 42, turn left, and look for the first Frank Lloyd Wrightish creation. You can't miss it. It's the one with the big mortgage."

Two-hundred-and-fifteen-pound Bill Zeckendorf is a shrewd, daring, and tremendously successful realtor who not only has visited all the states in the union but owns large segments of them personally.

His propensity for acquiring desirable real estate has made him a marked man. He has only to drive slowly down a street in any town in the country for values on either side to go sky-rocketing immediately. A messenger saw him step into an elevator recently with Bishop Fulton Sheen. As the door of the elevator closed, the messenger murmured sadly, "There goes St. Patrick's Cathedral!"

Fellow bought a house near a riverbank, despite the fact that the cellar seemed rather damp. "Snug as a bug in a rug," the realtor assured him. "This cellar is dryer than the Sahara Desert."

A month later the buyer charged into the realtor's office, prepared to wring his neck. "You and your Sahara," he cried. "I put two mousetraps in that cellar and when I went down to look at them this morning they had caught a flounder and a haddock!"

Are you looking for a distinctive name for that new place of yours in the country? A proud Tennessean has dubbed *his* dream house "Chateau Nooga." A Charles Addams monstrosity on the Jersey shore is called "Gruesome Gables." And a Baltimore minister, hoping his congregation will get the hint, lives in "The Wrecktory."

Eric Hodgins, author of *Mr. Blandings Builds His Dream House*, is understandably mystified about the vagaries of American suburbanites' architectural enthusiasms. "Why," inquires Hodgins gently, "do they select sites in the hottest parts of Texas to build Cape Cod houses, which are designed to keep you warm? Or put ranch houses, designed to keep you cool, in the coldest parts of Maine? Or build split-level houses, designed for perching on hills, in Iowa, where they have to build the hills to put them on?" The writer of the best answers to these questions will receive an extra copy of next week's real-estate section of his Sunday paper free of charge.

The sales manager of a fast-growing outfit sticks pins in a big relief map behind his desk to show where every one of his salesmen is located at a given moment. Ragsdale, of the Iowa sector, was not, in the opinion of the manager, living up to his early promise, and was summoned to the home office for a pep talk and reindoctrination. "I'm not saying you're in imminent danger yet of being fired," was the stern end of the sales manager's warning, "but if you'll look carefully at my map, Ragsdale, you'll note I've loosened your pin."

A tax collector was examining the books of a defiant—but slightly worried—supermarket proprietor when the clerk, climbing aloft to fetch a can of preserved peaches, upset a whole pyramid of same. Cans came tumbling down on the tax collector's noggin, sending him sprawling to the ground.

"Be careful, Irving, you fool," cried the proprietor. "Supposing that had been a customer!"

McTavish had been in America only a few days when he made his first sortie into a supermarket. An attendant opened the door for him, another provided him with a big pushcart. Before him was an array of fruits, vegetables, breakfast foods, and canned delicacies of every description. The enraptured visitor piled his cart high and headed for the exit.

There, effectively blocking his path, stood the cashier. "The devil take it!" cried McTavish, abandoning his cart. "I knew there'd be a catch in it."

The salesman for the forty-four-volume encyclopedia climaxed his pitch with a hearty "Yes, ma'am! You just put a tiny deposit down, and don't pay another penny for six months!" The prospect looked surprised and demanded, "Who told you about us?"

The most unusual salesman he ever met, avers Herb Shriner, is a fellow who made a modest fortune purveying lightning rods. Suddenly he lost interest in his work, however. He got caught in a storm with a bunch of samples in his arms.

A smart jewelry salesman took one look at the beautiful blonde and the sugar daddy acting as her convoy, and trotted out his most expensive item—a diamond-ruby-and-sapphire-encrusted clip depicting the American flag.

The blonde fondled it with an adding-machine look in her eyes and cooed, "It's positively scrumptious—but doesn't it come in any other colors?"

After weighty consultation with innumerable salesmen, John Straley has discovered why, month by month, their figures aren't quite what their bosses expected them to be:

January: People spent all their cash for the holidays.

February: All the best customers have gone South.

March: Everybody's preoccupied with income taxes.

April: Unseasonable cold—and people spent too much on Easter clothes.

May: Too much rain: farmers distressed.

June: Not enough rain: farmers distressed.

July: Heat has people down.

August: Everybody away on vacation.

September: Everybody back—broke.

October: Unseasonable heat—and customers are waiting to see how fall clearance sales turn out.

November: Everybody too upset over elections.

December: Customers too busy with holiday shopping to see any salesmen.

AFTER-DINNER SPEAKER   PRE-DINNER GUZZLER   ALL-DAY WORKER   ALL-NIGHT DRIVER

One exasperated boss, fed up with the alibis of lackadaisical salesmen, tacked the following notice on his bulletin board:

"It has been brought to the attention of the management that many salesmen not only are dying while on duty, but refusing to fall over when the act is completed.

"This practice must stop at once.

"Hereafter, when a salesman has not moved in several hours, department heads are ordered to investigate. Because of the close resemblance of death and the ordinary gait of our sales personnel, the investigation will be made quietly, so as to prevent waking the salesman if he is sleeping.

"If some doubt persists, extending a check to cover entertainment expenses is a fine test. If the salesman does not reach for it, it may be assumed he is dead. In that case, fifteen copies of a formal report should be typed at once, three of which are to be dispatched to Washington, and two to the deceased. The others will be promptly lost in the office files."

How do salesmen strike back at this kind of needling? One of them took it upon himself to compile this list of requisites for full membership in the selling fraternity:

"Must be a man of vision, ambition, and iron endurance, an after-dinner speaker, before-dinner guzzler, work all day, flatter all evening, drive all night, and appear fresh as a daisy the next morning.

"Must be able to entertain customers, wives, sweethearts, and receptionists, be a man's man, a lady's man, a lover like Gable, a diplomat like Churchill, a good sport, a Plutocrat, a Democrat, a Republican, a New Dealer, a Fast Dealer, a mathematician, and a mechanic.

"Must belong to all clubs and fraternal orders, and pay all expenses on 5 per cent commission plus 2 per cent excise tax, 1½ per cent old-age pension, and 2 per cent lost-sales tax.

"Is it any wonder 'good' salesmen are hard to find?"

A big manufacturer of dog food summoned his entire sales force to Los Angeles for a convention. The sales manager generated vast enthusiasm with his glowing account of prize-winning ad campaigns, sensational promotion gimmicks and revolutionary packaging. Only the company president remained unimpressed.

"If all you men are doing such a wonderful job," he demanded, "why are our sales off fifteen per cent—and dropping steadily?"

"There's one thing we haven't been able to lick yet," admitted the sales manager, considerably subdued. "The dogs simply won't eat our product!"

CHAPTER SIX

THE CREAM OF THE GUESTS

Extra men—presentable ones, at least—are so scarce in most circles these days that they can make their own rules. They demand a list of other guests, the names of their dinner partners, details of the menu and form of entertainment—and, in general, are the selfish, spoiled gents that have kept them single in the first place.

One insisted on a small additional service that struck my wife Phyllis and me as so reasonable, we now accord it to every weekend guest we invite: his own newspaper, fresh and unsullied, on his Sunday-morning breakfast tray.

"When there's only one paper in the house," grumbled the pampered fellow who made us see the light, "the host's fourteen-year-old son invariably has chewed it to bits hours before I wake up. Funny that the same host who thinks nothing of serv-

ing you the best victuals and imported beverages will boggle at a few cents extra to buy his guests their own newspapers!"

Clare Jaynes, Chicago authoress and socialite, thinks it's important that the guest room be furnished with appropriate literature. Her own guests, for instance, are confronted with the following titles:

THAT MAN IS HERE AGAIN
NOT AS A STRANGER
INTRUDER IN THE DUST
LOOK HOMEWARD, ANGEL
THE LOST WEEKEND
DEATH IN THE AFTERNOON
SO LITTLE TIME

and, after considerable urging on my part,

BENNETT'S WELCOME

63

A nearsighted society girl in New York, too vain to wear glasses, was at a dinner party when the butler handed her a note from the hostess. She gave it to Lord Doodlesworth on her left, beseeching, "Won't you read this for me, Your Lordship? I have something in my eye." His Lordship read, "Be nice to old Doodlesworth. He's a terrible bore, but we're hoping to be asked to his estate in England next summer."

Sam Levenson has an Aunt Beckie who is convinced this is the worst of all possible worlds.

The last time he came home from a weekend at her house he decided to shoot the works and sent her a magnum of champagne and a pound of caviar. A few evenings later he phoned her. "How are you, Aunt Beckie?" he asked. "Dying, of course," she moaned. "You never acknowledged my gift," he accused her. "Didn't you like it?" "I'll tell you," said Aunt Beckie thoughtfully. "The ginger ale wasn't so bad. But that huckleberry jelly . . . ! You must have left it standing next to some fish in the icebox all night!"

Leo Kaufman of Houston, Texas, in a reminiscent mood, tells of some of the rules one Ezra Kendall posted in an old Pittsburgh hotel years ago:

"To prevent patrons taking fruit from the table, there will be no fruit.

"In case of fire, jump out of the window and turn to the left.

"Do not clean your shoes with a towel—unless it has been stolen from another hotel.

"Notify us if you see a mouse in your room and we will send up the cat.

"Guests without baggage will leave their wives with the room clerk."

A plump gentleman ate a fine meal at the Waldorf with obvious relish, topped it off with some rare Napoleon brandy, then summoned the headwaiter. "Do you recall," he asked pleasantly, "how just a year ago I ate just such a repast in your excellent hotel and then, just because I couldn't pay for it, you had me thrown into the gutter like a veritable bum?" "I'm very sorry," began the contrite headwaiter. "It's quite all right," conceded the plump gentleman, lighting a cheroot, "but I'm afraid I'll have to trouble you again."

Ed Buckley, manager of New York's Hotel Roosevelt, was approached recently by the wife of a prominent publisher who asked him to donate the grand ballroom for a charity dance. Buckley explained to her that this was the peak season for rental of such space, and that it would be impossible to give it to her free. "But this is such a worthy cause," she protested. "All these wonderful but penniless authors and their broods . . ." Buckley again expressed regrets, then, remembering that she was the mistress of a sumptuous estate in the suburbs, suggested that she hold the dance in her own house. "What!" was the lady's indignant rejoinder, "and have all those bums cluttering up my living room?"

A stalwart mountaineer entered the lobby of a swank Huntington hotel, after a certain amount of difficulty with the revolving door, and signed the register with a big "X." The room clerk noticed that the new guest had left muddy tracks clear across the marble floor. "When you patronize a hostelry of this caliber," he remarked coldly, "you might at least wipe half the mud of West Virginia off your shoes." The mountaineer regarded the room clerk with honest amazement and asked softly, "*What* shoes, bub?"

The glamorous blonde, ambling through the lobby of Houston's finest hotel, was inclined to be hoity-toity, until she encountered the town's number-one oil driller. Then she became charm itself and inquired coyly, "How much did you say your name was?"

A group of very pious—and very frugal—gentlemen recently attended a conclave in a Chicago hotel. When they decamped, a waiter sadly told his wife, "Dem gentlemen arrived wid ten dollars in one hand and ten commandments in de udder—and neither wuz broken when dey left!"

The vast old Grand Union Hotel in Saratoga is but a memory now, but native son Frank Sullivan recalls the days when society packed the premises, Victor Herbert conducted the orchestra, and Monty Woolley's dad was the manager. That was years ago, of course—before young Woolley's chin bore even a remote hint of the sassafras that was later to become his trademark in Hollywood.

Sullivan secured a room for Marc Connelly once at the height of the season, but, instead of being grateful, Connelly reported it was so far down the corridor that, "even on a clear day, I can't see the lobby." As for his bed, Connelly declared it more uncomfortable than a slab of concrete, with spikes protruding therefrom. "That's a historic bed, you unfeeling lout," protested Sullivan. "George Washington definitely slept in it." "Hmphh," mused Marc Connelly. "Now I know why he never complained when he got to Valley Forge."

Gal from a local editorial office—the athletic type—went up to a highly publicized ski lodge for a weekend of risking life and limb on the glistening slopes. The morning after her arrival she complained to the manager that twice during the night she had to get dressed and go to the lobby for a carafe of ice water. "My dear young lady," said the manager, "why didn't you simply press the buzzer beside your bed?" "The buzzer?" exclaimed the girl. "The bellboy told me that was the fire alarm!"

To celebrate their fiftieth wedding anniversary, a dignified lawyer took his wife to Europe. Neither had been abroad before, but a more worldly and sophisticated junior partner volunteered to make their Paris visit a breeze. "I know the manager of the

finest hotel on the Champs Élysées," he assured them. "I'll write him that you're coming." He did too. "This gentleman has done a lot for me," is what he dictated, "so I want to be sure that you give him the best of everything: corner suite, room service, tips on where to go, etc., etc., etc."

The manager himself greeted the lawyer in Paris, and though he seemed a bit surprised to meet the wife, shrugged his shoulders and conducted the couple to their suite. Everything was lovely—including three young ladies, very scantily clad, who sat demurely in a row in the sitting room. "Who are they?" gasped the lawyer, blushing violently. "Ah, monsieur," the manager assured him, "it is as your friend requested. Those are the three et ceteras."

A waitress in a beanery was serving a customer when a bald-headed gent entered and planted himself at a table in the rear.

"That's old Professor Snead," vouchsafed the waitress. "He's got a twin brother and they're alike as peas in a pod, only this one's stone deaf. Watch me have some fun with him." She minced over to him, smiled prettily, and said in a loud voice, "Well, you bald-headed old baboon, what kind of food are you going to pour into that fat stomach of yours today?" The bald-headed gent answered softly, "I'll have ham and eggs, toast, and coffee. And by the way, my brother is the deaf one."

An editor of many years' standing couldn't help scanning the menu of his eating club for typographical errors, and one day he was convinced he had found one. "Oh, Adolph," he observed, "I note that you are featuring homburger steak today. You mean hamburger steak, don't you?" "Not at all," maintained Adolph. "This morning our new English cook dropped his hat in the meat grinder."

James McNeill Whistler, the celebrated artist, rather prided himself on his knowledge of French. In a fashionable Paris restaurant one evening he insisted upon ordering the dinner and got very angry when a friend tried to help the waiter understand everything that was being said. "I am quite capable of speaking French without your assistance," he grumbled. "That may well be," soothed his friend, "but I just heard you distinctly place an order for a flight of steps."

The late Bob Benchley's son, Nat, tells of a time his father was showing some friends around Paris and insisted they dine at a restaurant where he had eaten some memorable pressed duck. But he couldn't remember where the restaurant was located. Over the friends' protests, he continued his quest for hours and finally stumbled on the place.

It was only when the orders of pressed duck were being placed before his guests that Benchley remembered what had made it so memorable. It was the worst pressed duck he had ever eaten.

A shrewd restaurateur in Milwaukee has plastered a huge sign on his window proclaiming, "T-bone, 25 Cents!" When you get close enough to read the small print, however, you note this reservation: "With Meat, Four Bucks!"

Munro Leaf, author of the immortal *Ferdinand the Bull,* was driving his car across the country, and made it a practice to stop for chow at railroad inns where big trucks were parked in front. "Those truck drivers," he told his wife, "know these roads in their sleep—and they've learned by experience where the best eats are to be found." Once, however, the lead proved false. Despite the presence of four monster trucks in the parking space, the food served inside was virtually inedible. A waitress noticed Leaf's discomfiture. "I know what's bothering you," she whispered. "The boss bought those old trucks at a salvage sale. He figures they bring in more customers than an electric sign. There aren't even any motors in them!"

On Fourteenth Street in New York there is an old German restaurant named Luchow's, which grows more popular, it seems, as time goes on. Broadway and Hollywood celebrities flock there in particular on Sunday nights. One promising starlet was making her first appearance in the Big Town and her publicity-conscious agent said, "The place in which you'll attract the most attention tonight is Luchow's." "That suits me fine," enthused the starlet. "I haven't been to an honest-to-goodness Chinese eatery in heaven knows when!"

E. M. Statler, who founded the chain of hotels that bore his name, understood the psychology of waiters perfectly. Rufus Jarman, in his engrossing book about the Statler Hotels, *A Bed for the Night,* asserts that, not only Mr. Statler, but every experienced waiter in his employ, knew the approximate size of the tip almost before a guest sat down at the table.

Indications: (1) Guests who study the menu at great length are usually not good tippers. (2) Men who wear inexpensive gaudy neckties or loud striped shirts are poor prospects. (3) The type of drink ordered is particularly revealing. "Beer for everybody" ranks lowest, closely followed by "rye and ginger ale." "Scotch and water" is most promising. (4) Also suspect are pipe smokers (oh, come now!).

Waiters figure that pipe smokers are likely to be the nonconformist type, and if there's one thing a waiter hates, it's a nonconformist.

A motorist stopped at a big roadside tavern for a bite of supper. His waitress had eight tables to take care of, but only one customer seemed to find fault with the service. He became so noisily abusive, in fact, that the motorist chivalrously volunteered, "If that lout is bothering you, I'll be happy to toss him out on his ear." "Lay off, mister," the waitress whispered. "That's my husband and we've worked this act down to a science. He makes the other customers feel so sorry for me that they all give me extra-large tips."

Up to the porte-cochere of an ultraswank summer hotel drove a gleaming Rolls-Royce, replete with liveried chauffeur and footman. In the back seat lolled a lady swathed in mink and diamonds, and next to her sat a very little girl, also dressed to the teeth. The doorman bowed low to the lady and lifted the little girl out of the seat. "Beautiful child," he observed. "Can she walk yet?" The lady cast her eyes skyward and said fervently, "Heaven willing, she'll never have to!"

Old Mr. Gotrox was even grumpier than usual as he stomped up and down the veranda of his summer hotel. The reason for his irritation finally was revealed when he admitted, "For two solid hours last night I had to listen to that blithering bore Allister telling me about his confounded rheumatism." "That's not like you, Gotrox," one old crony was emboldened to say. "Why didn't you trump his story with the account of your diabetes?" "Shucks," scoffed Gotrox. "I led with that."

70

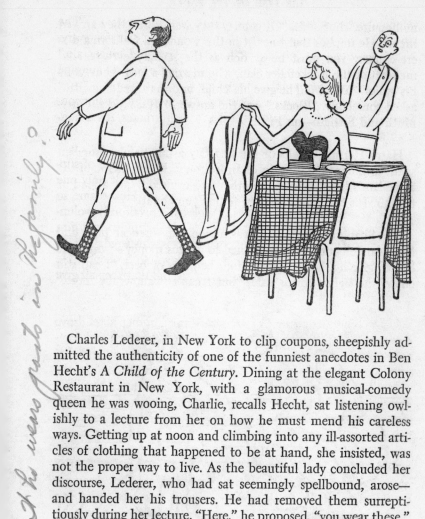

Charles Lederer, in New York to clip coupons, sheepishly admitted the authenticity of one of the funniest anecdotes in Ben Hecht's *A Child of the Century*. Dining at the elegant Colony Restaurant in New York, with a glamorous musical-comedy queen he was wooing, Charlie, recalls Hecht, sat listening owlishly to a lecture from her on how he must mend his careless ways. Getting up at noon and climbing into any ill-assorted articles of clothing that happened to be at hand, she insisted, was not the proper way to live. As the beautiful lady concluded her discourse, Lederer, who had sat seemingly spellbound, arose—and handed her his trousers. He had removed them surreptitiously during her lecture. "Here," he proposed, "you wear these," and walked coldly out of the restaurant in his shorts.

Of Palm Springs, the California desert resort, Cleveland Amory reports, "Not everybody you see at the lavish hotels is a millionaire," but adds, "Of course, they were when they arrived there." He implies that to exist in this wonderful California desert country you must be as rich as the seventy-seven-year-old member of the Rockefeller clan, who married a lady many years his junior. "What did he give his 'child' bride as a wedding gift?" asked somebody. "Blocks," was the answer. "Yes, blocks. Forty-ninth and Fiftieth—on Fifth."

Harry Hershfield tells of the first day a night-club comedian spent in the invigorating air of an Adirondack resort. One of the comedian's lungs tapped the other and exulted, "Get a load of this air. It's the stuff I've been telling you about!"

The Shangri-La-by-the-Sea was run on the American plan, and Mr. Mandelbaum was determined to get his money's worth. He had to give up, however, after four helpings of beef. "I can still chew," he sighed to his wife, "but I can't swallow any more."

Mr. Gans rubbed the sand out of his eyes in time to observe his son dragging the top half of a bikini bathing suit along the beach. "Now, sonny," he wheedled, "I want you to show Daddy *exactly* where you found it."

If old Jake Keim, who promoted the first boardwalk in Atlantic City, could see the throngs of today, the hotels, and the annual "Miss America" jubilee, he probably would gasp, "What did I start down here anyhow?"

Mr. Keim wasn't aware that his boardwalk was revolutionary. His little rooming house, prospering in the aftermath of the Civil War, had been protected from the waves by a sand dune. When it was removed, the tide changed his hostelry into a swimming pool. Keim talked the city into building the boardwalk.

It was a mile long and collapsible—sometimes unintentionally. Each fall the planks were disconnected and put away for safekeeping. In every Atlantic City budget from 1870 to 1879 there was one item of seventeen dollars, expense for "rent of barn for storing boardwalk."

Those tides were responsible for another Atlantic City institution too. In 1883, a lad named Bradley opened a candy kitchen on Mr. Keim's boardwalk, and was selling a very superior brand of taffy there. Then a giant wave whooshed over the place, and Mr. B. found himself with a mess of water-soaked confectionery.

A less enterprising soul would have quit and gone home. Bradley, however, evolved a new principle on the spot. "Salt water is *good* for taffy," he proclaimed, with a note of desperation in his voice.

To his amazement, the public believed him. "Salt-water taffy" has been a staple of the community ever since.

For years a mecca for visitors to "the nation's playground" was Captain John Young's Million Dollar Pier. It featured a nine-room Elizabethan cottage intended for the owner's personal dwelling. Since it was at the very end of the pier, seventeen

73

hundred feet from shore, it was ruled out of the jurisdiction of the state of New Jersey. So the captain gave it the address of "No. 1, Atlantic Ocean."

Captain Young fished by merely sticking a rod or net out the window. Soon he was advertising a daily net haul which visitors could witness at two bits a head. The catch included various fish, horseshoe crabs, empty beer bottles, and an occasional unwary swimmer.

They say one shark became so mesmerized by the "ohs" and "ahs" greeting his daily capture and release that he turned up in the net for seventeen consecutive performances.

CHAPTER SEVEN

THE DANCE OF LIFE

A young mother-to-be visited her gynecologist for a routine check-up, and was told that she would be blessed with twins. The doctor decided the husband should know immediately, too, so had the nurse drag him out of the front seat of his car below. "What's the big idea?" he protested. "I'm liable to get a ticket for being double-parked outside." "Well, son," said the doctor gently, "your wife's in the same situation inside."

75

"Doc" Sherman tells about the youthful couple who entered his Madison Avenue drugstore in search of a potent new baby tonic. "Here's one," promised Doc, "that will make your youngster husky, handsome, and happy." "That's just what we want," said the young lady, "but who takes it, my husband or I?"

Tax-conscious Bob Hope sees nothing surprising in the fact that babies start bawling the moment they are born. "In the first place," points out Hope, "they're hungry. And in the second place, by the time they're five minutes old, they owe the Department of Internal Revenue $1,900!"

A thoughtful pediatrician reminded a comparatively new father, "Never spank your child on an empty stomach. Be sure to eat something first." Then he noticed that the baby's hair had turned white. "This kid worrying about something?" he asked. "It's not the kid at all," the father answered him. "It's my near-sighted wife. She keeps powdering the wrong end."

Opening gambit of a sad, sad recital: "No sooner had we sold Junior's buggy than . . ."

When the wife of a high-powered copy writer in Westport gave birth to a baby daughter, he proudly announced by wire to his friends, "We have skirted the issue."

A year later, the mother made the mistake of leaving the baby in her husband's care while she closeted herself in the library to pay the month's bills. Pa buried himself behind his newspaper and forgot about the baby until he heard a series of thumps, followed by a horrendous wail. Clearly baby had fallen down the stairs.

"Martha," called the father excitedly. "Come quick! Our little girl just took her first forty-eight steps!"

If your kids are anything like mine, they dearly love receiving presents—but hate even more having to write thank-you letters therefor. My Jonny got around to thanking his Uncle Herbert for a Christmas gift along about March 25. What he wrote was, "I'm sorry I didn't thank you for my present, and it would serve me right if you forgot about my birthday next Thursday. . . ."

That note ranks with the intercepted correspondence of a boy and girl who sat next to each other in a third-grade class.

Wrote the boy: "Dear Judee: I luv you. Do you luv me? Jimmy." Answered the girl: "Dear Jimmy: I do *not* love you. Love, Judy."

A little girl, born and bred in Anderson, Indiana, had never seen the ocean and looked forward to her initial vacation in Florida. Arrived in the Southland, her daddy enfolded her in his arms and treated her to a first taste of the surf. She was squealing with joy when she rejoined her mother on the beach. "I just love the ocean, Mommy," she enthused, "except when it flushes."

A Boston six-year-old, obviously impeccably reared, came home from a party in fine spirits, to be asked by his mother, "Were you the youngest one there?"

"Not at all," he answered loftily. "There was another gentleman present who was wheeled in in a baby carriage."

"Gee, Pop," implored a youngster. "Why can't I go out in the green fields and play and run around like all other boys?" The father's terse reply was, "Shut up and deal!"

✓ A reader in North Carolina reports that her three-year-old son was having trouble unfastening the back button of his underwear. He interrupted a hot canasta session to ask her, "Hey, Mom, how about opening my bathroom door?"

Taxicab driver in Washington had a unique experience one day last week. A lady signaled him to stop, then lifted four wee kiddies into the back seat. "Be with you in a mo," she promised,

77

then disappeared into a house. She was back in about ten minutes, calmly hustled the kids out of the cab, and asked, "What do I owe you?" "I don't get it," confessed the mystified driver. "Just an inspiration," she explained. "I had to make an important long-distance call and it was imperative that I get the children safely out of the house."

Eight-year-old Claudia was packed off to Waterbury for a visit with her old-maid aunt. Her last minute instructions were, "Remember, Aunt Hester is a bit on the prissy side. If you have to go to the bathroom, be sure to say, 'I'd like to powder my nose.'" Claudia made such a hit with Aunt Hester that when the time came for her to leave she was told, "I certainly loved having you here, my dear. On your next visit you must bring your little sister Sue with you." "I better not," said Claudia hastily. "Sue still powders her nose in bed."

Little Mary Brown went walking with her dad in the park and came home to report that she had seen a great big lion gamboling on the greensward. Her mother promptly chastised her for lying and made her go upstairs to ask God to forgive her. Mary came down again after a while, and her mother asked, "Well, Mary, did you ask God's pardon for lying?" "I did," reported Mary, "and do you know what He said? He said, 'Don't even mention it, Miss Brown. I often mistake those great big yellow dogs for lions Myself.'"

In his autobiography, the late Vice-President Alben Barkley told of the lad who asked his father, "What's an ancestor?" "Well," said Pop, "for example, I'm an ancestor." "Yeah?" was the reply. "Then how come people brag about them?"

The famed Kentucky legislator also reminded us that "a child enters your home and makes such a racket for eighteen or twenty years that you scarcely can stand it, then departs, leaving the house so dismally silent you think you'll go mad."

78

The proprietor of a children's specialty shop in a New England shopping center was so busy dreaming up slogans like "Kwality Klothes for Kute Kiddies" that he neglected to pay his help a living wage. The long-suffering employees finally were goaded into picketing the establishment, but they showed a fine appreciation of the sensibilities of their clientele.

The picket signs read, "We'the out on thtwike."

Somebody asked editor Herb Mayes's younger daughter, "Does your old man have a den?" "He doesn't need one," was the answer. "He just growls all over the house."

Young Chris was diligently practicing away on the piano when there came a determined banging on the door. It was the cop from the corner, looking very formidable indeed. "Gotta investigate a call from the lady who lives next door, Chris," he said severely. "She swore two fellers named Chopin and Debussy was being murdered in here."

Observed Don McNeil to an appreciative audience at his TV Breakfast Club show: "It used to take an uncommonly strong man to tear a telephone book in half. Now that feat is easily—and frequently—accomplished by the average father of a teen-age daughter."

Ralph Moody, author of the award-winning book for boys and girls, *Little Britches*, receives a lot of fan mail from youthful admirers, but one letter he particularly cherishes came from a forthright lad in a Wyoming rural school.

"There is five of us in our class," it disclosed. "Our teacher just read us your book and I like it. You rite such bad English I can understand it. Love."

Reverend Otis Moore of New York reports on the predicament of eight-year-old Clara, who unfortunately was receiving a richly deserved spanking from her exasperated mother. In the middle of the proceedings, a little boy from across the way marched in and gave evidence of remaining till the bitter end. Clara stopped howling long enough to twist around and say very clearly, "Scram, John. Can't you see that Mother and I are busy right now?"

John was manly enough to admit later that he also was subjected to the humiliation of an occasional paddling in the woodshed. "Pop always proposes a toast before he whops me," added John. "He says, 'Bottoms up!' "

"When I was but a lad," recalls Duke Ellington, "I put books inside my pants for padding when a good spanking was evidently in the cards for me. Ever since, I've known the value of a literary background."

A chronic bachelor with a pronounced dislike for children became so smitten with a curvaceous blond widow that he up and married her, despite the fact that she was encumbered with an eight-year-old son.

A few weeks after the honeymoon, the kid was asked how he was getting along with his new daddy.

"Great," enthused the lad. "He's really fun. Thinks up new games for us to play all the time. Every day this week, for instance, he's been taking me out in Long Island Sound about two miles—and then I swim back."

"A two-mile swim every day sounds like pretty rough going for a kid your age," was the comment. "Doesn't it tire you out?"

"Nah," said the kid. "The swimming part is a cinch. I must admit, though, it isn't always easy getting out of that darn sack!"

"The trouble with our school system nowadays," explains educator William Brish, of Maryland, "is that the teachers are afraid of the principals, the principals are afraid of the boards of education and the boards are afraid of the parents. But the children of today—they're afraid of nobody!"

Of course children are not all quite so obstreperous as the little monster who crawled all over Tallulah Bankhead one afternoon. "Our little Philip is certainly a problem," admitted the mother. "We don't know what to make of him."

Miss Bankhead seized a moment when Mama's head was turned the other way to give Philip a hearty cuff on the ear and suggest, "How about a nice rug?"

Small fry, avers Basil Davenport, are having a hard time keeping their TV Wild West programs and adventures by rocket ship separate in their minds. One boy decked out in a space helmet hailed his dad with, "Put 'er thar, you ornery old horned toad, or I'll plug you with my six-shooter."

"You've got the wrong cue," corrected Dad. "You're talking Western, not space."

"I," said his son with considerable composure, "am from *West* Mars."

Mrs. Abernathy's eleven-year-old daughter, Nell, came home from camp with a gold medal for packing her trunk more neatly than any other girl. "How did you do it," marveled Mrs. Abernathy, "when at home we can never clean up the mess you leave behind?"

"It was cinchy," explained Nell complacently. "I just never unpacked it all summer!"

A new teacher suddenly appeared to take charge of a fourth-grade class in a fashionable Chicago suburb.

At the conclusion of her first session, the teacher was handed a note by a shy little girl who had been sitting in the front row. "I think you are going to be a wonderful teacher," it read, "and I have fallen in love with you already. P.S. The girl sitting next to me thinks you're a fat slob."

There's a little boy at a Beverly Hills school who poses quite a problem for the teacher every day. Because his father is a movie producer with an income estimated at something like eight thousand dollars a week, the son's sense of values is not the same as the other students'. One composition he turned in, for instance, has become a genuine collector's item in the school. It began, "This is the story about a very poor family. The father was very poor, the mother was very poor, the children were very poor, and the three butlers were the poorest of all."

Asked to recount the story of Noah in his Bible class another day, the lad began, "Well, it seems that God told Noah it was going to do some tall raining, so he'd better build himself a yacht. . . ."

Dr. Frank Littleton was on duty in a state medical bureau in the Blue Ridge Mountains district when a mother entered with a husky, tough-looking son of about three, and promptly proceeded to nurse him, to the consternation of the entire staff.

"My dear lady," sputtered Dr. Littleton, "that boy is too big to be nursed. You should have weaned him long ago."

"I know," admitted the mother sadly. "But every time I try, he throws rocks at me."

I never quite believe the stories I hear about boners pulled on eighth-grade examination papers, but even if this one isn't quite true, it bears repetition:

"One beautiful evening in the twelfth century, Queen Eleanor of Aquitaine entered Coventry, and after removing all her

clothes, rode through the streets astride a snow-white stallion. On her way, she bumped into Sir Walter Raleigh, who was embarrassed by her appearance and threw his cloak around her, crying, '*Honi soit qui mal y pense*,' which means, 'You need it more than I do.' The Queen graciously responded, '*Dieu et mon droit*.' ('By golly, you're right.')

"The entire incident is known as the Magna Charta."

And these three quotes allegedly come straight from exam papers in a progressive school near New York:

1. My teacher told me the name of the ruler of Ethiopia is Hail Silly Assy, but frankly I don't believe it. 2. Gothic architecture is easy to spot by virtue of its use of flying buttocks. 3. The safest kind of girl to take out is one who wears glasses. If you breathe heavily on them, she no longer can see what you're doing.

Eileen Bernard, an editor of American Cyanamid's house magazine, has come up with a definition of a grade-school teacher that will do until a better one comes along. "A teacher," she says, "is Courage with Kleenex in her pocket, Sympathy struggling with a snow suit, and Patience with Papers to grade. A teacher really does not mind sniffles, squirmings, stomach-aches, spills, sloth, and sauciness. Neither does she disintegrate before tears, trifles, fights, futility, excuses, parents who spout, little boys who shout, and little girls who pout. Most of all, a teacher is one who likes somebody else's children—and still has strength left to go to the PTA meeting. Thank Heaven for the Teachers."

(Editor's postscript: How about seeing to it that she gets a living wage?)

The transition from prep-school adolescent to sophisticated college freshman, of course, gives the average boy or girl a new sense of responsibility, depth of character, and awareness of world problems.

Typical examples:

1. The Princeton freshman who, when asked, "Are you familiar with the works of Sigmund Freud?" answered brightly, "No, but I think I know his brother, French."

2. The precocious Vassar babe who boasted, "I had a date last weekend with a general." Her roommate, impressed, inquired, "Major general?" "No," was the reluctant reply. "Not yet."

3. The wise lad at Northwestern who was asked for the feminine of "bachelor," and answered, "Lady in waiting."

4. The prodigy from Stanford who came home for his first Christmas vacation as a college man. His mother unpacked his trunk, and discovered a sports jacket with a hock-shop ticket attached thereto. The prodigy explained, "I checked it at a dance one warm evening, Ma, and I guess I forgot to remove the tag." A minute later his mother found a similar ticket on a pair of pants. "Oswald," she demanded sharply, "just what kind of a dance was this, anyhow?"

A successful banker, back on his college campus for a class reunion, visited his old economics prof, and picked up the current semester's final exam. "Holy smoke," he exclaimed, "these are precisely the questions you asked our class fifteen years ago. If you always ask the same questions, don't you know the students will get wise, and pass them on from class to class?"

"Sure," answered the prof blandly, "but in economics, you see, we're constantly changing the answers."

At Kansas State College, Professor H. W. Davis mourned, "The worst thing about being a professor is that after a while you begin to look like one." Another Davis on the faculty, first name Earl, cited as his idea of perfect graphic description, Carl Sandburg's line, "Lincoln crossed his right leg over his left knee, and planted both feet solidly on the ground."

A married lady on the Kansas State teaching roster had a rather unnerving experience just before I visited there. Not being able to locate a sitter, she brought her baby with her to an afternoon tea, and carried under her arm a toidy seat in pink plastic. Her hostess reached for the seat and boomed, "Welcome! Let me hang up your darling new hat!"

Residents of Chapel Hill are partial to a tale of D. C. Jacobsen's about an extremely frugal member of the University of North Carolina faculty. This worthy gent, it appears, had just drawn thirty-five dollars from his bank, bent upon acquiring some reference tomes at Paul Smith's Intimate Bookshop. No sooner had he turned away from the paying teller's window, however, than his path was blocked by the formidable figure of native son Kay Kyser, the popular band leader, who retired while he was about three millions ahead.

"I'm bound for lunch," announced Kay. "How's for coming with me?"

"Love to," agreed the professor. Then, glancing down at the

seven crisp five-dollar bills in his hand, he added hastily, "I'll join you as soon as I've made this deposit."

Latest story from one of those jerk-water colleges with outrageously overpublicized basketball teams is that the coach asked his assistant, "What's biting our all-star center? He's been moping and sulking for two whole days." "It's his father," explained the assistant, "who keeps writing him for money all the time."

"Wimpfheimer," said the philosophy pro sternly, "I'm sure you can tell us who wrote *Critique of Pure Reason*." Wimpfheimer, who had had a hard night carousing at the Williamstown Book Shop, admitted sadly, "Professor, I. Kant." "Amazing," said the professor. "This is the first correct answer you've given me in your five years as a freshman!"

Blasé undergrads today may not take college rivalries as seriously as their granddads were wont to do, but the very sound of "Yale vs. Harvard" still brings the light of battle into the eyes of any true son of Eli or Cambridge.

There was the day, for instance, when an ex-football gladiator from Yale, 214 pounds of All-American, got himself married to a rich and beautiful girl, the catch of the season. Society turned out en masse for the nuptials.

When the bride and groom knelt before the bishop, the congregation gasped.

Painted by a Harvard rascal on the sole of the groom's No. 16 left shoe, in brilliant crimson, was "To Hell," and on the right, "with Yale!"

Some new definitions whipped up for California freshmen by the ever-helpful Jim Marshall:

Alaska: A prelude to "No"
Aspersion: A burro in Teheran
Automaton: A person who eats in the Automat

Amazon: First part of a sentence (Example: Amazon of a gun!)
Buccaneer: Current price of corn
Flattery: An apartment house
Gubernatorial: A peanut in swimming
Incongruous: Where the laws are made
Lemon Juice: An introduction: Lemon juice you to Miss Lyon
Pasteurize: Something you see moving
Pseudo: Counterfeit money
Syntax: What the author of stuff like this has to pay the government.
Weasel: It blows at noon

Not long ago, a college on the Atlantic seaboard found itself in urgent need of two million dollars for a special project. Fortunately, a fabulously wealthy young heiress was lined up to supply the necessary funds. But alas, the college comic magazine chose that moment to publish what the editors believed was a hilarious parody of her social career. The heiress tore up her check, and the editors were kicked out of college.

This incident underlines the fact that there is no more hazardous job than editing an undergraduate humorous publication. Ever since the distant era when I narrowly averted disaster editing the Columbia *Jester*, entire boards have been given the heave-ho at regular intervals for getting too fresh with the faculty, treading on the sensitive toes of trustees, or, most often, printing jokes that might best have been saved for fraternity smokers.

In the latter instance, the offending issues promptly sell at a premium, and old grads who haven't been heard from in years pop up suddenly to renew subscriptions.

Undergraduate humor has a comforting sameness about it through the years. Barring one dismal stretch when ultra-sophistication was the order of the day, and every collegian was trying to imitate the style of *The New Yorker*, the editors have adhered to a dependable, earthy formula wherein boys will be boisterous and girls live up to the most eye-opening of Dr. Kinsey's belated discoveries.

If the following selections from this season's college comics sound vaguely familiar, it is only because the same stories, or reasonable facsimiles thereof, were appearing when the editors sported handle-bar mustaches and you still could snag a free lunch with a ten-cent schooner of beer:

"I can't stand necking," she protested softly, "so what do you say we sit down?"

She talked in her sleep so he sent her home to mutter.

"I'm knee-deep in love with that dame. You see, she has a wading list."

Statistics prove that blondes make the best students.

"You're looking great. What happened to that pain in the neck?" "Oh, she's at the bridge club."

"Doctor, what's your favorite sport?" "Sleighing." "I mean apart from business."

"That's a pretty dress you have on." "Yes. I only wear it to teas." "Whom?"

"Did you go to the Junior Prom this year, dear daughter?" "No, Mom. I ripped my shoulder strap playing tennis."

Coed to druggist: "You heard me. I want a green lipstick. I'm entertaining a railroad man this evening."

"I wouldn't say for sure that my girl was hungry tonight, but it was the first time I ever saw sparks fly from a knife and fork."

"Have you heard about my friend Kerch?" "Kerch who?" "Gesundheit!"

Freshman to English prof at end of term: "Thanks. You was a very good teacher."

"Doctor, did you say eating radishes would make my skin break out?" "No. I never make rash promises."

Randy: "I'll stick to you like glue, my love." Elly: "The feeling's mucilage."

Stuff like that!

A balding and paunchy gent, back from a vaguely disappointing thirty-fifth reunion of his old college class, decided he needed a complete check-up, and went to his doctor. "I just haven't got my old pep any more," he confessed sadly. The doctor examined him fore and aft and assured him, "There's nothing wrong with you that carrots, and plenty of them, can't cure. Take as many as you like." A month later, the doctor noted a distinct improvement. "Just go on eating carrots," he prescribed. The patient jumped from his chair, crying, "Carrots! Good Lord, Doc, I thought you said claret. I've been drinking a bottle a day!"

"I set out in life," reminisced the old grad sadly, "to find that pot of gold at the end of the rainbow. Now I'm fifty-eight, and all I've found is the pot!"

THE LIFE OF THE PARTY

An old moneybags latched onto a provocative blonde of twenty at Palm Beach—or could it be that she latched onto him?—married her, and brought her home to his Fifth Avenue mansion, where the butler eyed her with all the warmth and fervor of a dead codfish. "Isn't she a humdinger?" whispered the old goat triumphantly. "Could be, sir," ventured the butler, "but I do hate to see a man begin a full day's work so very late in the afternoon."

A cranky old party invested in one of those new hearing gadgets that are so small they are practically invisible, and was assured he could return it for full credit if it didn't prove twice as effective as the cumbersome device he had been wearing for years. He came back two days later to express his delight with the new aid. "I'll bet your family likes it too," hazarded the clerk. "Oh, they don't know I've got it," cackled the old party. "Am I having a ball! Just in the past two days, I've changed my will twice!"

Classified ad in a New England newspaper: "For sale: handsome second-hand tombstone. Outstanding bargain for a family named Perkins."

Tucked away in serene, windswept graveyards all over the country are old tombstones in varying states of preservation that bear epitaphs far out of the usual and expected patterns. Interest in them is such that there are over fifty full-sized volumes on the subject catalogued by the New York Public Library. One of the newest and liveliest of the compilations is *Stories on Stone*, by Charles L. Wallis (Oxford University Press).

Politics, points out Mr. Wallis, is such a serious business to some citizens that they seek to re-echo their convictions even from beyond the grave. There was a dedicated Republican named Grigsby, for instance, in Attica, Kansas, who insisted that this epitaph be inscribed on his stone: "I hereby enter my dying protest against what is called the Democratic Party. I have watched it closely since the days of Jackson and know that all the misfortunes of our nation have come to it through the so-called party. Therefore, beware of this party of treason." Mr. Grigsby, incidentally, expired in 1890.

The gravestone of B. H. Norris, of Montgomery City, Missouri, on the other hand, exhorts, "Kind friends I've left behind, Cast your votes for Jennings Bryan."

A monument to the family of Robert Hallenbeck in Elgin, Minnesota, records, "None of us ever voted for Roosevelt or Truman!"

The grim humor of the pioneers found expression in such still-existent gravestones as "Here lies John Coil, a son of toil, who died on Arizona soil. He was a man of considerable vim, but this here air was too hot for him"; "Here lies George Johnson: Hanged by Mistake"; and (in Rapid City, South Dakota):

Here be the bodies of Allen, Curry, and Hall
Like other horse thieves they had their fall.
So be a little cautious how you gobble horses up,
For every horse you pick up adds sorrow to your cup.
We're bound to stop this business, and hang you to a man,
For we've hemp and hands enough in town to swing the whole
* damn clan.*

There's a tomb in New Orleans' Metairie Cemetery that bears not a Bible verse, but the unusual inscription, "See Louisiana Reports, 1905. Page 39." It seems the lady who had ordered the tomb was lost at sea, but the Louisiana Supreme Court ordered the executors of her will to build the tomb anyway.

The thrifty executors, protesting to the end, had the last word. They obeyed the court order but they also had the tomb marked to show precisely why it was erected.

The ladies' dress business had been in the doldrums so long that Mr. Lapidus reversed his field and became an undertaker.

"Things are humming," he told a customer, and to prove his point, showed him four open caskets, all filled. Suddenly two of the corpses sat up, and the customer recoiled in horror. "Take it easy," soothed Lapidus. "Those are just my partners trying to make the place look busy."

Epitaph suggested by an Oklahoma student:

> *Weep a bit*
> *for E. Z. Lott:*
> *He was lit;*
> *His lights were not.*

Wes Laurence has a new "Little Willie" poem to add to your collection:

> *Playing his wooden oboe, Will*
> *Swallowed the horn at the top of a trill.*
> *Said Mother, watching Willie go:*
> *"What mighty aches from oak horns grow."*

I am indebted to the *Detroit Athletic Club News* for the story of a widow lady near the Vermont border who hadn't been known to smile or show a vestige of sentiment for twenty years. When she suddenly informed her regular summer boarders from

Detroit that she'd like to visit her husband's grave, they accordingly were overcome. Nevertheless, they drove her to the cemetery.

She dutifully began looking for the proper headstone, pausing occasionally to make a disparaging remark about the deceased, but finally she threw her flowers onto the ground.

"The heck with him," she decided. "I never knew where the so-and-so was while he was alive, and it ain't a bit different now!"

CHAPTER EIGHT

"THE FARMERS AND THE COWBOYS . . ."

The Farmers . . .

A farmer, paying his first visit to the state insane asylum, discovered one inmate propped up against a tree, blissfully watching the grass grow. The inmate idly inquired, "What's your racket, bub?" "I'm a farmer," was the answer. "Do tell," said the inmate. "I once did some farming too. Darn tough work. Ever try being crazy?" "I certainly did not," said the farmer heatedly. "Well, you ought to," concluded the inmate, relaxing even more completely. "It's got farming skinned seven ways."

Janet Peters tells about the time she persuaded the old carpenter from a Maine summer resort to pay his first visit to New York. He observed the traffic and general hubbub of the big town without comment, but when he reached Fifth Avenue and Thirty-fourth Street, he walked purposefully to the edge of the curb. Raising his thumb at arm's length, shoulder level, he squinted intently up at the great Empire State Building and commented, "Got it pretty plumb, didn't they?"

When the city slicker's foreign racing car got stuck in the mud and ran out of gas in the bargain, Ebenezer hitched his mule to it and after two hours' heaving and shoving under the broiling August sun, extricated the car and hauled it four miles to the nearest garage. When Eb returned, his wife said, "I hope you charged him good for all that work." "Two dollars," said Eb complacently. "Two dollars!" screamed his wife. "I swear, Pa, sometimes I wish you'd do the pullin' and let that mule handle the executive end of your business!"

Having spent his own youth on a farm, a big-city banker was determined that his spoiled young son should get at least a whiff of the same sound training, so he persuaded his old neighbor, Seth Parsons, to take the lad on as extra hand for July and August. About July 15 he called up Seth to ask, "How's the boy making out?" "I ain't the one to bandy words with you," declared the forthright farmer. "If that boy of yours had one more hand, he'd need a third pocket to put it in."

Vrest Orton tells of two ancient Vermonters who were reminiscing around "Pop" Johnson's old cracker barrel. "I never been licked but once in my life," boasted one, "and that's when as a boy of ten I made the mistake of tellin' the truth." His companion whittled quietly for a moment, then remarked, "Well, Sam, it suttinly cured ye."

A farm hand in Kansas ambled up to the owner of the place and drawled, "Thought ye might like ter know the bull's got loose and been chasin' yer wife around the pasture fer the past half hour or so." The owner jumped to his feet in panic and shouted, "You blasted fool! Why have you waited so long to tell me?" "What's the matter, boss?" asked the farm hand in some surprise. "Your wife short-winded?"

My old Uncle Herbert from Vermont was visiting New York recently, and was frankly appalled by the heavy traffic choking every thoroughfare. "You gotta nice town here," opined Uncle Herb, "but it looks to me like you fellers let yourselves get quite a bit behind in your haulin'!"

Main route Number 66 went through the very heart of Goosecreek Hollow, and the natives fumed when tourists tore through at about ninety miles an hour. Sheriff Deveen was finally prevailed upon to put up a couple of warning signs.

A week later he demanded of the chief agitator, "Well, Howie, them signs you hollered for had any effect yet?" "Sure did," replied old Howie glumly. "All the cars what used to go through at twenty miles an hour has slowed down to ten!"

Two typical Bucks County farmers met at a tavern around haying time, and the first one asked the proverbial question, "How's crops?" "Waal," allowed the second, "the gas station and the cheeseburger concession is just about holdin' their own, but durned if they ain't holdin' over *Springtime for Henry* for a second week in my barn."

Everybody in Herb Shriner's home town, he admits, always knows what everybody else is doing, but they read the local paper anyhow, to see if anybody's been caught at it. There are three sources of news: INS, the UP, and the A. & P.

February is about the coldest month. "Sometimes," recalls Herb, "the temperature goes to twenty below—and that's where you feel it most. In April, sprucing up begins. We're sort of in-between folks, though: too poor to paint and too proud to whitewash."

Comes summer and there's some trouble over insects getting into the corn. "But shucks," concludes Herb, "we just fishes 'em out and drinks it anyhow."

Walter Lonnergan tells about a backwoods stalwart who made his first trip to the big city, and was conducted to the vestibule of a new skyscraper. One door seemed to fascinate him. An old, weather-beaten lady stepped in, a red light flashed, and off she went. Seconds later the elevator descended, the door opened, and out stepped a magnificently beautiful girl.

"Gee whillickers," marveled the backwoodsman. "I should have brought my wife with me!"

Harry Hansen, distinguished critic, and editor of the *World Almanac*, recently undertook to show the sights of New York to a Nebraska farm girl who had never in her life been east of the

97

wide Missouri River before. A trip to the top of the Empire State Building would prove an eye opener, figured Harry, so up they went. "Observe!" ordered the distinguished cicerone. "Down there is J. P. Morgan's house and the Chrysler Building. Northward looms Radio City and, beyond it, Central Park. There are Macy's emporium and the Great White Way. And yonder the *Queen Elizabeth* is picking her way down the Hudson, headed for the open sea!"

The Nebraska lass observed all, then contributed her first remark to the festivities. "I guess," is what she said, "all towns look pretty much alike, don't they?"

"Yes, I'm the man who advertised for a top-notch lion tamer," nodded the owner of a small-time carnival. "Are you applying for the job?"

The husky farm hand before him nodded briefly, patted the gun in his holster, picked up a chair and a whip, and said, "Let me at him!"

"Not so fast," warned the owner. "There was one application in ahead of yours. We'll have to give her first whack."

"Her?" echoed the farm hand incredulously.

"Yes, it's a girl," admitted the owner. "I was surprised too. Here she comes."

With that a beautiful blonde hove upon the scene. She had a full-length fur coat wrapped around her, but not one bit of the usual lion-taming equipment—no gun, no whip, no chair.

"You're not going into the cage like that!" gasped the owner. "My lion is the meanest, most savage beast ever brought back alive."

"I don't scare easy," yawned the girl. "I've handled bulls; I can handle a lion." With that she unlocked the door and strode unconcernedly to the center of the lion's cage. There she flung open her fur coat. Underneath it, she was wearing nothing at all!

The lion's eyes bulged, it gave a deep M-G-M roar—and leaped at her. But there was no bloodshed. The lion swabbed his great red tongue across her cheek, gently kissed her hands and feet, licked her face again—and climbed back on his stool in the corner!

The carnival owner shook his head unbelievingly, and demanded of the farm hand, "Do you think you can do better than *that?*"

"Hell, yes," boasted the farm hand. "You get that damn lion out of there and I'll show you!"

The Hillbillies . . .

Jeb Russell contributes this bit of Ozarkana:

Couple of Eastern tourists were driving along a back road in Arkansas, when their right of way was disputed by a rootin', tootin' band of mountaineers, some on horseback, others on muleback, their whiskers streaming in the wind as they urged on their mounts with bloodcurdling war whoops. The tourists noticed a native woman eying the pack without too much interest, and inquired, "Sheriff's posse, ma'am?" "Nope," she answered. "Possum hunting?" "Nup, not that neither." "Well, then, what on earth are those fellows chasing?" "It's like this, strangers," explained the woman. "Buzz Wetherby's son Lance is twenty-one years old today, and the boys is tryin' to run him down to put pants on him."

Census takers in remote sections of the Arkansas hills have special problems to cope with. One, for instance, encountered a rugged girl—not more than twenty—with four children. "May I have their ages?" he inquired. The girl knitted her brows. "Let's see if I can recall," she mused. "One's a lap child, one's a floor creeper, one's a porch child, and the oldest is a yard young one."

Jack Lait, Jr., has discovered that hillbilly records have one virtue their severest critics cannot deny. When they're worn out, you can't tell the difference.

99

Latest hillbilly story concerns the poor fellow who had to spend a night in Little Rock and saw an electric light for the first time in his life. Returned to his mountain shack, he sank into his favorite chair and told his wife, "Don't know how them city folk catch any sleep. There was a big light burning in my room right through the night." "Why didn't you blow it out?" asked the wife. "Gol dang it—I couldn't," grumbled the hillbilly. "It was in a bottle!"

A moonshiner in West Virginny felt called upon to emphasize the potency of his brew. "All I kin tell you fellers," he said, "was that yesterday I spilled a coupla drops in front of a cow that had a bell round its neck. While I was in the house eatin' lunch, a coupla mosquiters buzzed up and sampled my likker. Whin I come out, them damn mosquiters had et up the cow and was ringin' the bell for the calf!"

In Crane, Missouri, Margaret Lucas tells about a city fellow who was rash enough to buy a mule, but soon realized he didn't have the faintest notion of how to make it obey his commands. So he hired a professional mule trainer.

That worthy approached the mule with a murderous gleam in his eye and a heavy wooden board in his hand. He took a round-house swing and socked the mule's back just as hard as he could. The mule didn't even blink. The trainer whacked him again.

"Gosh a'mighty," protested the owner, "are you fixing to murder my mule?"

"It's easy to see you know nothing about these critters," said the trainer grimly. "First thing you gotta do is win their attention."

Clem Hatfield's general store in the Blue Ridge country was located halfway down a steep hill. One day the regular assemblage of old gaffers on the porch saw a cloud of dust coming down the hill, and identified it as old Zim, a moonshiner from the backwoods. "Yep," nodded the postmaster. "Bet he's after that letter I told him was waitin' fer him three or four weeks back."

To the amazement of the audience, old Zim suddenly stopped shuffling and broke into a trot. By the time he passed the store he was positively galloping down the hill. The postmaster shifted his chewing terbacky and commented disgustedly, "Lookut the old fool! Too durn lazy to hold back!"

A hillbilly bride went off gaily to the other side of the mountain with her masterful new bridegroom, but when she discovered how much he liked his moonshine she trudged all the way home again to her pappy. That worthy was sitting in front of his cabin, scratching himself and lapping up the contents of a hefty whisky jug.

"Don't stand thar blabbering, gal," he told his daughter sternly. "Drinkin' ain't the wust thing thar be. How much does your man consume a day?" The daughter thought a moment, then guessed, "I bet it comes to a full quart a day, Pappy." "Lan's sake," chuckled Pappy. "You ain't got a thing to worry about. I *spill* more than that every day!"

Oil and gas men in the South are using a new type of aluminum pipe with a simplified coupler that has reduced costs and speeded up operations amazingly. Demonstrating the pipe at key meetings is Keen Johnson, former governor of the state of Kentucky.

At one meeting, Johnson recalled to Jim Clark a day when he was still governor. A mountaineer had been convicted of a feud killing—on circumstantial evidence—and sentenced to die. Petitions and pleas from interested parties had failed to impress the governor, but a note, scrawled in pencil on a piece of old scratch paper, from the prisoner himself, won him a commutation to life imprisonment.

"Dear Guvnor," it read. "I is skeduled to be execooted on friday and heer it is wensday. Yores trooly, Joe D."

. . . and the Cowboys

Lucius Beebe, official historian of Nevada's fabulous Virginia City, and all surrounding territory, tells of two cowpokes who recently revived the code of the Old West and opened fire on the broad highway in the best Jesse James tradition. The cowpokes were not very good shots, and bystanders sought shelter hastily beneath such incongruous shelters as hot-dog stands, 1956 two-toned sedans, and a delivery wagon full of laundry. Several bullets lodged in the laundry bundles, and one local wit declared that, for the first time in laundering history, the proprietor had a legitimate excuse for the condition in which he returned his customers' shirts.

Life in Nevada, says Beebe, is like this: One ancient met another who was toting under his arm two loaves of bread and six bottles of whisky. "Land's sake, Lem," he marveled, "what in heck you gonna do with all that bread?"

In a frontier town in West Texas, a cowboy rushed out of a saloon, essayed a running broad jump, and landed kerplunk on his sit-spot in the middle of a puddle in the roadway.

"Hurt yourself?" asked a bystander languidly.

"Reckon I'll live," allowed the cowboy, dusting himself off, "but I'd sure like to get my hands on the varmint who moved my horse!"

Trouble clearly was indicated in a Wild West saloon when a rootin', tootin' cowboy got into a hassle with a foreman from a rival outfit. Suddenly guns were blazing and everybody ducked for cover—everybody, that is, but one mild-mannered galoot who calmly maintained his position at the bar, sipping his drink. When the commotion died down, the proprietor of the saloon said, "I certainly admire your nerve, young feller. You're the coolest proposition we seen around these parts in a month of Sundays." " 'Twarn't nothing," deprecated the mild-mannered one. "I knowed I was safe. I owe everybody in the place money!"

Ray Harris of Albuquerque, commenting on the wild rush to discover uranium in New Mexico and thereabouts, says one city chap he knew, never before away from asphalt pavements in his life, mooched out into the desert with a newly purchased Geiger counter. "Did he find any uranium?" Harris was asked. "Not one ounce," reported Harris, "but he found four other prospectors named Geiger."

The Desperate Daltons

It's over sixty years since the infamous Dalton gang met its Waterloo in the town plaza of Coffeyville, Kansas, but to hear the proud citizens of that bustling community tell it, the bloodshed and excitement might have happened yesterday.

Coffeyville, seventy-five miles due north of Tulsa, and about one hundred miles from Wichita, also boasts of late-resident Walter Johnson, immortal pitching ace of the Washington Senators, and of America's greatest wit, Will Rogers, born in the nearby village of Oologah in 1879. It furthermore points with pride to the high school where a raw-boned fledgling named Wendell Willkie taught briefly in 1913.

But on the day when I visited Coffeyville, conversation inevitably veered back to the liquidation of the Dalton outfit.

In light of actual records, the fearsome reputation of the Daltons is difficult to understand. Their career of crime covered less than two years, and consisted principally of a series of clumsy, singularly unimaginative train robberies, featured by wanton killings and piddling booty. Bob Dalton was the leader, with his brothers Emmett and Grat for chief accomplices. A variable retinue of desperadoes completed the roster.

The Indian territory where they operated was thinly settled by farmers and cattlemen, and casually policed, else they would have been halted much sooner.

The Daltons were related on their mother's side to the four most dreaded—and publicized—outlaws of the day, Jesse James and Cole, Bob, and Jim Younger. Lurid paperbacks and the yellow press had built these criminals up to be glamorous and romantic fellows (how different is it these days?), and it is reasonable to suppose that Bob Dalton was seeking only to carry on the noble family tradition.

The raid on Coffeyville must have struck him as the epitome of daredeviltry, for this was his home town, where everybody knew him. His own father lay buried here, and so did his brother Frank, shot down, ironically enough, fighting bandits as a U.S. deputy marshal.

On the morning of October 5, 1892, Bob, Emmett, and Grat Dalton, plus two accomplices, galloped into Coffeyville and held up two banks on opposite sides of the plaza: the First National and Condon & Co. The Daltons' flimsy disguises—prop mustaches and goatees—fooled nobody, eyewitness Henry Isham least of all.

Isham dashed into his hardware store and passed out shotguns and revolvers in jig time to everybody in sight.

There followed a furious, five-minute exchange of shots, in which four bandits were killed outright (along with four inno-

cent townsfolk), and Emmett Dalton was seriously wounded. And the loot? Though the bandits had seized over twenty thousand dollars in cash from the two banks, they dropped it when the shooting started.

Despite the confusion, when Condon & Co. balanced their books that night, there was a shortage of only twenty dollars! More remarkable still, the First National had an unaccountable surplus of $1.98!

Survivor Emmett Dalton probably would have been strung up on the spot, had it not been for the quick wit of Dr. W. H. Wells, who bandaged his wounds. "Do you think the varmint will die?" the doctor was asked.

"Hell yes," he replied. "Did you ever hear yet of a patient of mine recovering?"

As a matter of fact, Emmett lived a full forty-five years longer, fourteen years in jail and the rest in California, where he made more money talking and writing about his brief career of crime than the Dalton gang netted on all its raids put together!

To a publisher and author, at least, the moral is clear.

CHAPTER NINE

THE GOOD OLD DAYS

Two Roman gladiators startled Nero and his court with their valiant exploits. Forty to fifty competitors at a time perished under their swords. Crowds cheered their every move. In no time flat, you might say, they were the Joe DiMaggio and the Willie Mays of gladiators.

Finally officials decided to give the two boys a real test. They were scheduled to take on eighty soldiers on horseback. They had massacred the lot of them in fifteen minutes and were

THE GOOD OLD DAYS

calmly sipping Cokes when Nero himself burst into their dressing room. "Next Sunday," he gloated, "we're putting you up against a hundred hungry lions! They've been eating up all the prophets anyhow. And just so you can't plan any strategy in advance, we won't let you even see each other again until you march into the arena."

The big day dawned bright and clear. The arena was sold out. Speculators were getting fifty gold pieces a ticket. And as the two gladiators were reunited, one began, "You should have been with me Wednesday night! I'm sitting in my studio when who should come barging in but the Empress. She was alone—and had on a slinky dress and wore some intoxicating perfume." "Holy smoke!" exclaimed the other. "Go on, go on!" "I'll have to finish the story later," yawned the narrator. "Here come those silly lions!"

A couple of noble Romans decided the time had come to burn down the city, but one said, "Maybe we're too late. I hear Nero himself harbors a similar notion." "Let's hurry and beat him to it," urged the other. "I'm all for eliminating the fiddle man."

Champion optimist of the world, nominated by David Green, is the general in Caesar's army who, when forced to flee before vandal hordes, sent this report to headquarters: "According to preconceived plan, we have proceeded to a point of vantage which lay eighty miles behind us."

A lad at Harvard claims to have discovered a bit of unrecorded dialogue between Julius Caesar and his false friend, Brutus. The latter asked Caesar, "How many bagels with lox did you consume this morning, Julius, old boy?" The answer, as you may have suspected, was, "Et tu, Brutus."

Diogenes, the story goes, decided to return to earth a short time back to resume his search for a really honest man. Holding his lantern aloft, he journeyed from California to New York, and

on to England and France, but his efforts went for nought. And the worst was yet to come. He finally crossed the border of Hungary and tarried in Budapest. There he not only failed to find an honest man—but somebody stole his lantern!

One of the perils of reading a lot of books when you're an adult is that some of your most cherished childhood illusions are likely to be shattered. Gory tales of pirates and buccaneers, for instance, who buried millions of pieces of eight, made off with beautiful princesses, and forced other captives to walk the plank ——they're all malarkey, insists Patrick Pringle in a volume called *Jolly Roger* (Norton).

He's done an infinite amount of research in piratical lore, says Pringle, and has never come upon a single instance where anybody "walked the plank." Pirates were too anxious to collect ransoms or put their prisoners to work to polish them off for mere bravado.

And Captain Kidd, most celebrated pirate of them all? Strictly a phony, sneers Pringle: a small-time operator who ended on the gallows, penniless.

In fact, most pirates, after dividing spoils with their crews and paying hush money to rascally officials, didn't have enough loot left to fill a single chest. What a blow to anybody who grew up thinking *Treasure Island* was the real McCoy!

Prepare yourself for another shock. Could it be that all the stories we learned in school about the intrepid patriots who masterminded the Boston Tea Party are mostly bunk? That's what John Hyde Preston stoutly maintains in his *A Short History of the American Revolution* (recently reissued by Pocket Books).

As Preston tells it, the East India Company, faced with an enormous loss on millions of pounds of tea, won the Crown's permission to send, duty-free, three shiploads, valued at seventy-five thousand dollars, to Boston, where they proposed to sell the cargo at a far lower price than tea had ever been offered to the colonists before.

Why was the price of tea so high in Boston? A group of leading citizens, says Preston, had built up a whopping business in tea smuggled from Holland. Now, suddenly, their monopoly was threatened. The tea merchants, led by none other than the wily Samuel Adams, had to convince the other merchants that if British tea was allowed in, other goods would follow and push the local merchants right off the map.

How would they like that? Not at all, roared the merchants, and a party of the most respectable of them promptly painted and dressed themselves like Indians and dumped the British tea into the harbor.

Personally, I don't like that version at all. Preston can have all his facts; I'll go along with the legend of the Boston Tea Party I always believed. How about you?

Another memory of the American Revolution dear to us all is the famous painting of George Washington crossing the Delaware on Christmas Night, 1776, just before his victory at Trenton.

Now there comes along an old meanie named Elsie Hix who, in *Strange As It Seems* (published by Hanover House), points out that the picture was painted in Germany by an artist named Leutze who never got closer to our shores than Hamburg. Furthermore, the river he depicted was the Rhine, and every one of the soldiers a hundred-per-cent German model. And the American flag waving over Washington wasn't even in existence at the time. It was not adopted until six months later!

Yes, we pick up all sorts of stories about the great and the near great in our schoolbooks and, later, in our newspapers, radio and TV shows, and gossip columns.

It's well to bear one thing very much in mind, however: they ain't necessarily so!

Cal Whipple's *Yankee Whalers in the South Seas* is chock-full of salty anecdotes, and should sell particularly well in Philadelphia, the city of blubberly love. I particularly liked the story of the cautious whaling captain from Nantucket who became embroiled with a British skipper, and found himself challenged to a duel. The American, having the choice of weapons, decided on pistols, and proposed a dueling spot which he knew and his opponent did'not. It turned out to be the crest of a hill. After the antagonists marked off their twenty paces, they couldn't even see each other, much less shoot!

When the whaling ship *Essex* was sunk in 1820, writes Whipple, only eight members of the crew lived to tell the tale, and all of them carried for the rest of their lives the memory of having become cannibals in order to survive. Captain Pollard, one of the eight, was challenged years later by a writer who claimed relationship to a member of the *Essex* crew who had not returned. "I wonder if you remember him?" inquired the writer. "Remember him?" cackled Captain Pollard. "Hell, son, I et him!"

Peter de Vries tells a story about the time Stephen Douglas was a young man debating in the political campaigns in Illinois. There was always a lanky, raw-boned lad sitting up front, watching his every move, listening to him intently. Douglas finally asked him point-blank, "Why do you come to hear me debate so regularly?" "Because," answered the boy, "some day I hope to be up there on the platform myself."
"That's fine," Douglas enthused. "What's your name?" "Abe," said the boy. "Abe what?" persisted Douglas. And the boy answered, "Abe Feldspar."

Abe Lincoln once attended the theater in Springfield, and arrived just as the curtain rose. His eyes riveted on the stage, he thoughtlessly placed his tall silk hat on the seat next to him, open end up.

Entered a lady of very bountiful proportions, headed straight for the empty seat. She sat. There was a crunch. She jumped up.

The hat was now a black silk pancake. Mr. Lincoln picked it up ruefully. "Madam," he declared, "I could have told you my hat wouldn't fit you before you tried it on."

Even Abraham Lincoln didn't always succeed in what he was trying to accomplish, but he seldom failed to admit his occasional failures. Robert Yoder recalls that he had one story that helped a lot at such times. It concerned a farmer who was confronted with a tree stump too big to pull, too wet to burn. "I'll tell you how I got rid of it," the farmer explained, "if you won't divulge my secret. I plowed around it."

Ted Dealy, Dallas journalist, likes to memorize the last words of famous men, and these, he says, are four of his favorites:

Goethe: Let there be light!

Nathan Hale: I regret that I have but one life to give for my country.

Stonewall Jackson: Carry me over the river, boys, and let me rest under the trees.

General Custer: Where did all those blank blank Indians come from?

112

From downtown San Francisco, today's businessman looks up to the rugged eminence of Telegraph Hill, now topped by a tower given by Lilly Hitchcock Coit. In pioneer days there was a semaphore there to let merchants know that a ship from the East was in sight, and due to drop anchor in an hour's time.

A ham actor in the eighteen-fifties once spread his arms dramatically on stage and rashly spoke the line, "What does this mean?" The entire audience, well versed in the semaphore signals, bellowed as one, "Side-wheel steamer coming in!"

In the very middle of an impenetrable Appalachian forest, an explorer came upon a mighty oak with these words carved upon it: "I was the first person to travel through these wilds. Daniel Boone." Directly underneath, however, was inscribed: "That's what you think! Eleanor Roosevelt."

In the early part of the nineteenth century, English Court circles were enlivened by the wit and wardrobe of a wealthy young gadabout named George Bryan Brummell—Beau Brummell for short. His bons mots were quoted from Bath to Vienna; his waistcoats and pantaloons were of such vivid hues that only a Lucius Beebe or Alfred A. Knopf would dare to appear in modern-day counterparts.

The trouble with Beau Brummell was that he didn't know when to leave well enough alone. Tiring of wasting his devastating wisecracks on pushovers, he began to cut the then Prince of Wales (afterward George IV) down to size. This was a formidable undertaking, since the Prince weighed 240 pounds. The payoff came one day when the Prince made what he considered a most impressive entrance to Court, only to hear Beau Brummell whisper to the Prime Minister, "Who's your fat friend?" The fat friend responded with the royal equivalent of "Throw that bum out of here," and soon Beau Brummell was an exile in France, where he gambled away his inheritance and came to a very bad end indeed.

To this day, of course, Beau Brummell's name is used to denote a fashion plate. By the same token, romantic males are labeled Don Juans and Casanovas. General A. E. Burnsides' side whiskers are still called sideburns, a Vandyke is a chin decoration similar to those depicted in paintings by the Flemish artist, and a Mae West life belt is—well, rather inflated.

The word sandwich comes to us from John Montagu, fourth Earl of Sandwich; a punched theater pass is an Annie Oakley, in honor of the gal who could shoot a hole in a jack of spades from a distance of a hundred yards; and a signature is a John Hancock, the first name affixed to the Declaration of Independence.

Gat comes from Gatling gun, perfected by R. J. Gatling. John Loudon McAdam introduced the type of road surfacing known as macadam. A malapropism is a ridiculous misuse of words, the title coming from the "old weather-beaten she-dragon" in Sheridan's famous play, *The Rivals*. The saxophone derives its name from the inventor, Antoine Joseph Saxe, and people who play the instrument after midnight in apartment houses are often treated to a drink known as a Mickey Finn, also named after its inventor.

Finally, let us not forget that Napoleon bequeathed us a pastry, Lord Derby a hat, Nellie Melba a toast, Amelia Bloomer a singularly unglamorous lady's garment, William Morris a chair, Mary Tudor a "Bloody Mary," Lord Zwei a back, and Joe Miller many of the jokes "originated" by columnists today.

Unauthenticated but intriguing is the tale of a journey made by Queen Victoria by train to London from a holiday at Balmoral Castle in the Scottish Highlands. The special train that bore her, Prime Minister Disraeli, and other important members of her entourage had been delayed by a heavy storm, and the engineer had his throttle wide open in an effort to make up lost time.

Suddenly he gasped with dismay. A figure loomed up on the track ahead, shrouded in black, waving its arms frantically. Every movement was outlined by the headlight of the onrushing locomotive.

The engineer jammed on his brakes and brought the train to a grinding halt. The Queen and Mr. Disraeli were hurtled from their chairs. The terrified train crew piled out into the night.

Just fifty yards ahead, a bridge had been washed out. Few seconds more, and Queen Victoria and everyone else aboard would have been lost—an irretrievable disaster that might well have changed the history not only of England but of the entire world.

Everybody breathed a silent prayer of thanks—and then looked for the mysterious figure that had flagged the train. It had vanished completely. The crew was about to reboard the train, when, in a flash, the figure reappeared on the track ahead, again waving its arms grotesquely. And then the engineer gave a shout—and pointed.

Imprisoned in the headlight of the engine was a tiny moth. The mysterious figure was nothing more than the reflection on the snow of its frenzied death dance as it zigzagged crazily closer and closer to the consuming beam!

In one of the rambling, low-ceilinged, early-nineteenth-century houses still found in northern Westchester County, New York, I have come upon a book that must have been a godsend to young ladies bothered by the niceties of behavior in what some folks still insist were the good old days. The book is called *Hill's Manual of Social and Business Forms*, and it was published about 1870 in Chicago by Moses Warren and Company.

Was a girl unfortunate enough to lose her heart to a fellow

addicted to use of that vile weed, tobacco? This, insisted arbiter Hill, was the way to brush him off:

"Dear Sir: I am in receipt of your courteous letter containing a declaration of love and, to make a candid confession, I reciprocate your affectionate regard. But you have one habit which makes it imperative that our further correspondence should cease.

"I have reference to the use of tobacco. 1. This addiction would impoverish my home. Only ten cents a day expended for a cigar, in a lifetime of forty years, with its accumulation of interest, amounts to over four thousand dollars! 2. It might wreck my happiness. The use of tobacco deadens the sense of taste, so that the user involuntarily craves strong drink in order to taste it. 3. It would surround me with filth. I am immediately faint at the thought of dragging my skirts through the spittle of a smoker; I turn with disgust at atmosphere tainted with the stench of tobacco smoke. In any room in which vulgarity and obscenity prevail, there is always tobacco smoke in the air.

"Nevertheless, I remain, your friend and well-wisher. Marietta Wilcox."

Of course, this was long before cigarettes became popular. Chances are that Marietta Wilcox's great-granddaughter gaily smokes two full packs a day.

Poor old Pa still had something to say about his daughter's matrimonial plans in the '70's. Mr. Hill suggested that an unwanted suitor be polished off as follows:

"I am compelled to inform you that, though my daughter has treated you with much friendliness, she will be unable to continue with you a love acquaintance, owing to a prior engagement with a gentleman of worth and respectability, which contract she has no occasion to regret."

Oswald, my coat and gloves!

Ladies who visited the better hotels in the old days found signs posted in bedrooms warning them to keep their menfolk from spitting on the carpets, lying in bed with their shoes on, or driving nails into the furniture. In New England, some guests who used cuss words in the public halls were either fined, or made to accompany the proprietor and his family to church services.

One hotel owner in New Hampshire with a sense of humor added, "Lady guests must not criticize the cooking. If you don't like it, go out to the kitchen and try to do better," and, "In case of fire, please do not call the Fire Department. Our local fire fighters usually do more damage than the fire."

Teddy Roosevelt's political trade-marks were a big stick and a wide-brimmed black sombrero. He came by the sombrero, asserts Hermann Hagedorn, in *The Roosevelt Family of Sagamore Hill*, purely by accident. Just before the nominating convention of 1900, one of T.R.'s children bopped him on the side of the head with a rock. The kid went out to work on his control, and T.R. went in to apply lotions. The lump just grew and grew, however, so Teddy seized the sombrero to conceal his condition from the public. When he saw the hit that it scored, he wore a sombrero for the rest of his life!

They say that the handwriting of the late Joe Cannon, onetime Speaker of the House of Representatives, was so illegible that a fellow congressman once told him, "This letter you sent me yesterday, Uncle Joe, really takes the cake. I showed it to about fifty acquaintances, and between us we managed to figure out everything but the last four words." "Let me see it," exclaimed Uncle Joe angrily, and seized his own scrawl. After a minute's scrutiny, he hollered, "You durn fool, those last four words are 'Top Secret and Confidential!'"

Here is what I believe to be a brand-new Cal Coolidge story and, since it comes straight from Herbert Hoover, there is no question about its authenticity.

Mr. Hoover, then Secretary of Commerce, was alone with

Coolidge in the President's study at the White House one evening when a phone began ringing. There were seven or eight phones on the desk, and Cal picked up all the wrong ones first. He was reasonably exasperated by the time he happened upon the right one, explaining in an aside, "This is a direct wire from the State Department. Hasn't rung in three years." (Editor's note: Those were the days!) "No wonder I didn't recognize the sound of the bell!" Into the phone he rasped, "What on earth are you calling me for at this hour of the night?"

The caller was Secretary of State Charles Evans Hughes and he explained, "We've just had word that Queen Marie of Rumania is planning a visit to the United States and I presumed you would want to know about it." Mr. Coolidge had only one comment to make before he hung up. "Hmphh," he mused. "I hope you'll see to it that she pays her own expenses!"

The late Calvin Coolidge, retired from the presidency, became even less talkative than when he was in the White House. Skeptics doubted Henry Newsome, therefore, when he swore he had persuaded Cal to make a speech—for nothing too—at a local banquet in Vermont. "I will admit," conceded Mr. Newsome, "that when Cal first opened his mouth dust flew out."

Mr. Coolidge even refused to speak at one whistle stop when he was campaigning for President. He looked over the crowd and stamped back into his private railroad car. "This crowd," he explained succinctly, "is too big for an anecdote and too small for an oration."

Dayton, Ohio, was the scene of one of the first press interviews ever given by the late Wendell Willkie. He held it in his hotel suite, after a banquet, and still wore his dinner clothes. Nervous at the outset, he quickly regained his confidence, and when the reporters and photographers departed, Mr. Willkie was well aware that he had made an excellent impression. Although he didn't know it, there was still one reporter on the scene: John Moore, now managing editor of the Dayton *Journal-Herald*, had gotten caught behind the door when the others trooped out. That's how he happened to be on deck when Mr. Willkie clapped his open hat on his head, waltzed gaily over to the mirror, and exclaimed happily to himself, "Well, Wendell, I'll be gosh-darned!"

That proverbially crusty politico, Harold Ickes, was stopped one day on his way to an important confab at the Pentagon Building by a silly old socialite who cooed, "If it isn't dear Mr. Ickes! And how do you find yourself these brisk wintry mornings?" Dear Mr. Ickes, striving to break loose from her iron grip, barked, "I just throw back the comforter, madam, and there I am!"

In *Say It Ain't So*, Mac Davis tells the story of a small-town kid in Missouri who loved to play ball. "It's no use," he was always told. "You can't see well enough. We don't want anybody on our team who has to wear glasses." "There must be something I can do," the kid insisted. "All right," he finally was told. "Since everybody seems to like you around here, you can go out there and umpire."

So the kid went out and umpired and got himself into a lot of hot water. But he managed to get by, and most of his decisions stuck. It was good training for him. The kid was Harry Truman.

Harry Truman likes to tell about the time a visitor called on his mother just a few weeks after he had been inaugurated as President. "My, but you must be proud of your boy Harry," gushed the visitor. "Of course I am," said Mrs. Truman, "but I've got another son just as fine—right out there in that field, plowing."

Mrs. Bess Truman, back in her modest Independence, Missouri, home after all those glittering years at the White House, took the change characteristically in stride. So did her distinguished husband. Mrs. T. did experience considerable difficulty in persuading the ex-President to resume operation of the power mower. "I spent the better part of our first summer back home trying to induce Harry to get out there and use it on the lawn," says Mrs. Truman. "Finally he heeded me—at exactly eleven o'clock on a Sunday morning, with all the Methodists and Baptists in town going by our house on the way to church. When I saw Mr. Truman cutting the grass on that lawn in his shirt sleeves, I was horrified. 'Harry! Come in here this minute!' I cried. There's not a doubt in my mind he planned the whole thing deliberately to save himself from ever touching that mower again. And he hasn't."

CHAPTER TEN

GUYS AND DOLLARS

In the hope that this will be the year in which you will accumulate all those American dollars that have eluded you heretofore, the next few paragraphs will be devoted to some facts about U.S. currency. They were supplied by Miss Dorothy Steinberg, of the Treasury Department.

Our currency notes include twelve denominations, all but one of which bear portraits of a former President or Secretary of the Treasury. Before reading further, can you tell what guys adorn our various dollars? There's some excuse if you do not readily recall the ones aboard the bills for $500, $1,000, $5,000, $10,000 or $100,000, since I imagine you don't get to handle more than two or three such bank notes a week, but you should be observant enough to recall the others.

The one-dollar bill glorifies George Washington, the two-dollar bill Thomas Jefferson, the five-spot Abraham Lincoln, the tenner Alexander Hamilton. On the twenty you'll find Andrew Jackson, on the fifty Ulysses S. Grant, on the hundred—the one exception to the general rule—Benjamin Franklin.

Then, ascending in our space ship to the wide green yonder, there's William McKinley on the $500 bill, Grover Cleveland on $1,000, James Madison on $5,000, Salmon Chase (Lincoln's Secretary of the Treasury from 1861 to 1864) on $10,000, and Woodrow Wilson on $100,000. Wilson doesn't get around much these days! Seriously, the $100,000 note is not in general circulation—even in Texas. It is a gold certificate and is issued only to Federal reserve banks.

Currency notes of the present size (2.61 x 6.14 inches) were issued in July, 1929. These notes, when new, will stack 233 to one inch. They cost about one cent per note to produce and the average life of $1.00 (unless Jack Benny gets hold of it) is approximately ten months.

The old series bills (3.15 x 7.4218) are now virtually extinct, for the most part in the hands of collectors.

All U.S. coins, except those minted in Philadelphia, where the government began the coinage of money in 1793, carry a letter to identify the city of their origin (and to keep the record absolutely straight, Philadelphia used a "P" on wartime alloy nickels coined there from October, 1942, to December, 1945).

Coins minted today in Denver bear a "D," and in San Francisco, an "S." Mints no longer in operation were located in Carson City (CC), Charlotte (C), Dahlonega, Georgia (D), and New Orleans (O). Any other initials on U.S. coins represent the designer's signature.

A young assistant in whom J. P. Morgan had great faith became involved with a chorus girl and his name suddenly was being bandied about in the headlines. "I'm disappointed in you," Morgan told him bluntly. "But, Mr. Morgan," protested the young man, "it's just that I'm not a hypocrite. I haven't done a thing that most other young men as fortunately situated as myself haven't done behind closed doors!" "You may be right," admitted Morgan, "but dammit, that's what doors are for!"

Just graduated with high honors from Harvard, young Smathers sought a job in one of Boston's swankiest banking establishments. Awaiting one of the vice-presidents, Smathers idly struck up a conversation with a freckle-faced office boy in short pants. "Tell me, Buster," he inquired loftily, "do you think there's an opening in this musty institution for a sharp young college graduate?" "There certainly will be," Buster assured him, "unless they raise me to twenty bucks a week by this coming Friday."

A millionaire banker (self-made) sent his kid brother to Harvard, where his real studies were devoted to the girls in the chorus at a night club in Boston. He fell madly in love with one of them and finally proposed marriage. "You're a darling," she replied pensively, "and you must be brave when I tell you I cannot marry you. I will always be a sister to you, however." And the next day, true to her word, she married the millionaire banker.

How many of you remember Samuel Insull? His spectacular career began when he was in his teens, in England. The Thomas A. Edison Company installed telephones in London, and employed him as their first switchboard operator. For a man of Insull's ability it was just a hop, skip—and a swim from there to the presidency of the Edison Company in Chicago.

Once established in Illinois, Sam Insull built up a fantastic empire, pyramiding his holdings, and fitting great utility companies into a jigsaw puzzle even he must have found it difficult, eventually, to decipher. Before the bubble burst in 1932, the market value of Insull-controlled securities totaled four billion dollars! (The gory details can be found in Emmet Dedman's *Fabulous Chicago*.)

After the crash, the once-mighty financier found himself not only bankrupt and jobless, but a fugitive from justice as well. He turned up, in disguise, in Istanbul, Turkey; and among the star reporters rushed over to cover his extradition was Jim Kilgallen, newshawk for INS and father of panelist Dorothy.

Until Kilgallen's arrival, Insull had managed to duck the photographers, but Jim cornered him, hiding in an Istanbul fruit shop, and persuaded him to talk. Coming back to America with him on the same boat, Jim sent home some exclusive interviews that made his rivals gnash their teeth with envy.

The day before the boat landed in New York, however, Jim Kilgallen suddenly realized that he had neglected to make out his expense account—the list of payments known in every newspaper office as a "swindle sheet." He sauntered into the writing room on the top deck, sat down at his portable and started his compilation.

He had reached almost the bottom of the page, and the total was reaching interesting proportions, when he became aware of someone staring over his shoulder. It was Insull.

He read Kilgallen's list to the end, shook his head, then commented wonderingly, "And they indicted me!"

Millions of other investors and speculators had suffered the same fate as Insull by the time the depression hit rock bottom in 1932. The memories are still too painful to probe—particularly to anybody who had common stocks in his portfolio at the time—but I do like to recall the crusty old Wall Street man who was dolefully reading about the latest drop in prices when his little boy tugged on his sleeve and reminded him, "You promised to buy me a toy railroad set."

The father assured him solemnly, "If you'll wait just a few days longer, I'll give you the whole New York Central."

Those were the times when advertisements grew so scarce that great national monthly and weekly magazines shrank from the pre-depression average of 250 pages to a mere shade of themselves.

One suburbanite in Ohio who stubbornly had maintained that

the gloom was unwarranted finally admitted to his wife that things had gone to pot. "What has convinced you at last?" she asked.

"A mild gust of wind," he told her sadly, "just blew our *Saturday Evening Post* off the front porch."

That's when the Wall Street boys really were jumping—and from pretty high up, too. Financial geniuses were turned back into washroom attendants overnight. Deals were no longer worth the tablecloths they were written on. They had to invent a new kind of ticker which automatically changed from tape to rope every time the market took another dive.

Happy days came back to Wall Street, however, and the bull market roared so lustily that even some of the customers made money.

The pages of recent issues of the *Bawl Street Journal,* an annual burlesque of the dignified and impeccable *Wall Street Journal,* reflect the deep contentment of the financial community. For wily editor John Straley and his coupon-clipping staff, the goose hangs high.

Their jokes are like their own securities: uninterrupted dividend payers for many years. No companies or institutions are too mighty to escape being targets for their parody ads.

Sinclair Oil regrets, "We cannot fuel all of the people all of the time." Beekman Hospital promises, "Our doctors will keep you in stitches." The Bureau of Internal Revenue's message is simple: "Thanks, fellas!"

R. W. Pressprich & Co. "would like to get their hands on an attractive young secretary." A. M. Kidder & Co. inquire, "Looking for an active, undervalued stock? So are we!"

The Fulton Fish Market proclaims, "Our market is always strong. Smelts to high heaven." Acme Exterminators boast, "Our clients have millions." J. P. Morgan & Co. assure "Small accounts ($100,000 and up)," that they are "cordially invited."

The only bank teller they've caught defaulting in the past two

years made the fatal error of putting back too much. He was sentenced for being generous to a vault.

One stockbroker has chalked up such profits that in Las Vegas he didn't even peep when he lost $115 in a stamp machine. He just strode manfully up to his hotel bar and demanded, "One for the road, brother: an asphalt and soda."

A banker in Phoenix, Arizona, read a number of surveys, all of which indicated that women control the greater part of the nation's wealth. "Apparently," he commented, "the hands that rock the cradle also cradle the rocks."

This is the story of an opportunity that was missed. In 1905, John P. Burkhard was the publisher of a new magazine for sportsmen called *Field and Stream*. Hearing that an ex-bicycle maker named Henry Ford had turned to the production of automobiles in Detroit, Burkhard hastened to assure him that full-page ads in *Field and Stream* would attract the moneyed customers he was seeking.

"How much?" asked the cautious Mr. Ford. The price was set at $60 a page for a twenty-month contract. Mr. Ford offered in payment $1,200 worth of stock in the Ford Motor Company or a new Ford coupé which retailed at the same figure. The publisher, just as cautious as Mr. Ford, unhesitatingly took the car and turned it over to his printer for credit.

Just how many millions that $1,200 of stock in Ford Motors would be worth today is something I'll let statistically minded readers figure for themselves.

Equally fabulous is the story of General Motors stock. The corporation came into existence in 1908. Let's say you also were in existence by that time and had the foresight to have bought ten original shares at the issue price of $100 per share and held on to them through thick and thin. Today, by virtue of various exchanges and successive stock split-ups, you would own 15,141 shares with a market value of something in the neighborhood of $700,000. Furthermore, you would have received dividends and rights totaling close to $400,000 more. In other words, a $1,000 investment would have netted you well over a million dollars. Buy America!

Bernard Baruch was asked once for an opinion on the stock market. He refused to single out any one stock, but did vouchsafe two rules he observed scrupulously himself: 1. Never pay any attention to what a president of a company ever tells you about his own stock. 2. When the market's gyrations on the up side hit the front page of the New York *Times*, sell! . . . Broker Washington Dodge remembers a Japanese trader who picked the very bottom of the market in 1932, and advised his customers to go in and buy (how right he was!) in a message unique among documents of its kind: "Here is a good omen: the elevator which seemed impatiently has now hit bottom and will quickly express without its hat and coat. All traders must not miss boat, now that castor oil season is over, and beautiful flowers and bugles will be blowing heartbreak for damfool amateur bearish."

The wife of a big Wall Street trader gave their gangling, thirteen-year-old son a significant glance and told her husband, "Irving, you've been evading your duty long enough. It's high time you explained to your son the facts of life." Dreading every minute of it, Irving herded the lad into the study, cleared his throat nervously, and began, "My boy, I'm going to tell you all about the bulls and the bears."

FRANÇOIS MARIE AROUET DE VOLTAIRE HIS CLOUD

GENEVA BIBLE SOCIETY AUTREFOIS LA MAISON DE VOLTAIRE

CHAPTER ELEVEN

HEAVENS ABOVE

One of the skeptic Voltaire's pronouncements was, "In a hundred years the Bible will be a forgotten book found only in museums." When the hundred years were up, the home in which Voltaire made his prediction was occupied by the Geneva Bible Society.

Dr. Alexander, whose sermons electrify thousands in Oklahoma every week, reports that the severe water shortage in those parts has made radical changes necessary in the baptismal rites of all sects. The Baptists of Oklahoma, insists Dr. Alexander, are now using the sprinkling system. Methodists and Presbyterians use a damp cloth. And the Episcopalians and Congregationalists are just passing out rain checks.

From Dr. Otis Moore comes the story about a pastor friend of his who shifted his base of operations from Springfield, Massachusetts, to Worcester. A member of his new flock stopped the pastor's daughter one Sunday morning and inquired, "Does your father preach the same sermons here that he did in Springfield?" "Yes, he does," admitted the daughter, "but he *hollers* in different places."

Dr. Leo Green tells about an architect who promised to build a badly needed new auditorium for the church if he could be allowed to keep the construction plans a secret until the inaugural ceremonies. A record crowd turned up for the opening. The preacher, scheduled as usual to speak only until noon, was, as usual, just getting warmed up when he should have signed off.

But that's when the new plan became operative. At twelve-three sharp, a trap door opened, the preacher dropped into the basement, and the happy congregation went home to Sunday dinner.

In Glendale, California, writes ace columnist Matt Weinstock, a husky lad entered John Valentine's bookstore and purchased two leather-bound Bibles. "One of them," he explained, "is for myself, the other for a guy at our shop I'm trying to convert. Gambling is rampant there and this fellow is the ringleader." As the clerk wrapped the volumes, she remarked, "I hope you succeed in converting him." "I do too," said the purchaser. "They've laid me five to three I can't."

A little girl in Idaho had a novel excuse for not having prepared her Sunday-school lesson. "There's only one Bible in our house," she explained, "and that one is the reversed version."

Recommended to intemperate witch-hunters is A. Gayle Waldrop's story of a religious sect called the Doukhobors. Many years ago they emigrated from Russia to escape the tyranny of the czars, and found the freedom to worship as they desired in Canada. Unfortunately, however, the Doukhobors have one cherished ritual which puts them in definite conflict with the accepted Canadian way of life. They believe that, on a certain day every spring, it is appropriate that they give homage to the Lord in a state of complete nakedness.

On the chosen day this spring, accordingly, a good Doukhobor appeared in the market place of a Canadian town and proceeded to divest himself of all his clothing. An outraged constable came to arrest him, but the Doukhobor fled and, being unencumbered by clothing, soon outdistanced the pursuing arm of the law.

The constable decided he could run faster without his coat. Then, in rapid succession, he discarded his shirt, shoes, and finally his trousers. When at last he was naked as a jay bird, he managed to collar the fleeing Doukhobor.

The trouble, alas, was that when the two nude figures re-entered the market place, not a single soul could tell which was the Doukhobor and which was the constable.

The six-year-old son of a Protestant lady in Bronxville had for a steadfast playmate the little Catholic girl who lived at the end of the block. One afternoon the two children were soaked to the skin by a flash thundershower, and the boy's mother, without further ado, stripped them and propelled them into a hot tub to prevent sniffles. An hour after the little Catholic girl had been packed off to her home, the boy came to his mother and announced with vast satisfaction, "Well, at last I understand the difference between Protestants and Catholics!"

Hollywood pictures in which nuns have figured as heroines have proven popular with general audiences, but are viewed with some doubts by the nuns themselves. Sister Mary Jean Dorcy, a Dominican nun from the School of St. Peter Martyr in California, notes wryly in her book, *Shepherd's Tartan:* "Hollywood found that the ignorance most people have about convents makes for good box office, so they created nuns in celluloid. We are now expected, not only to keep our rules and promote the active good works of the Kingdom of God, but also to be as beautiful as movie stars, to be experts at boxing and baseball, to emote in the grand manner at a moment's notice, and to frolic around in jeeps!"

Does that remind you of any pictures you've seen in recent months?

A young priest was hearing confession one Saturday evening when there appeared before him an unfamiliar young girl. "I've been away in another city for the past two years," she explained, "studying acrobatics. May I show you what I learned?" "By all means," said the young priest. The girl thereupon proceeded to do a complicated series of back flips and pinwheels, ending by standing on her head. During the course of her exhibition, two older ladies of the parish entered. "Glory be!" gasped one of them. "Would yez look at what the good father is giving for penance today—and me in me old last year's bloomers!"

There was great rejoicing in church circles of a town in Arkansas when the leading reprobate and liar of the county announced that he had seen the light and desired to be baptized. They doused him in the icy waters of the creek while all the town watched and applauded. As he came up with his teeth chattering, a friend hollered, "Hey, Tom, that water cold?" "No, sir," the prodigal son cried bravely. "Better duck him again, Parson," advised the friend. "He ain't quit lyin' yet!"

A minister, trying to impress his young daughter with the necessity of silence while he was writing his Sunday sermon reminded her, "You know it's the good Lord who really tells me what to say." "If that's true," demanded the daughter, "why do you scratch so much of it out?"

Herb Shriner tells about the minister in his home town who warned his congregation that alcohol and gasoline don't mix. One skeptic insisted on finding out for himself, and reported later, "The reverend's wrong. They mix all right—but they sure taste terrible."

The pastor of a church in a small town was loved and respected by his congregation, but his salary was necessarily small, and when a prosperous congregation in a large city offered him double the fee to shift his allegiance, the localites could not possibly match the offer.

"I suppose," mourned a member of the flock to the preacher's son, "your father will accept the call to that big city."

"Dunno," admitted the boy. "Dad's on his knees in the study at this very moment praying for guidance."

"And your ma?"

"She's upstairs packing the trunks."

An orthodox Jewish lad broke the news to his mother one evening that he intended marrying little Maggie Kelly, who had lived next door all his life. Mama was shocked into silence for a moment, but soon rallied her forces. "That's fine, Morris, my boy," she declared. "Only if I were you, I wouldn't tell Papa just yet. You know he has a heart condition. And I wouldn't tell your sister Sarah. Remember how strongly she feels on religious questions. I wouldn't mention it to your brother Abe for a while either. Such a temper he's got! He might break your jaw. Me, it's all right you should tell. I'm going to commit suicide anyhow."

In the Bronx, Helen Goldblatt saw a throng lining the Grand Concourse to cheer Cardinal Spellman. Loudest of the cheerers was a little old Jewish lady holding her granddaughter aloft to catch a glimpse of the passing prelate. "It's very nice of you to get so excited over Cardinal Spellman," observed Miss Goldblatt. "Cardinal Spellman?" echoed the startled old lady. "I thought it was Mischa Elman!"

A young man graduated from an orthodox rabbinical college and came home proudly wearing his long black alpaca coat, skullcap, prayer shawl, and ringlets—all badges of his calling. His mother looked him over carefully when he entered the room, then exclaimed, "Well, Papa, look who's here: *Joe College!*"

In Chicago, Dr. Morris Fishbein, warning businessmen who never took time out to rest, reminded them of the harassed merchant who came to his rabbi and mourned, "I'm in terrible trouble. I can't support my wife and seven children, and every year there comes still another baby. What should I do?" The wise rabbi told him, "Don't do anything at all."

Lewis Browne, a famous and successful author when he died, began his career as a rabbi on the West Coast. When an envious competitor heard this, he inquired sarcastically of Browne at a dinner, "A rabbi once, eh? Were you defrocked?" "Not at all," answered Browne calmly. "I was unsuited."

Three progressive, high-powered rabbis were boasting to one another about the advanced views of their respective congregations.

"We're so modern," asserted the first, "we've installed ash trays in every pew so members can smoke while they meditate."

"Pah," minimized the second, "that's nothing. We now have a snack bar in the basement that serves ham sandwiches after services."

"You boys," advised the third, "aren't even in the same class with *my* congregation. We're so reformed we close for the Jewish holidays!"

A Protestant minister entered the Pearly Gates when his appointed time arrived, and was presented with a spanking new Chevrolet by St. Peter. He went tootling all over heaven in it very contentedly, though he was a bit put out to observe Father Flanagan, his old neighbor from the Catholic church, whizzing by in a new-model Buick convertible. When Rabbi Goldstein, however, drove up in a sleek Cadillac limousine, with a liveried chauffeur and footman, the Protestant was so annoyed he marched back to St. Peter to register his protest. "This is rank favoritism," he pointed out. "Why should I get just a Chevvie and Rabbi Goldstein that snazzy Cadillac?" "S-s-sh," whispered St. Peter. "You don't seem to understand. He's related to the boss!"

The minister of a small town was awakened in the dead of night by a suspicious noise. Out of the darkness came a voice: "One move, and you're a dead man. I'm hunting for your money." "Let me get up and turn on the light," begged the minister, "and I'll hunt with you."

In a little flat in London one Christmas Eve, writes Edmond

Segrave, not a single gift had been purchased for the bright lad
of the house. It was not that his parents didn't love him—they
just didn't have a penny to spare.

"He's always loved to read," recalled the unhappy father,
clutching at straws. "I know a grumpy old publisher who always
entertains his authors and staff in high style the day before
Christmas. Maybe he'll be in good enough humor to give me a
damaged book or something from his overstock." The father's
hunch paid off. "Help yourself in the shipping room," said the
publisher indulgently.

And so on Christmas morning there was no pile of toys to
confuse the boy—just one small package. But his eyes shone
with joy when he opened it, and the parents shared in the glow.

A few days later, the publisher received a note from the boy.
"Thank you," it read, "for the magic carpet, the elixir of life,
and the beautiful golden key."

"What's all this folderol?" grumbled the publisher. "I just gave
the fool boy a book!"

A tragic moment in the life of a fading Broadway star comes when he finally must face the fact that the parade has passed him by.

No longer is he offered the choice of a half dozen fat parts at the start of the season. Stony-eyed autograph hounds gaze blankly into his face. Columnists have forgotten even how he spells his name. If he has neglected to save for this very rainy day while the cash was pouring in, the awakening is doubly painful.

One such disillusioned Thespian, recalls Eddie Cantor, had fallen so far from glory that he didn't know where his next month's rent was coming from and, with the Christmas season approaching, gratefully accepted the one job that was offered to him, playing Santa Claus in a big department store. He donned the traditional costume and whiskers and, with a brave attempt at joviality but a sinking heart, climbed to his seat in the toy department.

A long line of children was waiting to be dandled on his knee and to whisper lists of all the presents they craved. One little boy was so much gayer and more charming than the rest that the actor felt a sudden surge of warmth in his heart. "I'd like to have a look at your mommy," he told the boy. "Here she comes for me now," was the reply.

The actor looked up and caught his breath—he was gazing straight into the eyes of the glamorous woman who once had been his leading lady. More, she had once been his wife; but their marriage had failed years before, and he had read that she married a respected and prosperous businessman.

Fortunately she did not appear to penetrate his disguise. "You have a fine boy here," he said, summoning all his courage to keep his voice from breaking. "He wants a space suit, a rocket ship, and an autographed picture of Captain Video."

The lady winked gravely at Santa and said, "I know you'll get them for him, won't you?" "But, Mommy," interrupted the boy, "how will Santa Claus find me? Give him our address!"

The mother indulgently went to a nearby desk to fill out a

card, which she placed in an envelope and left in Santa's hands. He sighed with relief when she disappeared down the corridor. Then he opened the envelope.

The card read, "Merry Christmas to the greatest actor I ever knew." Clipped to it was a check for one thousand dollars.

CHAPTER TWELVE

THE HIGH AND THE FLIGHTY

Cleveland Amory's sparkling *The Last Resorts*, a book about the decline and fall of onetime society strongholds, such as Newport, Bar Harbor, Saratoga and Palm Beach, is a hilarious saga to such as you and me, but to surviving members of the snobbish and outrageously spoiled plutocracy who once held sway there it is nothing short of a dirge.

One old dragon who read it threatened to sue Amory for attributing a statement to her which she swears she never uttered. "Better keep your mouth shut," counseled a friend. "It's the only clever thing I've heard you say in thirty years."

Amory attributes the decay of the once-glittering resorts to an offshoot of Gresham's inexorable law: bad millionaires drive good millionaires out of circulation.

The phonies, the nouveaux riches, and the show-offs move in; the dignified old parties flee for their lives. "These newcomers," mourned one die-hard, "have marked the '400' down to $3.98." Taxes and the scarcity of servants have taken their toll, too, of the show places that once cluttered the landscape at spas and beaches.

"Today we're living on capital," mourned one blue blood, "and that's that. I can't even remember when I wore a white tie last!"

And, oh, how morals have changed in the once-hidebound domains of Old Society! In the days of Edith Wharton's *The Age of Innocence,* the "right people" looked askance at a divorcée. Today, one generally accepted man and wife boast eleven ex-spouses between them!

A Mrs. Messmore at East Hampton sighs for the days "when it was considered fast to play net at tennis."

Another dowager recalls a time when society debutantes would hesitate to show their insteps. "Today," she adds grimly, "they usually show their step-ins!"

Newport, Rhode Island, once was the summer home of Edgar Allan Poe, Bret Harte, Oliver Wendell Holmes, Henry Wadsworth Longfellow, Henry James, and Julia Ward Howe, but when the millionaires started building their now-obsolete hundred-room "cottages," the literary set folded their tents and stole

silently away. The society folk remained dimly aware that a few of them were still lurking around, however. Mrs. William Astor, queen bee of the colony, announced one day that she was planning a really "Bohemian" party. "How daring," exclaimed the late Lady Mendl. "What extras are you inviting?" Mrs. Astor pondered a moment, then answered, "J. P. Morgan and Edith Wharton."

The pampered rich don't feel quite so defenseless when they're surrounded by other unfortunates like themselves. One heiress from Toledo, for instance, took up residence for the season in Paris, but it failed to meet her expectations. An indefinable something was missing. Suddenly she discovered what it was.

"Paris is wonderful at last," she confided in a letter home. "You have no idea how many people from Toledo have suddenly begun passing through!"

The headwaiter at one of Chicago's nobbiest hotels still

trembles when he recalls the evening four unmistakable V.I.P.'s
—Dorothy Thompson, Vincent Sheean, and Mr. and Mrs.
Henry Luce—popped up at the height of the dinner rush.

There was no table free and the foursome milled about, somewhat miffed, in the lobby for some minutes. A friend of the
management spotted them, and pulled anxiously at the headwaiter's sleeve. "Do you know who those people *are?*" he
whispered hoarsely. "I do indeed," said the headwaiter. "I have
been told four times, sir."

The dry cleaner had promised to return Mr. Backer's trousers
in time for the Harriman ball, but at 6 P.M. of the evening in
question they were nowhere in evidence. Mrs. Backer got the
cleaner on the phone and threatened, "If those pants aren't here
in fifteen minutes, I'm going to sue you for promise of breeches!"

In *My Philadelphia Father,* socialite Cordelia Biddle tells how
Colonel Anthony Biddle once decided to become a concert

singer and hired the famous Philadelphia Academy of Music for his debut. The audience consisted almost entirely of Biddles and Biddle employees, but, even so, they soon remembered urgent engagements elsewhere. Biddle was so outraged he jumped on a train for Florida. When he returned home he was accompanied by a dozen live alligators. In the middle of a blizzard, he burst into the office of a strange doctor, bellowing, "Damn it, I've been bitten by an alligator." The doctor looked out at the snow and said soothingly, "Just sit down there till you get hold of yourself."

Colonel Biddle and his family were immortalized by King Edward VII of England. "In Philadelphia, when I was the Prince of Wales," His Majesty recalled one day, "I met a large and interesting family named Scrapple. They served me a rather delicious native food, too—something, I believe, called biddle."

A Boston society matron who didn't know what she was up against once tried to persuade the late W. C. Fields to speak at a garden-club-federation banquet. "Surely you believe in clubs for women," she exclaimed. "I most certainly do, madam," Fields assured her with immense dignity, "but only if every other form of persuasion fails."

The hopelessly spoiled son of a multimillionaire suddenly discovered that money couldn't buy everything. The girl he adored flatly refused to marry him. Disconsolate, he climbed into his imported eighteen-cylinder automobile, and ordered the chauffeur, "Drive off a bridge. I'm committing suicide."

A new maid turned up at the Vanderbricks to help at a big dance. "From seven to eight," Mrs. Vanderbrick instructed her, "you are to stand at the ballroom entrance and call the guests' names as they arrive."

"What jolly fun that will be," enthused the maid. "I know a couple of beauts!"

Two gardeners met at the village seed-and-implement depot. "I hear you're up at Golden Acres this year, working for that banker fellow Rockerbilt," said one by way of greeting. "Me working for Rockerbilt? You've got it all wrong," the other assured him. "Rockerbilt gets up at six-thirty every morning to get aboard an overcrowded, rickety train to commute to the hot city so he can keep up his estate and pay us all our weekly wages. *Rockerbilt is working for me!*"

John Gunther, whose *Inside Africa* is the sixth of an amazingly successful series, was weekending recently at a luxurious Long Island estate. The Japanese butler, Mitzumo, was an especial admirer of Mr. Gunther's talents. On Sunday morning a neighbor, coming to pay his respects, asked, "Is John Gunther available?" Mitzumo giggled and reported, "No, Mr. Inside out!"

Servant problems are pressing, the country over, but Las Vegas housewives (sure, there are some!) have something extra to contend with. One of them told a new cook to dice some beets for dinner. Two hours later the cook reported, "Ma'am, cutting up them beets was no trouble at all, but putting all those black dots on them is plumb driving me crazy."

A resident of the fashionable Nob Hill section of San Francisco hired an affable new Chinese houseboy, but found his name too difficult for everyday use. "I can't go around calling you 'Fu Yu Ling Tsein Mei' all the time," she exclaimed petulantly, "so I'll just label you Russell, if you don't mind." "O.K., lady," beamed the Chinese lad, "but please to tell me your name again." "I," said the lady loftily, "am Mrs. Eustace Tewksbury Foppingham." "You're too damlong too," decided the lad. "I just call you Charlie."

Mrs. Commins summoned her new chambermaid and told her angrily, "I was able to write your name this morning in the dust on the mantelpiece." "Yes," agreed the maid, "and you're not half as smart as you think. You spelled it wrong."

Gone for good in Hollywood is the ostentatious gambling for excessive stakes. They still tell of one maid who never had worked for picture folk before, and was initiated on an evening when one of the most fabulous of the oldtime stars was hosting a wild and woolly all-night poker game.

Her eyes popped when one player threw a red chip in the middle and announced, "I open for one hundred dollars." She dropped the tray with a crash when another tossed in a blue chip and said, "I raise you five hundred dollars." But the climax came when a third player produced a single yellow chip and declared, "Let's make it one thousand dollars and keep out the pikers."

When the last guest had gone, the maid tiptoed into the game room, stole all the chips, and took the next train back to Elmira.

The old plutocrat, his wheel chair pulled up to the window of his Fifth Avenue mansion, smacked his lips as a lovely young nursemaid wheeled her charge toward the park entrance. "Quick, Tague," he cried to his butler. "Bring my teeth! I want to whistle."

The directors of an exclusive Fifth Avenue Club were discussing an unfortunate occurrence involving two prominent members. It seems member Number One had returned home unexpectedly, and finding his wife in the arms of member Number Two, had tattooed the latter's anatomy with a load of buckshot. "What awful publicity for the club!" groaned the secretary. "Can you think of anything worse?" "I certainly can," admitted the president. "Had he come home just an hour earlier, he'd have shot *me!*"

"I thought I was drowning for sure," droned Smithers, the club bore. "I was going down for the third time, mind you, and suddenly my whole life passed before my eyes. In sharp, clearly delineated pictures, it all came back to me."

"Hmphh," snorted Old Man Perkins from the depth of his leather chair. "I don't suppose one of those sharp pictures was one of me lending you that ten spot back in the fall of 1932?"

An eagle-eyed underling at *Tide* magazine spotted this catastrophic typographical error in the rules book of a very doggy women's club: "Officers must limit all announcements to three minutes. If they exceed their time, the president should use her navel to silence them." Muses the *Tide* man: "We hope Madame President has the stomach for that sort of thing."

A press agent for the Copacabana night club insists that a lady accosted another in the powder room, inquiring, "Haven't we met in Cannes?" "Which one?" said the other. "This one— or the one at the Colony?"

After a troupe of Spanish dancers had completed their act at the Shamrock Hotel's night club in Houston, a Texas oilman from the wide-open wells tapped the star on the shoulder and told her, "I shore liked them castanets, ma'am. My wife and I was wondering if you could show us how you wind them up."

Those dresses Marlene Dietrich wore in her personal-appearance junket at Las Vegas weren't as revealing as the papers would have had you believe. Marlene had them lined with flesh-colored silk, with necklaces and bracelets cleverly concealing the materials' ends. She had three gowns, all the same model, but different colors. "I told them: 'Put nothing on top,'" laughed Miss Dietrich. "Always when I appeared on a stage, people looked down at my legs. I got tired of seeing only the tops of people's heads, so this time I tell my designers I want people to look up. So they designed this dress. People looked up all right!" Each dress set Miss Dietrich back $3,000—but, since her weekly stipend was just ten times that amount, she took the bill in stride. She also admits she lost, gambling. "I was at those slot machines every spare moment," she told me, "and I lost constantly." "How much in all?" I asked. "A lot," said Marlene. "Fifteen dollars!"

This may help explain why Marlene Dietrich is not only America's sexiest grandmother—but also its richest.

A famous dive near the Loop in Chicago was raided by the police, and such guests and entertainers who hadn't effected their escape via the windows were hustled into the patrol wagon. Miss Veronica Vere de Vere pushed everybody aside in her obvious desire to be first into the wagon. "What's the rush?" asked a cop. "I know what I'm doing," replied Miss Vere de Vere. "The last four raids I had to stand!"

Two of the moving spirits at a convention banquet drank so many toasts that finally they scarcely could move at all. "Lucky for me," one congratulated himself. "When I'm in this condition, I let somebody take me home and then I fall sound asleep the minute I hit the old bed."

"My trouble," confessed the other, "is hitting the old bed."

Two stories about intoxicants that seldom miss:

1. An intrepid explorer set out singlehanded for the Amazonian jungle in Brazil. Authorities equipped him with all the necessary gear, topped off with a miniature bottle of gin, another of vermouth, and a tiny mixer.

"What's this for?" asked the explorer. "You know I don't drink."

"That's in case you're hopelessly lost, without another human around for miles," was the answer. "Mix yourself a martini. Somebody's absolutely certain to pop up and tell you, 'Don't make it *that* way: make it *this* way.'"

2. A gent stepped up to a bar and asked for a martini compounded of twenty-four parts gin, one part vermouth. The bar-

tender, startled but game, said, "Yes, sir. Like a slice of lemon peel twisted in it?"

The gent grumbled, "If I want a lemonade, I'll ask for it."

Don Haggerty watched firemen extinguish a blaze in a Forty-fourth Street boardinghouse, and carry to safety the intoxicated gent in whose room the fire had originated. "Confound it," roared the chief, "haven't you got sense enough not to smoke in bed when you're in this condition?" The drunk protested mournfully, "Honest, Chief, I didn't set fire to that bed. It was burning already when I got into it!"

In his invaluable new treatise, *Never Say Diet*, Corey Ford claims that the following elbow exercise is bound to produce results: "Stand in vertical position, with elbows braced on edge of mahogany bar and right foot resting firmly on rail eight or ten inches above floor. Grasp glass in right hand and bend slowly until rim of glass touches lips. Lower elbow, refill glass, and repeat routine until chin is level with bar. Once proficiency has been attained, this exercise can even be continued in a horizontal position."

Fellow a little the worse for wear—and gin—stumbled into a taxi and ordered, "Take me over to Broadway and Forty-ninth Street." The driver informed him, "You're at Broadway and Forty-ninth Street right now." "Splendid," was the response. "Jush splendid. But next time, don't drive so fast!"

Fenwick suddenly planted his nineteenth highball on the bar, reeled dizzily across the saloon, and collapsed unconscious in a heap at the door. "That's the best thing about good old Fenwick's drinking," chirped a crony in admiration. "He always knows when to stop."

Far off in Switzerland, the touring proprietor of a bar and grill and an experienced guide were climbing up the Matterhorn, when they were caught in a snow slide. Ultimately a Saint Bernard dog toiled through to them, a keg of brandy tied under his chin. "Hurrah," cried the guide. "Here comes man's best friend."

"Yep," agreed the barman, "and look at the size of the dog that's bringing it!"

In an obscure gin parlor on Third Avenue, two gentlemen who were several sheets to the wind discovered, not only that both were Yale graduates, but were members of the same class. After many tearful embraces, and just before they both passed out cold, they swore to meet at this same bar, come hell or high water, ten years later to the day.

The first of them actually kept the date. He entered the gin parlor sheepishly, not believing there was one chance in a million the other would remember. But by all that was holy, there was Yale man Number Two propped up at the bar on the very stool he had occupied ten years before!

"What do you know!" marveled Number One. "I never dreamed you'd even be able to find this joint after ten long years!"

Number Two turned a bleary eye on him and growled, "Who left?"

150

A Wall Street broker encountered an old classmate who had fallen on evil days. Automatically he reached into his wallet and handed the down-and-outer a five-dollar bill. "What's this?" sneered the ungrateful recipient. "Two years ago you met me and gave me fifty bucks. Last year you retrenched to twenty. And now you hand me a measly five spot."

The trader, embarrassed, explained, "Two years ago I got married. Last year we had our first child. All those extra expenses and mouths to feed . . ."

"So that's it," roared the down-and-outer. "Raising a family on my dough, eh?"

"Has anybody ever offered you dinner in exchange for a respectable lick of work?" asked a Peoria lady as she regarded the seedy-looking tramp at her back door with obvious disapproval.

"Only once, ma'am," said the tramp hopefully. "Aside from that I've been shown nothing but kindness."

A wandering hobo had discovered through the years that doctors were comparatively soft touches, and his spirits rose when he saw a medico's shingle outside the door he was approaching. A beautiful young lady answered his peal on the bell. The hobo, looking as woebegone as possible, wheezed, "Do you think the good doctor could find an old pair of pants for an old fellow who's down on his luck?" The girl chuckled and replied, "Quite possibly, but I doubt that they'd do you much good. You see, I happen to be the doctor."

CHAPTER THIRTEEN

IT'S A BIG COUNTRY!

The Capital

At the height of the social season in the nation's capital, Senator Theodore Green of Rhode Island, a bachelor still at eighty-six, seemed a bit confused by it all. Over cocktails at a foreign embassy, a writer asked him how many parties he was attending that evening.

"Six," confessed the senator, and pulled out his pocket diary. "Trying to figure out where you're going next?" joshed the writer. "Not at all," replied the senator. "I'm trying to figure out where I am now!"

Another senator was buttonholed by Detroit industrialist Harvey Campbell, who demanded, "Look! I have the face of Claudette Colbert, the torso of Marilyn Monroe, and the legs of Betty Grable. Who am I?" "What do I care who you are?" cried the senator. "Kiss me!"

A passel of kids from one of those mammoth new city-housing projects was taken for a tour of Washington as an Easter-vacation treat. At Mount Vernon the guide announced, "This is where the father of our country made his home."

One youngster wasn't content with any such loose generalities. "On which floor," he demanded, "was his apartment?"

Secretary of Agriculture Ezra Benson found a small boy wandering disconsolately about the lobby one day, awaiting his father, who had business to transact with a minor executive in the Department. Benson told the lad, "If you've nothing to do for a while, why not go up that flight of stairs and have a look at the forty-foot mural on the next floor? I think you'll find it interesting."

The youngster bounded up the stairs three at a time, but a few moments later Secretary Benson's assistant came in, wondering, "Who could have sent an eight-year-old kid upstairs a few minutes ago to look for a forty-foot mule?"

Paul Pearlman, Washington's perennial handball champion, has a real tale of woe to unfold. It seems he followed a figure in a slinky black gown for ten blocks before he found out it was a Supreme Court justice.

153

Overworked girls in the Pentagon Building are circulating chain letters of their own:

"Fellow slaves! This is a plan to bring happiness and steak dinners to tired government working girls. It won't cost you a nickel. Simply send five copies of this letter to girls as underprivileged and neglected as yourself. Then tie up your boss and send him to the girl on the top of the list. When *your* name reaches the top, you will receive 12,938 bosses.

"Have faith! Don't break the chain! The last girl who did got her own boss back!"

New England

In his slightly biased *History of New England*, Will Cressy points out:

"New England consists of six states and Boston, which is frequently in an awful state."

"They do not 'till' the soil in New England. They blast it. The crops are planted in among the rocks with a beanshooter or a gun. They harvest them with search warrants."

"The Down-East Yankee has a keen gift of humor, because it is a gift."

"Statisticians have figured that, judging from the amount of furniture brought over in the *Mayflower*, the boat was slightly more than three miles long."

To which the late Fred Allen added, "Many typical New England seashore resorts are so dead, that the tide went out one day some years ago and never came back."

A poet on the *Old Farmers' Almanac* staff has a low opinion of Maine weather, if you can judge by the following:

> *Dirty days has September,*
> *April, June, and November.*
> *From January up to May*
> *It's pretty sure to rain each day.*
> *All the rest have thirty-one*
> *Without much chance of any sun*
> *And if one of them had two and thirty,*
> *They'd be just as wet and twice as dirty.*

In the old days of enormous country houses, there was one monster of a place in Lenox, Massachusetts, called "Shadowbrook." To show you how big it was, there's the story of the owner's son wiring from Yale, "Arriving this evening with crowd of seventy-six classmates." The owner wired back, "Sorry, but many guests already are here. Have room only for fifty."

It wasn't a very large motel and the smartest thing about it, apparently, was the live-wire bellboy. "What part of the country do you hail from?" asked an approving visitor. "Cape Cod, sir," said the bellboy. "I just knowed you was one of those shrewd Down-Easters," chuckled the visitor. "Only thing that surprises me is that you don't own the motel by this time." "There's one thing stopping me," explained the bellboy glumly. "The owner—he's from Cape Cod too."

Boston society folk, especially those living on or adjacent to Louisburg Square, dwell in a world of their own.

One old blue blood, for instance, eighty-five if she was a day, insisted on swimming at Bar Harbor far into September, though the ocean water by that time was absolutely freezing. Her friend saw her bobbing about in the surf one day when a big seal splashed right by her. When she finished her swim she was neither frightened nor even titillated by the unusual experience

—just very, very angry. "That Mr. Abernathy," she grumbled, "gets ruder every day. He swam right by me and never even said 'good morning.'"

Ted Weeks, editor of the *Atlantic Monthly* and authority on all matters pertaining to Boston, swears this happened. Two old Brahmins from Louisburg Square were dining in the Harvard Club and discussing the career of an old classmate who had defied tradition and gone down to Washington to assume a post in the Cabinet. "They say Bob is doing quite well," allowed the first Bostonian. "Making quite a reputation for himself." "I suppose he is," conceded the other grudgingly, "but purely in the national sense."

"Harvard graduates," observed Clip Amory, "are a conservative lot. Twenty years after a Harvard man has left the campus, you can tell by his suit he's from Cambridge." "Sure," agreed a Yale alumnus nearby, "because it's the same suit."

A group of hidebound old blue bloods in Boston were invited to a formal garden party one day this summer, and were startled to discover that the host, who had acquired a New Hampshire wild-animal farm without their being told about it (a sin in itself), had brought a few beasties down with him to help entertain his guests. One of the beasties, for instance, was a baby elephant! John Marquand relates that the most conservative and dignified of the guests so far forgot himself as to essay a playful slap on the elephant's rump. Unfortunately he was not familiar with the toughness of an elephant's epidermis. Result: several broken blood vessels in his right hand. He had to wear his arm in a sling for weeks.

The South

Lewis Gannett, distinguished book reviewer for the New York *Herald Tribune* put down with a sigh the sixth long novel about the Civil War he had read in two weeks. "The old question of who really won the War between the States has been settled at last," he said. "Clearly, it was the National Association of Book Publishers!"

Nobel Prize-winning novelist William Faulkner, however, enters this demur from an unreconstructed rebel in Mississippi: "Confound it, suh, if the South had had that atom bomb, we'd have cleaned out them damyankees in two weeks flat!"

The late Joe Palmer told about a newly elected senator from Tennessee who was making his way through Kentucky at a time when horseback was the only mode of travel in those parts. He tarried for the night at a stately plantation near Harrodsburg, where he was offered some delicious home-brewed bourbon, served neat in a water glass.

The Tennessean inquired tactfully if his host was acquainted with a delicious concoction called a julep, and learning with surprise that it was unknown in that part of Kentucky, dispatched flunkies forthwith to pick some mint from the banks of a neighboring stream. He thereupon made some of the darndest juleps in the history of choice beverages.

This was in April. The senator came back that way again in October, but though the servants greeted him ecstatically, the master of the house failed to put in an appearance. "No, suh, he ain't here no mo'," reported the head servant mournfully. "He took to his bed right after yo' teached him to put grass in his whisky and jus' plain drunk hisself to death."

Marion Montgomery passes along a story about the old family retainer of the president of a small college down South. The prexy's wife discovered that a cherished friend was moving into the neighborhood and asked the family retainer to go over and help her get moved in properly.

The retainer, her mission accomplished, returned to announce emphatically, "I ain't nevah goin' there no more. Dem folks just ain't quality. Dat friend of yours eben washes her own windows."

"But, Lucy," protested the prexy's wife, "you've seen me wash my windows too."

"Yes'm," admitted the retainer, "but dat woman knows *how*."

Reports an English visitor to Charleston, South Carolina: "On my way to the hotel, I decided to pick up a couple of American shirts, so I told my taxi driver to stop at the first haberdashery he encountered. 'Yes, sir,' said the driver, but when we were stopped by a red light, inquired, 'What was that you said, boss?' 'A haberdashery,' I repeated. 'Yes, sir,' he agreed again, 'a haberdashery it is.' We rattled along a couple of blocks and then he stopped once more. 'Listen, boss,' he assured me. 'With me there's no use beating round the bush. What is it you want? Liquor—or women?' "

In Red Springs, North Carolina, Flora Perry, librarian of the exclusive Flora McDonald College for the cream of Southern womanhood, noticed that an old Negro in the beautiful gardens always was on the job a full hour before any of his fellows. It was no urge to better his position in life, he hastened to explain to Miss Perry. "No, *ma'am*," he continued. "I just likes to breathe air early before other folks have a chance to be sniffin' off'n it."

Pastor Johnson preached long and earnestly about Jonah and the whale at an old colored Baptist church in Mississippi but made little impression on Sister Abernethy. On her way home, she scoffed, "What's so wonderful 'bout dat Jonah spendin' three days in de stummick of a whale? Mah husban' spent longer dan dat in de stummick of an alligator." "Sure 'nough?" asked an incredulous stranger in town. "How long would you say?" Sister Abernethy did some hasty calculating, then announced, "It's goin' on three years now."

The late Lyle Saxon was slaving over a manuscript on the

plantation of a friend outside Baton Rouge one day when the old mammy who kept his quarters in order inquired, "How come, Mr. Saxon, you spend all yo' workin' hours peckin' away at dat typewriter 'stead of bein' out huntin' and golfin' wid yo' friends?" "Because I'm an author, Mammy," explained Saxon. "Writing books is my business. This is my fifth I'm working on now. Right here on the shelf are the other four I've written."

Mammy's face was a picture of commiseration. "You poor soul," she clucked. "You never sold a one of dem, did you?"

Carl Carmer tells about a great big husky farm hand on an Alabama plantation who had a fantastic reputation with every lady within a radius of thirty miles. One day his boss said, "Mose, I'd like for you to visit my friend Colonel Parker's place over in Louisiana. He's got seventy-three gals working for him and nary one man, and I told him you'd be just the man to remedy a situation like that." "Just how far from here," inquired Mose, "is that place of Colonel Parker's?" "Two hundred and forty-two miles," said the boss. "Anything you say," declared Mose dubiously, "but that's a mighty big distance to travel for just one day's work!"

Colonel Worthington appeared on the veranda of his Alabama mansion and announced emphatically, "There are two things, suh, we don't stand for in the sovereign state of Alabama. One is sectional prejudices and the other is damn Yankees."

Miss Jeannie-Mae Beaufort, belle of a Mississippi town, was walking to the beauty shop when she became aware that she was being followed. For a time she pretended not to notice, but finally, becoming really perturbed, she wheeled to face the offender. To her surprise, it was gallant old Colonel Trombley, the town's only authentic military hero.

The colonel was in no way flustered. "Good morning to you, Miss Jeannie-Mae," he said with a flourish of his fedora. "I've been having a debate with myself for six blocks: whether to catch up with you and enjoy the repartee, or linger behind and enjoy the view."

A Northerner insulted a South Carolina bartender by asking anxiously, "Are you quite sure you know how to mix a very dry martini?" The bartender gave him a withering look and drawled, "Mister, ah been mixin' martinis heah fo' nine yeahs—an' in that time ah've used exactly two bottles of vermouth!"

Time was when only millionaires sneaked off to Florida and California when the snow began to fly. Today everybody's doing it. They tell of a meeting, for instance, that took place on the sands of Miami Beach between the wives of two rival cutters in the cloak-and-suit industry. "I'm here for the whole winter," boasted one. "Four months solid! And you?" "Five weeks, I'm afraid," was the answer, "is all I can manage this year." "Tsk! Tsk!" clucked the first with mock sympathy. "So your husband isn't working again?"

In Miami Beach, the aging author of a half dozen inspirational novels turned up with a ravishing if gaboring miss in tow, explaining she was his "niece." The niece walked out on him three days later, disillusioned with the literary life. "Not only did he lie to me about the size of his yacht," she complained to newsman Jack Kofoed, "but he made me do the rowing."

A successful young lady designer of men's sportswear, vacationing at Daytona Beach, was delighted to see a stalwart youth approach, sporting a pair of print bathing trunks she had originated. Becoming conscious of her stare, he flushed slightly, and asked, "Have we met somewhere?" "I never saw you in my life," chuckled the young lady. "I just have designs on you."

The Florida real-estate boom in the twenties provided shoestring operators and gold brickers a field day the like of which they've never enjoyed since. At its height—just before the boom

THE LIFE OF THE PARTY

was lowered—any subdivision that cost less than five million (all on paper) was regarded as smalltime stuff.

Kenneth Roberts tells of one impressive group who engaged a sign painter to erect a billboard proclaiming, "A five-million-dollar hotel and golf course will be erected on this spot." Unfortunately, the impressive group couldn't raise the eighteen dollars to pay for the sign, so the painter carted it away and sold it to another bunch of capitalists on the next beach.

"How much," asked Mr. Lapidus, "is that new hotel at Miami Beach?"

"I'll tell you, Joe, how to estimate your bill," advised a friend who had just flown back to New York. "Guess the highest you can imagine—then add 25 per cent! I myself pulled a boner when I asked for a forty-dollar suite. They handed me a Hershey Bar.

"There's a seven-piece orchestra in the men's room! That was too much even for a big spender like Jack Benny. He said a pianist and violinist would be plenty.

"The barbershop looks so elegant, I didn't dare go in until I had shaved in my room. All the signs are in French. Nobody understands what they mean, but it adds class. And in every room they have wall-to-wall carpeting!"

"So what," interrupted Lapidus. "New York hotels have that too."

His friend demanded, *"On the ceilings?"*

Comes the end of summer and residents along the Atlantic seaboard start watching anxiously for hurricane warnings, ready to batten down all hatches if the big winds begin to blow. In early fall the hurricanes—furious winds swirling counterclockwise over a diameter of fifty to three hundred miles—sweep up from the West Indies. Most of them spend their force harmlessly at sea, but occasionally they are diverted over Florida and up through New England.

That spells trouble—and plenty of it. A 1938 hurricane, for

instance, left about five hundred deaths and a quarter of a billion dollars' worth of damage in its wake.

One "native son" in Florida refused to be discouraged when a hurricane carried his whole house away. He rebuilt on the old foundations, maintaining stoutly, "This is the world's greatest spot—especially when it's standing still."

They have "big blows" in Oklahoma too. Legend has it that one "twister" blew a farmer off his buckboard, and pinned him flatter than a pancake to the side of the barn. Relatives scraped him off, but while they were carting him into the house, another gust blew him out of the wheelbarrow and back into natural shape.

Why do vicious hurricanes bear lovely girls' names, with no Tom, Dick, or Harry having the ghost of a chance to get into the act? It all started in 1941, when a University of California professor named George Stewart wrote a rousing novel called *Storm*. An immediate best seller and still widely read in a reprint edition, *Storm* tells how a minuscule weather disturbance off the coast of Japan could develop into a raging torrent by the time it swept across the U.S.

A junior meteorologist in Stewart's novel called the particular storm he was tracing after a girl he knew: "Maria." U. S. Weather Bureau operatives followed suit. So did military personnel in World War II. The practice was made official in 1953. Now the names of hurricanes are solemnly chosen at the beginning of each year by the big brass. It was hurricanes "Carol" and "Edna" that caused such devastation in the late summer of 1954.

Most of the public approves of designating hurricanes by girls' names, though malcontents still clamor for other systems, such as numbers (1,2,3), letters (A,B,C), animals (Antelope, Bear, Coyote), and Lord knows what else.

Movie star Zsa Zsa Gabor (or her press agent) also demurred at the selection of "Zelda" for the tag end of a recent line-up. "Zelda indeed," she pouted. "Why not Zsa Zsa? Anyhow, by the time they reach 'Z' there won't be any wind left. For next year, I demand that they start the list backward."

Texas

At a dinner party down South, Peter Lind Hayes refereed a hassle between a proud daughter of Kentucky and an equally proud son of Texas. The fur—and the boasts—flew in all directions.

"Why, we have so much solid gold stored in Kentucky," concluded the young lady, "we could build a wall of the stuff, ten feet high and four feet thick, clear around the borders of Texas."

The Texan smiled tolerantly. "Go right ahead and build it, honey," he urged, "and if we like it, we'll buy it!"

It's tough to get the last word in with a Texan, regardless of the circumstances. Jerry Coleman, for instance, back in big-league baseball after a distinguished tour of duty as a pilot in Korea, tells about a group of GI's over there who came upon a remarkably small horse tethered to a post.

"Gosh all hemlock," said one soldier, "I'll bet that's the smallest horse in the whole wide world."

"You're crazy," contradicted a recruit from Texas. "In the Lone-Star State, man, we got horses that's as little as two of that one!"

A Texas zillionaire decided to bestow a modest gift of $500,000 upon a university not far from Houston. One newspaper, however, made a slight mistake in its report of the bequest. It said that the gift was five million.

Fortunately, the zillionaire and the owner of the paper are friends. So there was not too much anger in the voice of the zillionaire when he phoned.

"I don't suppose I can make a liar out of that sheet of yours," he grumbled. "Since you said so, I'll make the gift five million this time. But confound it: don't let this happen again!"

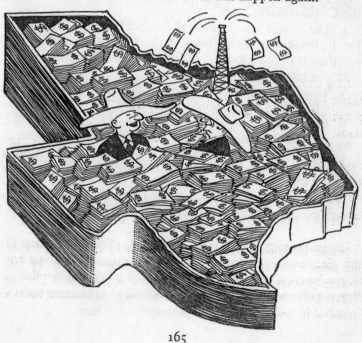

Another tycoon from Texas drove his air-conditioned limousine up to New York, but rebelled at paying a fifty-cent toll to cross the George Washington Bridge. "Son," he informed the attendant, "I never carry anything less than a $500 bill. *How much do you want for the bridge?*"

No collection of stories about Texas is considered official unless it includes at least two of these time-honored stand-bys:

1. The Texas governor who decided to collect miniatures and announced, "I'm agoin' to start with Rhode Island." (Alternate: the kid from San Antone who was put out in the final round of a spelling bee. He couldn't spell S-M-A-L-L.)

2. The oilman from Tyler, Texas, who got his first look at the Eiffel Tower and conceded, "Right purty. How many barrels does it produce?"

3. The Dallas school kids who sing, "The butcher, the baker, the Cadillac maker."

4. The farmer who consulted the Lubbock weather bureau for the latest reports on a hurricane he had heard was threatening the area. "Be specific," ordered the harassed weatherman. "Do you mean the eastbound or the westbound hurricane?"

5. The old judge in Pecos who recalled the day he gave "an ornery hoss thief twenty-four years to leave Texas."

6. The Houstonian who was having a cocktail atop the Mark Hopkins Hotel in San Francisco. "How do you like that sunset over the Golden Gate?" enthused his host. The Texan made a mighty effort to be polite. "It's really not bad," he conceded, "for a small town."

7. The luckiest Texan of them all. His fifty thousand head of prize blue-ribbon cattle suddenly started gushing oil!

From Houston a husband returned to Flatbush and dazzled his bride with the gift of three sable coats, two Jaguars, and $30,-000 in tax-exempt bonds. "It's really nothing, lambkin," he deprecated. "Remember I was in Texas over Halloween. For the heck of it, we spent an hour playing trick or treat."

Deep in the part of Texas near Waco, there's a town that boasts one of America's few remaining hand-set newspapers—a journal, furthermore, whose running battle with the demon rum has caused reverberations as far away as the Cork Club in Houston's Hotel Shamrock and the Bucket of Blood Saloon in Virginia City, Nevada. Here's one of the doughty editor's most recent blasts, which has become so popular that some people carry it around in their pockets in mimeographed form:

"If you must sully our community's fair name by guzzling liquor, why not start a saloon in your own home? Be the only customer and you won't have to buy a license.

"Give your wife twelve dollars to buy a gallon of whisky. There are one hundred and twenty-eight snorts in a gallon. If you pay your wife the prevailing exorbitant rate of forty cents a snort, in four days, when you've lapped up the gallon, your wife will have thirty-nine dollars and twenty cents to put in the bank, not to mention twelve dollars to start up in business again.

"If you can hang on in this fashion for ten years, before dying from D.T.'s, your wife will have approximately thirty-five thousand, seven hundred fifty dollars and fifty cents on deposit—enough to bury you respectably, bring up your children, buy a house and lot, marry a decent man—and forget she ever knew you!"

John Henry Faulk once roomed with a Texan who was deeply religious—but lazy as they come. He had a prayer framed right over his bed, so every night he could slide blissfully between the sheets, point to the prayer, and say, "Yep, them's my sentiments."

The West

Not long ago, the editors of the *Farmer-Stockman* printed a picture of a deserted farmhouse in a desolate, sand-swept field, then offered a prize for the best hundred-word essay on the disastrous effects of land erosion. A bright Indian lad from Oklahoma bagged the trophy with this graphic contribution:

"Picture show why white man crazy. Cut down trees. Make too big tepee. Plow hill, water wash. Wind blow soil. Grass gone. Door gone. Window gone. Squaw gone. Whole place gone to hell. No pig. No corn. No pony.

"Indian no plow land. Keep grass. Buffalo eat grass. Indian eat buffalo. Hide make plenty big tepee. Make moccasin. All time eat. Indian no hunt job. No work. No hitchhike. No ask relief. No build dam. No give dam.

"White man heap crazy."

The Indians out West finally were convinced the white men were plumb loco when they imported a herd of camels to the deserts of Arizona and California. That was back in 1856. Harlan D. Fowler tells the story in a book published by the Stanford University Press. The camels were the bright idea of the U. S. Army, when Jeff Davis was Secretary of War, and, until the railroads supplanted them, did quite a job hauling heavy freight across barren desert stretches.

In 1864, a wily promoter in Sacramento rounded up ten of the camels and staged a race on which white men wagered thousands. The Indians knew that nothing under the sun could make a camel run when he wasn't in the mood. The animals broke from the barrier briskly enough, but, as the Indians had predicted, soon lost interest and, while the gallery jeered, stopped dead in their tracks.

The race was won by a resourceful rider who abandoned his camel and crossed the finish line in triumph astride a spavined mule.

Giving a penny back on every empty beer can, surmised Orville Reed, could do more for the scenic beauty of America than three new national parks.

There is just one spot in the U.S.A. where it's possible for a person to stand in four states at the same time. Look at a map and you'll see that it's at the southwestern tip of Colorado, with New Mexico to the south, Utah to the west, and Arizona to the southwest. (This is the kind of knowledge that wins thousand-dollar jackpots in TV quiz programs!)

Arizona is one state where most of the citizens are a little smarter than the average. They have to be, a man in Phoenix explained to me, because they've got Californians bang up next to them on one side and Texans mighty close to them on the other —not to mention city slickers like author Bud Kelland, architect Frank Lloyd Wright, columnist Westbrook Pegler and publisher Ed Meredith in their midst every winter. Wright is the man who once defined a New Yorker as "an Arizonian with an ulcer."

Arizona's population is soaring percentagewise faster than any other state, since new and needed underground water supplies were developed a few years ago. Where water exists, the natives tell you, "All you've got to do is plant a seed, spit on it—and duck." Newcomers are pouring in so fast that the latest census revealed an increase of over 50 per cent in ten short years!

The spanking new airport at Phoenix cost seven million dollars—and looks it. It's a far cry from an old field nearby where Clark Gable some years ago made a picture about the then fledgling Air Force.

They gave him his part when he appeared for the first day's shooting. He read the trite lines with mounting dismay, then begged, "Have a heart, boys. Don't make me go up in a script like this!"

Since Palm Springs and adjacent California desert land have become a favorite vacation spot for Hollywood's "elite," some hundred miles to the westward, less spectacular visitors from other parts of the country blow in expecting almost anything to happen—and it often does.

Instead of "getting away from it all," the movie folk generally bring it with them. None of their didos, however, seem to startle the casual tourist more than a pamphlet freely distributed at all shops and roadside barbecues. It is called *The Sex Life of the Date*.

It is a strange fact that a date-palm grove is very much like a sultan's harem, with one "male" tree supporting as many as seventy "female" trees. The latter carry clusters of flowers that look lovely, but are for some reason repellent to bees and other insects. The date trees require, therefore, man's help in the rite of pollination.

Then they produce a fruit so dainty it carries a parasol during the ripening season, so sweet it is called "the candy that grows on trees," so nourishing that millions of desert dwellers, from biblical times to the present, have made it the principal item of their daily diet.

This information proved particularly surprising to one famous motion-picture producer. "A sex life for dates!" he echoed unbelievingly. "I always thought they grew on fig trees!"

An old soldiers' organization held its annual powwow in sunny San Diego this year, with headquarters at the commodious U. S. Grant Hotel. One veteran from Alabama found himself in something of a dilemma. "I cain't send mah friends a picture post card even," he wailed. "If they all saw the name of the hotel ah'm patronizin', they'd run me out of the county when ah came home!"

Bob Campbell has preserved a typical weather report from a tourist-conscious resort in southern California: "Rain and heavy winds all yesterday and today. Continued fair tomorrow."

Just before Goodwin Knight took office in Sacramento as governor of California, he found himself aboard a train with a group of lunatics being carted off to an asylum. The guard was counting them off. "One, two, three, four," when he stumbled into Goodie Knight. "Who are you?" demanded the guard. Knight drew himself up and announced proudly, "You are addressing the next governor of California." "Okay," said the guard. "Get in line. Five, six, seven, eight . . ."

When the Shriners convened in Los Angeles one year, a main boulevard was roped off for their climactic parade, and only official cars, prominently marked "Potentate," "Past Potentate," and the like, were permitted to use the thoroughfare for hours preceding the big march. One smart lawyer, anxious to avoid a detour that would make him thirty minutes late for his golf game, devised a sign for his car that got him right through the police barrier and enabled him to sail majestically up the empty boulevard. His sign proclaimed: "Past Participle!"

California boosters take a dim view of tall claims made by their neighbors in Texas. "That's why I'm so anxious for Alaska to win statehood," explained a California politician to me recently. "It will make Texas only the *second* largest state!

"I suppose you know what our flag will look like if they make Hawaii a state?" continued the politician. "Forty-eight stars and a pineapple!"

When a new lighthouse was erected on a dangerous shore off a wild stretch of coast in the Northwest, a couple of Eskimos appointed themselves "sidewalk superintendents." They studied every detail of construction and, when the lighthouse began functioning, were on hand day and night to watch operations. Then a heavy fog blew in. The light revolved and the foghorn tooted continuously. One Eskimo turned triumphantly to the other. "I told you white igloo builder big bum," he exulted. "Light shine, bell ding-dong, horn woo-woo, but fog come rolling in just the same."

CHAPTER FOURTEEN

KEEP MOVING

Automobiles

A kindly Cadillac owner spied the driver of an old Model-T Ford in difficulties at a roadside and offered to tow him to the nearest garage. Along the way, he forgot all about his tow, and ran his speed up to ninety miles an hour with the Ford careening madly in his wake. A state trooper set out in pursuit, but was soon outdistanced. He phoned a side-kick twenty miles ahead and warned, "Get the driver of a green Cadillac coming your way. I'll bet he's doing a hundred." "Okay," was the reply. "And that isn't all," added the first trooper. "I don't expect you to believe me, but

173

there's a loon in a Model-T Ford right behind that Cadillac, blowing his horn like crazy and trying to pass."

"I hear you picked up another beautiful girl this evening," said one motorist enviously to another. "How on earth do you do it?" "Simplest thing in the world," boasted the successful Romeo. "A mere case of winkin', blinkin', and nod."

"What is the thing I'm most anxious to get out of my new car?" grinned a businessman in answer to an advertising expert's question. "That's easy! My seventeen-year-old son!"

One of the big automobile companies had just unveiled its new models for the year, and the Long Island distributor cunningly displayed the most expensive one in his beautifully decorated showroom to its fullest advantage. An insurance underwriter was one of many whose power of resistance was broken down completely. He walked in, made out a check, and announced, "I want that one in the window." "Splendid," enthused the salesman. "Do you want to drive it home immediately or shall we deliver it?" "Just leave it where it is," requested the buyer. "I'll never find such a fine parking space for it again!"

Two taxis banged into one another in front of the CBS Building on Fifty-second Street. "Wottzamatter?" hollered the driver of one. "Ya blind?" The other promptly countered, "Blind? I hit ya, didn't I?"

Fifty years ago, when an automobile still made people come running blocks to gape and horses shy in their traces, Colonel H. Nelson Jackson made the first transcontinental motor tour in history. He set out from San Francisco on May 23, 1903, and wound up on Fifth Avenue, New York, exactly sixty-three days later, after a series of adventures that included mudholes, unbridged mountain streams, and journeys across untracked and uncharted desert wastes.

One of Colonel Jackson's most unnecessary detours was near Marysville, California, when a girl's misdirection sent him on a fifty-mile wild-goose chase. After he had retraced the ground, he asked the girl, "Why did you send us the wrong way?" "It was so my paw and maw could get a look at you," she told him shamelessly. "They never seen an automobile. And if you're aiming to go clear to New York, a few more miles ain't going to hurt you none!"

Lady Drivers

How quickly can a joke get round the whole U.S.A.?

A Boston columnist, with some space to fill, made up a story about a motorist whose car stalled on the Merritt Parkway. He stopped a lady driver and asked her to give him a push, telling her, "You'll have to get up to about thirty-five miles an hour to really get me rolling." He thereupon climbed into his jalopy, took the wheel, and waited for the push. It was a bit tardy in coming, so he stole a look behind him. There was the lady—bearing down on him at thirty-five miles an hour! "The damage to the man's car," concluded the imaginative columnist, "was approximately three hundred dollars."

Well, there wasn't too much real news that day, and the Associated Press sent the story out over its wires. Result: about five hundred newspapers printed it as gospel, and about fourteen radio and TV comics made it famous inside of a single day from Connecticut to Oregon!

The State Farm Mutual Automobile Insurance Company, of Bloomington, Illinois, has a terrific jolt in store for complacent male drivers who explain every mishap on the open road with a condescending, "I'll bet there was a woman at the wheel!"

Vice-President Tom Morrill writes me, "In the past three years, housewives have ranked twenty-eighth best in a list of sixty-four occupational classes in the safe handling of private passenger cars—and we have the statistics to prove it."

Morrill pours salt into male wounds by adding that auto salesmen trail in thirty-second place, doctors in thirty-ninth, truck drivers in forty-third, lawyers in fiftieth, the clergy (whose minds obviously are on higher things) in fifty-fifth, and traveling salesmen and students near the end of the pack in sixty-first and sixty-second places respectively.

The only cheering note I can find in these doleful tidings is in the standing of editors, reporters, and photographers: twenty-sixth.

I'll have to take Mr. Morrill's word for it that lady drivers have become more proficient than was their wont, but their tongues certainly get sharper all the time.

Take the case of the reckless speeder who was hauled before a judge in a Los Angeles traffic court recently.

The judge delivered quite a sermon, but the lady driver wasn't having any of it.

"Aren't you the eloquent one?" she sneered. "I'll bet you can recite Lincoln's Gettysburg Address by heart, too."

"I'm proud to say I can," admitted the judge, "and I hereby fine you fourscore and seven bucks."

A Boston policeman waved a lady motorist over to the curb and complained, "Madam, why have you no red light on the rear of your car?" "Officer," she answered angrily, "it is not that kind of a car."

"Our new power brakes are out of this world," a salesman for the Indestructible Eight told a prospective lady customer. "Now with that equipment, instead of running over a victim, you can stop squarely on top of him."

Vic Flanders, of Norfolk, Virginia, writes that his wife insisted upon taking driving lessons despite his strenuous objections. The first day she was alone at the wheel, he spotted her at a distance of three blocks wobbling uncertainly toward their residence. He rushed inside, double-locked the door, ran up three flights of stairs to his private study, and took refuge under the desk. "It wasn't any use," he admits. "She got me anyhow."

Mr. Flanders adds that, despite the snapshot enclosed with his letter, his car is not a foreign make—when his wife got through with it the steering wheel was on the right side.

M. Kadison, the millionaire broker, is another roads scholar who seems to be in trouble as soon as his wife takes the wheel. One day she complained, "Just look how close to us that lunatic ahead is driving!" Another time she explained her erratic steering with "I washed the car a couple of hours ago, and now I can't do a thing with it."

After smacking head on into a parked moving van, she announced with some satisfaction, "This is one time I've beaten that fifty-dollar-deductible clause, anyhow!"

One kind of driver who is a perpetual menace is the lady gad-about who plasters stickers all over a car from every hamlet, waterfall, and nutburger stand visited en route. Charles Mabie, in New Orleans, has a neighbor who goes in heavily for such stickers. Notes Mr. Mabie:

> *She's been around, it's evident*
> *From all those stickers showing,*
> *But due to flaunting where she's been,*
> *She can't see where she's going!*

Aviation

A veteran pilot on one of the transcontinental air lines discovered early in his career that one gentlemen's washroom on a plane carrying over sixty passengers poses certain problems. He has solved them for himself very neatly, however. Now, whenever he wishes to wash up, he just lights up the panel reading "Kindly fasten all seat belts," gives the customers half a minute to comply—then saunters majestically to the convenience.

The hostess on a stratocruiser was saying good-by to the passengers at the end of the flight, when her eyes suddenly glazed with horror, and she grabbed by the arm one gent whose pants had fallen around his shoes. "*Mister* Goppelheimer," she said severely, "it was your *safety belt* I told you to unfasten."

Another passenger who experienced seat-belt trouble was a Montana cowboy. He just would not fasten his safety belt. "Missy," he informed the stewardess firmly, "for nigh on twenty years I've rode everything I ever mounted, and I don't aim to be saddle-tied at this stage of the game. Let 'er buck! I'll ride 'er!"

The pilot of a new jet plane was winging over the Berkshires and pointed out a pleasant valley to his second in command. "See that spot?" he demanded. "When I was a barefoot kid I used to sit in a flat-bottom rowboat down there, fishing. Every time a plane flew by, I'd look up and dream I was piloting it. Now I look down and dream I'm fishing!"

In the flight kitchen of United Airlines in Chicago, they estimate that passengers travel approximately 25 miles while they toy with their appetizer, 110 miles while they eat the main course, 40 miles for the salad, and 55 more during dessert. In other words, a single dinner goes a long ways—230 miles!

The publication of Charles Lindbergh's *The Spirit of St. Louis* calls to mind a story that was popular in publishing circles just after Lindbergh had completed his epoch-making flight to Paris. George Palmer Putnam was smart enough to sign him up for a "quickie" book about his exploit, and the hastily written *We* became a great best seller overnight. Lindbergh, shy and reserved, wouldn't let his publisher become overfriendly. "In fact," recalled Mr. Putnam, "I couldn't get the time of day out of him until I came round with his first royalty check. It was for an even hundred thousand dollars. This will unbend him, I told myself. I was partly right too. He glanced at the check, smiled briefly, and commented, 'On this basis, you can come around more often.'"

Dr. Morris Fishbein knows a man in the luggage business who has a unique system for enjoying his vacation. "I drive out to the airport," he said. "Just to see the planes take off and arrive?" asked Dr. Fishbein. "Nah," scoffed the luggage man. "Who cares about planes? But I get genuine pleasure from seeing the redcaps scuff up the suitcases."

A huge air liner, with all sixty seats occupied, zoomed over the state insane asylum, and the pilot burst into loud laughter. "What's so funny?" demanded the hostess. "I was just thinking," replied the pilot, "what a commotion there'll be in that joint when they discover I've escaped!"

179

Mr. Gordon was dreaming of a play with two characters and one set that would run for eight thousand consecutive performances—while on a plane making a routine flight from New York to Chicago. Suddenly he looked up to see a parachutist drift past his window. "Care to join me?" hollered the parachutist. "Think I'm nuts?" responded Mr. Gordon. "I'm staying right here." "Have it your way," conceded the parachutist. "I'm your pilot."

General Jimmy Doolittle shared a seat in a transatlantic passenger plane with a young fellow who had been in the parachute troops throughout World War II. As the plane prepared to land at Paris, Doolittle noted that the paratrooper grew increasingly nervous. "What's the matter, my boy," scoffed the general. "Forgotten that you've been in a thousand planes before?"

"It isn't that, General," said the paratrooper earnestly. "This is the first time I've ever landed!"

George Jessel flew out to the Nevada desert, firmly convinced that after years of effort he finally had lined up a job for his Cousin Max—in the H-bomb tests. At the last minute, however, officials decided to use goats.

Georgie also reported the singular case of the flying saucer that landed in a dairy farm. The weird occupants poured out, and the leader leveled a new-fangled shooting iron at the nearest cow. "No stalling now," barked the leader. "Take us to your president!"

Railroads

A mentally disturbed patient was discharged as cured by an expert and given a job as gateman at a railroad intersection where traffic was not very heavy. There were, in fact, only two trains a day. One, up from the south, sped past the crossing precisely at noon each day; the other, bound from east to west, rattled by thirty minutes later. The new gateman waved at the engineers of the two trains each day and spent the rest of the time in peaceful contemplation. So did an old man named Heimerdinger who came down every morning to keep him company.

One day the gateman's phone rang. The train from the south, reported a dispatcher down the line, was a half hour late. "Take the necessary precautions," he warned. "I will," promised the gateman.

Hurrying from the booth, he pulled Mr. Heimerdinger to his feet and suggested, "I think it will be safer watching from the top of the hill today. And keep your eyes peeled too—because at twelve-thirty on the dot there's going to be the gosh-darnedest train wreck you ever saw in your life!"

Colonel Sam Fordyce, president of the Cotton Belt Railroad, was once on an inspection trip when his special train came to a grinding halt. Stepping out on the platform, the colonel found a gun jabbed into his ribs, while a gruff voice commanded, "Stick 'em up!"

The colonel recognized the voice. It was that of an old two-by-four bandit named Shang Doland, whom the colonel had saved from jail on two previous occasions. "Why, Shang," said the colonel softly. "Ain't you ashamed to come over on the Cotton Belt and try to rob a road as poor as this one? Don't you know that folks with big bank rolls never ride the Cotton Belt? Why don't you go over and hold up the Iron Mountain?"

The bandit was truly abashed. He pulled off his mask and said, "Colonel, I never would have held up this here special if I'd known it was yourn." He rounded up his accomplices, and off they galloped into the night. He took the colonel's advice, too. Couple of nights later he and his boys held up a northbound Iron Mountain train out of Texarkana, and got away with the haul of a lifetime.

A historian for the New York Central Railroad asserts that it was at Montrose, New York, back in 1870, that the line tried out the first device that enabled locomotives to pick up water without stopping. Employees soon referred to the process as "jerking water," and consequently Montrose became known as a "jerk-water" town. Today, of course, a jerk-water town is any pleasant little place where somebody you don't like happens to live.

Jim Barnes recalls a day when multimillionaire J. P. Morgan had to interrupt an Adirondack vacation to resolve a sudden crisis in Wall Street. He telegraphed the president of the New York Central Railroad that the ten twenty-four train was to be flagged for him at Paul Smith's station.

Arrived at the station, Mr. Morgan noted that the one man on duty had his feet planted unconcernedly on his desk, and was

reading a sports gazette. "How about getting up and flagging that ten twenty-four like you've been ordered?" thundered J. P. "Not me," said the unconcerned railroad employee.

So J. P. dug up a red flag and waved it furiously at the oncoming train. After it had ground to a stop, he discovered that Paul Smith's was a regular scheduled stop for the ten twenty-four.

A New England miss, visiting in Richmond, asked an outstanding citizen of those parts, "What sort of plant is a Virginia creeper?" Sadly he replied, "It is not a plant, miss. It's a railroad."

An old settler from Arkansas vows that his paw once decided to commit suicide, so he lay down on the tracks three miles ahead of the fastest express train in the state—and starved to death before it got there.

The engineer of this express, incidentally, made one unscheduled stop every day to pick up a dozen fresh-laid eggs from his cousin, who ran a farm ninety miles north of Little Rock. One day his cousin hailed him with the usual, "Hi, Cousin Abernathy," but this time added, "Ye'll have to keep them passengers waitin' a few minutes extry today. I got eleven eggs so far, but one hen is on the nest now, and that twelfth one ought to be along right soon."

In Wall Street they're telling about the commuter who saw the gate to the four-fifty train slam in his face, but was consoled to note that a darling little blonde had missed the train too. "What say we spend the time until the six thirty-one together?" he proposed. "Delighted," said she. "Let's go up to my place. It's cool and quiet, and I'll fix you a better drink than they serve in this neighborhood!"

Eventually the commuter arrived home, feeling no pain. "Well," said his wife, "what's the alibi this time?"

"No alibi," he protested. "I missed my train, that's all. But a darling little blonde let me idle the hours of waiting away in her duplex apartment."

"Ha, ha," jeered his wife. "Some dreamer! Now tell me who you played cards with—and how much you lost."

Commuters on the Long Island and New Haven railroads will lend a particularly sympathetic ear to a tale unwound by Robert J. Casey in his new book, *Chicago Medium Rare*. A trainload of passengers aboard a Northwestern Elevated Express was suddenly stranded at the Addison Street station. Seems the motorman heard a wild burst of cheering from the Cubs' baseball park as he brought his train to a stop and, unable to resist the temptation, unhooked his control, opened the door, and hotfooted it for the bleachers, where he arrived for the climax of a wild seventh-inning rally. The elevated line, meanwhile, was tied up for forty-five minutes while the management sought frantically to dig up a new motorman who cared only for the White Sox.

"So all right, things are going to pot," answered a commuter to a fellow who occupied a seat with him on the eight twenty-eight, and never stopped kicking about conditions from White Plains to Grand Central Station. "Why don't you write your congressman?" "What good would *that* do?" countered the kicker. "*I'm* my congressman."

CHAPTER FIFTEEN

LIMERICK LANE

Limerick is a lively Irish town on the banks of the River Shannon, just west of Tipperary, but if you as much as hint that its proud citizens have anything to do with the persistently popular five-line verse form that bears the name of their birthplace, any one of them is likely as not to tear you limb from limberick.

In case you're interested, the limerick form actually was popularized some years ago by the English artist and humorist, Edward Lear. He composed dozens of them—very clever too—for *The Book of Nonsense,* then, when he realized what he had started, grabbed a steamer and fled to Greece to get away from it all.

A quick survey of the specimens that follow will make his panic all too understandable.

1. At a bullfight in sunny Madrid
   A tourist went clear off his lid.
   He made straight for the bull
   While the crowd yelled, "The fool
   Will go home on a slab"—and he did.

✓ 2. There was a young belle of old Natchez
   Whose garments were always in patchez.
   When comment arose
   On the state of her clothes
   She drawled, "When ah itchez, ah scratchez."

3. There are plenty of people in Md.
   Who think that their state is a Fd.
   It seems odd to find
   That they don't seem to mind
   That Wis., not Md., is Dd.

4. A venerable dame in Nic'raguar
   Had her back hair nipped off by a jaguar.
   The lady gasped, "Ah,"
   The jaguar, "Bah,
   What a false, artificial old haguar!"

✓ 5. A lady who rules Fort Montgomery
   Says the wearing of clothes is mere mummery.
   She has frequently tea'd in
   The costume of Eden,
   Appearing delightfully summery.

6. There once was a lady named Psyche
   Whose love was a fellow named Yche.
   But the thing about Yche
   That the girl didn't lyche
   Was his beard, which was dreadfully pspyche.

7. A jolly old Southern colonel
   Has a humorous sense most infolonel.
   He amuses his folks
   By laughing at jokes
   That appear in the Ladies Home Jolonel.

8. A certain young pate who was addle
   Rode a horse alleged to be saddle,
   But his gust which was dis
   For his haps which were mis
   Sent him back to his lack which was Cadil.

9. A budget I knew who was flutter
   Lived the life of a fly which was butter.
   But ker which was po
   And girls that were show
   Turned him into a snipe that was gutter.

10. A nice patch of golds that were mari
    Belonged to a dan who was harri.
    When cals who were ras
    Filled their kets that were bas,
    She put up a cade that was barri.

✓ 11. Two eager and dashing young beaux
    Were held up and robbed of their cleaux.
    While the weather is hot
    They won't miss a lot,
    But what will they do when it sneaux?

✓ 12. A naughty old colonel in Butte
    Had a habit his friends thought was cutte.
    He'd slip off to Spokane
    And proceed from the train
    To a house of distinct ill reputte.

13. There once lived a teacher named Dodd
    With manners arresting and odd.
    He said, "If you please,
    Spell my name with three D's,"
    Though one was sufficient for God.

14. A gent with a drooping mustache
    Chewed some hair out while eating his hache.
    The phrases profane
    That he shrieked in his pain
    We shall represent here with a dache.

✔15. There was a young lady from Lynn
Who happened to sit on a pynn.
But to add to her contour
She'd stuck so much ontour
The point didn't puncture the skynn.

16. A doughty young private of Leeds
Rashly swallowed six packets of seeds.
In a month, silly ass,
He was covered with grass,
And he couldn't sit down for the weeds.

✔17. There was a young girl from St. Paul
Wore a newspaper dress to a ball.
But the dress caught on fire
And burned her entire
Front page—sporting section—and all.

18. While watching a game of croquet
A lady got caught in the wuet.
She was struck in the eye
By a ball that went beye
So she wears a glass orb to this duet.

✔19. There was a young girl in the choir
Whose voice went up hoir and hoir,
Till one Sunday night
It vanished from sight
And they found it next day in the spoir.

20. The kings of Peru were the Incas
Who got to be known as big drincas.
They worshiped the sun
And had lots of fun,
But the peasants all thought they were stincas.

21. A rascal far gone in lechery
   Lured maids to their doom by his treachery.
   He invited them in
   For the purpose of sin
   Though he said 'twas to look at his etchery.

22. A strip-tease named Cubbard in Kansas
   Said, "Mine's a routine that entrances."
   But when censors got there
   Miss Cubbard was bare
   She explained, "I don't know where my fans is."

23. A near-sighted fellow named Walter
   Led a glamorized lass to the altar.
   A beauty he thought her
   Till some soap and hot water
   Made her look like the Rock of Gibraltar.

24. There once was a scholar named Fressor
   Whose knowledge grew lessor and lessor.
   It at last grew so small
   He knew nothing at all,
   And today he's a college professor!

25. A student from dear old Bryn Mawr
   Committed a dreadful faux pas
   She loosened a stay
   In her new décolleté
   Exposing her je ne sais quoi.

It was in a Limerick saloon, incidentally, that a broth of a lad, decidedly under the influence, objected violently when the barkeep would serve him no more drinks. "I'll have yez all know," he hollered, "that I'm the featherweight champion of the Imerald Isle." "Be you now?" replied the barkeep grimly. "Well, one more peep out of you, me lad, and out you go—feathers and all."

CHAPTER SIXTEEN

THE LONG ARM OF THE LAW

There are lots of folks who subscribe to the theory that a lawyer's sole motto is "Let us have fees." I'm not one of them. I've noticed that the people who complain loudest about lawyers' fees are the ones who are bothering them oftenest to extricate them from some mess into which they've plunged themselves.

Legal lights have become used to abuse. Even Shakespeare, in *King Henry VI*, proposed, "The first thing we do, let's kill all

192

the lawyers." And Lloyd Lewis told about a bleak, wintry night when General Ulysses S. Grant strode into a tavern in Galena, Illinois. It was during the court session, and a passel of lawyers was huddling about the fire. One of them noticed Grant and commented, "Here's a stranger, gentlemen, and by the looks of him, I'd say he's traveled through hell itself."

"I have," agreed Grant.

The lawyer chuckled and demanded, "How did you find things there?"

"Just like here," admitted Grant. "Lawyers all closest to the fire."

Adlai Stevenson, who returned to practice of the law when certain of his plans miscarried in 1952, is one legal light whose sense of humor never has deserted him. In 1937, for instance, while still a private citizen, he built a fine house just outside Lake Forest, Illinois, only to see it burn to the ground shortly after its completion. Stevenson was ruefully watching the debacle when a piece of flaming debris landed at his feet. He picked it up and lit his cigarette with it. "Anyhow," he told the fire chief, "I'm still getting some use out of the house!"

In 1911, the Wisconsin Supreme Court awarded the owner of a shy heifer named Martha the sum of seventy-five dollars for unwelcome attentions paid her by an errant bull. Justice Barnes, his voice quivering with emotion, explained the decision as follows: "This plebeian bull, lowly born and nameless, had aspirations far beyond his humble station in life, and forced his society on adolescent, unsophisticated Martha—contrary to provisions of Section 1482, Statutes of 1898. The sinister birth of the hybrid calf that resulted from the union was ineligible to become a candidate for pink ribbons at county fairs, and was sold in the end to a Chicago butcher for a low price."

Under the circumstances, seventy-five dollars seemed like a very light penalty—but, at least, justice prevailed and outraged virtue in Wisconsin did not go unavenged.

A rather melancholy story comes by way of Boston. A successful and formidable old jurist lingered over the breakfast table reading his *Law Review*, with his wife sitting silently across the table from him—just as she had done every weekday morning for the past thirty-seven years. Seized by a sudden daredevil impulse, she spoke up. "Henry," is what she said, "is there anything interesting in the *Law Review* this morning?" The jurist frowned and answered gruffly, "Don't be silly!"

William McDermott, extolling the merits of simple psychology, cites the case of a woman who came to the family counselor, declaring, "I hate my husband! I not only want to divorce him, but I want to make things as tough for him as I possibly can."

"I know just how you should proceed," the old counselor assured her. "Start showering him with compliments and indulging his every whim. Then, just when he knows how much he needs you—you start divorce proceedings. You'll fracture him!"

The wife decided this was sound advice. Six months later the counselor met her at a dinner and asked, "Are you still following my suggestion?" "I am," said the wife. "Then how about filing your divorce papers?" pursued the counselor. "Are you out of your head?" countered the wife indignantly. "We're divinely happy! I love him with all my heart!"

George Allen tells how a lawyer friend of his accomplished the acquittal of a notorious purveyor of moonshine whisky in West Virginia some years ago. The lawyer, obviously destined for big things in Washington, pointed dramatically at his bleary-eyed, crimson-beaked client and exclaimed, "Look at him, gentlemen of the jury. Can any one of you possibly believe that if this defendant ever got his hands on a bottle of hard likker he'd sell it?" The jury voted for acquittal without leaving the box.

Another George Allen story concerns the day early in his own career at the bar, when he settled a twenty-thousand-dollar lawsuit for thirty-five dollars. "Your honor," he told the judge, "I'm just in no mood to quibble."

Steve Allen knows a girl who has a Supreme Court figure: no appeal!

The judge frowned when he looked at the defendant and demanded, "Haven't I seen that face of yours before?" "Indeed you have, your honor," said the defendant hopefully. "I gave your son violin lessons last winter."

"Ah, yes," recalled the judge. "Twenty years!"

Accused in court of waltzing off with a motorist's tool kit, the defendant maintained stoutly that he'd taken it only as a joke. "How far," asked the judge gently, "did you carry that kit?" "Just over to my home," answered the defendant. "About four blocks." "Thirty days," snapped his honor, "for carrying the joke too far."

The witness was a starlet who didn't care how much of her understandably famous chassis was exposed to the jury. As her dress crept higher and higher, the prosecuting attorney cried, "Point of order, your honor! I've just thought of something!" "Of course you have," said his honor sympathetically. "So has every other man in this courtroom!"

An absent-minded attorney rose to defend a client, and, intent on winding up the proceedings promptly and reaching the country club, got off on the wrong foot.

"This man on trial, gentlemen of the jury," he bumbled, "bears the reputation of being the most unconscionable and depraved scoundrel in the state . . ."

An assistant whispered frantically, "That's your client you're talking about."

Without one second's hesitation, the lawyer continued smoothly, ". . . but what outstanding citizen ever lived who has not been vilified and slandered by envious contemporaries?"

The terrified citizen assured the police lieutenant he had been felled in the dark outside his back door by an unknown assailant.

195

A rookie cop was dispatched to the scene, returned in due course with a big lump on his forehead and a woebegone look on his face.

"I solved the case," he reported. "Quick work," complimented the lieutenant. "How did you accomplish it?" The rookie cop explained, "I stepped on the rake too."

An upstate police commissioner staunchly defends the practice of abandoning license plates on the front of cars, and confining them to the back of automobiles. "Remember," he adds, "that nine out of ten pinches are made from the rear."

A gang of robbers, out to make a killing, broke into a home for old actors by mistake. The retired, supposedly decrepit Thespians put up such a battle, the robbers were happy to make their escape. Bruised and bloody, they re-formed ranks at the gang hangout. "It ain't too bad," philosophized one. "We got twenty-two dollars between us." The leader silenced him with a glance and snarled, "I told you lugs to steer clear of actors. We had twenty-four when we broke in!"

Some thoughtful friend on the Coast sent John Straley a clock recently. When the post-office officials in New York heard the ticking, they suspected a bomb plot, and threw the package into a bucket of water. It didn't help the timepiece any, but Straley refuses to part with it. He explains it's probably the only clock in the world where every hour on the hour the cuckoo comes out and gargles.

Scheduled to die in the chair the following morning, with not a mourner in sight, a notorious killer, in line with the immemorial custom, was allowed to order anything he wanted for his last dinner. The huge scowling desperado smacked his lips, and demanded cream of mushroom soup, mushroom patty, three portions of mushrooms under glass, and, for a dessert to top things off, a succulent mushroom pudding.

196

To the surprised warden the doomed man explained, "All my life I've loved mushrooms—but was convinced I'd get poisonous toadstools by mistake. Tonight's the first time I don't have to be afraid to eat them."

Do you think all motorcycle cops are heartless monsters? They tell of one up New England way who bagged two speeding cars at the same time, ordered the drivers to pull up at the side of the road. The lead car had a dazzlingly pretty girl at the wheel, and the appreciative young man in the second car whispered, "Go easy on her, bud," as the cop strode by, summons book in hand. A few moments later the girl drove off, and the cop approached the young man. He handed him a slip of paper. It contained the girl's telephone number. "Get going," he ordered, "and no more of that sixty-five-miles-an-hour stuff, or you'll never live to use this!"

CHAPTER SEVENTEEN

LOVE AND MARRIAGE

A very pretty girl in Altoona, Pennsylvania, had a persistent but unwanted suitor in New York. When she refused to see him any longer, he resorted to an intensive mail campaign, sending her a special-delivery letter twice a day for forty-seven days. On the forty-eighth day his strategy produced results. The girl eloped with the mailman.

Wilfred was notoriously bashful in the presence of the opposite sex, so his parents were pleased but surprised when he announced he was headed downtown to see a girl. He was back, however, within the hour.

"You're home mighty early, son," observed his mother. "Didn't you see her?"

"Sure did," enthused Wilfred, "and if I hadn't ducked down an alley she'd have seen me!"

Young Spooner, fortified by two stiff drinks, asked for the hand of crusty old Mr. Walker's only daughter. "Take her," snorted Walker. "I'm sure you're not making enough to support her—but, on the other hand, neither am I!"

Nobody ever expected that the Nuthalls' gangling, ambitionless young son would ever amount to a darn, but on the day he was nineteen, he staggered the neighborhood—his parents most of all—by getting the daughter of the richest man in town to say she'd be his. The wedding actually took place, too, causing skeptics to lose a couple of injudicious bets, and the lad slipped a ring on his betrothed's finger, mumbling, "With all my worldly goods I thee endow." "Well," whispered one of the skeptics, "there goes young Nuthall's bicycle!"

The office vamp reported, "I went out with a millionaire from Detroit last night, and what do you think he gave me? Five hundred dollars!" "Zowie," jeered the girl at the next desk. "That's the first time I heard of a $498 tip!"

The entire course of a young man's secret love affair was revealed to his mother when she came upon a sheaf of letters from the girl and noted this sequence of salutations:

Dear Mr. Carmichael
Dear Bill
Bill Dear
Dearest Bill
You Wonderful Guy
My Own Sensational Lover
You Wonderful Guy
Dearest Bill
Bill Dear
Dear Bill
Dear Mr. Carmichael

A young blonde who spent hours every day before a mirror faithfully apeing the mannerisms of Marilyn Monroe mournfully reported to a school chum, "Every time I pass a group of boys in front of the drugstore you should just hear the loud whistle —but darn it, the boys never whistle back."

Art Carney tells one of those stories about the smart young brother who always was underfoot when his pretty sister wanted to pitch a little woo with her boy friend. To get rid of him one afternoon the b.f. suggested, "Why don't you go down to the street, Willie, and count the men who are wearing red hats. I'll give you a quarter for every one that goes by." To the surprise of both lovebirds, Willie, usually very cagey, fell in with this suggestion. Fifteen minutes later, however, they heard his triumphant voice from below. "I don't know how you two are doing up there," he hollered, "but my ship is about to come in. Here comes the Shriners' parade!"

"I hear," said an aspiring young model to her roommate, "that your fiancé is doing settlement work." "Yes," agreed the roommate sadly. "His creditors caught up with him."

A daughter explained to her ma, "I can't marry that handsome young millionaire after all. I just found out he doesn't believe in hell!" "Don't let that stop you, gal," ordered Ma. "You just marry him—and we'll convince him!"

John Barrymore, who had good reason to know as much about the rocky road of love as he did about acting, remarked ruefully one evening, "Experience is what you have left after you have completely forgotten her name."

When Johnny Baxter proposed to little Wynnie Sukes, she resolved to become the perfect mate and learn to do everything he could do. First came the problem of driving his convertible. She signed for a full course of instruction, but what with all the prenuptial parties and hubbub, was barely able to merit a beginner's permit by the time she tripped down the aisle.

The wedding over, the toasts drunk, the bridal bouquet thrown, Johnny and Wynnie chugged off in a shower of rice. Ten minutes later, however, everybody was amazed to see Wynnie come tearing madly back into the house. "What's the matter?" cried the guests. "Oh dear," wailed Wynnie. "I almost spoiled everything. I drove off without my beginner's permit!"

A Mr. Floogle in South Bend had a brand-new washing machine that went on the fritz. Mr. Floogle had bent over to probe deep into the mechanism of the machine when Mrs. Floogle entered and turned on the switch. There was a whirr, and Mr. Floogle's legs shot up into the air. Mrs. Floogle watched him threshing wildly about and observed happily, "Fine, Sam! You've got it working again!"

In the Aga Khan's memoirs, he recalls a journey to Paris he made with one Sir George Greaves. "Tell me," said the Aga Khan, "is Lady Greaves accompanying you?" Sir George answered coldly, "When I go to a banquet, I don't take a ham sandwich in my pocket!"

One of the stories that, judging by the number of times it's been submitted, must be among the most popular extant, concerns the old man explaining the secret of seventy years of serene, fight-free married life. "Driving home from our honeymoon," is the old man's story, "my mare stumbled. 'That's once,' I noted. Then it stumbled again. I said grimly, 'That's twice.' When that mare stumbled a third time, I just naturally pulled out my gun and shot that mare dead. My new wife got mighty riled about all this and bawled me out plenty. I just sat there quiet till she ran down. Then I said, 'That's once!' Son, I ain't had a bit of trouble with her since."

Rosita Quarles's summary of the difference between lovers and husbands: day and night.

"How long are you going to let your wife henpeck you?" sneered the companion of a typical Mr. Milquetoast. "How's for reasserting your mastery of your own home?"

Milquetoast strode into his apartment and hollered, "What time's dinner?" "Seven-thirty, like always," answered his wife without thinking, but she recoiled when he announced, "Nothing doing! Tonight it's seven sharp. And I want a steak, not that canned slop you usually serve me. And put out my dinner jacket. I'm going to take that little blonde in my office out dancing."

Mrs. Milquetoast froze with astonishment. Drunk with power, her husband continued, "And when I'm ready to have my black tie fixed in a neat little bow, do you know who's going to tie it?"

Mrs. Milquetoast recovered her voice. "I certainly do," she announced grimly. "The man from the Riverside Funeral Parlor."

Ten husbands who are more to be pitied than censored:

1. The husband who discovered that, though his wife sure could dish it out, she couldn't cook it.

2. The husband whose wife told him to pull in his stomach—after he already had.

3. The husband who returned for credit a book entitled *How*

to Be Master in Your Own Home, explaining sheepishly, "My wife won't let me keep it."

4. The husband whose wife made him drink thirty cups of coffee a day to cure his dreadful snoring. After six months she boasted, "He never snores at all any more. He just percolates."

5. The husband who was caught shaving at the border of Central Park Lake. A cop protested, "Haven't you got a bathroom of your own?" "I certainly have," answered the husband bitterly. "I also have a wife and four daughters."

6. The husband whose neighbor boasted, "I got a cute little cocker puppy for my wife this morning." "Gosh," sighed the husband, "I wish I could make a trade like that."

7. The husband whose son, a freshman at college, reported, "I've landed my first part in a varsity show. I play a man who's been married for twenty years." "Good work, son," enthused Father. "Keep this up and first thing you know they'll be giving you a speaking part."

8. The husband who brought his boss home for dinner, explaining, "You're about to meet the finest little helpmate, the swellest cook, the best little housekeeper a man ever had—that is, of course, if she's home."

9. The husband whose wife was so concerned about his happiness that she hired three detectives to discover the reason for it.

10. The husband who reported this division of his income: 40 per cent for food, 30 per cent for shelter, and 50 per cent for his wife's clothing and amusement. "But that makes 120 per cent," protested his accountant. "You don't have to tell me," sighed the husband. "I know it."

Two successful Chicago businessmen, who hadn't met since they were classmates in a little southern Illinois schoolhouse, met in the Loop one afternoon, and after the usual wistful reminiscences, one persuaded the other to try "potluck" for dinner at his home. "Potluck" wasn't very good that night. An unco-operative and bored wife served up some cold ham and a can of preserved peaches and disappeared huffily toward her bedroom. The host gulped down his last bite of peach and boomed, "Well, Joe, now that you've broken bread at my house you'll have to ask me to dine at yours some time soon." "Not a bad idea," agreed Joe sourly. "How about tonight?"

It was the morning after Father's Day, and editor Norman Cousins, parent of four, was sipping a cup of coffee thoughtfully. "Did they give you anything for Father's Day?" asked a member of the staff. "They did," admitted Cousins. "They gave me all the bills from Mother's Day."

The team of Pedro and Pancho had been inseparable since boyhood, but the day came when Pedro took unto himself a blushing bride. The affair had blossomed so suddenly that Pancho never even met the girl before the evening of the wedding. There was a great feast for the occasion, and the tequila flowed like water. The guests waxed happier and happier. In the midst of the uproar, however, Pedro suddenly discovered that both his friend Pancho and his lovely bride were missing. He instituted a private search, and soon discovered them locked in each other's arms in the bridal chamber. Pedro reappeared at the party in a paroxysm of laughter. "Come look," he demanded. "That fool Pancho so drunk he think he's me!"

While Mrs. Erskine vacationed in the Adirondacks, Mr. Erskine turned their Park Avenue apartment into something of a club for his male friends, with one poker game setting some kind of endurance record by lasting from Friday evening clear through to Monday morning. Mrs. Erskine surveyed the wreckage rather grimly when she returned home, but less than twenty-four hours later she was able to report to her sister, "Well, I've swept out every nook and crony."

"My darling," murmured a husband to his bride of twenty years, "as I always tell anyone who will listen, you have the face of a saint." Under his breath he added, "A Saint Bernard."

Eddie Cantor goes a long way back for his story of the housewife who protested, "I don't like this apartment, Joe. There are no curtains in the bathroom, so every time I take a bath, the neighbors can see me." "That's all right, Rachel," soothed her husband. "When the neighbors see you, *they'll* buy the curtains."

A harassed young bride served her husband only a plateful of graham crackers for dinner. "And I had such a lovely meal planned," she wailed. "But when the steak started to burn and fell into the lemon pie, I had to throw the tomato soup on them to put out the fire!"

Sticking her head into Mrs. Rodgers' East Hampton bungalow, a neighbor asked solicitously, "How's old Morty feeling this morning?" "He can't complain," said Mrs. Rodgers. "Land's sake," clucked the neighbor, "I had no idea he was *that* sick!"

The *Wall Street Journal*, undertaking something of a Kinsey investigation of its own, has determined that a man's relationship with the opposite sex can be divided roughly into seven stages:

1. Whaaa! I want my mama!
2. G'wan, beat it. We don't want any old girl playing with us.
3. Gee, Myrtle, you're beautiful!
4. If you don't marry me, I'll shoot myself.
5. Go on home to your mother. See if I give a darn.
6. She's considerably younger than I am, Alice, I'll admit, but she understands me.
7. Kitchy-kitchy-koo! Did you hear that, Alice? She said "Grandpa!"

The classified-ad section of an Ohio newspaper betrayed an odd desire on the part of one reader. He sought an old-fashioned wooden potato masher, explaining, "I want it for my mother-in-law." It turned out that absolutely nobody in the community had a wooden potato masher he wanted to part with, but one helpful reader wrote, "A wire potato masher will suffice nicely for your mother-in-law. Just hit her a little harder!"

Mr. Goodman was the kind of husband who believed he was entitled to a night off every week. What's more, he sold Mrs. Goodman on the proposition. So every Wednesday, regular as clockwork, he pedaled off by himself. Only one Wednesday, he neglected to come back home. For seven years he was among the missing. Then, one Wednesday afternoon, he suddenly re-appeared. His wife, overjoyed, began calling all her friends. "Hey," protested Mr. Goodman, "whassa big idea?" "I thought I'd whip up a little welcome-home party for you this evening," she explained. "What?" roared Mr. Goodman. "On my night out?"

One friend listened to another explain his difficulties with his wife, most of which resulted from staying out nights. He said that he had spent one whole Saturday oiling the garage door to keep it quiet, had put graphite in all the locks, and had perfected a system for silent home-coming and entrance into the bedroom, but there she was, whether he was drunk or sober, and no mat-ter what time—blazing away at him. He invariably got mad, spoiled his whole night, and felt terrible the next day—and this was one of those days.

The patient friend explained that he had the wrong system and that his was better—worked nine times out of ten. He said, "Drunk or sober, no matter what time, I slam into the driveway with the horn blowing and the brakes shrieking, bump into the back of the garage, slam the doors with all my might, fall into the front door of the house, and slam that too. Then I stumble upstairs, kick my shoes around, get my clothes off, and step into the bedroom, turn on all the lights, and yell, 'Move over, dear, here I come.' Nine times out of ten she pretends she's asleep."

An attractive young honeymoon couple boarded a train for Niagara Falls, and indulged in the traditional billing and cooing. Suddenly, however, the baffled bride found herself hurling hate-ful insults at her husband, with his rejoinders matching hers in bitterness and venom.

And then she discovered a total stranger sitting next to her in the drawing room. "How did you get in here?" she gasped. "Who are you?"

The stranger answered softly, "I'm ten years from now."

CHAPTER EIGHTEEN

THE PRINTED WORD

Author, Author!

"Be brief," was George Bernard Shaw's unfailing advice to aspiring writers. I was walking down the Embankment in London with him one day when a young writer held out his hand and announced, "My name is Rothschild, Mr. Shaw." Shaw, without so much as breaking his stride, answered, "Good-by, Mr. Rothschild.

"That," he told me with some satisfaction when we were out of earshot of poor Mr. Rothschild, "is *brevity*."

Brevity is not always so simple to attain. The French author Pascal P.S.'d to a friend, "I have made this letter rather long because I have not had time to make it shorter." Woodrow

Wilson once remarked that it would take him two weeks to prepare a ten-minute speech, one week for a speech of an hour. Asked how long he would need to prepare a two-hour speech, he replied, "That I can do—right now."

Arnold Bennett once visited Shaw in his apartment overlooking the Thames Embankment in London and expressed surprise that not a single vase of flowers was in evidence. "I thought you were so fond of flowers," chided Bennett. "I am," responded Shaw abruptly. "I'm very fond of children too. But I don't cut off their heads and stick them in pots about the house."

Gabriel Pascal, the late motion-picture magnate, recalls one of his early dealings with Mr. Shaw. Shaw, it appeared, wanted eight thousand dollars for the screen rights to one of his lesser plays. "I'll give you four thousand," was Pascal's cabled reply. "You must have misunderstood my original demand," protested Shaw (collect). "What I asked was eighty thousand, not eight." Pascal answered promptly, "Excuse error. I'll give you forty thousand!"

Erich Remarque, author of *All Quiet on the Western Front* and *Arch of Triumph*, tells about a cousin of the same name who paced a hospital corridor awaiting the arrival of his firstborn. A nurse finally ended his anxiety by informing him he was the father of an eight-pound boy. A few moments later she was back to say, "You now have another son." The father had not been expecting twins. He stammered, "That last Remarque is uncalled for!"

Hale and hearty at the age of eighty, George Moore, the famous Irish novelist, startled everybody by his continuing clarity of thought and physical well-being. "To what do you attribute your great good health in your eightieth year?" asked a reporter. Moore replied cheerfully, "It's because I never smoked, drank, or touched a girl—until I was eleven years old."

Harry Kurnitz, mystery writer and Hollywood bigwig, was in London one summer with Moss Hart and Kitty Carlisle (Mrs. Hart in private life), and it was this trio that prevailed upon novelist Edna Ferber, rather against her intuitive judgment, to embark upon an excursion boat bound up the River Thames. The day was hot, the small boat was overcrowded, and the captain, a pasty-faced youth of about twenty with an unlighted cigarette glued to his lips, unprepossessing, to say the least. The boat wasn't fifty yards from its mooring place when it got stuck in the mud, where it remained three solid hours until derisive urchins on the shore began skimming pebbles at the marooned excursionists. Miss Ferber then turned to Hart with a martyred expression and sighed, "And now, dear Moss, they're stoning us." Dear Moss tried to bribe a passing oarsman to remove his party and row it ashore, but the pasty-faced captain roared, "'Ere now, there'll be no desertions from this ship. These currents are dangerous." The only other diversion before they all returned safely to port came when Mr. Kurnitz buried his head in his hands and groaned, "I never should have shot that albatross." Miss Ferber promises to confine future maritime ventures to the *Queen Elizabeth* and the *United States*.

A well-known literary figure on the West Coast recently made headlines with a spectacular suicide gesture. The fact that it obviously was designed to be unsuccessful brought to mind a famous lady friend of the late Robert Benchley. She made so many abortive attempts to do away with herself that Benchley finally told her, "You'll have to cut this sort of thing out, my dear. It's ruining your health!"

Hostesses who went in for literary parlor games never got very far when Robert Benchley was around. In a piece called "Ladies Wild," Mr. Benchley confessed, "In the exclusive set (no diphtheria allowed) in which I travel, I am known as a heel in the matter of parlor games. I will drink with the ladies, wrassle with them, and leer at them, but when they bring out the bundles of pencils and the pads of paper and start putting down all the things they can think of beginning with 'W,' or enumerating each other's bad qualities (no hard-feeling results, mind you—just life-long enmity), I tiptoe noisily out of the room and say, 'The hell with you.'

"For this reason, I am not usually included in any little game that may be planned in advance. If they foresee an evening of 'Consequences' coming over them, they whisper, 'Get Benchley out of the house.' For, I forgot to tell you, not only am I a non-participant in parlor games but I am a militant non-participant. I heckle from the sidelines. I throw stones and spit at the players. Hence the nickname, 'Sweet Old Bob,' or sometimes just the initials."

In his foreword to *The Benchley Roundup*, a selection of Robert Benchley's funniest pieces, his son Nathaniel recalls: "One time, during World War II an Air Force sergeant accosted my father in a bar and announced, 'I might as well tell you I don't like your work.' Benchley replied that he had moments of doubt himself. The sergeant then explained that he had hitched a ride from Africa to Italy on a cargo plane, and that the only available sleeping space had been on bags full of overseas editions of Benchley's books. By the time they passed Sicily, he said, he was so stiff and sore he hoped never to even hear the name of Benchley again. 'Try it yourself sometime,' he concluded. 'That stuff isn't so hilarious when you have to sleep on it.' "

Frank Sullivan, the Socrates of Saratoga, met a disturbed young lady who complained that she could never live, or even tarry briefly, on an island. "Islands," she said, "give me claustrophobia." Father Sullivan, who has learned by experience that the surest way to calm a phobia-ridden friend is to trot out phobias of your own, told her, "I know exactly how you feel. I have somewhat the same trouble." "You get uneasy on islands too?" she asked eagerly. "Not islands exactly," Sullivan admitted gravely. "I'm uneasy on continents."

The young lady seemed comforted.

Frank Sullivan boasts, incidentally, that he remains a rebel to the bitter end. He always sails, for instance, under true colors instead of false, leaves no stone turned, and, when angry, never dreams of hitting the ceiling. He hits the floor—and just lies there screaming. He carries a bag around with him, letting cats into it, and when he casts discretion it certainly isn't to the winds. "You might also mention," he concludes, "that I do not cast any pearls before swine, either. I save *my* pearls to cast before pretty girls. The reaction is far more gratifying." On my own, I'll mention that Frank Sullivan remains, year in and year out, one of the greatest and most consistent humorists in America.

One of the most popular American humorists a hundred years ago was Josh Billings—(real name, Henry Wheeler Shaw [1818–85])—who wowed the populace with his homely philosophy, deliberately misspelled. Josh began his career as an auctioneer in Poughkeepsie, but made the big time with gems like the following:

"Konsider a postage stamp: it sticks tew the job til the goods is delivered."

"It's better to know nothing than to know what ain't so."

"The wheel that squeaks loudest is the one that gets the grease."

"A sekret ceases tew be a secret if once it's confided. It is like a dollar bill: once broken it's never a dollar again."

"Love is like the measles: we kan't have it bad but oncet, and the later in life we have it, the tuffer it goes with us."

Cut from the same cloth was the droll commentary of Kim Hubbard (1868–1930), who, some seventy years later, made the towns of Gnawbone, Bear Wallow, and Weedpatch Hill famous the country over.

Hubbard created the character "Abe Martin," a single-gallused cracker-barrel philosopher not unlike Herb Shriner—with a dash of George Gobel thrown in for good measure.

It was Kim Hubbard who coined the oft-quoted, "What the country needs is a good five-cent cigar," though V. P. Tom Marshall usually gets the credit. Other Hubbard observations:

"A restaurant waiter allus lays your check on the table upside down so you won't choke t'death."

"Nothin' makes a poet as mad as a late spring."

"A warnin' is all the average American needs t'make him take a chance."

"The hardest thing t'stop is a temporary chairman."

"Speakin' of the high cost o' courtin', who remembers when all a fella needed wuz a narrow buggy an' a sack o' red cinammon drops?"

Wall Street was buzzing the other day with the story of a slaphappy hostess at a cocktail party who collared a bewildered author to tell him, "I read your book as a magazine serial, in book form, and as a condensation, and now I've seen it in the movies and on television. Frankly, Mr. Ingold, just what the hell are you trying to say?"

At the same party, an authoress whose tongue is feared on three continents was heard assuring an old, old friend, "Enjoy yourself while you can, my dear. After all, you only live nine times."

Author Ben Hecht takes a very dim view of celebrities. "A roomful of them," he writes in his autobiography, *A Child of the Century*, "depresses me, possibly because I have learned at first hand the wretched things that make a celebrity—the pain of almost constant defeat, the arrows of a thousand critics forever sticking out of your rump, the fact that your name has become a magnet for irritation, malice, or calumny. And worst of all, the fact that a celebrity cannot, like luckier folk, drop out of sight when he is ripened with age. He must stay on the vine and rot—for all to see and disdain."

Budd Schulberg, who writes wonderful books, but drives his publisher crazy by never delivering them on time (I know, because I'm the publisher!), explained his technique to reporter Ed Wallace. "First," said Budd, "I clean the typewriter. Then I go through my shelves and return all borrowed books. Then I play with my three children. Then, if it's warm, I go for a swim. Then I find some friends to have a drink with. By then, it's time to clean the typewriter again."

And that's why Schulberg's books are so few and far between. But they're worth waiting for!

A well-known but improvident author was toiling over a new novel when there came a ring on his doorbell. His caller proved to be a comely young woman who announced, "I represent the Federated Community Charity Fund." "You've arrived in the nick of time," enthused the author. "I'm starving."

James Branch Cabell, whose novel *Jurgen* was considered very daring stuff back in the 1920's, likes to tell of a note he received from a rabid fan some years later. "Dear Mr. Cabell," it began. "I have chosen you as my favorite author. Please write to me immediately and tell me why."

When F. Scott Fitzgerald's novel, *The Beautiful and Damned*, was published, everybody asked his wife Zelda how closely the heroine was modeled after her own career. "It seems to me," replied Mrs. Fitzgerald after some thought, "that on one page I recognized a portion of an old diary of mine which disappeared shortly after my marriage, and also scraps of letters which sound to me vaguely familiar. In fact, Mr. Fitzgerald—I believe that is how he spells his name—seems to believe that plagiarism begins at home."

An author in Kankakee found himself in something of a predicament recently. A magazine accepted a short poem and sent him a check for thirty-five dollars. The only man who could identify him at the bank, however, was his liquor dealer—whom he owed a hundred!

Agatha Christie, famous writer of detective stories, returned to London after a long visit to Bagdad with her husband, a renowned archaeologist. Asked how a woman with great creative talent felt about being married to a student whose eyes were turned always to antiquities, Miss Christie replied warmly, "An archaeologist is the best husband any woman can get. Just consider: the older she gets, the more he is interested in her!"

There was a time when John Gunther and his beautiful wife, Jane, in their interminable search for the "inside" of some place or other, arrived in Tokyo, Japan. They had been in primitive villages for a month and were therefore specially delighted to find a bath attached to their new hotel room. It was a highly polished wooden tub already filled to the brim with boiling hot water. "They must roast elephants in here," commented Jane, and sought a "cold" faucet to bring down the water's temperature.

There was none to be found, so she finally gritted her teeth and inched her way tortuously into the tub, where she enjoyed a veritable picnic. When she climbed out (red as a lobster), she summoned an attendant to mop up. It was then that the Gunthers discovered that Jane had used the week's bath water for the entire hotel. Each guest, explained the indignant manager, was supposed to take only a pitcher full of the steaming hot water for sponging-off purposes.

It cost Mr. Gunther twenty-five dollars to pay for the emptying and refilling of the tub. I presume he charged it off to research.

If you ever hope to get along with an author, there is one

thing you must understand from the outset. Every word that he sets down on paper automatically becomes a priceless gem, and the merest suggestion that he alter or condense his text is an unforgivable insult. Nor is this an occupational disease acquired after long apprenticeship. It manifests itself at an appallingly early stage of a writer's career.

When my son Jonathan, for instance, was eight years old, he and a favorite classmate named Judy Goetz (whose parents fashioned the dramatic versions of *The Heiress* and *The Immoralist*) were assigned to write a play. Jon had captured a live frog the week previous and this was very much in the minds of the collaborators when they set about composing their play.

The next day Jonny was home with a cold. Judy stormed in about five, crying. "That teacher has rewritten our whole first scene!" "Wha-a-at?" roared Jonny. "She can't get away with it!"

"Let me see this scene that your unfeeling teacher has desecrated," I suggested.

The manuscript was handed over to me, and I now give you, in its original and unabridged form, the scene as Judy and Jonny wrote it:

The curtain rises. A frog is on the center of the stage.
Frog: I don't think I'll go to school today. *Curtain.*

The World of Books

There is a man in New England, supposedly sound of mind and body, who has devoted virtually his entire life and fortune to a collection of recognized classics in unrecognized languages. His treasures include *Uncle Tom's Cabin* in Ukrainian, *Ben Hur* in Hebrew, and *Hamlet* in Hindustani.

Another collector seeks only first editions of books Abraham Lincoln was known to have read in his leisure hours.

A third buys volumes printed on black paper. No other color interests him.

A fourth seeks odd-shaped volumes: round, heart-shaped, fashioned after fruits and animals.

A fifth's sole craving is for books left unfinished because of their authors' untimely deaths—titles like Dickens' *Mystery of Edwin Drood*, Stevenson's *Weir of Hemiston*, and Hawthorne's *Dr. Grimshawe's Secret*.

These and other odd fish from the sea of literature are catalogued and dissected in bibliophile Walter Blumenthal's sprightly *Bookmen's Bedlam*, a Rutgers University Press publication. In its pages you will learn about the smallest, the largest, and the darndest books in all the world.

Smallest book: An edition of Omar Khayyam published in 1933 in Worcester, Massachusetts. Each copy, bound in full crimson morocco, weighs only a third of a carat. The whole edition of 150 would fit in an old-fashioned watchcase.

Largest book: Up the River Nile at Thebes, in the Temple of Rameses II. Its "pages" are walls 138 feet wide—"an ancient chronicle of triumph that has defied obliteration for more than three thousand years."

Most secure book: Bishop Lyndwood's *The Provinciale*, which, according to his will, was chained "for all time" to St. Stephen's Chapel, Westminster, to serve as the standard text of his work and discourage effectively both borrowers and abridgers.

An Englishman, Augustine Birrell, ordered a nineteen-volume set of the works of Hannah More buried deep in his garden. "The books take up too much room on my shelves," he explained, "and they are just as likely to be dug up from the garden as to be picked out for reading up here."

His countrywoman, Lady Gough, insured immortality among the literati by forbidding in her library the placing of books by male authors alongside those by female authors—unless, of course, they were married.

Mr. Blumenthal also claims to have unearthed the longest and shortest plays ever published. The longest, he says, is called *The Spanish Bawd* and runs a mere twenty-one acts. The shortest is Tristan Bernard's *The Exile*, and concerns a mountaineer and an exile. Here is the complete text:

Exile: Whoever you are, have pity on a hunted man. There is a price on my head.
Mountaineer: How much?

The revival of Sherlock Holmes by A. Conan Doyle's son, Adrian, and John Dickson Carr, is a source of deep satisfaction to the rank and file of detective-story addicts, and even the exacting members of the Baker Street Irregulars have reacted favorably. Discrepancies they have discovered, but theirs is an allegiance best expressed in the lines composed by Conan Doyle's brother-in-law (himself the creator of Raffles), Mr. E. W. Hornung:

> *Tho' he might be more humble,*
> *There's no Police like Holmes.*

In Great Britain, furthermore, they've launched a comic strip involving the intrepid Sherlock and his faithful Dr. Watson. It is carried in the *Evening Standard,* and in that sheet's letters column there recently appeared the following: "I rejoice to see the decline of that cursed interfering fellow Holmes to a mere comic-strip feature on a rather obscure page." The letter was signed, "Yours joyfully, Professor Moriarty."

The publishers of the Modern Library received a note from a young lady in Arkansas, which read, "I enjoyed your publication, *Les Miserables,* very much indeed, but would you mind telling me which character is supposed to be Les?"

Another reprint publisher received this fan letter from a satisfied customer: "Your book, *How to Win Friends and Influence People* ought to be read by every private in the Army. A week after I finished it, I got promoted to corporal. P.S. Have you got any books on sex technique?"

In a big marble mansion just off Fifth Avenue dwells the mother of a prominent publisher. She's so old that her family has been worrying about her keeping the place going all by herself. Her son, in fact, called in a high-priced analyst (one of his authors) and said, "Mama's taken to puttering about the kitchen. I want you to question her and tell me of her mental condition, but please be quite sure she doesn't know you're probing her mind."

"Trust me," the analyst assured him. "If you've read my book, I don't have to tell you I know exactly how to proceed in cases of this sort."

He found Mama happily engaged in roasting a leg of lamb and soon had her babbling away unreservedly. When he deemed the moment ripe, he suddenly held up a spoon and asked, "Mama, what's this?" "A spoon, of course," she replied. Then he held up a fork, which she identified just as readily. Finally he held up a knife. "And this, Mama: what's this?" he inquired.

Mama crinkled her tired old eyes, cocked her head to one side, and asked mildly, "A phallic symbol, maybe?"

In London, Peter Windsor encountered a man who had read a Charlotte Brontë novel eight times—obviously the perfect octo-Jane-Eyrian.

Commentator Sam Himmell, in *Printing News*, indicated that a lot of the tears shed over vanishing village smithies might have been saved for more deserving unfortunates. There are still 18,-215 blacksmith shops in the U.S., but only 7,368 bookstores!

At the last booksellers' convention in Atlantic City, a disconsolate purveyor of priceless literature sat in a hotel lobby, his head heavily bandaged and a pair of crutches across his knee. To a solicitous confrere he explained, "I fell out of a window."

"Obviously," commiserated the confrere, "you will be out of commission for the balance of the convention—so how's for slipping me the phone number of the little blond authoress you had draped over your arm the first evening we were in session?"

"With pleasure," agreed the bookseller, "but if a man answers the phone, I suggest that you hang up. It's probably the scoundrel who threw me out of the window."

Alan Green, discoursing on the importance of a novelist's engaging his readers' interests with his very first paragraph, cites two detective-story writers who remembered their lesson almost too well.

The first opened his book as follows:

"Was it necessary," asked the judge, leaning over the bench, "to produce this entire lake in evidence?"

Number Two came through with:

"It was nearly midnight before they had scraped Uncle Harry off the dining-room table."

A lady in Chicago sued for divorce recently. "I love detective stories," she told the judge, "and Field's automatically sends me every new one published. My husband gets hold of them first and writes the name of the murderer on top of page one!"

It appears the judge also liked whodunits. "Your husband obviously is a fiend," he ordained. "Divorce granted."

In Hollywood, William P. Dudley bought a limited edition of the works of Shakespeare from a temporarily impoverished Thespian, who assured him, "Parting with this treasure grieves me more than I can say. Each night before retiring I spent at least an hour reading and rereading the immortal bard's plays." When Mr. Dudley examined the set in his home, he found that none of the pages had been cut! "An unopened Shakespeare!" he thought to himself. "That's the uncuttest kind of all!"

Book-trade journals often ask publishers to supply summaries of forthcoming novels in "thirty-five words or less." Julien Dedman, of Scribner's, says that, had this practice been in vogue in the golden age of Athens, a preview of the *Odyssey* probably would have read something like this: "Strange goings-on in murky waters off the coast of Greece. Several wanton murders by a character named Ulysses. When he finally returns home, he rubs out the suitor of his wife, who was planning to divorce him for desertion."

Unhappiest librarian on record was the little man who set out to catalogue every volume in a famous English library. Because of his build, he had to raise the height of his chair by sitting on one fat volume.

When he completed his magnum opus, the index had only one glaring error—he forgot to include the single volume he had been sitting on for thirty years!

A student bought a desk dictionary from Bob Campbell's U.C.L.A. shop, reported later, "It's interesting—but I wish it didn't change the subject so often."

There's a bookseller up near White Plains who, convinced he never could support a wife and a Jaguar on the wages of a purveyor of the immortals, studied medicine in his spare time. He finally won his doctor's degree, and hung out his shingle next door to the bookshop. His first patient was a beautiful, beautiful girl (Westchester County is full of them). She complained of a stomach-ache. Our brand-new doctor examined the troubled area with a keen appreciation, then asked innocently, "Now do you mind if I browse around a little?"

Powers of the Press

When Horace Greeley made his famous pronouncement, "Go West, young man, and grow up with the country," he was not merely indulging in campaign oratory. He followed his own advice. Determined to push through his campaign for a transcontinental railroad, the great journalist set out by stagecoach in 1859 from Missouri, was deposited on the rolling prairie when a herd of buffalo stampeded the stage horses and overturned the coach, capsized again in the Sweetwater River where he lost a trunkful of manuscripts, persuaded Brigham Young to grant him a far-reaching interview in Salt Lake City, and wound up finally in a mad dash over precipice-bordering Sierra roads to Placerville, in the center of the California gold rush country.

According to the legend, Greeley was expected to speak in Placerville at seven in the evening, and the driver was instructed to get him there in time—or else. They set out at such breakneck speed that Greeley first cried, "I don't care if we arrive a bit late," then amended his statement to, "I don't care if we never get there at all." A final bump sent his head clear through the roof of the coach. The driver simply hollered, "Why don't you hang on to your seat, Horace?" scattered a welcoming brass band in nine directions, and arrived at the Carey House at one minute before seven. Greeley regained consciousness at one minute after nine.

By 1861, when Mark Twain covered the same territory, the story of Horace Greeley's wild ride into Placerville had become so familiar that Twain vowed he heard it "ninety-two times in eight days, flavored with every aroma including whisky, brandy, beer, cologne, sozodont, tobacco, garlic, onions, and grasshoppers." One guide promised to withhold it, but, says Twain, "in trying to retain the anecdote in his system he overstrained himself and expired in my arms."

A San Antonio newspaper featured this ad in its classified columns recently: "Wanted, big executive, from twenty-two to eighty. To sit with feet on desk from ten to four-thirty and watch other people work. Must be willing to play golf every other afternoon. Salary to start: $500 a week. We don't have this job open, you understand. We just thought we'd like to see in print what everybody is applying for."

There's a city editor on one of the Chicago papers who misuses words in a fashion with which no Hollywood producer possibly could compete. A reporter asked, "How much do you want me to write on that fire?" The editor answered, "About half a paragraph." He told his staff another time, "Here's our new policy. Do it if you can, but if you can't, don't worry. After all, it's mandatory." His top effort for the year, however, was, "They tell me we're printing too many old platitudes lately. Let's get rid of those old platitudes, boys, and go out and find some new ones."

When Ward Morehouse, now one of New York's best-known commentators on theatrical affairs, first broke into the newspaper field, he landed a job on the Savannah *Press*. For the princely wage of nine dollars a week he did city-news odds and ends and wrote a sports column under the pseudonym of "J. Alexander Finn." One day he picked an all-Savannah scholastic football team and was rash enough to omit the name of a stalwart named Bubber Bryson. Bubber did not take kindly to this discrimination. In fact, he sent a member of his retinue down to the *Press* office to beat the bejabbers out of young Morehouse. The editor in chief surveyed the damage to Ward's cherubic countenance and beamed. "This is a mighty fine thing to happen, boy! Shows your column's being read!"

There was a journalist in Chicago named Perlstein who suddenly changed his name to Paris. The latter, he explained, he now knew, as a result of careful investigation, had been the correct family name all the time. This gave author Emmett Dedmon the opportunity to tell all and sundry, "The last time I saw Paris —he was Perlstein!"

Pierre Lazareff, editor of the Paris newspaper, *Ce Soir*, summed up the life of a journalist in one sentence for a college class recently: "A journalist spends the first half of his career writing about things he doesn't understand, and the second half concealing the fact that he understands them only too well!"

Oh-so-true words from Bill Vaughan, of the Kansas City *Star*: "A favorite refuge of politicians, when caught in a crack, is to claim that they were misquoted in the press, and the chances are ten to one that they were. That is, they were misquoted in that the reporter cleaned up their rhetoric, supplied the missing verbs, and made sure that their predicates agreed in some gen'l way with their subjects.

"The nastiest thing a reporter could do to a politician would be to quote him absolutely accurately down to every uh, or, well, you see, that is, and so on."

John Wheeler, chairman of North American Newspaper Alliance, told fellow Sigma Chis of an early experience of Brother Kent Cooper of the Associated Press. When Kent was in his swaddling clothes, he played a fiddle in a theater orchestra near Indianapolis. The great Victor Herbert breezed into town, and Kent bagged an interview with him.

While Herbert chatted with Cooper, he hummed the beginning of a catchy melody, then paused to slip off one of his stiff, detachable cuffs and wrote the notes thereon. "May I have it?" asked Cooper eagerly. "You may copy it," said Herbert, "but I can't give it to you. After all, I can't arrive in Chicago with one shirt cuff."

Cooper kept his copy of the four bars Herbert had jotted down. He heard them many times over in the years to come. They were the opening notes of what was to be Victor Herbert's crowning composition—"Kiss Me Again" from *Mlle. Modiste*.

Richard Conte, assigned the role of a newspaper reporter in an upcoming motion picture, determined not to play it in the stereotyped, ridiculous manner followed slavishly by countless predecessors. To remind himself of his vow, he pasted this set of rules on his dressing-room mirror:

1. *No cigarette dangling from right side of lower lip.*
2. *No hat perched far back on head.*
3. *No loosened collar, and tie pulled far to one side.*
4. *No worn trench coat with turned-up collar.*
5. *No press card tucked in hat band.*
6. *No use of any of these phrases: "Stop the presses!"; "I have a scoop"; "Here's your headline!"; "Gimme rewrite"; "Tear out the front page!"*

Editor Sam Day tells a story of a cranky old head of a Philadelphia paper who liked to dash off his own lead editorials. He finished one in a white heat and slapped it into the copy basket with a great flourish. The managing ed, unfortunately, didn't know what he was talking about, and the boss had to admit, once he was challenged, that neither did he. Finally he decided, "Print it as is. It'll make them think, anyhow!"

Joe Patterson, one of the great newspapermen of all time, confessed to an interviewer, "I built the popularity of my paper on legs. When we got the circulation, we put stockings on the legs."

Early in his journalistic career, columnist Bob Considine toiled for "Cissy" Patterson on the Washington *Times-Herald*. Shortly after he left to seek greater fame in Manhattan, she phoned him to report that she had just had a whopper of a fight with her brother, Captain Joe Patterson, over a piece he had authored, and wanted Considine to ghost-write a full-page answer she proposed to run over her signature in the *Times-Herald*. Bob banged out a honey and air-mailed it to her. She phoned the next day and enthused, "It's exactly what I wanted, Bob, and I insist on paying you for it. How much do you want?" "Shucks," deprecated Bob, "I don't want anything at all. I did it for an old friend." "No, no," said Cissy. "Let's settle it this way. What did you get for your last article in *Cosmopolitan*?" "Seven hundred and fifty bucks," answered Considine, "but that hasn't anything to do with this. I beg you to forget all about it."

Two days later he got a check from Mrs. Patterson for five hundred dollars with a note in longhand attached that read, "Dear Bob: I called *Cosmopolitan*."

The cream of America's journalistic fraternity was assembled at Las Vegas for a series of highly publicized atomic-bomb tests, but heavy winds necessitated one delay after another. The cream did not take kindly to the postponements. "They don't seem to realize whom they've kept waiting," was their implied attitude.

About the fifth long afternoon, the youngest reporter in the crowd pointed to a red, setting sun and inquired, "That's the west over there, isn't it?"

A bored veteran yawned elaborately and assured him, "If it isn't, son, you've just scored the biggest scoop since the Johnstown Flood!"

Bill Nichols, of *This Week* magazine, describes a publisher as "a man who goes around with a worried look on his assistants' faces."

Advice from Richard Carlson to neophytes aiming for *The New Yorker:* "Write with *Collier's* in mind—then chop off the last two paragraphs."

Jim Thurber, reminiscing about his early days on *The New Yorker* magazine, says, "Editor Harold Ross gave me a job because he convinced himself I was an old pal of E. B. White. I tried to tell him I had met White for the first time on the way in to his office, but he wouldn't listen. I thought I was hired to be a writer, but for three weeks all I did was sign slips of paper they thrust under my nose. Finally, I asked, 'What am I signing here, anyhow?' 'That,' said my secretary, 'is the pay roll.' That's when I found Ross had made me managing editor. When I asked him why, he said firmly, 'Because everybody starts at the bottom here.' It took me eight years of solid writing to persuade Ross to make somebody else his confounded managing editor."

In *The Reporter,* Bill Mauldin confided the formula whereby Harold Ross, late and great editor of *The New Yorker,* managed to stay off radio programs. "I'm a profane *** by nature," he explained, "and whenever one of those *** round tables or something called up, I'd say, 'Hell, yes. I'll be glad to sit in on your *** panel, or whatever the *** you call it!' The word soon got around that I couldn't draw a breath without cussing and the *** hucksters never bothered me again."

An alert *Fortune* reporter spotted a very special classified ad the other day, inserted by an optimistic lady from Salzburg, Austria. "For sale," it proclaimed. "Palatial mansion in historic Salzburg. One hundred rooms, twenty-eight fountains, acres of courtyard. Price: one million dollars."

Here's how *Fortune's* house organ sized up the incident. The ad, it asserted, had been shipped in "uber der transom" by a "furuckte Frau who had been gestucken mit a weissen Elephant on her Hande." Her chances of getting out from under, it continued, were negligible, since "a million dollars heute is a lot of coconutten for ein Haus." In the old days, of course, sighed the *Fortune* sage, subscribers used to buy yachts and castles without "batting ein Auge," but there's a new order in vogue today, and that sort of extravagance is "raus forever"—or strictly "Keine Dice."

The personnel manager of a big paperback-book publishing outfit keeps a bowl of goldfish on his desk. "No, I don't give a damn about goldfish," he explains. "I just like to have something around here that opens its mouth without asking for a raise."

Most reassuring to timid souls who believe that the literary life of America is about to be snuffed out by television, is the revelation of what book publishers were fretting about back in the 1890's. Trolley cars, believe it or not, were what these short-sighted fellows foresaw as the ruination of the book business— trolley cars and tandem bicycles! "When young people," groaned one agitated publisher in 1894, "prefer bouncing down to Coney Island and back on a dangerously speeding trolley, to curling up in the library with a good novel, what in the world are we coming to?"

After the trolley and bicycle scares, of course, it was cheap automobiles, then movies, then radio that were going to sound the death knell of the book business. Television is only the latest of an endless series of bugaboos. But, as I repeat every time I get the chance, nothing—absolutely nothing—will ever take the place—or give the infinite satisfaction—of a really good book.

WARNING!
DOES PUNNING SEND YOU INTO RAGES?
IS WORDPLAY LESS THAN FUNFUL?
YOU'D BETTER SKIP THE NEXT FEW PAGES—
YOU'LL FIND THIS CHAPTER PUNFUL!

CHAPTER NINETEEN

THE PUN-AMERICAN CONFERENCE

The time having come to mete out some pun-ishment, we might as well begin with the singular story of a relative and name-sake of Syngman Rhee, doughty President of South Korea, who came to America to learn the magazine business and enlisted under the banner of Mr. Luce's *Life* magazine. Off on his very first assignment, he succeeded in getting lost completely, and it took New York's best private eyes to track him down.

When they finally spotted him in a Third Avenue café, one cried in relief, "Ah, sweet Mr. Rhee, of *Life*, at last I've found you."

A high Soviet commissar named Rudolph Mozoltoff was walking down a Moscow street with two friends—a man and his wife —when a drop of moisture settled on his blouse. "It's raining," he announced through his beard. "You're wrong," said the wife. "It's snowing." "Oh no," insisted her husband. "Rudolph, the Red, knows rain, dear."

An anthropologist in darkest Africa encountered one tribe whose dexterity with spears astounded him. The chief's aim was particularly unerring. When the anthropologist produced a half dollar from his tunic, the chief speared it from a distance of fifty yards. He achieved the same result with a quarter.

"Now," proposed the delighted scientist, "let's see if you can score another bull's-eye on this ten-cent piece." The chief demurred. "These tired old eyes of mine aren't what they used to be," he confessed. "Mind if I let my kid brother try it?"

With that, he cupped his lips and bellowed, "Brother, can you spear a dime?"

George Ansbarry tells about a twelve-year-old boy who was passionately devoted to his stamp album until the kid next door began collecting stamps, too. "He buys every stamp I do," the twelve-year-old complained to his father, "and has taken all the fun out of it for me. I'm quitting." "Don't be a fool, my boy," counseled the father. "You seem to forget that imitation is the sincerest form of philately."

There are any number of pun-icious characters in Peter De Vries' novel, *The Tunnel of Love*. One thinks a seersucker is a man who spends all his money on fortunetellers. A second keeps asking his analyst, "Have I told you about my aberration?" A third—my favorite—calls his place Moot Point (because there's a legal difficulty about the right of way), and, when asked if he ever heard of a dance called the czardas, asks dubiously, "That's by Hoagy Carmichael, isn't it?"

The captain of an undermanned sailing ship was offered a consignment of hardened convicts during the Napoleonic Wars. "Nothing doing," protested the wily captain. "Too many crooks spoil the sloop."

Jane Cannon's improbable story concerns a young miss who wanted to have her hair bobbed, but lacked the cash demanded by the town's only beautician. "My paw owns the biggest orchard in these parts," the girl reminded the beautician. "How's for letting me pay you in apples?" "Listen, toots," was the indignant reply, "I stopped bobbing for apples when I was twelve years old."

You will now kindly imagine that it is an unseasonably hot day in the spring of 1606, and that William Shakespeare and a friend from his Globe Theater staff are bent on a swim at a British beach resort. They're wearing last year's regalia, of course, and Shakespeare suddenly suspects that moths have been feeding on the back of his bathing trunks. "Wouldst investigate?" he asks his friend.

The friend makes a thorough, if unobtrusive, inspection, then reports cheerfully, "No holes, Bard."

An Irish literary critic was singing the blues, suffering, he explained, from a severe attack of new-writus. "You'd be happier," a supposed friend assured him, "if you'd just read Joyce and Synge."

And critic Jack O'Brian, upon hearing that the famous Dublin poet, George Russell (known universally as "AE"), had lost his temper in a debate, wrote, "You mean that AE's Irish rose."

That's what I think he wrote, anyhow. His pun-manship is not too legible.

Dick Rodgers, who obviously should stick to his inspired song writing, wagers that you can't list four islands whose names are complete questions.

The answers—and I advise you to start running before you give them to anybody—are: Hawaii? Jamaica? Samoa? and S'*tate*n Island?

Libby Noble, of Los Angeles, has an uncle who loves wandering to the far corners of the earth. He is known as the roamin'est Noble of them all. . . . Henry Allen, also of Los Angeles, is going to confine *his* traveling this year to a trip to Kansas City, believing that Missouri loves company.

A mighty North African potentate was wont to while away many a pleasant evening appreciating the gyrations of a native dancing belle named Bubbles. One night, however, a booking agent persuaded him to try Sari, a new importation from Paree. The potentate was so displeased with the substitution, he muttered the North African equivalent of "Phooey," phoned the agent, and announced curtly, "Sari wrong number."

The scene now shifts to Saudi Arabia, where according to Ken Suslick, of Chicago, an Arab sheik fell off the merry-go-round of a carnival and was promptly gobbled up by the second of three hungry sheep grazing nearby. (Sheep always graze in threes in those parts, it seems.)

The owner of the carnival, angry at losing a cash customer in this distressing fashion, seized the offending animal and exclaimed, "Middle lamb, you've had a dizzy Bey."

In the fair city of Rochester, New York, Howard Hosmer would have you believe that a young couple received from Australian friends a crated, two-month-old rary as a gift. The rary, not unlike a kangaroo in looks and habits, was cute as all get out, but its appetite was enormous and, as it matured, it showed every sign of eating the couple out of house and home.

The Rochester zoo had all the raries it wanted at the moment, and the young couple reluctantly decided to do away with their Australian beastie altogether. The husband knew a country road that skirted a steep bluff overlooking the Genesee River gorge, and, borrowing a dump truck for the purpose, dropped the animal over the edge.

Too late, the animal realized his fate. His last reproachful words, as he plunged into space, were, "It's a long way to tip a rary."

In England, a scamp named Sam Rollins became so expert in counterfeiting small coins that he avoided detection for years. Scotland Yard, however, finally caught up with him. On his way to jail, Rollins asked his captor disconsolately, "How did you track me down?" The Scotland Yard man, obviously a night-club devotee of Joe E. Lewis, hummed softly, "Sam, You Made de Pence Too Long."

Another counterfeiter's proud boast was, "I'm an expert with the bad mintin' racket."

The late Oliver Herford once visited a prominent nose and throat specialist, and found himself in the midst of a group of sinus patients who had had their treatments and were pulling themselves together in the waiting room. "They have come to cough," observed Mr. Herford, "but remained to spray."

Have you happened u-pun:

1. The chap at Coney Island who makes a pretty penny by being a habitué? He stands by a scale on the boardwalk, chanting to passers-by, "Habitué 168, habitué 184 . . ."

2. The young man in white who passed a pretty girl in a Los Angeles hospital corridor? He cauterize and winked. She interne winked back. (They were both attending a limping patient, who kept complaining, "My heel is Achille-ing me.")

3. The bridge game at the White House where a daring Eisenhower finesse failed and he went down two tricks? It was one of the few times anybody ever set a president.

4. The beautiful young lady who tugged constantly at her dress and wiggled uncomfortably? Obviously, a chafing dish!

5. The member of a Sanitation Department who was asked where he first had met his bride-to-be? Softly he hummed, " 'Twas on a pile of debris that I found her."

6. The disk jockey who lived on spins and needles? He won an Academy Award with his old plaque magic.

7. The maiden of sixteen who ne'er had been kissed? Summed up Bergen Evans: "A lass and a lack."

8. The big steel magnate who altered his will eleven times in two years? Obviously, a fresh heir fiend.

9. The two scoundrels in Casablanca who fleeced the town's

richest citizen? As they made off with the boodle, they muttered, "We must do this Moor often."

10. The Irishman who told his chiropodist, "Me fate is in your hands"?

11. The baker who perfected a new variety of doughnut? He calls it the "Phyfe." Soon, he hopes, every lover of antiques will be dunking Phyfes.

12. The postman who cut a big hole in the bottom of his pouch? His motto was, "The mail *must* go through!"

13. The harem-scarem heiress who invaded a Tunisian seraglio? She demanded a parlor, Bedouin, and bath.

14. The trusty at a state-prison farm? He routed the warden from his bed, shouting, "There's a character outside attaching an airplane propeller to his old jalopy. I think he's preparing to fly the coupe."

A butcher in the Bronx got along swimmingly with every tenant in his building except a mysterious swami who occupied the third-floor rear. How that butcher and swami loathed each other!

One evening, however, the swami found that his cupboard was bare and was forced to patronize his enemy's shop. "Give me a pound of liver," he ordered of a clerk. The butcher beckoned the clerk to the rear of the establishment. "Here's our chance to put one over on that fraud," he exulted. Then, pointing to his clerk's thumb, he sang, "Weigh down upon the swami's liver."

That same swami had a cousin who, understandably enough, was a whirling dervish in the Ringling Circus. One day an uncommonly handsome damsel picked up this dervish and took him out for a row on the lake in Central Park.

Suddenly the boat tilted, and the damsel quavered to her companion, "I'm afraid I've lost my oar, Derv."

Bruce Rogers, the famous typographer, traveled all the way from Danbury to tell me about a woman who enters bank, (1) greets the cashier, (2) declares she's in the bank's debt, (3) gives him the money, (4) says good-by, and (5) is grabbed at the door when the cashier shouts that her money is counterfeit— all in characters from Shakespeare: Othello, Cassio, Desdemona, Iago, and Caesar.

Writes Jerry Nedwick of Chicago, "Knowing how you like good corn" (where did he get a notion like that?), "I'm passing on an old vaudeville routine used by Harry Vokes and Hap Ward way back in 1902:

" 'Where did you get those pants?' 'Pantsylvania.'

'The coat?'	'North Dacoata.'
'The vest?'	'Vest Virginia.'
'The collar?'	'Collarado.'
'The hat?'	'Manhattan.'
'The shirt?'	'A fellow gave it to me.' "

Elizabeth Behymer, of Dallas, was in court when a drunk was handed a stiff fine and reprimanded by the judge. The drunk suddenly cussed out the court and made a break for freedom. He was apprehended and fined once more, with his honor pointing out, "Had you been chaste and refined, you'd never have been chased and re-fined!"

In my opinion, that judge was in contempt himself.

There's a pun concerning cats, too, but you have to know a little French (very little) to appreciate it. Seems there were three cats riding on a barge in the Seine when a river steamer rammed into it and sent it to the bottom.

The headlines in Paris papers the following morning read, "Un, Deux, Trois, Cats Sank."

A gardener attached to Buckingham Palace, chronicles writer Lee Rogow, stole a chair belonging to Queen Elizabeth and hid it in his greenhouse. He was speedily apprehended and sentenced to reading nothing but puns for ten years, an obvious vindication of the old maxim that people who live in glass houses shouldn't stow thrones.

Stout sea captain Peter Swanstrum (he says the crew is always having fun at his expanse) lost a sailor overboard in a storm and saw him swallowed by a whale. The resourceful captain took after the whale in a rowboat and, by judicious handling of an oar, managed to beat the tar out of him.

A special maestro was hired to conduct a concert of music by Bach and Mozart. In rehearsal he pushed the civic orchestra so intensely, he became known as a Bach Suite driver.

Clifton Fadiman, the pun-loving rover, has selected for special mention a few outstanding examples of the ancient art. He heads his list with Groucho Marx's irr-elephant hunting tale. In Africa, he grumbled, he found the tusks too firmly rooted, but in Alabama, of course, Tuscaloosa. Then there was the time George S. Kaufman got tangled up with the word "euphemism." He finally extricated himself by declaring, "Euphemism and I'm for youse'm."

Louis Untermeyer characterized composers plagiarizing from Debussy as "Debussybodies." Christopher Fry noted that a silver-tongued but opportunistic orator was "coruscating on thin ice." Max Beerbohm declined to be lured into a hike to the summit of a Swiss Alp. "Put me down," he said firmly, "as an anticlimb Max."

Fadiman himself, steering a party of friends to a little Italian restaurant he had praised to the skies, suddenly discovered he had misplaced the proprietor's card. "We'll have to go elsewhere," mourned Fadiman. "I seem to have lost my Spaghettisburg address!"

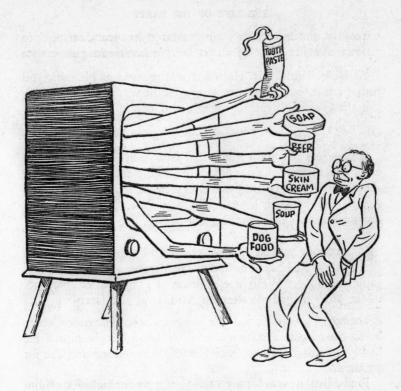

CHAPTER TWENTY

SOMETHING IN THE AIR

A really dyed-in-the-wool television addict these days, maintains Weare Holbrook, must be properly attuned to nose appeal. Mr. Holbrook valiantly kept his set turned up for one entire evening, and found his olfactory apparatus exposed to the following:

  8:00 *A coffee with that delicious aroma.*
  8:15 *A cigarette with that satisfying flavor.*
  8:30 *A toothpaste that keeps your mouth "kissing sweet."*
  9:00 *A bread with that home-baked fragrance.*
10:00 *A cigar with that rich Havana filler.*

10:30 A *shaving lotion with that tangy he-man scent.*
11:00 A *cedar chest with that built-in balsam breeze.*

At eleven-thirty, Mr. Holbrook was relieved at his post, and rumor has it that, some moments later, he was strolling through the stock yards, breathing deeply and pounding his chest delightedly.

A man in a television studio told Jack Paar, "My wife falls for every commercial she's exposed to. Before retiring each night she uses four face creams, two chin creams, and even one elbow cream." "I'll bet she's beautiful," mused Paar, "but tell me: how do you keep her from slipping out of bed?"

If somebody walked up and demanded the real first names of Red Barber, Red Skelton, Skitch Henderson, and Bing Crosby, could you oblige? Well, here, courtesy of Frank Farrell, they are, in the order named: Walter, Richard, Lyle, and Harry.

Allen's Sallies

Fred Allen was not only one of the authentic wits of the American theater but a generous, unassuming, and inspiring gentleman whose like will not soon be seen again. The half hours I spent with him in the dressing room every Sunday evening before we went on for "What's My Line?" will be among the memories I will cherish always.

Fred Allen's real name was John Florence Sullivan; he borrowed the "Fred Allen" from an agent when he broke into vaudeville after World War I with what he called, "The world's worst juggling act." A placard on stage read, "Mr. Allen is quite deaf. If you care to applaud, please do so loudly." Fred wore a suit obviously too big for him. "I had it made in Jersey City," he explained to his audience. "I'm a bigger man there than I am here."

His first chance to utter words on a stage came when he assumed the role of a Wise Man in a Christmas play at his Sunday school. The words were, "Myrrh is mine, its bitter perfume breathes a life of gathering gloom." Fred was six at the time.

Fred Allen's famous feud with Jack Benny was for stage purposes only. In private life they were firm and fast friends. At a Friars' dinner in honor of Benny, Fred's speech, by common consent, was the highlight of a memorable evening. "When Jack signed his new contract with CBS," confided Allen, "he was told he could have everything he wanted. To his everlasting credit, be it said he never took advantage of this. He left them the basement of their building at 485 Madison Avenue." Concerning

Benny's talent as a violin virtuoso, Allen added, "Jack is the only fiddler who makes you feel the strings would sound better back in the cat."

John Crosby recalls a day when Benny was appearing on the Paramount stage and Allen heckled him from a front-row seat. The audience was laughing so hard that Jack finally waved a twenty-dollar bill and offered it to anyone who could top Allen's last gag. Instantly, Allen was on his feet, topped his own sally with a better one—and claimed the twenty dollars!

Typical Fred Allen creations who reappeared in the pages of his nostalgic book, *Treadmill to Oblivion*, included the only armless sculptor in the world (he put the chisel in his mouth and his wife hit him on the back of the head with a mallet); Professor Gulpo, who swallowed umbrellas (he was putting something away for a rainy day); and an uncle who brought his goldfish to the aquarium every year for a two-week romp. One day, however, Uncle fell into the tank himself, and they couldn't tell him from the other fish. Finally, they threw a picture of Allen's aunt into the water—and when one of the fish recognized it and tried to escape from the tank, they grabbed him. For twenty years, claims Fred, his mother in Boston kept a light burning in the window for him. When he came home she gave him a royal welcome and a gas bill for $729.

Fred disposed of network executives with a caustic "If the United States can get along with one vice-president, I don't know why NBC needs twenty-six." Of his agent, he remarked, "He gets 10 per cent of everything I get except my blinding headaches."

One of his happiest conceptions was the Allen Relaxation Society, designed for tired businessmen whose doctors had prescribed a long rest, but who didn't have time to follow orders. Allen supplied substitutes to take the relaxation for these brilliant tycoons, thereby leaving them free to overwork themselves to death or their hearts' content.

"We took care of one magnate," recalled Fred, "whose doctor warned him to go off with his wife for a long, health-restoring cruise. We produced a man who not only took the cruise for him, overate for him, undertipped for him, and got seasick for him, but flirted so shamelessly with a cute blonde for him that his wife went into a huff all the way from Cherbourg to Juan-les-Pins."

One morning, Janet Kern sportingly printed in her column a letter from a reader lambasting her savagely—also ungrammatically—for daring to criticize a remark Fred had thoughtlessly made on "What's My Line?" Fred wrote consolingly, "Dear Janet; isn't it strange that people learn to hate before they learn to spell?"

Very few important comedians laugh at other important comedians. Very few, in fact, even bother to listen. A great exception is Jack Benny. George Burns and Danny Kaye can reduce him to helpless mirth merely by opening their mouths. In fact Jack not only laughs at his confreres, but cues them into repeating their best stories.

It was at his insistence that Jesse Block, of the famous team of Block and Sully, told us of their appearance at the London Palladium, where Miss Sully suddenly discovered that her necklace was missing. "Don't worry," soothed Block. "There are no gangsters over here. All we have to do is summon Scotland Yard."

In due course, exactly the kind of character they were expecting turned up from the Yard—complete with walrus mustache, derby, rolled umbrella, and black notebook. They heard nothing from him for twenty-four hours. Then Block was told he was calling. "What did I tell you?" he exulted.

When he returned to the dressing room, Miss Sully demanded, "Has he found my necklace?"

"On the contrary," answered Block glumly. "He's lost his umbrella."

Steve Allen, droll TV star, says that if you'll listen attentively enough you'll discover that a comedian always starts his next story with "And seriously," after the last one has laid an egg. "And seriously," he adds, "we've been packing the rafters at our own show. Of course there haven't been many people in the seats, but we sure are packing those rafters!"

When but a babe, recalls George Burns, his ma paid a nursegirl a dollar a day to wheel him around the park in his buggy—and he's been pushed for money ever since.

William Archibald Spooner was an Anglican clergyman and educator who became the dean of New College, Oxford, in 1876, a post which he occupied with distinction for thirteen years. What his students remembered with the greatest delight, however, was an unfortunate predilection for transposing the letters or sounds in two or more words.

For example, he startled one audience with, "Kinquering congs their titles take," told another, "Our chapel desperately needs funds with which to refurbish these beery wenches."

The official word in all dictionaries for such mix-ups always was "metathesis," but the dean erred so frequently in this direction that "Spoonerism" took its place, and is now accepted by scholars without question as definitive. (In China, of course, it's called a slip of the Tong.)

With announcers on the air working under continuous pressure, the wonder is they scramble words so seldom. But the best of them have perpetrated some "fluffs" that will be remembered for years.

Really smart announcers have learned never to attempt correcting a Spoonerism. Woe befell the unfortunate commentator who hailed "Hoobert Hever," then hurriedly bumbled on, "I mean 'Hervie Hoober.'" Another fellow got tangled up in "Visit your nearest 'A and Poo Feed Store.'" A third referred to "My dear friends, the Duck and Doochess of Windsor." Bill Leonard, evidently mindful of the ups and downs in an actor's career, once introduced Joe E. Brown as "currently starving in *Harry*." And a top reader of commercials is still trying to live down his prize Spoonerism: "For that extra thrill, try Buppert's Reer."

Two radio announcers got their tongues twisted with unfortunate consequences recently. One, speaking of a fragile movie star, declared, "Her breath will take your beauty away." The second attributed a news flash to "respected White House souses."

Today people actually are making a hobby of collecting TV bloopers. Some of the more glaring errors—including many no self-respecting publisher would print—have even been immortalized on a series of fast-selling phonograph records.

By common agreement, the TV master of ceremonies who won this year's award for the prize boner was the hapless soul who asked a small boy three times, in increasingly urgent tones, to name "the cereal you love to eat every morning, sonny." Sonny finally broke his silence by pointing out to the M.C.—and the coast-to-coast TV audience, "You're hurting my arm, mister."

It served the moderator of one of radio's innumerable quiz shows right! His jack-pot question was "Can you name the difference between amnesia and magnesia?" The audience howled with joy when the contestant, after a moment's deep deliberation, hazarded, "The fellow with amnesia has no idea where he's going."

A sportscaster was giving his all to a wrestling show in Knoxville, Tennessee, recently when the cops asked him to interrupt his rhapsody long enough to make an announcement. A 1955 Buick was parked illegally outside the arena, blocking all traffic. The sportscaster read aloud the model, make, and license number, with all the proper flourishes—then realized it was his own car!

On an unrehearsed TV show, a loquacious gob threw the M.C. off stride by maintaining that his girl had the most beautiful legs in the world. "How do you know?" ventured the M.C. The gob said, "I counted them."

With panel shows and quiz programs featured ever more prominently on TV, the spotlight has focused on Mark Goodson and Bill Todman, the ingenious young pair who concocted a half dozen and more of the most successful examples of the art. "What's My Line" is theirs, for instance, and so are "I've Got a Secret" and "Two for the Money." Somebody once saw a table with four empty chairs grouped around it and quipped, "If Goodson sees this, he'll have a new TV show by six this evening!" Another day, Bill Todman let a heavy chair slip out of his grasp. "Careful, Bill," admonished Goodman Ace, "or you'll lose your script."

When she appears on the panel of "What's My Line?"—or any of the many other television shows in which she stars— Arlene Frances invariably wears around her neck a gold chain and beautiful diamond-encrusted heart. One day she received a call from a young lady who explained that her boss had noticed the heart, loved it, and was anxious to get a replica to give his wife as an anniversary gift. Arlene, because she is a warm, generous girl, went to considerable trouble to arrange a meeting between the boss and the jeweler who had fashioned the heart for her, and the boss got his replica in due time and at a reasonable price.

A week later the secretary phoned Arlene Frances again. Her boss, she explained, was so grateful for her interest that he was sending one of his products to her as a gift. Arlene said "Thank you," without ever inquiring what the product was. The next morning she found out. The boss was one of the heads of the Dodge Motor Company. His gift—a shiny new Dodge sedan— was standing in front of her apartment house when she stepped out into the sunshine of Park Avenue.

Did you know that the principal radio announcer who told the nation the sad details of the funeral procession of Franklin D. Roosevelt in Washington was Arthur Godfrey? Godfrey tells of the man who took a taxi from a hotel, bound for Union Station, and instructed his driver to pull up while he, followed by the driver, alighted to watch the solemn procession file by. The two men stood bareheaded and mournful for a long time, then resumed the drive to the station. There the passenger asked, "What do I owe you?" "Two bits," said the driver. "Your meter must be out of kilter," said the passenger. "We must have been standing out there an hour at least." The driver reminded him, "Mister, he was my President too."

Groucho Marx met an honest-to-goodness bullfighter south of the border and asked him, "How many bulls do you figure you've met?" "At least two hundred, señor," smirked the bullfighter. "You must be the envy of every cow in Mexico," marveled Groucho.

An amateur radio ham went delirious with excitement when he caught a newscast straight from Moscow on his set. "Our great athlete, Ivan Skvitch," the announcer was booming, "has just smashed all existing world's records for the two-hundred-yard dash, the mile run, the five-mile run, and the hundred-mile run, overcoming such formidable obstacles as a blizzard, a range of mountains, and complete lack of water." There was a moment's silence, and then the announcer continued in more subdued tones, "Unfortunately, Ivan Skvitch's fantastic performance was in vain. He was captured and brought back to Russia."

John O'Hara, distinguished author of *Ten North Frederick* and *A Rage to Live*, has rallied to the defense of television. In his provocative column in *Collier's* he told of a friend whose sprawling household includes children by his first marriage, children by his present wife, and stepchildren whom his wife brought with her. There are, roughly, ten children in all.

"Before we bought a TV set," this friend assured O'Hara, "this place used to be a madhouse. Kids all over the house. But then we installed the set in our cellar. Now the kids spend their lives there, and once a week we throw them a couple of fish heads, and everybody's happy."

CHAPTER TWENTY-ONE

IT'S ONLY A GAME . . .

Baseball

Say Hey Willie Mays's "autobiography," *Born to Play Ball*, really was written by Charlie Einstein, who dogged the center fielder's footsteps faithfully for weeks, trying to assemble enough facts to justify a $3.50 price tag on the book. The first draft completed, Einstein contacted Willie on the phone, where, according to the always-accurate Harvey Breit, the following conversation ensued: Einstein: "Hi, Willie, this is Charlie Einstein." Mays: "Who?"

Einstein: "Charlie Einstein. You know—the fellow who wrote the book." Mays: "What book?" Curtain . . .

Another distinguished literary light from baseball circles, Casey Stengel, was persuaded to attend a performance of George Abbott's musical production, *Damn Yankees,* which is an adaptation of Douglass Wallop's sprightly (and wishful-thinking) novel, *The Year the Yankees Lost the Pennant.* Asked how he liked the show, Casey drew himself up in the best and haughtiest George Jean Nathan manner and declared, "I ain't gonna comment about a guy which made $100,000 writin' how my club lost."

Catcher Dixie Howell was chasing a foul pop one night at the Montreal ball park. It was headed right over the home team's dugout, and one of the players not in the game jumped out and grabbed Howell to prevent his falling down the step. Dixie ended up hanging onto the roof of the dugout while the ball bounced way up in the air.

"Did you see how high that ball bounced when it landed on the concrete?" demanded Howell.

"Concrete, hell," said his teammate. "It landed right on my head!"

Two rooters at a ball game were so engrossed in the contest that neither wanted to take time out to march back to the refreshment bar for hot dogs—and there wasn't a vendor in sight. They finally bribed a kid nearby to go for them, giving him forty-five cents and saying, "Buy a dog for yourself at the same time."

The kid came back with thirty cents change for them, explaining, "They only had *my* hot dog left."

Stan Musial, champion batter of the National League, is aptly described by Joe Garagiola, catcher on a rival team, but close friend of Musial's in the off season. "Stan," broods Garagiola, "comes sauntering up to the plate and asks me how my family's making out. Before I can answer him, he's on third base."

Charlie Grimm is equally renowned as a big-league baseball manager and a left-handed banjo player. He was acting in the former capacity in Chicago a few seasons ago, with no conspicuous success. In fact, his Cubs were floundering in last place, when one day a scout rushed into the clubhouse in great excitement to report, "Charlie, I just saw a kid in a sand-lot game fan twenty-seven batters in a row. He had such baffling curves and blinding speed that nobody even got a foul off him till two were out in the ninth. Should I sign him up?" "You're balmy," Grimm told him, strumming idly on his banjo. "It's hitters we need right now. Sign the fellow who got the foul off him."

Lou Boudreau, manager of the Boston Red Sox, snorts with disgust at recurrent rumors that there have been occasional clashes of temperament between him and his star operative, Ted Williams. Boudreau dismisses the rumors with a single sentence that might be tacked up over the desk of every big-league manager in baseball: "Any manager who can't get along with a .400 hitter ought to have his head examined."

Frank Graham tells this story about a typical, dyed-in-the-wool Brooklyn Dodgers fan. Gil Hodges, in the throes of a slump, stepped up to bat in the fourth inning. "Git dat bum outta dere," yelled the fan. "He can't hit his way outta a paper bag!" Toots Shor, sitting behind the fan, warned, "Lay off that Hodges. He's a pal of mine." "Okay," conceded the fan reluctantly, "but tell me, mister, how many udder bums on dis team is pals of yours too?" "Well," figured Toots, "there's Campanella, and Snider, and Erskine, and Jackie Robinson, to name only a few." "Holy mackerel," said the fan. "Lemme outta here, mister. You ain't gonna stop *me* from enjoyin' dis game!"

How many United States Presidents are real baseball fans,

and how many simply put on an act to win friends and influence voters? Sam Himmell has done some diligent research along these lines and comes up with the following. Abraham Lincoln was actually playing baseball when a committee came to his home to inform him he had been nominated for the presidency. William Howard Taft was a confirmed baseball fanatic; it was he who originated the now-standard procedure whereby the President opens every pennant race by tossing out the first ball at the Washington stadium (F.D.R. threw out more first balls, of course, than all the others combined; if practice makes perfect, he could have qualified for a job on the Senators' first-string mound staff!).

It was Benjamin Harrison, twenty-third President of the U.S., who tagged the New York club of the National League with its nickname, "The Giants."

The most avid fan among Presidents was Woodrow Wilson, the most apathetic, Calvin Coolidge. Harry Truman once yearned to be a professional ballplayer, but couldn't quite make the grade. William McKinley, on the other hand, turned down what was in those days a fabulous offer, from a big-league scout, to pursue his political career.

When Casey Stengel signed his first contract to manage the New York Yankees, Jimmy Cannon took him over to Toots Shor's celebrated bistro for a celebration of sorts. The ebullient Mr. Shor promptly produced a pencil and proved by mathematics that Casey's team was a shoo-in to cop the pennant. At closing time Stengel pulled off the tablecloth upon which Mr. Shor had made his computations and started to stuff it in his pocket. "Hey," roared Toots, "whassa idea of trying to bust up my joint?" "I just won my first pennant on that tablecloth," explained Stengel, "and I'd like to keep it as a souvenir."

In seventeen years as a stellar pitcher in the American League, "Lefty" Gomez of the Yankees didn't exactly knock down the fences with his bat. In fact, he averaged about four scratch singles a season. One day he closed his eyes, took a hefty swing and, to everybody's amazement, including his own, smacked a solid triple to left center. Poised on third, the triumphant "Lefty" boasted to Coach Art Fletcher, "Hey, Art, I think I can steal home." Fletcher shuddered, and begged, "It's taken you four months to get this far: don't blow it!"

Yogi Berra, the great catcher of the New York Yankees, is famous, too, for some of the classic remarks he makes far from the baseball diamond. He was describing, for instance, the deep friendship that exists between two other infielders on the team and summed it all up by insisting, "Why, they was as close as Damon and Runyon!"

Milton Berle discovered Tallulah Bankhead rooted to a radio in her dressing room one day, screaming her head off for the New York Giants. "Gosh," exclaimed Miltie, "I didn't realize you were so interested in the national pastime." "Dahling," snapped Tallulah, "I *am* the national pastime."

Incidentally, Tallulah wanted some new recipes for her chef to try. She called her favorite bookseller and ordered two copies of Fanny Farmer's Boston Red Sox Cookbook!

Leo Durocher, ex-manager of the New York Giants, is—or was —probably the most accomplished needler—or "bench jockey"— in big-league baseball today. He could get antagonists so angry with a couple of sarcastic barbs that they forgot all about the business at hand and actually came charging at him in the dugout to do him bodily injury.

A few springs back the Giants were playing a preseason exhibition game at West Point. The cadet corps began to ride Leo as he paced up and down the coaching box at third base. "Hey, Durocher," roared one leather-lunged upperclassman, "how did a runt like you ever sneak into the big leagues?" Leo, they say, silenced the uproar with a single retort. He just hollered back, "My congressman appointed me!"

The New York Giants once had a deaf-and-dumb pitching star popularly known as Dummy Taylor. Taylor thought it was safe to tell umpire Hank O'Day exactly what he thought of him with his fingers, but unfortunately, O'Day knew the sign language too. The episode cost Taylor a five-day suspension and a hundred-dollar fine. Another arbiter once cleared the whole Red Sox bench, including Coach Heinie Wagner. "I didn't say a single word," protested Wagner. "That's possible," admitted the red-faced ump, "but I know what you was thinking, and I didn't like it. Git!"

Entire pennant races have hinged on one tough decision by a harassed umpire. In 1908, Hank O'Day called Fred Merkle out for failing to touch second on a hit that ostensibly had beaten the Cubs, and the Giants lost the championship by that one game. The Brooklyn Dodgers, too, feel that a single wrong decision at the plate by umpire Dascoli in a late-September game in Boston cost them the 1951 championship. In both instances, of course, the umps simply were "calling them as they saw them."

Jerry Bruck is readying a novel about a baseball umpire named Gibbon, for publication about the time the new season opens. This Gibbon loses his glasses during a twilight game at Ebbets Field, spends the rest of his life in a futile search for them, and finally plunges to his death from the second tier of a grandstand in Kansas City. The title, of course, will be *The Decline and Fall of the Roaming Umpire.*

Umpire Bill Guthrie is responsible for two of the classic re-joinders in big-league baseball history. He told one batter who was kicking up an unholy rumpus about a called third strike, "Pipe down, son, and nobody but you and me and the catcher will know you can't see any more." And to another indignant athlete who had tossed his bat into the air in protest, Guthrie announced, "If dat bat comes down, mister, youse is outta da game!"

Riddle from Jim Albright: If two gals fortify themselves with a bottle of hooch, hie themselves to the ball park, and get magnificently plastered, what inning is it, and how many men are on base? Answer: It's the last of the fifth, and the bags are loaded.

Every once in a while some rawboned rookie from the hills turns up at a big-league training camp to evoke inevitable comparisons with Ring Lardner's famous "busher"—and to become the butt of endless practical jokes dreamed up by other members of the squad. One spotted a sign reading "Billiards" above a tavern entrance and actually asked, "What in tarnation is billiards?" A veteran on the team narrowly averted swallowing his chew of tobacco and answered, "Don't tell me you never had a slug of billiards, son! Best drink in the world! Guaranteed to put hair on your chest!"

The rookie was led into the tavern, and the veteran, with an elaborate wink to the barkeep, announced, "Give this lad a glass of the best brand of billiards in the joint." The barkeep scooped up a tall glass of soapy water from the sink, added a slug of gin, and slid the vile concoction across the bar. The rookie managed to down it, grimaced, and murmured weakly, "Them billiards is a powerful drink, all right, but did any of you fellers ever notice how much it tastes like dishwater?"

Laraine Day contributes the story about an elementary-school teacher who told his class to jot down the names of the nine men who, in their opinion, were the greatest in American history.

Everybody completed his list but ten-year-old Jerry, who sat with his brow furrowed, chewing on his pencil. "What's the trouble, Jerry?" inquired the teacher. "Can't you think of nine outstanding Americans?" "I've got eight, all right," answered Jerry, "but what I still need is a second baseman."

Golf

"Slamming Sammy" Snead, one of the all-time greats of golfdom, is an old buddy of another outstanding athlete, Ted Williams, outfielder of the Boston Red Sox. Ted invited Snead to sit on the Red Sox bench for a big game against the New York Yankees, and led his teammates in needling the golf star. Baseball, was the tenor of the remarks, was a man's game: tough, demanding, and complex. "Any old goof could hit a defenseless golf ball." But what about connecting with a baseball that was propelled toward the plate at blinding speed by a smart tricky pitcher? Snead took all the ribbing with perfect good nature, finally drawled, "Maybe all you boys say is true, but there's one thing in golf: when we hit a foul ball, we've gotta get out there and play it."

I don't think I ever saw a story sweep across the nation as quickly as the one about the man who interrupted a match-deciding putt on the eighteenth green, to stand respectfully, hat in hand, while a funeral cortege rumbled by on the road behind him. Then he sank his putt. "Congratulations," said his opponent grudgingly. "It took iron nerve not to let that funeral procession fluster you into missing your putt!"

"It wasn't easy," admitted the victor. "On Saturday we would have been married twenty-five years!"

There was a near tragedy at the water hole of the Century Club in Westchester last fall. An irate golfer plunked one new ball into the pond and threw his driver after it. When a second

ball landed in the same spot, he threw in his whole bag of clubs. Then his caddy made a grave mistake. He laughed. So the golfer threw in the caddy.

Ben Hogan, all-time golfing great, was foiled by fate one day when he tried to give a duffer the thrill of a lifetime. Ben and a friend were playing a practice round. They had just holed out on a short three-par hole whose green was partially surrounded by trees and traps when suddenly, out of nowhere, a ball plopped down and trickled within two inches of the cup.

Hogan playfully tapped the ball in, and when a red-faced player came puffing from the direction of the deepest trap, held out his hand and said, "Mister, you're in for the biggest kick you ever got out of golf. Just look in that cup." The player followed directions and then hollered to a partner still hidden from view, "Hey, Joe, whaddya know! I sank it for a seven!"

In Hollywood, actor John Payne had to grow a beard for one of his swashbuckling Western roles. With a three-week growth of foliage concealing his manly features, John essayed a round of golf on the toughest course in town and drove one ball into a deep sand trap. A member of a foursome on an adjoining fairway investigated the cause of the interesting language emanating from the trap. He watched John blasting away, then noted his whiskers flapping in the afternoon breeze.

"Good heavens, Payne," he asked, "how long have you been in this trap?"

George Burns, of Burns and Allen, playing golf on a strange course, studied the lie of his ball and asked the caddie, "What club would you use here?" "A number eight," said the caddie without hesitation. So Burns used a number eight, hit a perfect shot—and found himself still forty yards short of the pin. "That's a full spoon shot," he announced to the caddie angrily. "Why did you tell me you'd use a number eight?" "Because," explained the caddie, "that's the only club I've got."

It is estimated that a prominent attorney in our town has now taken golf lessons from thirty-seven different pros in the past four years. "I can't understand it," he wailed in the locker room one day. "Despite all the lessons, I played worse last year than the year before, and the year before it was worse than the year before that." "How are you doing now?" asked his friend, Dr. Morris Fishbein. "You shouldn't have asked," said the attorney sadly. "Already I'm playing next year's game."

A mild earthquake once settled a championship golf match in Arizona. A contestant had to sink a long putt on the eighteenth green for a win, but his ball stopped on the lip of the cup. He resigned himself to a play-off of the tie the following morning.

Just then the earth trembled, however, the ball plopped into the cup, and there being nothing in the rule book to the contrary, he was declared the new champion. His opponent had one more stroke too—apoplectic.

The last word on the royal and ancient game of golf was passed by two wealthy Chinese merchants of San Francisco, who were invited to spend a day at a country club outside of Berkeley and saw, for the first time, a couple of duffers trying to hack their way out of a sand trap. "Wouldn't you think," observed Ah Sing, "that men as rich as that could get servants to perform such arduous and unpleasant labor for them?"

Published by the Coats & Clark's Sales Corporation, located at 430 Park Avenue, New York 22, is a long-needed schedule of the going rates for (1) listening to stroke-by-stroke descriptions of interminable matches, (2) sympathizing with habitual victims of "lucky" and "unethical" opponents, and (3) helping to condemn rascally caddies who forget to hold pins, rake traps, and demur at searching for balls in the deep woods because of poison ivy or rattlesnakes.

Staying awake during recitals of this sort is difficult work, and it's high time it was properly compensated!

Hackers on the golf links will rejoice at the announcement that the Motorola Corporation is experimenting with an electronic ball. It is equipped with miniature batteries and a tiny transmitter which sends a radio-frequency signal strong enough to be picked up by a portable receiver in the pocket of the golfer.

Gone will be those dreary searches for lost balls! The duffer can whack one a hundred yards into the deepest rough and, by simply turning his receiver in the proper direction, recover what Charles Morton would call "his elusive white pellet" without a moment's delay.

Daniel E. Noble, vice-president of Motorola, warns that this revolutionary golf ball, unfortunately, has been developed for demonstration purposes only, so far.

May it be perfected in time to help an earnest but inept golfer in Hollywood who had his first chance to break 125 a few Sundays ago—but had to sink a ten-foot putt to accomplish the feat! Trembling with excitement, he crawled around the green for five minutes studying each blade of grass in the path of the ball, then fluttered a handkerchief to determine the exact direction of the wind.

Finally he appealed to a companion, Bob Sterling, who shoots in the low seventies. "How should I putt this, Bob?" he asked. Sterling answered, "Keep it low!"

Football

History records that in 1916 a young lieutenant, just graduated from West Point, was summoned from his post at Fort Sam Houston to coach the football team of a nearby school named St. Mary's. The coach, one Dwight D. Eisenhower, found the spirit at the school willing, but the material sparse. Desperately seeking reinforcements for the skimpy squad of eighteen, he suddenly spotted a husky specimen crossing the campus. "Look here, young fellow," he called sharply. "Why the heck aren't you out to play football for your Alma Mater?" The husky specimen replied, "Lieutenant, I'll have you know I'm the principal of this school."

Rotund and rollicking Herman Hickman, once all-American guard from Tennessee, then line coach of the greatest teams ever turned out at Army, then head coach at Yale, has, alas, quit active participation in football. He now does his all from press box and sound stage.

Solvent but sedentary, Herman the Erudite has wasted away to a mere 290 pounds—just small enough to fit in his entirety on a twenty-one-inch screen. When he was eating at government expense at the Point, Herman hit a high of 320, and there was talk of splitting him three for one.

In his youth Herman aspired to a career in the law. At the age of seven he was already sending for catalogues of legal tomes. At ten he was reading—and memorizing—them. When he graduated from college in 1932, however, jobs were nonexistent in law

261

offices and just about everywhere else. Herman became a wrestler for a time—the only pro in that sport ever admitted, says Jimmy Cannon, to the human race. Then he turned to coaching gridiron squads.

Competent football players were few and far between when Hickman finally landed at Yale. Some friends from his home town of Johnson City, Tennessee, decided to help him out and, for a birthday present, brought him a burly, barrel-chested tackle named Apidoupolos, who tossed the varsity squad around like a set of ninepins at his first scrimmage. "He's terrific," conceded Hickman, "but can he satisfy Yale's entrance requirements? For example, how's his Greek?"

"He *is* Greek," explained the friends. "It's his English we're worrying about."

In December 1952, Herman Hickman got lost in the hills of eastern Tennessee. "Mighty embarrassing, losing my way in practically my home territory," he told a mountaineer. "Home territory, my foot," scoffed the mountaineer. "You look like a big fat Yankee to me."

Herman convinced him, however, and the mollified mountaineer asked, "Who won that election last month?"

Herman knew that this section was solidly Republican, so he said, "You'll be glad to know that Ike Eisenhower sailed in. But don't you take any newspapers around here?"

"We take 'em," nodded the mountaineer grimly, "but the durn Democrats won't read 'em to us."

The trusting citizens of an Indiana town found out what happens if you elect a veteran football referee to the post of police commissioner. The very day he assumed office he arrested the community's outstanding strip-teaser. His charge: her back was illegally in motion.

Neal O'Hara tells about the football coach who started a brand-new backfield for the final quarter of a game safely won, consisting of Osscowinsinski, Yablanowicz, Palleofontack, and Bacjewobonwich. "Are they any good?" asked an old grad on the bench. "Heck no," barked the coach, "but, boy, will I pay back a score I owe a couple of those smart-aleck newspaper sports writers!"

Herman Massin tells of a time Lou Little, well-loved coach of the perennially undermanned Columbia football team, suggested to Frank Leahy, then at Notre Dame, "Suppose my Lions are playing Michigan State. We kick off and State returns the ball to our five. On the next play they pull the shift you invented. Wouldn't you say that shift was designed to pull my team offside?"

Leahy replied thoughtfully, "All I can say, Lou, is that if your team kicked off to Michigan State, and they returned the ball only to your five-yard line, your defense certainly must be improving."

Guided Muscles

A much-beaten pugilist announced his intention to retire from the ring, but his manager, sensing the loss of a fair-to-middling meal ticket, sought to dissuade him. "This ain't no time to quit, Spike," he protested, "just when you're beginning to improve. I've been noticin' right along that in every fight lately you come to much quicker!"

"The first lesson to remember in the gentle art of self-defense," advises Steve Allen, "is to keep your glasses on."

Fight managers aren't what they used to be now that television has entered the act, maintains Budd Schulberg. They used to yell, "Don't forget to duck, kid." Now they exhort, "Don't let him get away with that! He's trying to keep your back turned to the camera again!"

When a Brooklyn lad decided to become a professional pugilist, his mother was outraged and never ceased her lamentations —not even when he bagged the middleweight championship. "Now you're at the top," she begged him, "quit before it's too late. Promise you'll stop fighting right now." "But, Mama, you don't understand," the son protested. "I'm in the big money now that I'm champ. With TV and everything, I'm likely to gross a cool hundred thousand on my next bout." "A cool hundred thousand," gasped the mother. "My boy, promise me you'll stop fighting in nine or ten years."

The Idle Hour Athletic Club was putting on one of its better fixed fights, with the five-to-one favorite bribed in advance to let himself be knocked cold in the eighth round. The underdog, secure in the knowledge that he couldn't lose, let a couple of real punches loose and rattled every tooth in the favorite's head. "You dirty little double-crosser," hissed that gentleman in a clinch. "Just wait till I get you outside!"

Harry Ruby tells about the prize-fight manager whose inexperienced new middleweight was taking an unmerciful trimming in his first professional bout. Finally the manager propped up his unhappy charge and told him, "I don't care if it's bad luck or not—but this is the ninth round coming up, and, kid, you've got a no-hitter going!"

Fishing

In a Maine fishing camp, Hans Hinrichs, of New York, was served a beaker of orange juice whose flavor delighted him. "Emil," he asked his host, "where do you get your oranges? Never have I tasted such delicious juice." "In the little store down the road," answered Emil.

Mr. Hinrichs bought an entire crate on his way back to town. But when he sampled the juice, the taste definitely was not the same. He phoned Emil to register his disappointment. "I can't understand it," admitted Emil. "Your oranges are the same as ours. What gin did you use with them?"

At another fishing camp, deep in the Wisconsin woods, a group of vacationing city fellers dispatched an old guide once a week to canoe fifteen miles to the nearest village and back to collect newspapers and mail. When they checked out for the season, the old guide presented his bill. It read, "Three up and three down, at two dollars a went. Twelve dollars."

"Fishing is simplicity itself," explains Hamilton Clay, Jr. "All you have to do is get there yesterday when the fish were biting." One disciple of Izaak Walton picked the wrong day for sure. He was discovered by the father of a seven-year-old boy, pole discarded, hopping on one foot, caressing the other, and howling with anguish. "What happened?" demanded the father. "I guess it's my fault," said the seven-year-old. "This man told me he hadn't had a bite all morning—so I bit him."

If you'd like to hear about some of the darndest varieties of fish under the sun—or at least under the surface—Eugenie Clark's *Lady with a Spear* is the book for you. She tells about one fish that has double eyes, enabling it to see either in the air or in the water; another which, at full growth, is considerably less than one inch long; another that squirts poison at its enemies through a hypodermic-like syringe. Then there's the razor fish, which swims standing on its head, and, queerest of all, the pipe-fish, of which the male, believe it or not, has the babies!

One of the fishermen's favorite "tall tales" concerns the fellow who, impatient at his failure to pull in a single thing, impulsively dipped the minnow he was using as bait in a jug of moonshine and then lowered his line again. Seconds later he felt a strike and hauled in a huge sea bass, which was threshing about helplessly against the minnow, which had it by the throat and was choking it to death.

The parson, detained from his dearly loved weekly fishing expedition by a young couple who insisted upon being hitched immediately, regarded the bridegroom sourly, and inquired, "Do you promise to love, honor, and cherish this woman?" "I do," said the bridegroom fervently. "Good," boomed the parson, heading for the nearest exit. "Reel her in."

A fisherman in the Arabian Sea pulled in his net one day and found entangled therein a strange copper bottle with a golden seal. When he broke it open, a cloud of black smoke rushed out and turned into a monstrous genie. "I will revenge myself for my imprisonment in that bottle," roared the genie, "by killing everybody I see, and I will begin here and now with you."

The quick-thinking fisherman sneered, "Go ahead and kill me, you goon. Tear down that whole coastal range of mountains. And still I won't be convinced that a monster like you could be contained in that tiny bottle!"

"You won't, hey?" roared the genie. "Doubters like you *really* burn me up. Look at this, you twerp!"

Condensing himself in the twinkling of an eye, he poured himself back in the bottle. "Amazing!" chuckled the fisherman as he replaced the cork and threw the bottle back into the sea.

Hunting

Lest you think that hunting these days is a carefree and inexpensive diversion, Brother Bill Feather of Cleveland quotes these prices from a sports lovers' catalogue: "Duck shooter's parka: $55; Duckers' mittens: $10; Lambskin vest: $32; Alpaca-lined covert coat: $85; Paul Bunyan hunting boots: $38.70; Shotgun: $550; Sleeping bag: $98."

When Herb Wise, of Lengsfeld, goes duckhunting, however, he needs none of this highfalutin paraphernalia; just his trusty old double-barreled fowling piece. One day he took his nephew along to show how it was done. A solitary duck flew over the blind. "Down you go," chuckled Herb, and fired. The duck flew serenely on.

Herb scratched his head. "Son," he declared, "you are witnessing a miracle. There flies a dead duck!"

A prominent society physician was better equipped when he set out on a hunting trip, but he also returned empty-handed. "I didn't kill a thing today," he admitted. "That's the first time that's happened in years," said his unfeeling wife.

Some brand-new members of a hunting club were coming in from their first day's shooting. Since they were unused to handling guns, the casualty list was rather formidable. One had his hand in a sling, another was hopping on one foot, a third looked like the drummer boy in the old Revolutionary War picture. "Cheer up, fellows," urged an old member. "Judging by the bulge in your bag, you're not coming back empty-handed anyhow!" The one who was carrying the bag answered wearily, "That's our hunting dog!"

Joe Grizzly Bear, Indian scout at a hunting camp in the Black Hills, has a favorite picture. He carries it in his wallet, in fact. It shows a fat lady all togged up in fancy hunting clothes, with a smoking rifle in her hands, and a look of unholy glee on her face. "I must have hit something," she's exulting to her husband. "Just listen to that language!"

A party of hunters finally talked their faithful cook, old Mose, into going with them while they tracked down a huge grizzly. "All right, I'll go," he conceded reluctantly, "but if you gets wrestling with that bear and you looks round and don't see nobody, that's me."

In Colonel Weatherbee's Louisville trophy room there hangs a majestic moose head. A visitor's young daughter, fascinated by it, finally asked her father, "May I go into the next room and see the rest of it?"

One of the colonel's hunting forays produced no such imposing specimen. Blithely he sounded his moose-call horn, but no noble animal burst into the clearing. Instead, an army of mice scurried into view.

"Damnation," muttered the colonel. "I told my secretary to order a moose-call by mail, but, as usual, she made a typographical error!"

In Africa, three big-game hunters were resting by their campfire after a hard day in the jungle when one announced, "I'm restless. Think I'll go for a short hike before chow."

The other two didn't fret over his non-appearance for over an hour. Then one glanced at his watch and murmured, "Hmm! Wonder what's eating old Ernest?"

Racing

A race-track devotee of many years' standing, thoroughly versed in the lore and form sheets of horse racing, was astonished to note that two dear little old ladies picked the winner unfailingly in seven straight races—some of them fantastic long shots. Finally he whispered to them, "Divulge your system to me, ladies, and I'll show you how to pyramid your bets so you'll make a million." "There's really no trick to it," chuckled one of the little ladies happily. "We just bet on the ones with longest tails."

The late Joe Palmer had a prize story about a horse owner in Wyoming who showed up at a race meeting with an eight-year-old non-starter and put him in an important race. Since an eight-year-old maiden is hardly a betting attraction, he was off at $136.50 and galloped home first by a cool ten lengths. The stewards suspected dirty work at the crossroads and demanded of the owner, "Is this horse unsound?" "No, sir," asserted the owner. "Soundest horse you ever saw. Ankles like iron, and there ain't never been a pimple on him." "Well then," persisted a steward, "why haven't you raced him before?" "To tell the truth," said the owner sheepishly, "we couldn't ketch him till he was seven."

A racing habitué bought a broken-down filly in a claiming race. When he went to the paddock to examine it, he found it on its side, with two veterinary surgeons attending it. "Is my horse sick?" he asked. "She's not the picture of health," said the vets, "but we hope to pull her through." "But will I ever be able to race her?" persisted the habitué. "Chances are you will," one vet assured him, "and you'll probably beat her too!"

Two Jewish race-track addicts met on the way home from Belmont, and one began immediately to bemoan an unbroken streak of miserable luck. The other boasted, "Not me! I've gone right back to fundamentals. Every morning now I pray for fifteen minutes at the synagogue, and since I started not a day has gone by that I haven't picked at least two winners." "What have I got to lose?" said the unfortunate one. "I'll try your system."

Three weeks later they met again. "I followed your advice," began the steady loser. "Not only did I pray every morning, but every evening as well. All day Saturday I spent in the synagogue, too, not to mention a couple of holidays. And in all that time, believe me, not a single winner I picked." "I can't understand it," said his friend. "What synagogue did you pray in?" "The one on Grove Street," was the answer. "No wonder, you schmo," shouted the friend. "That's for trotters!"

Haggerty had had a miserable run of luck at the track and was down to his last ten-spot when, just before the last race, he happily caught sight of his parish priest anointing one of the horses entered therein. "With the holy father blessin' the craiture," reasoned Haggerty, "how kin he lose?" So he put the whole ten right on the nose to win.

There were eight horses in the race—and Haggerty's choice

finished eighth. A few days later he encountered the reverend gentleman on the street and grumbled, "It's been lettin' me down ye've done, that's what! I bet on a horse because ye stop to bless it, and begorra, it finishes last!" The priest told him sadly, "You should have more faith than that, my boy. I wasn't blessing that horse. I was giving him the last rites."

Gambling

A purveyor of lottery tickets always lay in wait for wealthy Baron Rothschild when he exited from a European spa, and tried to talk him into buying the equivalent of a fifty-cent chance. To get rid of him, Rothschild said one day, "Here's fifty francs. Pick out any one you want and don't bother me again." Some days later the ticket seller came up in great excitement and said, "The ticket I bought for you has won the grand prize—$250,000!"

"Well," said the baron, pleased in spite of himself, "I suppose I'll have to reward you. Which do you prefer: ten thousand dollars in cash, or three thousand dollars a year for the rest of your life?"

"I'll take the ten thousand," said the ticket seller without a moment's hesitation. "With your luck, I wouldn't live another six months!"

When the mighty Hoover Dam, harnessing the waters of the Colorado River, was completed in 1936, agricultural and industrial interest in the Southwest were protected for the first time from a recurring and devastating cycle of floods and droughts. Boom times ensued for southern California, Arizona, and Nevada, but nowhere were the results so immediate as in the town, twenty-six miles from the dam, called Las Vegas.

From a sleepy community of five thousand in 1925, Las Vegas has mushroomed into a feverish, brassy city of fifty thousand today, featuring high gambling, low taxation, easy marriage, and painlessly simple divorce. It has seven magnificent resort hotels

with more building—and virtually anything goes there, particularly a visitor's money.

Let's take the lush Sands Hotel as typical of this new vacation "paradise." The Sands, fronting the new and constantly expanding "Strip," cost four million dollars and it took the proprietors almost two full months of round-the-clock gambling by panting guests to recoup their investment. One gent who had lost three thousand dollars considered a sixteen-dollar charge for his room exorbitant. The benevolent desk clerk reduced it to fourteen dollars and the man went away happy.

Another guest—a lady whose lantern jaw won her the nickname of "Mme. Popeye"—held the dice for forty-five minutes. She made twenty-seven consecutive "passes" (sevens and elevens), but being a cautious soul, won only $132. Excited gamblers around her, however, backed her heavily, and her splurge cost the management $215,000.

Outside of the constantly crowded gaming rooms of the Sands, and other hostelries in its class, are lavish accommodations, elegant shops, and deserted swimming pools. For those who do not like fancy roulette or the galloping dominoes, there are slot machines in every nook and cranny.

I asked one busy lady, "Which way is it to the office of the Las

Vegas *Sun?*" Without breaking her rhythm (she couldn't lose her money fast enough at one machine, so was crouched over two), she answered: "Thirty slot machines straight ahead, then fourteen dice tables to the left."

Las Vegas night clubs don't care how much they pay their stars, figuring, no doubt, that the stars will probably lose their loot, and then some, right back at the gaming tables. At one time, luminaries like Bankhead, Lena Horne, Joe E. Lewis, and Melchior are likely to be appearing within the confines of a single mile along the "Strip."

To see them, you need only order a round of sodas for your entire party. The boys will get you on the way out. Joe E. Lewis ended his engagement by climbing atop a dice table and imploring, "Shoot any part of me." At the airport he added, "If I was alive today, I'd be a very sick man. But I'll be back to play Las Vegas again next year. I want to visit my money."

One of the characters who presides over the gambling activities in the Sands Hotel rejoices in the name of Sherlock Feldman. In his salad days, Sherlock was co-proprietor of a gambling casino in the Klondike, where they used chips made of ice. One night a lucky miner made twenty-two consecutive passes, with all his pals backing him to the hilt, and Sherlock's partner moaned, "They've broken the bank. We're ruined!" The resourceful Sherlock, however, merely turned up the furnace another fifteen degrees, and all the chips melted.

Another time, at the Sands, a patron who had taken a fearful shellacking wagered every last chip he had left, crying, "Shoot the works." He was so agitated that his upper false teeth fell out upon the table. Sherlock promptly planked down *his* lower plate and declared cheerfully, "You're faded."

Education is not neglected at Las Vegas. There's a new elementary school that Joe Lewis has christened P.S. 6-to-5. "How old are you?" Arlene Frances asked one of its cutest pupils. The little girl answered, "Four, the hard way."

273

Gambling parlors and slot machines are not the only hazards in Las Vegas with which to conjure. "Look out for the odd-shaped swimming pools too," warns Mel Torme. "They have a very high chorine content."

An officer of the law stopped short when he observed a man proceeding down Main Street clad only in a barrel. "Ah, ha," he exclaimed. "Been playing poker, eh?" "Not me," said the man in the barrel sadly. "But I just left six other fellows who were."

The man who was watching Mr. Guggenheimer play bridge was mildly puzzled when he failed to double an opponent's grand-slam bid although he held the ace of trumps in his hand. "A bit cautious, what?" he asked *sotto voce*. "Lordy," explained Mr. Guggenheimer, "I'd never dare double that lunatic. He redoubles at the drop of a hat!"

Indoor Sports

The wife of one of the forwards on the New York Rangers hockey team admitted, "It's really thrilling to be married to a big-time hockey star. Every time he comes home he looks like a different person."

Mrs. Nussbaum's and Mrs. Goldstein's first visit to a neighborhood bowling alley was not exactly a triumphal affair, but Mrs. Nussbaum derived a certain modicum of comfort from their performance. "I hope you noticed," she said on the way home, "that we didn't lose a single ball!"

Coaches all agree that something will have to be done about the height of basketball players. They've grown so tall and gangling on most squads, nobody under six feet is allowed to carry the towels and water bucket any more.

Players no longer shoot baskets; they drop in the ball while passing by, as though they were mailing a letter.

One Indiana team *averaged* six feet last season. Everybody was impressed except poet Carl Sandburg. "So what?" he pointed out. "Abe Lincoln was over six-three!"

Cartoonist Robert Day, six-six himself, depicts a guard who was so tall he merely had to stand under the basket with his head protruding therefrom. Enemy shots, of course, bounced harmlessly off his noggin.

No wonder his coach watched him, chuckling happily and enthusing, "Best darn guard in the country!"

Milton Berle rashly planked down a bet on William and Mary College near the close of the basketball season—and lost. "Dawgone it," he complained, "how was I to know they were going to let Mary play?"

From basketball-mad Indiana comes the story of two Scottish fans who attended a championship game. One was equipped with a pint, to which he resorted with increasing frequency—but alone. Meanwhile, he regaled his arid companion with tales of his own triumphs as a center on the Glasgow Globetrotters.

"Fifty per cent o' yer gab I can persuade myself to credit," grumbled the arid one at long last. "I can see ye're an unco' fine dribbler. But, mon—yer na gude at all at passin'!"

The Russian temperament is peculiarly suited to chess. They say that a Russian named Droskycharnoff invented the greatest defense in the history of the game. He grew whiskers so long that they hid all sixteen of his pieces.

When it came to self-confidence, another Russian chess champion named Bogolyubov took the cake. Asked the secret of his success in game after game, he explained calmly, "When I have the white pieces and move first, I win because I am white. When I have the black pieces, I win because I am Bogolyubov."

Sylvia Fine, Mrs. Danny Kaye in private life, tells the story of a West Coast chess master whose five-year-old son loved to watch him play, and even accompanied him to Sacramento for the state championship. At a crucial point in the final match, the father reached out to move a knight.

The five-year-old tugged urgently at his sleeve and whispered, "Papa, don't move the horse." The father reconsidered, suddenly discovered that the move he had contemplated would have cost him the match, reoriented his strategy, and ultimately triumphed.

On the way home he gazed proudly at his son and asked, "What made you warn me not to move the horse?" The boy explained simply, "He looked hungry."

CHAPTER TWENTY-TWO

TRAVEL IS SO BROADENING . . .

(Around the World in 28 Pages)

A Philadelphia socialite, returning home with his family from a two-month tour of Europe, was asked by reporters when his ship docked at Quarantine, "Did you see many signs of poverty abroad?" He answered bitterly, "Not only did I see signs of it, but I've brought some back with me."

The socialite's new English chauffeur was stopped by an immigration officer who explained, "We have a tip that you are smuggling in a quantity of pornographic literature." "It's a lie!" sputtered the chauffeur. "I haven't even got a pornograph!"

277

Sailing across the Atlantic aboard the *Queen Mary*, the traveler is apt to hear this story, intriguing even if it isn't true, about how the liner got its name:

Since time immemorial, Cunard ships always had names ending in "ia" and, in keeping with this tradition, the new addition to the fleet was scheduled to be called the *Queen Victoria*. When the Cunard chairman called on King George V, however, to acquaint him with this fact, and began by saying, "We're pleased to tell you our new liner will be named after one of Britain's greatest queens . . ." the King interrupted happily, "Good, good! Her Majesty, I know, will be simply delighted!"

So, the *Queen Mary* it became, and the good lady herself christened the ship as it slid down the ways.

The English

Riding up to London in a first-class railroad compartment with Winston Churchill, a man on the seat opposite stared at him for a full half hour, finally tapped him on the shoulder and inquired, "I say, would your name possibly be Churchill!" "It would," grunted the great "Winnie." "*Winston* Churchill?" persisted the stranger. "Right again," said Mr. C. The stranger slapped his hand on his knee and boomed, "Then I do believe we went to Harrow together in 1888!"

The late Harold Laski was dispatched one day to secure an interview with Winston Churchill. When he returned, his editor said, "Well, did you get in to see him?" "Not only did I get in," Laski assured the editor, "but I sat for two hours and listened to his thunderous and well-rehearsed improvisations."

Here's a story that highlights the special quality that makes the English different from all other folks. An elderly lady was riding down to London in a first-class railway compartment when she suddenly confided to the young lady across the aisle,

"I saw a splendid play the last time I visited London. Gielgud starred. He was superb. The direction and lighting also were perfect. Only fault with the play was the girl in the leading role. Marguerite Chapman I believe her name was. Shocking performance. I wonder how she got on to acting for a living in the first place."

The young lady's eyes flashed. "It may interest you to learn," she snapped, "that I happen to be Marguerite Chapman."

The elderly lady nodded. "Yes," she said softly, "I know."

Historians finally have discovered what Lord Godiva said to Lady Godiva when she returned from her famous ride. He was waiting at the door in a towering rage and demanded, "Where, exactly, have you been? Your horse got home two hours ago!"

And when a lovely young lady in waiting at King Arthur's Court sneaked into the castle, she whispered feelingly to Queen Guinevere, "What a knight!"

In Pierre Barton's lively *The Royal Family*, he recalls a sea trip Queen Victoria made to Ireland. The ship encountered dirty weather, and one monstrous wave almost knocked Her Majesty galley-west. Regaining her equilibrium with some difficulty, she commanded an attendant, "Go up to the bridge, give the admiral my compliments, and tell him he's not to let that happen again."

King George V, narrates Berton, was an avid stamp collector. A secretary commented one morning, "I see in the *Times* that some damn fool paid fourteen hundred pounds for a single stamp at a private sale yesterday." "I," retorted King George calmly, "was that damn fool."

In London, three Oxford professors of literature resisted the determined advance of a group of fancy ladies they encountered on Picadilly, then sought to find a phrase best describing them. The specialist in the Barchester novels voted for "A chapter of trollops." The Shakespearian scholar clung to "A flourish of strumpets." The collector of short stories carried the day, however, with "An anthology of pros."

Two crooked, but very formal, Londoners had shared the same cell in jail for over six years. One's reserve finally broke down and he assured the other, "No need to call me 'Number 855625' from now on, old chap. Henceforth, to you, I'm plain '855'!"

A wealthy Londoner sought to purchase an expensive American convertible car. "But, my dear fellow," expostulated the dealer, "we've been allotted only two of this model all year, and there are already one hundred seventy-four orders ahead of yours." "Too bad," murmured the Londoner, seemingly not too dismayed. As he left he ostentatiously tossed a large bundle of ten-pound notes into the trash basket.

The very next morning the precise model he was seeking was delivered to him. A few days later the dealer called him on the phone. "Those ten-pound notes," he roared, "are all counterfeit."

"Exactly," agreed the Londoner blandly. "That's why I threw them in the trash basket."

British pride in native products has not dimmed.

A London plutocrat was driving his fine new Rolls-Royce over the Alps when he heard a disquieting "twang." His front spring had broken.

He called the Rolls plant in London by long distance, and, in what seemed like no time flat, three gentlemen arrived by plane with a new spring—and off went the plutocrat on his interrupted jaunt.

Now comes the really interesting part of the story. After six months the plutocrat had received no bill from the Rolls people. Finally he appeared at the plant in person and asked that the records be checked for "the repair of a broken spring in Switzerland." After a brief delay the manager of the plant appeared in person, gazed at him rather reproachfully, and announced, "There must be some mistake, sir. There is no such *thing* as a broken spring on a Rolls-Royce."

Tom Driberg, Member of the British Parliament, is authority for the fact that several London "pubs" have taken to featuring a new drink they call "The Clothes Brush." When this concoction is served to a customer, the barman puts an actual stiff-bristled clothes brush beside it. The customer usually downs the drink in a single gulp, then falls flat on his face. A few minutes later he comes to, gravely brushes the dust off his clothes with the brush, pays his check, and goes about his business. Driberg avers further that in a Soho pub where he was watching the clothes-brush routine in its finest flowering, one customer, at least, had the strength of mind to order something else. "Just whip up something long and cold and full of gin," he commented. The man alongside him promptly volunteered, "Take my wife here."

The Scottish

A thrifty old Scot named MacCrindle stayed with a business associate in London and became deeply attached to the latter's black cocker spaniel. The dog returned his affection and kicked up such a fuss when MacCrindle was leaving that the Londoner insisted he be taken home as a gift.

"This is uncommon kind of ye," declared MacCrindle, "and as soon as I get back to Scotland, I'll be sending ye the biggest finest turkey ye ever did see."

Several months passed before MacCrindle ran into his English friend again. The latter remarked in passing, "By the way, that turkey you were going to send me never did arrive."

"I forgot to tell ye," replied MacCrindle. "The turkey got well."

On a lake steamer in Scotland, a lovely young girl fell overboard. The waters were very choppy, and the girl had already gone under twice when a middle-aged Scot, extremely well dressed, kerplonked into the lake and dragged the girl aboard the steamer. The girl's father threw his arms around the drenched Scotsman and enthused, "You're a great hero, sir. How can I ever repay you?" "Just tell me one thing," said the Scotsman grimly. "Who pushed me?"

Houdini, the wily escape artist, made one of his rare miscalculations when he fought his way free of a supposedly foolproof police straight jacket and heavy handcuffs from the top span of a big bridge in Scotland. The stunt was widely advertised, and a traffic-stopping throng was expected. Yet only a corporal's guard turned up. "Don't they like me here in Scotland?" the disappointed Houdini asked a city official. "They're crazy for you," was the reassuring reply. "But, mon, you performed on the wrong bridge. That's a toll bridge!"

McGregor lay breathing his last. He roused himself to whisper to the assemblage round his bedside, "Tannish owes me fifty pounds." "It's a great mind the man has," marveled his wife. "Clear as a bell to the very end." McGregor spoke again: "I believe I owe Sandy Mollinson a hundred pounds." "Ach, the poor mon," sobbed Mrs. McGregor. "Take no notice of his delirious meanderings!"

The song of a generous Scotchman:

> Oh, I hand out cash with a lavish hand
> In a philanthropic fury.
> Ask, and I'll give to you fifty grand—
> That is, while I'm on the jury.

An English commercial traveler found himself stranded for the weekend in a small Scottish town whose amusement list was limited, to say the least. In desperation, he asked the innkeeper, "What on earth can a poor soul do in this town after dark?" The innkeeper considered the query gravely, then replied, "I'm not sure, sir, but the fancy lady walks at eight!"

Another salesman, representing the Highland Kilt Company (he had a kilt complex), ran into a spell of dirty weather in the Midlands and notified headquarters, "Likely to be marooned here for several days. Wire instructions." Back came a telegram—collect—which read, "Begin summer vacation as of this morning."

Scotch joke variation Number 68414: Excavators in Aberdeen have come upon a Scottish penny dated 1588. A few feet away they then unearthed three skeletons, all on their hands and knees.

The Irish

Irish prerogatives, claims author Frank O'Connor, are in jeopardy. It was galling enough when he read in *Variety* that the music for the two St. Patrick's Day dances staged in Omaha last year was furnished, respectively, by Adolph Urbanovsky's Bohemian ensemble and Toothless Simon and his Five Cavities. But Frank really needed an outlet for his Eire escape when he picked up a fine old sturdy shillelagh and found brazenly stamped thereon, "Made in Japan"!

In an opening-round match for the duffers' booby prize at a Dublin golf club, says Frank, one Timothy O'Brien demanded of his opponent, "How many strokes would you be takin' on that last hole?" "Let me see now," mused the opponent with a fine show of concentration. "I'd say I took eight. No, 'twas only seven." "I'll put you down for nine, you spalpeen," announced O'Brien severely. "You'll recall there's a penalty of one stroke here for improvin' your lie!"

Mr. Doolan caught his old friend, the bartender at Moriarty's saloon, in an unguarded moment and begged, "Mike, me mother-in-law has gone to her just reward, and it's a ten spot I'm needin' to supply a wreath that will uphold the Doolan standards. Can ye advance me the ten?"

The bartender emptied his pockets and the cash register, but the combined total came to only nine dollars and thirty cents.

"That'll do for the moment," said Doolan hastily. "I'll take the other seventy cents in drinks."

During a tour of America, the distinguished Irish wit, speech maker, and parliamentarian, T. P. O'Connor—fondly known as "Tay Pay" to his constituents—was asked repeatedly, "What is the state of Ireland today?"

"Status quo," "Tay Pay" would reply cheerily. "In the South of Ireland we have the Catholics, and in the North the Protestants, and they're at each other's throats as usual all the time.

285

. . . If only they were haythen so they could live together loike Christians!"

Clancy sidled into the back of the Shamrock Bar and Grill with his right pocket bulging. "It's a stick o' dynamite I've got there," he confided. "I'm waiting for Finnegan. Every time he meets me he wallops me side and breaks me pipe. This time, begorra, he'll blow off his hand."

Maureen O'Hara, as fair a colleen as ever whipped up a blintz in County Cork, tells about an Irish sea captain who became temporarily confused on the bridge one day and narrowly averted ramming the admiral's flagship. A rash of signal flags broke out on the admiral's vessel. "It's a message for you, sir," an ensign told the befuddled captain. "It says, 'You blank blank landlubber, what the blank do you think you're doing with that blank blank tub of yours?'" "H-m-m-m," mused the captain. "Better take that down to the signal room and have it decoded immediately."

A candidate in the recent Irish elections displayed a candor some of our own politicians would do well to emulate. "All we ask," he declared from the platform, "is another two years to complete our program." "And what," demanded a voice from the rear, "*is* your program?" The candidate answered forcefully, "To stay in for another two years!"

The French

There once lived in France a whimsical couple who named their first-born son "Formidable." All his life, he was the butt of assorted jibes because of this ridiculous name, especially since he grew up to be a skinny unimposing wisp of a man.

Nevertheless, Formidable found himself a beautiful wife—the

catch of the town—and what's more, lived with her in utter tranquility for a full fifty-seven years.

At eighty-five, Formidable came to the end of the road. His dying request to his wife was, "Do not put that awful name of mine on my tombstone. It would prevent my resting in peace." Tearfully the wife promised, and was good as her word. His epitaph read simply: "Here lies a man whose wife was absolutely faithful to him for fifty-seven years."

And so every Frenchman who passes that grave exclaims, "*Regardez! C'est formidable!*"

Anatole Litvak tells an enchanting tale about a young Parisian who was wheeling his baby son's carriage through the Bois. The son was howling with rage. The Parisian contented himself with repeating softly, "Control yourself, Bernard. Just be calm, Bernard."

A child psychologist watched the scene approvingly and tapped the Parisian on the shoulder. "Congratulations, monsieur," he said warmly, "for keeping your temper so admirably. You know instinctively how to handle the little fellow. Gently does it! So he's named Bernard, eh?"

"Not at all," corrected the Parisian. "He's named André. *I'm* Bernard."

Author Harry Kurnitz achieved the impossible: he happened upon a restaurant in Paris where the food was positively terrible. What's more, the waiter cheerfully admitted the fact. "Monsieur would be wise," he whispered, "to get out of here fast. There's a really fine little restaurant right across the boulevard." "Are you sure?" asked Kurnitz. "Sure? *Certainement*," said the waiter vehemently. "I own it." Then he added, "This miserable place is where I find my customers."

The maître d'hôtel at one of those intimate side-street French restaurants assured Irwin Shaw that snails were the specialty of the house. "I know," sighed Shaw, "and you've got them dressed as waiters."

A Wall Street banker took his wife to Paris, where he closed a big bond deal. Final signing of the papers took longer than he had expected, so he called the Ritz Hotel and told the French maid, "Please tell madame to go to bed and wait for me." "*Bien,* monsieur," answered the maid, "but who shall I say called?"

An heir to millions, native of Cincinnati, was dining alone in Paris when he thought he detected a "come hither" look in the eyes of the prettiest girl he had ever seen. "She jumped into a cab," he told his friends when he returned to America, "and I jumped into another. 'Follow that girl,' I commanded. Down the Champs Elysées we raced, across the Seine, and up the Boulevard Raspail. When she alighted at a studio building in the heart of the Left Bank, I was only a few steps behind her. I caught her on the landing of her apartment, and with a happy sigh I never will forget, she melted into my arms." "What happened after that?" his friends asked breathlessly. The excitement died down in the heir's voice. "After that," he admitted, "it was just like Cincinnati."

An old French farmer was walking through his pasture with an American tourist and his eager-beaver wife. "I notice," said she eagerly, "that some of your cows have horns and some haven't. Why is that?" "There are three cases in which they lack horns," explained the farmer carefully. "Some are born without them, some are dehorned, and some have their horns knocked off fighting." "And what about that different-looking one over in the corner?" persisted the wife. "Ah," murmured the peasant. "That is case Number Four. That is a horse."

Two Americans met on the Champs Élysées on their first visit to Paris. "This sight-seeing sure takes a lot of time," grumbled one. "I've been here nearly four days and I still haven't visited the Louvre." Suggested the other, "Maybe it's the water."

Sacha Guitry, long-time favorite of the Paris theater, had a father, Lucien, who was equally famous in his day. Lucien, among other things, was noted for the perfection of his make-up for various of his starring roles. For example, he had a photo of Pasteur pasted on his mirror and, while visitors gaped, he would make up for the role, looking so *exactly* like the photo when he was finished that no one could detect any difference whatever. Nor was there any. For what the wily Guitry had done was to make himself up first as Pasteur, then have himself photographed—then substitute the result on his mirror in place of the original!

In Paris, Frank L. Rand was fortunate enough to be there or thereabouts when a lady tourist saw her sight-seeing group riding away in a bus without her. After frantically consulting her pocket English-French dictionary, she took off in pursuit, shouting, "Hey, garcon! Wait! Attendez! Stoppez at once! Je suis gauche derriere!"

Sunny Italy

Sunrise over St. Peter's and the Tiber, an Italian nobleman assured a beautiful young tourist from the States, was a memory of Rome she would cherish the rest of her life. "We will sit in my garden," he proposed, "and watch the dawn together." "But, Count," she protested, "what about the dew?" "My dear," said the count firmly, "when in Rome, dew as the Romans dew."

A lady from Indiana got her first view of the Colosseum, clutched her guide's arm, and gurgled, "It's perfect! Don't let them change a thing!"

The night Gina Lollobrigida was the mystery guest on "What's My Line?" panel moderator John Daly observed appreciatively, "There's one Roman who wasn't built in a day." Victor Borge estimated, "She's about five and a half feet tall—lying down on her back." Steve Allen had the last word. "Only two good things have come this way from Italy all season," he declared, "and Gina's got both of them."

Darkest Africa

Two shipwrecked Broadway characters, marooned on a dinky and deserted island off the coast of Africa for months, shrieked with joy when a bottle came floating in on the tide. With trembling hands one of the castaways extracted a note from the bottle. Then his face fell. "Nuts," he exclaimed. "It's from us!"

From an installation in the Sahara Desert, a big oil refinery got a letter complaining that the personnel's water rations were inadequate. The president pooh-poohed, "Those spoiled so-and-so's are always complaining they haven't enough water." "This time," answered his aide, "I think they mean it. Their postage stamp is attached with a pin."

Several telephone maintenance men were assigned to stretch a new line across a remote district in the Zulu country. A Zulu chief and his advisers watched the work in silence for a while, then the chief pointed out disgustedly, "White men damn fools. Put wire so high, livestock can walk right out under it."

An intrepid British sportsman invaded the African jungle in search of big game (he was driving a Jaguar, of course), but ran afoul of a blazing native insurrection. Whipping out his service revolver, he emptied all barrels point-blank at the enemy, returned to his base to report happily, "I guess I've just shot the last of the red-hot Maumaus!"

An Irish sailor wandered up the beach while his ship was anchored at an obscure African port, and was promptly captured by a band of cannibals.

Each day the fiends would prick his arm with a spear and drink some of his rich Hibernian blood. The day came when he could stand this no longer. Thrusting his lower jaw out at the chief, he hollered, "Kill me and eat me if ye will, ye heathen rascals, but this is positively the last day ye're going to stick me fer the drinks!"

In far off Nigeria, Africa, the owner of one of the few movie emporiums has found out exactly what his patrons want and, by golly, he gives it to them. On every Monday, Tuesday, and Friday, for the past six years, writes a magazine correspondent, he has packed them in with *King Kong,* and on Wednesdays, Thursdays, and Saturdays, he turns them away with *The Mark of Zorro.* It's on Sundays, however, that he really hits the jack pot with a double bill consisting of—you guessed it—*King Kong* and *The Mark of Zorro.*

One of the great cartoons of recent years was drawn by Ed Fisher for *The New Yorker* magazine. It shows a cannibal chieftain happily advising his assembled board of strategy: "Now here's the plan. We let word out that we're in a state of political ferment. Russia smells an opportunity and makes overtures. The West gets worried. *They* make overtures. Russia asks to send cultural ambassadors, and we let them. The West asks for equal representation, and we invite them. Then, when we've got them all here, we eat them."

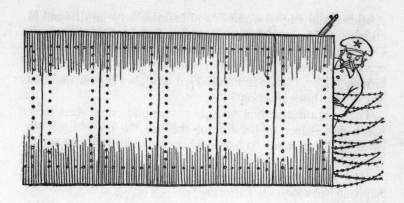

Behind the Iron Curtain

Here are two paragraphs about the Russians. Can you guess who wrote them?

"Let it be clearly understood that the Russian is a delightful person till he tucks in his shirt. As an Oriental he is charming. It is only when he insists upon being treated as the most easterly of Western peoples instead of the most westerly of Easterns that he becomes a racial anomaly extremely difficult to handle. The host never knows which side of his nature is going to turn up next."

". . . Asia is not going to be civilized after the methods of the West. There is too much of Asia and she is too old. You cannot reform a lady of many lovers, and Asia has been insatiable in her flirtations aforetime. She will never attend a Sunday school or learn to vote save with swords for tickets."

No, dear reader, the author was neither Winston Churchill nor John Foster Dulles, but Rudyard Kipling, in a story called "The Man Who Was," written way back in 1890!

During the Kremlin's abortive campaign to provide more consumer goods for the Russian people, one farmer got fed up with another set of empty promises and had the nerve to demand in an open meeting, "Where is the white flour and the new shoes Comrade Malenkov has been promising us?" "What is your name?" countered the visiting delegate. "Petrovsky," said the farmer. "Okay, Comrade Petrovsky, I will answer your question at our next open meeting."

The next meeting had scarcely gotten underway when there was a disturbance at the rear of the hall. "I know," said the delegate. "You want to know what's happened to the white flour and the new shoes."

"Not at all, Comrade," was the reply. "I want to know what's happened to Comrade Petrovsky."

Two strangers stopped to admire a handsome new automobile parked at a curb in Prague. "Beautiful model!" enthused one. "Another great triumph for Soviet initiative and ingenuity!" The other protested, "But that's an American car. Don't you know one when you see one?" "Of course I do," snapped the first stranger. "But I don't know *you!*"

A German in the Western Zone of Berlin, suspecting that letters to his son in Warsaw were being read by Communist operatives, declared in one, "I'm enclosing herewith a hair, which will fall out, no doubt, if some censor opens the envelope." The son replied, "Stop your foolish worries. The hair was still there when your letter arrived." The German now had all the information he wanted. He had not put a hair in the original letter.

Another German, in East Berlin, was assigned to labor in a factory which was supposed to ship parts for baby carriages back to Moscow. Having a baby himself, he resolved to pilfer enough parts to construct a carriage of his own. A fellow workman, aware of his scheme, asked him a few days later, "Well, have you got that carriage rolling yet?" The German scratched his head and said, "It's the most astonishing thing. I've got all the parts—but no matter how I assemble them, it comes out a machine gun!"

A story currently circulating in Budapest concerns two political prisoners who were trying to console one another before they went to trial. "If only I hadn't confessed," mourned one, "that I bought sugar on the black market." "That was a mistake," admitted the other. "Why did you confess that?" "What could I do?" was the answer. "The man who interrogated me was the one who had sold me the sugar."

"What a man, that Krubnovkivich!" enthused a Russian delegate to the U.N. "He invented radio, airplanes, and the electric light. In fact, I'd say he's almost as great a genius as Yibishiv."

The American looked puzzled. "Who was Yibishiv?" he asked.

"Ha," chortled the Russian. "Yibishiv invented Krubnovkivich!"

An alert factory worker in Budapest sidled up to the lady foreman and implored, "May I leave at the end of eleven and a half hours this evening instead of twelve, Madam Director? I'd like to go to the state opera."

"You may," decided the director. "I'm happy that our workers appreciate culture. But cut out that 'Madam Director' business. Now that we have been liberated, remember we are all comrades! By the way, what opera are you attending?"

"*Comrade Butterfly*," said the worker.

In the Soviet heaven, the Communist equivalent of St. Peter stopped one applicant at the gate (made of ersatz pearl) and demanded, "State your qualifications for entering here." "Well," said the applicant, ticking off the reasons on his fingers, "on earth my father was, first, a rich industrialist. Second, my mother came from a family of middle-class tradesmen. Me, I was a writer. And, finally, after inheriting a large sum of money, I married a baroness."

The Soviet St. Peter was choking with rage by this time. "And are those your only claims for entering the Soviet heaven?" he spluttered.

Meekly the applicant added one claim more. "I thought my name might help me," he murmured. "It's Karl Marx."

Oriental Flavor

A reporter known to Nunnally Johnson was present in Tokyo when a very small Jap was hanged for doing in several members of his family. The reporter's comment—heard all too distinctly by Mr. Johnson—was, "Oho, there's a little nip in the air this morning."

The Japs are great ones for imitating American and British products, but the labels they paste thereon are often dead giveaways. In Tokyo, for instance, a New York newspaperman delightedly displays a bottle of so-called "Scotch whisky" whose label proclaims, "These whisky is made from choicest grape, as by appointment to His Majesty King Elizabeth."

Chinese factory workers, to the accompaniment of city-wide fanfare, were accorded a rare treat in Communist-dominated Shanghai recently: an election with secret ballot to choose a new workers' committee! Each man, upon approaching the ballot box, was handed a sealed envelope and told to deposit same through the slot at the top of a cardboard box.

One rash worker flipped open the envelope and began to examine his ballot. "Hey," shouted a supervisor. "What do you think you're doing there?"

"I want to know who I'm voting for," explained the worker.

"You must be mad," decided the supervisor. "Don't you realize that the ballot is *secret?*"

An engaging Chinese myth concerns an artisan who, eager for wealth and fame, determined to cast a very special bell. Effort after effort proved fruitless however. There always was a flaw. Finally the artisan said, "Wealth and fame obviously are not for me. They're overrated anyhow. But before I quit, I shall cast one more bell—just for my own satisfaction and enjoyment."

The tone of this last bell was so glorious that people thrilled everywhere when they heard it. "Who cast this perfect bell?" they asked. And so the artisan became rich and famous.

Another oriental legend tells of a traveler who strayed from his caravan and was lost in a trackless wilderness of sand. Two days of aimless plodding left him exhausted and about to perish from thirst. Suddenly his eyes lit on what looked like a waterskin. Reaching it on his knees, he tore it open. Alas, it was only a bag of gleaming flawless pearls!

Hearts are no longer so light or life so bright in "dreamy Chinatown" on the tip of lower Manhattan since the families who stayed in the homeland were swallowed up by Communist hordes.

But the show must go on for out-of-town visitors who wouldn't dream of leaving New York without a sight-seeing tour of the missions and hostels on the Bowery, and the joss houses—carefully preserved replicas of Chinese temples—on Pell Street.

In one teashop every bus load of tourists is regaled with the story of old Loo Ching, the Chinese laundryman, who violated a fundamental law of his powerful Tong soon after his arrival in New York and was condemned to death in a secret conclave. American law permitted no violent carrying out of the sentence, so the Tong leaders simply decreed, "We pronounce Loo Ching a dead man."

From that moment on, not one soul spoke to Loo Ching or revealed the slightest awareness of his presence. Shopkeepers ignored his attempts to buy or beg food. Children turned the other way when he shuffled down the street. His room was rented to another and his belongings deposited in a back alley. Loo Ching spoke not one word of English and knew nothing of American ways.

So each day he grew thinner and more desperate, until finally his wasted body was found in the snow outside the teashop. His death sentence had been carried out.

Gallagher strolled into his favorite saloon and was rather surprised to find the floor strewn with rice. "What's this?" he exclaimed. "Had a wedding in here today?" "Naw," explained the barkeep. "I just knocked the stuffings out of a Commie Chinaman."

A San Franciscan had just decorated a grave in the public cemetery with a garland of roses when he noticed a venerable Chinaman placing a bowl of rice on a mound adjacent. "What time," whispered the American, "would you be expecting your friend to come up and eat that rice?" "About same time," answered the Chinaman, "yours comes up to smell the flowers."

Columnist Irving Hoffman, bound home from Hong Kong, visited Bombay, India, and was shown the city by a high police official. "Maybe you'd like to hear about the most dangerous political fanatic in the country," suggested the official. "At this very moment he's probably constructing a bomb to hurl into police headquarters. If you'd like to meet him in person, that, too, can be arranged. He's my brother-in-law."

Three salesmen who had dined sumptuously at a Chinese chop-suey emporium were now studying the "tell-your-fortune" slips of paper that are wrapped in a certain kind of crisp little Chinese cooky. The paper in the first man's cooky read, "You are about to embark upon a business venture that will net you millions." The second man's read, "You will soon meet a tempestuous redhead whom you will take on a long journey." Then the third man opened his little slip. This one read, "Help! I'm trapped in a Chinese bakery!"

"Hello, Hawaii"

Hawaii has become a movie maker's paradise. The natives have become so used to Hollywood shenanigans, in fact, that a Clark Gable or Hank Fonda can wander, entirely unmolested, the length of Kalakaua Avenue. *Time's* apt line about Esther Williams ("a lot of water has flowed over this dame") was duly appreciated by the Waikikeyhole set, but when the ravishing Esther appeared on the coral sands in person, she attracted no more attention than a local *wahine* waddling by in her shapeless *muu-muu*.

For uninitiated souls on the mainland, *wahine* means "woman," and a *muu-muu* is a garment patterned after the unflattering covering that appalled missionaries, some hundred years ago, hastily draped over native maidens who were blissfully ambulating with all their abundant charms fully exposed. One maiden is supposed to have flung the covering angrily hence. It landed on a cow, which registered even more vociferous indignation; hence the name, *muu-muu*. The missionaries, meanwhile, their purity assured, proceeded to do mighty well for them-

selves in a material way. Their descendants are the recognized aristocracy of the islands.

The recent eruption of Kilauea Volcano in Hawaii came as no surprise to natives of that area. Well they know that Pele, tempestuous and all-powerful red-haired fire goddess, after wanderings more extensive than Eleanor Roosevelt's, finally settled down to housekeeping in that volcano. Every now and then she is expected to flex her muscles to keep the franchise.

Madam Pele (Hawaiians pronounce her name "Paley," to conform with a Madison Avenue god of comparable stature at the Columbia Broadcasting Company) controls the warmth of the earth and the ocean currents, and woe betide anyone rash enough to thwart her desires!

In 1935, for instance, you are told solemnly, two American Army planes flew a dangerous mission over erupting Mauna Loa and, by pin-point bombing, diverted a flow of lava that imperiled Hilo City. Everybody knew that Pele would have her revenge. Sure enough, some months later these very planes collided in mid-air, and only one occupant parachuted to safety.

Furthermore, that survivor proved to be the single member of both crews who had not participated in the mission over Mauna Loa!

How, I asked, could one interpret the moods of Madam Pele and perhaps forestall her? The *kahunas* know, was the answer. The *kahunas* are a rough equivalent of the witch doctors in other civilizations.

There is at least one accredited *kahuna* in every sizable community, and even white residents (*haoles*) from the mainland soon learn to seek their counsel.

When U. S. Navy engineers constructed the first dry dock at Pearl Harbor, the story goes, they ignored the warning of *kahuna* that the site they had chosen was a graveyard for subjects of Madam Pele. What happened? When the scaffolding was removed, the dry dock collapsed (this fact, at least, can be verified), and imbedded in the bottom of the structure was found the skeleton of a whale.

Next time out, the Navy listened carefully to what the *kahuna* had to say—and there hasn't been a particle of trouble with dry docks at Pearl Harbor since.

Do you know why so many Hawaiian words sound and look alike to the uninitiated? There are only twelve letters in the Hawaiian alphabet. The vowels A, E, I, O, and U, and the consonants H, K, L, M, N, P, and W.

Although the luxury liner *Lurline* sails from Hawaii every fortnight, its skipper, Commodore Gillespie, still gets a kick out of the band blaring native airs and the hula maidens swaying in the breeze. He even shows passengers how to scale their flowered leis into the sea as the ship rounds Diamond Head, in a scene reminiscent of the finale of *From Here to Eternity*.

Tradition, quotes the commodore gravely, dictates that if the lei floats ashore, the tourist is destined to return to Hawaii another day. And since, because of the tide, the lei invariably does, everybody is happy. Aloha!

The Amazon

With its thousand tributaries, ten larger than the Rhine, author Willard Price points out, the Amazon contains a tenth of the world's running water and drains an area equal to 85 per cent of the United States. The main body of the river, of course, is in Brazil, but it sends feelers into Bolivia, Peru, Ecuador, and Venezuela. It is navigable for over 2,400 miles, at which point it is still 120 feet deep.

Nearing the Atlantic, the Amazon is more than 150 miles wide. Aboard Price's plane, a hostess told him, "We are beginning to cross the Amazon"; a half hour later she added, "We have finished crossing it." (A man I know calls his wife Amazon—because she has such a big mouth.)

At the end of the rainy season, the Amazon's waters roar down to the sea in a mighty torrent that upends trees and sends them hurtling into the air. Not a single bridge spans the river, because nothing made by man could resist its unleashed fury.

Heaven help any human caught in the Amazon's swirling waters! If he is not speedily drowned, he falls prey to the alligators or the piranhas, relentless little fish with razor-edge teeth and a taste for blood. Thirty-eight-foot anacondas slither along the river's banks to mop up what's left.

No place for a punster.

Ezio Pinza had an enchanted evening of his own in the Amazon country a few years ago when a Brazilian rubber magnate flew him a thousand miles and back, to give a single concert at a place outside Manáos.

Pinza was led in complete darkness down a narrow path, into a darkened building, and onto a dimly lighted stage. He felt that there was a large audience, but could see nothing beyond the footlights. He sang his heart out, but there was no applause. "They hated me," he remarked ruefully as he was driven back to Manáos.

"On the contrary, they adored you," said the impresario.

"Now that you have completed your performance, I can tell you that you have just rendered a great service. You have brought a little beauty to one of the largest leper colonies in the world."

The first known descent of the Amazon by a white man was made in 1541 by Francisco de Orellana, whose bug-eyed reports of the beautiful, seven-foot female warriors he encountered gave the river its name. Pinza confirms the fact that these ladies, alas, exist there no more. The theory is that the last of them long since were snapped up by model agencies, musical shows and soft-ball teams.

South of the Border

Life for public officials in the smaller South and Central American republics continues hazardous. News flashes always recall the late Willie Howard's summary of a south-of-the-border politico's career: "He run for mayor; he make it. He run for governor: he make it. He run for president: by golly, he make that too. But then he run for border: poor Manuelo, he no make *that!*"

The difference between tamales in the States and in Mexico, explains Pepe Montiguez, is that in the States they're merely hot; in Mexico, they're still sizzling ten minutes after you've eaten them. There's one place in Mexico City, swears Pepe, where, if three people are eating hot tamales at the same time, the automatic sprinkler system goes on.

A veteran cattleman from the Southwest was taken to his first bullfight in Mexico City, and was obviously fascinated by the various tricks of the picadors and matadors. Finally the big star of the show strode into the arena. A savage bull made straight for him, but the bespangled hero, armed only with a gorgeous cape, twirled it about in the air and avoided the animal's lunges by a fraction of an inch.

The crowd roared its approval, but the old cattleman did not join in. Obviously disgusted, he finally hollered, "Mister, if you don't hold that sack still, how in heck do you expect the critter to run into it?"

It was in Mexico City, too, just outside the magnificent new university that a señora said to her luscious friend, "Pepita, you must be mighty proud of your husband Juan. He is so big and strong."

"Pah," sneered Pepita. "You should have seen the Juan who got away!"

CHAPTER TWENTY-THREE

UNACCUSTOMED AS I AM . . .

After delivering an interminable speech to a vanishing audience, an English author, beginning a cross-country tour, asked a Town Hall chairman, "How do you think it went?" "Smooth as silk," was the tactful answer. "For the first two hours you had them glued to their seats."

A speaker at a Detroit function, confides Harvey Campbell, couldn't get his audience to settle down in silence for his address. Finally he thundered over the loud-speaker system, "Mr. Chairman and Gentlemen-so-called: Your committee assured me I would be greeted here by a vast audience. As I look out into this great auditorium and see every other seat empty, I realize that what I have instead is a half-vast audience!"

This story was told in Kansas City by a prominent Democrat once stationed in Washington (you guess!). A garden specialist, in the course of a lecture at a women's literary club, mentioned blandly that one of the best fertilizers is old cow manure. At the conclusion of his talk, one of the richest ladies in the community told him that she had enjoyed his talk and meant to heed his suggestions. "But tell me," she pleaded, "where can I find an old cow?"

Suggested opening for a lecture by a gossip columnist: "Accustomed as I am to public peeking . . ."

A prominent speaker recently was engaged to address a women's club in Chicago. An ardent cigar smoker, the speaker lit one rich Havana cigar after another before he rose to make his address. A friend wrote him the next day, "I suggest that you smoke fewer stogies hereafter, when you are completely surrounded by ladies."

The speaker wrote back: "Where there are angels, clouds are nearby." They've hired him to talk again next season—at double the fee.

In Cleveland, David Dietz, famous science editor, received an invitation to deliver the annual address at a very exclusive club. He accepted and added that the subject on which he meant to discourse was "Adventuring through the Universe." When the club's dignified president arose to introduce Mr. Dietz, he began to read to the members a list of the speakers at fifteen previous annual meetings, along with the topics they had chosen. The fifth name on the list stopped him cold. "In 1943," he announced, "our speaker was David Dietz, and his subject—dear me!—was 'Adventuring through the Universe'!"

"I'm afraid it's the same old speech," began Dietz, "but by the same token, it's the same old universe."

In a class by itself as a road attraction on the lecture circuit at the turn of the century was the joint appearance of Mark Twain and James Whitcomb Riley. Nothing comparable to it, in fact, came along until fifty years later, when Charles Laughton and his troupe triumphed in *Don Juan in Hell* and *John Brown's Body*. Twain would read from his own works. Riley would tell folksy anecdotes and recite his poems ("When the Frost Is on the Punkin" and "Little Orphan Annie" wowed them in particular), and the goose generally hung high—except on such occasions when Mr. Riley got higher than the goose. Horace Gregory, in *Poet of the People*, tells of some of the subterfuges to which Twain resorted in his efforts to keep Riley on the straight and narrow. One day he even locked the Hoosier poet in his room and kept both keys in his own pocket. Riley proved equal to the occasion however. When Twain finally released him for their walk to the local athenaeum, he was, if possible, more intoxicated than at any previous moment of the tour. He had imbibed a whole bottle of whisky through a keyhole with a straw, the bottle reverently held by a bellboy on the other side of the door.

To watch one of the nation's leading statesmen spellbind an audience with the greatest of ease, one would never suspect that just a few short years ago he was terrified at the mere prospect of opening his mouth in public.

Yet I happen to know that when nomination for his first important governmental post was offered to him, he almost refused because he knew acceptance entailed an endless series of after-dinner speeches to crowds of total strangers.

One story saved him and made possible his subsequently brilliant career, and because it may bail out timorous readers of *The Life of the Party*, too, if ever they are called upon to deliver a few impromptu remarks, I think it is worth repeating.

"If ever you sit trembling while the chairman is delivering the usual flowery introduction," the teller of the tale counseled his candidate (and how I wish I could tell you the candidate's name!), "just close your eyes for a few seconds and imagine that every blessed member of the audience is sitting there *in his un-*

derwear. Suddenly what you have imagined to be a sea of angry hostile faces will lose all its frightening aspect; they'll simply look ridiculous. Addressing them after that will be a breeze."

One man who heard the statesman recall the incident remarked, "Of course, if the underwear fantasy had failed to work, you might have gone one step further!"

Undoubtedly the most famous and adroit after-dinner speaker of our time is Georgie Jessel, who has been dubbed, with good reason, America's Toastmaster General. Georgie speaks because he loves to—at the drop of a hat, or even the wiggle of an ear. George Burns said of him, "Spring is the season when the birds and the bees follow Jessel—taking notes." And the immortal Will Rogers added, "George has only to see half a grapefruit and he's on his feet saying, 'Ladies and Gentlemen, we have with us tonight . . .'"

He confesses that one day he made four public appearances —at the christening of an infant, the launching of a destroyer, a funeral, and a screen writers' dinner.

"What's more," he adds, "I made the same speech at all four occasions!"

Spyros Skouras, of Twentieth Century-Fox, is an outstanding American today and a great philanthropist, but he never has lost his rich Greek accent. Introducing Mr. Skouras at a big convention, George Jessel observed, "Spyros sailed here from Athens over forty years ago, but judging by the way he speaks English, he doesn't land till next Tuesday."

At a dinner honoring New York's Governor Harriman, Jessel remarked, "Life's been good to Ave from the very beginning. He was born with the Union Pacific in his mouth."

I point with pride to one record I have compiled in the past three months. Invitations received to testimonial dinners and fund-raising banquets: thirty-one. Invitations declined: thirty-one. Batting average: one thousand. As far as I am concerned, banquets are an abomination.

I am convinced that most people would cheerfully double their donation to the worthy charity involved if they were permitted to stay home with their slippers, easy chairs, a good book —or even a fixed wrestling match on television.

Consider the average public dinner. The food is cold, badly served, and indigestible. Table companions usually are total strangers, even less interested in you than you are in them. The one fate worse than being planted at a table in the far corner next to the kitchen, is to be seated on or near the dais, where strategic retreat is completely cut off.

An internationally famous scientist became so irked by the series of bumbling long-winded speakers who preceded him at one banquet that, when he finally was called upon, he declared, "It seems I finally have been asked to give my address. Gentlemen, it's the Belvedere Hotel, and that's where I'm headed this very moment, since it's two hours past my usual bedtime. I thank you!" And with this, he strode out of the hall.

When Calvin Coolidge was Vice-President of the United States, Washington chairmen soon discovered that he promptly accepted all banquet invitations. Once present, however, it was well-nigh impossible to pry a word out of him.

The effervescent Alice Roosevelt Longworth volunteered to draw him out one evening, but she never had a chance. Finally she snapped, "I wonder why you come to all these affairs, Mr. Coolidge, when obviously they bore you so."

"Well," observed the frugal Cal, "a man's got to eat."

Because everybody appreciates words of sound advice, especially when you have to look up many of them in the dictionary, I pass on to you the admonition of a Florida jurist, memorized faithfully by A. B. Clark, of Jacksonville:

"Beware of platitudinous ponderosity. Let your communication possess coalescent consistency and concatenated cogency. Eschew all flatulent garrulity and asinine affectations. Use intelligibility and veracious vivacity without rodomontade or thrasonical bombasity. Sedulously avoid all prolixity and psittaceous vacuity."

In other words, "Be intelligible, think for yourself, and be brief."

An English magazine recently listed six rules for a good talker that are worth remembering:

1. Never tell funny stories about your own children unless you are certain you would be amused if Mrs. Whoop-te-do told them to you about hers.

2. Never try to start a long conversation with someone who obviously is busy, with his mind on something else.

3. Never talk to yourself in the middle of talking to others. (Let's see: was it really the last week in August? Maybe it was the first week in September. I know it was after Aunt Minnie left. Yes—it was August.)

4. Never describe the plot of a film your victims haven't seen, or a book they have not yet read.

5. Never apologize for something you're really proud of (I don't know anything about art, music, or poetry—*but . . .*).

6. Above all, *never* forget that other people also prefer *talking* to *listening*. Allow others to get in the last word—or the last laugh—occasionally. You'll be better liked for it—and may learn something besides. Incessant talkers learn *nothing!*

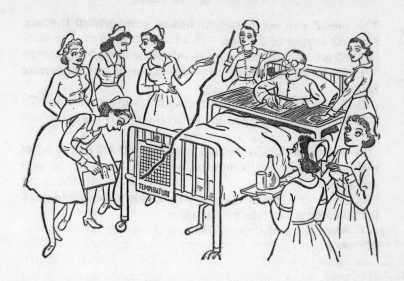

CHAPTER TWENTY-FOUR

WHERE THERE'S AN ILL

In virtually every office there is one deluded soul who takes fanatical pride in slaving twelve hours a day, and hasn't had a vacation worth mentioning in years. For good measure, he usually bolts down a sandwich at his desk at lunch time and takes home a portfolio full of documents and reports to foul up his weekend too.

If you'd like to help one of these benighted souls, hell-bent for a breakdown, you might tell him you've nominated him for A. S. Kettunen's mythical "Coronary Club." Mr. Kettunen, himself the victim of a heart attack, compiled this list of eligibility rules for candidates:

1. Your job comes first. Forget everything else.
2. Saturdays, Sundays, and holidays are fine times to be working at the office. There'll be nobody else there to bother you.
3. Always have your brief case with you when not at your desk.

This provides an opportunity to review completely all the troubles and worries of the day.

4. Never say "no" to a request. Always say "yes."

5. Accept all invitations to meetings, banquets, committees, etc.

6. All forms of recreation are a waste of time.

7. Never delegate responsibility to others; carry the entire load yourself.

8. If your work calls for traveling—work all day and drive all night to keep that appointment you made for eight the next morning.

9. No matter how many jobs you already are doing, remember you always can take on one more.

——And the next stop, of course, is the hospital!

The patient in Room 726 was apopleptic with rage when the doctor stopped in on his morning rounds. "That idiot nurse that came on at 8 P.M.," he roared, "plugged my electric blanket by mistake into the automatic toaster on my night table—and every four minutes I kept popping out of bed!"

A very rich lady loved to read a very successful magazine because every month it gave the details of a rare new disease, which the rich lady immediately imagined she was suffering from herself. Several doctors made a handsome living out of this. Up in Maine for the summer, however, she suddenly ran into one old country doctor who wasn't having any of her nonsense.

"You couldn't possibly have this disease you say is destroying you," he told her gruffly. "In the first place, if you did have it, you'd never know it. It causes absolutely no pain or suffering whatever."

"Just as I suspected," crowed the rich lady triumphantly. "Those are my symptoms precisely!"

A doctor in a Milwaukee maternity ward was making his morning rounds. "Nurse," he inquired, "on what day does this little lady expect her bundle from heaven?" "May fourth," was the answer. "And the next lovely patient?" "May fourth." "And this one?" "May fourth also, Doctor." The doctor appeared mildly surprised. "What a coincidence," he mused. "Don't tell me this other charming soul is also expected to be a mother on May fourth." "I wouldn't know, Doctor," admitted the nurse. "She wasn't at the picnic."

Mr. Haydn admitted to his wife that he was feeling much better since his operation, but couldn't account for the enormous bump on the back of his head. "Oh, that," chuckled Mrs. Haydn. "In the middle of your operation they suddenly ran out of ether."

The Mayo Clinic, in Rochester, Minnesota, is not only one of the biggest and best equipped in the world, but it cures minds as well as bodies. A friend of mine went out there to lose his arthritis, and managed to get rid of an inferiority complex and habitually harassed expression at the same time. One of the young doctors on the staff gave him a bit of philosophy from the Deep South which he claims has changed his whole life: "When you works, work easy; when you rests, rest loose; when you worries, roll over and go to sleep!"

Groucho Marx was so impressed with the daily routine at

Mayo's that he went around himself for weeks feeling people's pulses. He frightened the wits out of one poor lady by dropping her wrist like a hot potato and solemnly assuring her, "Madam, you have mice!" Her reaction, in fact, was so satisfying, the line was inserted in his next picture.

The biggest shot seen in Rochester in many a day, they say, was a coot who had made a couple of quick millions in the Williston Oil Basin, and arrived at the clinic in a big limousine with solid-gold trimmings and platinum ash trays. He was about as near-sighted as it's possible for a man to be, so a fellow townsman was astonished to see him driving through heavy traffic without glasses. "Don't tell me," cried the townsman, "that they cure acute myopia at Mayo's too!" "Not so's I know about it," admitted the big shot, "but you don't have to worry about my driving, son. I've got my prescription built into the windshield."

The whole Mayo Clinic owes its inception to a tornado that swept over Minnesota some sixty-six years ago. The two Mayo brothers, William and Charles, had just graduated from medical school, and in their own words, were "greener than grass," yet they pitched in with their father, who was one of the pioneer surgeons of the Northwest and, through three sleepless days and nights, and with inadequate equipment, saved the lives of scores of victims of the big blow. Impressed both with their skill and their dedication, Sister Albert, Mother Superior of the Convent of St. Francis, offered to finance a new clinic if the Mayos would undertake its direction. It opened its doors in 1889, with a policy still in effect: no set fees. A patient is billed according to his ability to pay. At first the clinic specialized in surgery, but long before both Mayo brothers died in 1939, it had spread all over the medical map. One enthusiastic patient insisted, "They've got drugs out there so new they haven't even discovered diseases for them yet."

A delectable Virgil Partch drawing shows a surgeon performing a delicate operation before a gallery of enthralled spectators. But one important thing is missing: there's no patient on the operating table, just a long piece of cord! The explanation is whispered into the ear of one spectator by the nurse: "Poor Dr. Goldbrick is operating on a shoestring!"

The phone rang at Polyclinic Hospital the other morning, and a voice demanded a connection with the nurse in charge of the seventh floor of the private ward. "I'm calling to find out about Julius Schwartz," this nurse was told when she picked up her receiver. "How's he progressing?" "Just fine," said the nurse. "And when will he be allowed to go home?" the voice continued. "Saturday morning," said the nurse, "and may I ask who this is calling?" "You may," said the voice, with a chuckle. "I'm Julius Schwartz. Nobody would tell me a damn thing around here!"

A doctor's most important patient demanded his presence at her bedside just when he was whooping it up at a class reunion. He endeavored to sober himself sufficiently to take her pulse, but gave it up, muttering disconsolately, "Blotto! Boiled to the ears!" The following morning he received a fat check, with a note reading, "Thank you for your prompt and expert diagnosis. It will be appreciated if you keep it strictly to yourself."

Mr. Jones had been tossing nervously in his hospital bed for an hour when he had his first visitor. There was a knock on his door. He called, "Come in," and in walked the prettiest nurse he ever had seen. "We'll just give you a little preliminary check-up," she announced cheerfully. "Remove your pajamas, please." Mr. Jones complied a bit sheepishly, and the nurse then examined him carefully. "That's it," she said finally. "Hop back under the covers. Any questions?" "Just one," said Mr. Jones ruefully. "Why did you knock?"

Never in my life have I actually seen a beautiful night nurse, but I know they must exist because they keep bobbing up all the time in funny stories.

Authors, too—to hear them tell it—have always been singularly

315

fortunate in drawing pulchritudinous hospital attendants, and it's probably just my bad luck they're never on duty when I happen to be around.

It was Heywood Broun's proud boast, for instance, that he was the only paying guest ever asked to leave a certain expensive rest home favored by overtired writers. "My trouble was I couldn't sleep," he explained. "So I took a turn for the nurse."

Irvin Cobb also had tales to tell of frolics in hospital corridors. One smart nurse soon put a stop to his marauding, however. She took the tires off his wheel chair.

In Rochester, Nelson Winter's nurse confessed to him that she had kissed every doctor in the hospital. "Intern?" queried Winters. "No," she giggled, "alphabetically."

There's a story about an Arab lady who didn't return to her husband's bed and board until the gray of the dawn. Her explanation: "I was sitting up with a sheik friend."

Offhand, I can recall the names of only four nurses who achieved world fame in modern times, though I am sure readers of this book will come up with many more nominations. My four: Florence Nightingale, Edith Cavell, Clara Barton, and Sister Kenny.

And I guess everybody's ideal of what a nurse should be was Ensign Nellie Forbush of *South Pacific*—especially when she was portrayed by Mary Martin!

There is no end to the situations in which a nurse is continually embroiled. There was the case of a much-publicized railroad official, for instance, who was rushed to the hospital following an exceptionally gay celebration, moaning with anguish.

Don't ask me how he did it, but he had swallowed a big gold watch his father had given him for his twenty-first birthday.

When his nurse showed him the X-ray, the railroad man leaped from his bed of pain, crying, "Let me out of here! I'm three minutes late!"

When I addressed an audience of doctors in San Diego, one

of them assured me he was the hero of the story, widely circulated, about an operation on a bad-tempered old lady of eighty. She came through with flying colors despite all her dire prognostications, but set up a new clamor when the doctor told her that, in accordance with the rules of the hospital, she'd have to walk ten minutes the very first day after her surgery and would have to get out entirely in a week, since beds there were at a premium.

Well, she had her ten-minute walk the first day, tottering but under her own steam, lengthened it to twenty minutes the second day, and by the time she went home was stomping all over the hospital—including rooms where she had no right to be.

Later, her family tried to pay the doctor a premium for his "wonderful job." "Nonsense," he laughed. "It was just a routine operation." "It's not the operation we're marveling over," said a grandson. "It's her walking. The old girl hadn't taken a step in six years!"

The patient shook his head gingerly and slowly regained consciousness. "Well, Doc," he said weakly to the face bending over him, "was the operation a success?" "Sorry, son," was the gentle answer, "but I'm St. Peter."

In London, a new reviewer has appeared who will bear watching. She signs herself "Jersey Lily," and her first efforts were devoted to appraising the merits of a book, published by the National Association for Mental Health, called *Do Cows Have Neuroses?* Miss Lily's review, in its entirety, read, "As a cow, I did not find this book very helpful."

A worried, twitching little man signed up for the full treatment with a prominent psychoanalyst. On his first visit he lay on the couch for thirty minutes without opening his mouth. The second visit was a replica of the first. Halfway through the third session he finally spoke. "Say, Doctor," he inquired, "am I allowed to ask you a question?" "Ah, ha," thought the doctor, "the floodgates are about to open!" To the patient, he said encouragingly, "I hope you'll tell me absolutely anything that enters your mind." The patient admitted, "I'm curious to know what you charge me for every visit here." "Fifty dollars," answered the doctor. The patient was silent again for ten minutes. Then he asked meekly, "Say, Doctor, wouldn't you like a partner?"

Even kiddie stories have a different twist when psychiatrists tell them. What do you think, for instance, of this one, included in the after-dinner speech of a famous analyst recently: A mother was entertaining three other ladies at tea when her nine-year-old son burst into the room, decked out in a shimmering white evening dress, a flowered hat, rouge on both cheeks, and his mouth smeared with lipstick. "Wilfred!" cried his horrified mother, "you nasty boy! Go upstairs and take off your father's clothes this very minute!"

Two roommates in a compassionately run nuthouse were comparing ailments. "I'd be all right," mourned one, "if I didn't have a hole in my head." "You're lucky," disputed the other. "I have *two* holes in my head." "Ba-a-h," grunted Number One. "You and your holier-than-thou attitude!"

A famous psychiatrist grimly informed one of his most difficult patients, "No, it is *not* all right for you to marry an octopus." "Drat it," grumbled the mortified patient, "then here I am stuck with eight engagement rings."

Dave Antman would have you believe that a banana sought out a psychoanalyst and wailed, "Doc, you've got to help me. A soda jerk has been trying to tell me I have a split personality."

Professor Harold Rome has come up with the proper distinction between a psychotic and a neurotic. A psychotic, avers the good professor, says, "Two and two are five and I'll fight any man who says me nay." A neurotic says, "Two and two are four, and I simply can't stand it."

The analyst stroked his chin and admitted to the tortured-looking character across the desk, "You're one of the most difficult cases that ever came here seeking my help. Is there any insanity in your family?" "There must be," maintained the character. "They keep writing me for money!"

A prominent Chicago psychiatrist told a patient, "Ridiculous that you should still be frightened of thunder at your age. Thunder is a mere natural phenomenon. Now the next time it storms, and you hear a couple of claps of thunder, just you do like I do—put your head under a pillow and stuff your ears until the thunder goes away."

Two old friends, lunching together for the first time in months, suddenly discovered that they were being analyzed by the same doctor. "Let's give him a problem that really will floor him," proposed one. "We'll make up an elaborate dream with all kinds of ramifications that I'll describe at my morning session tomorrow. Then you'll tell him you had precisely the same dream when you hit the couch in the afternoon."

With fiendish glee, the conspirators perfected their plot, and in accordance therewith, patient Number One reeled off the gory details the following morning while the analyst filled his pad with notes. At four-thirty patient Number Two gave an identical report. The analyst said not one word until the recital was completed. Then, however, he slapped down his pencil, jumped from his chair in great agitation, and exclaimed, "This is the most remarkable coincidence in my professional career." "What has disturbed you, Doctor?" inquired his tormentor innocently. "You won't believe this possible," answered the analyst, "but you're the *third* patient who has had that exact dream in the past twenty-four hours!"

Are you one of those timid souls who shudder at mere mention of a dentist's chair and regard his exploratory apparatus as far too bitter a drill to swallow? Drink a toast then to Max Grogle and Arnold Roe, of Barranquilla, Colombia, whose device— patent Number 2,648,043—enables any unfortunate in the chair to holler at will the electrical equivalent of "Ouch," though his jaws be jimmied wide apart and his mouth be cluttered with cotton, machinery, and the dentist's left arm. By merely pressing a switch in his hand he automatically shuts off the power that operates the drill—there's nought the dentists can do about it.

Dentistry, of course, has made vast strides in the past twenty years, and most of the pain inflicted is now anticipatory rather than actual. False teeth fit so well and look so natural that one of Hollywood's most glamorous stars has been fooling the public with a set through ten features and more.

In Revolutionary days, however, false teeth were so painful and cumbersome that George Washington refused to wear his set while posing for his celebrated portraits by Gilbert Stuart. It was only when the foremost dentist in the colonies, John Greenwood, took him in charge that he achieved some degree of comfort.

(Another gentleman who practiced dentistry as a sideline in those days was Paul Revere.)

A set of choppers Greenwood made for General Washington, incidentally, is still on display in the museum of the Baltimore

College of Dental Surgery and is said to have inspired one practitioner to drop his implements, seize a set of golf bags, and call over his shoulder as he headed for the exit: "That reminds me! I've got eighteen cavities of my own to fill this afternoon!"

How much time do *you* spend cleaning your teeth? Devote just five minutes to that task immediately after every meal and the chances are you'll seldom need a dentist at all.

The catch is that most of us are dreaming about something else while we go through the motions—and what we think is five minutes of polishing the molars is probably closer to thirty seconds.

"Put it this way," Dr. Ed Pullman once told me. "The blood circulating in your gums is like trains coming into Grand Central Terminal. The old trains must be shunted back to the yards so that new trains can come in. And the old blood has to be massaged out of the gums so that fresh blood can circulate there. Isn't that clear?"

"You ought to write a book," I told him.

"I have," he announced cheerfully as he drilled off the tip of my tongue. "My assistant will give you the manuscript on the way out. I call it: *The Yanks Are Coming.*"

CHAPTER TWENTY-FIVE

WORDS AND MUSIC

Perfection is a rare and wonderful thing, separated from mere competence by an unbridgeable gulf. It takes no trained eye to thrill instinctively when a Fred Astaire or Gene Kelly executes a dance routine, or a Joe DiMaggio drifts back to haul in a towering fly, or a Sonja Henie does a hula on ice skates, or a Judy Garland or Mary Martin bangs out a popular tune.

They represent the nearest to perfection any human can approximate. All of them will tell you, however, that perfection is only nine parts God-given talent. The tenth—and absolutely essential—part is painstaking practice and dedication.

When Lynn Fontanne, Alfred Lunt, and Noel Coward, perfectionists all, were co-starring in the latter's *Design for Living*, Miss Fontanne never succeeded in mastering one unimportant piece of business to her own satisfaction.

In the course of the very last matinee, however, she rushed off stage and hurled herself into Coward's arms. "That letter bit!" she exclaimed triumphantly. "I've just learned exactly how to play it."

"Rather on the late side, aren't you, my pet?" laughed Coward. "Have you forgotten this is our last day?"

Lynn Fontanne glared at him. "We still have a performance this evening, have we not?" she inquired coldly.

That's my idea of perfection.

Do you think the team of Alfred Lunt and Lynn Fontanne are a sure-fire draw in every big city in the U.S.A.? Not so, says Lunt. For some reason he cannot fathom, they've never fared well in Pittsburgh, Pennsylvania. The last time they were penciled in for a week there, Lunt decided to do something about it. "I'll take over in Pittsburgh next week," he informed the company manager. "Somebody has not been doing his job here properly in the past."

When the week was over, Lunt sought out the company manager. "I told you I'd fix everything," he announced triumphantly. "Look at these figures, man! Thirty-five hundred dollars net profit!"

"Uh-huh," agreed the manager coldly, "but there's one thing I must point out. You forgot to pay the Lunts!"

Graphic commentary on the present state of show business by Mike Connolly: Two actors passed each other on Route 66, one going from New York to Hollywood, the other from Hollywood to New York. As recognition dawned in both their faces, they jumped to their feet and hollered frantically to each other, *"Go back!"*

It is comic Bert Wheeler's boast that he never has told a joke he wouldn't tell in front of his own mother. "Where is your mother?" Fred Allen asked him one time. Confessed Wheeler, "She's with a burlesque show."

Robert Harris, known to millions for his TV characterization in "The Goldbergs," once played a season in support of the Yiddish star, Maurice Schwartz. Harris played the part of Schwartz's attorney. One scene called for him to sit down at a table and breathe a heavy sigh. Opening night he sighed so heavily he blew out eight candles on the table. As the curtain dropped, Schwartz whispered angrily, "Stop padding your part!"

Feel a bit depressed once in a while? Next time the blues overtake you, think how much better off you are than the actress who, in the space of a few hours, lost a wonderful part she had been gunning for, had her new convertible stolen, and learned that her daughter had run away with a married man. Just then the janitor yelled up through the dumb-waiter, "Any garbage today?" The actress answered wearily, "Okay. Send it up."

The old Shakespearean actor cupped a hand over his ear and apologized, "You'll have to speak a bit louder, my good man. I've become a wee bit deafened. All that applause, you know . . ."

In many a notable London stage production, Sir Ralph Richardson has co-starred with that dazzling pair, Sir Laurence Olivier and Vivien Leigh. The three are firm friends, bound together by the memories of shared theatrical adventures and misadventures. And yet the Oliviers, like other hosts in England, hesitate to invite Sir Ralph for a weekend—or even for dinner.

Not, heaven knows, because he's dull. It's just that when Sir Ralph puts in an appearance, things begin to happen. Thereby hangs a tale, imported and partially vouched for by publicist Irving Hoffman.

It seems that the Oliviers had just finished furnishing a new home in the London suburbs, complete with expensive decorations and invaluable mementos of their careers. The housewarming party was the event of the season—but Sir Ralph found something missing. "Where are the Roman candles, old boy?" he protested. "No housewarming is complete without one!" To prove his point, Sir Ralph produced a Roman candle forthwith. It popped up a single fireball and then sputtered out.

"Bad show," grumbled Sir Ralph, and angrily picked up the Roman candle. That's when fireball Number Two went off. It zoomed past the spectators through an open window of the new house and promptly ignited the drapes. It then plowed a furrow through the rug, ricocheted off an old master, and sizzled upstairs to the master bedroom.

In less time than it takes to tell, the Oliviers and their guests were warmer than ever—but there was no house left. "To think," ruminated Sir Laurence, "that the insurance policy would have gone into effect at nine tomorrow."

Miss Leigh's comment was more to the point. "Sir Ralph," she decreed, "get off these premises and see that you never come back."

In due course the Oliviers once more were ready to resume light housekeeping—this time in a fifteenth-century castle they had restored with the profits from three years of slaving in the theater and Hollywood. Sir Ralph remained in banishment, but he looked so wistful that Miss Leigh, against her better judgment, relented. "Come for the day," she conceded, "but it must be distinctly understood that you don't set foot outside the library."

Sir Ralph stuck to his bargain straight through dinner, and it was Olivier himself who precipitated the next disaster. He led Sir Ralph on tiptoe to explore the treasures in the attic. Both men carried candles and Sir Ralph was so afraid of causing another conflagration that he proceeded as though he were walking on eggshells.

Of course he lost his balance. It was while he was negotiating a stretch on an open rafter. He crashed headfirst through the ceiling of the room beneath (it happened to be Miss Leigh's silk-lined boudoir) and on through *that* floor, bringing up, bloody but unbowed, at the very feet of Miss Vivien.

"Ah ha," he observed to that properly outraged lady, "here we are, right back in the library!"

The Oliviers refuse to be panicked by stories of Russia's growing war potential.

"If worse comes to worst," they reason to friends, "we can always send Sir Ralph for a fortnight of repertoire in Moscow."

The leading man in a touring Feuer and Martin musical show recently behaved so shabbily to a young lady in the chorus that he was dismissed summarily by telegram. That night he phoned the producers long distance and wailed, "How could you do this to me? Wasn't I giving a satisfactory performance?" "Your performance on stage couldn't have been better," they told him, "but we fired you because in private life you are the most unmitigated scoundrel we have ever encountered." "Thank heaven," exclaimed the actor. "You've made me feel like a new man again!"

George S. Kaufman recently characterized a familiar stage personality as "the most painsgiving director in the New York theater."

Variety recalls the time in World War I when a ham actor was attempting to sell Liberty Bonds from the steps of the Sub-Treasury in Wall Street. Not a soul had bought a bond and the actor was getting desperate. Finally one man came to the rescue and subscribed for a five-hundred-dollar bond.

"What town are you from, mister?" asked the actor.

"Topeka," said the man.

The actor turned to the crowd and declaimed, "Think of that! A man from a lousy little town like Topeka takes a five-hundred-dollar bond and you Wall Street pikers won't put up a dime!"

One of the most frustrating telephone conversations in history is recorded by *Theatre Arts* magazine.

A subscriber dialed "Information" for the magazine's number. "Sorree," drawled the lady, "but there is nobody listed by the name of Theodore Arts." "It's not a person; it's a publication," insisted the subscriber. "I want *Theatre Arts.*" The operator's voice rose a few decibels. "I told you," she repeated, "we have no listing for Theodore Arts." "Confound it," hollered the subscriber, "the word is 'Theatre': T-H-E-A-T-R-E." "That," said the operator with crushing finality, "is not the way to spell Theodore!"

Three typical debonair New Yorkers—director Josh Logan (born in Texarkana), author Sam Behrman (born in Worcester), and composer Harold Rome (born in Hartford)—were on their way to a rehearsal of their new musical play, *Fanny,* when Logan suddenly opined, "There's a spot in Act I that's made to order for a good, red-hot, talk-provoking belly dancer."

While Behrman and Rome were looking up yellowing press clippings, detailing the triumphs of a former torso gyrator who called herself "Little Egypt" at the Chicago World's Fair way back in 1893, Josh phoned Istanbul to sign up a Turkish delight named Nejla Ates for his new production.

Nejla (pronounced "Nella") Ates had as much to do with the plot of *Fanny* as my aunt Ruby, but there is no question that she stopped the show cold—or rather, hot. When this harem-scarem lassie goes into her act, all of her four-feet-eleven is moving—and what's more, it's moving in several different directions at the same time. Maybe it's something she Ates. Nor did her costume materially hinder her plan of campaign. Josh Logan certainly did right by his little Nejla.

With *Fanny* ensconced at the Majestic Theatre for what obviously was to be a long and well-deserved run, I felt that I owed it to my readers to seek an interview with Miss Ates. My arrival backstage prompted Walter Slezak, one of the big attractions of *Fanny*, to comment bitterly, "This wraps up the woes of the Broadway stage show in a nutshell. Here we have a great new musical, starring people like Ezio Pinza and Walter Slezak—and everybody comes to write a story about the belly dancer!"

Miss Ates, however, refers to her specialty as a *danse orientale*. Even off stage, she's an active miss. She speaks nine languages, she says, though I'd hardly call English one of them. In a few short weeks in America she acquired a mink coat and a diamond ring, both contributed by a love-smitten Texas gallant. When his ardor cooled, he made an effort to retrieve the loot.

"This fellow," reported Nejla dreamily, "is American, so okay he Indian giver. But Nejla Turk, not Indian. No give back!"

Nejla takes her new fame in stride, likes to stand in front of a flamboyant twelve-foot mural of herself that is plastered on the wall of the theater, and assure bedazzled passers-by, "Is me. Crazy, no?"

The first time that producer David Merrick, Logan, Behrman, and Rome actually saw Miss Ates do her number in costume, they remained rooted to their front-row seats for a full minute after her exit.

Author Behrman broke the silence: "Gentlemen, that's the best dialogue I have ever written!"

A couple of beaten-up old acrobats had been closing bills at vaudeville houses so long with the same act, they could go through their routines in their sleep. One week they finally made the Palace and, at the opening Monday matinee, stood in the wings while the late John Barrymore gave his magnificent rendition of the soliloquy from *Hamlet*. The audience went into raptures. One acrobat turned to his partner and muttered angrily, "If that's the kind of junk they want today, I guess we better work out a new act for next season!"

Charles Frohman, the famous theatrical producer and "star maker," was the man who discovered Billie Burke and developed her into one of Broadway's all-time box-office champs. When it became evident that she was falling for the charms of his bitter rival, Florenz Ziegfeld, however, he flew into a rage. Invading her dressing room one day, he declared, "I am off for London and, to remind you not to get married, I'm going to leave my hat here. Don't do anything idiotic while I'm gone." He had not yet reached London when Miss Burke and Ziegfeld slipped across the Hudson and were married in Hoboken. Frohman cabled her, "Send me my hat." She never saw or heard from him again.

When David Belasco produced Eugene Walter's *The Easiest Way*, he chose for his leading lady the relatively unknown Frances Starr. In rehearsal she did everything that was expected of her except in one scene, where her hysterical scream was several pitches below the result desired by the "Master." In the dress rehearsal Belasco tiptoed behind her, and Miss Starr gave a shriek that stood everybody's hair on end.

"That's what I want," exulted David Belasco, throwing the

329

safety pin he had used into the wings. "It's the effect I've been working for these last three weeks!"

One of the few failures produced by John Golden was a gambling story by Winchell Smith called *The Wheel.* The second-act climax was a dramatic scene in which the hero lost his last cent playing roulette on a crooked wheel. On the morning of the premiere, Golden realized that the balcony audience would be able to see the numbers into which the ball finally plopped. He called his friend, the police commissioner, and wailed, "Where can I get a rigged roulette setup before sundown?" "Leave it to me," said the commissioner. He raided a well-known gambling joint, and Golden had his crooked wheel three hours before curtain time.

P. G. Wodehouse, creator of the famous English comedy butler, Jeeves, recalls a theater manager who discovered one day that his box-office treasurer had been shortchanging him for years. He sent for the culprit and asked, "What's your salary here?" "Sixty a week," was the answer. "It's raised to a hundred. No, by George, make it two hundred," said the manager. "Thank you," burbled the treasurer. "I'm overcome." "There's just one thing more," added the manager cheerfully. "You're fired!"

"You see," he explained to Wodehouse later, "I wanted to fire the crooked so-and-so from a really *good* job."

One of the funniest backstage mishaps in theatrical history occurred during rehearsals of an old Bolton and Wodehouse musical at the Century Theatre. The Century, like the show's producers, Messrs. Ziegfeld and Dillingham, is, alas, gone forever, but in its day it was a beautiful structure with the biggest revolving stage in the country.

The plot called for an Italian tenor, and a gent who called himself "The Neapolitan Nightingale" showed up for an audition. He barely had launched into "Ridi Pagliaccio" when the revolving stage suddenly started off at Number Three speed and swept him into the wings.

"Why he didn't jump off, or at least stop singing," laughs Bolton, "we'll never know. Maybe he sang with his eyes closed. Maybe he thought the spinning turntable was part of his big test. At any rate, he suddenly popped into view at the other end of the stage, singing lustily, and after being seen briefly, whirled off on his second journey. By this time everybody in the theater was in convulsions. He ended the song out of sight, back of two tons of scenery, and everybody cheered. Unfortunately the part was cut out of the show and 'The Neapolitan Nightingale' got nothing for his pains but a magnificent run-around."

On the Bowery in New York there still exists the dilapidated restaurant in which, many years ago, a penniless lad named Irving Berlin waited on tables and picked out tunes on the piano for a living. Every guide includes the spot in his itinerary. The night I made the trip, our informant even declared that it was on that very battered piano that Berlin had composed "White Christmas."

One evening Irving Berlin himself decided to visit this haunt of his early days. In a nostalgic glow, he seated himself at the old piano and began to hum "Oh, How I Hate to Get Up in the Morning." In the middle of the rendition, a bus load of sightseers shuffled in, and their gravel-voiced guide began his spiel.

"Yes, sir, folks," he declared, "this is the very place the great Oiving Boilin began his career—singing songs on that same pianner you see standing in the corner. As a matter of fact, the song that Bowery bum is playin' this minute happens to be one of Boilin's own songs!"

The guide then walked over to the piano and dropped a heavy hand on Berlin's shoulder.

"Fella," he announced, "if Oiving Boilin could hear the way you're moiderin' one of his greatest songs, he'd toin over in his grave!"

331

Today plutocrat Berlin is one of those fellows who's firmly convinced he never sleeps a wink. One night he was a member of a big houseparty at cinema-magnate Joe Schenck's house when the family Saint Bernard created a tremendous uproar by falling into the swimming pool about 4 A.M. By the time he had been rescued, not only the entire household but neighbors for half a mile around had been aroused—that is, everybody but Berlin, who slept like a babe throughout the hullabaloo. Next morning somebody asked him innocently, "How did you sleep last night, Irving?" "Same old story," mourned Berlin. "I took four sleeping pills and still didn't catch a wink."

Another time he was forced to admit he had slept a few hours. "But," he added triumphantly, "I dreamed I didn't!"

In *Fun with Musical Games and Quizzes*, David Ewen and Nicolas Slonimsky quote two excerpts from contemporary reviews of musical compositions that later became famous. You wouldn't guess what pieces were on the griddle in a thousand tries! Number One: "It has no more real pretension to be called music than the jangling and clashing of gongs and other uneuphonious instruments with which the Chinaman, on the brow of the hill, fondly thought to scare away our English bluejackets." (From the London *Musical World*, June 30, 1855.) Number Two: "This music is only half alive. How trite and feeble and conventional the tunes are, how sentimental and vapid the harmonic treatment, under its disguise of fussy and futile counterpoint! Weep over the lifelessness of its melody and harmony, so derivative, so stale, so inexpressive." (Lawrence Gilman in the New York *Tribune*, February 23, 1924.) Well, the London *Musical World* was reviewing Wagner's *Lohengrin*; Mr. Gilman was polishing off George Gershwin's *Rhapsody in Blue*.

There was a composer in Munich one time, continues Slonimsky, named Max Raeger, who felt that a derogatory critic had overstepped all bounds. Raeger wrote him as follows: "Sir: I am sitting in the smallest room of my house. I have your review before me. In a moment it will be behind me."

Can you name the fourteen biggest popular-song hits of the past sixty years? The list, as compiled by historian Richard B. Morris, contained some surprises for me, and it will, I think, do the same for you. Here it is:

"The Sidewalks of New York" (1894), "The Stars and Stripes Forever" (1897), "Sweet Adeline" (1903), "Take Me Out to the Ball Game" (1908), "Ah! Sweet Mystery of Life" (1910), "End of a Perfect Day" (1910), "When Irish Eyes Are Smiling" (1912), "St. Louis Blues" (1914), "Dinah" (1925), "Ol' Man River" (1927), "Star Dust" (1929), "Easter Parade" (1933), "God Bless America" (1939), and "White Christmas" (1942).

The great Maestro Arturo Toscanini is noted for his temperamental outbursts, but his good friend Sam Chotzinoff has learned that he can dispel the wildest of Toscanini's rages by producing some childish practical joke. Wine glasses with a hole in the bottom, trick knives that collapse, fake "butlers" who spill things on purpose send him into gales of laughter. He concentrated for an hour on playing with a seven-year-old boy's toy magnet.

Another sure-fire way to restore his radiant good humor is to question him on his encyclopedic knowledge of music, or the countless other greats of the musical world he has known through the years.

"I will tell you all about Richard Strauss," he announced on one visit with the Chotzinoffs. "In 1906 I wrote to him for permission to give the first performance of *Salome* in Italy at La Scala. He replied yes. Very good. Then one day I read in the newspaper that Strauss *himself* would give *Salome* in Turin one week *before* my performance in Milan. I was crazy. I could not eat. That night I took the train for Vienna and confronted him in his own house. 'Strauss,' I told him, 'as a *musician* I take off my hat to you. But as a *man*, I put *on* ten hats.' "

As the maestro finished his story, Chotzinoff recalls that "his face shone with scorn and he feverishly put on ten imaginary hats."

The classic Toscanini story concerns the day he passed a hurdy-gurdy man, half asleep, who was lazily droning through the Toreador song from *Carmen*. Toscanini shook the startled player violently and commanded, "Faster, you fool! You play that as if it was a funeral dirge."

The next day the hurdy-gurdy man had a new sign on his battered instrument. It read, "Pupil of Toscanini."

Joan Carr attended a concert at Carnegie Hall that ended in a spontaneous ovation for the conductor. Applauding more madly than anybody else were a couple of uniformed ushers. Miss Carr had just whispered to her partner, "Those boys appreciate music more than all the frauds who pay seven dollars a ticket," when she heard one usher say happily, "If we can keep this applause going five minutes more, we'll collect overtime!"

A famous orchestra concluded the season with its usual deficit some years ago and the management went to Andrew Carnegie for help. "I'm getting a bit weary of being the patsy every season," grumbled Mr. Carnegie. "Somebody else will have to carry part of the load. You get him to make good half the deficit, and I'll give you my check for the rest."

The management called the very next day to report success. Mr. Carnegie made out his check and asked, "Mind telling me who coughed up the other half?"

"Not at all," he was assured. "It was Mrs. Carnegie."

An old and broken-down orchestra conductor made an ill-starred farewell tour in America. After the debacle at Carnegie Hall, the first violinist was asked, "What did he conduct tonight?" The violinist answered, "Lord knows what he conducted —but we played Tschaikowsky's Fifth."

Rumor is that a pedestrian on Fifty-seventh Street, Manhattan, stopped Jascha Heifetz and inquired, "Could you tell me how to get to Carnegie Hall?" "Yes," said Heifetz. "Practice!"

An amateur musician was making horrendous sounds on his saxophone in the middle of the night when the outraged landlord burst into his apartment, yanked the instrument out of his hands, and roared, "Do you know there's a little old lady sick upstairs?" "I don't think I do," admitted the amateur. "Would you mind humming the first few bars of it?"

Ad in a Providence newspaper: "For sale cheap: my son's collection of be-bop and rock-and-roll records. If a fourteen-year-old's voice answers the phone, hang up and call later."

Titian-haired Lucy Monroe has sung "The Star Spangled Banner" so often that several legislators have discussed admitting her as the forty-ninth state. From the Supreme Court to Milwaukee —home of the plea to the land of the Braves—she's warbled our national anthem in fair weather and foul, and become so identified therewith that every time she appears with a new male es-

335

cort, wits immediately presume his name is Francis Scott Key.

When Lucy gives with the high notes the lyrics come across as clear as a bell. Obviously there was nobody like her around when columnist Franklin P. Adams was a lad. He confesses that, until he reached the age of twelve, he was convinced that the first line of our anthem was, "Osage, Kansas City."

When Mama made up her mind that little Nathan was destined to become a great violinist, Papa's complaints about the racket and the expense fell on deaf ears. Finally on the music teacher's recommendation he bought Nathan one of those "half violins" specially designed for the kiddies.

To the surprise of everybody but Mama, Nathan turned out to be a born fiddler. First thing you know, the teacher demanded that he have a full-sized violin.

Complaining at every step, Papa hied himself to the music store, where his eye fell on a big violoncello. "There's the one I'll take," he announced happily. "Let the little so-and-so learn to outgrow that!"

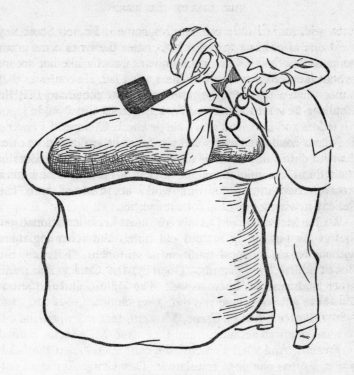

CHAPTER TWENTY-SIX

THE GRAB BAG

Pet Peeves

There are certain minor irritations in workaday life in the city that make everybody fume. It takes no terrible-tempered Mr. Bangs, for instance, to start spluttering at impatient motorists forever tooting their horns in a hopeless traffic snarl, or fat ladies who block aisles in theaters, resolutely refusing to pull in their feet or their middles an eighth of an inch, or ill-mannered oafs who shamelessly try to barge into the front of a line that's been queuing for an hour.

In addition to universal annoyances of this sort, however, every one of us has a special list of private peeves that make our gorge rise. Often they are inconsequential and irrational, but we cannot laugh ourselves out of them.

Less than a year after he retired from the presidency, Calvin Coolidge flew into a tizzy when a hat-check girl wouldn't put his fedora and his friend's on a single check. Columnist Franklin P. Adams conducted a personal war for years against house owners who didn't display their numbers plainly on the outsides of their doors. As mild-mannered a matron as ever I've known works herself into a tantrum when her husband tears the Sunday newspaper apart and leaves sections all over the floor.

Walter McConkle of Detroit is aroused because national syndicates are buying up famous old hotels and renaming them without regard for local tradition or sentiment. "Farewell, the Book-Cadillac," he mourns. "Good-by, the Copley Plaza and other landmarks we knew so well. The Hiltons and the Sheratons have got you 'cause you didn't watch out!"

Mrs. Porter Lucas of Crane, Missouri, sees red when she enters an American restaurant and they hand her a menu printed in French. "And what French!" she continues. "Even the headwaiter is often unable to translate it. They charge American dollars; let them print American menus!"

Compton Brooks of Paoli, Pennsylvania, waxes indignant at the mere thought of commuters who hog double seats for bridge games on crowded trains.

"Although no seats are reserved and they have no justification whatever, these buzzards take it for granted that that cardboard which they have bribed the conductor to throw across the seat is enough to hold four places for them, while other passengers are already standing in the aisle, and not one player has put in an appearance.

"The other evening I said to myself, 'Tradition be blowed.' I threw the board aside, sat down, and opened my newspaper. Believe it or not, I not only had to take abuse from the four bridge players when they finally showed up just before train time, but the other passengers took their side!"

Here are a few of my own pet peeves: Elevator starters who engage in long social conversations with the operators while I'm itching to keep an appointment on the twenty-ninth floor . . . TV-conscious baseball managers who interrupt a game five times to whisper advice to pitchers or batters, or dispute every close decision with umpires . . . Wives who won't let you put the top of a convertible down on a perfect summer day because they "don't want my hair to blow" . . . Advertisements—usually for autos—showing fascinating stretches of scenery without identifying them . . . Water taps in bathrooms that must be held on to keep them running . . . Proverbial and incurable no-check-grabbers . . .

There must be a special space in Hades reserved for people who solicit funds from strangers over the phone for unknown charities, using names of well-known figures to assure attention. Author-actor-producer Howard Lindsay has a wonderful way to stop such miscreants dead in their tracks. The moment he hears, "Judge Goofenswoggle was sure you'd be interested in the bazaar he's whipping up for——" he interrupts in a deceptively silken tone: "I'm sorry, but haven't you heard? I've just been elected president of the Anti-Solicitation-by-Telephone Association!" Then he hangs up.

A definite menace to society are the goons who persist in confronting comparative strangers with a simpering "Guess who this is," or "I'll bet you don't remember who I am." A few can be squelched with an emphatic "I most certainly do not." Most hang on, however, until it finally develops they sat next to you at a football game nine years ago, or had some equally intimate relationship with your cousin at prep school in 1928.

Habitual "Guess-who-I-ammers" ought to be marked with a

warning red light or a tolling bell buoy. They obstruct navigation.

It's a different kettle of fish, however, when you fail to identify or recall the name of somebody you've known perfectly well for years. We can't all be like the late Wendell Willkie, who never forgot even the first name of a person he had met in an elevator or at a crowded cocktail party. Jim Farley and Groucho Marx are blessed with similar total recall, though Groucho was moved to inform a pest, "I never forget a face, but I'm willing to make an exception in your case."

At the opposite end of the picture was the mighty Babe Ruth, who never remembered *anybody's* name. Five years after he joined the New York Yankees, he was still referring to everybody on the bench, including his roommate, Lou Gehrig, as "Kid" and "Whatchamacallit."

I'm not always so good at remembering names myself. In theater lobbies, I attempt to cover up with a hasty, "You know my good wife, Phyllis, of course," which suffices unless the little woman, in a perverse mood, counters demurely with, "What did you say the gentleman's name was, Bennett?" This leads to some interesting conversation after we get home.

One day a passer-by grabbed me and demanded, "Why haven't you answered all my phone calls?" Not knowing him from Adam, I replied heartily, "I've tried a dozen times, but you're never in. How much longer will you be in town?" This proved to be the wrong gambit. "What are you talking about?" he demanded. "I'm your dentist!" All I could manage was a weak "Why aren't you wearing your white coat?"

Sign Language

"Silly standardized country—America," grumbled a distinguished English author recently as he completed a U.S. lecture tour, his pockets bulging with silly standardized American dollars. "Your cities look so much alike, I had to consult my itinerary to see whether I was in Milwaukee or Memphis, Sioux City or Spokane. Same hotels, same stores, same signs . . ."

Same signs, my eye! This land of ours abounds with individualistic merchants who would rather be caught dead than hang a conventional sign outside their place of business. They'll stew for weeks thinking of a new twist—and one in a hundred is worth the effort! For instance:

Outside a Phoenix auto-repair shop: "May we have the next dents?" and "Second-hand cars in first-crash condition." A Dallas dealer has a more subtle approach: "Be a wealthy pedestrian. Sell us your car!" The shop next door displays clothes for debutantes, featuring "Convertible sun dresses. Very sporty with the tops down."

Offered by a dry-goods emporium in Allentown, Pennsylvania: "Bath towels for the whole damp family"; by a chicken incubator in Vermont: "Cheepers by the dozen."

A furrier in Kalamazoo begs, "Be our miss in lynx," and an alert fortuneteller in Asbury Park promises, "Your problem solved, or your mania cheerfully refunded."

Owners of restaurants and grogshops are in the forefront when the whims blow. A tavern keeper in Lexington advises, "If you drive your husband to drink, drive him here." A sign on the wall of a diner along Route 101: "What foods these morsels be!"; on the gas pump outside: "Four gals., one buck. May we suggest Ethyl?" In Hollywood, one proprietor cautions, "Not responsible for ladies left over thirty seconds."

And a Broadway delicatessen advertises: "Today only! Homemade imported caviar." Another sign inside the store warns, "If you don't smell it, we ain't got it."

Designed for motorists: In New Jersey: "Crossroad 200 yards ahead. Better humor it." In Connecticut: "Give our children a brake." At the bottom of a precipitous hill in West Virginia: "Resume breathing." On the back of a massive furniture van: "Watch my rear, not hers." On the water tank of a small college north of St. Louis: "This university was founded by our beloved president, William Johnson. Born 1855. Died 1911. Capacity, 150,000 gallons."

Humorists commandeered a paintbrush at the San Diego air base and indulged in some gay signing off. Outside a phone booth, they hung a placard reading: "Please limit calls to six girls"; on the bulletin board: "For sale cheap: one slightly defective ten-inch TV set. For details, see Lt. Squinty." And near a runway: "Absolutely no flying permitted over nudist camp 8.3 miles SSW on a true course of 177 degrees."

Atop California's seven-million-ton Shasta Dam some wag planted the sign, "U. S. Government property. Do not remove!" At Wellesley, a bright miss hung over a dormitory bathtub the reminder, "Don't forget your ring." And for several weeks (an unimaginative cop removed it) a sign above the entrance to the New York morgue advertised, "Remains to be seen."

A haberdasher in New York ran a chain of stores whose windows always were plastered with big signs proclaiming, "Going out of business," "Must vacate," and "Positively last twenty-four hours." One day he told his lawyer, "My son graduates from college tomorrow. Should I take him into business with me?" The lawyer suggested, "Open a new store for him and let him go out of business for himself."

Tall Tales

I've heard a lot of very tall tales in my day (my office is located smack in the middle of the highest-powered advertising agencies on Madison Avenue), but the yarn told with a perfectly straight face by David Vikomerson certainly takes the cake.

David insists that he and some convivials were prowling for sailfish in the Gulf Stream off Miami when suddenly one of them felt a tremendous strike. "It's a whale," he gasped, while his reel began to whip around like an airplane propeller. By turning on this cruiser's full power, they managed to tow the monster to shore and anchored him momentarily near the naval station at the edge of the causeway.

Then several fourteen-story hotels nearby, finished that Tuesday, began to sway ominously, and an admiral, experimenting with an electric razor, was hurtled clear across the base. "It's the Soviet Navy attacking," he hollered wildly. "Don't shoot, boys, till you see the eyes of their Reds!"

"So we cut the line pronto," concludes David. "If we hadn't, the whole of Miami Beach undoubtedly would have been towed to somewhere near the Azores.

"We did manage to get a snapshot of the monster before he headed for the open sea—and, believe it or not, the snapshot alone weighs thirty-one pounds."

That fish story reminded British author Eric Partridge of another whopper wherein a carpenter made and painted three wooden decoy ducks so lifelike that a deluded cat promptly bit the heads off two of them. The third one? He flew away!

343

"It was on my last safari in the jungle," recalled another tall taler at the Explorer's Club, "that a man-eating tiger sauntered into our camp at sundown. One of my trusty beaters just threw a glass of water in his face, and he slunk away with his tail between his legs.

"You doubt my veracity? Strolling later in the moonlight, I encountered this very tiger and playfully stroked its whiskers. Gentlemen, those whiskers were still wet!"

Mr. Bee McIntyre prevaricated his way to a hard-won championship of the Burlington, Wisconsin, Liars Club with his account of a wind so powerful that it picked up his brass wash kettle (which weighed two hundred pounds) and blew it clear out of the county.

"Furthermore," was his clincher, "that wind blew the kettle

so fast that, while it was sailing across our front yard, lightning struck at it five times—and missed!"

And yet that wind of Bee McIntyre's was but a gentle zephyr compared to the one that smote a blooming liar named Honest Dick McCardle, of Athens, Georgia. "It blew so hard," avers Honest Dick, "that our local creek ran backward, threw the mill wheel into reverse, and unground a thousand sacks of flour so fast that when the bags were opened the wheat wasn't even ripe enough to harvest."

There was a bit of a breeze out Lew Owens' way in Independence, Missouri, too. It picked up all the telephone poles and set them down in the same order—along with the operators —clear out in California. A subscriber, unaware that she, too, had been wafted over a thousand miles off base, asked for Kansas

City 0080. "Have to change the exchange, dearie," the operator told her. "We're just three miles out of Beverly Hills now."

The son of one of Minnesota's hardy Swedish pioneers was visiting a friend out West. The Westerner began to brag about the wonderful echo in his valley. "If you stand and call 'John Smith,'" he declared, "you will hear no less than thirteen echoes of it." "That's nothing at all," belittled the man from Minnesota. "Just outside of Minneapolis there's a high hill. If you climb to the summit and call 'Ole Oleson,' you'll immediately hear the echo saying, 'Which one?'"

The late Wilson Mizner was a wonderful storyteller, with no particular regard for the truth. Coming back from the Yukon gold rush—owning, alas, precious little of the gold himself—Mizner read in a Chicago paper that turkeys were in short supply that year and were bound to bring fifty cents a pound by Thanksgiving Day.

So, avowed Mizner, he bought five hundred baby turkeys from an Oregon farmer for a dime apiece, invested twenty dollars more in feed, and started driving them across country on foot. He figured he'd reach the Windy City in ten weeks flat—just in time for the holiday market and fortune.

"I got the turkeys clear through to Chicago too," he mourned, "but with the stockyards in sight, and a flock of five hundred nicely fattened fowl bound to net me five bucks apiece, cruel Fate stepped in.

"The turkeys developed sore feet and flew away."

In a mammoth and extensively publicized liars' contest in Milwaukee, a man named Butler was unanimously declared in a class by himself. The chairman noted, however, a certain reservation when the winner walked up to claim his prize.

"What's the matter?" demanded the chairman. "Gold cup not big enough to suit you?"

"It isn't that," confessed Mr. Butler. "I'm deeply honored.

346

But it's taken so long to get this meeting over with. *What will I tell my wife when I get home?*"

Tongue Twisters

Probably the two best-known tongue twisters in the English language are, "She sells sea shells by the seashore," and "Peter Piper picked a peck of pickled peppers." But there are hundreds more, as Duncan Emrich, chief of the folklore section at the Library of Congress, discovered when he appealed to listeners on an NBC radio program to send in any they happened to remember.

At last reports, Chief Emrich still was trying to dig out from under the bags full of mail that descended upon him, but he managed to list some of the twisters that popped up most frequently for an article in the historical bimonthly, *American Heritage.*

Take a deep breath, suggested Dr. Emrich, and see how quickly you can say "Sarah saw a shot-silk sash shop full of showy, shiny shot-silk sashes." Or: "She sawed six slick, sleek, slim, slender saplings." Or:

> *Bitty Batter bought some butter*
> *"But," said she, "this butter's bitter."*
> *So she bought some better butter,*
> *And she put the better butter in the bitter butter.*
> *And made the bitter butter better.*

When Duncan Emrich got himself straightened out, he added that several informants wrote about a tongue-twisting game they had played in their youth—a game that consisted of concocting long sentences whose every word began with the same letter.

Examples were "Six sick soldiers sighted seven slowly sinking ships," and "Frivolous fat Fannie fried fresh fish furiously Friday forenoon for four famished Frenchmen."

During World War I, Al Jolson popularized a song in similar

vein that called for a deal of rehearsing. It was called "Sister Susie's Sewing Shirts for Soldiers."

Tongue twisters work particular hardships on stutterers. In the speech department at the State University of Iowa, writes Gilbert Barnhill, it was decided that one way to help stutterers overcome their reticence in speaking to strangers was to send them to an Iowa City establishment in quest of an item obviously not carried in stock. They then were instructed to ask where it might be found and how to get there.

This season, every stutterer was sent to a campus bookstore to ask for ping-pong balls. The first dozen were turned away empty-handed, of course, but the thirteenth, to his amazement, found enough ping-pong balls on the premises to outfit the whole country. "I don't know why a bookstore should be expected to carry anything like this," admitted the clerk, "but we've never disappointed our customers before and we're not going to start now.

"What gets me, though, is this," he added. "Why does everybody who plays ping-pong *stutter?*"

Shaggy Doggerel

Today's wave of prosperity has swept the animal world, too, if the headlines in leading zoospapers can be trusted, but as is so often the case, the wealth has not been evenly distributed. Complains one disgruntled orangutan, "Bull markets may be great for bulls, but what the heck good are they for orangutans?"

Another disturbed soul is a leopard of my acquaintance. He sought the advice of a neurologist. "You've got to help me, Doc," he pleaded. "Every time I look at my wife, I see spots before my eyes." "Of course, dear boy," soothed the neurologist. "You're a leopard, aren't you?" "Sure, I'm a leopard," was the answer, "but my wife is a zebra."

A calf-é society columnist reports that a curvaceous piggy from Paree is sporting the season's most dazzling wardrobe, just for saying "oui, oui, oui" all the way home.

Night-club favorite, Joe E. Lewis, in an improbable foray into the animal world, tried crossing one rooster with another rooster. All this netted him was two very cross roosters.

A confrere of Joe's, meanwhile, wangled a date with a musical-comedy producer to exhibit his trained dog—a creature who could add, subtract, mambo, and recite "Casey at the Bat." The performance concluded, the dog's owner said, "Amazing, what?" "Not bad," conceded the producer. "Let's see her legs."

A couple of pigeons flew over the Bowl at New Haven just before the annual Yale-Harvard football game. "Who do you like?" asked one pigeon. "Well," replied the other with a knowing wink, "I've just put everything I have on Yale."

A cowboy once rode into town on his favorite pinto mare and reined up to watch a poker game in progress on the porch of Ray "Two Gun" Washburne's book, liquor, and grocery emporium. One of the players looked up and asked, "Like a little stud?" The mare answered, "Sure! Where is he?"

Walter Carroll tells about a prisoner sentenced to ten years in solitary confinement. The first year, he found an ant in his cell and determined, "I'll keep myself occupied teaching this ant some tricks, so that when I get out I can make a fortune with it."

By the time the prisoner was released, he had taught that ant, by exercise of infinite patience, how to do somersaults, speak fluent Greek and Latin, and explain the Einstein theory. He put it in a little box and headed for his first drink in ten years.

Here was his chance to show off his miraculous ant! He placed it carefully on the bar and called the barkeeper. "Hey," he cried. "Have a look at this!"

The bartender nodded grimly. He brought the flat of his hand down with a squash and complained, "That's the third darn ant I've killed on this bar today."

A cocker spaniel from the country was trotting down a busy street with a companion from the city and paused at what he thought was a mere hitching post. Too late he discovered it was a parking meter. He barked disgustedly and asked, "Do you mean to say you've got to pay now?"

There was the devil to pay when Pat Knopf's singing canary fell into the meat grinder. All week the family ate nothing but shredded tweet.

A thirsty gentleman entered a saloon with the peaceful intention of buying himself a beer, when he noticed that the bar was being tended by a horse. "Whassa matter?" snarled—or neighed —the animal, as he deftly flicked the collar off the beer. "Ain't you never seen a horse before?" "It's not that," the man assured him hastily. "I just never thought the cow that used to own this gold mine would sell."

Stanley Jr. and Livingston Jr. were having a hot toddy in their tent while shooting an African adventure film for M-G-M. "I think I'll go out and shoot a lion before dinner," boasted Stanley Jr. "I've got five says you can't do it," scoffed Livingston Jr. Stanley seized his rifle and exited. About an hour later a lion poked his head in Livingston's tent and asked, "Do you happen to know a screwball named Stanley?" "I do," said Livingston. "Well," said the lion, "he owes you five dollars."

An octopus became entangled in the propeller of an ocean liner, causing a sympathetic observer to murmur, "Crazy, mixed-up squid!"

A pig in California had to be taken to a mountain cleanery. He splattered himself with purple oink.

A cat presented the family tennis racket to a psychiatrist, who quickly diagnosed, "Your brother is too high-strung." This probably was the same analyst who made such a name for himself in the laboratory, pulling habits out of rats.

And in a garden, two caterpillars were lazing in the sun when a lovely butterfly fluttered by overhead. Declared one caterpillar firmly, "You'll never catch *me* going up in one of those things!"

Farmer Klopfer bought a perky young rooster in Flemington, with the thought that it would add vigor to his flock. The new rooster started out being courteous indeed to the old one on the job, but the old one wasn't having any of his soft ways. "Divide the harem 50-50?" he snorted, when the new rooster mildly suggested this solution, "I should say not!" He even turned down an 85-15 split.

Finally, the old rooster put forward a suggestion of his own. "See that tree across the field?" he asked. "I'll race you to it, and the winner takes the entire flock. I ask only that in view of my rheumatic condition you stake me to a modest ten-yard handicap."

"Done and done," agreed the newcomer, confident that youth would have to be served.

The race started. For a few seconds the young rooster let his rival maintain his lead. Then he lit after him in earnest—but just as he was about to catch him, Farmer Klopfer upped with his shotgun and decapitated him.

"Dunno why," mused Farmer Klopfer as he hung the gun back on its pegs, "but that's the third queer rooster to show up in my flock this month!"

A Scotch terrier took his wife and puppy to see a dog show and promptly was pulled out of the audience to receive first prize in his class. Startled and gratified, the Scottie stopped off at a tavern on the way home to celebrate his good fortune and inadvertently left his prize on the bar. He discovered his loss the moment he got home and sent the puppy to retrieve it.

The puppy ran briskly to the tavern and nudged his way through the swinging doors. The bartender noted his entrance and, pointing a long finger at him, demanded, "What'll *you* have?" The pup, of course, answered, "Pap's blue ribbon."

And for an appropriate tailpiece to this volume, there's the story of young Jonathan, who had been promised a new puppy for his tenth birthday, but had a tough time choosing between a dozen likely candidates at the neighborhood pet shop.

Finally he decided upon one nondescript shaggy pup who was wagging his tail furiously.

Explained Jonathan, "I want the one with the happy ending."

TRY
AND STOP ME

A Collection of Anecdotes and
Stories, Mostly Humorous

By Bennett Cerf

ILLUSTRATED BY CARL ROSE

Printed in the United States of America

CONTENTS

CONTENTS

FOREWORD

I have always had a hitherto useless knack for remembering hundreds of unrelated anecdotes about unrelated people. In the minds of some this has constituted me a "raconteur"; in the mind of my wife, who has had to listen to the same yarns a hundred times, it has inspired justifiable thoughts of mayhem. It is not always possible to avoid her eyes and put boyish zest into a "That reminds me of a funny thing that happened just yesterday" at the same time. If it does nothing else, this book may persuade Mrs. Cerf that remembering stories isn't a complete waste after all.

To supplement my own memory, I have pored through countless issues of The New Yorker, Time, Life, Newsweek, Variety, Reader's Digest, *and* Coronet *in quest of additional anecdotes. I have devoured reams of columns by Winchell, Lyons, Sobol, Wilson, Skolsky, Hoffman, and their fellows. I have listened to radio programs until I thought that one more singing commercial would destroy my sanity entirely. Some of the choicest material comes from new books and old ones. I have tried to give credit wherever possible, but anecdotes are bandied about so generally and new stories sweep the country so quickly that it is often impossible even to discover who put a story into the public prints first, let alone find out who actually originated it.*

Column conductors and radio comics are engaged in a highly competitive business, and their anxiety to establish the originality of their material is thoroughly understandable. It has always struck me as faintly ridiculous, however, for them to cry "Thief! Thief!" at rivals who very possibly overheard the gem in dispute at the same night-club table or in the same gentlemen's room. They seem to forget that they actually create very few of the bright quips and amusing anecdotes they chronicle, and that the people who tell them their stories probably repeat them to a dozen others that very evening.

One of the most amusing features of my research for this volume was the frequency with which certain classic yarns bobbed up with entirely different casts of characters. In one instance,

357

Bernard Shaw had said something to H. G. Wells; in another, Ilka Chase had delivered the same bon mot to Hedda Hopper. An identical witticism was credited to Oliver Wendell Holmes, Winston Churchill, and Charles Boyer. A Dorothy Parker sally of 1936 found its way into a feature story about Gypsy Rose Lee in 1944. Columnists and "raconteurs" (odious word) discovered long ago that the public laughs harder and is more impressed when a line is delivered by somebody whose keen sense of humor is already established. Any honest celebrity who subscribes to a clipping service will admit that he learns about some of his cleverest punch-lines for the first time when he reads that he has delivered them. This is a harmless and amiable practice and generally flattering to the beneficiaries, but it makes the business of tracking anecdotes to their actual source complicated indeed.

Many of the paragraphs in this volume appeared originally under my name in my weekly "Trade Winds" column in the Saturday Review of Literature, *and in* Esquire, Coronet, Liberty, American Mercury, Reader's Scope, *and* Town and Country. *You will recognize dozens of them. For every new anecdote, I have included two that are hoary with age. I did not make them up; I collected them. If they remind you of some good ones you had forgotten; if they add a few more to your repertoire; above all, if they provide a few honest thrills and belly-laughs, this volume will have achieved the purpose for which it was compiled.*

BENNETT CERF
New York

Chapter One

SHOW CASES

HURRAH FOR CAPT. SPALDING AND

THE OTHER MARX BROTHERS

What this country needs is a new show for the Marx Brothers. It's all very well to recall their patter of years gone by, and chuckle reminiscently over it, but something fresh along the lines of *The Coconuts* or *Animal Crackers* would give Broadway an unbelievable fillip. The funniest lines usually fell to Groucho. He revived on the radio the other night his "I never forget a face —but I'm willing to make an exception in your case."

One of his funniest routines concerned his African hunting

trip which began with "Did I ever tell you how I shot a wild elephant in my pajamas? How he got into my pajamas I'll never know. Getting his tusks off was quite a problem. In Alabama the Tuscaloosa." He came home in a rickshaw. The meter registered $11.40. "Confound it," he roared to the driver. "Didn't I *tell* you not to go through India?"

Then there was the skit where Groucho and Chico served as opposing lawyers. Chico became tongue-tied when it was his turn to question the witness. The judge thundered, "Well, ask your witness some questions." "All-a-right," said Chico. "What's a big-a da animal wid four legs an' a trunk in da front?" "That's irrelevant," screamed Groucho. "Dat's a right," agreed Chico. Groucho crossed the stage, planted his portfolio on the judge's bench, and declared, "I rest my case."

And the time when Groucho proposed to that wonderful foil, Mrs. Rittenhouse. "Your eyes shine," he told her, "like the seat of my blue serge pants." "But you'll have to get out of that house you're living in," he added. "I don't like Junior crossing the tracks. In fact, come to think of it, I don't like Junior."

The weak sister of the Four Marx Brothers on the stage was Zeppo, but when he quit the grease paint and became an agent, he ended with more pelf than the other three put together. Harpo, who never says a word on the stage, is the wittiest conversationalist in private life, and was one of Alexander Woollcott's favorite companions. Harpo once flew all the way from Hollywood to Bomoseen, Vermont, for a week-end to surprise Woollcott. He painted himself from head to foot with hideous hues, paddled to the island, and howled like a banshee. Nobody was frightened, however. In fact, nobody was on the island. Another time, Harpo appeared in a broken-down Model-T Ford. "What on earth do you call that?" scoffed Woollcott. "This is my town car," said Harpo grandly. "Yes," answered Woollcott, "and the town is Pompeii."

Chico's wife invited an elderly relative to spend a few weeks at his house one time. The visitor was very charming, but her English was on the sketchy side. When Irving Thalberg and his wife, Norma Shearer, were coming for dinner, Chico took the old lady aside. "When Mr. Thalberg says 'pleased to meet you,' " he instructed her, "all you have to do is answer with one word: 'likewise.' " The old lady repeated the word several times, and swore that she would uphold her end without mishap. The Thalbergs arrived. "Pleased to meet you," said Thalberg as expected. The old lady beamed at him. "Wise guy," she said.

The Marx Brothers once became the managers of a prizefighter. He was a lumbering giant named Cohen, and richly earned the nickname of "Canvasback" by an invariable custom of getting himself knocked cold in Round One of every fight. The boys had a great time with Canvasback Cohen until one day, according to legend, Groucho knocked him out in a gymnasium workout. That was too much. Harpo claims that Canvasback started as a lightweight, but was hit so many times that he swelled out into a heavy.

As long as I have rambled on this far about the Marx Brothers, I'd better quote a few other of their more famous lines, if only to avoid the wrath of thousands of enthusiasts who remember their dialogues almost word for word and are ready to fight at the drop of a wisecrack. In *Horse Feathers*, Groucho informed his son, "I'd horsewhip you—if I had a horse."

His secretary interrupted him to announce, "Jennings has been waiting to see you for hours, and he is waxing wroth." Groucho's reply to this was, "Tell Roth to wax Jennings for a change."

When Chico entered the scene, Groucho commented, "Hey, you look a lot like a guy I know by the name of Ravelli." "I am Ravelli," declared Chico. "Aha," said Groucho, "that accounts for the resemblance."

In *Monkey Business*, Groucho discovered a large automatic pistol and near it a few small pearl-handled revolvers. "This gat," announced Groucho, "had gittens." Almost immediately after that deduction, the ship's captain hove into view. "I've got a complaint," roared Groucho. "What is it?" said the captain testily. "Last night when I was in bed in my cabin, who do you think came tiptoeing along the corridor and tapped on my door?" The captain said he didn't know. "Nobody did," declared Groucho, "and that's my complaint."

Marx Brothers addicts will never forget their burlesque of Madame Du Barry. Groucho, essaying the role of high minister, was feverishly embracing Du Barry when Chico came charging into the scene. "Who are you?" snarled Groucho. "King of France," averred Chico. "What?" said Groucho. "You the king? And I the prime minister? France is certainly in one hell of a fix!"

★ ★ ★

Vaudeville lovers remember with some affection the old comedy team of Sweeney and Duffy, which invariably brought down the house—whenever Duffy, a rather vague character, remembered to show up. A distraught stage manager found him luxuriating in a Turkish bath one afternoon when he should have been on the Orpheum stage. "For God's sake, Duffy," he spluttered, "what are you doing here? You're on now!" "I am?" said Duffy. "How'm I going?"

Sweeney and Duffy's act didn't please the burghers of Memphis, Tennessee, on one memorable occasion. Joke after joke fell flat as a pancake. Duffy stood the chill silence just so long. Then he strode to the footlights and declared, "Citizens of Memphis! This is one of the proudest and happiest moments of our lives! Your tumultuous reception has overwhelmed us! And now, if you all will just remain seated a few moments longer, my partner, Mr. Sweeney, will pass down the aisle with a baseball bat, and beat the be-Jesus out of you."

That was the end of the act known as Sweeney and Duffy.

★ ★ ★

During a rehearsal of a John Barrymore play, the leading lady aroused the star's ire, an incautious procedure, to say the least. Barrymore gave a pungent lecture on her paternity and nocturnal pursuits. "Kindly remember," interpolated the actress, "that I am a lady!" "Madam," snapped Barrymore, "I will respect your secret."

★ ★ ★

John Barrymore once confounded an audience with a somewhat similar stunt—right in New York, at the height of the run of *Redemption.* There was an epidemic of coughing throughout the first act. When it broke out again in the second, Barrymore was all set. He suddenly yanked a five-pound sea-bass from under his coat and flung it over the footlights. "Busy yourselves with *this,* you damned walruses," he bellowed, "while the rest of us proceed with the libretto!"

★ ★ ★

John Barrymore and Richard Bennett, reports Gene Fowler, spent an evening together in London that included liquid refreshments of many descriptions and copious quantity. Bennett woke up the next morning, gingerly felt his head, and wondered if Barrymore had gotten to his home without bodily injury. He phoned him, and, when several seconds passed without an answer, called angrily into the instrument, "Hello! Hello!"

Barrymore's voice, very sleepy, replied, "Hello."

"Are you all right?"

"I'm fine. How are you?"

"Fine. But I've had the devil of a time getting your room. Are you in it, or down in the lobby?"

"I don't know."

"What in hell do you mean, you don't know? Where *are* you then?"

"Here, I suppose," said Barrymore, poking his head out from beneath Bennett's own bed.

★ ★ ★

June Havoc, musical comedy star, and, incidentally, sister of Gypsy Rose Lee, was taken to a tea at the sedate Columbia Faculty Club by a learned and curious admirer. Miss Havoc took a despairing look at the venerable professors who decorated the premises and sighed, "My, my! I've never been with such a lot of extinguished gentlemen before in all my life."

★　★　★

One of the costliest musical comedy failures of recent years was a show called *Allah Be Praised!*, produced by Al Bloomingdale, a scion of the well-known department-store magnate. During the Boston try-out, an experienced "play doctor," Cy Howard, was summoned to give first aid to a palpable crack-up case. He watched the show in silence. When the final curtain fell, Bloomingdale asked anxiously, "Well, what do you think?" Howard put his hand on the other's shoulder. "Al," he advised, "close the show, and keep the store open nights."

★　★　★

Eugene O'Neill, America's leading dramatist, has long since completed his brilliant new play entitled *The Ice Man Cometh*, but has forbidden its production until he is on the scene to check every detail. He has a sound reason for this decision. Only once in his career was a play done without his personal direction. That was *Dynamo*, in 1929, and, says Mr. O'Neill bitterly, "The only thing anybody seems to remember of the entire production is that Claudette Colbert wore a red dress and had beautiful legs." *The Ice Man Cometh* will have to wait until the author is good and ready to come to New York and brave once more the rigors and heartbreaks of rehearsals and out-of-town try-outs.

The new play is based on that period of Mr. O'Neill's turbulent youth when he lived in a grubby little rooming-house over a saloon just off the Hudson River waterfront. It was known as "Jimmy the Priest's." Those were the days when he sailed before the mast, and underwent the experiences that were poured into *The Long Voyage Home* and his other early plays of the sea. A little later they were produced by the Provincetown Playhouse. George Cram Cook, Eleanor FitzGerald and Jimmy Light ran the Provincetown then. They remember the day when O'Neill appeared in tow of a burly chap who was no less self-conscious because he was temporarily out of funds. He was Howard Scott, but his magic Technocracy was still around the corner.

O'Neill never could stand the ordeal of his own first nights. On the memorable occasion of the premiere of *Strange Interlude*, he wandered unrecognized down Broadway. Unrecognized, that is, by all but a single passer-by, who clapped him on the back and boomed, "Eugene O'Neill, by all that's holy! Haven't seen you since we shipped together on the *Southern Cross!* What on earth ya been doin' with yourself since?"

★ ★ ★

Joe Cook spent an entire season in a musical revue that co-starred the oft-married Peggy Hopkins Joyce. His billing for her was "that somewhat different virgin."

★ ★ ★

365

One of the sharpest and most devastating wits in the theatre is the property of Beatrice Lillie, in private life Lady Peel. She was virtually unknown in America in 1924 when an unpretentious musical called *Charlot's Revue* opened, and made stars overnight not only of Miss Lillie, but of her co-players Gertrude Lawrence and Jack Buchanan.

Years later Bea Lillie was being fitted for a number of dresses by a leading Chicago modiste. A lady who had married into the Swift hierarchy was next on the appointment calendar, and fussed and fumed because she was being kept waiting. "Tell that actress in there," she said very loudly, "that she is delaying Mrs. Swift!" This tactic, of course, resulted only in Miss Lillie's taking a half hour longer in the fitting room. Finally she tripped blithely out and, as she passed the fuming Mrs. Swift, said airily to the modiste, "Tell that butcher's wife that Lady Peel has finished now."

The only time Miss Lillie's *sang-froid* deserted her behind the footlights was at the final New York performance of *The Third Little Show*. The revue had enjoyed a long and prosperous run, and both the cast and the management were in high good humor. Howard Dietz, who had composed the lyrics, bought the entire first row of the orchestra that night, and distributed the tickets among mutual friends of Bea Lillie and himself. She was in the middle of a solo number when, by prearranged signal, everybody in the row, men and women alike, bent down and donned long whiskers of every conceivable shade and pattern— bright red, green, pink, zebra, plaid, and polka dot. The sight was too much for Bea Lillie, who stopped in the middle of her song, pointed helplessly at the solemn and oblivious first row, and ran howling to the wings. By the time Dietz reached her dressing room she had regained control of the situation. "Nobody can appreciate my voice anyhow," she reminded him, "when I sing above a whisker."

★ ★ ★

Phil Baker, master of ceremonies of the popular radio show called *Take It or Leave It*, recently received a letter—possibly from his press agent—which read, "Dear Phil: Here's a real $64 question for you. Will you lend me $64?"

THE GREAT NOSEPIECE

Jimmie "Schnozzola" Durante's recent ascent to heights he had never before known is one of the most soul-satisfying comebacks in show business. The "Schnoz" had been bogged down for years by atrocious Hollywood material, but once he turned back to his own wacky song creations, and the inimitable routine that had first won him favor, he was back in lights in no time flat.

Durante is a product of the sidewalks of New York and beer joints in Coney Island. There he learned to maltreat a piano, make capital of a nose Cyrano would envy, and warble ditties like "I Ups to Him," "Could Broadway Do Widout Me" and "The Hot Pertater" in a voice that sounds like a foghorn off Sandy Hook. For years, his partners were Clayton and Jackson. Then he had a girl stooge for a while. Her name was Martha Raye. Regardless of his associates, the backbone of his act involved storming about the floor of a night club, throwing hats at the musicians, mangling the King's English, and working himself up into a monumental dudgeon at nothing in particular. The trumpeter was "playin' wid only one lip." The waiters were "tryin' to horn in on the act." The customers were walking out at the wrong time. "Remember, mister," Jimmie told one of them, "I never fergits a back!" "I know dere's a million good-lookin' guys," he explains, "but I'm a novelty."

At the Copacabana, Jimmie packed them in so deep that, he declared, the star customers had to be satisfied with a table behind a *small* post. He dropped a collar-button one night, and before he could recover it, "a waiter threw a table cloth over it and seated five people." "Dose waiters," he ranted. "Assassins! Twelve-fifty for a load of ice wid three olives! If you don't tip 'em five dollars more, de Union calls 'em out on strike! Let 'em touch dis nose, however! I'll sue de jernt and turn it into a bowlin' alley!"

Some years ago Russel Crouse and Howard Lindsay, producers of *Life with Father* and *Arsenic and Old Lace*, signed Jimmie Durante to co-star with Ethel Merman in a musical play called *Red Hot and Blue*. When the day for the first rehearsal came round, they were horrified to learn that the "Schnoz" was

in Italy. They called Lou Clayton, now acting as Durante's manager. "What's this about Jimmie being in Italy when he ought to be here rehearsing?" they demanded. "Naw, he's not in Italy," said Clayton patiently. "He's in Rome. Tomorrow he gets to Italy."

Jimmie came home exuberant about the sights he had seen. "Dat day in Rome was de best of all," he reported. "How could you possibly do Rome justice in one day?" asked Lindsay. "One day?" said Jimmie. "Why, I didn't know what to do wid myself all afternoon!"

A great fuss developed over which name was to go first on the billing: Mlle. Merman's or Monsieur Durante's. The agents kicked up more of a row than the stars themselves. "Merman's got to go first," said her representative. "The lady's name *always* goes first." "Yeah?" said Jimmie. "How about 'Mister and Missis'?" For a while it looked as though the whole show would be called off. Eventually a settlement was effected. The names were crossed:

Jimmie's wartime experiences were "humiliatin'" and "colossial." He volunteered to drive his neighbors to work but "Share-the-Ride Schwartz" and other rotund guests kept crowding him over farther and farther in his jalopy. "Suddenly I'm standin' on de corner waitin' for a streetcar!"

In Congress, he saw senators pass a bill voting eighty millions to the Army and sixty to the Navy. "Den I hears a great commotion. A Senator starts tearin' around screamin', 'I dropped a nickel out of my pocket, and not one Senator leaves dis room till I finds it.'" He met a Colonel and cried, "Hello, chum." "Hello, chump," was the answer. "De Colonel," Jimmie explained, "speaks more distinct dan I do."

In private life, Jimmie is so friendly, unassuming, and generous that everybody in show business loves him. Fred Allen calls him "The Riff-Raff's Caruso." "His voice," reports Allen, "can only be described as a dull rasp calling its mate, or an air-raid signal blasting through two layers of gravel." He hasn't much hair left, and refers to himself as "The Surrey with the Fringe on Top." He wears glasses now ("to read de racin' form"), plays piano duets with men like Professor Einstein and Deems Taylor, and explores esoteric dishes at exclusive restaurants. He had his first cheese soufflé at an expensive French eatery not long ago.

After one bite, he registered ecstasy, and summoned the head waiter. "Where has dis been all my life?" he demanded. The waiter looked very pained. "I do not know, sir," he apologized.

★ ★ ★

Drama critics have to see so many horrible "turkeys" in the course of a season that they may be excused if they occasionally forget their manners in print.

Brooks Atkinson wrote the shortest review on record. It read: "Such-and-such opened last night. Why?" Another critic declared that a musical "arrived in town after an insufficient number of postponements." "The picture version of *Panama Hattie* needs a certain something," wrote David Lardner, and added pensively,

*Actor's-eye view of three dramatic critics**

"Possibly burial." Burton Rascoe announced that a certain actress' performance "sickened him." The next day she sent him a bottle of castor oil.

Percy Hammond closed a review with "I have knocked everything except the knees of the chorus girls, and nature anticipated

* (Left to right) Brooks Atkinson, Wolcott Gibbs, Kelcey Allen.

me there." David Lardner is credited with "The plot was designed in a light vein that somehow became varicose." A Detroit music reviewer contributed: "The Blank Quartet played Brahms last night. Brahms lost."

Somebody met George Kaufman after a particularly gruesome opening. "What did you think of it?" ventured the stranger. "It's not quite fair for me to say," Kaufman assured him. "I saw it under peculiarly unfortunate circumstances. The curtain was up."

★ ★ ★

Kelcey Allen, the dean of New York's present-day dramatic critics, composes his essays on the theatre for a paper called *Women's Wear Daily*. His reading audience is composed chiefly of the garment trade and buyers in town to have a time for themselves, and he guides himself accordingly.

A woeful production of *Macbeth* in modern dress once came close to turning New York into a one-night stand. Somebody in the audience was heard to mutter, "Lay on, Macduff; lay off, McBride." For years this witticism was credited to Kelcey Allen, but now Wolcott Gibbs comes along to say that it really was coined by Harry Hershfield.

One afternoon Russel Crouse was sitting in the Astor lobby when Allen approached with a man whom he identified as a doctor. "Don't bother getting up," he added hastily. "He's only a dentist." The play *Amphitryon 38* was always "Amferon 56" to him. Allen has an amiable habit of falling sound asleep in the middle of a show. One evening he began to snore in a spirited tempo. Walter Winchell whispered, "I see that Kelcey is writing his review early."

Allen was one of the prime spirits in the founding of the New York Critics' Circle. He makes no bones about his motives. "It's the only way," he says, "that I thought I might ever get to meet George Bernard Shaw in person."

★ ★ ★

371

Paul Muni, whose real name is Muni Weisenfreund, served his apprenticeship in the Jewish theatre. One of the roles that brought him stardom was that of a coal miner. In the second act finale, he led a delegation to plead for higher wages from a flint-hearted mine owner, who threw him out, but got what he deserved in a rousing third-act climax. One night Muni's entire family attended the show, and the young star put everything he had into the performance. So eloquent, in fact, was his description of the starving wives and babes of the miners that, at the height of his plea, the actor who was playing the owner suddenly burst into tears, and cried, "Stop! Stop! You're breaking my heart. Of course, you can have a raise!" They got the curtain down somehow or other, and the manager had to explain that just before the third act began the wicked owner had experienced another change of heart, and decided to lock the miners out after all.

★ ★ ★

When William Collier died, his old friend, Joe Laurie, Jr., jotted down a few reminiscences. It was Collier who originated a now-familiar theatrical jibe when, asked how he had liked a newly opened show, he replied, "The play was a success but the audience was a failure."

He met Al Wilson, a German comedian, at a railroad station and noted that Wilson was at one end of the platform, his company at the other. "I never speak to my company," explained Wilson. "I saw your show," said Collier, "and I don't blame you."

Collier opened one of his own plays, *The Patriot,* in New York on December 30th. January 2nd he advertised: "Second Year in New York." Meeting the oft-married DeWolf Hopper at the Friars Club, he grumbled, "Wolfy, I wish you'd invite me to one of your weddings now and then."

He was toastmaster at a banquet where first an admiral, and then a general, talked on and on while the audience writhed. Collier restored everybody to good humor by his comment: "Now I know what they mean by the Army and Navy Forever."

★ ★ ★

372

Ilka Chase's first husband was the actor, Louis Calhern. Miss Chase describes their brief romance very frankly in her autobiography, *Past Imperfect*. After their divorce Calhern married Miss Julia Hoyt. A month or so later Ilka found in her trunk a box of beautiful calling cards engraved, "Mrs. Louis Calhern." "It seemed a pity to waste them," relates Miss Chase, "so I mailed the box to my successor. But, aware of Louis' mercurial marital habits, I wrote on the top of one, 'Dear Julia: I hope these reach you in time.' I received no acknowledgment."

★ ★ ★

Louis Shurr, the corpulent theatrical agent, is the hero of many Broadway fables. Shurr is said to own a sable coat and an emerald necklace with which he adorns his lady of the evening. When he bids her good night, he takes the wrap and necklace home with him.

Shurr is hard to impress. An actor is said to have burst into his office one day; when he took off his hat, Shurr observed that four daisies and a stalk of asparagus were growing right out of his head. "I think I've got something for Ripley," said the actor. "Why?" said Shurr.

A vaudevillian proposed a novel turn to him on another occasion. "I dive off a gallery box onto the stage," he explained, "committing suicide right in front of the audience. It'll wow them." "Could be," agreed Shurr, without too much enthusiasm. "But what'll you do for an encore?"

★ ★ ★

There was a scene in Sherwood's *Reunion in Vienna* that Alexander Woollcott particularly loved. It was played by the returning Hapsburg (Alfred Lunt) and the old beldame who ran the Vienna restaurant (Helen Westley). Lunt speculated idly as to whether she still wore her old red flannel drawers, and at an opportune moment lifted her skirt to see. One night the unpredictable Miss Westley forgot to put the red flannels on. Lunt gazed in horror, and choked over his next line, which read, "Well, thank God there is one thing in Vienna that hasn't changed!"

KAUFMAN AND HART

The combination of Kaufman and Hart has become as familiar to Americans as ham and eggs. In the theatre it is the hallmark of themes so timely, dramatic construction so instinctively perfect, and dialogue so crackling that in their particular field the collaborators are simply beyond competition. One magazine or another is always writing pieces about them. They are wonderful copy; both have said so many funny things that a writer has only to string a lot of them together to convince himself—and his editor—that he has turned out a sparkling and highly original piece of work.

Kaufman has been called "the gloomy dean of Broadway wits." He is nervous, short-tempered, abrupt. "I'm never sure," said one famous actress, "whether George is smiling at me or baring his teeth." Moss Hart soon discovered, however, that beneath his acidulous manner there beats a heart of purest marshmallow. Hart himself looks like a benevolent Mephistopheles. His warmth and charm of manner have endeared him to hostesses all over the country. A hundred highly eligible girls have set their caps for him, but when it comes to matrimony, elusive is the word for Mossy. He entered the Stork Club one evening with Miss Jane Doe, a charming actress whom he was squiring at the moment. Somebody remarked, "Here comes Moss Hart with the future Jane Doe."

Kaufman and Hart are ideal collaborators, close neighbors in Bucks County, and inseparable companions. For a long time their lives were so closely interwoven that nobody even talked about them separately. In the past couple of years, however, they have gone about some separate affairs of their own, Hart to write *Lady in the Dark* and *Winged Victory*, Kaufman to direct *Doughgirls* and *Over Twenty-One* and to collaborate with J. P. Marquand in a dramatization of *The Late George Apley*. Before they intertwine again in an inevitable future collaboration, let us take gun and camera in hand, and explore a few of their vagaries:

GEORGE S. KAUFMAN . . .

George Kaufman is allergic to vegetables, dogs, hats, and typical New York first-night audiences. He favors bright-hued neckwear from Charvet, snappy bridge and gin rummy games, croquet, and being by himself. He can disappear from crowded cocktail parties and stuffy dinner groups with the speed of a meteor. "He shies at the slightest display of emotion," confides Hart, "as most men flee from smallpox. At our first meeting I was wide-eyed with hero worship; Kaufman recoiled in horror. Later, however, everything worked out fine; we married and had several beautiful children."

Kaufman was born in Pittsburgh in 1889, studied law for a few months, loathed it, sold hatbands and ribbons on the road for a year, and loathed that even more. He then settled down for a spell as a newspaper columnist, under the aegis of Franklin P. Adams, who had been deeply impressed by contributions he had received from "G.S.K." In 1917, he journeyed to Rochester to act as best man at a wedding. Another member of the bridal party was Beatrice Bakrow. Kaufman married her on the spot. The young couple were short on cash but long on hope, good humor, and friends who, like themselves, were bound for places in a hurry. Furthermore, Kaufman caught the press agent of a swank metropolitan hotel cadging his material; in retribution the hotel boarded the Kaufmans free in an elegant suite for the first months of their married life. Mrs. Kaufman's introduction to the literary and theatrical set that she now rules in queenly fashion (they were known as "the Algonquinites" in those days) came

when George and Frank Adams took her to a cocktail party, introduced her to numerous persons who said "hello" and then forgot her, and deposited her on a cane-bottom chair in the corner. The cane-bottom collapsed, and the new Mrs. Kaufman found herself imprisoned in the framework, her posterior drooping to the floor like a loose coil of rope. There was a sudden hush while everybody turned to stare. Adams added to her confusion by remarking, "I've told you a hundred times, Beatrice: that's not funny!" Today Mrs. K. would take a thing like that in her stride. Not long ago, Mrs. Kaufman met so many relatives and friends from her home town in a walk up Fifth Avenue that she reported, "All Rochester seems to be in New York this week." "What an excellent time," commented George, "to visit Rochester."

From columning, Kaufman drifted into the drama department of the *New York Times*; he clung to his well-loved job of drama editor long after his plays were netting him a fortune on Broadway. His first smash hit, *Dulcy*, was written with Marc Connelly; so were *To the Ladies* and *Merton of the Movies*. Before he met Hart, he also collaborated with Edna Ferber, Katherine Dayton, Ring Lardner, Alexander Woollcott, Morrie Ryskind, and Herman Mankiewicz. On the side he became one of the best directors of our time, and turned many an indifferent entry into a solid success by adroit doctoring during the out-of-town try-outs. In all his spectacular career he has written only one play alone: *The Butter and Egg Man*, produced in 1925.

Kaufman traces his ancestry back to Sir Roderick Kaufman, who, he claims, went on the Crusades—as a spy. After the playwright's success was assured, he was plagued with the usual swarm of stock salesmen and insurance agents. One gold-mine promoter told him his stake was so rich that it was unnecessary to dig for the gold; it lay around right on the surface. "What?" grumbled Kaufman. "You mean I'd have to stoop over to pick it up?" He and his cronies used to play cards once a week above the swanky Colony Restaurant in New York. Harpo Marx ordered a ham sandwich; roared indignantly when his bill came to $1.50. "Isn't there *anything* you can get for a quarter in this restaurant?" he inquired. "Sure," Kaufman assured him. "Twenty cents." When his daughter Anne informed him that a friend of hers at Vassar had eloped, George remarked, "Ah! She put the heart before the course."

When Kaufman is in the throes of composition, a slow and careful picking of lint from the carpet, Moss Hart discovered, is generally the forerunner of the emergence of a particularly effective line. Sometimes he removes his shoes and stretches full length on the floor. Then he performs gymnastics that would make "The Daring Young Man on the Flying Trapeze" turn green with envy. He is afraid of genuine satire, which he defines as "something that closes Saturday night," and does not welcome suggestions from outsiders. "Possibly you don't realize who I am?" grumbled one self-appointed critic when he was brushed aside. "That's only part of it," Kaufman assured him.

On an opening night, Kaufman broods in the rear of the orchestra, and glares at the limelight-hoggers who arrive late on purpose so that everybody may see them parade to their seats. He says that his farewell to the theatre will be a production of *Noah's Ark* in modern dress. The curtain won't go up until the last straggler is in his seat. Then Noah will appear and say, "Now it's going to rain for forty days." At this point the audience will be drenched with water from the ceiling of the theatre. Kaufman promises to stand at the door with a hose to catch any stray who may have escaped the general inundation. Another of his whimsical notions is *Othello* in blackface. Every character will be black except Othello himself, who will be played by somebody like Clifton Webb or Frank Sinatra. His will, he swears, provides that he be cremated and his ashes thrown in the face of a certain Hollywood producer.

Ruth Gordon once described a new play to him. "There's no scenery at all," she explained. "In the first scene, I'm on the left side of the stage, and the audience has to imagine I'm eating dinner in a crowded restaurant. Then in Scene Two I run over to the right side of the stage and the audience imagines I'm home in my own drawing room." "And the second night," nodded Kaufman, "*you* have to imagine there's an audience out front." During the abbreviated run of *Let 'Em Eat Cake*, an unsuccessful sequel to *Of Thee I Sing*, a disappointed backer spied Kaufman in the lobby and mistook him for George Gershwin. "How could you let a thing like this happen, Mr. Gershwin?" he complained. "My score is perfect," answered Kaufman, suddenly restored to high good humor. "The whole trouble is with Kaufman's book!"

He keeps a close check on his productions, lest the actors let down, as they do so frequently in long-run successes. Late in the run of *Of Thee I Sing* he sent a wire to one of the stars, William Gaxton, which read, "Am watching show from rear of orchestra. Wish you were with me." In another hit, the leading actor began to change his part to suit himself. Kaufman brought him back to scratch with a note that began, "Your performance grows more scintillating every evening. Sorry I can't say the same about the lines."

The Kaufmans recently went in for chicken-raising on a substantial scale at their country place. George made an inspection tour, and fourteen hundred chicks, expecting to be fed, came flocking toward him. He remarked: "I believe these chickens expect me to say a few words." He mounted a crate and exclaimed, "Chickens of the world, unite!" At this point a Connecticut bantam bit him on the ankle.

379

A guest expressed concern at the fate of all the women war workers when the boys came marching home. George had a ready solution. "Keep the women on the job," he suggested, "and let the men stay home and have the babies. All that is necessary is a certain amount of retooling."

Brooks Atkinson sums up George Kaufman's contribution to the theatre: "He has done the best work he could on every occasion; he is master of the destructive jest; he has made the wisecrack part of our language; he has given something distinctive, compact in form, dynamic in tempo, to American drama." Furthermore, George Kaufman is one of the few important figures in the theatre who have resisted the blandishments of Hollywood. Except for the briefest of intervals, he has declined fantastic offers from picture studios, in order to stay in the legitimate theatre, where he belongs. He has helped to keep the American drama on its course when it was floundering desperately.

. . . AND MOSS HART

"I was born on Fifth Avenue," says Moss Hart grandly, but adds in a whisper, "at the wrong end." It was 107th Street as a matter of fact, and the whole family was desperately poor. He went to public school in the Bronx. At the pinnacle of success he couldn't resist going back to impress his old principal, who had not regarded him too highly as a scholar. The principal looked him over coldly. "Moss Hart?" he mused. "Oh, yes, I'm sorry, my good fellow, but I can't do a thing for you." "This prodigal son business," concluded Hart, "is strictly bunk." He got his first look at Broadway one November day in 1918. People were dancing in the streets and embracing one another indiscriminately; ticker tape was cascading from every window. Young Hart decided then and there that Broadway was his oyster, a conviction that remained unshaken even after he learned that what he had witnessed was the Armistice celebration. The Astor

Hotel looked to him like a palace in fairyland; he spent the night there after the opening of *Once in a Lifetime;* it was a dream come true. So many others of his boyish dreams have come true that you'd think Moss Hart would be the happiest man in the world. He isn't. Vague and undefined fears dog his waking hours, a result, possibly, of early privations and inhibitions. Psychoanalysis is gradually ironing out the kinks in his unconscious. Such treatment costs most men a fortune; it's characteristic of Hart that he turned it to a handsome profit. He can patronize psychoanalysts to his heart's content for the rest of his life on the royalties from *Lady in the Dark.*

From the Bronx, the Hart family drifted to Brooklyn, and then to Sea Gate, on the fringe of Coney Island. Moss became a director of amateur theatricals, and a "host" at summer resorts on the "Borscht Circuit." It was his job to keep the guests happy. This involved whipping up entertainments, strumming guitars, crooning love ballads, and donning grease paint himself. It soon developed that he was a willing donner. A half-inch beneath the suave Hart exterior is a layer of pure ham. To this day he is ready to dash on-stage at the drop of an understudy.

When he wrote the first draft of *Once in a Lifetime* the Hart exchequer was in its usual state of non-existence. Irving Berlin read it and suggested that it be made into a musical with music and lyrics by himself. Ninety-nine out of a hundred struggling young writers would have swooned at an opportunity like this. Not Moss Hart, however. "Nothing doing," he declared. Berlin was flabbergasted but impressed. He told George Kaufman of the minor miracle. A meeting was arranged. Kaufman and Hart became a going concern. At first Moss was scared to death by his famous collaborator. His terror increased when Kaufman visibly shuddered every time he entered the room. Later he found that it was because of the aroma of his five-cent cigars. Today he smokes a pipe so regularly that several people have mistaken him for a book publisher.

Once in a Lifetime opened at the Music Box Theatre on September 24, 1930. George Kaufman was a member of the cast, so he couldn't moan around the back of the theatre, convincing himself and Hart that the show was a failure. It was so evident a smash hit, in fact, that after his ecstatic night at the Astor Hotel, Moss taxied out to Sea Gate, rounded up his family, and moved them en masse into a suite in the Ansonia Hotel, on upper Broadway. The furniture and everything else were left behind in Sea Gate; for all Hart knows, they are still there. Life began anew for the Harts, with no leftovers from the seedy days. Papa Hart, who came to be known as "the Commodore" for no apparent reason, decided he was a song-writer. He has written a song for every one of Moss' plays, *The Man Who Came to Dinner* being his favorite. Irving Berlin, uncowed by his previous rebuff at the hands of an impetuous Hart, ventured to suggest a variation in one of the Commodore's melodies. "You stick to your songwriting," spluttered the Commodore, "and let me stick to mine." He called up Moss from Florida last winter to sing his latest composition, a little number called "Carrie from Toledo, Ohio." Moss told him it wasn't quite up to his usual standard. "Don't forget," said the undaunted Commodore, "that I'm singing it without my teeth."

With Moss' theatrical star steadily in the ascendant, his brother Bernie became a Broadway fixture too. At the moment he is stage manager of *The Doughgirls* and one of the best in the business. Moss' mother, until her death, gloried in her son's success, and couldn't keep up with the gifts he showered upon her. Once he phoned her from California that a friend was coming East to lie low in his apartment until a front-page domestic entanglement blew over. Mrs. Hart entered the conspiracy with the zest of a Borgia. The following morning she wired him, "Coast clear. Have left K. with the J." Moss Hart finally figured out that she had left the key with the janitor. "We Harts," he boasted, "rise to our greatest heights in other people's crises."

Moss Hart was now fully embarked upon what he terms his "gold garter period." All the things he had dreamed of owning when he was a penniless kid he bought—usually in triplicate. His

wardrobe became so varied and authentic that his impeccable
butler consented to patronize the Hart tailor and bootmaker.
Edna Ferber remarked that he was "monogrammed in the most
improbable places." Probably his greatest extravagance—but one
that gave him the most genuine happiness—was the remodeling
of an old brick house on a tract he purchased in Bucks County,
Pennsylvania. With a prodigal hand, he turned a run-down old
farm into a model estate. Whole forests were uprooted and re-
planted with gay abandon. "Look," he said to Wolcott Gibbs,
"I've moved this oak so that it shades my library." "It just goes
to show you," muttered Gibbs, "what God could do if He only
had money."

Bucks County merchants are accustomed to bargaining over
their transactions; when they quoted Moss a price of ten dollars
on an article, they fully expected to be beaten down to five.
Moss usually confounded them, however, by exclaiming, "Only
ten dollars! How can you afford to sell a thing like that for so
little?" A landscape artist gave him an $11,000 estimate for a
particular job. Moss would have okayed it without question, but
fortunately Beatrice Kaufman was on the premises that day.
"Mr. Hart will give you exactly $7000 for this job," she said
firmly. "Done and done," agreed the landscape man without a
second's hesitation. Hart had a beautiful swimming pool constructed on the grounds; it was quite finished before he discovered that there wasn't enough water to fill it. His guests that
first summer dodged enough drilling equipment to supply a
Texas oil field; water finally was uncovered about three hundred
feet down.

All these didoes confounded the simple Bucks County folk for
a while, but he soon won their hearts with his unfailing friendliness and kindnesses. Now they stand and gape at the steady
succession of Hollywood stars and Broadway celebrities who
come to visit him. A typical bowling expedition to the near-by
alleys at Lambertville will include Moss, Barbara Stanwyck,
Robert Taylor, Darryl Zanuck, Gertrude Lawrence, his butler
Charles, and his general supervisor Raymond. "What's your

score?" Moss asked Taylor at the end of four frames one evening. "Forty-seven," said Taylor. "Hah!" exulted Hart. "I'm sixty-three." "You look it," said Taylor. The neighbors liked it, anyhow.

In fourteen years of successful playwriting, Moss Hart has

earned over a million dollars. In the same period, he has spent over a million dollars. His *Winged Victory*, written as a noble contribution to the Army Air Forces Fund after a 28,000-mile air

tour of the country's training centres, has netted him untold glory but left him strapped. Nobody—least of all himself—doubts that his next effort will put him right back in the big money. About him is the ineffable aura of success. He does everything in a big way. When he goes to the dentist, he stays in the chair for fifteen hours and has three experts tinkering with his molars. He has their signed affidavit to prove it. At the moment, happier than he has ever been, he is the spiritual guide of the boys in the cast of *Winged Victory*. When he goes to a party he takes sixty or seventy of them with him. They sing Army Air songs, eat and drink everything in sight, go their way with the blessings of their startled and unprepared hosts. Kaufman calls him "Forked Lightning." Broadway is waiting for him to strike again.

★ ★ ★

S. N. Behrman, whose plays contain some of the wittiest and most polished dialogue in the American theatre, has been called "the Boswell of the overprivileged" by Irving Drutman, "a man who writes like a silk herring" by Fanny Brice. Not for Behrman the problems of the lowly proletariat; in *The Second Man, Biography, No Time for Comedy, The Pirate,* and a half-dozen other successes he has probed the neuroses and peculiar problems of the well-heeled, putting wittier dialogue into their mouths than ever was heard in Newport or Palm Beach. Ina Claire, who often appears in his plays, once heard that she had only three weeks to learn a new Behrman part. "Three weeks!" she echoed in horror. "I can't even learn what some of Sam's lines *mean* in three weeks!"

Behrman is now a famous personage in Hollywood. The first script that he wrote there, however, failed to win the approval of the tycoon who had hired him. "It stinks," he pronounced flatly. "Ah," said Behrman, "a master of innuendo." His greatest admirer on the Coast today probably is Greta Garbo. One day when he had finished his current Hollywood stint, he interrupted Garbo on her set to say good-bye to her. She embraced him passionately, and cried, "Come back soon, my darling!" He was just closing his luggage when she burst wildly into his room. "You're going to New York!" she accused him. "Sure I am," said Sam. "Why do you think we had that great farewell scene?" "Oh, darling," she sobbed, "I thought you were just going down to the beach for a swim."

385

Another time in Hollywood, Behrman escorted the voluble Ruth Gordon to a small dinner with Somerset Maugham and Aldous Huxley. When he returned home, he commented bitterly, "It certainly gives you a thrill to dine with two of the world's greatest writers—and hear Ruth Gordon talk."

Behrman's social habits sometimes puzzle his friends. "The minute Sam makes a date," explained one, "he's already trying to find a way to break it." "Never pick up a telephone receiver," he once counseled. "The minute you do—you're trapped." One day he bade farewell to all his friends, announced that he was off for a visit to the fjords of Norway. A week later, however, Elmer Rice found him dining comfortably at his favorite table in the Plaza. "Ah, Sam," said Rice pleasantly, "I see you're forgotten, but not gone."

Behrman, an infrequent patron of New York night spots, popped up at the Stork Club one evening last winter, where he noted the presence of Tallulah Bankhead, Irene Dunne, George Jean Nathan, and of course, William Saroyan. Resolved to make a night of it, he taxied over to "21" a little later, where the first people he saw were Tallulah Bankhead, Irene Dunne, George Jean Nathan, and of course, William Saroyan. "Good heavens," exclaimed Behrman, "there seem to be two sets of everybody!"

There's only one Sam Behrman, however.

★ ★ ★

George Jessel, whose telephone conversations with his "Mama" have made millions laugh, has a huge income, but about forty-one relatives seem to live on it. One day, says Jessel, his Uncle Rafael went too far. "So," said the uncle, "I see you got on a fine new necktie, you loafer! Me you won't even buy a grand piano!"

At a party Jessel rushed up to greet an old sweetheart, but she was making a great play for a South American millionaire, and gave Jessel a haughty stare. "I don't believe I got the name," she said coldly. "No, you certainly didn't," agreed Mr. Jessel, burning, "but baby, you certainly tried hard enough!" In 1940 he did marry a beautiful young lady of seventeen. When the draft began he predicted, "The Army will soon get me. My wife was born after Pearl Harbor!"

Jessel is one of the greatest after-dinner speakers in the country—incredibly quick with quotable repartee. A toastmaster introduced him as "an unusual specimen—you have only to put a dinner in his mouth and out comes a speech." Jessel snapped right back with, "I want to call attention to your toastmaster, who is also unusual. You have only to put a speech into his mouth—and out comes your dinner." True, Joseph Choate had said the same thing fifty years ago.

Here are three of Jessel's sure-fire after-dinner stories:

A Hollywood "wolf" noticed a beautiful girl sitting by herself in a hotel lobby. Infinitely sure of himself, he registered "Mr. So-and-so and wife," and then strolled over to make her acquaintance. Two days later they handed him a bill for six hundred dollars. "What's the idea?" he sputtered. "I've only been here two days." "That's right," said the clerk smoothly, "but your wife has been here for a month and a half." . . .

An irate lady, seeking a divorce in court, told the judge, "My husband is an out-and-out loafer who thinks of nothing day and night but horse-racing. He doesn't even remember our wedding day." "That's a lie!" shouted the outraged husband. "We were married the day Twenty Grand won the Wood Memorial." . . .

A young playwright, suddenly in the chips, bought a small sea-going yacht, and a uniform to match. Anxious to impress his old mother, he invited her for a sail, and, pointing to his cap, said, "Look, mama, now I'm a captain." She put her hand on his arm. "Sammy," she said, "by me, you're a captain. By you, you're a captain. But by captains, Sammy, you're no captain." . . .

★ ★ ★

Helen Hayes, along with Katharine Cornell, is generally considered First Lady of the American stage today. Miss Hayes made her debut back in 1908, at the age of seven. The place was the old Herald Square Theatre, opposite Macy's, and the occasion was the premiere of a musical comedy called *Old Dutch*. Lew Fields was the star, John Bunny, Vernon Castle, and Ada Lewis were in the supporting cast, and Victor Herbert was the composer of the score. The following year, Fields transferred them all to another musical named *Summer Widowers* and Helen had a scene of her own for the first time.

She entered with a little boy who had gotten a raspberry tart for a present. Helen said, "How do you know it's raspberry?" The boy said, "Take a bite and see." Helen carefully ate the entire tart and admitted, "You were right. It's raspberry." Then she wiped her hands on the little boy's sleeve. The audience loved it. Charles Frohman sent for her and put her in a play with John Drew. Her career was launched.

Helen Hayes was playing in stock at Poli's Theatre in Washington, at the age of sixteen, when Fritz Kreisler gave a concert there. He had been disabled in the War and came to America to raise money for Austria, his homeland. We were not yet in the War, of course. President Wilson and his wife were in the Washington audience at the concert in question.

Suddenly there was a great commotion. Kreisler was late in arriving, and was taken through the front of the theatre to the stage entrance just back of the President's box. He was talking excitedly to his accompanist in German, and some secret service men thought he was a spy, come to assassinate Mr. Wilson. By the time explanations had been made all around, the concert was an hour late and Mr. Kreisler was in no shape to give his best performance.

The sight of Helen Hayes' shining young face in the wings seemed to restore his composure. When the concert was finished, he asked her if he could play something specially for her. "*Poor Butterfly*," said Helen promptly. Somebody brought him the music, and while the audience in front was still crying for encores, the great Fritz Kreisler played *Poor Butterfly* for Helen Hayes in his dressing room backstage.

★ ★ ★

Helen Hayes' first great dramatic hit in New York was in support of William Gillette in Sir James Barrie's *Dear Brutus*. She left the company after many months to tour under the management of George Tyler. Gillette was furious. "What did Tyler do for your daughter that we did not?" he asked her mother. "Well," she said, "he has given her a tremendous raise in salary and we are to have a drawing room on every train." "You should be very happy, Madam," said Gillette coldly. "You have sold Helen for a couple of Pullman tickets."

★　★　★

Miss Hayes met her husband, Charles MacArthur, at a cocktail party at the home of Neysa McMein. According to legend, MacArthur had a bag of peanuts in his hand. He took one look at Helen and handed her the peanuts. "I wish they were emeralds," he said. (In January 1944, MacArthur, now a major in the U. S. Army, flew with a mission to India. He came upon a couple of small but perfect emeralds and sent them to his wife. The accompanying card read, "I wish they were peanuts.")

Helen Hayes' daughter Mary was not quite five when she saw her mother on the stage for the first time. MacArthur took her to a rehearsal of Maxwell Anderson's *Mary of Scotland*. Mary watched Miss Hayes in silence while she played a stormy and dramatic scene with Queen Elizabeth. Then she turned to her father. "Mama's angry," was her comment.

During the run of *Mary of Scotland*, Miss Hayes noticed that after five or six consecutive matinees, a little boy stood at the stage door waiting for her to come out. He never spoke to her, and when one afternoon she smiled and said "Hello there," he turned brick red, and ran. After the next matinee he was waiting for her again. He thrust a little box into her hand and was gone. Inside the box she found a silver medal. The inscription read, "For scholarship. Public School 42. 1933."

★ ★ ★

The Hayes-MacArthur home is situated in Nyack, New York —about fifty miles from Broadway.

Gilbert Miller was playing host to an elaborate party at the Waldorf one evening a few years ago, when Miss Hayes took him to one side.

"Charlie is a bit high," she said, "and is having too much fun to leave now. I've got an early rehearsal tomorrow, and want to slip away. Won't you see that Charlie gets to bed O.K.?"

Miller promised. When the party broke up, he dutifully bundled MacArthur, now sound asleep, into his car and drove the full fifty miles to Nyack. When he got there, he was surprised to find that the house was boarded up and padlocked. There was nothing left to do but drive back to town and deposit MacArthur on a spare couch in the Miller apartment.

The next morning Miss Hayes called in a panic. "What have you done with Charlie?" she demanded. Miller explained that he had taken him all the way to Nyack and back.

"Good heaven," said Helen Hayes. "I forgot to tell you. We're living at the Waldorf for the winter."

★ ★ ★

Isabel Leighton, the writer, once aspired to be an actress, and landed a bit in *Deburau,* which starred Lionel Atwill. She reported her new job triumphantly to the "round table" crowd at the Hotel Algonquin. "All I do is walk once across the stage," she said. "But it's a start!" "What theatre do you open at?" asked Marc Connelly. "The Belasco," answered Miss Leighton. "Too bad it isn't the Hippodrome," said Connelly. "Your part would be twice as big."

"THE YANKEE PRINCE"

If you would like to preserve your illusions about George M. Cohan, the Prince of the American Theatre, I'd advise you to pass up Ward Morehouse's fascinating and carefully documented biography. In many ways it is the most unusual book about a legendary figure in theatrical history I ever have seen. I don't believe the author himself realized what a devastating portrait he was drawing. Morehouse, like the reader, evidently began his task in a roseate glow of hero worship, but the halo began to crumble as the evidence piled up. There were a lot of wonderful things about George M. Cohan; as he grew older, unfortunately, the meaner side of his nature came to the fore. He lost touch with the theatre that had done so well by him. He turned on the actors and associates who had worshipped him. He resolutely refused to understand important new playwrights and theatrical trends. Their language was "objectionable," their preoccupation with the thornier side of life "lamentable." The glamorous and exciting part of Cohan's career ended in 1919, when the actors struck for their rights, and Cohan flabbergasted them by spearheading the opposition. Up to that time he was indeed "The Yankee Doodle Kid"; from then on he began more and more to resemble the very model of a modern postmaster general.

George Michael Cohan was born in Providence, Rhode Island, on July 3, 1878. "His father Jerry," says Morehouse, "with a keen sense of the future publicity of an Independence Day birth, did a little understandable adjusting of the birth record." George's real name was "Keohane," and his ancestry was Irish through and through. The name "Cohan" (accent always on the last syllable) caused some amusing mix-ups in his later life. "George gets 'em coming and going," grumbled an envious competitor. "The Jews think he's Jewish and the Irish *know* he's Irish!" In a little hostel in Ireland Cohan once asked for his breakfast in bed. "Go tell that Jewish gentleman," said the irked proprietor to a bellboy, "that in this place, if he wants his breakfast he can come right down to the dinin' room an' get it!" "There's a mistake somewhere," said a man at the desk. "That man's name isn't Cohen—it's Co-han. His grandfather was born right here in County Cork." "The divil!" said the proprietor. "Why didn't you say so in the first place? Boy, tell the poor lad he'll have his breakfast in bed just as soon as we can fetch it to him."

George was a fresh, cocky kid from the very beginning. His first love, which he never got over, was baseball; his pet aversion the violin lessons his parents made him take. After he had become a great success he took his father one day to a modish and expensive restaurant. A violinist played a fancy solo. "See, George," said his father jokingly, "if you had paid more attention to your violin lessons, it might be you who was playing here now." "So it might," agreed George readily, "but then you wouldn't be eating here."

George and his sister Josephine soon were incorporated into their parents' act; "The Four Cohans" became a standard headliner on the Keith and Proctor circuits. Gradually young George took over from his father the task of supplying new material for the act. In 1899 he married a dashing young actress named Ethel Levey; in 1901, his first full-length play, *The Governor's Son*, opened in New York at the Savoy Theatre on 34th Street. (That theatre is still standing. It is opposite R. H. Macy's, and has long been a second-run motion-picture house.)

In 1904 Cohan got the luckiest break of his career. He met

Sam Harris, and formed with him the producing firm of Cohan and Harris, destined to sponsor a series of the most fabulous successes ever seen on Broadway. Their first whopping hit was *Little Johnny Jones*, written by George, featuring the Four Cohans in the cast. The song hit was "Give My Regards to Broadway." Cohan had only the vaguest notion of the plot for his play when he started to promote the cash to back it; he made up the details while he sat at a luncheon table with a prospective backer. (Years later, Ben Hecht and Charles MacArthur employed the same tactics with Sam Goldwyn. In urgent need of ten thousand dollars, they rushed into Goldwyn's office, outlined a colossal melodrama to him and pocketed his check. Months later, when Goldwyn demanded a finished script, neither Hecht nor MacArthur could remember a single detail of the plot they had improvised for him.)

At any rate, *Little Johnny Jones* knocked 'em off their seats—everywhere but in George's native town, that is. The Providence critic was so severe that Cohan swore he would never play there again. And he didn't—not for six years. Cohan himself knew that he wouldn't live up to the threats and promises he made in the course of his frequent outbursts. His partner Harris caught him one day firing an actor, so enraged that he could scarcely talk. After the actor had effected his escape, Cohan turned to Harris and said, "Remind me, Sam, never to hire that such-and-such again—unless we absolutely need him."

After *Johnny Jones* Cohan enjoyed twelve years of almost uninterrupted glory. *Forty-Five Minutes from Broadway, The Talk of New York, Get-Rich-Quick Wallingford, The Little Millionaire, Seven Keys to Baldpate* followed one another in dizzying succession. George M. Cohan was the most popular figure in the American theatre. His mere appearance on a stage anywhere from Boston to Seattle was the signal for such an outburst as only a Frank Sinatra can achieve today. His proverbial generosity made him a veritable god in the eyes of young actors and actresses. One sick, down-and-out trouper sold advertising space in a book to promote funds to finance a cure in a Western sanitarium. "How much is half a page?" asked Cohan. "Fifty dollars," said the actor hopefully. Cohan wrote out a check, drawled, "Take care of yourself, kid." The check was for $10,000.

On January 31, 1914, after the final performance of *Broadway Jones* in Detroit, Cohan presented fifty percent of all of his varied interests to his mother and father. The day after America went to war in 1917, George Cohan sat down at his desk in Great Neck, Long Island, and on two sheets of paper dashed off a song that was destined to become the greatest of his career. *Over There* was written in little over one hour. "All I wrote was a bugle call," said Cohan later. But it sold almost two million copies, eventually won him a Congressional medal. They're still looking for a song that can match it in the war that's going on today.

Over There marked the peak of George M. Cohan's career; from then on the sour notes began to mar the rhapsody. Cohan fought the actors' strike in 1919 tooth and nail; the scars that were left from that ill-advised fight never healed. He broke with Sam Harris; wrote and produced a succession of mediocre plays on his own. He scored acting triumphs in *Ah, Wilderness!* and *I'd Rather Be Right,* but his heart wasn't in his work. He quarreled with his associates, shunned the Broadway he had loved. "They don't seem to want my plays any more," he said once. "You have to give them filth these days or it's no good." In his eyes, Eugene O'Neill's chief claim to fame was that he was the son of "that grand old trouper, James O'Neill." He knew in his heart that the parade was passing him by, became infuriated when a critic called his work "corny." "Anything," he wrote, "that hasn't to do with West 52nd Street night life is 'corny' to those smart-alecks in their ready-made dinner suits. Gosh, how I hate that word!"

Ward Morehouse loved George M. Cohan very deeply; I have nothing but admiration for his having resisted the temptation to sugar-coat his biography (as was done in the recent motion picture of his life), and having dared to set down the damning facts with the laudatory ones. His book should—but probably won't—serve as a model for future life stories of American idols.

★ ★ ★

Howard Cullman, Broadway's most popular—and successful—play angel, has the annoying habit of calling his theatrical friends at nine in the morning—which is three hours, on the average, before their rising time. "Listen," expostulated Russel Crouse, "the only reason I got into this show business is because I like to sleep late." Cullman is a bearcat for efficiency. "He's a nice man," said his secretary, "but he wants everything done yesterday."

Cullman has developed a neat technique which may give executives who read these lines an idea. At eight-thirty sharp he calls his office and has his secretary read the mail to him over the phone. He dictates his answers before he hangs up. Recipients of these notes think "Jiminy cricket, but that Cullman is a ball of fire." Frequently the ball of fire has meanwhile turned over and peacefully gone back to sleep.

★ ★ ★

The latest riser of all, probably, in the playwriting fraternity, is Ferenc Molnar, Hungarian author of *Liliom* and *The Swan*. Molnar rarely stirs before one in the afternoon. He was summoned as a witness in a court action in Budapest one time, and when he saw that the case was called for nine in the morning he almost collapsed. Two servants finally got him out of bed and dressed on the day in question. As he left the house at eight-thirty, crowds of working people were passing on the way to their offices. "Good heavens," blinked Molnar in astonishment, "are *all* these people witnesses in that fool case?"

A compatriot of Molnar's in those carefree days was Alexander Inze, who later became the publisher of *Stage Magazine* in America. Inze loved the theatre from boyhood, but rarely could promote the price of a ticket. He developed the amiable habit of mingling with the audience in the lobby at the end of the first act of a play and slipping back into the theatre with them to catch the last two. Last year Gilbert Miller sent him the script of a play and asked for his opinion of it. "The latter part is fine," reported Inze, "but I don't think much of the first act." "What do you know about first acts?" chided Miller. "You never saw one in your life."

I met another debonair Budapest playwright at the once gay Donapalota Hotel there, dining with his current and very beautiful wife. "Which wife is this, my friend?" asked an unabashed companion. The playwright frowned in puzzlement, and turned to his bride. "Which one are you, darling?" he asked. "The fifth or the sixth?"

★ ★ ★

The first time that Grace Moore aired her voice professionally was for an agent of the old Aborn Opera Company. "The voice is O.K.," he opined. "Now lift your skirt, girlie, so I can see the legs." Miss Moore got the job. "Now that I look back on it," she reminisces, "I've had quite a bit of leg trouble. Managers seemed never to consider the voice as important as what there was below."

★ ★ ★

Harry Ruby, the famous song writer, hired a new cook the very day that a large dinner party was scheduled at his home. The cook spoiled the soup, the entree, and the dessert; only the meat course was even fit to be brought to the table. After the ladies had left for the powder room, a disconsolate butler appeared with liqueurs. "Tell me," Oscar Hammerstein inquired gently, "is it all right to take brandy on an empty stomach?"

★ ★ ★

Charles W. Couldock was a distinguished stage star some years ago. He was noted both for his excellence as an actor and for his personal irascibility. In one of his plays, the opening scene was between himself, another actor, and a third actor, who

397

played Mr. Couldock's elderly father. One night the actor playing the elderly father didn't show up. The stage manager hastily put a long white beard on a super and seated him on a chair at the fireplace, telling him just to sit there and that he, the stage manager, would speak the lines from offstage through the fireplace. There was time only to tell Mr. Couldock that there was to be a different actor playing his father and to assure him that everything would be all right.

The stage manager rang up the curtain, then hurried down below the stage to reach the fireplace on the other side of the set. In his haste he ran into a beam and knocked himself unconscious. Over his head, the play progressed to the point where Couldock was asked how old his father was. Couldock answered: "I don't know exactly. I shall ask him." He went over to the bearded super and said, "Father, how old are you?" There was no answer. Couldock stared at him, ad-libbed a line about father's being a little deaf, kicked the super in the shins, swore at him under his breath, and repeated the question, "Father, how old are you?" Again the answer was complete silence.

Couldock marched down to the footlights and addressed the audience. "Ladies and gentlemen, my father is so goddam old he can't even talk."

★ ★ ★

Howard Dietz is publicity chief of Metro-Goldwyn-Mayer, as well as the author of such successful plays as *The Band Wagon*, *The Little Show*, and a half-dozen other top-notch musicals. One day Louis B. Mayer, head of MGM, complained that Dietz was giving too much time to outside activities. "Howard," he chided, "I think you're getting to your desk too late every morning." "But you seem to forget, Mr. Mayer," Dietz reminded him, "that I also leave very early every afternoon." By the time Mayer had figured it out, the crisis was over.

Howard Dietz and Arthur Schwartz once accepted a radio job that kept them turning out a new song every day for thirty-nine weeks. "Doesn't that take a lot out of you?" asked an interviewer.

"Yes," said Dietz, "but it also takes a lot out of Bach, Beethoven, and Brahms."

Of the Hollywood columnist, Louella Parsons, Dietz once declared, "Lolly can spell everything but words. She has a magnificent sense of Reno and a sense of Yuma." His own title for L. B. Mayer is "czar of all the rushes." At a banquet presided over by the impeccable Lucius Beebe, replete with the richest foods and just the right rare vintages to go with them, Dietz made a sudden rush for the washroom. When he came back, still pale and shaken, he found the host regarding him with deep disapproval. "Everything is perfectly all right, Lucius," Dietz reassured him. "The white wine came up with the fish."

Chapter Two

BACK TO
THE HOLLYWOODS

THE GOLDWYN SAGA

Of all the movie producers in Hollywood, the most famous is undoubtedly Samuel Goldwyn. Part of this fame he has achieved by a series of outstanding and notable productions, part by a collection of weird statements and a misuse of the English language. Some of the sayings are undoubtedly authentic; more of them are pure inventions by Hollywood wits like Howard Dietz and Jock Lawrence, who pinned remarks on Mr. Goldwyn that he probably hasn't heard to this day. Gradually he became a legend. So many people said that a book could be written about him that Alva Johnson actually undertook one. He called it *The Great Goldwyn*; it was serialized by the *Saturday Evening Post* and published by Random House.

Mr. Goldwyn demanded advance proofs. The *Post* editors got uppity and refused; Random House, all in the spirit of good,

clean fun, did likewise. Lawrence, at that time Goldwyn's publicity chief, phoned frantically from the Coast. "If there is one
libelous word in that book," he threatened the publishers, "we're
going to sue the *Post* for two million dollars, and you for one
million." The book publishers declared that this was unfair discrimination; if the *Post* was going to be sued for two million,
they wanted to be sued for two million also. Eventually, the
book delighted Mr. Goldwyn so much that he distributed hundreds of copies to his friends. It developed, however, that Mr.
Goldwyn's fame—like that of all picture producers and directors
—was more or less limited to New York and Hollywood. Citizens
at large seemed to care only about the stars themselves. Countless booksellers in the South and Middle West asked the salesmen, "Who *is* this 'Great Goldwyn' anyhow?" When this fact
was reported to Mr. G., he thought they were kidding him.

The Nineteenth Century greets the Twentieth.
(left to right) Mrs. Malaprop, Mr. Goldwyn

There follow a handful of the choice Goldwynisms. It is impossible to say how many of them actually sprang from the lips
of Sam Goldwyn. For a time he was suspected of actually encouraging their manufacture and circulation. In those days, any

kind of publicity was considered good publicity. Shrewd and intuitive character that he is, however, Goldwyn sensed that a new mantle of dignity and artistic consciousness was about to descend upon the cinema, and he began to disavow these tales in increasingly testy tones. Recently, upon reading a prediction on the future of Hollywood, signed by himself, in a Sunday supplement, he is said to have remarked indignantly, "This fellow has no idea of my literary style. Tell him to read the piece my last man wrote for me."

Mr. Goldwyn's most famous dicta undoubtedly are his "Gentlemen, kindly include me out," and the matchless "In two words I tell you my opinion of that picture: im-possible." In an argument over possession of a big star's services, a Paramount man suggested that the decision be left to arbitration. "O.K.," said Goldwyn reluctantly, "if it's understood that I get him."

Another time he called up L. B. Mayer, of MGM. "Louis," he said sadly, "both of us are in trouble." "How come?" asked Mayer. "It's this Clark Gable," said Goldwyn. "You got him; I want him." When he was introduced to Aldous Huxley he beamed, "I understand you are practically a genius." He counseled a friend, "Keep what I'm telling you under your belt." A cousin told him he had named his new baby William. "What did you do that for?" disapproved Goldwyn. "Every Tom, Dick, and Harry is named William." The first time he saw a sundial, and learned what it was, he murmured, "Tsk! Tsk! What won't they think of next!"

When Goldwyn's lovely wife, Frances, persuaded him to forsake movie-making long enough to sail to Hawaii for a vacation, a farewell party was whipped up in his honor at the studio. Every one of his employees was there. His press agent whispered in his ear, "They expect you to say a few words." Goldwyn cleared his throat, and the crowd fell silent. "Well, fellows," said Sam, "bon voyage!"

His secretary complained that the files had grown so cluttered that it was growing impossible to find anything. "At least," she begged, "let me destroy the letters that are ten years old or more." "O.K.," said Sam reluctantly, "but don't forget to make copies." He asked a newly signed actor where he hailed from. "Idaho," said the youngster. "Out here, young man," Goldwyn advised him, "we pronounce it Ohio."

Goldwyn loves to play games of any description, but he can't stand losing them. The money, obviously, does not trouble him, but he feels that a defeat at golf, or gin rummy, or backgammon is a slur on his ability that is too painful to bear. He took countless golf lessons without graduating from the duffer class. One day on the practice tee, he took a mighty swipe at the ball, and sent a low liner whistling down the fairway, to land *plunk* on the green two hundred and sixty yards away. Goldwyn gaped for a moment, then wheeled on the professional and demanded, "What did I do right?" On a round with Harpo Marx he was putting so abominably that at the sixth green he hurled his putter furiously into the woods. When he wasn't looking, Harpo sent his own caddy back to redeem the club. Harpo was putting like a streak that day. Several holes later Goldwyn asked him how he explained his new-found skill. "It's this new putter," Harpo told him. "It's balanced so delicately that the ball practically rolls into the hole by itself." Goldwyn tested it, approved—and bought back his own putter for ten dollars. At the end of the round, Harpo was thirty dollars ahead. "I'll match you double or nothing," said Sam grimly. He lost. That made it sixty. "One more," he demanded. He lost again. When the debt had risen to $960 Harpo begged off. "Look," he said, "I didn't come out here today to win all this money. I came out for eighteen holes of golf. Pay me the thirty dollars you lost on the game and let's call it quits." "That's very sporting of you," conceded Goldwyn. "Now I'll match you just once more: sixty or nothing."

In a bridge game, Goldwyn drew Connie Bennett as a partner against two experts. The men wanted to play for fifty cents a point, but Connie sagely declared that her limit was a penny. Goldwyn volunteered to carry her. That meant that he was playing for ninety-nine cents a point. Everything went reasonably well until one hand when, with both sides vulnerable, the man at Goldwyn's right bid "one heart." Goldwyn, in a voice that spoke volumes, said "I pass." The third man also passed. Connie said "one spade." "Two hearts," declared the first bidder. "I pass," said Goldwyn a little more loudly. Connie went to two spades; the man next to her bid three hearts. "I pass," Goldwyn virtually shouted. Eventually Miss Bennett bid four spades, was doubled, and went down four tricks—eleven hundred points. Goldwyn was apoplectic. As the last card was played, he leaped to his feet, pounded on the table, and screamed at his partner: "Damn it, couldn't you HEAR me keeping quiet?"

Many years ago, George Oppenheimer assured Goldwyn, then his employer, that *The Wizard of Oz* would make a fine motion picture, and finally persuaded him to read the book. It is a juvenile, consisting of about a hundred and fifty pages of very big type. The next morning Goldwyn was enthusiastic. "I sat up till two reading it," he said as he disappeared into his office. A day later he summoned George. "You're ruining my whole social life with that book," he declared. "I was up till past midnight again with it." "Well," said George eagerly, "what do you think?" "I'm not sure yet," Goldwyn answered. "I'm only half through with it so far." He eventually bought the story, kept it on the shelf for years, and then sold it at a small profit to MGM, whose not too imaginative version of it netted millions and made a star of Judy Garland.

A lesser effort on the Goldwyn schedule was made in his absence. The night he returned, the director brought it to his house to run it through for him on his private machine. Goldwyn sat through the picture glumly, and declared at its conclusion, "It's terrible. I myself don't know what it's all about, and if I don't know what it's about, what do you think the moving picture audience will make of it?" "Maybe you don't understand it," said the mortified director, "but I'll bet your twelve-year-old son would." "We'll prove it," cried Sam, and called his boy down from his studies while the picture was run off again. "Well, son, did you understand it?" said Goldwyn confidently, but his jaw dropped when the answer came, "Of course, I understood it. It's simple as A B C!" The director's triumph was short-lived. Goldwyn wheeled on him angrily and demanded, "What do you think I'm doing in this business? Making pictures for twelve-year-olds?"

Goldwyn's nerve sometimes reaches awe-inspiring proportions. Dining at the house of a famous playwright, he declared that in all of his hectic Hollywood career, not one person ever had had occasion to sue him. His host felt obliged to remind him that two of the five gentlemen present (one being himself) were suing him at that very moment. "Present company," said Sam blandly, "is excepted." He has created more stars than any other producer because he is willing to risk millions on a brand-new personality. One of his recent pictures, for instance, called *Up in Arms*, featured Danny Kaye, a stage favorite in the key cities but virtually unknown to movie audiences. Goldwyn gambled over two million dollars on the production, and cashed in handsomely, because Kaye was a sensational hit.

One time he stubbed his toe with a foreign beauty named Anna Sten. Goldwyn starred her in a version of Zola's *Nana* and lost a fortune on the venture. Some time previously he had signed a new director and assured him, "I don't want 'yes men' around me. I want you to 'no' me once in a while—even if it costs you your job." This intrepid soul took him at his word, told him the script of *Nana* was terrible and Miss Sten was miscast, and refused to have anything to do with the project. Goldwyn fired him. For years thereafter, if anybody suggested that this director be used on another picture, Goldwyn would shake his head vigorously, and declare, "No, *sir!* That man was connected with my greatest failure."

Goldwyn wants top-flight men working for him and will pay any price to get them. He is responsible for the presence of some of the world's greatest authors in Hollywood. He hired Louis Bromfield at a huge salary, greeted him upon his arrival with, "It's good to have you with us, Mr. Bloomberg." One of his earliest importations was Maurice Maeterlinck. "I know you don't understand picture technique," Goldwyn assured him. "You don't have to. Just go home and write your greatest book over in the form of a scenario. I don't care how long it takes you." Some weeks later Maeterlinck came back with a finished script. "Now we'll see something," beamed Goldwyn, and took it into his sanctum sanctorum. Two minutes later he rushed out tearing his hair. "My God," he screamed. "The hero is a bee!"

I hope that all of the foregoing stories have not deceived you about Samuel Goldwyn's ability to make outstanding and profitable motion pictures. For years he has been a lone wolf in Hollywood, the one big producer who never had to go to a bank to pull him out of trouble. He has blazed many a new trail in a community where innovations are far and few between, and every penny that went into his costly experiments was his own. He is a stickler for detail, and spares neither time nor expense to make the tiniest prop authentic, the most fleeting shot exact. Most of the people who scream loudest against him end up by coming back to work for him. In his fashion, he plays the game straight; as long as he continues to turn out such screen classics as *Wuthering Heights, Arrowsmith, Stella Dallas, Street Scene,* and *The Little Foxes,* his envious competitors will know only too well that there's Samuel Goldwyn in them thar Beverly Hills.

★ ★ ★

Hollywood has lifted eyebrows over the marriage of Victor Moore, the 67-year-old comedian, to a girl of 22. "What's wrong with that?" queried Buddy de Sylva. "When she is 100, he will only be 145."

★ ★ ★

This is an incident that could happen only in Hollywood. A zealous policewoman bagged three frowsy gypsy fortune-tellers, herded them into a squad car, and laughed merrily while they predicted disaster for her. The sun shone brightly through the evidence, a sizable crystal ball, and set fire to the upholstery and her crisp new uniform.

Possibly the police lady has grounds for a sibyl suit.

★ ★ ★

Somebody asked Bob Hope what went through his mind when he got his original view of Dorothy Lamour in a sarong. "I never gave it a second thought," he averred. "I was too busy with the first one."

★ ★ ★

Van Cartmell tells the story of a housewife who asked a little grocery boy his name. "Humphrey," answered the boy, and added that the last name was Bogart. "Humphrey Bogart, eh?" said the housewife. "That's a pretty well-known name." "It darn well ought to be," the boy agreed. "I've been delivering groceries in this neighborhood for four years."

★ ★ ★

W. C. Fields is certainly the greatest juggler in the world, and some folks will swear he's the greatest comedian too. His real name is Claude William Dukenfeld, which he signs to an original scenario every now and then just for the hell of it. He was born in Philadelphia, but ran away from home when he was eleven. Some very tough years followed. "I was a big city Huck Finn," he says. Constant colds and hacking coughs gave him his husky and rasping voice, repeated punches in the nose from older and heavier aggressors swelled and reddened his proboscis to an extraordinary degree. These two characteristics have become a sort of trademark; he keeps them up to snuff with frequent libations of Irish whiskey, a liquid to which he is not allergic. A lad came to see him last year who declared he was a long-lost son. Fields was skeptical, but asked him in. "Drink?" he inquired. "Coca-Cola," said the lad. Fields ejected him with a roar of rage. "An obvious impostor," he explained. Another time he returned from four weeks of location work in a town that was bone-dry. "Can you imagine me subsisting all those days," he marveled, "on nothing but food and water?"

Fields' first professional job was a combination of juggler and drowner at an Atlantic City beer joint. When business slackened, he would dive into the briny, and be saved just as he was going down for the third time. The crowd was expected to order beer and wienies while the waiting emergency squad restored him to consciousness. One July Fourth he "drowned" seven times.

His first great hit on Broadway was scored in the Ziegfeld Follies. He did a combination juggling-and-hokum act with a trick billiard table that simply defies description, and that would

bring just as many howls of laughter today as it did then. One night Fields got a laugh where he didn't expect it. Upon investigation, he found Ed Wynn hiding under the table, mugging at the audience. Fields, whose temper was not improved by his years of hobo camps and slow freights, hauled off and conked

Wynn with a billiard cue. The crowd roared appreciatively, and laughed again every time Wynn clasped his sore head and moaned in agony. Fields calmly continued with his act, and later suggested that they include the routine every night. Wynn never butted into his number again.

"When I was a tot," confessed Fields, "I swore that if I ever got in the chips, I'd help kids who were homeless waifs like I had been. For years I couldn't afford it. Then came Hollywood and riches." "Did you start a foundation as you had planned?" asked a girl interviewer eagerly. "No," said Fields, "I'm afraid I didn't. I said to myself, 'To hell with them.'"

Every time Fields goes to the theatre he writes a note to the house manager. It reads, "My wife and I will be in your theatre tomorrow evening. We will occupy seats number G-108 and 110, where my wife will lose a pair of white silk gloves."

★ ★ ★

Edgar Bergen tells about an old ventriloquist who had no Charlie McCarthy to turn his act into a headliner. In fact, he became so convinced that there was no future for the act he had been presenting for years that he decided to set up shop as a crystal-gazer in Hollywood, a mecca, he had been told, for cultists and mesmerizers of every description. Business, unfortunately, was virtually nonexistent in his new stand, and when one morning an uncertain young woman, dressed in black, appeared upon the scene, he determined that she should have the works. "Can you put me into communication with my dead husband George?" she inquired. "You bet I can," promised the ventriloquist, and the young lady thereupon had such a satisfactory conversation with George that, instead of paying the five-dollar fee requested, she insisted on paying ten. "This is mighty white of you, lady, mighty white," he said. "And to show my appreciation, the next time you converse with your dead husband George, by golly, I'll drink a glass of water at the same time."

★ ★ ★

In Hollywood, where many a benighted soul has been coasting along on a three-thousand-dollar-a-week salary on Friday night, only to find himself out on his ear on Saturday morning, names are painted on the outside of office doors in a substance that can be scraped off very easily. Mr. A's office today may be Mr. B's tomorrow, and Mr. C's a week from Tuesday.

When Dorothy Parker was first assigned her own little cubicle in a writers' studio her fame was not yet universal, and not a soul dropped in to see her for days on end. Panting for company, Miss Parker took steps one evening after the other hired help had departed. First she scratched the "Dorothy Parker" off her door. Then she replaced it with the simple legend, "Gents' Room." The next day her problem was solved.

Gene Fowler suffered from the opposite complaint: too many visitors barged into his private office to exchange quips and keep him from work. The sign *he* painted outside his door read "Horace Witherspoon, Jr.: Famous Polish Impersonator." Nobody came near him for weeks.

★ ★ ★

Cecil B. De Mille once produced a motion picture allegedly based on E. Arnot Robertson's story of the Indo-Chinese jungle, *Four Frightened People*. The star was Claudette Colbert. De Mille took the author to a preview. "How did you like it?" he asked when the lights went on again. Miss Robertson reflected a moment. "Mr. De Mille," she said slowly, "do you remember the roar of an off-stage lion that came in somewhere about reel three? Well, I do believe that you took that straight from my story."

★ ★ ★

Jesse Lasky has been toying with the idea of filming a life of James Audubon with Errol Flynn slated to play the noted ornithologist. "Audubon," said Lasky, "often pursued a specimen for weeks." "You sure picked the right man to play him," said a friend.

★ ★ ★

One of the Glamour Colony's greatest stars gave a party last year for the crème de la crème. White ties, strapless gowns, and all the emeralds and sables in town. At the height of the festivities, a well-known agent weaved in, dressed in shapeless slacks and plastered to the gills. The hostess froze and remarked acidly that she did not remember inviting him. "Not only did you not invite me, but I *declined*," he replied, and fell on his face.

★ ★ ★

Two agents sat together watching a preview of an important picture. One happened to be the agent for the male star of the piece, the other for the female lead. They sat silently while several reels were unwound and then one nudged the other in the ribs. "Look at those two hams up there," he said with some disgust, "getting eighty percent of our dough."

★ ★ ★

Another agent story concerns a flourishing coast agency named Feitlebaum & Garfinkel. One morning Feitlebaum came to Garfinkel and explained that he was sick and tired of his cumbersome and harsh-sounding name. "With your permission," he explained, "I have changed my name this morning to O'Brien." Garfinkel said nothing, but a few mornings later he came to his partner with the declaration that he too was tired of the name he had been bearing all his life. "With your permission," he said, "I have also changed my name to O'Brien." Thereupon, the old sign was taken down and a resplendent new one, reading "O'Brien & O'Brien," was put up in its place. A few mornings later the telephone rang and a voice demanded to be connected with Mr. O'Brien. "Very good, sir," said the cheery-voiced operator, "but which Mr. O'Brien do you want: Feitlebaum or Garfinkel?"

★ ★ ★

A few years ago a new edition of Thackeray's *Henry Esmond* was published in the Modern Library series. To the amazement of the editors, there arrived a letter some days later from a prominent Hollywood agency addressed to William Makepeace Thackeray, Esq. It read as follows:

"We have read your recent book *The History of Henry Esmond, Esq.* and believe it possesses material adaptable for motion pictures.

"We are recognized agents for writers at all studios and as such would like to represent you in the sale of both your own personal services and your literary products.

"In the event you have already made a commitment to some agent for the above book, we nevertheless are impressed with your potential possibilities as a screen writer and would be interested in both your services and future stories.

"We would appreciate your advising us by return mail whether or not you are represented here in Hollywood; and in the event that you are not and desire us to represent you, we would be happy to forward to you a copy of our agency agreement with writers for your information and guidance."

A busy publisher always has time to enter into the spirit of an affair of this sort, so the following note was promptly sent back:

"Thank you for your letter telling me that you believe that my recent book, *The History of Henry Esmond*, possesses material adapt-

412

able for motion pictures. This effort is a rather crude attempt, I fear, but I am now working on a new novel which I think will be a natural for pictures. I am thinking of calling the new book *Vanity Fair*.

"I will be interested in hearing what you think of this title.

Sincerely yours,

William Makepeace Thackeray"

Three days later another letter arrived from the agency:

"Acknowledging receipt of your letter of December 28, in reply to our previous communication, we feel that the title which you are thinking of giving your new book, namely *Vanity Fair*, is a good one. We would greatly appreciate receiving a manuscript on this story. Perhaps you could also send us a manuscript at this time, or if not, a copy of the book, *The History of Henry Esmond*.

"We would like to submit this, if we are authorized to do so by you, to the studios for their consideration."

There the matter rests.

★ ★ ★

When Gloria Swanson's mama heard that she had married a titled gent in Paris, she hastily phoned her lawyer. "What's a markee?" she demanded. "It's one of those things," he explained, "that you hang in front of a theatre to keep the rain off customers." "My God!" cried the good lady. "Gloria married one of them this afternoon!"

★ ★ ★

Major studios register new titles for contemplated productions with the Hays office, which promptly reports any conflicts with previous registrations. When the Fox organization recently announced its picture based on the life of President Wilson, titled, with unusual simplicity, *Woodrow Wilson*, the Hays office dutifully reported that it had on file one title that might conflict. It was Mark Twain's *Pudd'nhead Wilson*.

★ ★ ★

"THE BEARD"

There was a time about ten or fifteen years ago when the most
famous beard in the literary world adorned the countenance of
a reasonably distinguished Irish critic who could be heard pon-
tificating practically any afternoon near the bar of whatever publisher's cocktail party chanced to be in progress. He would stroke
his beard with a gentle and tentative gesture comparable to a
movie star milking a cow for a publicity photograph, and emote
at length on any subject from Abyssinia to Zoroaster. One unkind critic hinted that the beard concealed a pocket-size encyclopedia; another, more acidulous, withered him one day with,
"What you need, my man, is a good shave. You look like an
armpit."

At any rate, the fame of this critic's beard was long ago
eclipsed by that of Monty Woolley, Yale professor, bon vivant,
wit, and motion-picture star, whose whiskers are his trademark

and have been impressed in the pavement of Grauman's Chinese Theatre alongside Charlie Chaplin's shoes and Betty Grable's legs. Woolley was one of the guests at a Cole Porter party some years ago where the composer introduced a new number he had written called "Miss Otis Regrets She's Unable to Lunch Today, Madam." The burden of this lugubrious chant concerned an urgent appointment that Miss Otis had with the public hangman, necessitating a complete curtailment of her social activities. Woolley fell passionately in love with the song and sang it constantly at every party he attended for the next year. He sang it so well, in fact, that people began to suspect he was wasting his time at Yale. He was talked into a substantial part in a musical comedy called *On Your Toes* where he held his own against such accomplished show-stealers as Ray Bolger and Louella Gear, and then really reached the heights when Kaufman and Hart had the happy inspiration to cast him as Alexander Woollcott in *The Man Who Came to Dinner*. He played the part in Hollywood, too, and will probably be there from now on.

Woolley is reported to have summoned his butler one morning (this story is also credited sometimes to J. S. Bache) and said, "I'd like to know what my household expenses really amount to out here. If you will be good enough to leave out of the bills your rake-off on food, liquor, laundry, gasoline, and God knows what else, I will be happy to add it to your salary at the end of the month." "Mr. Woolley," said the butler gravely, "you couldn't afford it."

On one of his visits to New York between pictures, Woolley gave a party for his old friends. It was a very formal affair, and Woolley didn't consider it amusing at all when Cole Porter showed up with a bearded lady from the circus as his escort. Porter listened to Woolley's remonstrances for a moment, then turned to the bearded lady and remarked, "Madam, your son has atrocious manners."

At a bond rally in Hartford, Woolley sat toying with his famous beard, next to a prominent lady author, waiting for his turn to address the assemblage. Suddenly he belched. The lady author gave him a horrified look. Woolley bridled. "And what did you expect, my good woman?" he inquired. "Chimes?"

Woolley was so pleased with this line that he insisted it be written into his next role in Hollywood.

★ ★ ★

There is a coterie in Hollywood that plays the game of hearts for very high stakes. The card to avoid in this game is the queen of spades, and when one evening Mr. Rufus Lemaire was caught with it four hands running, he accused his friends of unfair discrimination, and sticking him on purpose. The very next hand he got the queen of spades again. He jumped out of his chair, cried, "I will never enter this house again," and stamped angrily out into the night. He was back ten minutes later, however, looking rather sheepish. It was his house.

Lemaire was host at a buffet supper another evening. The servants had forgotten to pass napkins. "It's on account of the war shortages," Oscar Levant explained. "Instead of napkins, from time to time a woolly dog will pass among you."

★ ★ ★

Mankiewicz en riposte

One of the sharpest and most unsparing wits in Hollywood is that of Herman Mankiewicz, the writer. "You are a composer after my own heart," he once told Sigmund Romberg. "You write the kind of music people whistle as they go *into* the theatre." A friend burst into his house and reported the sale of an original script for five thousand dollars. Mank turned to his wife and commanded, "Dance for the gentleman." In a poker game he told Harry Ruby, "There are two ways I always can tell when you have a good hand: your face lights up, and you play it wrong." He also told Ruby, "You look like a dishonest Abe Lincoln." "It's conditioned my whole life," admits Ruby. "I'm afraid to sit in a box at theatre." Mank is also credited with summing up a producer's career as "Poland to polo in two generations." He says, however, that the phrase was coined by Irving Caesar.

Mankiewicz's own game of bridge is on the sketchy side. Playing with George Kaufman one evening, he butchered a hand inexcusably. "When did you learn this game, Mank?" asked Kaufman. "Now don't tell me it was this afternoon. I want to know what *time* this afternoon."

★ ★ ★

Triumph of tact: Miss Marlene Dietrich had her picture taken, and fumed at the result. "I can't understand it," she said. "The last time I posed for you, the photographs were heavenly." "Ah, yes," sighed the camera man, "but you must remember that I was eight years younger then."

★ ★ ★

Two of the best-known motion-picture magnates in Hollywood are Louis B. Mayer, of MGM, and his talented and headstrong son-in-law, David Selznick. The Selznicks were in New York on the day that the President suggested a $25,000 ceiling for executives' salaries. "Golly," said Mrs. Selznick, "I wish we were in California this evening so we could hear papa holler." "Just open the window," suggested her husband. "You can probably hear him from here."

Chapter Three

THE LITERARY LIFE

Dorothy Thompson, most overpowering and awe-inspiring female commentator in America, was anything but that when she first met Sinclair Lewis at a dinner party in Berlin. Lewis was so enchanted that in the middle of the dinner he leaned past a couple of startled guests and asked her to marry him.

They spent their honeymoon on a trailer trip through Britain. Later Adolf Hitler personally ordered Miss Thompson bounced out of Nazi Germany, an indignity for which she has never forgiven him.

The Lewises had a tranquil married life until Miss Thompson became so engrossed in column-writing, lecturing, radio work, and general reshaping of the world that she had no time left for anything else. Somebody asked "Red" Lewis where she was one

evening. "She disappeared into the NBC Studios three years ago," answered Red, "and nobody has seen her since." Another time he heard that she was being mentioned for a presidential nomination. "I wonder," he said wistfully, "if they'll let me write 'My Day.'"

Heywood Broun wrote that Miss Thompson was greater than Eliza. "She not only crosses the ice but she breaks it as she goes. What's more, she's her own bloodhound."

Miss Thompson is quite ready to fight for her beliefs. A female patron of a famous East Side café made a couple of cracks in favor of the Nazis in her presence; Miss Thompson marched her outside and nailed her one on the button. She attended the disgraceful Bund rally at Madison Square Garden and gave them the old Bronx cheer until they got her out—with the aid of the police. That took guts.

It's a lucky thing for a certain bookseller in Louisville, Kentucky, that Miss Thompson never heard his comment when a Houghton Mifflin salesman showed him an advance copy of her newest book. "Dorothy Thompson. Let's see now," he mused. "Wasn't she the principal character in that show called *Rain?*"

★ ★ ★

One of the colossal nuisances of the publishing industry is the annual taking of inventory. Books are scattered among a dozen warehouses, binderies, branch depositories, and the various departments of the publisher's office itself. Each title, of course, must be tabulated separately. During the course of the year, hundreds of odd copies are given away to visitors—or filched—without review slips being made out. If the individual totals come out within a hundred copies each of the indicated records, everybody is reasonably satisfied.

All this is a preamble to a tale about the final day of inventory-taking at a downtown publisher's plant. The pair who were tabulating the figures waited until Saturday to count the books in the president's private office. The president himself was out counting strokes in every bunker on the Creek Club course. On

Monday morning he bustled in bright and early (ten-thirty) and was mildly astonished to find the inventory records scattered on the floor of his inner sanctum. All of the figures were in apple-pie order except the notations on the last page. This was headed "president's office." The first notation read: "One set Encyclopædia Britannica; one Roget's Thesaurus; one Fannie Hill; one unopened bottle of Scotch." A wavering cross had been drawn through these lines and a second notation added that listed the same books, but concluded with the item, "one-*half* bottle of Scotch." This, too, had been scratched out, however, with a series of blotches and hieroglyphics, and one last line recorded in barely legible penmanship. It read: "One revolving encyclopædia."

★ ★ ★

An advanced student of literature unearthed from *Spicy Western Stories* a gem that read: "She was silent a long time. He could smell the perfume wafted upward from between her proud breasts, placed so cleverly on the lobes of her ears." *The New Yorker* snapped it up, of course, and added the perfect comment: "Novel, but we wouldn't like it as a steady thing."

★ ★ ★

Some years ago, the Hotel Ambassador played host to the first International Crossword Puzzle Tournament. This was a purely spontaneous affair and the fact that the entire executive board of Simon and Schuster and the publishers of Webster's Dictionary happened to be buzzing around was purely coincidental. The winnah and undisputed champeen turned out to be a legal gentleman named William Stern, who was not quite prepared for the prize that rewarded his great effort. It was one of those walloping big dictionaries that should come equipped with their own electric hoisting machines. The chairman managed to deposit it in Mr. Stern's outstretched hands. Mr. Stern thereupon fell flat on his face, closely followed by the chairman. The defeated contestants cheered mightily.

★ ★ ★

Harold Ross, editor of *The New Yorker*, once tried to stop private telephone calls in his office and went so far as to install a public coin booth in the reception room. The next morning he found the booth torn loose from its roots, on its back in his own private office. Stretched out inside it, a calla lily clutched in his hand and a wreath on his head, lay James Thurber. When Ross

Harold Ross (right)

once complained, "Thurber's women don't have any sex appeal," Marc Connelly reminded him, "They do for Thurber's men."

Thurber's definition of humor will do until a better one comes along: "Humor is a kind of emotional chaos told about calmly and quietly in retrospect."

★ ★ ★

When Simon and Schuster published a book called *The Ten Commandments,* somebody suggested that it be one of the publications of the Armed Services paper-bound books intended for men in the services abroad. "It is much too long," opined one director. "Wait a minute," urged Philip Van Doren Stern, who was originally trained by Simon and Schuster. "How about using only five of them and calling it A *Treasury of the World's Best Commandments?*"

HEYWOOD BROUN (1888–1939)

Heywood Broun died in 1939. The multitude of friends who loved and admired him from the bottom of their hearts find it hard to believe that it's as long as that since they saw him shambling into his favorite haunts, sloppily attired, tardy for appointments, but welcomed with shouts of joy wherever he appeared. His name bobs up in conversations as frequently as though he were still alive, turning in his daily columns. And what columns the doings of these past years would have inspired in him! By a stroke of cruel irony, the space they once occupied was turned over to the outpourings of Westbrook Pegler, who represents everything Broun detested most. "The trouble with Peg," he explained once, "is that he was bitten early in life by an income tax."

Broun's classmates at Harvard included John Reed, Walter Lippmann, and Hamilton Fish—an omen, possibly, of the later conflicts between his political convictions and his sybaritic personal habits. Foreign languages were his nemesis. An irate German professor shied an inkwell at him, but missed. His habit of fulfilling assignments at the last possible moment, if at all, failed to enchant the Harvard authorities, and he was not graduated. His classmates watched in awe while he threw all of his belongings helter-skelter into a trunk, and then climbed in himself and trampled them down after the fashion of a Burgundy grape-presser.

Broun got a job with the *Tribune*, and turned in some of the greatest baseball and football stories that have ever been written. Then he was transferred to the drama department. The day of the transfer, he acted as official scorer at a Giant-Cub ball game in the afternoon, and covered Ethel Barrymore's opening in an Edna Ferber play called *Our Mrs. McChesney* in the evening. At the ball game, he scored a close play as an error for the visiting shortstop, thereby depriving the Giant batter of a base hit

in the records. That evening, he roasted Miss Barrymore's performance to a fare-thee-well. The next day the *Tribune's* managing editor received two indignant communications. One, from the Giant batsman, read, "What's the big idea of sending a lousy dramatic critic up here to be official scorer?" The other, signed by Miss Barrymore, concluded, "How dare you assign a cheap baseball reporter to cover the opening of a Barrymore play?"

Broun loved the theatre, and the majority of his reviews were gentle and encouraging. One evening, however, an actor named Geoffrey Steyne gave a performance that displeased him. Broun allowed that Mr. Steyne was the worst actor on the American stage. Mr. Steyne sued. The whole principle of dramatic criticism was at stake in this suit; if the actor won it, obviously, a dangerous precedent would have been established. The case was dismissed, and it remained only to see what Heywood would say about Mr. Steyne on the occasion of his next New York appearance. The big night finally arrived, and the next morning initiates turned eagerly to Broun's review. He did not so much as mention Geoffrey Steyne until the last sentence of his last paragraph. This read simply, "Mr. Steyne's performance was not up to his usual standard."

Heywood was a war correspondent in France in 1918. General Pershing saw him in uniform and asked him if he had fallen into a ditch. A fellow worker once dubbed him "Six Characters in Search of a Laundry." Heywood usually forgot to put laces in his shoes. When he took them off for bowling—which he loved—he disclosed socks with such enormous holes that they looked like ankle supporters. His first wife, Ruth Hale, was just as careless as Heywood. The first time I visited their home, a step in the back staircase was broken; three years later it had not been repaired. Everybody just hopped over it, while Ruth would remark placidly, "Somebody's going to break his neck on that step some day." I had come to collect an introduction for a book that Heywood had promised to deliver some two months previously. He wrote it while I waited. Then we lunched together in his kitchen. We vaulted the broken step, and found that the icebox contained a single can of peaches. Heywood punctured the lid with a beer opener, and emptied the peaches into two saucers that he salvaged from a pile of dirty dishes in the sink. We ate standing up.

When Dorothy Parker and Beatrice Kaufman visited the Broun Home Front, Mrs. K. is reported to have discovered a couple of deep brown, bedraggled old toothbrushes hanging in the bathroom. "Good heavens," she cried, "what are those things?" "Don't you recognize them?" said the ever-helpful Miss Parker. "Those are the broomsticks the witches ride on every Hallowe'en."

The last tenant of the Brouns was Ed McNamara, who plays every Irish cop role in Hollywood. "Mac," Heywood told him, "it's a shame that with a rich, resonant voice like yours, you don't ever know what the hell you're talking about!" One night Mac came home to discover his trunk on the doorstep, and a note from Heywood written on the tag. "Dear Mac," it read, "I forgot to tell you that I sold the house."

In 1921, Heywood joined the staff of the morning *World*, where he became scared to death of the editor, Herbert Bayard Swope. Years later, although they now were close friends and met night after night at various people's houses, he still held Swope—not to mention Swope's wife, Margaret—in something like awe. When Winston Churchill's son, Randolph, wangled a job on the *World* at the tender age of eighteen, and called Swope "Herbert" the day he joined the staff, Heywood practically dropped in his tracks.

Some of Heywood's quips at this time are still quoted and collected in anthologies. The depression had not yet come along to toughen our fibre and sharpen our consciousness of social inequalities; everybody drifted along in a happy haze of bathtub gin and Wall Street profits. Heywood lost more money at poker games and the race track in a single day than he had had to his name a few years previous. At a Bankhead opening, he whispered into the star's ear, "Don't look now, Tallulah, but your show's slipping!" Invited to a poker game by Ring Lardner, he reported over the telephone, "I can't come, Ring. It's my son Woodie's night out, and I've got to stay home with the nurse." He made a disparaging statement about a fight manager in Syracuse. "You wouldn't dare come up here and repeat that," taunted the Up-stater. Broun answered, "I'll be up there and say it next Friday at half-past five." "And were you?" asked the man to whom Broun was telling the story. "Of course not!" he replied. At the Baer-Carnera fight, Grantland Rice remarked, "Golly, that big fellow sure can take it." "Yeah," answered Broun, "but he doesn't seem to know what to do with it." On the day that Babe Ruth smacked out two home runs in a World Series game, and con-tributed a couple of sparkling catches as well, Broun's account began, "The Ruth is mighty and shall prevail."

Heywood's dawning preoccupation with the class struggle manifested itself clearly in the Sacco-Vanzetti case in 1927. He regarded the execution of these two men as a flagrant miscar-riage of justice and he wrote two burning and devastating col-umns about the case that belong with the great pieces of invec-tive of all time. Ralph Pulitzer of the *World* asked him to write no more on this controversial subject, and Broun staged a one-man strike. Swope patched up the quarrel, but two years later, the wound still rankled, and Heywood accepted a fabulous offer from Roy Howard of the *Telegram*. This was when Broun first began to tell us, "You can't sit on the fence much longer. It's time to choose your side for keeps." Events of recent years have been his vindication. Referring to one fence-straddling commen-tator, Heywood remarked, "His mind is so open that the wind whistles through it. Nothing sticks. He's afraid to stay on any side if self-aggrandizement beckons to the other." Heywood knew an appeaser when he saw one—years before any of us had occasion to use the word.

The last years of Heywood's life were devoted principally to the organization and promotion of the American Newspaper Guild. His customary carelessness disappeared like magic when he embraced this cause; newspapermen will never forget what he did to improve their pay and working conditions. Heywood respected all labor unions. It was against his principles to cross a picket line. One noon, however, the waiters at his favorite hangout were out on strike, and Heywood, lost in thought, passed the pickets. "Mr. Broun," said one of the waiters reproachfully, "we're on strike." "Tell me who your favorite customer is," said Broun contritely, "and I'll write him a letter and tell him to stay away." The waiter replied, "Why, you are, Mr. Broun." Heywood stormed into the restaurant, sent out luncheon to the pickets, and effected a settlement of the strike on the spot. He didn't know until much later that the proprietors had been dying to settle for days, and awaited only some face-saving device to get them out of an embarrassing situation. At the height of the celebration, Broun cried, "My God, I'm due at a meeting of the Book-of-the-Month Club judges!" and rushed out, leaving behind, as usual, the galleys that were to be the subject of discussion that day. The other judges can't remember one occasion when Heywood arrived at a meeting on time.

Over Thanksgiving week-end in 1938, the Averell Harrimans were hosts to a gathering of sixty at their estate in Arden. The house is located at the top of a steep hill. Heywood looked down from the summit and recalled that the year the house was built, he had eluded the guards at the outer gate, and crawled up the hill, intent on getting an exclusive interview with the ailing Edward H. Harriman, of the Union Pacific. He was caught the moment he emerged from the shrubbery, however, and hustled down to the bottom again. "Today," said Heywood, ruefully considering his build, "it's all I can do to get up the hill in an automobile." That evening, Heywood was very late to dinner. "I was down in the kitchen," he explained cheerfully to Averell Harriman, "trying to persuade the butler to strike for higher wages."

This was the week-end that Broun and Swope decided to cross-examine Duff Cooper, another of the distinguished guests. We all gathered round expectantly, and Swope asked the first question, which Broun promptly answered—at considerable length. Then Broun essayed a query, which Swope answered. It gradually dawned on us that the interview was destined to be an exclusive dialogue between Swope and Broun. Their rhetoric flowed on, while Duff Cooper sat blinking in complete silence, like a tortoise with lumbago. Later he confided to a friend that we were the rudest people he had ever met.

Two years later, we all spent another Thanksgiving with the Harrimans in Arden—all, that is, but Heywood, who was dead, and Quent Reynolds, who was reporting the Blitz from London. Swope proposed a toast that night to the two who were absent. "One," he said, "is in Heaven, and the other is in Hell."

Heywood had a genius for discovering strange methods of throwing his money away. Once he ran for Congress on the

Socialist ticket. Another time he edited a local newspaper called the *Connecticut Nutmeg*. His greatest extravagance was a play called *Shoot the Works,* which he wrote, financed, and appeared in personally. Indirectly, this play provided him with the greatest happiness in his life. One of the girls in the chorus was named Connie Madison, and Heywood adored her at sight. They were married in 1935. She spruced him up almost beyond recognition. Heywood's friends accepted Connie without qualification the first time they met her. George Kaufman gave her a part in *Merrily We Roll Along.* She crossed the stage once, and had a single line which read, "I wouldn't dare bob my hair. My father would throw me out." Broun, in his review, remarked, "Miss Madison was adequate."

★ ★ ★

The technical term for the transposition of letters or sounds in a word, or series of words, is metathesis, but the more familiar designation is "Spoonerism." The Rev. W. A. Spooner, Warden of New College, Oxford, achieved this dubious claim to fame when he announced to his congregation: "Let us now sing the hymn 'Kinquering congs their titles take.'" Another time he caused a mild commotion in church by demanding "Is this pie occupewed?" A radio announcer created two classics of his own when he referred to New Juinea gungles instead of New Guinea jungles, and topped it with slote flulo for flute solo. Emily Wedge of Baltimore's famous Enoch Pratt Library quotes a gentleman who declared, "My wife says I have had tee many martoonis, but I am not so much under the alfluence of incohol as some pinkle theep. I mean *thinkle peep.*"

★ ★ ★

W. Somerset Maugham urged a young friend of his to try his hand at writing a book. "But I haven't anything to write about," demurred the young man. "My boy," said Maugham, "that is the most inconclusive reason for not writing that I have ever heard."

★ ★ ★

A charming but long-winded professor spent a full hour outlining a project for a major opus to Alfred Knopf. The latter listened in growing impatience and, when he was finally able to get a word in edgewise, he propelled the professor firmly to the door, and said, "Why don't you get all this down in a written outline? Then submit it to me, and we'll consider it carefully at the next editorial meeting." "Why, Mr. Knopf," said the professor reproachfully, "what are you talking about? I have been describing a project for which you gave me a contract, and a two-thousand-dollar advance, seven years ago."

★ ★ ★

Whit Burnett, the editor of *Story Magazine*, was opening a pile of manuscripts one morning when a note fluttered out of one of the manila envelopes. "Dear Editor," it read, "you will find me a combination of Hemingway, O'Neill, Faulkner, and Saroyan, with a certain something peculiarly my own added for good measure." "This lad's father," grunted Whit, "must have been an anthology."

The Burnett son and heir has been exposed to writers and writers' shop-talk exclusively since birth. The garbage man found him alone in the kitchen once and said, "Hi, sonny! Whatcha got to say for yourself?" The little boy eyed him gravely and answered, "Have you finished your novel yet?"

Burnett had a young editorial assistant who had a Harvard accent but little else to offer, and was slightly overpaid at fifteen dollars a week. At the end of a day's work, he stopped Burnett on the way out, and said, "My wife and I are throwing a little cocktail party this evening. How's for dropping in for a couple on the way home?"

Burnett accepted. To his amazement he was taken to a fourteen-room duplex with chromium furniture, a Rodin statue, and Metro-Goldwyn-Mayer drapes. It developed that the young man's wife had six or seven million dollars in her own name.

The next morning Burnett summoned his aide. "Bill," he said, "I've been worrying about you all night. A man who lives in the style that you do has no right to be working for fifteen dollars a week. As of today, old man, I'm raising you to sixteen."

Before *Story Magazine* came to America, it was edited in the island of Majorca, off the coast of Spain, by Whit Burnett and Martha Foley, and printed on the local press. The typesetter was a worthy and painstaking fellow, but unfortunately his font included no "w"s. Issues of *Story* brought out during that period have little holes scattered all through the page where the "w"s should have been. In the spirit of good, clean fun, Miss Foley once wrote a short story that did not contain a single "w." Edward O'Brien reprinted it in his anthology of the best stories of the year.

★ ★ ★

Duell, Sloan and Pearce engaged a commercial photographer to take a picture of their serious-minded young Hindu author, Krishnalal Shridharani (*My India, My America*), at the feet of the venerable Rabindranath Tagore, with whom he studied in his youth. The commercial photographer, whose knowledge of Indians seems to be confined to the Cleveland Baseball Club, submitted his bill: "24 glossy 5 x 7. SHRID WITH TARZAN." Du sent him his ten dol.

★ ★ ★

Cass Canfield of Harper's was approached one day in his editorial sanctum by a sweet-faced but determined matron who wanted very much to discuss a first novel on which she was working. "How long should a novel be?" she demanded. "That's an impossible question to answer," explained Canfield. "Some novels, like *Ethan Frome,* are only about 40,000 words long. Others, *Gone with the Wind,* for instance, may run to 300,000." "But what is the average length of the ordinary novel?" the lady persisted. "Oh, I'd say about 80,000 words," said Canfield. The lady jumped to her feet with a cry of triumph. "Thank God!" she cried. "My book is finished!"

★ ★ ★

Max Schuster received a wire reading: "How big an advance on a novel of sixty thousand words?" He wired back: "How big are the words?"

★ ★ ★

Senator Oliver St. John Gogarty, noted wit, statesman, limerick reciter, and author of *As I Was Going Down Sackville Street*, has been paying a prolonged visit to our shores, and being in general the most thoroughly Irish Irishman ever seen on a lecture platform. Mr. Gogarty's makeup, brogue, and blarney make Pat O'Brien, Jim McNamara, and Barry Fitzgerald look like character men in the Jewish Art Theatre.

Gogarty was a character in James Joyce's *Ulysses*; "Buck Mulligan," Joyce called him. They met in 1903, when Lady Gregory, patron saint of the Abbey Theatre in Dublin, ran out of "geniuses" and advertised for more of same. She was dismayed at the poverty-stricken flood of applicants and fled. Joyce wrote the following limerick:

> There was a kind lady called Gregory,
> Said, "Come to me, poets in beggary."
> But found her imprudence
> When thousands of students
> Cried, "All we are in that caTEGory!"

Gogarty sniffs at England's time-honored sport of fox-hunting as "the pursuit of the uneatable by the unspeakable."

★ ★ ★

A very, very up-to-the-minute young lady in one of Raymond Weaver's literature classes at Columbia asked him whether he had read a best-seller of the moment. When he confessed that he had not, she cried reproachfully, "Oh, you'd better hurry up; it's been out for over three months!" "Young lady," said Weaver severely, "have you read Dante's *Divine Comedy*? No? Well, you'd better hurry up; it's been out for over six hundred years."

THE WOOLLCOTT MYTH
A MINORITY REPORT

The temptation to forget a man's faults after his death, and to overemphasize his deeds and contributions, is understandable enough. "Do not speak ill of the dead" is a maxim to which almost everybody subscribes. In the case of Alexander Woollcott, however, this glorifying process, it seems to me, is assuming the proportions of deification. His letters have been collected by loving friends (who took good care to leave out the more waspish and vitriolic variety), his family are composing elegies for sundry magazines, and now Samuel Hopkins Adams, his old fellow alumnus and sponsor from Hamilton, is writing a biography which may be expected to give the great Woollcott myth another shot in the arm.

Not even Woollcott's worst enemies—a goodly assemblage with representatives in every city and hamlet that the Master hit in the course of his wanderings—will deny that he was an extraordinary man, who made a genuine contribution to the gaiety of the nation. He was a superb story-teller, although he often padded his tales with whimsy-whamsy of the most appalling variety. He fought with no holds barred for the things he believed in, although he could become as much aroused over a defense of Minnie Maddern Fiske as over an all-out campaign against fascism. He truly loved the theatre, and his unbounded enthusiasm helped some really good plays to catch on with the public. He turned several books into best-sellers single-handed, although a summary of the titles reveals all too clearly a taste that was most erratic, if not downright oversentimental and second-rate. (A few of his more violent enthusiasms: *Beside the Bonnie Briar Bush, The Chicken Wagon Family, Lost Horizon,* and *Goodbye, Mr. Chips.*) One prerequisite for his idea of a masterpiece was its discovery by himself. A new play or book that was recommended by somebody else was usually doomed in

434

advance. When he raved about something and the whole world did not echo his sentiment, Woollcott became truly convinced he had discovered a classic and embarked upon a crusade that stopped at nothing. George Macy had the temerity to appoint him a co-judge of The Readers Club with Sinclair Lewis, Clifton Fadiman, and Carl Van Doren. He never agreed with them on anything; the oftener they rejected some of his weird proposals, the harder he would thump for them at the next meeting. Because of him, they finally changed the whole procedure governing selections.

Woollcott's manners, atrocious to begin with, became progressively worse when he discovered how much people were willing to take from a great celebrity. *The Man Who Came to Dinner* crystallized and enhanced the Woollcott myth a hundredfold; it turned his insults into high comedy, and undoubtedly prevented his being socked in the jaw at least twice a week. His closest friends forgave him his rudeness, his bad sportsmanship, his failure to understand the very fundamentals of fair play. True, Harpo Marx dubbed him "just a big dreamer with a remarkable sense of double-entry bookkeeping." Noel Coward addressed him as "Little Nell of Old Dreary." Robert Benchley called him "Louisa M. Woollcott." To George Jean Nathan he was a "Seidlitz Powder in Times Square." Charlie Brackett swore that he wouldn't even talk to a man who wouldn't make a good magazine article; Heywood Broun added that an exception might be made for sycophantic souls who would play Ghost to his Hamlet—and *never* step out of character. Edna Ferber averred that he was just "a New Jersey Nero who mistook his pinafore for a toga." These, mind you, were Woollcott's friends. What some of the myriad of people he had insulted in one way or another called him may be left to the reader's imagination. Woollcott rather liked being called bad names by his friends; common salutations among the little set he bullied and bell-wethered were, "Oh, it's you, you faun's behind," or "Who is this harpy standing here like the kiss of death?" or "Get out, repulsive. You are beginning to disgust me." Such shenanigans he considered the height of humor. Let somebody outside the charmed circle take a swipe at him, however, and Woollcott reacted like so many other people who specialize in lampooning and mocking others. When his old friend Harold Ross, editor of *The New Yorker*, ran a profile of him by Wolcott Gibbs that told a few unpleasant truths, Woollcott went into a monumental rage, and didn't speak to him again for years.

Alexander Woollcott was born in 1887, in Phalanx, New Jersey, in a settlement that had once been dedicated to community or cooperative living. The experiment hadn't worked, and Woollcott's grandfather had taken over the property. In 1889, the Woollcotts moved to Kansas City, where, according to Gibbs, little Alec developed such a knack for bellowing when he was hurt that a group of bullies formed a syndicate to exploit his talent. When they saw an adult approaching, they would throw Alec off the veranda of his home onto his head. He bawled so hard that the passer-by frequently gave him a nickel as hush money. The gang then took the nickel. Woollcott swore that this story was a malicious lie from beginning to end.

In 1897, the Woollcotts moved to Philadelphia, and Alec attended Central High School there. Classmates were Ed Wynn and Harry Scherman, the guiding genius of the Book-of-the-Month Club. The three lads had little in common. Woollcott chose Hamilton College, in Clinton, New York, as his alma mater because he had been impressed by the worldly manner of a graduate of that institution he met one summer. He had a fine time there, and Hamilton, along with the Seeing Eye, Mrs. Fiske, the Marx Brothers, Laura Richards, Ruth Gordon, Rebecca West, Sibyl Colefax, Dr. Eckstein, and a few assorted articulate murderers and yegg-men, became the greatest enthusiasm of his declining years. As an undergraduate, he edited the college magazine, and starred in female roles in the dramatic club productions. To a snowbound group in his dormitory he introduced the game of choosing for each person on the campus the one adjective which fitted him more perfectly than any other. He pointed out that, if the proper selections were made, everybody could be identified from the list of adjectives. For himself he selected "noble," but admitted later that "this was voted down in favor of another which reduced the whole episode in his memoirs to the proportions of a disagreeable incident." When he graduated, Sam Adams gave him a letter of introduction to Carl Van Anda of the *New York Times*, where, after vain efforts to attune his expanding bulk and personality to the requirements of news reporting, he was given a whack at drama reviewing as a last resort. That was in 1914. It was the beginning of Woollcott's period of glory. A new despot came into his own.

Following a brief interlude as reporter for *Stars and Stripes* in France in 1918, where he wrote stories in the manner of Ernie Pyle with an interlarding of Elsie Dinsmore, Mr. W. settled down for an indefinite run as the country's most respected drama critic, most relentless and feared gossip, and infinitely most accomplished raconteur. All three qualities made a radio career inevitable, and as "The Town Crier" Woollcott became famous, wealthy, and more ruthless and domineering than ever. His social life was unbelievably complicated. He summoned whomever he willed to his home on East 52nd Street (named "Wits' End" by Dorothy Parker); surprisingly few refused. He spent weeks at the White House, and told the Roosevelts whom to have in to dine with him. He spoke at department-store book fairs, autographing copies of his own anthologies, and insulting his audience and other authors who appeared with him. He bought an island in Vermont, charged his guests hotel rates, and banished them when they wouldn't play croquet, cribbage, or hearts according to his own special rules. He installed a big double bed in the ground-floor guest room of this island retreat. It was comfortable but creaky, and let out a tell-tale groan when anybody moved in it. Woollcott called it the "informative double." His opinions became more and more didactic, his prose style more lush and untrammeled.

The Man Who Came to Dinner was the direct result of a typical Woollcottian sojourn at Moss Hart's new Bucks County estate. He bullied the servants, condemned the food, invited friends of his own from Philadelphia to Sunday dinner, and wrote in Hart's guest book, "This is to certify that on my first visit to Moss Hart's house I had one of the most unpleasant times I ever spent." He also suggested that Moss write a play in which he could star. The next day Hart was describing Woollcott's behavior to George Kaufman. "Wouldn't it have been horrible," he ruminated, "if he had broken a leg or something and been on my hands the rest of the summer!" The collaborators looked at each other with dawning delight in their faces and took the cover off the typewriter.

Some months later, Woollcott filled a lecture date in Newark, and wheedled Hart into driving him over and back. "I'll do it on one condition," proposed Hart. "I once clerked in a bookstore in Newark and I'd like to show them that I'm a big shot now. I want you to let me sit on the platform with you, and be introduced to the audience." When they entered the hall there was a single folding chair, sure enough, to the left of the speaker's table. Hart sat down, and began crossing and uncrossing his legs, while Woollcott delivered his lecture without making the slightest reference to him. At its conclusion, he said, "I usually have a question period at this time but tonight we'll dispense with it. I'm sure you'd all want to know the same thing: who is this foolish-looking young man seated here on the platform with me?" With this he retired, leaving Hart to get out of the hall as best he might.

Woollcott's last years were devoted principally to playing himself in a road company of *The Man Who Came to Dinner*. The rigors of the trip, coupled with the heart strain induced by a strenuous diet that lopped off over fifty pounds, weakened him to such an extent that he was prey to the slightest ailment. When he felt death approaching, the spluttering vindictiveness went out of his writing; he began to make peace with the world, and to write conciliatory notes to long-time enemies. He even made up with Harold Ross. This lent weight to the contention of his friends that at heart he never was quite the irascible, ill-mannered tyrant he pretended to be. He was stricken in the midst of a broadcast in New York; his last words were a bitter denunciation of weak-minded sentimentalists who were willing to make a soft peace with Germany.

While George Kaufman and Moss Hart were working on *The Man Who Came to Dinner*, Hart went to stay with Woollcott to study him once more at first hand. Hart has an insatiable curiosity for reading messages not intended for his eyes, an idiosyncrasy that did not escape Woollcott's attention. One morning Hart was busy devouring several of Mr. W.'s missives, not yet stamped and addressed, when he found one that read, "I'll ask you up here just as soon as I can get rid of that nauseating Moss Hart, who hangs on here like a leech, although he knows how I detest him." Hart was beginning to quiver with rage when he came to the postscript, which read, "Moss, my puss: I trust this will cure you of the habit of reading other people's mail!"

Woollcott was a confirmed bachelor, whose only known romances were of a literary variety, or the plain hero-worship he bestowed on great ladies of the stage. Edna Ferber, departing for Europe one summer, declared, "I want to be alone on this trip. I don't expect to talk to a man or woman—just Alec Woollcott." When he returned from a lecture in St. Paul and reported to Frank Sullivan that he had spoken to ten thousand women, Sullivan replied, "And what did you tell them? 'NO'?" Rebecca West jestingly wrote in a copy of one of her books that she sent him, "I append my married name to remind us both to keep our passion in bounds."

The paucity of his own love life did not prevent his superintending the amours of his little circle, or suggesting the steps to be taken in the bringing up of his four nieces. When one of them, Nancy, was twelve, her friends whipped up a magazine and rejected her every prose and poetry contribution promptly and firmly. Alec was as indignant as Nancy. He heartily approved when she inserted a paid advertisement (cost: six cents cash) which read as follows:

Miss Nancy B. Woollcott

THE MOST CHARMING WOMAN

IN THE WORLD

Call Between 2:30 and 3

When Nancy and her sisters visited their uncle, his grand manner and famous friends awed them completely. They reported to their horrified mother that he had a portrait of himself reading on the toilet set right into the tiles of his bathroom, entitled "Laxation and Relaxation." They also were present when Harold Ross, who has a lamentable gap between his front teeth, asked Woollcott's man for some dental floss. "Never mind floss," said Woollcott airily. "Bring him a hawser!" Woollcott was very proud of these nieces until they began to criticize him. One winter he sent his friends one of his slushy, raving notes—not about a book, play, or favorite charity this time, but a brand of whiskey. He was paid handsomely for the effort. The Lord knows what he would have said had any of his friends stooped to such commercial prostitution. The nieces sent him a note reading, "Buy stocks on margin if you must, But don't trail the family name in the dust!" In a sharp note to their father, Mr. W. remarked that if he could discover which of the nieces had dared perpetrate such sacrilege, he "would break her goddam neck."

Woollcott accompanied Edna Ferber to an auction one afternoon. Suddenly she spied her mother, and made the mistake of hailing her by an uplifted hand. There was a crash of the auctioneer's hammer, and Miss Ferber discovered that she had become the owner of a particularly hideous grandfather's clock. Every time Woollcott told the story, the price of the clock was a little higher. On the George Kaufmans' fifth wedding anniversary (in 1922) he wrote them, "I have been looking around for an appropriate wooden gift, and am pleased hereby to present you with Elsie Ferguson's performance in her new play." When Gertrude Stein visited New York in 1933, she dared to dispute a statement of the great Mr. W. "I will forgive you this once," he said grandly. "You have not been here long enough yet to know that *nobody* disputes me." "Woollcott," said Miss Stein with a hearty laugh, "you are a colossal fool." The host, who happened to be myself, was delighted.

One evening I brought to a dinner party a lovely young lady whose aunt and uncle are both well-known California novelists. Woollcott was playing cribbage with Alice Duer Miller, and couldn't be bothered with rising from his seat. He inspected her coolly, however, and deigned to remark, "I know your aunt and uncle, of course. Your aunt is a splendid woman. Your uncle is an obscenity." (I borrow here a Hemingway device to indicate a four-letter word that is not used in Simon and Schuster books.) The young lady won my heart by replying, "My definition of that word, Mr. Woollcott, is a man who uses it to a lady he is meeting for the first time." I'll say for Woollcott that he threw back his head and roared with approving laughter.

My own relations with him were severed by the Random House edition of Marcel Proust. C. K. Scott-Moncrieff, the translator of the first six parts, died before he could complete his task. After long deliberation and consultation, we selected Frederick A. Blossom to translate the seventh and last of the Proust novels. Every critic approved his work but Woollcott, who launched into a tirade in *The New Yorker,* and made statements that enabled us to prove publicly that he didn't know what he was talking about. This was the sort of thing Woollcott couldn't forgive. One thing led to another, and finally I struck his name from the Random House review list. I made a perfect picture of a man cutting his nose to spite his face—because Woollcott's enthusiasms could make a book a best-seller more surely than anything else. I think it only fair to tell this story here, to indicate that this report is not exactly impartial, and that my recollections of Mr. Woollcott are not set down with what might be termed Olympian detachment.

In the early thirties, Woollcott visited Russia, where he created a great commotion because of his striking resemblance to the bloated capitalist invariably depicted in Soviet cartoons. He weighed over two hundred pounds at the time; Soviet citizens had seen nothing like him since the fall of the Czars. Their hoots of laughter did not increase his love for the Russian experiment. ("Hoot" is apt; one Moscow journalist declared that Woollcott looked exactly like an owl.)

In England, Woollcott attended a small dinner given in honor of Edward, then Prince of Wales. He was deeply flattered when the Prince called him into private consultation after the ladies had left the room, but his elation vanished when the reason became apparent. "Woollcott," said the Prince, "you've got something to do with that blasted *New Yorker* magazine, haven't you? Well, why the devil do my copies reach me so irregularly?"

Later he visited Japan, where he was made so much of that he came back home with an overflowing heart. He raved about their "neatness and love of flowers—the sweet hum of their voices and the occasional deep boom of a vast gong at a temple on a hill." He then ventured an opinion on our "future war with Japan," of which "he heard nothing from the Japanese—but in the bar of the Shanghai Club, or in the veranda café of a Pacific liner, or among our own Army and Navy officers who are stationed in the Far East and have a lot of time on their hands. I only hope," he concluded, "that if there ever is such a war and we win it, we shall remember that we won it because we are larger, richer, and more numerous, and not feel too proud about it. For I have seen just enough of Japan and the Japanese to suspect that such a victory might be only another of history's insensitive triumphs of quantity over quality." Well, more profound folk than the ingenuous Mr. Woollcott were taken in by the wily little Japs, and maybe it isn't quite fair to bring the matter up. At least, Woollcott lived to learn how wrong he had been.

All of his life, Alec Woollcott raged because people insisted on confusing his beloved Hamilton College, at Clinton, with Colgate University, at Hamilton, New York, not many miles away. When he died, he stipulated that his ashes be deposited in the Hamilton cemetery. By the irony of fate, they were shipped first to Colgate, and had to be readdressed.

★ ★ ★

The book business today is enjoying a wave of unparalleled prosperity, but one little store in downtown New York never did share in the general increase in business. In fact, it was bankrupt. One partner was sadly surveying the premises just before the final padlocking. "I can't understand it," he mused. "Here we go busted, and only yesterday I read where the President was saying that business was never better."

"Maybe," suggested his brother, "the President had a better location than ours."

★ ★ ★

An agent tried to dissuade a client from chucking a big-salaried studio job to go back East and write a novel. "Why do it?" wailed the agent. "You can't make any money that way. How much did you make from your last novel?" "Seventy-five thousand dollars," replied the writer with some pride. "See," said the agent, "what did I tell you?"

★ ★ ★

Another agent story: An author expressed the hope that he could promote a $500 advance on his new pot-boiler. "Just to show you how good I am," declared the agent, "I will get you $1500." He called several publishers and finally found one gullible soul who fell for his palaver and agreed to the terms. The agent hung up the phone, clapped his hand to his forehead, and groaned, "Oh God, why am I such a crook?"

★ ★ ★

Harry Scherman, president of the Book-of-the-Month Club, says he is getting a bit fed up with the recurrent story of the lady who looked like a fugitive from a Hokinson drawing rushing up to him at a party and exclaiming, "I have always dreamed of meeting the president of my club." One day an employee of the Club heard that Hilary Saunders, author of *Combined Operations*, was trying to find a set of jacks to take back home to his young daughter in Britain. She brought them along with a ball to the BOMC offices and was quite put out when they disappeared. A search was instituted and the jacks were eventually recovered. Harry Scherman had sneaked them into his private office; when apprehended, he was trying vainly to get past threesies.

★ ★ ★

Richard Tregaskis, author of *Guadalcanal Diary* and *Invasion Diary*, has the most enormous eating capacity of anybody in the

445

literary business or possibly any other business, if you get right down to it. I recently had occasion to take him out to lunch and, being in an experimental mood, ordered the same dishes as Tregaskis, course for course. When the more than ample repast was concluded, I boasted, "Well, Dick, you're certainly not the man I thought you were as far as food is concerned. I ate every

Richard Tregaskis caught between entrée and salad

single thing that you did. Frankly, I am disappointed in you." "Don't be," confessed Tregaskis. "Maybe I oughtn't to tell you this, but before coming up here to have lunch with you, I had lunch with Joe Connolly."

★ ★ ★

Thomas Craven, author of *Men of Art*, has a young son who was asked by his history teacher to name the principal contribution of the Phoenicians. The youngster's answer, given without hesitation, was "Blinds."

★ ★ ★

446

The accountant of a publishing house whose name you would recognize is reported to have burst into the office of the head of the firm in a state of wild jubilation one day last week. "After five long years," he chortled, "I am pleased to report to you that we now are no longer in the red!" "Glory be," cried his chief. "Make up five copies of the annual report at once so that I can wave them in the face of that so-and-so bank." "But I have no black ink," said the accountant. "We haven't needed any for so long." "Go out and buy a bottle," the chief said. "I should say not," was the reply. "In that case, we'd be back in the red."

★ ★ ★

Henry L. Mencken claims that his book, *In Defense of Women,* stemmed from his discovery that every bride he met was infinitely smarter than her somewhat befuddled bride-groom. One touching testimonial that he received for this book came from the death house of a woman's prison. It read, "If I had only known how smart I was, I would not be here."

★ ★ ★

In the summer of 1929 The Viking Press imported five hundred copies each of a couple of expensive, beautifully printed and bound editions of obscure, third-rate English poets. After the market crash in the fall of the same year, "limited" editions of this sort were a drug on the market.

George Oppenheimer, now of Hollywood, then an officer of The Viking Press, was visiting a young couple he knew in Buffalo when he spied copies of the special editions on the bookshelf. He roared with laughter, and exclaimed, "How did you ever get stuck with those lemons? We couldn't *give* them away." The lady of the house turned a cold eye on him. "They were your wedding gift to us," she reminded him.

Oppenheimer recently tried his hand at a ghost movie. It didn't quite jell, and when the preview was over, the producer said sadly, "This picture will never scare anybody." "Oh, yes, it will," said Oppenheimer. "It'll scare my agent plenty." Later they asked him if he could suggest any way of cutting the film. "Try straight up the middle," he murmured—and enlisted in the Army.

Oppenheimer once was invited for a week-end to the fabulous Hearst ranch in San Simeon, and his mother made him render a prompt and detailed report of the goings-on. The morning after his arrival she received the following wire: "Two things have happened to me here already that never happened to me before. My car was stopped by a camel and I fell downstairs in my own bedroom."

★ ★ ★

Counterpoints offers this comment on literature: A German novel is a book in which two people want each other in the first chapter but do not get each other until the last chapter. A French novel is a book in which two people get each other in the first chapter and from then on to the last chapter don't want each other any more. A Russian novel, finally, is one in which two people neither want each other nor get each other, and about this 1,450 very melancholy pages are written.

★ ★ ★

A recent biography of Hans Christian Andersen appeared under the title of *The Shoemaker's Son. The New York Labor News* requested a review copy.

★ ★ ★

Elizabeth Chevalier, author of the best-selling novel, *Drivin' Woman,* wrote in a letter to Macmillan, "Have you heard the one about the novelist who met an old friend? After they had talked for two hours, the novelist said, 'Now we've talked about me long enough—let's talk about you! What did you think of my last novel?'"

★ ★ ★

The solemn, almost mournful countenance of Robert Emmet Sherwood camouflages a playful nature that found expression at an extremely early age. His bedridden grandma was wheeled out on the porch in sunny weather; the boy Robert was discovered there, manipulating a rod and string, at the end of which dangled a live beetle. Grandma was ducking as best she could, and hollering for help. Robert saw no reason why he should be punished. "All I was doing," he explained indignantly, "was tickling up Grandma." He also emptied his Noah's Ark into Grandma's new flush toilet, gumming up the works one hundred percent. "This is a mighty fine watercloset," said the plumber later, "but I never

told you it would pass elephants." For several weeks Robert's apoplectic grandfather kept fishing up yaks and rhinoceroses. When his grandson left for home, he delivered a bon mot which Robert used years later in his capacity of editor of *Life* (the pre-Luceite *Life*): "Robert, if I never see you again, it will be too soon." The unrepentant Robert told his parents, "I am thoroughly sick of Grandpa."

Sherwood grew up to be a great playwright, a close adviser of President Roosevelt, the husband of a beautiful movie queen (Madeleine Hurlock), and a punster of the first water. Invited to sit in on a gambling orgy, he muttered, "Only the brave chemin de fer." When rich Spaniards sought to escape the Civil War via the international bridge leading to Hendaye, France, and were strafed unmercifully by "unidentified" warplanes, Sherwood read the reports and said, "That's what comes of putting all their Basques in one exit." At his English country home in Great Enton, he essayed a pun (unfortunately it cannot be quoted here) that caused the staid London butler to spill a platterful of mutton and gravy into the lap of an outraged guest. His wife diagnoses these moments as a throwback to the days when he edited the Harvard *Lampoon* and gave ample evidence that he was Pulitzer Prize timber by flunking Freshman English. The first time he burst across the literary firmament was with a novel called *The Virtuous Night,* which practically burst the publishers at the same time. They forgave him when the grosses on *Reunion in Vienna, Idiot's Delight, The Petrified Forest, Abe Lincoln in Illinois,* and *There Shall Be No Night* began piling up.

Robert Sherwood is a great power in the O.W.I. at the present writing. Insiders profess to recognize his touch in most of President Roosevelt's most important speeches. His tory Republican cousin asked him to bring back a souvenir from the White House. "What would you like?" asked Sherwood. "His scalp?" When the war is over, he probably will resume his practice of turning out new Pulitzer Prize plays every other year or so. His first winner, *Idiot's Delight,* gave the Goebbels propaganda machine a name for him. "You can ignore those short-wave broadcasts," hooted Goebbels. "They were written by a delighted idiot."

★ ★ ★

The librarian at Columbia University received a letter last year addressed, "Mr. L. I. Brarian. Dear Mr. Brarian."

★ ★ ★

The inmate of a St. Louis asylum borrowed three long books from the library each morning, returned them the same afternoon. The librarian tested him with the city telephone directory. Sure enough, he was back with it a few hours later. "Don't tell me you've finished that big book already," said the librarian. "I certainly have," answered the touched one. "The plot was rotten, but oh boy, *what a cast!*"

★ ★ ★

Fanny Hurst is the kind of lady who never does things by halves; when she decided to reduce, she made such a thorough job of it that some of her best friends found it difficult to recognize her. One such was the late Irvin Cobb who strolled down Fifth Avenue directly behind her for a half-dozen blocks without doffing his chapeau to her. "Well," she declared finally, "are you going to say hello to me or aren't you?" "Don't tell me you're Fanny Hurst," said the astonished Cobb. "The same Fanny Hurst," she assented coldly. "No, no," decided Cobb. "The same Hurst I will concede—but definitely *not* the same Fanny."

Mr. Cobb was also the gentleman who introduced Michael Arlen, creator of the almost-forgotten Iris March and her Green Hat, as "the only Armenian I ever met who didn't try to sell me a rug."

★ ★ ★

When Ludwig Bemelmans was meandering through Ecuador, he stopped in a dubious village café, where he was suddenly confronted by a burly, unshaven desperado who frightened him to death by plumping down into the seat next to him and demanding a double whiskey straight. Suddenly the stranger spied a tattered old copy of *Esquire* and pounced on it. He turned to a certain article, and began mumbling the words laboriously to himself. Then he was on his feet, bellowing with rage. "Those blankety-blank editors!" he roared. "They've cut out my best lines again!"

★ ★ ★

451

One of the most celebrated literary fracases in history had as its principals Ernest Hemingway and Max Eastman. Their highly publicized combat took place a little more than a decade ago. Hemingway had just written *Death in the Afternoon*. Mr. Eastman referred to him in a magazine article as the leading exponent of the "false-hair-on-the-chest" school of writing, not suspecting that he would bump squarely into the gentleman in the Scribner offices a few days after the piece appeared. Mr.

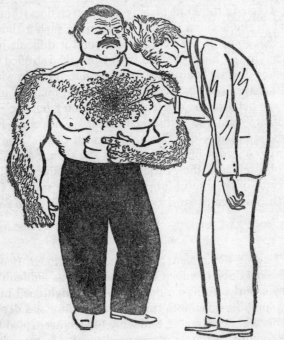

Hemingway rose to his feet. Mr. Eastman did not know what the look in his eye portended, but he had a rough idea. There are four authentic eye-witness accounts of what happened next, all of them completely different. Eastman scored a technical victory by getting his version into print first. He contacted a *World-Telegram* reporter faster than a GI answers mess call. His story did not impress anybody who had watched Hemingway work out in a gymnasium. Such cognoscenti figured that if Ernest had ever landed one punch on the willowy Max's epiglottis, there would have been no enjoyment of laughter for the Eastman family for the next six months.

A clause in Hemingway's contract with Scribner's provides that the publishers may not change a single word in his manuscripts. Scribner's brilliant editor, Maxwell Perkins, was reading the typewritten script of *Death in the Afternoon* when he encountered an old, four-lettered Anglo-Saxon word beginning with "f." He rushed frantically to the office of the elderly Charles Scribner, and read the offending passage to that dignified but flustered gentleman. "Remember," said Perkins, "that we're forbidden by contract to change a word." "Dear, dear," said Mr. Scribner, "we will have to discuss this fully when I return from lunch." Absent-mindedly he jotted down the word on a pad headed "What to Do Today."

It is rumored further that while Mr. Scribner was lunching, his secretary glanced at his pad, gasped, and exclaimed, "Holy smoke, is a secretary expected to remind her boss of *everything?*"

Cuban fishermen along the docks in Havana have grown used to the presence of the burly American who fishes with them in amiable silence and performs more important duties on the side that they know nothing about. "Señor Way" they call him, convinced that "Heming" is his first name, and there is evident affection in their voices when they speak of him. "Señor Way," one of them went so far as to declare to a visiting correspondent, "is a great American—as great as the other two most famous men in your history." "Which two do you mean?" the correspondent asked idly. "Señor George Washington and Señor Tom Collins," was the prompt reply.

★ ★ ★

Herbert Mayes, the editor of *Good Housekeeping Magazine*, is planning a mystery cook book. Every recipe will have one important ingredient missing.

★ ★ ★

453

Miss Josephine Austen, librarian at Forest Park, Illinois, declares that her profession provides a unique opportunity for souvenir-collecting. Readers use unbelievable objects for bookmarks, and frequently forget to remove them before they turn in the volumes. Miss Austen's collection includes violent love letters, nail files, playing cards, bobby pins—and most unexpected of all, a very, very thoroughly fried egg.

* * *

A recent literary dinner found Carl Van Doren in a richly reminiscent mood. He recalled a vacation time in Nassau when he and Marc Connelly stumbled over two obvious old maids, napping blissfully in the sun on Paradise Beach, a camera in the sands next to them. On an impulse, the distinguished gentlemen snatched up the camera, took it into the men's private solarium, and snapped an entire reel of photographs of luxuriating nude sun-worshippers. Then they put the camera back where they had found it. What the maiden ladies said when their films were developed—or what the kodak company said to *them* when the nature of their pictures was discovered—is something for one's imagination to toy with.

Another time, Carl and Logan Clendening found themselves on the same train, bound to fulfil lecture engagements in the same city. Another passenger was a generous and convivial soul with a full bottle of excellent bourbon. One thing, said Carl, led to another. "Did you deliver your lectures O.K.?" he was asked. "We certainly did," he replied. "But Logan delivered my lecture on literature, and I gave his on surgery."

* * *

It is rumored that W. C. Fields, the comedian, found cause to deplore the lack of an adequate bookstore near his California residence. He approached the leading intellectual of the community and gave him a high-powered sales talk on the advantages of opening such a store for the local trade. "Thirty thousand will do it, my boy," said Fields with conviction.

"Surely you can raise such an insignificant sum at the drop of a hat." The young man allowed that it was a fine idea and that he would like nothing better than to open a well-stocked bookstore. "I think I can get my hands on about $20,000," he told Fields. "As for that remaining $10,000, how about your putting it up for me?" "Under ordinary circumstances," Fields assured him, "nothing would give me greater pleasure, my boy. At the moment, however, I find myself in rather a strange predicament. All of my available funds are completely tied up in ready cash."

★ ★ ★

The late Max Harzof was one of the rare book trade's great "characters." There are countless anecdotes about him. Gabriel Wells tells how he once bought an Oscar Wilde manuscript for $1,040. "Why the odd price?" he asked, after the bargain had been struck. Harzof replied with commendable candor, "I wanted to make an even thousand-dollar profit."

★ ★ ★

There is a note at the back of H. Allen Smith's *Life in a Putty Knife Factory* which reads as follows: "The liveliness and grace of the typography are directly attributable to the craftsmanship of three printers named Sam, Terence, and Giambattista, one of whom was a little drunk and none of whom appeared to be amused. The paper on which the book is printed was made out of trees. Real trees."

★ ★ ★

At the height of the last Christmas rush, a slightly befuddled matron wandered into Dutton's Bookstore. "Is this Scribner's?" she inquired of a clerk. "No, Madam," was the reply, "it's Dutton's." "Oh," said the lady. "I saw the sign 'Dutton's' on the window, but I thought it might be Scribner's."

★ ★ ★

A customer approached the technical book department in Scribner's Bookstore and asked for "that Acetylene book." "Acetylene torches?" inquired the clerk. "No, Acetylene Encyclopædia Britannica," answered the customer. He turned out to be a Mr. Ben Huebsch of The Viking Press.

The manager of Scribner's, incidentally, was asked how he was handling the unprecedented rush of business these days. "We open the doors at nine," he replied, "and jump out of the way."

★ ★ ★

Vincent Starrett recalls one of the funniest incidents in the late Frank Harris' alleged autobiography, that amazing three-volume conglomeration of literary lore and sophomoric pornography that under-the-counter specialists peddle for as much as fifty dollars a set. Harris described a crucial international conference with all the wealth of detail that only a man who had not been present could supply. At the height of the confab an English munitions king let out a cry of anguish. His valuable timepiece had been hooked. The chairman—prime minister of a great European power—was properly outraged. "Gentlemen," he declared icily, "this will never do. The lights will be extinguished for five minutes. All of us will file out of this chamber in darkness. The thief, as he exits, will place the watch on the table there beside the door, where the buhl clock now stands." Thereupon, concluded Harris, the delegates filed out in silence and darkness. Five minutes later the room was relighted. Not only was the watch still missing; the buhl clock also had disappeared.

★ ★ ★

It was one of those gatherings of well-heeled, supersophisticated suburbanites with whom too many good writers have been spending too much of their time in recent years. The buffet disposed of, the guests began a furious round of parlor games, panicked lest a few precious minutes be squandered in conversation. Eventually, somebody proposed a game of charades and I must tell you the four that ended the proceedings just this side of mayhem:

1. Three matrons are gossiping idly about their children. Suddenly the Marx Brothers burst into the room, sling the bewildered ladies like sacks of meal over their shoulders and make off with them. Question: What famous novel does this represent? Answer: The Brothers Carry Mas Off.

2. A bon vivant complains that his new butler has not only forgotten to put studs in his shirt, but has laid out yellow Oxfords to be worn with his dress suit. Question: What best seller does this situation represent? Answer: How Green Was My Valet.

3. Mrs. Jones and her daughter operate a chicken farm. Mrs. Jones sends said daughter out to check on the number of eggs the chickens have laid one morning. Daughter reports in a speech of four syllables. Question: What distinguished living novelist does her answer represent? Answer: Some Are Set, Marm.

4. A man examines several packs of cigarettes; rejects, in turn, Lucky Strikes, Philip Morris, Chesterfields, Old Golds, Pall Malls. Question: What statesman does he represent? Answer: Mustafa Kemal.

★ ★ ★

The day that my publishing house decided to add the *Complete Works of Tacitus*, the Roman historian, to the Modern Library series, we chose as editor Professor Moses Hadas of Columbia University and persuaded that academic luminary to attend a conference in the Random House sanctum. We had a fine talk on the subject of Tacitus and agreed as to exactly what things were to go into the anthology. Just as he was leaving, the professor turned to me and asked with a most innocent expression: "Tell me, Mr. Cerf, exactly when did you read that encyclopedia article on Tacitus?" Caught red-handed, I admitted that I had read it exactly ten minutes before his arrival.

"Neat recitation," commented Hadas. "You see, I happened to write that article."

★ ★ ★

London's Savoy Hotel is where dull British author-lecturers will stay when the war is over, instead of coming over here to prey on the women's clubs, if a friend of mine on an English journal has his way. He doesn't mean *all* lecturers, of course— just the ones who have the following easily recognizable characteristics:

1. A standard costume of striped pants, frock coat, and stiff wing collars that look as though they were choking the speaker, but unfortunately never do.

2. Acute boredom while everybody else on the program is speaking.

3. Reference to the American Revolution in such jocular manner as "a bit of a show in which you chaps gave us a jolly good hiding"—accompanied by an expression intended to denote unutterable good will and sportsmanship, but that succeeds only in suggesting Arthur Treacher in his standard Hollywood role of gentleman's gentleman who despises his employer, his employer's family, and his employer's friends.

4. Repeated use of English words like "lift," "tram," "petrol," and "aluminium."

These are the babies who usually conclude by blaming any shortcomings in their speech on a snifter forced upon them by an overhospitable host just before they ascended the podium: "I believe you Americans call it a cocktail." (The last time this gambit was pulled, the comely publicity gal chaperoning the author for three horrible days whispered into my ear, "Cocktail, my eye! One more Scotch and soda and the old goat would have fallen clean off the platform!")

My English friend suggests that we, in turn, restrain Mickey Rooney from portraying Eton schoolboys and let English ladies be English ladies on the screen. In short, both nations are to keep their hams across the sea.

★ ★ ★

Russel Crouse refers to his friend Frank Sullivan as his "Pillar of Jello."

DARING YOUNG MAN

William Saroyan's calculated whimsicality and instinctive urge to plunge into action whenever there is the remotest chance to get his name into print have annoyed some of our more conservative and puritanical critics to a point where they deny him the homage that is his just due. They will not—or cannot—recognize that beneath Saroyan's cheap-jack shenanigans there throb an abundant and original talent and an imagination and love of life that have already made a rich contribution to American literature and drama. Meanwhile, with a Pulitzer Prize play and two successive choices by the Book-of-the-Month Club to his credit at the advanced age of thirty-four, Mr. Saroyan, product of the vineyards of Fresno, California, self-educated son of simple Armenian parents, has done right well for himself.

Saroyan attended a Fresno public school until he was fifteen. He began selling newspapers in his spare time at the age of eight, and became a telegraph messenger at thirteen. At harvest time, he pruned vines with Mexican and Jap laborers in his uncle's fields. He observed much and forgot nothing. He loved every minute of his work and every person he encountered in the doing of it. This is the quality that has illuminated every line he has ever written. He knew, at an early age, that he was going to be a writer. The first story that he sold was *The Daring Young Man on the Flying Trapeze*. Whit Burnett, of *Story Magazine*, accepted it in 1934. Saroyan's only surprise was that it had taken so long for the literary world to discover his talents. He made a package of all the other stories he had written and dispatched them to a publisher. Their publication was an unqualified success, and Bill has been flying through the air with the greatest of ease ever since. The day he received his six author's advance copies, he boarded the Oakland-San Francisco ferry, and descended upon reasonably startled passengers with a jubilant shout. "I'm the man who wrote this book," he cried. "Yes, sir, I'm William Saroyan himself. Don't you want to buy an autographed copy?" The books went so fast that the author suggested that the publisher send him a hundred additional copies for similar exploitation.

Rejection slips did not destroy Saroyan's ebulliency for too long a period. He changed the author's name atop a sheaf of unpublished stories to "Sirak Soyan" and submitted them to the late Edward O'Brien, high priest of the short story in Britain. "These tales," he wrote, "are different in substance from the stories of my cousin, William Saroyan, but, I believe, are rather related to his work." O'Brien announced his discovery of a new major talent to the editors of *Story* just as they were writing to tell him how they had found Saroyan. O'Brien stoutly maintained that *his* Armenian discovery was the more important; Burnett defended *his* man with equal vehemence. The argument continued for several months, until Saroyan could stand it no longer, and admitted that he and his "cousin Soyan" were one and the same. O'Brien's and Burnett's laughter did not ring out so heartily as Saroyan's.

Saroyan came East the following spring, and delighted columnists, reviewers, and lion-chasers speedily discovered that here was a young man who manufactured his own copy and distributed same with prodigal generosity. Reference to him or his work in the most obscure periodical evoked a four-page reply, banged out on his ever-ready typewriter even while he was being interviewed by somebody else. His love-life was conducted with similar reticence. I had introduced him to a pair of beautiful sisters at a cocktail party. He addressed the elder of the two (she was twenty, I believe) in front of a half-dozen of us and blandly suggested that she accompany him on a trip to Philadelphia.

Her indignant refusal startled him somewhat, but he rallied bravely, and called her back. "How about your sister?" he asked.

I took Bill to the very first play he ever saw on Broadway. I think the year was 1935. It was a play about the Newark Airport called *Ceiling Zero* and it starred that superlatively good actor, the late Osgood Perkins. "So that's New York theatre," said Bill at the end of two acts. "Why, for the love of Mike, I could write a better play than that in twenty-four hours!" And, by golly, he did. His first play, *My Heart's in the Highlands*, was produced

LAUREL
WREATH

RESERVED
FOR THE
WORLD'S
GREATEST
WRITER

as an experiment by the Group Theatre in April 1939. It was uneven and unpolished, but astute dramatic critics, notably George Jean Nathan, recognized that their prayer for a fresh and original talent in the theatre had been answered. His next play, *The Time of Your Life*, which was presented by the Theatre

Guild on October 25, 1939, won both the Pulitzer Prize and the New York Drama Critics' Award, the first play ever to receive both honors. Saroyan created a national furore by refusing the former prize. He claimed that wealth had no right to patronize art. The resultant publicity was worth not only five times the amount of the prize to Mr. Saroyan, but it took the high and mighty Pulitzer Committee down a number of pegs as well.

Saroyan's subsequent plays have not been successful, but he has found ample compensations in other fields. *My Name Is Aram* was a Book-of-the-Month Club selection in 1940. A year later, he sold an original script to Metro-Goldwyn-Mayer for $60,000. It was called *The Human Comedy*. He promptly distributed the bulk of this money among his relatives in California, retaining something less than ten thousand dollars for himself to finance a season of Saroyan repertory that he proposed to institute in New York at the beginning of the current theatrical year. The repertory survived for exactly one week, and accounted not only for all the money he had left, but for several thousand dollars more. This did not faze Mr. Saroyan. He promptly declared the entire New York theatrical season a wash-out, and sat down to transform his motion-picture script into a novel. The result was a book that became his second successive Book-of-the-Month selection. It was a leading best-seller for months. The picture also was a whopping success. Saroyan is back in the chips again and is also in the United States Army, at the present writing in Europe with the Signal Corps. What the Army will do to William Saroyan and vice versa is anybody's guess. The last time I saw him, Army discipline had not weighed too heavily upon his ebullient spirit. Our phone operator announced, "A man who says he is the world's greatest author is here to see you." "Send Private Saroyan in," I answered.

★ ★ ★

Allan Ullman, of the *New York Times* advertising department, was the recipient of a copy of Lin Yutang's *Wisdom of China and India*. His five-year-old son was attracted by the colorful jacket, and grabbed the book. Allan grabbed it back. "Lay off, you oaf," commanded his wife. "Stop taking Gandhi from a baby."

★ ★ ★

The late G. K. Chesterton was over six feet tall and weighed upward of 300 pounds. When he tried his hand at the drama with the unusual comedy called *Magic*, Bernard Shaw referred to it as "Fatty's First Play." "It must be wonderful," a young girl once gushed to him, "to be so famous that everyone knows who you are." "If they don't," replied Chesterton sadly, "they ask."

His voice had an irritating habit of escaping from control and breaking into falsetto. When he gave his first lecture in America, Edwin Markham, author of *The Man with the Hoe*, was in the chair. The distinction of introducing so notable a visitor evidently unhinged Markham's reason; he embarrassed the speaker of the evening by a florid eulogy that went on indefinitely. Chesterton was red with embarrassment. He heaved himself to his feet, shuffled to the centre of the platform, looked plaintively around him, and murmured, "After the whirlwind, the still, small voice."

On the same visit, he was led forth to see the nightly spectacle of Broadway ablaze with those myriad glamorous lamps, now not so bright as in pre-war days. "How beautiful!" exclaimed Chesterton. "How beautiful it would be for someone who could not read!"

★ ★ ★

Two distinguished publishers marked up one of Caesar's best linen tablecloths in the exclusive Oak Room of New York's Hotel Plaza one day in an endeavor to assemble a team of bearded literati, with the inspired notion of challenging the House of David to a ball game next season. The tentative line-up worked out as follows: Chris Morley, first base; Rex Stout, second; Ernest Boyd, third; Will Durant, shortstop; Georges Duplaix, left field; Elliot Paul, centre field; Ernest

463

Hemingway, right field. The starting battery was a foregone conclusion: Charles and Mary Beard. A kibitzer suggested Bernard Shaw for hot-dog vender; his vegetarian principles would remove all temptation to consume the stock personally.

★ ★ ★

Not many years ago ex-Governor Alfred E. Smith complained that his autobiography, *Up to Now*, was not being promoted vigorously enough. "But, Governor," remonstrated his publishers, "we planted your book in every bookstore in the country." "Bookstores," snorted the Governor, unconsciously summing up every publisher's grievance for the past five generations. "Who in hell goes to bookstores?"

★ ★ ★

A bibliophile was poking around a second-hand book shop and came across a rare old quarto that he wanted. "I'll give you fifteen dollars for it," he said. "Take it," sighed the dealer, "but I paid twenty-five for it myself." "How can you stay in business on any basis like that?" scoffed the customer. "Sssh," cautioned the dealer. "I make a wrong entry in the ledger."

★ ★ ★

How many readers remember Trader Horn? "Zambesi Jack," as he liked to call himself, cut quite a swath when he arrived here in the early thirties. His preposterous memoirs were kited to best-sellerdom by one of Simon and Schuster's most ingenious publicity campaigns. His long gray beard, his picturesque cape and sombrero, and his unbelievable capacity for liquor in any form added lustre to the legend. Zambesi autographed hundreds of copies of *Trader Horn*. When his manager protested that he was sapping his strength needlessly, he made a remark that has become famous in book circles. "It's been my experience," he declared, "that people never lend an autographed book." He swore that he once had a pet tiger who liked to sleep across the foot of his bed. One night he kicked the tiger in a moment of absent-mindedness. "Do you know that one kick broke the poor tiger's spirit? Shows how careful we must be of the other fellow's feelings." Another time he claimed that he shot a mother gorilla. Just before she died she reached out her hand to her little baby gorilla. "I tried to make amends to outraged Nature. . . . I took the baby gorilla and paid a slave girl thirty shillings to nurse it." To hear Trader Horn tell it, women fell for him just as hard when he was eighty as when he was eighteen. He credited this to a love potion a beautiful witch in Zululand brewed for him.

★ ★ ★

In London, Liddell Hart said to Bernard Shaw, "Do you realize that 'sumac' and 'sugar' are the only two words in the English language that begin with 's-u' and are pronounced *shu?*" "Sure," answered Shaw.

★ ★ ★

In Oxford, Mississippi, a young lady offered William Faulkner a crystal-clear distinction between "like" and "love": "If I like 'em I lets 'em. If I loves 'em, I helps."

★ ★ ★

In Elmira, H. K. Arthur persuaded a modest lady author to visit a nudist colony, assured her there was a story to be written about its survival. A member, noticing that she was fully dressed, inquired, "Are you one of us?" "Oh, no," the novelist assured her. I'm only aghast."

★ ★ ★

Early in life, says Ben Hecht, his Aunt Chasha taught him that self-apologies usually make an unholy mess of things. In a theatre mix-up, Aunt Chasha lost her temper, and dressed down a couple of ushers in no uncertain terms. The fat little manager rushed up and blustered, "I am afraid, Mrs. Swernofsky, I must ask you to apologize." Aunt Chasha teed off, smacked the manager over the head with her umbrella, kicked him in the shin, and whisked the enchanted Ben into the sunshine. "Remember what I tell you," she said cheerfully. "That's the only way to apologize so they remember it."

Ben Hecht is the most fascinating story-teller I have ever met. The very extravagances that mar his written works serve only to enhance his effectiveness when his audience literally can sit at his feet. I have seen a whole roomful of people, all fond of talking themselves, held spellbound while he wove his fantastic stories. About the person of his old friend Maxwell Bodenheim, poet, novelist, Bohemian of sorts, Hecht constructed a running history, possibly fifty percent true, that interrupted a roaring stud-poker game for three solid hours.

When they were lads together in Chicago, explained Hecht, they went in for a bout of amateur theatricals. Hecht wrote a one-act play that called for Bodenheim's death in an early scene. To save the cost of a policeman's uniform it was arranged that Bodenheim was to die at the edge of the stage with only his feet showing when he fell. Hecht could then pull him off while one of the other actors indicated to the audience that the police had come for the body. Rehearsals went splendidly, but on the opening night, Bodenheim succumbed to the lure of the footlights, and after staggering about the scene for a full minute, collapsed in the exact centre of the stage. Hecht had to rush to the corner and give the cop on the beat a dollar to come in and haul him off.

A misguided lecture manager in Milwaukee once offered Hecht and Bodenheim fifty dollars apiece to stage a literary debate on any subject that appealed to them. They took the precaution of collecting their fees in advance, and strode onto the platform. "The subject of this debate," announced Bodenheim, "is, 'Resolved: that any person who pays good American cash to hear a literary debate is a blithering idiot.' I will uphold the affirmative, Mr. Hecht the negative." "I concede," cried Hecht.

Then the two of them fled before the outraged audience could get to its feet. They haven't played Milwaukee since.

★ ★ ★

A poet came into the Doubleday office recently and asked, "What do you pay for blank verse?" The telephone operator had the proper reply: "Blank checks."

MISS PARKER'S PEN

Until a few years ago, Dorothy Parker was looked upon as one of the brightest and most scintillating wits in the country. Her bons mots were quoted from Atlantic City to Del Monte, and even if she never did say thirty percent of the things she was given credit for, the residue was sufficient to insure her place among the humorists of the ages. Then, suddenly, she stopped being funny. At the same time her output of brilliant short stories and trenchant verse dwindled into a mere trickle. Some people said it was the war. Others ascribed it to a happy marriage. "Dotty," they explained, "can only do her best work when her heart is breaking." Whatever the reason, the best Parker quips all date back to 1938 and earlier; you may judge for yourself how wonderfully they have withstood the ravages of time. (The average sally, or wisecrack, is stale and flat a week after its utterance.)

Dorothy Parker was born in a Jersey summer resort, and educated, in a manner of speaking, at a convent, which she left abruptly amidst mutual rejoicing. The first marks of her fingernails began to appear on people when she was dramatic critic of *Vanity Fair*, but her acidulous comments provoked such wrath along Broadway that a petrified management, fearing lynching parties and tar and featherings, bade her be gone. Two other lights, just beginning to shine, went with her in protest. Their names were Robert Sherwood and Robert Benchley. Miss Parker had polished off Channing Pollock's *The House Beautiful* in a single sentence. "*The House Beautiful*," she reported, "is the play lousy." When Katharine Hepburn opened in a little thing called *The Lake*, Miss Parker's comment was, "She ran the whole gamut of emotion from A to B." Hepburn made her eat those words later. They were milk and honey, anyhow, to the literary reviews she turned out later for *The New Yorker* when she hit real midseason form. Her review of Margot Asquith's biography began "The affair between Margot Asquith and Margot Asquith is one of the prettiest love affairs in literature." The caption on her dissection of Edith Wharton's life-story read, "Edie Was a Lady." Of Lucius Beebe's *Shoot If You Must*, she commented, "This must be a gift book. That is to say, a book which you wouldn't take on any other terms." She polished off one scientific volume with the dictum, "It was written without fear and without research." A. A. Milne was not exactly her meat. "Tonstant Weader," she reported, "fwowed up." There was something about the face of Harold Ross, the editor, she explained, that made her go into her office and slam the hell out of the first book that came to hand. The office was shared with Benchley, and was known as "The Park Bench" to favored patrons of the Algonquin Hotel. At a round table in the Algonquin dining room, Miss Parker gave birth to many of the sallies that won her fame.

Somebody asked her if she had enjoyed a cocktail party at

which she was seen. "Enjoyed it!" she purred. "One more drink and I'd have been under the host!" At a society dinner she entered the dining room alongside a beautiful and catty lady-playwright. The playwright stepped aside. "Age before beauty," she said sweetly. "Pearls before swine," responded Miss Parker, just as sweetly, and sailed in to as hearty a dinner as ever she ate. Over the coffee, she asked her dinner partner, "Where on earth do these people come from? I bet when the evening is over, they'll all crawl back into the woodwork."

Miss Parker spent a summer in England. Upon her return she explained that she had devoted the better part of her time to sliding up and down barristers. A drunk on the boat developed an unrequited passion for her; Dorothy referred to him as a "rhinestone in the rough." On one occasion he assured her, "I simply can't *bear* fools." "Apparently," said Miss Parker, "your mother did not have the same difficulty." Her report on a Yale prom did not endear her to the New Haven authorities. "If all those sweet young things present," she declared, "were laid end to end, I wouldn't be at all surprised."

Miss Parker could scarcely be considered the ideal week-end guest. Her hostess at one such gathering was described as "out-

spoken." "Outspoken by whom?" rasped Miss Parker. That evening she wired a friend in New York, "For heaven's sake, rush me a loaf of bread, enclosing saw and file." She is unfailingly polite to people's faces—so darn sweet and gracious, in fact, that some sensitive souls cannot watch her performance without a convulsion—but her angelic smile can dissolve into an angry snarl at the turn of a back. One of her victims analyzed her as one-tenth critic, nine-tenths hypocritic. Think what you will of Miss Parker in person, there is no gainsaying the fact that her short stories and verse rank with the very best. The ever-moderate Woollcott summarized her work as "so potent a distillation of nectar and wormwood, of ambrosia and deadly nightshade, as might suggest to the rest of us that we write far too much." Somerset Maugham contented himself with, "It is as difficult to say anything about Dorothy Parker that has not been said as it is about the Venus of Milo. Helen could make a scholar famous with a kiss; she can make a fool immortal with a jibe."

Two full-length plays have been written around the complex characters of Dorothy Parker. One was *Here Today,* by George Oppenheimer; the other, *Over Twenty-One,* by Ruth Gordon. "I suppose that now if I ever wrote a play about myself," commented the heroine bitterly, "I'd be sued for plagiarism."

★   ★   ★

A beminked young matron asked a clerk in one of Brooklyn's biggest department stores one day for a copy of a birth-control book called *Rhythm.* Shown the regular dollar edition she expressed a desire for a ritzier format. When she heard that it came only in the one-dollar binding, she took it reluctantly and declared, "Well, I guess it's good enough for every day."

★   ★   ★

Evelyn Waugh's *Decline and Fall* is back in print in this country after a long lapse. This is the book of which one critic said, "It has the desperate jauntiness of an orchestra fiddling away for

dear life on a sinking ship." Connoisseurs remember it lovingly
for one priceless sentence that might be called the epitome of
British humor: " 'Meet my daughter,' said the Bishop with some
disgust."

★ ★ ★

Channing Pollock, in his autobiography, *Harvest of My Years*,
tells the story of a train acquaintanceship made on his first journey, when he was fourteen. His fellow passenger, a stockily built
man, took an interest in his youthful views on Byron and Dickens. Finally he inquired, "Have you ever read *Sherlock Holmes?*"
"Don't you think," said Pollock pontifically, "that detective
stories are a waste of time?" "No, I don't," said the stranger.
"You see, I write them. My name is A. Conan Doyle."

★ ★ ★

S. J. Perelman had an even more astonishing encounter one
time aboard a train, to hear him tell the tale. A loquacious conductor confided to him that he had been riding on trains for so
long that he had begun to smell like one. "Sure enough," adds
Mr. P., "two brakemen waved their lanterns at him a short time
later and tried to tempt him down a siding in Kansas City. It
came as a blow when I heard the next morning that he had
fallen off the train during the night. The fireman said that we
had circled about for an hour trying to find him but that it had
been impossible to lower a boat because we did not carry a
boat."

★ ★ ★

When Quentin Reynolds completed the manuscript of one of
his many best-sellers, *Only the Stars Are Neutral*, he dispatched
it to his publisher from London by clipper plane. The postage
bill was for $16. "What on earth was your hurry?" his publisher
cabled him. "You know we are not going to publish the book
for three months. Stop throwing your dough around that way."

The cable office called up a few minutes later. "We sent Mr. Reynolds your message," they said. "The charge is $20.81."

Reynolds reports he has given up the practice of drinking two cups of coffee at breakfast. "I found," he says, "that they kept me tossing around all morning."

★ ★ ★

Some time ago Russel Crouse promised to write a foreword for a reprint edition of *Life with Father*. Pressed for delivery of same, he wired, "My understanding was that this foreword was to be a joint contribution of Lindsay and Crouse. Now you'll have to wait until I get Lindsay in a joint."

Mr. Lindsay, meanwhile, got himself involved in a "word game" at the home of Lewis Browne. Everybody was playing except Russell Gleason, who declared firmly, "No word games for baby! I'm anti-semantic!"

★ ★ ★

Don Marquis' favorite story had to do with revenge of a subtle kind back in the Blue Ridge range in the rootin', tootin', feudin' country. An ornery sprout of the McGregor family plugged a member of the Larrabee family in the back one day. The victim never knew what had hit him. One old Larrabee buck pointed out that a simple killing was too merciful for the varmint. His ingenious suggestion, promptly passed unanimously, was that once every day a shot be fired at McGregor that would *just miss him*. For twenty years, this amiable pastime was put into effect. When Marquis saw the victim, his hair was snow-white, his face and hands twitched continuously, his glance darted madly from one side to another. He was reaching for a bottle of soda pop when a shot rang out. The bottle was shattered into a thousand fragments. McGregor howled like a coyote. "They'll do it every day to him," commented a villager dispassionately, "till the poor b—— hangs hisself."

★ ★ ★

A ladies' club in New Jersey invited a femme book reviewer to speak at its May meeting. She told the plot of a triple-A tear jerker, and the entire assemblage broke into tears. All but one, that is—a lady who sat dry-eyed and unmoved through the entire recital. After the lecture, the reviewer asked her why she hadn't cried. The lady's answer stopped her cold. "Oh, I'm not a member," she explained.

★ ★ ★

When Elliot Paul, whose antics make hard-pressed columnists chortle with delight, completed the manuscript of his best-selling book, *The Last Time I Saw Paris,* he exceeded all previous records by insisting that Random House send daily proofs to him at his farm in Connecticut via a pair of carrier pigeons that he brought home with him from the West. Everybody at the publishing office became very fond of the pigeons except Robert Haas, the vice-president. He was on vacation when Mr. Paul brought the pigeons in and naturally their coop was installed in his private office.

This formality attended to, Mr. Paul summoned a taxicab at Madison Avenue and 57th Street and drove to Boston for a haircut.

Before the war, Elliot Paul maintained an apartment in Paris. One day his friends learned that he had rented desk space in the restaurant on the first landing stage of the Eiffel Tower. An incredulous reporter from the *Paris Herald* found him there, typing away contentedly on a story. "Well," said the reporter, "you certainly must be attached to the Eiffel Tower!" "Attached to it!" snorted Paul. "This is the only place in Paris where I can avoid seeing the damn thing!"

In New York Paul once bought a grand piano by telephone. He had the Knabe salesman wheel the instruments up to the phone one by one, and strike a few chords. Finally he heard one whose tone pleased him. "Send it along," he commanded. Another day he convinced a *Telegram* reporter that he had been appointed Professor of Drinking at a famous Midwestern university. "At last they realize that a gentleman must learn how to carry his liquor. I'll teach the whole student body," he asserted solemnly. There was hell to pay when the story appeared.

In Boston, he spent six months compiling figures on various types of employment in Massachusetts. The next job they gave him was connected with statistics on health and diseases in the Commonwealth. He disappeared for some weeks and then turned in the employment figures with new headings. Nobody ever complained; for all he knows, they are still part of the official records.

Paul's prize achievement was the hiring of a private office in New York where he could work undisturbed. He found just the place he wanted, paid three months' rent in advance, hired a secretary, paid her a month's salary, and arranged to start work the following Monday. Unfortunately, when Monday came around, Paul couldn't remember the address of his new office. He hasn't found it to this day.

Hollywood finally captured Elliot Paul. A big executive asked him how well he knew Europe. "I know every country there intimately," said Paul, "with the exception of Sweden, where I never have visited." A week later he was sent for by telegram. The locale of the story they wanted him for, of course, was Stockholm.

★ ★ ★

Overheard in a theatre lobby: "Saroyan isn't his real name, you know. It's a pseudonym. Saroyan is NATURE'S spelled backwards."

★ ★ ★

Professor Harold Laski is an Englishman, but he knows more about American law and American history than ninety-eight percent of the people who were born here. Every few years, he comes over to tell us about ourselves or to write a book about us. His recent *The American Presidency* was a Book-of-the-Month Club selection. He lectured at Harvard for a while but quit after a fight about the Boston police strike in 1920. He is a close friend of Supreme Court Justice Frankfurter, and calls the Justice's disciples "the little hot-dogs." A facile phrase-maker, Laski is best known for: "A liberal is a man with both feet planted firmly in mid-air," "A big nation can take a lot of ruining," and "England sat on the fence so long before 1939 that the rust got into her soul."

Laski's memory rivals those of John Kieran and Herbert Swope. At his lectures he answers questions unhesitatingly with, "You will find that on the eighth line of page 134 of Bryce's *Commonwealth*," or, "Suppose you check the facts in the September 8, 1937, issue of *Time*." Several listeners who thought he was bluffing took the trouble to check some of these references. He was never wrong.

A young girl who was hearing him for the first time asked where he gave regular courses. "At the London School of Economics," his American publisher answered. "I believe he has been referred to there as 'the Wild Bull of the Campus.'" The girl said "Moo!"

* * *

A suburban bookstore ordered a copy of the *Encyclopedia of Sexual Knowledge* from a New York bookstore. Two days later the volume was returned. The notation read "Customer couldn't wait."

* * *

Harry Kurnitz, author of most of *The Thin Man* scenarios, relates that when he was a struggling young reporter in Philadelphia, the gay blades with whom he associated acquired, one by one, raccoon coats. They were a badge of distinction in those happy days of John Held flappers and bathtub gin; Kurnitz was extremely mortified that he could not afford one. Then one day he spied a coat made of wolf skin in a second-hand shop. It was barely within his means, but he bought it without a second's hesitation. "Did this end your inferiority complex?" I asked. "Could you once more dally with your fellow creatures on an even footing?" "It was superb," answered Kurnitz. "I wore it all winter, rain or shine. I had only one bit of trouble with it. It seems that every time there was a severe snowstorm, I found myself running madly after sleighs."

★ ★ ★

A rather down-at-the-heels magician went from one publisher to another trying to land a contract for his proposed autobiography. "I need the money," he confessed. "For ten years straight I have been sawing a woman in half and, with my luck, I always end up with the half that eats."

OH, SHAW!

Any man who, at the age of eighty-eight, can dismiss a visitor with a chirpy "Get along with you now; I'm fully two years behind in my work as it is," is still a force to be reckoned with. That's what George Bernard Shaw told Lawyer Morris Ernst in London a few short weeks ago. Casual observers who construed some of his more ridiculous remarks of recent seasons as a sign of approaching senility neglected to take into account Shaw's increasing propensity for deliberately playing the clown, and being cute for visiting journalists and celebrity hunters. He still loves to see his picture in the papers, and will be just outrageous enough to corral the front page of a literary supplement. At heart, he remains one of the shrewdest horse-traders in the world.

Less than a year ago, Shaw pointed out that writers made a mistake in working twelve months of the year in Hollywood, regardless of how big their salaries might be. "The work you are doing," he reminded them, "becomes the sole property of your employers. When you write successful plays or novels, you may reasonably expect royalties on them every year for the rest of your lives—and the taxes aren't so big." Today, one prominent author after another is arranging to stay in Hollywood six months at most in the year, and is coming back to New York to write novels or plays—properties in which he can retain a vested right. It is amusing to note that a man going on to eighty-eight led the way.

I first met Bernard Shaw in his London apartment, facing the Thames Embankment, in the spring of 1936. Random House was planning an anthology of hit plays produced by the Theatre Guild, and, of course, we wanted to head off the volume with Eugene O'Neill's *Strange Interlude* and Shaw's *Saint Joan*. Our written request elicited one of his customary "Absolutely no" cables, but Lawrence Langner gave me a note of introduction, and when Shaw consented over the phone to see me I knew that all was not lost.

He opened the door himself. The sight of that ruddy face and expanse of silvery whiskers in the doorway almost floored me. Miss Patch, his secretary, was away that day. We had the house to ourselves. First he showed me a photograph of himself with his arm around Marion Davies. He had received it that morning, and obviously fancied himself in it. This led to a brief dissertation on William Randolph Hearst. "I cannot understand," said Shaw, "why so many Americans shudder at the thought of Hearst. Doesn't he represent everything you worship most: success, power, fortune? Why don't you elect him President?" My reaction must have been just what he was angling for, because he threw back his head and roared with laughter. Then he dropped the picture of Miss Davies. I made the mistake of reaching down to pick it up. Shaw snatched it angrily out of my hands. "I'm not as old as all that," he said sharply. "I do nicely for myself here without a soul in the house."

"And now about *Saint Joan*," he said finally. "What will you pay me?" I told him what we planned to pay for each play in the proposed anthology. "You can have *Saint Joan*," he said, "if you give me twice as much as anybody else. Without me, of course, you have no book."

He had me dead to rights on that. "I can't give you more than I do Eugene O'Neill," I protested. "*Strange Interlude* is just as important as *Saint Joan*." "Ah yes," he agreed, "but I know

477

very well that you are Mr. O'Neill's own publisher in America, and he gets the entire payment. I must split mine with Dodd, Mead. That evens it."

I was very happy to settle things on that basis. Tea was brought up from the restaurant downstairs, and I said good-bye. He had a last thought just as I was stepping into the lift. "If a book club takes your collection," he called, "I shall have to ask double." Sure enough, the Book-of-the-Month Club chose the *Theatre Guild Anthology* as a dividend, and Mr. Shaw cashed in very handsomely. In acknowledging the check he wrote, "I owe part of my success to the fact that I never had a partner in anything I did. If you wish to be a successful publisher, for heaven's sake, never take a partner." "I already have two," I answered, "but I'm not sure that all three of us together could cope with a city slicker like yourself."

Shaw's acknowledgment was a clipping of an apocryphal interview with Samuel Goldwyn. That gentleman was supposed to be imploring Shaw for permission to film *Pygmalion*. "I don't care if the picture loses money," he declared. "It's the contribution to art I'm thinking of." "That's the difference between us," Shaw assured him. "You think of nothing but art, and I think of nothing but money."

As a matter of fact, Shaw finally consented to a screen version of *Pygmalion*, but a Hungarian named Gabriel Pascal was the producer, not Goldwyn. The story goes that Pascal won Shaw by an approach that certainly was novel. "Not only do I want your permission to make a picture of *Pygmalion*," was his proposition, "but I want you to help me to raise twenty-five thousand pounds to finance it. The fact is, I'm broke at the moment." Mr. Shaw attended the preview, and signed autographs that one night as happily as the veriest Hollywood ham. He even consented to appear on the stage at the conclusion of the picture. Somebody in the gallery cried "boo." Shaw waved merrily, and said, "My friend, I quite agree with you, but what are we two against so many?" The picture was very successful both in England and America, largely due to a sensitive and characteristic performance by the late Leslie Howard. Shaw claimed that the picture netted him twenty-nine thousand pounds, but that it cost him fifty thousand in war taxes. "Another success like that," he grumbled, "and I am ruined."

Baiting Americans is an old pastime of Bernard Shaw's. "Why should anyone want to visit the United States?" he once said. "I do not want to see the Statue of Liberty. I am a master of comic

irony, but even *my* appetite for irony does not go as far as that." He boasted to Hesketh Pearson (whose biography, G.B.S., is superb reading): "I am always careful never to say a civil word to the United States. I have scoffed at their inhabitants as a nation of villagers. I have defined the one-hundred-percent American as ninety-percent idiot. And they just adore me." It is barely possible that Mr. Shaw has been reading the wrong newspapers.

When Cornelia Otis Skinner opened in a revival of Shaw's *Candida*, he cabled, "Excellent. Greatest." Miss Skinner, overwhelmed, cabled back: "Undeserving such praise." Shaw answered, "I meant the play." Miss Skinner bristled, and replied, "So *did* I."

Shaw's romance with the actress, Ellen Terry, has been the subject of an infinite number of anecdotes and conjectures. When she requested permission to publish some of the voluminous correspondence he had addressed to her in the course of a lifetime, he refused indignantly, saying, "I will not play the horse to your Lady Godiva." "Ours was an ideal love affair," he explained, "because it was conducted principally by post. Ellen got tired of five husbands, but she never got tired of me."

He became a vegetarian in 1881, although H. G. Wells had hinted darkly that he drinks liver extracts on the sly. When his friends predicted that abstinence from meat-eating would be the death of him, he retorted that at least his coffin could be followed by a procession of all the animals he had never eaten. "They will look better than most pallbearers I have seen," he added. Mrs. Pat Campbell, in the heat of a particularly exasperating Shavian rehearsal, cried, "Shaw, some day you'll eat a pork chop, and then God help all womankind."

Shaw is a favorite subject of caricaturists, but he doesn't like any of them. He has a vast collection of photographs of himself, but I noticed nary a caricature in evidence when I visited him. He explained to a writer on *The Manchester Guardian:* "A photograph is eighty percent sitter, twenty percent photographer. A painting is seventy-five percent artist, and only twenty-five percent sitter. Caricatures? Bah! Child's play! Caricatures are never like me. Low's aren't like me at all. One day I went into a friend's flat and I did at last see a caricature of me that seemed to be good. It was cruel, of course, but still it was what a caricature should be. I thought I would bring Low to see it. Then it moved and I saw it was a mirror."

Mr. Shaw has unpleasant memories of his school days, and is determined that his plays be excluded from scholastic curricula. "I lay my eternal curse," he wrote, "on whosoever shall now or at any time hereafter make schoolbooks of my work and make me hated as Shakespeare is hated. My plays were not designed as instruments of torture." He does most of his reading standing up, often dressing or undressing at the same time. "I never shut a book," he told Mr. Pearson, "but put the next book on top of it long before it's finished. After some months there is a mountain of buried books, all wide open, so that my library is distinguished by the stain of dust or soot on it."

In an unusual burst of modesty, Shaw confessed: "In moments of crisis my nerves act in the most extraordinary way. I size up the situation in a flash, set my teeth, contract my muscles, take a firm grip on myself, and without a tremor, always do the wrong thing." "When I die," he says, "I want to be thoroughly used up. The harder I work, the more I live. Life is no brief candle for me. It is a sort of splendid torch, which I have got hold of for the moment. I want to make it burn as brightly as possible before handing it on to future generations."

★ ★ ★

It's difficult to keep up with the adventures of the absent-minded publisher of the *Saturday Review of Literature*, Hal Smith. His latest exploit took place at the corner of Fifth Avenue and 23rd Street. While the traffic light was red, a man planted himself directly in front of Hal's jalopy. The light turned to green, but the gent moved nary a step. Finally Hal leaned out of the car, and gently reminded him, "Say, bud, the light is green. How about getting the hell out of my way?" "Sorry, I can't oblige," replied the character. "Your car is on my foot!"

★ ★ ★

In 1887, an obscure young English doctor named Conan Doyle needed money badly, and whipped up a short story about a detective as a likely way to get it quickly. He named the detective Sherlock Holmes. Almost sixty years later, three new books about Sherlock Holmes were published in America within a few weeks of one another. A one-volume edition of his exploits was selling at the rate of thirty thousand copies a year. A group of solid, responsible citizens calling themselves "The Baker Street Irregulars" were dedicated to the task of "turning the Sherlock Holmes legend into a living being, incomparable and ageless." Anybody who dared to remark that, in the light of present detective-story standards, the Holmes-Watson sagas were pretty stuffy and obvious, ran the risk of being flayed alive by a Christopher Morley, or a Vincent Starrett, or an Elmer Davis.

Doyle himself didn't even like Sherlock Holmes. To him the creation of a great sleuth was just a stunt. He tried his darnedest to kill him off. In the last story in *The Memoirs of Sherlock Holmes*, published in 1894, Holmes met his arch-enemy, Professor Moriarty, face to face on the edge of an abyss, and Doyle made it abundantly clear that the two had perished together.

The author reckoned without his public, however. The outcry was so terrific that Sherlock Holmes simply had to be brought back to life. If the stories that followed were halfhearted and inferior, one would never guess it by the public reaction. Connoisseurs were not taken in. Several people wrote angry letters to the newspapers claiming that the new Dr. Holmes was an obvious impostor. A Cornish boatman told Doyle himself, "It is possible, sir, that when Holmes fell over that cliff he may not have killed himself, but he was never quite the same man afterwards."

Not many people know, incidentally, that Holmes was named after the American poet, Oliver Wendell Holmes, whose son could still recite most of the Sherlock Holmes stories by heart when he retired from the Supreme Court at ninety-odd.

At the first dinner of the "Baker Street Irregulars," Alexander Woollcott turned up in the cloak and fore-and-aft cap that William Gillette had worn in his great stage impersonation of the intrepid sleuth, and kept them on all through dinner, although the temperature of the room was over eighty. Another guest was a Mr. Laurence Paine of Boston, who had a fine time but discovered when he got home that an unsentimental loafer had taken advantage of the occasion to burglarize his apartment. He was afraid to tell the police where he had been.

When General Mark Clark went to North Africa to discuss details of the American invasion at Casablanca with loyal French officers, the rendezvous was very hush-hush, of course. The French officers detailed to meet the Clark party grew more and more tense as the night wore on without a hint of the prearranged signal. Suddenly the little boat which held Clark and his men glided silently into view. One French officer, a Colonel Watson (his father was English), could wait no longer. He waded waist-deep into the water, and extended a hand to the American officer in the prow of the boat.

"Watson," he identified himself.

"And I," said the American, "am Captain Holmes. I think, my dear Watson, that we have met before." The tension was broken. The vital business of the evening proceeded in an atmosphere of mutual amity and trust.

Logan Clendening tells a story about Sherlock Holmes' arrival in Heaven. The angels turned out en masse to meet him; the Lord Himself descended from his throne to bid him welcome.

"Holmes," He said, "to be perfectly frank, We have a little mystery of Our Own up here which you may be able to help Us solve. Adam and Eve seem to have disappeared. Nobody has been able to locate them for aeons. If you could possibly uncover them for Us. . . ."

Holmes darted to the fringe of the assemblage, and hauled two frightened, thoroughly surprised angels before the Lord. "Here they are," he said briefly. Adam and Eve readily admitted their identities. "We got tired of being stared at and asked for autographs by every darn new angel who came up here," they explained. "We assumed aliases and these simple disguises and got away with them for centuries until this smarty-pants ferreted us out."

"How did you do it?" marveled the Lord.

"Elementary, my dear God," said Sherlock Holmes. "They were the only two who had no navels."

★　★　★

Arthur Kober, author of the side-splitting *Dear Bella* stories and *Having Wonderful Time,* adores his mother. She, in turn, is so proud of him that she talks of little else. "His Bella stories must be wonderful," she says. "Even though he wrote them, it takes him twenty minutes himself to read one." At a party one day she met a lady who claimed that her son, too, was a writer.

"She says they want her boy should go to Hollywood and they would pay him twenty-five hundred dollars a week," she reported to Kober. "Honestly, I wanted to laugh in her face, but still I didn't say anything."

"Did you find out the lady's name?" asked Kober patiently.

"The name? I dunno. Kingsley-Schmingsley?"

"Why, that must have been Sidney Kingsley's mother," Kober told her. "Kingsley wrote *Dead End* and *The Patriots.* I'm sure he could go to Hollywood any time he wanted to for twenty-five hundred a week."

"Yeah?" said Mama Kober, somewhat deflated. "Well," she added brightly, "I didn't say anything."

Kober sent his mother to a hotel in the Catskills for a vacation, but she didn't like it much. "The food here is plain poison," she wrote, "and such small portions!"

When Arthur himself went to Hollywood, his lovely wife, Maggie, promised to keep an eye on Mrs. Kober. She phoned her one day and said, "How about going out with me this afternoon?" "What do you plan?" asked Mrs. Kober. "I thought we might go to see *Mrs. Miniver,*" said Maggie. "O.K.," said Mama. "I don't know the lady, but any friend of yours is a friend of mine."

★　★　★

When Clifton Fadiman was serving as editor for Simon and Schuster, he opened one manuscript that consisted entirely of nudes of a Miss Jones. She wanted to sell the idea of a series of Yogi exercises in book form. Fadiman's one-line report was, "I see nothing in this manuscript except Miss Jones."

STEIN SONG

Scarcely a day goes by at my office but somebody writes in to inquire about the safety and whereabouts of Gertrude Stein and her lifelong companion, Alice Toklas. Not many people even claim to understand the intricacies of Miss Stein's prose style, but millions admire her rugged and magnificent personality. When last heard from, the two ladies were safe, well, and reasonably happy at their villa in Bilignin, a bare thirty miles from the once fashionable resort of Aix-les-Bains. That was before the Germans took over unoccupied France, however. What's happened since then is anybody's guess.* When last heard from, the ladies were doing their own gardening, cooking, and housekeeping, but this worked no special hardship on them because they never could tolerate servants getting in their way and generally ended up by doing everything themselves anyhow.

Gertrude Stein's latest opus, a novel called *Mrs. Reynolds*, was smuggled out of France by a friend of the author, and brought to New York via Sweden and Great Britain. It now reposes in a publisher's safe, pending an end of paper rationing. The lady who brought the script over had one unpleasant moment in England when an alert customs inspector mistook it for a secret document, written in an ingenious and entirely undecipherable code. Finally he conceded grudgingly that it was the manuscript of a novel, all right, but added that it was the first one he had ever seen that seemed to read the same from back to front as it did from front to back.

The last time that I saw Gertrude Stein in person was in 1936,

* Southern France was liberated just before the book went to press. First person to tell her experiences over the radio: Gertrude Stein.

when Jo Davidson and I flew down for a week-end at Bilignin. In accordance with her instructions, we flew to Geneva, although we discovered later that the airport at Lyons was twenty miles nearer her home, not to mention an hour and a half airtime closer to Paris. Gertrude had just been reading some poetry by Pablo Picasso. "I read his poems," she told us happily, "and then I seized him by both shoulders and shook him good and hard. 'Pablo,' I said, 'go home and paint!'" Miss Stein was so

*Gertrude Stein composing prose,
Toklas taking notes*

pleased and engrossed in her characteristic monologue that we lost our way at least ten times on the way to her home. We went through one village three times. The last time the children waved to us as old friends. Arrived at long last in Bilignin, Gertrude stopped the car to greet every passer-by and ask them point-blank the most intimate questions about their loves and business affairs, all of which they answered cheerfully and in voluminous detail.

Gertrude Stein really won the hearts of the American public when she revisited the United States in 1931. It was just after the Dillinger case had been wound up, and Gertrude said that she was replacing Dillinger as the sensation of the moment. Reporters who came to scoff at her ended by giving her front-page publicity. When she made a short for the newsreels, Miriam Hopkins and Mary Pickford helped her make up. Broadway loiterers stopped her for autographs. In Washington she stayed at the White House as a matter of course. The morning that she arrived in Hollywood, she demanded that Dashiell Hammett, Charlie Chaplin, and Dorothy Parker be produced for a dinner party that evening. They not only came, but boasted about it later.

Nobody would ever have mistaken Gertrude and Alice for devotees of Bergdorf-Goodman. They were not interested in ensembles. Both of them were champion dawdlers. At the last moment they would dress themselves in whatever garments happened to be handy and sally forth. In those days there was an employment agency for domestics located directly below the Random House offices. Gertrude arrived for luncheon one day a full hour late and announced cheerfully, "That fool elevator boy of yours dumped us out at the employment agency. He thought we were cooks."

Moss Hart once asked her if she had written any other plays besides *Four Saints in Three Acts*. "Of course I have," answered Gertrude. "Seventy-seven, to be exact!" At a party at my hotel apartment one evening she demanded a pot of boiled water long after the kitchen downstairs had closed. "Let me boil it for you, Miss Stein," volunteered a lady standing alongside her. Later Gertrude expressed her appreciation. "Who are you and what do you do?" she asked. "Oh, I write too," said the lady meekly. "My name is Edna Ferber." One of the few people who refused to be overawed by Miss Stein's astounding flow of rhetoric was Mortimer Adler, the author of *How to Read a Book* and the pretentiously titled *How to Think About War and Peace*. He and Gertrude got into a terrific argument one evening. Miss

Toklas trembled on the outskirts of the battlefield, and was heard to remark, "Dear me! Gertrude is saying some things to-night that she won't understand herself for six months."

George Gershwin played the complete score of *Porgy and Bess* for the first time in public for the edification of Gertrude Stein. She sat beside him at the piano in a straight-backed chair, her arms folded, and said not a single word until he finished. Then she rose and threw her arms around him. "George, it's wonder-ful!" she cried. "Now I know it's right," said Gershwin. Ger-trude has a booming, infectious laugh. She throws her head back like President Roosevelt, and slaps her thigh when something pleases her particularly. More often than not, it is a remark that she has made herself.

In the last letter that came from Gertrude Stein before postal communications with unoccupied France were cut off, she calmly asked for eleven books. "You should be flattered," she wrote complacently, "that I want so many of your new publica-tions." The package was sent but, alas, it came back stamped "service suspended." Gertrude must have been very angry about that.

The usual print order for a new Gertrude Stein book is twenty-five hundred copies. The demand is constant. There rarely are fifty copies left over, but a second edition is never necessary. When *Mrs. Reynolds* is finally published, the manufacturing de-partment will order the usual edition without so much as con-sulting anybody. Gertrude's last book, *Ida*, was supposed to be about the Duchess of Windsor, and I sent a copy to Government House in Nassau. "It was nice of you to send me *Ida*," wrote the Duchess, "but I must confess that I didn't understand a word of it."

The Duchess had nothing on Miss Stein's faithful publishers.

★ ★ ★

The war has put a stop, for the time being at least, to the Book Fair craze, introduced innocently and legitimately a few years ago by a few large Midwestern department stores who went to infinite trouble and expense themselves to put on fine shows and really whipped up the community interest, but prostituted thereafter by chiseling, publicity-seeking phonies all over the country who wrote to the publishers literally demanding cash donations, autographed books, electric displays, prominent authors to make speeches and do fan dances, sixteen-cylinder Cadillacs and the front line of a *Mexican Hayride* chorus. "Play ball with us and we'll play ball with you," was their theme song. There were more ball-players in the book business than in the whole National League. One brave publisher, after much fatiguing brain work, finally evolved his now-celebrated Form Letter No. 891 to answer all Book Fair communications. "Your exceptionally modest request," it read, "would cost my firm only about $800, an admitted bagatelle that, if your current rate of business with us tripled as a result of your ball-playing, we could earn back easily in about two generations. Cordially and sincerely . . ."

In New York, *The Times* sponsored a fair to end all fairs at which practically every author in town took his turn on the platform, and thousands of dear little kiddies pilfered all the lovely catalogues that frantic publishers were trying to hold out for their elders. The official opener of everything in New York from a baseball season to a can of sardines is Mayor Fiorello La-Guardia, so it was taken for granted that the Little Flower would open the Book Fair. "At the Polo Grounds I throw out the first ball," mused the Mayor. "What do I do here?" "Throw out the first author," suggested an editor of the *Tribune*—a bon mot that has since echoed around the world and sent *The Times'* secret service on a frantic investigation to find out how a *Tribune* operative got into the opening ceremonies.

★ ★ ★

Robert Benchley was caught in a thunderstorm one afternoon, and came home soaked to the skin. "George," he called to his servant, "get me out of this wet suit and into a dry martini."

Benchley attended the opening night of a play called *The Squall*. After a dreary half-hour or so, a half-caste girl emoted,

"Me Nubi. Me good girl. Me stay." Benchley rose in his seat, announced, "Me Benchley. Me bad boy. Me go," and staggered out of the theatre. In a drama called *Rope*, a murderer dumped his victim's body into a cedar chest, and served tea on top of it to the detective who had interrupted his gruesome business. Eventually, of course, the detective discovered what was inside the chest. "That's what comes of eating on an empty stomach," Benchley pointed out. All this was when he was acting as drama critic for *The New Yorker*.

Benchley the
drama critic

Benchley the
author

Benchley the
movie actor

Benchley the
bon vivant

Four sides of a many-sided character

Benchley, who has more friends than almost anybody else in the world, describes himself as an "unstylish stout." Some of his most hilarious pieces are preserved in volumes with the provocative titles of 20,000 *Leagues Under the Sea, or David Copperfield, From Bed to Worse, My Ten Years in a Quandary,* and *Inside Benchley.* He says it is so easy to make money as an actor in Hollywood that he's never going to write again. Last year a movie queen whose love-life would have filled ten volumes passed away. Benchley suggested for her epitaph: "She sleeps alone at last."

★ ★ ★

The Junior Literary Guild recently distributed a book about penguins. "This book," reported a conscientious young subscriber, "told me a good deal more about penguins than I like to know."

★ ★ ★

Did you ever hear about the tiger who cornered Mr. Aesop and ate him for Sunday dinner? "Well, Aesop," said the tiger pleasantly, "I suppose you'll be making up a fable about *this* now, too."

★ ★ ★

A discouraged young novelist was fingering his drink listlessly at the Players Club a few days back. "I know I'll never win the Pulitzer Prize," he declared. "Of course you won't," responded his publisher cheerily, "but wouldn't you rather have the critics say 'Why *didn't* this writer get the Pulitzer Prize' than 'Why *did* he get it'?"

At an adjoining table the narrator of an anecdote found himself stumped for a name. "What *is* the name of that ham in Hollywood?" he appealed to Marc Connelly. "What *is* the name of that coal in Newcastle?" shot back Mr. C.

★ ★ ★

491

The Victory Book Committee arranged a noonday rally at the New York Public Library one day and announced that Gypsy Rose Lee and Clifton Fadiman would be the guests of honor. Two thousand people turned up. A script had been prepared for Fadiman, but Miss Lee declared that she preferred to stick to a few impromptu remarks of her own. Panicked at the last moment, however, by the seething throng before her, Miss Lee reached for a script at hand. It was Mr. Fadiman's, of course, and an enraptured audience heard her open her address with the sweeping statement, "All my life has been spent in the world of books." Two sponsors swooned.

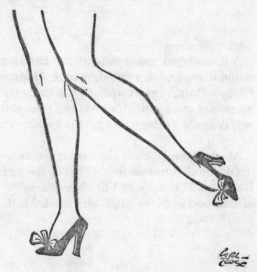

After her Victory Book address, Miss Lee was so visibly nervous that a bystander called out, "What's the matter, Gypsy, frightened of crowds?" To which she replied testily, "How would you like to stand up here before such a mob with all your clothes on?"

★ ★ ★

Another report concerns a day on which the lady was autographing copies of her book in a Midwestern department store. A customer came in and asked to see the best Bible on the market for two dollars. Suddenly he spied the callipygian Miss Lee and, after gulping once or twice, planked down his two dollars, got his autographed book, and made for the nearest exit. "How about that Bible you wanted?" asked a clerk. "Can't use it now!" he cried cheerily. "I done spent my book money."

★ ★ ★

Another tale about Miss Lee has it that she woke up fully dressed one morning and cried, "Good heavens, I've been draped."

★ ★ ★

One of William Lyon Phelps' students at Yale asked him this question in the middle of a lecture on Browning: "Professor, which gives you the greater thrill: a student who knows and appreciates Browning as thoroughly as you do, or that same student weaving through an entire Harvard team for a touchdown?" "Billy" Phelps replied without hesitation, "I thrill to either performance, young man. The only difference is that when a student understands Browning, I do not smash my hat."

★ ★ ★

At a recent dinner party, the eminent John Gunther found himself sitting next to Lily Duplaix, the orchidaceous wife of Georges Duplaix of Simon and Schuster. Mr. Gunther, with unfailing charm, set about winning Mme. Duplaix's heart, but unfortunately, when he was introduced to her, he caught her name as Lilly Daché, the famous milliner, and accordingly spent most of the dinner telling her everything that he knew or thought about ladies' hats. Mme. Duplaix listened in somewhat astonished silence, and directly after dinner sought out her host. "Your Mr. Gunther," she pronounced, "shouldn't drink so much."

★ ★ ★

Big reprint publishers who sponsor as many as fifty new titles in a single month obviously do not have time to read carefully the various additions to their line. Neither do the hapless wights who have to prepare the jacket copy. This sometimes leads to grim consequences. One eminent physician, for instance, nearly committed mayhem when he discovered that a reprint of his tome on anatomy bore on the back of the jacket an advertisement for a rival practitioner's treatise on the same subject. It seems that the book thus shamefully advertised included a paragraph that labeled the good doctor "a palpable quack" and his opus "a worthless collection of undigested nonsense." A brandnew jacket appeased him somewhat, but there is a definite feeling abroad that his next reprint is headed elsewhere.

Another morning, a visitor insisted upon meeting the president of the reprint house and demanded a copy of a particular book on the art of letter-writing. "Oh, we let that go out of print long ago," said the publisher cheerfully. "But how about this new one on the same subject? It's got that dreary old stinker skinned a mile." "I do not need your invaluable assistance in composing letters," the caller remarked coldly. "I happen to be the author of the dreary old stinker."

★ ★ ★

Henry L. Mencken has evolved a happy formula for answering all controversial letters. He doesn't even have to read the blast to which it replies. "Dear Sir (or Madam)," he types. "You may be right."

★ ★ ★

494

One of our bookbinders has a clerk who reported a painful domestic incident last week. He arrived home very late for dinner and explained to his irate wife, "I had to wait for mine boss." "You mean to standing dere and tallink me you are making a pal out of dot dirty keppitalist?" she cried. "You and him is going hum togadder now?" "Who's tukking about keppitalists?" groaned the clerk. "I had to wait for de crosstown boss!"

Chapter Four

RICH MAN, POOR MAN...

There lives a millionaire in Canada named Harry Falconer Mc-
Lean, whose amiable eccentricity consists in giving away money
from time to time as the fancy seizes him. One day he turned
up at a Toronto soldiers' hospital, and handed out hundred-
dollar bills to patients and nurses to the tune of about twelve
thousand dollars. Another day he enjoyed a musical comedy and
sent every member of the chorus a mink coat. Several of the
girls didn't have enough cash to pay the duty on the coats when
they came back to the United States, and had to sell them on
the Canadian side. A taxi driver got Mr. McLean to the Toronto
station in record time one evening. Mr. McLean sent the driver's
infant son a check for $2000. Canadian newshawks, intent upon
spotlighting a benefactor of this kind, were doubly dumbfounded when they discovered their subject's nationality. Harry
McLean is a Scotsman. Incidentally, he is a self-made man, and
loathes publicity. He distributes largess for the sheer pleasure of
giving. He is a rare and very swell egg.

Mr. McLean inevitably brings to mind another Scotsman who hewed more closely to the proverbial line. That was Sir Harry Lauder, who was so tight that he himself made a joke of it, and was the first to relate that when he opened his purse one day to take out a dollar, four moths flew out. He attended a dinner of twenty one evening. It was of the caviar-champagne variety, and when the check came, it was a whopper. Several guests reached for the check, but Sir Harry's voice rang out, "No, no, gentlemen! This dinner is on me!" The next morning's headline, avers Sir Harry, read, "Scottish ventriloquist murdered!"

I met Harry Lauder, near the close of his remarkable career, at the Gleneagles Hotel in Scotland. He was probably the wealthiest guest at the hotel, but he occupied one of the smallest rooms. "What would I be doing with a sitting room?" he asked. "I'll do *my* sitting in the lobby." It poured steadily for a week, but Sir Harry and a few of his countrymen had come to Gleneagles to play golf, and by everything holy, they wouldn't have let a flood and a tidal wave interfere with their program. As he came into the clubhouse thoroughly drenched one afternoon, I asked grumpily, "Does it *always* rain up here?" "Oh, no," answered Lauder cheerfully. "Sometimes it snows." Rumor had it that there were dangerous snakes in the rough to the left of one of the tees. To make the story binding, the caddy master swore that Sir Harry drove three balls in succession into the patch in question, *and didn't even look for them.*

★ ★ ★

Among the countless other tales of tight-fisted Scots, I like best the story Thomas Lamont told the first time he saw Christopher Morley with a beard. Mr. Lamont's Scot had gone over to America as a boy, and amassed a great fortune. Eventually he decided to go home for a visit, and notified his three brothers to meet him at the station. When he alighted from his train, he saw nobody that he recognized for an instant, but then spied three figures who seemed vaguely familiar. They were his brothers, all right, but each of them had beards that ran clear down to their waists. "Now what would the three of you be growing them bear-r-rds for, lads?" he asked. "We had to," answered the eldest. "When ye went to Amer-r-rica, ye took the razor wi' ye."

★ ★ ★

The stories of Harry McLean's largess sent J. P. McEvoy to the files for records of other super-spendthrifts. He comes up with the story of "Coal-Oil Johnny" Steele, who ran through two million dollars in a few years. He spent $8000 for clothes in a single day. A hotel clerk in Philadelphia failed to accord him proper deference. "Coal-Oil Johnny" leased the entire hotel for a day for $10,000—and fired the clerk. Then there was the Marquis of Hastings, who wagered his entire inheritance on a single horse race—and lost. And "Diamond Jim" Brady who had a separate, complete set of jeweled studs, rings, and cuff links for every day of the month, and gave chorus girls a thousand dollars apiece for attending his parties.

Most spendthrifts are living examples of the old adage "easy come, easy go." Starving prospectors who strike gold or oil and become millionaires overnight, shop clerks who inherit fortunes from unknown relatives, soda jerkers who become internationally idolized movie stars—these are the people who build incongruous palaces in the desert (you'll find a half-dozen of them in Oklahoma), or have their doorknobs made out of solid gold, or give banquets at which a dozen dancing girls step out of a huge blackberry pie. The big bull market provided dozens of such newly-rich exhibitionists in the Roaring Twenties; many of them were jumping out of windows when the bubble burst.

One man used his fortune to better advantage. He made a huge bequest to his old alma mater for the construction and stocking of a fine, model library. The crash wiped him out just about the time the last stone was put in place. The trustees met to ponder the situation. They offered him the post of assistant librarian in the building he had made possible. He accepted.

★ ★ ★

The lady with the sable coat lived in a luxurious hotel that faced the park. Her chauffeur called for her every morning at eleven. As he helped her into the car one day, she noticed a shabbily dressed man on a bench across the street gazing up at the hotel with a rapt expression on his face. He was there again the next morning—and the next. The lady's curiosity was aroused. She told her chauffeur to wait, ignored his obvious disapproval, and crossed over to the man on the bench.

"I simply have to know," she told him, "why you keep staring at the hotel that way every morning."

The man smiled apologetically. "Lady," he said. "I'm a penniless failure. I sleep on this bench when the cops don't chase me. And I dream that some day—just once—I'm going to spend a night in that swell hotel across the way."

The lady, feeling very pleased with herself, declared, "Tonight your dream is going to come true. I'm going to pay for the best room in the house for you."

She summoned him to her breakfast table the following morning. "Well," she said, "how did you sleep?"

The man proved most disappointing. "Never again, lady," he answered. "I sleep better on the bench than I did here."

"Good heavens, why?" she asked. "Wasn't the bed soft and warm enough for you?"

"It wasn't that," he explained. "You see, down there I can dream I'm in the hotel. Here, the whole night through, I kept dreaming I was back on the park bench."

★ ★ ★

One of the elder DuPonts of Wilmington has a collection of Ming china second to none in the world. He keeps it in a little museum on his estate, and allows occasional visitors to inspect his treasures.

A young couple were there by invitation. While waiting for their host, the girl picked up a delicate vase. To her horror, it slipped from her fingers and smashed into a hundred fragments on the stone floor. Just then little Mr. DuPont came pattering up.

"Oh, Mr. DuPont," wailed the girl, "I have broken the little vase that stood in this niche. I do hope it wasn't one of the valuable pieces."

Mr. DuPont took a quick look at the broken fragments. "Fortunately, my dear," he said, with a reassuring pat, "it wasn't valuable at all. Don't trouble your pretty head about it."

Then he fainted dead away.

★ ★ ★

When Heywood Broun III was about ten, his father decided that a progressive schooling was what the boy needed, and went to inspect one of the most prominent of such institutions in New York. As he approached the head of the stairs, a class was dismissed. One after another, the moppets dashed into Mr. Broun's ample frame, shoved him angrily aside with mutters of annoyance, and continued on their way. Only the last little boy to leave the room stopped long enough to say "I beg your pardon" when he stepped on a Broun toe.

The teacher watched the proceedings with absorbed interest. "You'll have to excuse that last student," she said to Mr. Broun. "He's only been in the school for three days."

Heywood Broun, by the way, blithely ignored small-time hecklers who poked fun at his theories on education and politics. When friends asked him why he didn't hit back at his self-appointed critics, Broun said, "Why use dynamite when insect powder will do?"

★ ★ ★

Walter Clark, author of *The Ox-Bow Incident*, visited a little New England town to get background material for a new novel. Everybody was friendly and helpful to him, particularly the editor of the local gazette, who supplied fascinating biographical bits about the inhabitants.

One afternoon he was walking down the main street with the

postmistress when a man he had not seen before approached from the opposite direction. Clark noticed that everybody averted his gaze when the man went by. One woman gathered her little girl into her arms and pointedly crossed the street to get out of his way. "Who is this fellow coming along here?" he asked. The postmistress literally froze. "His name is Eustace Barron," she said coldly. "We do not talk about him in these parts." Clark noticed that Barron was well dressed, but had a hunted, furtive look on his face. He asked the editor about him, but that worthy gave him a withering look, and stalked off to the press room without a word.

Clark was intrigued. Here was some dark mystery that might make perfect material for his book. That evening he came back to the newspaper office, with a jug of applejack to assure his welcome. The old editor expanded visibly under its influence. Clark bided his time. The old man was chuckling over an anecdote he had just retailed, when Clark suddenly said, "Now you simply have got to tell me about this fellow Eustace Barron. Why this conspiracy of silence? Did he commit rape, murder, incest, or what?"

The editor compressed his lips. "Do you think I'd mind any little thing like that, son?" he said.

"Well, then, what was it?"

"You asked for it," said the editor. He carefully pulled down every shade in the room, tiptoed to the door to make sure nobody was eavesdropping, and finally whispered his secret into Clark's ear.

"Eustace Barron," he said, *"dipped into his capital!"*

★ ★ ★

The most faithful and persistent Boswell of the foibles of the idle rich is Lucius Beebe, who writes so beautifully in the *New York Herald Tribune* every Saturday morning about a world that ceased to exist fully thirty years ago. A few die-hards are left, clinging to the outer raiment and obsolete rituals of the lost tribe; Lucius reports the details of their death throes with an absorbed fascination.

Beebe long ago was nicknamed "Luscious Lucius" by a jealous competitor who envied him his silk-lined evening cape, his pearl-gray top-hat, his ability to ride atop a tallyho in an Easter Parade as though he did it every morning in the week—and, above all, the deep and very obvious enjoyment that he got out of life. When he wasn't concocting drivel for his "This New York" col-

umn in the Saturday *Herald Tribune,* Beebe turned out several absolutely first-rate books on American railroading.

It was Beebe who told the story of Valentina, unbelievably

chic modiste of Fifth Avenue, who tried to sell a customer a sable coat. "But I already have a mink coat," said the lady. "Meenk! meenk!" echoed la Valentina. "Meenk is for football games!" Beebe reports that when this lady gave an Easter party she told each guest exactly what color dress to wear so that the general effect would be perfectly balanced. He also tells of Jack Miley's visit to the Pump Room in Chicago. In peace times, Miley is sports editor of the *News*. On the day in question, he was fried. The Pump Room specializes in flaming foods served on swords, spears, bayonets, and what have you. Miley watched the spectacle for a few moments and commanded, "Waiter, bring me a double order of scrambled eggs, extra soft, and listen, fellow, bring them on a *saber*."

"Cartier's," mourns Lucius, "isn't selling anywhere near the number of men's gold garters the shop usually does. Not because there is a declining demand; on the contrary, they aren't able to fill even the orders on hand because they can't get the good-quality elastic!" Isn't that terrible? When cruel war deprives people of the special wines, paté, caviar, and cuff links to which they are addicted, it's a lucky thing there's a fellow like Beebe around to record the ravages.

In private life, Lucius Beebe is the scion of a fine old New England family, so influential that when Lucius was requested to leave Yale, he was taken on at Harvard—a thing that isn't done every day in the week, I promise you. Legend persists that Lucius' precipitate exit from New Haven had to do with a ventriloquist whom he palmed off on the Yale Chaplain as a famous minister from the West. The minister was asked to deliver a sermon in the Yale Chapel, and progressed beautifully until the point where he stopped talking, cupped his hands about his lips, looked aloft, and called, "Am I right, Lord?" Down from the rafters (remember, he was a ventriloquist) came an answering "You certainly are, My Son!"

Beebe avers that he has the formula for a perfect summer garden: half mint, half marijuana! He awoke in his bed one morning with a bad hangover and rang for his man. "Send out the suit I had on last night for a cleaning," he ordered. "As I recall, an accident befell it." The valet hesitated. "Make it snappy," said Beebe. "All right," said the valet, "but do you want me to send it out as it is now—or would you like to take it off first?"

C. V. R. Thompson, the English humorist, sums up Lucius Beebe as "the only man outside of Warner Brothers' pictures who still says Zounds, Egad, and Oddsbodikins. . . . A crisis in Beebe's life is when he finds somebody wearing a wider lapel than his." Stanley Walker, on the other hand, predicts, "It is probable that in some happier time in the future when the sour-pussed young pipsqueaks of today are living off their social-security income and spending their old age writing their dreary memoirs, the journalists of America will do something handsome by Lucius Beebe, as the man who kept the faith during the dark years."

★ ★ ★

Stanton Griffis, head of Paramount Pictures, Madison Square Garden, the Brentano book chain, and Lord knows what else, is the man who signed Bob Hope for Paramount. That is like a publisher getting six Book-of-the-Month Club selections in a row. At a recent dinner, Mr. Griffis introduced Mr. Hope with these lines: "I want to present the funniest comedian in pictures, one of the screen's handsomest leading men, and the fellow who wrote this introduction for me—Bob Hope."

★ ★ ★

Speaking of dinners, E. Phillips Oppenheim says that he has one sure-fire formula for innumerable occasions on which he is called upon, without warning, for a few remarks. He clears his throat with a series of garrumphs, and declares severely, "As King Solomon remarked to the Queen of Sheba, 'Madam, I did not come here to speak!' "

★ ★ ★

There are a host of stories based on the penny-pinching habits of John D. Rockefeller. He got used to the sensation of signing away millions, but actual cash out of his pocket was something else again. His famous ten-cent tips were cause for hilarity the country over. His clothes concerned him little, if at all. One suit had a big patch on the coat, and a bright shine on the pants. "What's wrong with this suit?" he asked crankily when a friend urged him to discard it. "Everything," said the friend. "Your father would be ashamed of you. You know how neatly he used to dress." "But," protested Rockefeller triumphantly, "I'm wearing a suit of my father's right now."

Mr. Rockefeller spent his last winters in Florida. Down there they tell a story that one day he went to the dentist to have a tooth pulled. "How much?" he asked in advance. "Three dollars," said the dentist, who didn't even know who his client was. "Hmph! Three dollars to pull a tooth!" grumbled John D. "Here's a dollar. Loosen it a little bit!"

★ ★ ★

Bob Lovett, a mainstay of the War Department, was an important banker before the hostilities began. He was entertaining Bob Benchley and Donald Ogden Stewart, among others, at his Locust Valley home one evening, when he was called to the telephone. "Why, yes!" his awestricken guests heard him say. "*Let* Austria have eight million dollars." Next day Stewart sent him a telegram which read, "You have made me the happiest little country in the world." The signature was "Austria."

★ ★ ★

A young banker picked up the telephone. His end of the conversation went as follows: "No. No. *No.* No. No. No. *Yes.* No. No. No." Finally, with a last explosive "No" he hung up the phone. The vice-president of the bank overheard him and grumbled, "What d'ya mean by saying yes to that fellow?" "I had to," explained the other. "He asked me if I could hear him."

★ ★ ★

Mrs. Harrison Williams, frequently voted by modistes "the best-dressed woman in the United States," once bought a hat

505

from a Paris milliner for a rather staggering sum, but with the assurance that the model would not be duplicated. The very night she returned to America, she was dancing at the Stork Club when another woman appeared with the identical hat on her head.

Mrs. Williams was indignant for a moment, but then realized that the other woman must have been bilked the same way that she was. When they passed close to one another on the floor, she pointed first to her hat, then to the other's, and smiled. The other lady looked straight through her. "Maybe she didn't understand," Mrs. Williams said to her partner. "Dance me over next to her again." This time her gestures were so broad that no misunderstanding was possible. She pointed to both hats, shook her head, and then smiled again. The woman cut her dead.

Mrs. Williams was pretty miffed about the whole thing until she went to the powder room and took a look into the mirror. She was wearing a different hat altogether that evening.

★ ★ ★

Beardsley Ruml, creator of the pay-as-you-go tax plan, is allergic to magazine profiles. A friend of his told a *New Yorker* reporter, "Ruml hates physical exercise. If you ever find him on a tennis court, you'll know it's because he dropped dead crossing it on the way to a Scotch and soda." Two days after the article appeared, a Macy big shot accosted Ruml with a sharp, "What's this I hear about your being found dead drunk on a tennis court?"

★ ★ ★

At a dentist's office one day, Abel Green, the editor of *Variety*, heard a lady patient arguing over a bill. The gold inlay was $90. "Can't you make it $80?" begged the lady. The rest of the bill was $140. "Can't you make it $120?" she demanded. Finally she asked what time the doctor expected her on the following morning. "Eleven o'clock," said the doctor. Green answered for the surprised patient. "Can't you make it 10:30?" he asked.

A visitor from the sticks, whom Abel Green was entertaining at "21," asked if they have a regular $2 dinner there. "Sure," said Abel. "Do you want it on white or rye?"

SWEET ARE THE USES OF PUBLICITY

The high-powered (and higher-priced) "publicity counsel" of today represents billion-dollar businesses and self-made tycoons who want to be known as philanthropists and patrons of the arts. Basically, he is still the barker selling snake-oil remedies to the rubes at a carnival or the advance man of the old traveling one-ring circus. He is judged by the amount of free space he can wangle in the press, and the extent to which he can make a gullible public fall for his subtle, and often completely fictitious, propaganda.

One of the first press agents who turned publicity into a million-dollar business was the late Harry Reichenbach. This master of the art of exploitation has been called "the greatest single force in American advertising and publicity since Barnum." One of his earliest exploits was to salvage a little restaurant that had everything but customers.
He put a simple bowl of water in the window with a sign reading, "The only living Brazilian invisible fish." Increasing crowds gathered to observe this phenomenon. Some swore they could see the invisible fish make the water move. Reichenbach promptly hid a little electric fan in the corner to blow ripples on the water. "There it goes," the crowd would cry, and then, for no

OLD DR. SHMOO'S ORIGINAL INDIAN SNAKE OIL GOOD FOR MAN & BEAST apparent reason, would go inside to eat dinner. Business boomed for weeks. Reichenbach claimed later that the proprietor simply couldn't stand prosperity: he tried to serve the invisible fish as a course.

It was inevitable that Reichenbach and the expanding motion-picture business should discover one another. He was engaged to publicize a gruesome affair called *The Return of Tarzan*, after a preview indicated that its chances were nil. A few days later a bearded professor registered at the Belleclaire Hotel in New York as "T. R. Zann" and had a "piano" hoisted to his room by block and tackle. In reality, the piano box contained a toothless old lion. Mr. Zann then called room service and ordered fifteen pounds of raw meat. The puzzled waiter who brought it took one look into the room, and fled. "There's a live lion up there," he screamed. Mr. Zann then led the animal through the main lobby, causing (1) three old ladies to faint dead away, (2) the management to call the police emergency squad, and (3) Mr. "T. R. Zann" and his lion to get reams of front-page publicity in every paper in town. By the time red-faced editors discovered it was all a publicity stunt for a fifth-rate movie there was nothing they could do about it. When the picture opened, the crowds fought to get in.

Reichenbach next turned his attention to a little number called *The Virgin of Stamboul*. A Turkish potentate and staff of seventy took an entire floor at a swank hostelry. The potentate was reluctant to be interviewed, but finally consented to reveal that his brother, the Sultan, had dispatched him to find the dastardly American sailor who had stolen the Number One favorite from the Sultan's harem. It's hard to believe, but only one reporter in town saw through this incredible hocus-pocus. The exception was a former publicity man himself, who was so intrigued by the build-up that he held his peace until the story broke in the papers. Then *The Virgin of Stamboul* (which, by an odd coincidence, featured the abduction of a harem pin-up girl by a Yankee gob) swept triumphantly into New York, and the "Sultan's brother" went back to his dish-washing job in an Armenian restaurant.

As the picture industry prospered, its publicity methods became less crude and obvious. Reichenbach kept pace with their progress. When the Metro Pictures Corporation was formed, it had everything but a production department. Reichenbach kept exhibitors intrigued for a full year by a whirlwind campaign that featured the slogan "Can they keep it up?" What they were keeping up nobody, including themselves, knew; but in the end, perseverance won its just reward, and the Metro Corporation blossomed into Metro-Goldwyn-Mayer.

The press agent for one Broadway show hired a huge truck to tour the city. The name of the play was emblazoned on its sides, and a loud speaker within blared its virtues. At one of the most important intersections in the city, the truck broke down—accidentally, of course. Traffic was snarled in every direction for a full half-hour while the merits of a fly-by-night musical comedy were broadcast to a stalled and helpless populace. Another press agent evolved the notion of taking a native California boy who had been unable to get a break in the movies, and shipping him to England where he became the janitor of a well-known London theatre. In the dead of night, the two changed the electric sign above the marquee, and put the boy's name in lights. With the photograph of this sign as his only evidence, the agent then convinced a big Hollywood studio that his client was one of the most popular stars in Britain, and secured a signed contract for him. The boy really had talent, and is a genuine picture star today. The same technique has been followed a dozen times since. A lot of those exotic foreign sirens you see writhing around the screen drew their first breaths in such typically oriental oases as Wichita, Kansas.

One publicity man made a Broadway chop house nationally famous by the simple expedient of scattering sawdust on the floor. Another guided a shoe emporium to fame and fortune by persuading the proprietor to boost his fixed price from $6.95 to

$12.95. The shoe man was incredulous until the promoter proved his point by an actual experiment. He put two identical pairs of shoes in the show window, side by side. His sign read, "There is absolutely no difference between these shoes. One pair is priced at $6.95; the other at $12.95. We just want to see which price you prefer." Three women out of every four who entered the shop, suspecting chicanery of one sort or another, insisted upon paying $12.95.

Harry Reichenbach's most conspicuous achievement was connected with that third-rate, innocuous painting called "September Morn." The proprietor of a Broadway art store had seen the original in Paris, and thought it had commercial possibilities. He had ordered innumerable reproductions in assorted sizes at a cost of over sixty thousand dollars. The unpredictable American public, however, paid no attention to "September Morn" and the dealer seemed stuck with his entire investment. It was at this juncture that he enlisted the services of Reichenbach. He got results within twenty-four hours.

Reichenbach put the biggest available print of "September Morn" in the dealer's window. Next he hired a dozen high-school

510

kids and rehearsed them painstakingly in the routine he had decided upon. Then he burst into the office of Anthony Comstock,
ever-ready head of the Anti-Vice Squad and self-appointed custodian of the people's morals. "Mr. Comstock," cried Reichenbach, "there's a vile picture on display in a Broadway window,
and schoolchildren are ogling it this very minute!" Comstock
grabbed his hat and the two made a running dive for the dealer's
store. The kids saw Reichenbach coming, and, as previously arranged, began pointing at the picture, smirking, and making ob-
scene remarks about it. Comstock charged into the store like a
wounded bull and had the deliriously happy dealer clapped into
jail. By the time the excitement and nation-wide publicity had
died down, "September Morn" was undoubtedly the best-known
painting in the United States, and more than two million reproductions of it were sold.

Reichenbach employed a similar technique to turn Elinor
Glyn's atrocious *Three Weeks* into a rip-roaring best-seller. He
sent anonymous letters of protest to puzzled post-office officials
all over the country. Finally the Postmaster General barred the
book from the mails—and the stampede was on.

The methods of the highly organized "lobbies" that infest
Washington today are really little more than elaborations of the
technique perfected by Reichenbach and his disciples. Sometimes their tricks are just as crude. A sudden deluge of thousands
of taxpayers' letters on senatorial desks in the midst of debate
on controversial measures does not just happen spontaneously.
Some master publicity counsel is pulling the strings. There are
informed commentators who will tell you that the "spontaneous
public clamor" for Wendell Willkie at the 1940 Republican Convention had been planned step by step, and minute by minute,
at a banker's residence six months ahead of time.

Astute publicity men have extricated million-dollar enterprises
from many a jam. One of the funniest of them involved a magnate who "got in on the ground floor" of a new salmon-canning
project. The price of his stock was right, and the salmon was

delicious. Unfortunately, the color of the salmon was pure white, instead of the customary pink. It tasted just as good as the best, but the public was used to *pink* salmon, and would have no truck with any other kind. The inventory reached alarming proportions, and bankruptcy loomed. Then the high-powered "public relations counsel" was called in. By printing just one line in big type on every can of salmon in stock, he cleaned out the inventory in exactly four months, and, if rival canneries had not secured an ultimate injunction, would undoubtedly have put most of them out of business. The line that he suggested was simple. It read: *"This salmon is guaranteed not to turn pink in the can."*

★　★　★

There is a formidable blonde lady on the Bowery, according to Joseph Mitchell, who has achieved great local fame as cashier and proprietress of a movie "grind" house where ten cents gets you a double feature, newsreel, selected shorts, and a crack at a set of dishes. "Mazie" is the lady's name, and she keeps her house open from 8 A.M. to midnight. On cold days many a "bum" produces his dime early in the morning and sleeps peacefully until closing time. "Some days I don't know which this is, a movie theatre or a flop-house," sighs Mazie. "Pictures with shooting in them are bad for business. They wake up the customers." If one of the sleepers snores loudly enough to annoy the rest of the audience, Mazie charges down the aisle with a couple of copies of *True Romances* tightly folded as a bludgeon, and hollers, "Outa here on a stretcher, you big baboon! Every tooth in your head! Every bone in your body!" The women and children, reports Mitchell, enjoy this mightily, particularly when Mazie gets the wrong man, as she frequently does.

★　★　★

One day in 1929, Myra Hampton, now the wife of Paul Streger, the agent, gave birth to a baby boy. That night the Thanatopsis Poker Club, whose full membership knew and loved Myra, chipped in and bought the infant one share of United States Steel, then selling at something like two hundred and fifty dollars a share. Shortly thereafter Wall Street collapsed. At the next meeting of the club, Franklin P. Adams remarked casually, "I hear that Myra's kid has been clipped by the market."

NOT VULNERABLE

P. Hal Sims, one of the greatest card-players of our time, waxes suddenly compassionate when his victim is writing out a check for an evening's losses. "Maybe I play this game a little better than you do," he will admit. "Let's have a round of golf in the morning, and I'll give you a chance to get it back." He neglects to add that he negotiates an eighteen-hole course in an average 74. This remarkable man is also a championship billiard player and shot, and, before he took on weight, bagged a number of tennis trophies as well.

It is as a bridge-player, however, that he won national fame. Before he tired somewhat of the game, he played ten or twelve hours a day, seven days a week. He owned a house at the New Jersey seashore, where bridge sharks came for a week-end and stayed for the summer. Reporters began dropping in to cover the impromptu tournaments. No servant ever remained more than four days. The only guest who was ever thrown out was an Italian who chanted hymns. Sims grew suspicious when the Italian's partner made fourteen successful finesses in a row. He called in an interpreter who discovered that the hymns went something like

> "The King of Hearts is on the right,
> The Queen of Spades is by it."

Sims finally tired of feeding half of the nation's bridge experts and sold his house to Max Baer for use as a training camp.

Aboard a liner for England, Sims spotted a quartet of professional card sharps in the smoking lounge the first afternoon out and resolved to have some fun with them. On his way to their table, however, he was stopped by an English clergyman who proffered his hand and said, "Mr. Sims! I recognized you from your pictures! Please have a drink with me!"

Sims found the clergyman such stimulating company that he never did get over to the card sharps, either that afternoon or during the remainder of the voyage. Several weeks later, in the company of an official from Scotland Yard, he ran into the clergyman at the Savoy Grill in London, but was surprised to see him turn white and duck for the nearest exit. "I wonder what's gotten into Dr. Ogilvie," he said. "Dr. Ogilvie!" echoed his companion. "That's no doctor. He's one of the slickest card sharps in Britain." Sims then realized that he had been neatly decoyed aboard the steamer, and had left the field clear for the "doctor's" pals to lure more likely game into their little net.

The card sharps knew what they were up against when they confronted Hal Sims. He has the percentage of every game of chance figured to such a nicety that the slightest deviation finds him hot on the scent of skulduggery. He once picked an intricately marked deck of cards from a hundred regular ones in less than five minutes. He was kind enough to warn a friend not to play gin rummy with him for money. "No matter how carefully you mix the cards," he explained, "a few of them are bound to remain in the same order they turned up in for the previous hand. I remember the exact order of the cards for the last three."

Hal Sims has befriended many players who were down on their luck, although he knew that some of them were inveterate grifters. One notorious four-flusher phoned to say that if he didn't get a thousand dollars immediately, he'd be jailed as a confidence man in the morning. "A thousand is too much," said Sims, "but if you can get that banker we played with last night to put up five hundred, I'll make up the difference." "He gave it to me," the man reported happily an hour later, and Sims made out his check for the sum he had promised. The next time

Sims saw the banker, he said, "It was nice of you to let our poor friend have that money he needed." "Yes," said the banker. "He told me what a fix he was in, so I let him have the thousand."

Mrs. Hal (Dorothy) Sims is quite a character in her own right. Her father was Isaac L. Rice, successful industrialist who invented the Rice gambit in chess, and was a great patron of the game. Mrs. Sims' comment is, "They have another name for patron now." It is never warm enough for Mrs. Sims. I remember her bundled up in three sweaters during a Bucks County weekend that was so hot that the other guests spent most of the time in the swimming pool. She hustles her husband off to Havana every October and stays there until the following May. One July morning, her husband demanded his bathing suit. "It's all packed for Cuba," she reported. "What's the idea?" he asked. "We're not leaving for over three months." "I know," she said, "but I hate packing, so I hurried up and got it over with." Sims cheerfully calls her "the poorest bridge player in the world" and she just as cheerfully replies, "Well, then I can't get any worse." They have a standing rule that she is never allowed to bid "no trump"; Sims has finally convinced her that there is nothing "undignified" in stopping the bidding short of a game. Mrs. Sims is the inventor of the "sycic." She says it came to her in a flash. She picked up a hand one day with no spades in it—and bid a spade. Her partner nearly had a fit—until he discovered that her impulsive declaration had prevented their opponents from bidding—and making—a grand slam in the spade suit. That made her something of a heroine. She wrote up her experiment for a magazine and meant to call her new system "Psychological Bidding," but her sense of spelling, never too clearly defined, failed her in the clutch—and "sycic" it became. It was Dorothy Sims' great moment.

★ ★ ★

New York's Cavendish Club has been the scene of some of the most dramatic bridge contests of our time. Through its corridors flit the elite of bridgedom: "The Four Aces," Culbertson,

Sims, and a host of others only slightly less talented. Even the hat-check girl keeps the members strictly classified. A guest couldn't find his coat one night, and started searching a rack on the right. "Oh, it wouldn't be there," the girl told him. "I distinctly remember hanging it with the two-cent-a-point players."

Some of the experts—Count Von Zedtwitz, for example— have been known to ponder a full twenty minutes before playing a certain card; others, like Hubert Boscowitz, play so quickly that even their partners are confused at times. Sir Cedric Hardwicke played a few friendly rubbers as Boscowitz's partner. The latter had to leave to catch a train. As he stood waiting for the elevator he heard Hardwicke say, "I'll bet that blighter is in Chicago by this time."

There was a lot of bidding on a hand at the Cavendish one afternoon. Just before play started, George Kaufman requested, "May I review the bidding—*with the original intonations?*"

One gentleman, no longer associated with the club, sent a donation to Bundles for Britain when that was the thing to do. The committee was a little puzzled as to the disposal of four immaculate, stiff-bosomed dress shirts. A lady was handling one of them rather gingerly when four aces dropped out on the floor!

★ ★ ★

The average card-player hasn't got a chance when he mingles with ranking experts like Hal Sims, Ely Culbertson, or Oswald Jacoby. These men not only play their cards with superlative skill, but have learned to turn every personal peculiarity and facial expression of their opponents to their own advantage. This is perfectly legitimate, of course. When playing with one another, they never dream of arranging their cards in order, since every one of them automatically observes from what part of the hand each card is taken. If a player exposes any part of his hand to an opponent he has only himself to blame if said opponent takes advantage of it.

There's a tale told, probably fictitious, of a bridge game where Culbertson, seated at another expert's left, played a neat trick on his adversary. The latter had bid up to six clubs. Culbertson had the king of clubs and another small club in his hand. He purposely let the opponent see the king at the left end of his hand, but hid the small club among the cards on the other side. The opponent thereupon bid "seven clubs" which Culbertson doubled. The first time the opponent had the lead, he confidently planked down his ace of clubs. When Culbertson plucked the little club from its hiding place, instead of the expected king, the opponent bellowed with rage, threw his cards on the table, and cried, "I refuse to play with crooks!"

★ ★ ★

When John Mulholland, one of the great prestidigitators of our time, was a youngster, he was added as an afterthought to a program at the National Arts Club, and forthwith gave a very creditable performance. When it was over, however, an old killjoy with a perverted sense of humor asked if the young magician could do the same tricks with any old pack of cards. Mulholland brazened it out, and found an unopened pack of cards, with the National Arts device on their orange backs, thrust into his hands. To the astonishment of the members, he performed some tricks with the new cards that eclipsed any he had done with his own prepared deck—more mystifying, indeed, than any he has been able to do since. It appears that when Mulholland unwrapped the deck he noticed (although he did not see fit to call it to the attention of the members) that a singular error had occurred at the factory in the assembling of that pack. It was made up of fifty-two aces of spades.

★ ★ ★

In London, a certain lord married a woman forty years his junior. Adele Astaire preserved for months the London *Times'* account of the ceremony, which ended with, "The bridegroom's gift to the bride was an antique pendant."

★ ★ ★

Clarence Darrow delivered the funeral oration at the bier of a friend who, after an unparalleled streak of bad luck, had committed suicide. "My friend," said Darrow simply, "decided, in a moment of temporary sanity, that his life was no longer worth living."

★ ★ ★

John M. Weyer, reports Leonard Lyons, gave a dinner for gourmets, and told a new maid, "Please remember to serve the fish whole, with tail and head, and a slice of lemon in the mouth." The maid appeared surprised, but said nothing. That evening she bore the fish triumphantly to the table, complete with tail and head. And in her mouth she carried a slice of lemon.

★ ★ ★

A maharajah who was entertaining Neysa McMein in India some winters ago queried a servant on the progress she was making in hunting. "The beautiful lady shoots divinely," reported the impeccable Hindu, "but Providence is merciful to the birds!"

519

Chapter Five

STRICTLY PROFESSIONAL

RELATIVE TO EINSTEIN

One sultry afternoon this summer, I discovered a famous figure trudging complacently ahead of me up Sixth Avenue, puffing on his pipe, and carrying a huge package in his arms. It was Professor Albert Einstein, discoverer of the theory of relativity, Nobel Prize winner, American citizen by grace of Nazi stupidity and intolerance. I followed him for a full block. Not one soul recognized him. "Aren't you surprised that nobody stops to gape at you?" I asked when I caught up with him. "If Lana Turner walked up this same block, a thousand people would turn to stare." "Lana Turner," replied the professor sagely, "has a great deal more to show than I have."

Professor Einstein, by this time, has become a familiar and accepted part of the Princeton family. When he and his wife first arrived from Germany, however, he knew little English, and was frankly dismayed by the homage paid him by a strange people who didn't understand beans about his mathematical theories, but plagued him for his autograph and demanded to know what he thought of American womanhood. On the dock, a reporter assured him that he looked just like Kringelein in *Grand Hotel*. "I never stopped there," said the professor.

The general public first heard about the Einstein theory of relativity when some savant proclaimed that only twelve men in all the world understood what he was talking about. This intrigued the American people in much the same way that *Information, Please* and other radio quiz programs do. Jokes about relativity, most of them awful, became part of every comedian's repertoire. The best of them was the conversation between Ginsberg, who demanded to know what relativity was, and Garfinkel, who brazenly attempted to explain it to him. "It's like this," says Garfinkel. "You go to the dentist to get a tooth pulled. You are in the chair only five minutes, but it hurts so much that you think you are there for an hour. Now on the other hand, you go to see your best girl that same evening. She is in your arms for a full hour, but it is so wonderful to have her there that to you it feels like only five minutes." Ginsberg nods dubiously. "I see," he says, "but tell me, Garfinkel—from dis he makes a *living?*"

Professor Einstein had been famous in Europe for years before he came to this country; his definitive paper on relativity had been published in 1915; he did not arrive in New York until 1933. He and his family, however, had always assiduously avoided the limelight. One story has it that at the first lush banquet at the Waldorf given to honor him, an orchid was placed on the plate of every lady before she sat down. Mrs. Einstein thought it was something to eat, and was stopped in the nick of time from cutting it with her knife and fork. Some weeks later the Einsteins were taken to the Mt. Wilson Observatory in California. Mrs. Einstein was particularly impressed by the giant telescope. "What on earth do they use it for?" she asked. Her host explained that one of its chief purposes was to find out the shape of the universe. "Oh," said Mrs. Einstein, "my hus-

band does that on the back of an old envelope." As a matter of fact, Einstein has often said that he could write everything basic that he knows about relativity within three pages.

Princeton University offered him a lifetime post in the Institute for Advanced Study. He accepted gratefully, and has lived comfortably near the campus ever since. After Mrs. Einstein died in 1936, the professor moved into his present home at 112 Mercer Street. It is furnished with Spartan simplicity. That's how he wants it. The hand-made furniture was shipped to him from Germany; he considers it very good luck that he managed to salvage what he did. Some of his rarest books and manuscripts were burned by Nazi vandals. But he saved enough for a fresh start. His couch is the nearest thing to a fakir's bed of nails that I have ever felt, but the professor sleeps like a log on it. His companion is a coal-black cat. Dr. Einstein believes that this cat's nightly forays are spent in "soliloquizing," and has named him "Hamlet." But the neighbors, who have different ideas, call him Casanova.

Perhaps you have heard of the twelve-year-old girl who fell into the habit of dropping in on the professor every day on her way home from school. Her parents were gratified, but somewhat mystified too. One evening the mother found an opportunity to ask the professor, "What do you two talk about every day?" "Oh," laughed the professor, "she brings me cookies and I do her arithmetic for her."

Einstein's simplicity and imperturbable good humor have won him the love of the entire Princeton faculty and student body. At a faculty meeting one day, he was importuned to explain his theories in a brief lecture. He said it was impossible. A brash associate volunteered to do it for him. After floundering around for twenty minutes, the dean begged him to desist. "Maybe twelve men can understand Einstein," he said, "but certainly *nobody* understands you." Einstein comforted his crestfallen friend. "In Germany once," he said, "a hundred Nazi professors collaborated on a book to prove that my theories were poppycock. Imagine! If I really was wrong, one would have been quite enough."

Professor Einstein became an American citizen in 1940. He loves everything about his adopted country, and is particularly fascinated by American slang. He listened carefully three times to the story of the employer who told his secretary, "There are two words I must ask you never to use in my presence. One of them is 'lousy,' the other is 'swell.'" "That's all right by me," said the secretary. "What are the two words?" When he finally comprehended, the professor threw back his head and roared with laughter. In a seminar one afternoon, he ran out of pipe tobacco. None of the students had any either, but one of them taught him to break up several cigarettes, and fill his pipe with cigarette tobacco. "Gentlemen," he said gravely, "I think we have made a great discovery." The experiment, however, as you will know if you have ever tried it yourself, proved a failure.

Oddly enough, Professor Einstein is not exactly a wizard at the simplest forms of arithmetic. Income-tax blanks dismay him, too. A clerk at the Princeton Bookstore caught him glancing at

an income-tax guide recently, and asked if he would like one. "Good heavens, no," cried the professor. "It's terrible enough to have to figure out the tax without having to read a whole book about it!"

When Professor Einstein visited Palm Springs last year, another distinguished guest at his hotel was James "Schnozzola" Durante. One day the manager called Jimmie and said, "Professor Einstein has his violin with him, and is dying for somebody to accompany him at the piano for a little while. I told him you might oblige." Jimmie agreed, and there followed possibly the most incongruous duet in the history of music. "I don't play classical music so good," confessed Jimmie. "Every time I made a really terrible mistake the professor gave me a hurt look like I done it on purpose." As an afterthought, he said, "The professor made plenty of mistakes too."

Einstein was really stopped cold at a recent Princeton function by Jascha Heifetz's irrepressible sister Pauline. "Tell me, Professor," she said with deadly seriousness, "is this mathematics racket really on the level?"

★ ★ ★

M. F. Ashley Montagu's book, *Man's Most Dangerous Myth: The Fallacy of Race*, includes the story of the wife of a Worcester Cathedral Canon who listened to the first announcement of the theory of evolution with consternation. "Descended from the apes!" she exclaimed. "My dear, we will hope it is not true. But if it is, let us pray that it may not become generally known!"

★ ★ ★

Those two eminent scientists, the Doctors Piccard, are exact twins, as identical, to coin a phrase, as peas in a pod. This fact enabled them to play a harmless prank on a barber in their native Switzerland.

The stratosphere flier assured the barber that he had the toughest, most stubborn beard in captivity, and offered to bet that the best shave in the world would only last him a few hours.

The barber angrily offered him another shave free if he should need it within twenty-four hours. He spent an hour giving him the closest shave possible without skinning him alive.

An hour later, the other brother arrived with a formidable beard and collected a free shave—after the bewildered barber had been given a strong restorative.

★ ★ ★

The late Cardinal Hinsley of Great Britain and the Archbishop of Canterbury attended the same dinner party and later shared a taxicab into town. "It is quite fitting that we take the cab together," smiled the Archbishop. "After all, we both serve God." "Yes, yes," agreed the Cardinal heartily. "You in your way; I in His."

Cardinal Hinsley liked to tell the story of two brothers who studied for the ministry. One was a little too flippant and whimsical to reach the heights; the other, a pompous and heavy-handed party, became a Bishop in due course. "My brother," the whimsical one explained, "rose because of his gravity; I was held down by my levity."

Another story always credited to Cardinal Hinsley features a lecturer who told his audience that the world would probably end in seven billion years. "How long did you say?" came a terrified voice from the rear. "Seven billion years," the lecturer repeated firmly. "Thank God," said the voice. "I thought for a moment you had said seven *million*."

★ ★ ★

A Bishop of Texas visited London and was taken to a fashionable soirée at which the ladies' dresses were cut very low. His hostess asked condescendingly if he had ever beheld such a sight. "Not," said the Bishop, "since I was weaned."

This same Bishop made a great hit with some English churchmen with a story that most of them probably have been using to advantage ever since. It concerned a colored preacher whose sermon emphasized free salvation, but who later complained about the paltriness of the collection. "Didn't you done say, Parson," protested a parishioner, "that salvation is free—free as the water we drink?" "Salvation *is* free, Brother," replied the minister. "It's free and water is free, but when we pipe it to you, you has to pay for the piping."

★ ★ ★

Irwin Edman, brilliant author and professor of philosophy at Columbia University, is that stock comedy character, the absent-minded pedagogue, in actuality. Beloved by his students for his wit, erudition, and uncanny ability to make the most abstruse subject sound easy, he is also the source of a whole saga of campus humor. One day he stopped a student on Riverside Drive and asked, "Pardon me, but am I walking north or south?" "North, Professor," was the answer. "Ah," said Edman, "then I've had my lunch."

ALMA MATER

Unable to enter his classroom, he summoned the janitor, complained that the door was broken. The janitor turned the key that was already in the lock, and opened the door. "That's what keys are for, Professor," he explained gently. Irwin spent an evening with a colleague and his wife, and the conversation was spirited until about two in the morning when, after several elaborate yawns had been ignored, the colleague said, "Irwin, I hate to put you out, but I have a nine o'clock class in the morning." "Good lord," said Irwin, blushing violently, "I thought *you* were at *my* house!"

At Columbia, a warning bell sounds three minutes before the end of a classroom hour. Edman was lecturing on Santayana one afternoon when the warning bell sounded, and several students stirred in their seats. "Just a moment, gentlemen," said Edman. "That was not the final bell. I wish to cast a few more pearls."

His looks are deceiving. A stranger could be excused for thinking him an undergraduate rather than a professor of international repute. Early in his pedagogical career he met his former professor, Felix Adler, on the campus. "What are you doing now, Irwin?" asked Adler. "I'm teaching here, too," said Irwin. "How cute!" exclaimed Adler. In a Munich beer-hall, years before the war, Edman fell into conversation with a portly Bavarian who was impressed with his store of knowledge and inquired, "What do you do in America?" "I am a professor of philosophy at Columbia," was the answer. The German roared with laughter. "If that were true," he said, "we would be colleagues." There is a sequel to this story. Irwin was so indignant that he rushed back to his hotel for his credentials and a letter of introduction signed by Columbia's president, Nicholas Murray Butler. The abashed German admitted that *he* was the one who had been bluffing; he was only an instructor at the local high school.

Edman came back home from that visit on an Italian boat. "Put me at a table," he told the purser, "with some native Italians. I'd like to practise talking the language." The purser gravely led him to a tableful of eight nuns. When the voyage was completed, they asked him for his autograph. Edman likes to tell this story. In fact, he likes to tell any story. He is an accomplished raconteur, and can disguise the hoariest Joe Miller chestnut with Platonic double-talk.

The tale of the nuns reminds him of the Frenchman on the *Normandie* who was assigned to a table where a bushy-browed stranger was already in the midst of his dinner. The Frenchman bowed and said, "Bon appetit!" The stranger also bowed and said, "Ginsberg." This happened every night for four nights. On the last night of the voyage, the stranger came to the table and said, "Bon appetit!" The Frenchman got up, bowed himself, and said, "Ginsberg."

★ ★ ★

A magazine called *The War Doctor* ran a cartoon that showed a group of physicians surrounding a patient on an operating table. From an incision in his stomach issued a stream of moths and butterflies. "By God," ran the caption, "he was right!"

★ ★ ★

The learned but unworldly head of the department devoted to the study of comparative religions at Harvard invariably asked the same question on every final examination: "Who, in chronological order, were the Kings of Israel?" Students came to count on this procedure as a sacred institution and prepared accordingly. Some crabby misanthrope tattled and, one precedent-shattering spring, the professor confounded his class by changing the question to: "Who were the major prophets and who were the minor prophets?" The class sat dumbfounded and all but one member slunk out of the room without writing a word. This sole survivor scribbled furiously and deposited his paper with the air of a conqueror. "Far be it from me," he had written, "to distinguish between these revered gentlemen, but it occurred to me that you might like to have a chronological list of the Kings of Israel."

★ ★ ★

Elihu Root liked to have aggressive and independent people working for him, but one promising young office boy sometimes went too far. There was the day, for instance, when he sauntered into the office, propped his elbows on Mr. Root's desk, and said, "Say, boss, there's a ball game at the Polo Grounds today I'm dying to see. Will you give me the afternoon off?"

"James," said the courtly Mr. Root, "that is not the way to ask a favor. Now you sit down in my chair and I'll show you how to do it properly."

The boy thought this was a delightful idea. He settled himself in his employer's chair. Mr. Root went outside. Then he entered softly, cap in hand, and said meekly, "If you don't mind, sir, there is a ball game today that I would like to see. Do you think you could spare me for the afternoon?"

In a flash the boy answered, "Certainly I can, Jimmie—and here's fifty cents to pay your way in."

Another time Mr. Root's firm had occasion to send an emissary to an important business conference in France. One of the bright young men in the office was selected for the trip, and was sent in to receive Root's final O.K. "I take it," said Root, "that you speak a fluent French."

"Hardly fluent," replied the young man. "But I've never had the slightest trouble making waiters and taxi drivers understand me."

"Ah, yes," said Mr. Root, "but suppose that no waiters or taxi drivers turn up for the conference?"

A distinguished scientist, says Louis Sobol, who probably saw him, was observing the heavens through the huge telescope at the Mt. Wilson Observatory. Suddenly he announced, "It's going to rain." "What makes you think so?" asked his guide. "Because," said the astronomer, still peering through the telescope, "my corns hurt."

★ ★ ★

A Harvard professor spent his vacation on a canoe trip in the Maine wilds. Shooting a series of rapids, he expressed concern at the growing fury of the swirling water, and the jagged rocks on every side. "Don't worry for a minute," the guide reassured him. "I know every rock in these rapids." Just then the canoe smacked into one of the rocks head-on and capsized. The bookman found himself floundering in the current, his equipment scattered in every direction. "You see," said the guide, trying to salvage his paddle, "there's one of the damn things now!"

That story reminds me of the guide who was showing some American tourists through Oxford. "I'd like to see Jowett's study," said one of them. "You know, the fellow who translated Plato." "Easiest thing in the world," said the guide, and led his party to a cloistered square near by. "That open window on the second floor, my friends, is Mr. Jowett's diggings. I say, would you like to see the Professor himself?" The Americans assured him that they would like nothing better. The guide thereupon picked up a sizable rock and hurled it with deadly accuracy through Jowett's open window. A moment later a face purple with rage appeared in the aperture. "Aha!" said the guide triumphantly. "That always gets him. There's the old boy himself!"

★ ★ ★

In Bernard Newman's *The New Europe*, he tells the story of a professor at a cosmopolitan university who set his class to writing a thesis on the general subject of "The Elephant." The Englishman devoted his essay to "The Elephant and How to Hunt Him." The Frenchman considered "The Strange Love Life of the Elephant." The German entitled his tract "Are Elephants Aryan—and Can They Be Eaten?" The Russian produced "The Elephant—Does It Exist?" The Pole, whose piece was as long as all the others put together, wrote on "The Elephant and the Polish Question."

★ ★ ★

531

In the Westchester County Court in White Plains, Joseph H. Choate once drew as opponent a local lawyer who tried to sway the jury by advocating that they "disregard the Chesterfieldian urbanity of the distinguished and expensive lawyer from Fifth Avenue." Choate quietly hazarded a guess that "his Chesterfieldian urbanity" might be preferable to his opponent's "Westchesterfieldian suburbanity."

★ ★ ★

When Judge Samuel Leibowitz was a criminal lawyer, his stratagems and wiles made him nationally famous. One that other lawyers like to tell about to this day was in connection with a gent named Romano, who tried to shoot his wife, but plugged a passing policeman instead. He retained Leibowitz. The prosecution produced five witnesses. Romano had none—nothing but a flimsy alibi. He had been working that day in a fish store, he said.

The prosecutor sent for a basket of fish. He held up a halibut. "What is it?" he asked Romano. "A flounder," declared Romano. He then identified a bluefish as a perch, and a sea-bass as a trout. There were twenty fish in the basket; the unhappy Romano guessed wrong twenty times. The prosecutor rubbed his hands gleefully—but then Leibowitz swung into action.

"Fraud," he claimed. "Was there in that array of fish a single pike, a pickerel, or any other fish that can be made into gefüllte fish? There was not. My client told you that he worked in a fish store in the heart of a Jewish neighborhood; the prosecutor very carefully avoided showing him a single fish that would be sold there. What a travesty on justice! My client is an Italian that works in a Jewish fish market, and they try him on Christian fish."

The jury laughed long and loud. They also acquitted Romano.

Leibowitz is credited with telling one jury, "My client talks like an idiot and acts like an idiot. Do not be deceived, gentlemen. He really *is* an idiot."

★ ★ ★

The law firm of Stanchfield and Levy once won an important action for Sir Joseph Duveen, who called to thank Stanchfield and to find out what his bill would be. "You'll have to see Levy on that," Stanchfield told him, and, while Sir Joseph was en route, buzzed Levy on the inter-office system and said, "Duveen's on his way to see you. He's tickled pink. I think he'll stand for twenty-five thousand."

That was the fee that Levy demanded. Sir Joseph never batted an eye. "Pounds?" he asked. "Certainly," said Levy.

★ ★ ★

Martin Littleton, the attorney, was the second of two scheduled speakers at a barristers' banquet not so long ago. The first guest orated at such length that everybody was ready to go home by the time Littleton, justifiably enraged, got the floor. "I'll confine my remarks to a single story," he declared. "One day when I was a boy, my father was throwing whole carrots to his hogs by the barrelful. A neighbor criticized this procedure. 'Don't give 'em whole carrots, you fool,' he said. 'If you'd cut them up and cook them, the hogs could digest them in half the time.' My father's simple retort was, 'What's time to a hog?'"

Mr. Littleton believes that his fellow speaker got the point.

★ ★ ★

Judge Ben Lindsey, of Denver, was another illustrious but long-winded jurist. He was passing sentence on one offender who listened glumly for twenty minutes, and then interrupted, "Say, Judge, is this a sentence or a filibuster?"

At a dinner in his honor, the Judge was not exactly flattered when the toastmaster recalled a famous jibe of Henry Clay. A long-winded chest-thumper cried, "I speak not only for today, but for posterity." "But it is unnecessary," called out Clay, "to talk until the arrival of your audience."

★ ★ ★

Morris Ernst has resurrected the story of an attorney who journeyed to California to try an important case, promising to wire his partner the moment a decision was announced. At long last the wire came and it read, "Justice has triumphed." The partner in New York wired back, "Appeal at once."

★ ★ ★

Oscar Levant tells about the minister in New York who phoned a minister in California. "Is this a station-to-station call?" queried the operator. "No," replied the reverend. "It's parson-to-parson."

IN THE MIDST OF LIFE . . .

I have carefully cultivated the friendship of an undertaker in my neighborhood who combines a rare skill and tact in his trade with an objective and documented appreciation of its occasional unexpectedly humorous ramifications. This gentleman preserves in his back office an intriguing file of his fraternity's trade papers, *The Embalmer's Monthly* and *The Mortician's Digest*, and a scrap-book into which he has pasted countless witticisms relevant to burial ceremonials. He surely may be forgiven for trying to find an occasional ray of sunshine in a profession so generally steeped in sorrow and unhappiness! On the door of his retreat is tacked a poster I had made for him two Christmases ago: "Fun in an Undertaking Parlor."

My friend has been embalming in a professional way for twenty-five years. "My ideals got a jolt right after I started," he told me. "There was a hot fight going on in Congress and the newspapers as to whether or not the American soldiers who had been killed in France in 1917 and 1918 were to be brought back to the States. I found out that an undertakers' association was helping to finance the drive to bring back the bodies. Then I discovered that the cash for the other side was coming from a French wine-growers' group who wanted the bereaved parents to visit France. Just went to show me things aren't always what they appear on the surface."

One of the big funerals he was in on was that of Tex Rickard, the fabulous sports promoter. The body was put on public view at Madison Square Garden, and thousands shuffled by to look at it. Paul Gallico quotes one sports writer as saying, "Boy, I'll bet they've got him lashed down so he can't spin. Would he be revolving in that box if he saw this mob all coming in here on the cuff!"

My friend's favorite story concerns an elderly soul named Pincus who decided it was time to buy himself a coffin, and broached the point to his fellow lodge-member Nussbaum. "For a pal like you," conceded Nussbaum, "here is my best mahogany number, with sterling silver handles, lined in genuine satin, for three hundred dollars." Pincus retired for meditation, returned a half-hour later with fire in his eyes. "Hah, a fine pal!" he cried. "A stranger, Shlepkind, down the street, who don't know me from Adam, you understand, offers me the same number, with the same mahogany, silver handles, and satin lining, for fifty dollars less." "All right, all right," roared Nussbaum, "you buy your coffin from Shlepkind. But I tell you right now that, six months

after they bury you, your behind will be sticking out through the bottom."

Another story in the scrap-book enlarges on the sorrow of the laborer Pietro as the body of his young wife was lowered into the ground. In the carriage on the way back from the cemetery, his friend tried to console him. "Sure, it's-a tough, Pietro; Rosa she was a fine girl. But pretty soon another pretty girl she come along and in six-a month, maybe, you get married again." "Six-a month!" wailed Pietro. "What I gonna do tonight?"

One that I had heard before told of the German who wandered down the bomb-scarred Unter den Linden eagerly scanning the front pages of every newspaper on sale at the various kiosks. "What are you looking for?" he was asked. "The death notices." "But the death notices aren't carried on Page One." "The death notice I'm looking for," said the German confidently, "will be on Page One all right!"

My friend swears that he is the hero of the story of the four chance acquaintances who launched a bridge game on a midsummer run of the Empire State Limited. They ordered frequent rounds of drinks, but finally the steward reported that the ice had run out. "I think I know where I can get some," volunteered my friend, and supplied the party until the train was well past Schenectady. "I'm afraid this is the last pitcherful," he said then. "If I take one more cube of ice, the body won't keep till Buffalo."

Death affects people in varying ways. Some are resigned, others hysterical. Most stoical on record is old Lord Higginbottom, who was reading the London *Times* in his club when a friend remarked, "Understand you buried your wife this morning." "Had to, old chap," drawled Lord H., without looking up. "She was dead, y'know."

There are nasty little rats who have devised all sorts of petty rackets designed to take advantage of people whose sensibilities and perceptions have been dulled temporarily by sorrow. One such operated an umbrella shop in Oxford Street, London. He would con each morning's obituary notices with an eagle eye, and promptly send the estate a bill for an expensive umbrella. He was always prepared to swear that the deceased had purchased it, but ninety-nine times out of a hundred, even that wasn't necessary; the executors paid small bills of this sort automatically. This particular buzzard was caught red-handed when he sent a bill to the estate of a man who had been a helpless paralytic, strapped to a bed, for fifteen years.

My friend has a great collection of epitaphs saved up. I liked the one Ben Franklin suggested for his own tombstone:

The Body of
B. Franklin, Printer,
(Like the Cover of an old Book,
Its Contents torn out,
And Stript of its Lettering and Gilding)
Lies here, Food for Worms.
But the Work shall not be lost;
For it will (as he believ'd) appear once more,
In a new and more elegant Edition
Revised and corrected
By the Author.

Here are a few epitaphs dreamed up by celebrities whose whistlings in the dark aren't fooling anybody:

LIONEL BARRYMORE: "Well, I've played everything but a harp."

NUNNALLY JOHNSON: "I thought there was a funny taste about that last one."

W. C. FIELDS: "On the whole, I'd rather be in Philadelphia."

LEWIS STONE: "A gentleman farmer goes back to the soil."

PAUL WHITEMAN: "Gone to look for the lost chord."

WALLACE FORD: "At last I get top billing."

CONSTANCE BENNETT: "Do not disturb."

EDDIE CANTOR: "Here in nature's arms I nestle,
Free at last from Georgie Jessel."

FONTAINE FOX: "I had a hunch something like this would happen."

H. G. WELLS: "I told you so, dammit!"

DEEMS TAYLOR: "Here lies Deems Taylor—under protest."

WARNER BAXTER: "Did you hear about my operation?"

HORACE BROWN (dentist): "Stranger, approach these bones with gravity;

Doc Brown is filling his last cavity."

WILLIAM HAINES: "Here's something I want to get off my chest."

EDWARD EVERETT HORTON: "A nice part—only 'four sides'—but good company and in for a long run."

My undertaker friend has framed on his walls a reproduction of what, with good reason, he considers the most modest and significant epitaph a famous man ever composed for himself. Thomas Jefferson died on July 4, 1826—on the fiftieth anniversary of the Declaration of Independence. For his tomb he chose this inscription:

"Here was buried Thomas Jefferson, author of the Declaration of American Independence, of the statutes of Virginia for religious freedom, and father of the University of Virginia."

538

Chapter Six

FUNNY BUSINESS

A tale that may take a few of our high-powered traveling salesmen down a peg concerns the visit of a man in quest of a bottle of catsup to Finkelstein's Grocery Store. The shelves of the entire store were solidly lined with bags of salt—hundreds upon hundreds of them. Mr. Finkelstein allowed as how he had a stock of catsup, but had to go down to the cellar to fetch a bottle. The customer went with him, and there, to his surprise, found another huge stock of salt stacked on all sides. "Say," commented the customer, "you certainly must sell a lot of salt in this store!" "Nah," said Mr. Finkelstein with resignation. "I can't sell no salt at all. But the feller who sells *me* salt! Can *he* sell salt!"

★ ★ ★

The late Arthur Kudner, advertising tycoon, had a single framed quotation hanging in his office. It was made by the 1936 world's champion hog caller: "You've got to have appeal as well as power in your voice. You've got to convince the hogs you have something for them."

★ ★ ★

539

In a little shop down on 14th Street, New York, an ingenious chap named Irving Klaw has built up a substantial business in movie stills. He has thousands of them in stock, dating way back to the days of Theda Bara and Valentino, but the bulk of his sales is concentrated, of course, on the pin-up girls who make with the legs and terrific torsos.

"Ann Sheridan," reports this authority, "in her clothes is just another actress. Put her in a bathing suit and I can't keep her in stock. Dorothy Lamour in a sarong is dynamite, but in her clothes she's a dead duck. You may be surprised, but the face is not very important in a pin-up picture."

Klaw gets most of his stock direct from the picture companies, who consider his sales good publicity. He sells them for ten cents each and up. A Rita Hayworth or Betty Grable in unmentionables is like two seats down front for *Oklahoma!*

★ ★ ★

Lewis Miller is the sales manager today of a sizable enterprise. In his salad days he covered New York State in a Model-T Ford and made his daily collections from customers en route. He was heading for home one evening with seven hundred dollars in his jeans when, just outside of Ossining, a man in shabby, ill-fitting clothes beckoned for a hitch. Miller stopped for him, and soon learned that his companion had just completed a ten-year stretch at Sing Sing for robbery. Suddenly he remembered the seven hundred dollars in cash in his pocket.

With what he considered a master-stroke of ingenuity, he pushed the accelerator all the way to the floor. The old Ford could still do sixty. A motorcycle cop could not be far behind; Miller would have police escort to the nearest station house.

The motorcycle cop arrived on schedule, bawled the daylights out of him, and wrote a ticket calling for his appearance in court the following Monday! In vain, Miller pleaded to be arrested on the spot. His passenger pulled his cap over his eyes and said nothing. Reluctantly, Miller started his car again. As they approached the darkest Bronx, he had already written off the seven hundred dollars in his mind.

Suddenly the passenger announced, "This is it, brother." Miller stopped the car. His moment had come. The man in shabby clothes stuck out his hand. There was no gun in it!

"Thanks for the lift," he said. "You've been very good to me. This is the least I could do for you."

He handed Miller the motorcycle cop's black leather summons book.

★ ★ ★

The village idiot bought a book describing inexpensive fabricated houses and became so fascinated with the subject that he drew his last penny out of the bank and ordered a house by mail. Some weeks later he wrote a bitter note of protest to the manufacturer: his house was a complete failure. An inspector came to investigate, and roared, "You loony, you've put up the whole thing upside down!" "Oh, that's the trouble, is it?" pondered the befuddled customer. "No wonder I kept falling off the porch!"

★ ★ ★

There is one night club in New York that has made a fortune out of insulting its patrons. It is called the Club Eighteen, and one Jack White guided its destinies until he died in 1942. Since then a group of underlings, well trained in his ego-demolishing methods, has carried on. Across the street from the unostentatious, badly ventilated, but always jammed Club Eighteen is the exclusive "21," dining spot of Hollywood celebrities and socialites."We send them our overflow," explains the maestro of Club Eighteen, with a lordly flick of his cigar ashes.

One of the club's champion insulters spotted J. Edgar Hoover at a ringside table. He was asked to take a bow, and then introduced, successively, as "a former President of the United States," "a bum who invented the vacuum cleaner," and "a flatfoot from an outlying Flatbush precinct." Mr. Hoover took it all with high good nature. It is a tribute to the exquisite skill of the hecklers that only one victim out of twenty stalks out of the place in a dudgeon. One patron who couldn't take it was a moneyed race-horse owner who resented being spotlighted while a master of ceremonies shouted, "Hey, you bum, that horse you gave me in the second race at Hialeah yesterday—there's a reward out for him!"

A standard act at the Club Eighteen is an actor who is bathed in a sickly green spotlight and begins reciting Longfellow's "I shot an arrow into the air. It fell to earth I know not where." Suddenly he stops and ruminates sadly. "I lost more damn arrows!"

If you are interested in more details of this fantastic club, and can't stay up late enough nights to inspect it yourself, I refer you to Maurice Zolotow's piece about it in his lively *Never Whistle in a Dressing Room*. A famous star summed up his experience at the club: "After I had ordered some food, they heckled me until in self-defense I had to take the floor. I went there to be entertained and ended up entertaining myself. When I returned to my table one of the actors had eaten my sandwich and the waiter had finished my drink."

★ ★ ★

There is a humorist in charge of the Complaint Department of one of New York's biggest dry-goods emporiums. Tacked to his door is a sign that reads "Come in and grouse." A lady took him at his word a few weeks ago. It appears that some months before she had buried her beloved spouse and bought several packets of carnation seeds with which to decorate the grave. Then she went off to Mexico to pull herself together. Several months later, all hell broke loose in the Complaint Department. It seems that when the lady came home and visited the cemetery she found her husband's grave completely covered with rhubarb. "I don't know what she was screaming about," said the Complaint Manager. "We were perfectly willing to refund her the price of the seeds."

★ ★ ★

This "pearl necklace" story has been told at one time or another about every big department store in the country, although most narrators insist angrily that it happened "to their own cousin."

A lady and her daughter are sauntering down Fifth Avenue. In front of Tiffany's the young girl's "pearl necklace" breaks, and the pearls roll all over the street. She reclaims them, and suggests giving them to Tiffany's for stringing.

"We can't ask Tiffany's to restring things like that," protests the mother. "After all, the whole necklace cost only $12.98 at Blank's." Anyhow, they enter Tiffany's. The man at the repair desk takes one look at the loose pearls, asks to be excused for a moment, and returns with the general manager, who offers the startled lady fifty thousand dollars for the lot.

The explanation? The president of Blank's has smuggled in the strand of pearls for his wife by hiding them with a shipment of cheap imitations addressed to the store's bargain jewelry department. The special marking on the real pearls has been lost, and the strand mixed up with all the others. The honest lady brings them back to Blank's just in time to clear the saleswoman, who has been accused by the president of stealing the pearls for her own purposes.

Of course, a story like this *could* have happened in real life. Reasonable odds against it: 4000 to 1.

★ ★ ★

Most jewel thieves and smugglers are apprehended sooner or later, but one clever fraud has gotten away scot-free. He came into a famous New York jewelry shop and said he was looking for a special pearl for his wife's birthday. The price made no difference, he declared; he was a Texas oil millionaire, and had credentials to prove it. He finally picked out a beautiful pearl and paid $5,000 cash for it.

A few weeks later he was back. His wife was crazy about the pearl; wanted to match it for a pair of earrings. The manager of the store said he doubted whether a duplicate could be found.

"Advertise," suggested the customer. "I'll pay up to $25,000 for a duplicate of that pearl." It developed that a lady in Chicago had just such a pearl, which she was willing to sell for $20,000. The store bought it from her—but is still waiting for the "Texas millionaire" to claim it. What he had done, of course, was to sell back the store's own pearl for four times the purchase price. Even if they find him, they'll have a hard time convicting him of any crime.

★ ★ ★

A Georgetown fortune-teller gazed into his crystal ball and told his young lady client that something very amusing was about to happen to her. Then he burst into uproarious laughter. The young lady rose and smacked his face. "Why did you do that?" asked the astounded clairvoyant. "My mother," she said firmly, "always told me to strike a happy medium!"

★ ★ ★

William Faulkner tells about the time that a little Mississippi bank suddenly found itself insolvent. A Negro depositor was just about to withdraw some cash when the frightened teller got the bad news and gulped, "I am sorry, we won't be able to give you the money you want. Our bank has gone broke."

The Negro was a philosopher. "I'se heard of lots of banks failing," he lamented, "but dis am de fust time one has gone bust right in my face."

★ ★ ★

George Perry tells of the Texas lady who aimed to sell her old plow. "What you plannin' to ask for it, Miss Edna?" asked a neighbor. "Oh, I reckon 'bout thirty or forty dollars," said Miss Edna. "But you can git a new one out of the mail-order catalogue for eight-fifty," the neighbor protested. "I'm tired of this hagglin' over pennies," decided Miss Edna. "Gimme a dollar an' take the plow!"

★ ★ ★

There was a Dr. Munyon many years ago who sold a powerful lot of patent medicine by direct mail. His slogan was "There Is Hope." His ads always carried an impressive photograph of himself, revealing a senatorial phiz with a huge mop of snow-white hair.

"How much do you spend every year in advertising?" asked a visitor. "About a quarter of a million," said Dr. Munyon. "If I show you how to save fifty thousand of it," proposed the visitor, "without losing a sale, will you give me five thousand for myself?" "I will," said Munyon. "Get a haircut," said the visitor.

★ ★ ★

John Wanamaker told of meeting a boyhood friend who had experienced nothing but hard luck in his career. He had been locked out of his meagre hotel room, and he was half starved. Deeply moved, Mr. Wanamaker fed him in his own restaurant, and urged him to order every delicacy on the menu. Then he handed him enough to pay his hotel bill, and ordered him to report for a good job the next morning.

The man never came. The hotel clerk, to whom the jubilant fellow had related the whole incident, called Mr. Wanamaker about noon. The man had died during the night—of acute indigestion.

★ ★ ★

There was a total eclipse of the sun in 1932, and a newsreel company sent two expeditions to South America to get authentic pictures of it. Bad weather prevented their getting any shots worth exhibiting. The company had to have a picture, however, and put the problem to its technical expert. "I'll manufacture a picture of an eclipse for you right in my laboratory," he promised, and he was as good as his word. There was one flaw. When the picture was run off, the word "Mazda" appeared on the face of the sun.

★ ★ ★

545

In front of an East Side delicatessen, a well-known art connoisseur noticed a mangy little kitten, lapping up milk from a saucer. The saucer, he realized with a start, was a rare and precious piece of pottery.

He sauntered into the store and offered two dollars for the cat. "It's not for sale," said the proprietor. "Look," said the collector, "that cat is dirty and undesirable, but I'm eccentric. I like cats that way. I'll raise my offer to five dollars." "It's a deal," said the proprietor, and pocketed the five-spot. "For that sum I'm sure you won't mind throwing in the saucer," said the connoisseur. "The kitten seems so happy drinking from it." "Nothing doing," said the proprietor firmly. "That's my lucky saucer. From that saucer, so far this week, I've sold thirty-four cats."

★ ★ ★

Major Corey Ford brought back from Iceland the story of the salesman who ran from igloo to igloo trying to sell electric fans. "Fan?" each resident would exclaim in amazement. "What do we want with a fan? It is 60 below zero here now." "Sure, I know," soothed the salesman. "But you never can tell. Tomorrow it may jump to zero."

★ ★ ★

A school that taught playwriting by mail received a script from a student whose opening curtain rose on a little old French lady knitting in her chair. Her husband entered, visibly fatigued, and placed his black instrument bag on the table. "Oh, Pierre," said the lady, "you have been away all night. Was it a difficult accouchement?" "Yes," answered the weary doctor. "But it was worth it. History was made last night. The baby's name was— Victor Hugo." The author wasn't able to keep up that pace for long.

Another script began with these lines: "Time of Act One: 7000 years ago. Act Two: One day later."

★ ★ ★

Joe Brooks delivered a check from his insurance company to the widow of a deceased client. She was apparently inconsolable, and had been weeping three days without stopping. A glance at the amount of the check—it was for fifty thousand dollars— stilled her tears. "You may not believe it," she told Brooks soulfully, "but I'd give twenty thousand of this to have him back."

★ ★ ★

On a recent radio program, Fred Allen introduced one character as his "molehill man." "Every morning," he vouchsafed by way of explanation, "this fellow arrives at his office and finds a molehill on his desk. It's his job to make a mountain of it before 5 P.M. comes around."

Allen says his next sponsor will be the manufacturer of Lumpo Soap: "It doesn't lather. It doesn't float. It contains no secret oils. It is designed solely to keep you company in the tub."

★ ★ ★

A traveler for a big publishing house couldn't wait to get to St. Louis, where his oldest friend owned a prosperous bookstore. "Sam," he said to the owner the moment they were alone, "I want you to lend me $2000." "The answer, Joe," said Sam, "is positively no." "But, Sam," protested the salesman, "in 1929, when Bond and Share broke from 189 to 50, who gave you ten thousand dollars to keep you from being wiped out?" "You did," admitted Sam. "And in 1931, when your daughter Shirley had that tropical disease, who took her down to Florida because you couldn't get away from business? Who did, Sam?" "You, my friend, you did." "And in 1933, when we were fishing together, who dove into the rapids and saved you from drowning at the risk of his own life?" "You did, Joe. It was wonderful!" "Well, then, Sam, in Heaven's name, why won't you lend me $2000 now when I need it?" "All the things you say are true," said Sam, nodding his head slowly. "But what have you done for me lately?"

Chapter Seven

POWERS OF THE PRESS

The phenomenon of present-day journalism is the vogue of columnists. Political pontificaters, military analysts, Washington insiders, keyhole experts, Hollywood Boswells, and night-club rounders with sharp ears are syndicated in hundreds of papers all over the land. News space may be cut and pages of advertising omitted, but let an editor omit one signed column and the readers' wrath descends upon him forthwith. "Harriet Beecher Stowe," Charles Fisher points out, "reached a meager million of her contemporaries with *Uncle Tom's Cabin*; Winchell reaches ten million of his with a note upon Miss Rogers' nightwear. Forty thousand pre-Victorians awaited the latter numbers of *Pickwick Papers*; seven million moderns wait for 'The Washington Merry-Go-Round' each day. The columnist is the autocrat of the most prodigious breakfast table ever known. He is the voice beside the cracker-barrel amplified to trans-continental dimensions. He is the only non-political figure of record who can clear his throat each day and say, 'Now, here's what I think' with the assurance that millions will listen."

One of the pioneers and by all odds the most influential of

the columnists in the land, of course, is Walter Winchell. Future histories of American journalism will have to devote an entire chapter to this amazing man. Starting as a straight gossip columnist, he developed into a force whose opinions on national affairs and characters carry incredible weight. Important enemies of the United States landed behind bars because Walter Winchell put them there. H. L. Mencken credits Winchell with adding all of these now more-or-less familiar expressions to the American language: making whoopee; shafts (for legs); veddy (for very); welded, sealed, merged, and middle-aisled for married; on the verge, phffft, and curdled for blasted romance; that way (about someone); infanticipating; debutramp; moompitcher; Park Rowgue (for newspaperman); and The Hardened Artery (for Broadway).

Early in Winchell's columning career, when he was employed by Bernarr MacFadden's puerile and short-lived tabloid, *The Graphic*, he printed a story about the Brothers Shubert which incensed them. The producers, said Winchell, summoned the manager of one of their most dismal failures and demanded, "Why did we ever buy that lousy play?" The manager said it just hadn't worked out. The playwright was not to blame. Every business had occasional flops. Look at the Sesquicentennial Exhibition in Philadelphia; there was a real flop! "Did he write that too?" groaned Shubert.

The producers promptly barred Winchell from all their theatres. It was a spectacular feud. "I can't go to their openings, eh?" said Winchell. "Okay. I'll wait three days and go to the closings." The Marx Brothers disguised him in false whiskers, dark glasses, and a putty nose one night and introduced him to Lee Shubert backstage as their long-lost uncle. The Shuberts finally gave up the battle. They couldn't take it any more.

★ ★ ★

There is a daily columnist in Hollywood who just dotes on printing long lists of notables seen at important picture premieres. She missed the opening of *Going My Way*, but a supposed friend volunteered to supply her with a list of big shots in the audience. She printed his story unedited. It began with a bang. "Among those present," it read, "were Miss Lizzie Borden, Mr. Marcus Aurelius, Mr. Ethan Frome . . ." Most readers got no farther.

★ ★ ★

A newspaper in Georgia awards an annual prize to the champion liar of the year, although we understand that ex-governors are barred. This year's winner averred that "Georgia soil is so rich that when they throw corn to the chickens, they have to catch it on the fly or eat it off the stalk." Nunnally Johnson, the smartest producer on the Twentieth Century-Fox lot, if not in all Hollywood, is a Georgia product. So is Erskine Caldwell. One evening an indignant Atlantan confronted Johnson. "I ask you to bear me out, suh, that our fair state of Geo'gia has never known perverts and morons like the characters in those libelous abominations, *Tobacco Road* and *God's Little Acre!*" "Why, in the part of the state I come from," answered Nunnally softly, "we regard the people Mr. Caldwell writes about as the country-club set."

★ ★ ★

Screwball journalism of the type portrayed so hilariously in the Hecht-MacArthur play *The Front Page*, and more recently in Robert J. Casey's *Such Interesting People*, is a thing of the past. Rip-snorting reporters whose motors ran strictly on alcohol, who were as likely to wind up in the local hoosegow as the city desk, but who brought in the scoops that sent circulations soaring, went out with Prohibition and Babe Ruth. They have been replaced by "boiler plates" and syndicates, and less colorful but infinitely more efficient wire services that supply hundreds of papers at a time with last-minute news, impersonal, impartial, and prosaic.

Journalism was a rollicking profession in the twenties, however, if you happened to be on the right papers. Casey happened. Most of the time he operated out of Chicago, where feature reporters, influential lawyers, and gun-toting hijackers seemed to be somewhat interchangeable. The title of his colorful collection of yarns stems from the time-honored observation of the yokels who meet gentlemen of the press: "Gee, it must be wonderful to be a journalist. You meet such interesting people!" Winchell once answered, "You certainly do, and every one of them is in the newspaper business."

Casey went to bat with lots of outsiders, however, not all of whom were rank. There was a queer customer in Cairo, for instance, named Captain Eddy, who talked in telephone numbers, and was listed as a phony. One day he remarked in passing that he had three of the world's greatest pearls in his possession, and was looking for more. Eager to show up the Captain at last, Casey's companion summoned the greatest pearl expert in Egypt. Captain Eddy nonchalantly tossed his three pearls on the table. The expert studied them a moment, looked at the rumpled and unshaven Captain in amazement, and said in slow, careful English: "If you would sell them, I shall give you fifty thousand pounds for them. . . . They are worth more but that is all I can afford." "No, siree," said the Captain. "I'm saving those pearls for my daughter." He stuffed them back in his pocket, and shuffled off into the night.

Casey was there or thereabouts when the episode occurred that may explain Charles Lindbergh's consuming and unrelenting hatred of the press. You may remember the time when a man named Floyd Collins got trapped by a rock in a Kentucky cave. Miners drove a shaft to the cavern where he was pinned down. They worked frantically night and day while the whole country watched breathlessly to see whether or not they would reach him in time. As a matter of fact, they did not, but that isn't the point of this story. One Chicago paper, Mr. Hearst's *Examiner*, decided to put one over on its competitors by flying pictures by plane from the shaft head to the main office. Lindbergh, as you have probably guessed, was the pilot. He was a raw-boned and inexperienced kid. When he arrived on the scene of action, he had the misfortune to encounter a Mr. Steeger of the rival *Chicago Tribune.* "Ah, yes," said Steeger, "Lindbergh of the *Examiner!* Where have you been all this time? I've been waiting for you! Get these plates back to Chicago just as fast as you can make it." Lindbergh flew back to the *Examiner* office post-haste and duly delivered a box of blank, unexposed plates. Casey probably isn't exaggerating when he suggests that the smile with which young Mr. Lindbergh favored Mr. Steeger of the *Tribune* was the last he ever gave to anybody connected with a newspaper in any capacity whatever. Lindbergh got partial revenge some years later when, at a national air meet in Cleveland, he whizzed his plane so close to a group of camera men that they dove in panic into a huge mud puddle at the edge of the field to get out of his way.

* * *

"Newsmen are simple boys at heart"

Newsmen, swears Casey, are simple boys at heart. They treasure clippings with typographical errors for months, particularly when the result verges on the pornographic. They play infantile tricks on one another. They wake up outraged strangers by 4

A.M. phone calls. In Chicago they found an unfortunate innocent named "Upjohn" in the directory, and called him in relays
all night long to inquire sweetly, "Are you Upjohn?" A Boston
group found a Paul Revere in the book, and yanked him from
bed with a phone call to demand, "Why aren't you on a horse?
The British are coming!" I myself know of a sophisticated group
spearheaded by no less a personage than Harold Ross, editor of
The New Yorker, who spent a deliriously happy afternoon calling Long Island society matrons, and saying that they spoke for
a nationally-known yeast manufacturer. They offered five thousand dollars for a signed testimonial, and further played on their
victim's vanity by adding: "Of course, you won't keep this
vulgar money yourself. We will leave it to you to pass it on to
your favorite charity." The matron would coo with pleasure and
then the tormentor plunged in the harpoon. "We simply want
you to say," he would murmur into the mouthpiece, " 'A year
ago, before I discovered Blank's yeast, my face was an unholy
mess of pimples and unseemly blotches.' " . . . There usually
was a violent click at the other end of the wire at this point.

★ ★ ★

In Fort Smith, Arkansas, the mayor's wife died and the old
icehouse burned on the same day. The local gazette printed a
two-column portrait of the deceased lady on page one with a
caption that made the issue a rare collector's item: "Old Eyesore
Gone at Last!" The *Chicago Journal* got a society column and
a shipping report all mixed up in the press room with the following results: "Mrs. So-and-So of the Chicago Beach Hotel has
had a pleasant summer visiting friends in Bar Harbor and Ken-
nebunk. After encountering heavy weather off the Virginia
Cape, she put into Hampton Roads to have her bottom scraped."
A novice on the *American* once asked Casey, "How do you spell
pinochle?" Casey told him. The next day his story appeared in
print. "Adolph Klepperman," it began, "has reached the pinochle
of success."

★ ★ ★

Casey's prize story of transposed headlines concerns the *New York Herald Tribune,* which ran big stories one day on an address by Mr. Hamilton Fish and a new formula for feeding tropical fish, issued by the Aquarium. It was George Dixon, on the night shift of the rival *Mirror,* who discovered that the headlines for the two stories had been mixed in the shuffle. He called the *Tribune* and announced himself as Mr. Fish. The managing editor himself came to the phone. "We know why you are calling, Mr. Fish," he said hurriedly. "It was a dreadful mistake." Then he launched into an elaborate explanation of how things like that sometimes could happen in the best-regulated newspaper offices. Dixon was extremely gracious, and accepted the apology.

At midnight Dixon was relieved by another bright young man named Dolan who also called up the *Tribune.* A brand-new voice, equally suave and apologetic, had gotten halfway through the same involved explanation, when the managing editor got back on the wire. "Mr. Fish," he asked, "didn't you call us about this mistake barely an hour ago?" "Oh, no," said Dolan haughtily. "That must have been Mr. Hamilton Fish. This is Mr. *Tropical* Fish."

Of particular interest to booklovers is the story of the time when a prominent denizen of the Chicago underworld, Big Tim Murphy, just back from a stretch at Leavenworth, decided that Bob Casey was just the man to ghost-write his autobiography. Big Tim had his own notions about publishing procedure. "We got to be reasonable about the price of this book," he said. "Ten bucks a bite is too much. Five is enough." Casey explained that the normal price for such a tome was two dollars, of which Tim would pull down ten percent in royalties. "Nix," decided Tim. "We'll take the five bucks and give the publisher ten percent. Don't forget there's five thousand garbage-haulers alone in my control and every one of them guys is going to buy my book or else! Then there's the electricians and gas-meter readers and street sweepers. I'll just go to their meetings and tell them where to kick in with their five bucks. The trouble with you long-haired fellows, you don't pay enough attention to the business side of book writing. Me, I see both sides. . . ." For all we know, Big Tim Murphy might have revolutionized the entire publishing industry in America. Unfortunately, he suddenly became involved in the opening of a new gambling house, and abruptly lost all interest in the pursuit of literature.

I have picked out only a few of Robert Casey's salty anecdotes to retell here. For an all-around picture of high-powered newspaper publishing in the days when rugged individualism still ran riot, you'll go a long way before you find anything better than *Such Interesting People*.

★ ★ ★

When "Bugs" Baer, ace humorist of the King Feature Syndicate, first landed a good job, his friend, Ward Greene, suggested that he acquire new raiment to match the job. "What's the difference?" said Baer. "Nobody knows me." Fifteen years later Greene caught him wearing the same old rags. "What's the difference?" repeated Bugs. "*Everybody* knows me!"

★ ★ ★

Charles Michelson, long-time press agent of the Democratic Party, remembers a "roly-poly little Englishman" who acted as war correspondent in Havana in 1898. "He invited his fellow reporters up to his room for a session of poker," recalls Michelson. "As the cards were being dealt, he ordered a bottle of champagne—and one glass. His American guests blinked, but conformed, and so they sat through the evening, every man with his own bottle and glass!" The English correspondent's name was Winston Churchill.

★ ★ ★

In the golden days when Victor Lawson was the proprietor of the *Chicago Daily News*, the staff at one time included such notables as Carl Sandburg, Ben Hecht, Vincent Sheean, Rube

Goldberg, and the inimitable Con Rourke. Rourke volunteered to represent the paper at the funeral of an obscure copy-reader. He had no relatives or church connections, and an amateur preacher from another paper was conscripted to conduct the services at the graveside. Unfortunately, it was raining cats and dogs, and in the middle of the ceremony the "preacher" slipped and shot under the coffin into the grave. "It was quite confusing," reported Rourke. "Half the mourners didn't see where this guy had gone and the other half were in favor of burying him with the corpse."

★ ★ ★

There was one Chicago reporter named Buddy McHugh who believed it was highly unnecessary to cover an assignment in person if he could get the information over the telephone. He didn't care who he had to say he was to get the party on the other end to divulge the wanted facts. One day he called the residence of a freshly slaughtered gangster and said, "This is Chuck Reynolds of the coroner's office." "That's funny," said the voice at the other end of the wire. "So's this." McHugh was a character in Hecht and MacArthur's hilarious *The Front Page*. He's the one who called up a lady and inquired gently, "Is it true, Madam, that you were the victim of a Peeping Tom?"

Another of the many episodes in *The Front Page* that was drawn directly from life depicted the reporters of one paper trying to hide an escaped murderer long enough to score a complete scoop in the following morning's paper. The authors did exactly that when they were feature writers on the old *American*. In the play, the shivering unfortunate begs piteously for air; the managing editor lifts the top a fraction of an inch, pushes in some ozone with the palm of his hand, and assures him that he's "sitting pretty"!

★ ★ ★

A London newspaper asked a noted British novelist and an equally distinguished American poet to record their choices of the ten most beautiful words in the English language.

The British selection was: carnation, azure, peril, moon, forlorn, heart, silence, shadow, April, and apricot.

The American choice was: dawn, hush, lullaby, murmuring, tranquil, mist, luminous, chimes, golden, and melody.

★ ★ ★

When Arthur Brisbane was about to complete fifty years of journalism, Mr. Hearst, his employer, urged him to take a six-months vacation with full pay. This magnanimous offer Brisbane refused to accept, saying there were two reasons for his doing so.

"The first reason," he said, "is that if I quit writing my column for six months it might affect the circulation of your newspapers. The second reason is that it might not affect the circulation."

On several occasions, Editor Brisbane was heard telling Windsor McKay, "You're the second greatest cartoonist in the world." Harry Hershfield asked him, "Who's the first?" "I don't know," said Brisbane. "But this keeps McKay on his toes."

★ ★ ★

Before Ralph Ingersoll won a commission in the Army and wrote his thrilling *The Battle Is the Payoff*, he was editor of the newspaper *PM*. Before that he toiled briefly for Harold Ross, the unpredictable editor of *The New Yorker*. He bearded the lion in his private den one day and talked himself into an assistant editorship, although some of his elation vanished when, after he had agreed on terms and walked happily to the elevator, he heard Ross screaming, "Damn it all, I seem to hire any nut that sticks his face in here."

The advance campaign for *PM* was so brilliant and high-powered that the appearance of the actual paper was bound to be a terrific anticlimax. Everything seemed to go wrong with it at the same time. The original capital disappeared in a few short months. The circulation dropped below 90,000. A disgruntled stockholder who couldn't even get in to tell the harassed editor what he thought should be done to improve the situation was

558

heard to exclaim, "The trouble with Ingersoll is that his failure
has gone to his head."

Ingersoll hadn't failed, however. He persuaded Marshall Field
to supply fresh capital and suddenly *PM* began to click.

WHERE THERE'S LIFE
THERE'S SWOPE

Sir Willmott Lewis, American emissary of the London *Times*,
recalls that when he first was ordered to this country, his editor
warned him, "You will hear two terrific noises when you get
there, but do not be frightened by either of them. They won't
hurt you. One is Niagara Falls. The other is Herbert Bayard
Swope." "A plausible fellow," is Swope's rejoinder—"but un-
sound."

Swope, an overpowering and dynamic personality, is a whole
Information Please board of experts concentrated into one unbelievable storehouse of facts, many of them useless. He is
never less than thirty minutes late for an appointment. He once
was responsible for getting a popular actress to her own husband's funeral an hour after the services had started. His manner of sweeping into a gathering of any kind is nothing less than
regal. "Swoping" was a word once applied rather generally to
confirmed table-hoppers and people who referred to international celebrities by their first names. He has a booming, foghorn sort of voice which frequently can be heard delivering
grandiloquent statements like, "I told Franklin I didn't agree
with him," or "Personally I am very angry at the United States
Navy." But even his severest critics will concede that the Swope
charm is irresistible, and that everybody from presidents to stable boys feels warmed and gratified at a sign of his imperial favor.
If there were more Herbert Bayard Swopes around, this would
be a gayer and more amusing world, although it must be conceded that certain nervous and supersensitive souls might be
quite unable to live in it.

Swope comes from a family whose ancestral seat was the tiny village of Lengsfeld in Germany, in the shadow of the Wartburg, steeped in the tradition of Tannhäuser and Martin Luther. Herbert himself was born in St. Louis in 1882, ten years after his brother Gerard. Both boys did well for themselves. Gerard became president of a little company called General Electric. Herbert rose to national prominence in 1912 by virtue of a sensational murder case. He was a star reporter on Pulitzer's *World*,

Mr. H. B. Swope holds an informal conversation with Winston, Franklin and Joe

and one of the first people to hear that a gambler named Herman Rosenthal had been bumped off outside a Broadway café called the Metropole. Insiders knew that Rosenthal had been scheduled to spill a sordid story of corruption in the police department to the District Attorney the following day. Swope sensed a great melodrama, routed the D. A. out of a sound sleep in a Turkish bath, stuck a pen in his hand, and had him sign an indictment naming Police Lieutenant Becker before he was fully awake. Swope then raced back to the *World* office and splashed a headline across the front page that he borrowed from Émile Zola: "I ACCUSE." The District Attorney's name was Charles Whitman. Before the echoes of the case had died away, he was Governor of the State of New York.

Swope's reporting from behind the German lines in the First World War won him a Pulitzer award. When America entered the fight, he became a Lt. Commander in the Navy. In 1919, he covered the Versailles Peace Conference. His manner and attire had achieved a distinction by this time that made flunkeys rush to open doors for him at sight. Thus he got hold of a copy of the first League of Nations Covenant hours before anybody else— the journalistic scoop of a lifetime. Jealous rivals claim he had Clemenceau running errands for him. He returned home a conquering hero, and was rewarded with the title of executive editor of the *World*, a post that he filled with signal distinction for nine years. He lashed out at social injustices and subversive organizations in campaigns that rocked the entire country. He created a "page opposite editorial" that employed at one time the services of Heywood Broun, Walter Lippmann, Alexander Woollcott, Laurence Stallings, Franklin P. Adams, Frank Sullivan, and Deems Taylor. The Swope salons, held nightly in his 58th Street home, were frequented by every celebrity in town. If a ship news reporter missed a visiting notable at the pier, he knew that his man could be found the same evening at Swope's.

Since 1929, Swope has occupied himself with innumerable directorships in first-line corporations, the chairmanship of the New York Racing Commission, and a position of ex-officio adviser to cabinet ministers and chiefs of staff. Probably the job he likes best is in connection with the racing. He took me out to the Tropical Track in Miami recently (he's chairman of the board) and gave me inside information on every race. Unfortunately it was so far inside that even the horses never heard it.

Swope's favorite outdoor pastime is croquet, which gives him a chance to practise strategy on a complicated scale. In one game his partner, the late Gerald Brooks, had the temerity to make a shot without consulting Swope. "Never do that again," warned Swope. "After this, you do exactly what I tell you, without question, and we'll win in a walk." A few turns later, Brooks' shot grazed another ball fifteen yards away. "Wonderful," exulted Swope. "Knock him into the lake!" Brooks took singular satisfaction in carrying out the order before he pointed out that it was Swope's own ball. Another morning Swope made one of his regal entrances three-quarters of an hour late, with a butler carrying his mallet and towel behind him. One man on the court was a stranger to him. "I'm Herbert Bayard Swope," he said. The stranger shook his outstretched hand gravely, and announced: "I'm Harpo Marx's chauffeur."

His family doctor once sent him to a famous specialist for a check-up, which was interrupted three times by interminable telephone conversations. Swope apologized, and explained that the first one had come from the Mayor, the second from Bernard Baruch, and the third from President Roosevelt. The specialist nodded gravely, phoned the family doctor when he had left, and said, "What did you send that man to me for? What he needs, obviously, is a psychiatrist." His frenzied concern about political, theatrical, and international complications reach their highest pitch at the precise moment he is scheduled to leave for a dinner or a show. He kept five people waiting in a car once for forty minutes. They heard him banging drawers upstairs and creating a terrific hullabaloo. When he finally appeared, he was astounded that the rest of the party was annoyed. "You knew very well," he reminded Mrs. Swope, "that I was counting our bottles of beer."

Herbert Swope's memory for names and faces is uncanny, except for a not-too-endearing habit of telling dinner partners stories that involve intimate details about their mates' previous wives and sweethearts. His own wife, a poker-faced lady full of unexpected kindnesses, is thoroughly conditioned to take almost everything he does as a matter of course, although she has been heard to declare that if she ever were to write a daily column like Mrs. Roosevelt, *hers* would be called "My *Damn* Day." One summer afternoon, a group of men stopped for a drink at his Sands Point estate on their way home from the Belmont track. Swope impulsively asked them all to stay for dinner. Mrs. Swope rang for the cook, and calmly announced, "Mae, there will be thirty-four extra for dinner this evening."

Swope always has time to dash off a line of commendation to any one of his innumerable friends who has accomplished something of note. Practically every book publisher in town has entreated him to cut down his voluminous correspondence and write a book of memoirs. What a story he could tell—although the editor might have to blue-pencil a few of the windier passages and the six-syllable words. One night a Broadway friend and his blue-eyed babe taxied Herbert Swope home from a theatrical party. Swope, as usual, carried the conversational ball. "The era of the economic royalists and predatory robber barons went out with the Hoover administration," he boomed. "I have told Franklin and I have told Wendell—I'm sure you agree with me—that if they ignore the portents and pussy-foot back to the tenets of the McKinley era, I will not be responsible for anything that happens to them." The little lady sitting next to him gazed at him in wide-eyed wonder, and said softly, "Hey, hey, Big Boy!"

★ ★ ★

A fearsome man is Colonel Robert Rutherford McCormick, publisher of the *Chicago Tribune*—especially when somebody dares to disagree with him. The Rhode Island legislature, for instance, passed a bill that displeased him. Out into the *Tribune* lobby strode the Colonel, and snipped one star from the American flag that waved there.

Colonel McCormick wrote a memorable letter to a subscriber

in 1942, in which he claimed credit for introducing the ROTC into the schools, and persuading the Army to take up machine guns, mechanization, and automatic rifles. He also noted that he was the first ground officer ever to go up in the air to observe artillery fire, was first to advocate an alliance with Canada, fought unsuccessfully to fortify Guam, and all but persuaded the Navy not to divide its fleet into a two-ocean affair. He also told the Administration that "airplanes could destroy battleships," "got the Marines out of Shanghai," but couldn't quite "get the Army out of the Philippines." What a man! Carl Sandburg read this extraordinary claim and murmured, "And on the seventh day He rested!"

Colonel McCormick is the man who thinks Rhodes scholars are undercover British agents out to make the citizens of Chicago stand up every time the band plays *God Save the King*.

★ ★ ★

George Antheil, former high priest of modernistic music, when last heard of was conducting a syndicated column of advice to the lovelorn in Hollywood. This is the most incredible transformation since the late Harold Stearns, brilliant young Harvard intellectual of the twenties and author of a highly regarded treatise on American culture, suddenly bobbed up in Paris as "Peter Pickum" with a daily dope sheet on the horse races for the *Paris Tribune*. Antheil was first brought to America by the energetic Donald Friede, then a publishing partner of Horace Liveright and now a successful literary agent on the Coast. The first Antheil concert packed Carnegie Hall and featured a number that was rendered on twenty-six pianos and four airplane motors. When the cacophony of sound was at its highest pitch, somebody whispered into his companion's ear a meek, "Isn't this simply horrible?" A harridan in the row ahead turned angrily and snorted a W. C. Fieldsian "Quiet, please!"

At the very time that Antheil's *Ballet Mécanique* was startling Paris, and Stearns was picking the day's winners at Longchamps for the *Tribune*, Bill Shirer, Elliot Paul, Jay Allen, and

Ed Taylor were fellow reporters on the same fabulous sheet. One day Elliot Paul announced that he was ready to begin work on the Great American Novel, and his confrères volunteered to give up their day off for a period of weeks so that Paul could devote his best efforts to the new book. For months thereafter Elliot only came to the office one day a week. "If this sheet was properly staffed," he grumbled one morning, "I wouldn't have to show up at all." After a long stretch of this routine, Paul, who is a consummate actor, staggered into the *Tribune* office one morning clutching at his heart and stammering that he had left the finished manuscript on a bus on the Boulevard Raspail. To this day nobody knows whether there ever was a manuscript at all; certainly the French police could find no trace of one.

When Stearns saw how gullible the staff was, he suddenly announced that somebody had given him a horse named Étoile Vert, and took frequent collections to help feed and stable him. The whole American colony was primed to back Étoile Vert in his first race and didn't discover until the very morning of the event that there had never been an Étoile Vert. Peter Pickum announced laconically that this horse had died of excitement in his stall the night before.

The staffs of both the *Paris Herald* and *Tribune* during those lush years of the twenties were populated by a score of talented authors who are today our most famous foreign correspondents and creators of some of our greatest best-sellers. Three young men seated at adjoining desks in a comparatively tiny city room were destined to write *Berlin Diary*, *The Strategy of Terror*, and *The Last Time I Saw Paris*. Around the corner was the office of the Paris correspondent of the *Chicago Daily News*. His name was John Gunther. Ernest Hemingway, Scott Fitzgerald, Whit Burnett, and Morley Callahan were on the Left Bank. This was the Paris that Americans remember and now will see again.

★ ★ ★

Clare Boothe Luce, the glamorous playwright and Congresswoman, tells this on herself. She and her important husband,

Henry Luce (*Time, Life,* etc., etc.), were walking through the lobby of a Washington hotel, and overheard somebody comment, "There go Arsenic and Old Luce."

Mr. Luce always looks pretty serious. *Time* co-founder, the late Briton Hadden, once remarked to him in their undergraduate days at Yale, "Look out, Harry. You'll drop the college."

Chapter Eight

MUSIC HATH CHARMS...

GEORGE GERSHWIN (1898–1937)

On an oppressively hot Sunday evening in July 1937, a group of people were gathered in a remodeled Bucks County farmhouse, engaged in various desultory pastimes. A spiritless bridge game was in progress in one corner of the room; a bout of cribbage in another. The host was tinkering aimlessly with the radio dials. Some of the guests were splashing about in the pool outside, although there was no moon, and the night was pitch black. The heat had everybody down. Suddenly the clear voice of a news commentator came over the air: "The man who said he had more tunes in his head than he could put down on paper

568

in a hundred years is dead tonight in Hollywood. George Gershwin passed away today at the age of thirty-eight."

Everybody at that party was a close personal friend of George. Two of them had collaborated with him on his brightest Broadway hits. We had seen him within the month—joshed him on his complaint of recurring headaches (he had been telling us details of his symptoms and disorders for years; nobody took them seriously) and on a front-page report that a little French picture cutie had entrusted him with a gold key to her front door. His unbelievable energy and vitality had astounded us for so long that we sat speechless at the thought that he was dead. Now seven years later, his music is played incessantly, and stories about him spring readily to mind. Because he graduated from Tin Pan Alley, it has taken all these years to convince some critics that George Gershwin was a great composer—one of the greatest we have produced in America. Because his monumental but strangely unobjectionable conceit encouraged his friends to circulate hilarious anecdotes about him, some of them did not realize until he was dead how deeply they liked and admired him. The stories that I have gathered for this piece are set down in loving memory. George laughed at all of them himself.

George Gershwin was born in Brooklyn on September 26, 1898. He was the second of four children. Ira, whose sparkling lyrics were so perfectly attuned to George's music, was the eldest. Another brother, Arthur, followed George. The youngest was their sister Frances, who married the inventor, Leopold Godowsky. The family moved as a unit, a mutual admiration society that was completely unaffected by temporary failure or dizzying success. Mrs. Gershwin was adored by everybody. "You must meet my mother," George would tell anybody who called. "She's the most wonderful mother in the world." On further reflection, he would frequently add, "and so modest about *me*." The father, Morris, was one of those restless souls who embark upon a new business career every year or so; the family was always ready to pull up stakes cheerfully at a moment's notice. George once figured that he lived in twenty-seven different houses before he finished school. Gershwin père was a lovable and loquacious soul whose accent lost none of its rich and indescribable flavor as the family fortunes rose. His son George was the apple of his eye. One day after the boys had hit the jackpot he was driving down Broadway in a roadster they had given him, when a cop flagged him for ignoring a red light. "But you can't do this to me!" he expostulated. "I'm Judge Gershwin's father!" "Oh, Judge Gershwin," said the copper, visibly impressed. "Pardon me for holding you up, sir."

When George was twelve, his mother bought a piano. The idea was for Ira to take lessons, but it didn't take long to discover that George was the one with music in his soul. At the High School of Commerce, he was pianist for the morning assembly exercises. At fifteen, he was a song plugger for the music-publishing house of Jerome Remick. One of his chores took him to Atlantic City, where he pounded out Remick melodies at the local five-and-ten. Down the Boardwalk, Harry Ruby was doing a similar job for a rival outfit. At night the boys would dine together at Child's and dream of writing songs of their own.

His first song was published in 1916. It was called "When You Want 'Em You Can't Get 'Em," and it earned him an advance of five dollars. His next few numbers began to carry lyrics by Arthur Francis. That was brother Ira making his debut as a lyricist, using the first names of his other brother and kid sister as a pseudonym. His first real clicks came in 1919, when he did his first complete score for *La La Lucille* (remember "Nobody But You": "Billie Burke—Alice Joyce—none of them were my choice"?) and wrote a couple of numbers for the opening bill of Broadway's biggest movie palace of its time, the Capitol. One of the numbers was "Swanee," and I've heard it twice on the radio this very week.

Beginning in 1920, George wrote the music for *George White's Scandals* for five consecutive years. A few of the hits of these scores were "Drifting Along with the Tide," "I'll Build a Stairway to Paradise," and "Somebody Loves Me." Most of the lyrics were contributed by Buddy De Sylva, now head man at the Paramount Studios. In those days, White was the great Ziegfeld's only serious rival. Gershwin didn't meet up with Ziegfeld himself until 1929, when he wrote the score of *Show Girl*. Working with Ziegfeld was perfect training for fighting on Guadalcanal, but that's another story. After the contract with Gershwin was signed, Ziegfeld went to Carnegie Hall to hear *An American in Paris*. At the symphonic poem's completion, Otto Kahn rose and made a brief speech in which he declared that George was well-nigh a genius. "In fact," said Kahn, "some day he will be a genius, but geniuses must suffer, and George hasn't suffered yet." Ziegfeld turned to Larry Hart, who was sitting next to him, and said, with a sly wink, "He'll suffer!"

George became internationally famous in 1924, when Paul Whiteman introduced his *Rhapsody in Blue* at a concert in Aeolian Hall. By now the family was located in a private house on West 103rd Street, where George worked imperturbably amidst a hubbub that suggested Grand Central Station on the eve of a Fourth of July week-end. The *Rhapsody* was written there in exactly three weeks; George had to meet a deadline! That year saw, too, the first of seven musical comedies produced by Aarons and Freedley, with music by George and lyrics by Ira. Five of them made Broadway history. They were, in order, *Lady Be Good*, *Tip Toes*, *Oh, Kay*, *Funny Faces*, and *Girl Crazy*. They made stars of Fred and Adele Astaire, Gertrude Lawrence, Ethel Merman, and Ginger Rogers. "Fascinating Rhythm," "Do, Do, Do," "Sweet and Low Down," "Embraceable You," "I Got Rhythm," and a dozen other wonderful songs followed one another in dizzy succession. In addition, *Of Thee I Sing*, which Gershwin wrote with George Kaufman and Morrie Ryskind, won the Pulitzer Prize in 1932. George moved to a Riverside Drive penthouse, which became headquarters for a series of wondrous Sunday evening delicatessen suppers that featured Barney Greengrass' sturgeon and attracted the greatest wits and socialites of the town. That's when the Gershwin saga really started. George, who loved to play the piano for hours on end, and naïvely—also justifiably—took it for granted that nobody wanted to hear anything but his music, would finally suspend operations to seek refreshments. His place would be taken by a surly young man named Oscar Levant, who played George's music just as well as the composer.

Oscar likes to tell the story of the night he and George journeyed to Pittsburgh to play with the symphony orchestra there. George took it for granted that the lower berth of the compartment was his proper due. Before turning out the light, Oscar peered over the edges of the upper to see George sprawled complacently below, puffing a huge cigar. "Do you know what this picture represents?" said George pleasantly, when he spied Oscar's face. "It's the difference between talent and genius." One day, Oscar, George, Ira, and I journeyed up to Baker Field to see a Columbia-Navy football game. We were late, and I weaved in and out of the trolley poles on Sedgwick Avenue rather recklessly. "For God's sake, be careful!" cautioned George. "You've got *Gershwin* in the car!"

George loved to go to parties, and thought nothing of playing the entire score of a forthcoming musical for his friends. This practice irked his canny collaborator, George Kaufman. "If you play that score one more time before we open," Kaufman once told him, "people are going to think it's a revival." Kaufman also deplored Gershwin's genial habit of inviting everybody he met to sit in on rehearsals. Kaufman left one run-through with a deep scowl. "It's going to be a prize flop," he predicted. "What makes you say that? I thought it went beautifully," protested Gershwin. "Not at all," grumbled Kaufman. "The balcony was only half filled."

I accompanied George on some wonderful vacation trips. They were a succession of hilarious adventures and beautiful girls. He banged out the *Rhapsody* once in the parlor of the Colonial Hotel in Nassau at seven in the morning to please a girl he had met on the boat, and was indignant when the manager made him stop. "I guess he didn't know I was Gershwin," he consoled himself.

In Havana, a sixteen-piece rhumba band serenaded him en

masse at four in the morning outside his room at the old Almendares Hotel. Several outraged patrons left the next morning. George was so flattered that he promised to write a rhumba of his own. He did, too. His *Cuban Overture* was played for the first time at the Lewisohn Stadium in August, 1932. In Havana George reached his greatest height of indignation. A lovely Cuban miss failed to keep a luncheon date with him. Later that afternoon he spied her on the Yacht Club terrace, and exclaimed, "Hey, do you know that you stood me up today?" "Oh, I meant to phone and tell you I couldn't meet you," said the contrite maiden, "but do you know something? I simply couldn't think of your name." George didn't recover for days.

He reserved one unpublished little waltz tune for affairs of the heart. "You're the kind of girl who makes me feel like composing a song," he would tell the enraptured lady of the moment, and lead her off to his suite. We would follow on tiptoe to hear him compose the familiar tune for her. "It will be dedicated to you," he would conclude soulfully.

One day, I happened to remark that the score of one of his infrequent failures, *Pardon My English*, was below par. George demurred. All of us were sun-bathing in the nude; George insisted that we all go inside while he proved his point by going through the score from opening chorus to finale. I can still see him sitting at the piano, stark naked, playing the songs and singing them, too, at the top of his voice. George belonged at a piano. I have never seen a man happier, more bursting with the sheer joy of living, than George when he was playing his songs. He would improvise and introduce subtle variations, and chuckle with childlike delight when his audience exclaimed over them.

The work that George Gershwin loved best was *Porgy and Bess*. He composed it in eleven months and orchestrated it in nine. Its initial production by the Guild in 1935, a bit too stuffy and pretentious, was only moderately successful. When it was revived seven years later, it really came into its own, and its songs seem destined to become part of America's richest musical heritage; the tragedy is that Gershwin wasn't living to see that come to pass.

George moved to Hollywood in 1936. He wrote the music for the Fred Astaire-Ginger Rogers picture, *Shall We Dance?* which included one of his best songs ("Oh, No, You Can't Take That Away From Me") and *A Damsel in Distress*. He was working on the *Goldwyn Follies* when he was stricken by a brain tumor.

The last years of George's life were almost equally divided between composing and painting. George took his painting very seriously, and indeed had a genuine talent for it. At a memorable dinner one evening he said, "A man told me today that I need never write another note; I could make a fortune with my palette and brush." "Isn't it amazing," said one awed lady, "that one man should possess a genius for two of the arts?" "Oh, I don't know," said George modestly. "Look at Leonardo da Vinci." At another dinner, apropos of nothing, George suddenly said, "Has anybody here seen my new cigarette case?" It was solid gold, and inscribed thereon were facsimile signatures of a score of famous men. It had been presented to him after a performance of his Concerto in F. The case was passed clear around the table. As George was putting it back into his pocket, his brother Ira produced a crumpled pack of Camels. "Anybody want a cigarette?" he inquired pleasantly.

But Ira, like everybody else who knew him well, adored George Gershwin. After his death, Ira wrote practically nothing for years. That he had lost none of his talent he proved, however, with the lyrics for *Lady in the Dark*.

George Gershwin expressed his credo in these words: "My people are American, my time is today. Music must repeat the thought and aspirations of the times." Seven years after his death his exciting songs are being played more frequently than they were during his lifetime. One critic recently remarked, "George Gershwin brought to serious consideration a new idiom in American music, and forever changed its future direction." Once every summer twenty thousand people gather in a New York stadium to hear a program dedicated to his memory. As the first familiar strains of the *Rhapsody in Blue* hush the expectant audience, it is hard to believe that the composer has been dead since 1937. It's such a little while since he sat beside me in Cuba listening to the same composition on the radio, and saying, "It *is* great, isn't it? But wait until you hear the one I'm working on now."

★　★　★

The character of "Sporting Life" was played in the original production of *Porgy* by a Harlem hoofer named Bubbles. He was one of the great dancers of the day, but had only the haziest notions of discipline and rehearsals. The conductor, Alex Smallens, had a terrible time perfecting him for the part. Once he suggested sarcastically, "Maybe the fault is in my conducting?" Bubbles mollified him completely when he said in all sincerity,

"Mr. Smallens, if I had the money of the way you conduct, I'd be a millionaire!"

* * *

About thirty years ago there was a lightweight boxer in Hoboken, New Jersey, who fought under the name of Marty O'Brien, and was a member of the town's fire brigade on the side. He was a clean, likable kid, completely on the level, and among the host of friends that he made was a rising young singer named "Bing" Crosby.

Marty O'Brien got married, and in time had a son who was too frail to become a boxer like his dad, but inclined toward a musical career. He could carry a tune like nobody's business. Marty wrote to his old friend Bing. Could Bing help the

kid get the musical education he craved? Bing Crosby could—and did. O'Brien's boy studied music and in due course turned professional.

The boy was Frank Sinatra—Bing Crosby's most formidable rival in the crooner ranks today.

★　★　★

That lovely and nostalgic tune, "Melancholy Baby," was written in 1912 and is still a sure-fire encore for any orchestra, sweet or hot. The legend goes that George Norton, who wrote the lyrics, was in a railroad station waiting for the arrival of his best girl. Word came through that the train was delayed. While the young man paced impatiently up and down the platform, the theme of "Melancholy Baby" began to take shape in his mind. Barely had he jotted down the last lines on the back of an envelope when the station master gave him sad tidings. The train he was waiting for had been wrecked; the girl was one of the victims. Neither Norton nor Ernie Burnett, who composed the melody, has written another song hit since that day.

★　★　★

One place where they really take their music seriously is aboard a certain British airplane carrier. Every afternoon at four, unless there's a heavy gale running or the enemy has actually engaged the ship, there is a concert on deck. The band sits on the principal plane elevator, which is depressed about two feet, so that the musicians may follow better the baton-wielding of the conductor. He stands at the edge of the deck above, his back to the audience, which is always ample, since every man who can be spared is there under official orders.

On the afternoon in question, the carrier was coursing lazily through Mediterranean waters, and the concert was in full cry. Suddenly a mechanic in the control room noticed the plane-elevator indicator, which registered the fact that it was not quite flush with the deck. Afraid that the mechanism was out of kilter, he pressed a button hard. The ship's band, in the middle of the overture from *Carmen*, suddenly disappeared from the view of the entranced audience and plunged into the bowels of the ship. The mechanic, horrified when he saw what he had done, hastily pushed another button. The elevator shot skyward. It came to the surface with a jolt that sent every musician bouncing at least three feet in the air. But ah, those imperturbable British! Not one man stopped tooting his instrument for a moment during the entire round trip. The leader never lost a beat. When the overture was concluded, the unsmiling ship's company applauded politely.

★ ★ ★

The musical fraternity has an unending fund of anecdotes which it never tires of repeating. Moriz Rosenthal, the noted pianist, is responsible for many of them. It was either he, or Godowsky, or Hofmann—authorities differ—who accompanied Mischa Elman to that never-to-be-forgotten debut of Jascha Heifetz at Carnegie Hall. A tumultuous audience roared its approval. Elman mopped his brow, and grumbled, "It's stifling in here." "Not for pianists, Mischa," was the gentle reply.

Rosenthal attended one of Paderewski's farewell performances with another distinguished pianist and composer, Abram Chasins. It was a lamentable exhibition, and Chasins murmured sadly, "The things that man has forgotten!" "What he forgets isn't so bad," said Rosenthal. "It's what he *remembers*."

★ ★ ★

One of Chasins' most successful compositions is a piano piece called *Rush Hour in Hong Kong*. "It was published only seven months ago," he told Rosenthal proudly, "and it has just gone into its seventeenth edition!" "I was never so crazy about that piece, Abe," was the answer, "but so bad I didn't think it was!" Back at Chasins' studio, he found the piano rack covered with compositions by Bach, Beethoven, and Schubert. "My, my," commented Rosenthal. "I was under the impression that you composed by ear."

★ ★ ★

Rosenthal was dragged reluctantly one afternoon to hear a third-rate string quartet go through its paces. After the recital, the second violinist rushed up to him. "Did you like it, maestro?" he asked eagerly. "Excellent, excellent," lied Rosenthal. "And our tempi, did they suit you?" persisted the violinist. "Ah," said Rosenthal, "they were simply marvelous—particularly yours." Another day, Rosenthal was listening to a friend's newest composition. He made no audible comment, but the composer noticed that he took off his hat several times, and then put it on again. "It's too hot in the studio here," the friend suggested. "I'll open a window." "No, no," Rosenthal assured him. "It isn't that. I was just bowing to all the dear old friends I recognized in your piece."

★　★　★

The story goes that Mrs. Vanderbilt once demanded to know what Fritz Kreisler would charge to play at a private musicale, and was taken aback when he named a price of five thousand dollars. She agreed reluctantly, but added, "Please remember that I do not expect you to mingle with the guests." "In that case, Madam," Kreisler assured her, "my fee will be only two thousand."

Another rich dowager was taken to a recital of the famed Budapest Quartet. Introduced later to the first violinist, she gushed, "It's a shame your little orchestra hasn't got money enough to expand. I'm going to write you out a check for five thousand dollars; we'll make that band of yours as big as Tommy Dorsey's!"

★　★　★

Toscanini had a painful experience one evening with a soloist who began his cadenza bravely enough but soon got into difficulty. Obviously flustered, he wandered farther and farther off key. The maestro and the entire orchestra held their breaths. Just before their cue to resume playing, the soloist managed to recover the original key. Toscanini bowed and said, "Welcome home, Mr. Ginsberg."

★　★　★

579

Oscar Levant once played with an orchestra whose conductor he detested. The conductor reciprocated the feeling and delighted in pointing out errors in his playing. Levant finally lost his temper completely and convulsed the other members of the orchestra—and also terminated his own association therewith—by shouting, "If you bawl me out once more, I'll follow your beat!"

A Hollywood notable attended a Beethoven festival with Levant because he thought it would emphasize his position as a patron of the arts. He nodded uneasily through the concert, but

perked up as the final number began. It was the C Minor Symphony, which has several false climaxes. At the first two, the producer half rose from his seat. At the third, he turned angrily to Levant and muttered, "The rat fooled me again!"

Levant played background music for a Parisian picture under the guidance of another brilliant producer. "It's good," said the connoisseur, "but it's not Frenchy enough." He thought a moment, and added, "I've got it, Oscar! Put in a few more French horns!"

★ ★ ★

Did you know that Cole Porter's first two song hits were those enduring Yale favorites "Bingo" and "Bulldog, Wow Wow Wow"? His first complete score was for a show called *See America First* that was produced by Elisabeth Marbury in 1916, but lasted only a fortnight. The book of that show was by Lawrence Riggs, who later became Catholic chaplain at Yale. Porter went on to write some of the greatest popular songs of our time; "Night and Day," "Begin the Beguine," "I Get a Kick Out of You," "Just One of Those Things," are only a few of them.

Porter comes from a wealthy and socially prominent family, and lives in a rather grand manner that baffles some of his Broadway associates. One summer the Porters had a cottage near Long Beach. The stage manager of one of his old shows noticed that twice a week the Waldorf-Astoria sent a truck out to the Porter abode. Consumed with curiosity, he finally knocked on Porter's door and said, "My wife wants to know what it is so special that you can't get it in Long Beach and have to have it sent out twice a week by the Waldorf?" "Oh," said Porter, surprised, "I guess it's our laundry. They call for it Mondays, and get it back on Thursdays!"

Producers never could find him when they needed him in the old days when the boats were still running. One of them wailed the length of Broadway: "I waste hundreds of dollars in cables trying to locate the guy, and where do I finally find him? He is faltbooting down the Rhine! First, I am sick and tired of chasing him around the world when anybody else is no farther away than Lindy's, and second, what in hell is faltbooting?"

★ ★ ★

Nora Bayes and her husband, Jack Norworth, were once doing their act under the management of Lew Fields. Their stipend was $750 a week. Norworth thought they were worth a lot more, and wired Fields that their pay ought to be doubled. Fields' answer put Norworth's nose out of joint for weeks. "Frankly," he wrote, "your wife isn't worth $1500 a week to me in her present act."

The same act was incorporated later into the Ziegfeld Follies of 1908. Norworth felt that it needed a shot in the arm, and riding downtown on the subway one afternoon, he decided that a new song about the moon might do the trick. He wrote one that very day. "Shine On, Harvest Moon" was its name.

Two other famous songs that were introduced professionally by Nora Bayes were "Over There" and "Has Anybody Here Seen Kelly?" She was a temperamental songstress and changed accompanists with great regularity. They usually quit in a huff. Two of them later achieved some success on their own. One was Edmund Goulding, the ace Hollywood director. The other was George Gershwin.

★ ★ ★

The Russian composer Stravinsky tells the story of an exchange between Gershwin and himself. "How much will you charge me to come over and give me lessons in orchestration?" said Gershwin. "How much do you make a year?" answered Stravinsky. "$100,000," said Gershwin. There was a moment's silence, and then Stravinsky said: "How about your giving *me* lessons?"

★ ★ ★

In New York, a five-year-old girl was taken to a concert, warned that she must remain quiet in her seat. She listened respectfully to two intricate pieces, then turned to her mother and asked gravely, "Is it all right if I scream now?"

★ ★ ★

In Cleveland, a guest conductor was driven crazy at rehearsals because at least one member of the orchestra was always missing. After the last rehearsal, he tapped for attention and said, "I want to thank the first violinist publicly for being the only man in the entire orchestra who had the decency to attend every rehearsal." The first violinist hung his head. "It seemed the least I could do," he said in a deprecating tone. "You see, I don't expect to show up for the concert tonight."

And of course everybody must have heard about the night that Stokowski was conducting the Philadelphia Orchestra in the rendition of Beethoven's *Leonore* Overture No. 3, and the offstage trumpet call twice failed to sound on cue. Directly the last note of the overture had been played, the apoplectic Stokowski rushed into the wings with murder in his heart. He found the trumpeter struggling in the clutches of a burly watchman. "I tell you you can't blow that damn thing here," the watchman kept insisting. "There's a concert going on inside!"

★ ★ ★

No collection of musical anecdotes today should conclude with anyone but Frank Sinatra, now known simply as "The Voice" in worshipful radio circles, and as "Frank Not-So-Hotra" by frustrated rival croonatics. When Sinatra inaugurated his own weekly program, Ginger Rogers was the guest star for the first show, and the rehearsal provided a field day for rabid autograph hounds. One of them carried off the signatures of both Ginger and Sinatra in triumph. A moment later Ginger heard her address a friend disdainfully. "Swap you Sinatra for an ordinary Roosevelt and Churchill? What kind of a dope do you think I am?"

Chapter Nine

THE GOOD OLD DAYS

When the Victoria Theatre occupied the present site of the Rialto at 42nd Street and Seventh Avenue, and Willie Hammerstein managed the vaudeville shows staged there, anybody in the public eye could get headline billing for a single week. Hammerstein particularly favored good-looking gals who had just beaten a murder rap. One such damsel shot a man on Friday and opened at the Victoria the following Monday at $1000 for the week. She tried to get a second week at the same figure. "Not until you go out and shoot somebody else," Hammerstein told her promptly.

★ ★ ★

There was an estimable Baron Fugger who lived in Germany many decades before Hitler—fortunately for the baron, who had an impeccable taste for food, drink, and pleasant living. He decided one day to make the Grand Tour of Italy and took the

585

precaution of sending a trusted servant ahead of him on his proposed route. It was the servant's duty to sample the wine at every hostel and monastery along the way. If he approved, he chalked up the word *est* on the outer gate, and the baron then knew exactly where it was safe for him to refill his tank. One sunny morning the servant pulled up at the monastery of Montefiascone, a bare fifty miles north of Rome, and called for a carafe of the native wine. It was so wonderful that he rushed to the gate and chalked up "EST! EST! EST!" A few days later, the baron reached Montefiascone, and marveling at this sudden extravagance on the part of a customarily imperturbable connoisseur, wheezed up the hill on the double and demanded some of the wine that was responsible. One sip was all he needed. He unpacked his duds, and promptly drank himself to death. Just before he expired—in a daze of complete happiness—he made a solemn pact with the good friars. He left half of his entire estate to the monastery on condition that once each year, a barrel of Est, Est, Est would be emptied over his grave. Until the outbreak of World War Two, at least, this ceremony was religiously performed every spring.

★ ★ ★

One of the most famous hotels in all the world was the original Waldorf-Astoria, which threw open its doors for the first time on March 13, 1893 (the Astoria part of the hotel was not completed until four years later) and was the centre of the New York hotel world until it was torn down to make way for the world's largest office structure, the Empire State Building. One of the most famous features of the old Waldorf-Astoria was Peacock Alley. It was said that if a person would simply sit there for two days, as at Shepheard's Hotel in Cairo, Egypt, he could see the rest of the world pass by. Another room that country folk flocked to see was the grill, which featured an honest-to-goodness trout stream. Young bucks were given a rod and reel and could actually fish for their dinner. Attendants unhooked their catch and bore it off to a sizzling grill near by; the bucks frequently filled in the moments of waiting by pushing each other into the stream. One of the memorable days in the history of the old Waldorf came when Sergeant York, hero of the First World War, made his first visit to Manhattan. He was major domo-ed by a Tennessee Congressman not yet very well known, named Cordell Hull.

★ ★ ★

Marquis James, whose biographies of Sam Houston and Andrew Jackson are about the last word on the subjects, and who insists that he is a "fifth or sixth cousin of Jesse James," once worked as a reporter on the *New Orleans Item*. It was there that he uncovered the story of the lady of the underworld whose only real ambition was to be buried in New Orleans' swankiest cemetery. She ran the biggest brothel and gaming casino in the South; important politicians changed their vote at a nod of her peroxide curls; a police commissioner who tried to raid her establishment was literally driven out of town. But the Bishop was her stumbling block. Her generous donations to his church were refused. Her efforts to buy a plot in the Bishop's cemetery were sharply rebuffed.

One day she sold out her extensive interests and sailed for France, where she turned respectable with a vengeance, and married a marquis who took up three pages in the French *Who's Who*. When the New Orleans Bishop received a huge contribution from the Marquise de Fourabonne, how could he be expected to know that she was none other than the madam he had snubbed so often? He accepted her gift with a warm note of thanks, and assured her that her request to be buried after her death in his cemetery would be carried out to the letter.

Eventually she died, and her body was borne in state to the vault that had been built at her order. It occupied a plot at the edge of the cemetery. A wire fence was all that separated the vault from the tracks of the Southern Pacific Railroad.

Some time after the burial services—conducted by the Bishop himself—a new signal tower was erected by the railroad. Today,

587

not ten feet from the body of the Marquise, there flashes a bright and powerful red light.

★ ★ ★

Some years ago, one of the bright young men who represented Standard Oil in China returned to America for a vacation, in the course of which he met and married a lovely girl from his home town.

"You'll just love Shanghai," he assured her again and again on the way out, "particularly my Number One Boy, Ling. You won't have to lift a finger. Ling runs the household beautifully. There is no detail he doesn't regulate."

In due course they arrived in Shanghai, the bride met Ling, the Number One Boy, and approved. The next morning her husband kissed her good-bye before reporting back on the job. "Sleep as long as you like, darling," he told her. "Ling will take care of everything."

A few hours later she awoke again, to find herself being shaken ever so gently by the Number One Boy. "Time to get dressed and go home now, Missy," he said.

Chauncey Depew told two railroad anecdotes so frequently— and so well—that somebody suggested engraving them on his tombstone when he passed away.

One concerned a grizzled old maintenance man at Grand Central Station whose task it was to check on the shoe brakes of all the cars after the trains were made up and ready to start their runs. Depew watched him plodding from car to car one morning and called down from the platform, "How long you been doing that job, my friend?" "Forty years," was the answer. "Exactly what are you looking for under all those cars?" persisted Depew. "I'm damned if I know," said the veteran.

The other Depew standby was the farmer who had been the only witness to a disastrous head-on collision on a lonely stretch of track in Texas. Asked to tell in court what he had seen, the farmer said: "Wal, fust I seen Number 48 roarin' down the track from the West at about seventy miles an hour. Then I turned and seen Number 17 bearin' down the same track from the East just about as fast. It was easy to see they was goin' to smash right inter one another."

"What did you think while you watched all this happen?" asked the judge.

"What did I think?" repeated the farmer. "I thunk, this is one hell of a way to run a railroad!"

Depew was sitting in a Savannah park one Sunday morning, listening to the church bells for which the town is famous.

"Wonderful bells," said Depew to an old gaffer sitting beside him.

"What's that?" said the other, cupping his hand over one ear.

"I said the bells here sound wonderful," said Depew in a louder voice.

"Can't hear you," returned the old man.

Depew's voice rose to a shout. "I say that you have beautiful bells here in Savannah," he bellowed.

"It's no use," said the gaffer. "I could probably hear what you was saying if it wasn't for them goddam bells!"

★ ★ ★

Wilson Mizner was a veteran of the Alaska Gold Rush of 1897—a burly, six-foot-four giant of a man, who dazzled Broadway for years as a dramatist, publicity expert, professional gambler, and wit. Some of his pals in the Klondike days were Tex Rickard, Jack London, Rex Beach, and Robert Service. He was a genuinely tough hombre—with a magnificent sense of humor. He is the man who coined the phrase: "Never give a sucker an even break." Cleaned out himself in a crooked roulette game, he explained without rancor, "Sure, I knew the wheel was crooked. But what could I do? It was the only one in town." He could only admire, he added, the skill and dexterity of the croupier. "That guy," he declared, "would steal a hot stove and come back later for the smoke. I know his brother, too. Blackjack dealer. He could do more with fifty-two soda crackers than most crooked dealers could do with a marked deck."

While he was in Alaska with Rickard, the latter pulled a gat and plugged a man through his sombrero. "What's the idea?" asked Mizner languidly. "You know my gal Goldie?" said the excited Tex. "Well, that rat insulted her!" "For God's sake," said Mizner, "*how?*"

A "big shot" approached a poker game that Mizner was banking. He asked to be declared in. "This game is too big for you," warned Mizner. The big shot was very much put out. "What do you take me for—a piker?" he rasped. "Cut me in here for ten thousand dollars." Mizner calmly slipped the ten one-thousand-dollar bills into his cash drawer. "Joe," he commanded, "give the gentleman a blue chip." At one time, Mizner persuaded all his fellow gamblers in New York to wear roses in their lapels as a means of identification. Times had gotten tough, and they had begun to prey upon each other.

During one of his intermittent periods of prosperity, Wilson Mizner owned a hotel in New York. A sign in the lobby read, "Guests must bury their own dead and will please not smoke opium in the elevator." He ordered a steak in his own dining room, snipped off a piece and put it in his pocket. "When I went out alone tonight," he explained, "that dame in 811 said I should choke on the first bite. This ought to fool her."

Invited to lecture before a women's club, Mizner got hold of an attendant and told her to be sure to place a pitcher of ice water and a glass on the speaker's table. "Do you want it for drinking?" she asked. "No," said Mizner, "I do a high-diving act." Another time he began tossing money about with unwonted abandon. "Where did you get it?" they asked him. "Playing a horse," he explained. "Where—in Saratoga?" "No—in vaude-ville." Once he persuaded his friends for a week that he was going to marry a beautiful girl. Then he announced that the engagement was broken. "I told her about my rich uncle," he explained mournfully. "Now she's my aunt!"

Jim Tully once persuaded Mizner to try his hand at a short story. He promptly sold it to *Liberty* for a thousand dollars, but wasn't satisfied. "It took me eight hours to write that thing," he complained. Later he made an observation on the writing game that has been quoted many times since: "If you steal from one author, it's plagiarism; if you steal from many, it's research."

In the hospital for a variety of ailments, Mizner submitted to a colonic irrigation with the worst possible grace. When it was finished, he inquired of the nurse, "Now how about checking me for oil and water?"

Mizner never minced words about his numerous sins of omission and commission. "They'll find out anyhow," was his philosophy. "There's something about a closet that makes a skeleton terribly restless."

Somebody once asked Mizner what he thought of Frank Case, of the Algonquin Hotel. "He's a prince," declared Mizner. "He's the kind of guy who'd give you—" He opened his coat, looked down, and finished, "My God, this *is* his shirt!"

★ ★ ★

Oliver Herford and a famous military man were joint guests of honor at a banquet. The hostess suddenly announced, "Mr. Oliver Herford will now improvise a poem in honor of the occasion."

Herford, a modest and retiring man, shriveled in his chair. "Oh, no," he protested. "Have the general fire a cannon."

★ ★ ★

Joe E. Lewis once spent a night at Saratoga's venerable Grand Union Hotel. He swears that at three in the morning he heard his closet door creak and saw a Confederate soldier step out to demand, "Who's winning?" Naturally, Joe couldn't sleep after that. Besides, the railroad station was directly below and a switching engine kept shunting cars back and forth incessantly. Finally Joe summoned the night clerk. "Maybe you can tell me," he suggested, "what time this hotel reaches Chicago?"

Lewis went straight from Saratoga to a hospital. His first bulletin read, "I've taken a turn for the nurse."

★ ★ ★

One of the first automobiles ever seen on Fifth Avenue was built personally by Vincent Astor's father, Colonel John Jacob Astor III. It was a converted surrey, with a steam-driven engine under the seat, and probably a fringe on the top. The Colonel took it out for its first and last spin one summer day in 1900; Mrs. Astor and the eight-year-old Vincent stood outside and watched the Colonel rattle by. Suddenly the crowd started shouting. The Colonel, gratified, took a bow. Then he realized that his car was burning under him. He leaped in the nick of time.

Undaunted, the Colonel tried again several weeks later at Newport. This time he drove a steam Locomobile, and several other pioneering blue-bloods entered cars to race him. The course was an old trotting track. The contestants struck up a dizzy pace for about four laps, but then the overtaxed boilers lost their pressure, and a wag in a pony cart drove onto the track and left the whole field behind in a cloud of dust. The Colonel suffered the crowning indignity of having to push his car over the finish line.

★ ★ ★

James Thurber has had a few motoring experiences quite as frightening, in their way, as Mr. Astor's. Once he was driving with a cherished aunt on Christmas Eve in Columbus, Ohio, and died a thousand anticipatory deaths while she tooted merrily through green and red traffic lights at forty miles an hour. "Why, honey," she explained later, "I thought the city had put up those lights for the Christmas festivities!" Another time he was driving himself, quite at peace with the world, when he suddenly noticed a gauge on his dashboard that registered "1650." Expecting the car to blow up any instant, he nosed it gingerly into a wayside garage, where the attendant reassured him: "That's your radio dial, Mac. You got her set at WQXR."

Thurber says his car harbors a definite grudge against him. Driving through a bleak little town out West, he mused aloud, "I'd hate to be stuck in this place." The car promptly burned out a bearing and he was stranded there for two days. Thurber hopes that engines are on their way out.

★ ★ ★

Edward R. Hewitt, in *Those Were the Days*, tells the story of the first time Mrs. Hamilton Fish took the controls of her shiny new electric runabout. She was hurtling down Third Avenue at a ten-mile-an-hour clip when a burly pedestrian stepped directly into her path. She tried to stop, but pushed the lever too far forward, thus increasing her speed. Her victim was just beginning to figure what had hit him when the flustered Mrs. Fish jammed her car into reverse, and got him again on the way back. Once more she jammed her lever forward too far. "Hit 'im again, lady!" cried an entranced onlooker. The pedestrian rolled out of her way. "Twice, madam, is sufficient," he informed her.

★ ★ ★

Judge John C. Knox recalls that when he was a boy he visited a courtroom in Greene County, Pennsylvania, presided over by a certain U. S. Circuit Judge Wilson, with the assistance of two associate "lay judges." The case had to do with a citizen who had gotten snarled up with the liquor laws, an act considered not too heinous in those parts.

The testimony was given haltingly, and then Judge Wilson asked his lay associates what they thought the penalty ought to be.

"'Bout ten days, I guess," said the first. "Ten days is what I reckon too," said the second. "I think ten days myself," remarked Judge Wilson. "And three times ten are thirty." That was the verdict.

This was the part of Pennsylvania, you may recall, in which the Whiskey Rebellion was staged many years ago by rugged individualists who wanted no traffic with U. S. revenue agents. Donald Ogden Stewart burlesqued the story in Thornton Burgess' bedtime manner. The opening lines, treasured by connoisseurs of humor, go as follows:

"Just the *day* for a Whiskey Rebellion," said Aunt Polly and off she ran, lipperty-lipperty-lip, to get a few shooting rifles. "Oh, goody goody," cried little Emily. "Now we can all shoot at those horrid Revenue Officers."

★ ★ ★

Here are a few stories about Texas from Boyce House's hilarious book, *I Give You Texas.*

594

There's no need to ask a man what state he's from. If he's from Texas, he'll tell you himself; if he's not, why embarrass him? The state is so big that El Paso natives refer to citizens of Texarkana as "effete Easterners" and Brownsville folk regard Dallasites as "Northern white trash." Roads leading South bear signs marked "This way to Texas." Those who can read keep on going; the others settle in Arkansas. They're the kind who think the Alamo is pie with ice-cream. . . .

Even Texas sandstorms, continues Boyce, are something special. A farmer went to town to borrow money on his farm. The banker said, "I'll have to ride out and look over your place." "That won't be necessary," said the farmer. "Here comes the place now." On his way out, the farmer's hat blew off. He just reached up into the air and pulled down another one. . . .

A Texas rancher shot a man dead and telegraphed a slick lawyer in Fort Worth, three hundred miles away, offering a $5000 fee. The attorney wired back, "Leaving for your town on next train, bringing three eye-witnesses." . . .

Four men, one of them minus an eye, were playing poker in a West Texas saloon. Suddenly one of them yanked out a gat and intoned, "I ain't callin' no names, but the next rat I see dealin' from the bottom of the deck, I'm gonna shoot his other eye out!" . . .

Sam Houston is the hero of a thousand Texas anecdotes. At a big outdoor dinner in his honor, somebody handed him a plate of sizzling hot rice pudding. In the midst of an oration, Houston lifted a huge spoonful to his mouth, let out a roar, and then spat the rice to the ground. "You see, folks," he explained, "many a durn fool woulda swallowed that!" . . .

The court house at Stephenville has a large clock that is the pride of the town. It is illuminated at night. One citizen staggered up to a mail box, dropped a penny in the slot, glanced at the clock, and exclaimed, "Jehoshaphat, I'm nine pounds overweight." . . .

★ ★ ★

"Gate-crashing" is the intricate art of getting into places without a ticket.

The most famous gate-crasher of recent years is a character known as "One-Eyed Connelly," who boasts that he has seen seventeen consecutive World Series baseball games and twelve heavyweight championship fights without paying his way in. His methods are a closely guarded secret. Maybe he is the authentic invisible man. He once sneaked out of a model jail where he was serving a thirty-day sentence, imposed by a judge who failed to appreciate the artistry of his gate-crashing proclivities. He broke back in the next night just to show he could do it.

History records a gate-crasher back in 1841. He was a dull-witted cockney named Jones who had a passion for sneaking into Buckingham Palace, where he was picked up time and again by mortified guards. The last time they found him hiding under Queen Victoria's royal sofa.

A more legitimate blood brother of the gate-crasher is the free-pass hound, who will spend ten dollars and countless hours to get a free ticket for a fifty-cent movie. There is something about complimentary theatre passes—and to a somewhat lesser extent, free review copies of books—that tickles the vanity of the most honorable and solvent citizens. In theatrical vernacular, a free pass is known as an "Annie Oakley." Annie was a famous shot in her day, the female counterpart of Buffalo Bill, and could plug an ace of spades full of holes from a distance of a hundred yards. If you have ever noticed how many holes are punched in a free ticket, you will understand why it is called an "Annie Oakley."

★ ★ ★

When William T. Jerome was district attorney of Manhattan he made a determined effort to drive out the crooked gamblers who infested the city. One band he exposed had perfected an ingenious racket. They rode on crack trains between New York and Boston, and lured prosperous-looking victims into "a couple of rubbers of bridge."

By the time the game was over, the "fish" was usually several hundred dollars in the hole. The winner agreed to take a check, but once he had it in his hands, became suddenly conscience-stricken.

"I never thought the game would get this big," he would say. "I bet you think we're a parcel of professional gamblers. Let's call the whole thing off." He would then tear the check into shreds. Nine times out of ten the loser, vastly impressed, would insist on writing out a new one. When his vouchers came back from the bank on the first of the month, of course, *both* checks were there. The crooked gambler had palmed his original one, and torn up a blank piece of paper.

★ ★ ★

Exploring the Dangerous Trades, by Dr. Alice Hamilton, reveals the true origin of the phrase "mad as a hatter." Dr. Hamilton explains that mercury is used in the making of felt hats, and the poison resulting from its use over a period of years eventually caused the unfortunate victim's muscles to jerk violently and involuntarily. The hatter's friends drew false conclusions.

Robert Briffault, in his novel *Europa*, declares that the origin of mourning lay not in the desire of the bereaved to show sorrow over the loss of the departed, but in a desperate attempt to prevent the ghosts of said departed from haunting them in the days that followed. They figured that by dressing completely in black, they might escape the attention of presumably near-sighted ghosts entirely.

If you crave still more fascinating information, Bruce Bairnsfather, creator of Old Bill and "The Better 'Ole," explains the origin of the little row of buttons on the sleeves of men's coats. It appears that His Majesty's troops in the old days didn't take very enthusiastically to the notion of wiping their noses on handkerchiefs, when a good sleeve served the same purpose. Buttons were added to the sleeve of the uniforms to introduce a keen element of hazard into this unfortunate procedure—and the custom stuck.

★ ★ ★

Edith Wharton, author of *Ethan Frome*, was what some people would call a first-rate snob. She explained that "only eight people in New York are worth dining with" and therefore had only eight chairs in her dining room. She was taken aback, however, when she learned that Mrs. William Waldorf Astor had referred to her as "that Bohemian."

★ ★ ★

James Whitcomb Riley became a poet via the unlikely route of purveyor of a cure-all patent medicine. In his early twenties he traveled all over the country with a quack doctor, and wrote poems on the backs of envelopes while the doctor was hornswoggling ruralites into buying bottles of his worthless elixir.

It was Riley who taught the doctor a routine that later became famous on the vaudeville circuits. The doctor would begin his spiel in a voice so hoarse and feeble that even the hicks in the front row couldn't hear him. Then, with a shaking hand he would pour himself a tablespoonful of his patent remedy. He would swallow it with evident relish, smack his lips, and then roar in a voice that could be heard three blocks away, "AND NOW, FOLKS . . ."

In later years, Riley liked to tell about the man with a dozen warts on his face who asked the quack if his medicine would remove them. "It can't miss," the doctor assured him. The next day, swore Riley, the man's wife followed the quack to the next town and demanded her money back. "Didn't it work?" asked the doctor in feigned amazement. "Work? Listen—Joe swallered that whole bottle of yours last night. This mornin' every one of them warts was still there—*but his face was gone!*"

★ ★ ★

Up for sale at Sotheby's famous London auction rooms recently was a letter described conservatively in the catalogue as "one of the most extraordinary" ever offered. Brief and to the point, and written by the noted English novelist Anthony Trollope to an Irish colleen in 1851, it said:

My Dearest Miss Dorothea Sankey:

My affectionate and most excellent wife is, as you are aware, still living—and I am proud to say her health is good. Nevertheless, it is always well to take time by the forelock and be prepared for all events. Should anything happen to her, will you supply her place— as soon as a proper period of decent mourning is over?

Till then, I am your devoted servant.

Trollope married a Miss Rose Heseltine in Dublin in 1844. When he wrote this letter to the mysterious Miss Sankey he was in "the dangerous forties." When he died at the age of sixty-seven, his "affectionate and most excellent wife" was still living, which left "dearest Dorothea" very definitely holding the bag— and the letter. Today it is a choice collector's item.

"THE ADVENTURES OF MARK TWAIN"

In 1857, when Samuel Clemens was twenty-two, he became a journeyman pilot on the Mississippi, charged with keeping his packet from running aground on the numerous shoals and mud banks. This necessitated continual depth soundings, and one of the calls used to warn of shallow water and submerged rock was "mark twain." He explained later, "I was a fresh, new journalist, and needed a nom de guerre, so I confiscated the mariner's one, and have done my best to make it remain what it was in his hands—a sign and symbol and warrant that whatever is found in its company may be gambled on as being the petrified truth."

The motion-picture version of Mark Twain's life is inaccurate, sugar-coated, and far too long, but at least it made me look up his actual biography. And before I knew it, I was rereading *Tom Sawyer* and *Huckleberry Finn*. For that I am grateful. Maybe you remember the story of the tactful Englishman who first non-plussed Mark Twain by remarking, "I'd give ten thousand pounds not to have read *Huck Finn*," but then made everything perfect by adding, "so that I could have the joy again of reading it for the first time."

Mark Twain made a fortune out of his books, went bankrupt when he turned publisher himself, and then paid every cent of his debts and became rich again by virtue of new writings and fabulously successful lecture tours. His financial troubles did not increase his affection for the banking fraternity. He defined a banker as a man who "loaned you an umbrella when the sun was shining and demanded its return the moment it started to rain." He invented the story of a bank president who was proud of a glass eye that had been made for him by the greatest artist in Paris. "Twain, you need $5000," he quoted this gentleman. "I'll give it to you if you can guess which of my eyes is the glass one." "It's the left one, of course," snapped Twain. "It's the only one with a glint of human kindness in it." On another occasion, Twain sought to borrow a book from a banker who lived next door to him. "You'll have to read it here," said the neighbor. "I make it a rule never to let any book go out of my library." The next night the banker asked for the use of Twain's lawn-mower. "Sure thing," agreed Twain. "But you'll have to use it on my lawn. I make the same rules you do."

Mark Twain is credited with the classic remark, "Everybody

complains about the weather, but nobody does anything about it," but Robert L. Cooke claims he can prove that Charles Dudley Warner actually coined the phrase. Twain *did* say, "If you don't like the weather in New England, just wait a few minutes." "Cauliflower," he said, "is nothing but cabbage with a college education." He told a lecture audience, "If you pick up a starving dog and make him prosperous, he will not bite you. This is the principal difference between a dog and a man." Acting

Mark Twain and mankind

as master of ceremonies at a dinner, he warned the speakers: "I once heard a preacher who was powerful good. I decided to give him every cent I had with me. But he kept at it too long. Ten minutes later I decided to keep the bills and just give him my loose change. Another ten minutes and I was darned if I'd give him anything at all. Then when he finally stopped, and the plate came around, I was so exhausted, I extracted two dollars out of sheer spite."

Mark Twain's wife, whom he adored, was a genteel and highly moral product of Eastern society. She disapproved highly of his picturesque Western vocabulary, and often persuaded him to censor some of the more outspoken passages in his manuscripts. Her intentions were the best, but her unceasing efforts to remold Twain's character probably were largely responsible for the inner tumults and confusions that assailed him in his declining years. Twain cut himself while shaving one morning, and cussed vociferously for five minutes straight. His wife heard him, and, intent upon shaming him, repeated every blasphemy he had spoken. Twain listened calmly, and told her, "You have the words, my dear, but I'm afraid you'll never get the tune." She had an appointment to meet him at the Waldorf for luncheon one day, but was very late. He left a note for her with the head waiter: "Never the Twains shall meet!" He wanted to take her to see Sarah Bernhardt, but when she heard that balcony tickets were three dollars apiece, she raised the roof. "And you're the man," she reproached him, "who told me you couldn't afford to raise our poor maids three dollars a month! You take that six dollars right out to the kitchen and give it to them!" Twain sheepishly did her bidding. The maids added four dollars of their own to the six he had given them, and went to see Sarah Bernhardt—in the orchestra.

One friend of Mark Twain (Mr. Miller Hutchison) invented both the Klaxon Horn and the Acousticon for the deaf. "Hmpfh," commented Twain. "Hutchison invented that confounded horn to deafen people so they'd have to buy his Acousticons." Another friend was the sort who would punctuate a story at least three times with, "Now stop me if you've heard this one before." Twain grew impatient one day and assured him, "I not only heard your damn story, I made it up!" Of his father he said, "When I was twenty, I thought him the stupidest man I had ever known. When I was thirty, I was amazed to learn how much the old man had learned in the past ten years."

Twain was a distinguished-looking figure in his later years. One day he was strolling in the park when a little girl pattered up to him and asked if she could walk with him. Highly flattered, Twain told her stories for an hour, then gave her a nickel and said, "Now run along home—and when you grow up you can tell your friends you once walked with Mark Twain." "Mark Twain!" echoed the little girl, bursting into tears. "I thought you were Buffalo Bill!" He received countless letters and photographs from harmless souls all over the world who insisted that they looked just like him. Twain finally composed a form letter to acknowledge such communications. It read: "I thank you very much for your letter and your photograph. In my opinion you are now more like me than any other of my numerous doubles. I may even say that you resemble me more closely than I do myself. In fact, I intend to use your picture to shave by. Yours thankfully, S. Clemens."

Speaking of Mark Twain's doubles, Fredric March's portrayal on the screen is a triumph of acting and make-up. While the picture was in production, March passed Jack Benny on the Warner Brothers lot, but didn't see him. "How do you like that?" commented Benny. "March is made up so good he doesn't even recognize me!"

★ ★ ★

Under Cover, the sensational exposé of American Fascists and Quislingites, was turned down by a dozen publishers before it was signed up by Dutton's. Every year, some manuscript that has been kicked around from pillar to post pops up as a huge best-seller. Publishers never know just where the next success is going to come from, what obscure little writer is suddenly going to blossom into another Sinclair Lewis or Ernest Hemingway. John Galsworthy used to tell about a luncheon he had with his publisher near the beginning of his career, just before he sailed to the Far East on a P. and O. steamer. "There is no new talent coming along in London," sighed the publisher. "The writing profession is going to the dogs." "Cheer up," said Galsworthy. "Maybe I'll run across something while I'm on my trip." Several days out of England, while his boat was steaming down the West African coast, Galsworthy was approached by a diffident ship's officer, with a manuscript under his arm. "Mr. Galsworthy," he said, "may I impose upon you to read this manuscript for me? English is not my native tongue, and I have never tried to write a book before. I won't be too disappointed, therefore, if you think I've been wasting my time." Galsworthy promised the officer he would glance through the script. The officer's name was Joseph Conrad. The book was *Almayer's Folly*.

★ ★ ★

In 1918 Blasco Ibañez's *The Four Horsemen of the Apocalypse* made publishing history in America in more ways than one. Its chances in this country were rated so unlikely that an agent sold the American rights outright for $500. Years later, after the book had sold hundreds of thousands of copies and the picture version had created a new idol in the person of Rudolph Valentino, Blasco Ibañez visited the United States, and was presented with a check for $10,000 by the fortunate publisher. The perfect ending of this little idyll of honesty and good will would be a tableau of the author swooning in gratitude. As a matter of fact, he squawked to high heaven.

★ ★ ★

Some years ago *Collier's* sent Julian Street on a countrywide tour to get background material for a series of articles on out-of-the-way American towns. Wallace Morgan accompanied him to provide the illustrations. One of their stops was the old mining centre of Cripple Creek, and the local Chamber of Commerce, duly honored by their visit, turned the town inside out for their amusement. The thing that stuck in the author's mind, however, was the Cripple Creek red-light district, and when his piece duly appeared in *Collier's*, it was devoted exclusively to that section of the town. The enraged Chamber of Commerce met at once, and officially renamed the crooked lane that led through the filthiest houses in the district "Julian Street."

I wonder if the signpost is still standing.

★ ★ ★

When Victoria Lincoln, the author of *February Hill*, was a little girl of ten, the garden of her Fall River home adjoined that of the aging Lizzie Borden, central character in New England's most famous murder case. One day her mother was horrified to spy her tagging happily behind Lizzie Borden while that lady was plucking a basketful of flowers. She was rushed into the house, and warned never, never to go near Miss Borden again. "But why, Mother?" Victoria asked. The answer to her query was certainly one of the greatest pieces of understatement in the history of English speech. "You see," her mother explained, "that lady was very unkind to her mother and father!"

Certainly you have heard the little rhyme:

> Lizzie Borden took an axe
> And gave her mother forty whacks.
> And when she found what she had done,
> She gave her father forty-one.

★ ★ ★

James Buchanan Duke, of Durham, North Carolina, the country boy who revolutionized the tobacco industry of the entire world, was an enigma even to his father. "There are three things I don't pretend to understand," said that gentleman: "women, electricity, and my son Buck." As long as he lived, Duke employed when he could boys who, like himself, had been born in a small village. "A country boy," he explained, "can learn everything a city boy knows in six months. A squirt who was born into soft city life, on the other hand, couldn't learn in ten years the things every country kid knows automatically." Duke was greatly influenced by his uncle Billy, a vociferous country evangelist on the lines of Billy Sunday. Uncle Billy prayed for rain

605

one day after a long dry spell. "And Lord," he concluded, "when you do send us rain, don't send one of those little gully-washers. Send us a regular sizzle-sozzle." Uncle Billy had to admit later that when it came to selling tobacco and cigarettes, his nephew Buck was a sizzle-sozzle of the first water.

Until the end of the Civil War, cigarette smoking was virtually unknown in America. Small quantities were imported from Turkey. About 1869, native American tobacco was used in a cigarette for the first time. By 1879, the annual output was in the neighborhood of a quarter of a billion cigarettes, all hand-rolled. It was at this point that Buck Duke stepped into the picture. He hatched the brilliant notion of including the picture of a pretty undraped actress or a popular ball-player in each package, developed the premium idea, and, most important of all, gained control of a new machine that could make cigarettes a hundred times faster than the most expert hand roller.

By the year 1908, Duke's American Tobacco Company had become a hydra-headed trust that enjoyed a monopoly not only in cigarettes, but in cigars, pipe and chewing tobacco, snuff, and even the boxes, cartons, and tin foil in which tobacco products were marketed. It also controlled the jobbers and the retail outlets (United Cigar Stores). The annual cigarette sale at this time was about nine billion. When the Government ordered a dissolution of the trust, its structure proved so intricate that only one man in the world could make head or tail of it. The world was treated to the irony of Buck Duke's being commissioned by Congress to break up his own trust!

Among the remains of the broken-up colossus was the Winston plant of R. J. Reynolds. In 1913, this company gave the world its first "blended" cigarettes—Camels. In two years Camels captured a quarter of the country's cigarette market. American Tobacco frantically countered (1916) with Lucky Strikes, Liggett and Myers with Chesterfields. Old Gold and Philip Morris came later. Backed by frenzied advertising, these brands kited cigarette consumption to the staggering annual figure of 200 billion. Probably half of the cigarettes are smoked today by women, although Duke himself wouldn't stay in the same room with a woman who lit one.

Not content with the huge fortune he acquired in tobacco, Duke built up a billion-dollar hydro-electric company, wangled a substantial interest in the Mellon aluminum monopoly, donated a hundred million dollars to Duke University, and fathered the Doris Duke Cromwell who has figured in so many page-one newspaper stories in the past decade.

When Buck Duke first came to New York in 1884, he lived in a hall bedroom that cost him two dollars a week. He died in his marble mansion on Fifth Avenue—one of the stateliest and most ornate in town. Duke himself was sometimes a little startled by his latter-day surroundings. He liked to tell the story of the first time he rode down Fifth Avenue on a horse-drawn rubberneck wagon. The spieler called attention to the palatial new residences. "There's the Morgan place," he said. "Pierpont?" asked Duke. "No, Junius," said the announcer. "And here's the home of the Vanderbilts." "Cornelius?" suggested Duke. "Wrong again," snapped the announcer. "William Henry." A moment later he pointed to a new church. "Christ Church," he announced, and when Buck Duke said nothing, added, "Go on, kid, take a chance!"

Chapter Ten

THIS, GENTLEMEN, IS HISTORY!

When Francis Meynell, the great typographer and founder of the Nonesuch Press, visited America, he was tendered a dinner by the American Institute of Graphic Arts. Aware that students of printing as far away as Kansas City were going to journey to New York to hear his talk, Meynell spent days in feverish preparation, and marched off to the dinner with a sixteen-page typewritten manuscript in his pocket.

Unfortunately, a preliminary "cocktail party," hosted by the genial Rockwell Kent, lasted a full two hours longer than had been anticipated, owing in part to Mr. Kent's discovery of a half-dozen bottles of prime Irish whiskey, in part to the fact that most of the guests began falling on their faces. When Meynell faced the Institute audience, he swayed a bit, forgot all about the prepared speech in his pocket, and told the following story:

In the time of Nero, when sport-loving Romans crowded the Colosseum every Saturday to see a Christian tossed to the lions (on some Sundays there were double-headers), there was one special victim who had given the authorities untold trouble before he was rounded up. Nero had eleven of his most ferocious lions starved for a full week to assure a neat performance when they were turned on this Christian the following Saturday. Eighty thousand spectators turned out, not including the press. The Christian stood alone in the centre of the arena, calm and unafraid.

The first lion was released. He made a bee-line for the Christian. The crowd wetted its lips. But then an amazing thing happened. The Christian bent down and whispered something in the lion's ear. The lion's tail went between his legs, he lowered his head, and slinked out of the arena. When the same performance was followed by six more half-starved kings of the forest, and the gallant crowd was beginning to holler for its money back, Nero, sore as a pup, summoned the Christian and curtly said, "If you will tell me what you say to those lions to make them act that way, I will grant you a full pardon." "It's very simple, Nero," explained the Christian. "I just whisper in their ears: 'Remember, you'll be expected to say a few words after dinner!'"

With this story, Mr. Meynell called it a day. He was so

conscience-stricken the following morning that he had a special edition printed of the speech he really had intended to make, and sent a copy with his compliments to every person who had attended the meeting. It's quite a collectors' item today.

* * *

Edgar Saltus, author of that lush chronicle of Roman times, *The Imperial Purple*, told another tale about Nero's simple efforts to keep his Romans amused. There came a time when there were no more early Christians left in captivity to feed to the lions, and other prisoners were pressed into the service. These poor wights were given a fifty-fifty chance. They were allowed to pull a slip from a helmet. If the one they selected read "no" they were sitting pretty; if it read "yes" it was a break for the lions.

One culprit was in the jug because he had an annoying habit of stealing friends' and countrymen's wives. Indignant cuckolded husbands were determined that he be erased from the picture once and for all; they marked both of *his* slips "yes." A female gladiatrix managed to tip him off in the nick of time. "Think nothing of it," warbled the irresponsible lady-killer. "I'll meet you at the Zeusevelt Bar in twenty minutes." He reached into the helmet, picked up a slip, read it, tore it into shreds, laughed merrily, and started to walk off. "Just a minute," cried the infuriated captors. "What did your slip say?" "Never mind that," said the prisoner. "Just read the one you have left!"

* * *

Lewis Galantière is fond of regaling dinner parties with this rich quotation from Gibbon: "With the venerable proconsul [Gordian], his son was likewise declared emperor. His manners were less pure, but his character was equally amiable with that of his father. Twenty-two acknowledged concubines, and a library of sixty-two thousand volumes, attested the variety of his inclinations, and from the productions which he left behind him, it appears that the former as well as the latter were designed for use rather than ostentation."

★ ★ ★

The famous Lady Godiva was born way back in 1040. I didn't believe it until I checked the date in the Encyclopædia Britannica. She took her famous ride through the streets of Coventry, astride a white charger and clad only in her luxuriant golden tresses, as a protest against her husband's oppressive tax levies. Everybody refrained from looking at her with the possible exception of her husband (so contrite that he slashed the tax rate in half) and a tailor, henceforth known as Peeping Tom, who was promptly stricken blind. That's the legend, anyhow. A later historian named Fred Allen declared that another errant citizen considered peeping too but changed his mind when he heard the final arrangements. "Gadzooks," he exclaimed, "I've seen plenty of white horses before. What's all the shooting about?"

★ ★ ★

✓ Henry IV, who ruled England from 1399 to 1413, was a puritanical soul. Persuaded that his subjects wore too many jeweled and golden ornaments, he decreed that such personal adornments be prohibited. Nobody paid any attention to the law until he added one amendment: prostitutes and pickpockets were exempted. The next day there wasn't a jewel or gold ornament to be seen in the city of London. His French wife soon put a stop to this nonsense; she appeared at court one day looking like a show window at Tiffany's. The law was stricken from the books.

★ ★ ★

When Sir Walter Raleigh was imprisoned in the Tower of London, he decided to while away the interminable hours by writing a history of the world. He had covered about two hundred pages of foolscap when, one morning, he was interrupted by a great noise in the prison courtyard. Two prisoners, working there, had become involved in a violent argument. Blows were struck. Inmates clung to the barred windows of their cells and yelled gibes and encouragement until the guards tore the men apart just in time to avoid mayhem.

When the prisoners were assembled for mess that noon, nobody talked about anything else. Eight prisoners gave the attentive Sir Walter their version of the fracas. No two stories were the same.

As soon as he was back in his prison apartment, Sir Walter took the manuscript of his history of the world, tore it into pieces, and threw it into the fire.

★ ★ ★

The original draft of George Washington's Farewell Address —a priceless document—is one of the treasures belonging to the New York Public Library. The privileged souls who are allowed to examine it are told also the surprising fact that this address never was actually delivered; it was just printed in a newspaper.

The original draft was prepared by James Madison in 1792, but pigeonholed when Washington was re-elected that same year. Four years later, Washington decided that two terms were enough for any man, thereby establishing a precedent that was not broken for 144 years. He pondered over Madison's original draft, reworded it to suit himself, and by arrangement with Editor David Claypoole, it was published in the *American Daily Advertiser* on September 17, 1796.

★ ★ ★

Neal McNeil of the *New York Times* tells how the most edible kind of wild rice was first introduced into America. (This delicacy is not to be confused with the coarse wild rice that was an important part of the Indians' diet in the Minnesota region centuries before.) It seems that the special grain was developed accidentally in the Pontine marshes in Italy; when the local authorities became aware of its delicious taste and nutritive value, they slapped a complete embargo on its exportation. Thomas Jefferson was our Minister to France at the time. He was taken on a tour of the Italian marsh region, and, as he ambled along, cannily plucked off heads of the grain and pocketed them. Back in America, he pondered on the best place to plant his prized grains, and settled on the marshy shoreline of the Carolinas. The wild rice flourished there, and was the original lure for the myriad of wild duck and other fowl that have migrated to those parts ever since.

A Tammany jurist who heard McNeil's story remarked, "This is just one more blessing we can credit to the Democrats." Another member of the party was the publisher, Max Schuster, who confessed that one evening he had broken a tooth on a grain of wild rice. His rueful comment at the time was, "Well, sir, I have seen wild rice in my day, but this is certainly the wildest yet."

★ ★ ★

Samuel Johnson blundered into a musicale at Mrs. Thrale's house one night; registered acute nausea when a soprano mutilated an aria. "Come now," said Mrs. Thrale, "make some allowances. You don't realize how very difficult that piece is." "Difficult, Madam," snorted Johnson. "I wish it were impossible!"

★ ★ ★

Voltaire was invited one night to participate in an orgy by a notoriously dissolute group of Parisians. He went, and gave such a satisfactory account of himself that the very next night he was asked to come again. "Ah, no, my friends," said Voltaire with a slight smile. "Once: a philosopher; twice: a pervert!"

★ ★ ★

Voltaire had a visitor who remarked that he had encountered another literary notable of that era on the way. "Ah," said Voltaire, "a very able man, a fine character." "That's very kind of you," said the visitor, "because he said that you were a villainous old wretch." "Well," said Voltaire with a smile, "perhaps we are both mistaken."

When Rousseau wrote his ode "To Posterity" he sent an advance copy to Voltaire. Voltaire read it with a frown and remarked, "This poem will never reach its destination."

★ ★ ★

Stories of the clashes in Parliament between Benjamin Disraeli and William Ewart Gladstone are legion. "Disraeli," shouted his enraged adversary once, "you will come to your end either upon the gallows or from some loathsome disease." "That depends," replied the unruffled Disraeli, "upon whether I embrace your principles or your mistress!"

Disraeli defined the difference between a misfortune and a calamity: "If Gladstone fell into the Thames, that would be a misfortune; if anybody pulled him out, that would be a calamity."

"Mr. Disraeli cannot possibly be sure of his facts," thundered Gladstone in one debate. "I only wish," was the reply, "that I could be as sure of anything as my opponent is of everything."

Disraeli's friends assured him that, despite his persistent efforts, he could never eliminate Gladstone as a factor in the government of England. "Have you ever watched a stone-cutter at work?" answered Disraeli. "He will hammer away at a rock for perhaps a hundred times without a crack showing in it. Then, at the one hundred and first blow, it will split in two. It is not alone that blow that accomplishes the result—but the hundred others that went before, as well."

★ ★ ★

Senator Barkley told the Washington Press Club that just after President Grover Cleveland allowed a tax bill to become law without his signature, Mrs. Cleveland woke up in the middle of the night and thought she heard burglars in the house.

"Not in the House, my dear," said Cleveland. "In the Senate."

★ ★ ★

In the McKinley Administration, John Hay was Secretary of State. China was represented at Washington by Minister Wu. The latter visited the State Department one day. Mr. Hay, asked about the conference, waxed jocular. "Oh," he said, "I talked until the Minister was 'hazy,' and then he talked until I was 'woozy.' Anything else, gentlemen?"

★ ★ ★

One of the most famous and most respected of the colleges that make up the great university of Oxford is Balliol. For some reason the venerable institution attracts African potentates and Indian nabobs in addition to eminent white students; its alumni include more black-skinned men, probably, than all the rest of the colleges combined. This gave rise to a story that has a very high rating in British circles.

An explorer was going about his business in darkest Africa when a hungry cannibal tribe bagged him in full flight and considered its Sunday-dinner problem solved. He weighed about two hundred on the hoof and there were murmurs of genuine

satisfaction when they seasoned him with salt and lowered him into the pot. He was just beginning to simmer when the cannibal chief remembered his manners.

"Jove," he ejaculated, "you sound like an Oxford graduate. What college?"

"Balliol," gasped the half-baked explorer.

"Release this man," cried the chief. "Balliol men never eat one another!"

★ ★ ★

When General Pope was named to command the Union Army of Virginia in 1862, he issued a proclamation threatening the Southern forces with many dire catastrophes. The proclamation was headed "Headquarters in the Saddle." Stonewall Jackson is credited with the perfect retort: Why pay any attention to a general who obviously didn't know his headquarters from his hindquarters?

★ ★ ★

One day President Lincoln journeyed to the front to inspect the Union defenses; the task of piloting him fell to young Oliver Wendell Holmes. Holmes pointed out their enemy; the President stood up to look. Wearing his high plug hat, he made a magnificent target. A snarl of musketry fire came from the enemy trenches. The young officer dragged him under cover. Later Holmes remembered to his horror that he had muttered "Get down, you fool!" He was relieved, however, when Lincoln came to him before returning to the capital. "Good-bye, Captain Holmes," he said. "I'm glad to see you know how to talk to a civilian."

★ ★ ★

An excited supporter burst into the private chambers of the old tiger Clemenceau one day and cried, "Your son has just joined the Communist Party." Clemenceau regarded his visitor calmly and remarked, "Monsieur, my son is 22 years old. If he had not become a Communist at 22, I would have disowned him. If he is *still* a Communist at 30, I will do it then."

★ ★ ★

William Allen White, lifelong Republican, was inveigled into attending the 1928 Convention of the Democratic Party. Senator

Jim Reed of Missouri asked him to give the invocation. White hesitated, then begged off. "I'd better not, Jim," he said. "I don't want God to know I'm here."

★ ★ ★

Some years after he had been President, William Howard Taft had to make a sudden trip to Chicago. Only an upper was left. Taft noticed that the lower of his section was assigned to an insignificant Casper Milquetoast, and resorted to a bit of psychology. "Last time I occupied an upper," he announced cheerfully, "it collapsed. I certainly hope this one will hold me." Then he went off to the club car. When he returned the little man was neatly buttoned up in the upper berth.

★ ★ ★

✓ Dr. Hugh Hampton Young, eminent surgeon, attended the unveiling of a bust of himself at the University of Virginia. After the ceremony, a fluttery Southern belle came up to him and remarked: "Doctah, Ah hope you appreciate that Ah've come fifty miles in a station wagon to see your bust unveiled." The gallant doctor replied: "Madam, I would gladly return the compliment."

★ ★ ★

President Coolidge, "Honest Cal," apostle of normalcy, owed his success to a happy combination of Vermont shrewdness and extraordinary good luck. When, for example, after holding office through such a boom as America had never before experienced, he made his famous announcement, "I do not choose to run," and eased out of the White House just in time to let Mr. Hoover weather the crash in 1929, he was probably guided to some degree by instinctive caution and knowledge that a piper was going to demand payment one day; he also was a lucky, lucky man.

Most of the amusing anecdotes concerning Mr. Coolidge relate to his taciturnity and respect for his bankroll. In Northampton one day his wife fell for the blandishments of a traveling book salesman and bought one of those 1800-page "home medical advisers" for something like fifteen dollars. Misgivings assailed her the moment the salesman's hypnotic presence was removed. "What will Calvin say?" was the thought that plagued her. "How am I going to tell him?" Finally, she decided to put the book down on the centre of the library table, and await the explosion when her husband discovered it. To her amazement he said nothing about it at all—either the first evening or for several days thereafter. Mrs. Coolidge couldn't understand it—until one morning she opened the book and found that he had written a note on the fly-leaf. "I have looked carefully through all 1800 pages of this work," it read, "and find no cure whatever for a sucker."

One day Mr. Coolidge fell asleep while the presidential yacht was cruising down the Potomac. He awoke with a start, grinned sheepishly at his guests, and remarked drily, "Is the country still here?" Another time he found himself addressing a tribe of Indians on a reservation where there had been no rainfall for months. Native medicine men and professional "rain-makers" had practised their wiles in vain. Skies remained cloudless. Crops were going to ruin. The Great White Father rose to address a pretty depressed array of Indians. "Do not think that I in Washington," he said, "have not been worrying too about your lack of rain, and wondering what I could do to help you." Just then a veritable cloudburst descended upon the astonished and delighted audience. The President was soaked before he got under shelter. He watched the rain pour down and said, half to himself, "Gosh, I didn't know I had it in me."

The ambassador of a great nation called at the White House one day for an important and private conversation with the President. Mrs. Coolidge came in as the ambassador was preparing to leave. "Why don't you offer the ambassador a drink?" she suggested. "He's already had one," said the President testily. The next day, correspondents asked if he had anything to say about the conference. "No," said Coolidge. "I have nothing to say to you about anything else either." As they were leaving, he called after them, "And don't quote me!"

President Coolidge once visited the Emily Dickinson house in Amherst, and was shown the poetess' original manuscripts. He examined them casually and made a single comment: "Wrote with a pen, eh? I dictate!" There is a famous anecdote about a Sunday when Mr. Coolidge attended church without his wife. When he returned to the White House, she asked what the subject of the sermon had been. "Adultery," said the President. "What did he say about it?" she persisted. Coolidge thought for a moment. "He's against it," he reported finally. (That always reminds me of the sinner who sat in church, bored and dejected, while the pastor rumbled on about the Ten Commandments. Suddenly he reached Number Seven, and intoned

"Thou shalt not commit adultery." The man snapped to attention, brightened visibly, and exclaimed with satisfaction, "*That's where I left my umbrella!*")

When Dorothy Parker heard that Calvin Coolidge was dead, she remarked cruelly, "How can they tell?" Clarence Darrow spoke his perfect epitaph: "The greatest man who ever came out of Plymouth Corner, Vermont!"

★ ★ ★

When Cundliffe, the Australian economist, was notified that he had been appointed a professor at Oxford, he went to his children's Australian nurse, and asked if she could accompany the family to England. "England?" she echoed in horror. "Where all the convicts come from? Never!"

★ ★ ★

Eamon de Valera, the Irish political leader who was born in Brooklyn, is a serious man today, but in his youth showed flashes of typical Irish wit. Returning to Dublin from a visit to Paris many years ago, he was asked by a friend to give his impression of the French mesdemoiselles. "Gentlemen," de Valera is said to have replied, "I may safely say that sex in Ireland is in its infancy."

Another time, he was arrested in the middle of an inflammatory political tirade, and clapped into prison for a full year. When he was released he went right back to the scene of his arrest, summoned his followers, and began another speech, "As I was saying when I was so rudely interrupted."

★ ★ ★

The Governor of Iowa has a name that makes rather a neat mouthful: Bourke Blakemore Hickenlooper. He himself tells about a drugstore clerk who refused to charge ten cents' worth of asafetida to the Hickenlooper account. "Take it for nothing, boss," said the clerk. "I wouldn't write both asafetida and Hickenlooper for a dime."

During President Hoover's last year in office, he was walking down Pennsylvania Avenue with his Secretary of the Treasury, Andrew Mellon. "Andy," said the President, "I came out this morning without a cent in my pockets. Lend me a nickel, will you? I want to call up a friend." "Here's a dime," volunteered Mellon. "Call both of them!"

★　★　★

Jane Addams, the famous social worker and founder of Hull House, told this story on herself. She met an old friend on a train one afternoon, and greeted her cordially, but simply couldn't remember her name. "The conversation is bound to give me a clue," she thought, but for a half-hour she got nowhere. Then the friend said, "My poor brother is working himself to death these days." Miss Addams felt that her moment had come. "Ah yes, your dear brother," she exclaimed. "And what is he doing now?" Her companion glared. "He is still President of the United States," she remarked coldly.

★　★　★

Somebody once asked the late Huey Long if he thought we would ever have fascism in the United States. "Sure we will," predicted Long, "only *we'll* call it anti-fascism!"

★　★　★

The last time Thomas Lamont was in London he checked on the story that Lenin, many years ago, spent a long period of study in the British Museum. Mr. Lamont challenged an aged and fragile attendant of the Museum. "Do you remember seeing a little man named Lenin around here several years ago? He had a small, reddish beard, and he probably spent most of his time in the sociology and political philosophy alcoves." "Lenin? Lenin?" mused the old attendant. "Why, yes, now that you mention it, I do remember a gent by that name, sir. Read a powerful lot of deep books, 'e did, sir. You know, I've often wondered what became of that little man!"

★ ★ ★

Only in China could a thing like this happen, said Ilona Sues, who wrote *Shark's Fins and Millet*.

Two mighty war lords, an uncle and his nephew, both of whom bore the name of Lieu, were engaged in a bloody fight for the supremacy of Szechuan Province. That was several years before the United Front in China. The country's greatest tennis player, Gordon Lum, arrived at the nephew's headquarters. The latter was delighted. His enthusiasm for tennis was matched by that of his uncle. He promptly dispatched an emissary to his uncle's camp, and a three-day truce was arranged to celebrate Lum's visit, and stage an honest-to-goodness tennis tournament.

A couple of hundred soldiers from both camps were detailed to build a first-rate tennis court in the middle of the wilderness. The two armies fraternized, Lieu and his nephew sat side by side at the edge of the court, and everybody got beautifully drunk on the best wines that could be found in the province. When the tournament was over, both armies went back to the exact positions they had occupied, and resumed the war where they had left off.

Gordon Lum said that just as he was about to serve one afternoon, he spotted a human head nailed to a tree behind the court, and became so unnerved he missed one ball completely.

"Why didn't you ask them to take it off?" asked Miss Sues.

"Not on your life," said Lum. "Such a request might have offended either the uncle or nephew or both of them, and spoiled the whole feast. A trophy is a trophy, and must remain where it is put. As a guest of honor, I could not make such a tactless remark. So I pretended that I hadn't even noticed the thing."

★ ★ ★

623

On the day that be-ribboned, be-medaled Higinio Morínigo achieved the presidency of the Republic of Paraguay, his aged mother is quoted as saying, "Hmphff! If I had known they were going to make a president of him, I would have sent him to school."

* * *

John Collier, Commissioner of Indian Affairs, gives some surprising facts in *The Changing Indian,* a new publication of the University of Oklahoma Press. Mr. Collier, no one for vague generalities, avers that there are now 350,397 Indians in the United States, and that this represents an increase of thirty-four percent over the 1890 tabulations; 153,993 are full-blood. Some tribes, notably the Dakotas and the Cherokees, are more numerous today than when the white man first encroached upon their territory, and many reservations are becoming overcrowded.

Maybe you have heard the story of Mrs. Lapidus who saw an honest-to-God Indian for the first time in her life at a basket-weaving exhibition at Wanamaker's. "Is it true dot you are a real, one hundred percent Indian?" she asked him. "Ugh," affirmed the Indian affably. "My, my!" mused Mrs. Lapidus. "How do you like our country?"

* * *

A male penguin proposes, according to Sir Hubert Wilkins, who was in the Antarctic long enough to find out, by placing a pebble at the feet of the lady penguin who has captured his heart. If she is inclined to accept, she picks up the token and carries it to a spot she has no doubt lined up well in advance; the nest is promptly built there and connubial relations established without further folderol.

There was a painter on one of Sir Hubert's expeditions who was sketching on the rocks when a female penguin came waddling along and rather pointedly deposited a pebble at his feet.

"Did he marry her?" laughed an interviewer. "No," said Sir

Hubert pensively. "But don't forget, we had been there only four months at the time!"

★　★　★

In Hollywood, Carl Sandburg was shown the wonders of the MGM lot and met the most glamorous stars without uttering a syllable. The guide, in desperation, led him to the dressing room of a freakish show girl and said, "Just think, Mr. Sandburg. This girl is six foot two!" Sandburg spoke at last. "Lincoln," he said, "was six foot three and a half."

★　★　★

The correspondent John Whitaker reports that Mussolini openly sneered at his own lieutenants in the final years that he ruled Italy. Pointing to a painting in the Palazzo Venezia of Count Volpi standing arrogantly with his hands thrust into his pants pockets, Mussolini remarked bitterly to Whitaker, "That is the only time I have caught my own Finance Minister with his hands in his own pockets."

★　★　★

Within three months of Pearl Harbor, ninety percent of the famous authors in America had journeyed down to Washington trying to get jobs of one sort or another in furtherance of the war effort. Edna Ferber was one of the group. "I want to help the Government in Washington," she is said to have told Archibald MacLeish, "but I don't want to be a writer. I want to do something else. What can I be?" "Well," said Mr. MacLeish, "you can always be a battleship."

★　★　★

Astute diagnosing by John Gunther in his latest book, *D Day*: "The worst thing about war is that so many men like it. . . . It relieves them of personal responsibilities. . . . There is no worry about frictions at home or the dull necessity of earning a living. Military life is like a perpetual camping trip. I heard one officer say, 'How nice all this would be if only you could eliminate the bloodshed and the killing.'" "Perhaps," adds Orville Prescott, "peace planners who debate problems of frontiers and economics had better give a little more attention to eliminating the pleasures of soldierly comradeship and vast cooperative endeavor, the drama and excitement and the fun of war also."

★ ★ ★

The mayors of New York in recent years have supplied copy for every newspaper in the land. First there was John Hylan (called "Red Mike" behind his back) who escorted Queen Marie of Rumania on a tour up Fifth Avenue. "What a wonderful avenue," exclaimed Her Majesty. "You said a mouthful, Queen," agreed His Honor. Hylan seldom bothered to read speeches that trusted ghosts prepared for him ahead of time. In the middle of one speech he came to the phrase, "That reminds me of one of my favorite stories about a traveling salesman." It developed that the Mayor had never heard the joke before, and when he finished reading it, he laughed so hard he broke his glasses. The chairman of the dinner had to finish the speech for him.

Jimmie Walker brought color and gaiety to City Hall, although later he had a little trouble explaining what he took away from it. A pretty girl was once led into his office, worrying audibly whether she should address him as "Your Honor," "Mr. Mayor," or plain "Mr. Walker." Jimmie settled all that by pulling her down on his lap and crooning, "Come to baby, Beautiful," while the camera men clicked away in delight. Asked by a publisher to name his ten favorite novels, the Mayor laughed and declared, "Son, I never read a book in my life!"

A battered wreck of a man accosted Mayor Walker outside the Central Park Casino one night. "Jimmie," he pleaded, "gimme a quarter for something to eat." "Have a Corona," said the Mayor, reaching into his vest pocket. "Don't smoke," asserted the hooligan. "I just want a quarter for something to eat." "Come inside with me," suggested the Mayor, "and I'll stand you to a couple of whiskies. They'll buck you up!" "Don't drink," was the answer. "It's food I want." "I tell you what I'll do," persisted Walker. "I'm going to Belmont tomorrow. I happen to know of a horse that's a sure thing at twenty to one. I'll put a couple of dollars on it for you!" "No, no," cried the beggar. "I wouldn't think of gambling. Please stop all this nonsense and slip me a simple two bits for something to eat." "All right," conceded the Mayor reluctantly. "But first you've got to come over and meet my wife. I want her to see what happens to a guy who doesn't smoke, drink, or gamble."

Tammany Hall decided that New York needed a mayor to follow Walker who would be a different character in every re-

Hizzoner Jimmie Walker and Hizzoner John P. O'Brien,
or an illustration of the old political dictum,
"Never follow a banjo act with another banjo act."

627

spect. Jimmie agreed. "Never follow a banjo act with another banjo act," was his dictum. So they bobbed up with John P. O'Brien, who, in his own words, was "a thousand percent different." Mr. O'Brien early endeared himself to his constituents when he referred to "that scientist of scientists, Albert Weinstein," and told delighted reporters that he was "a slave to literature." Mr. O'Brien's first interview consisted mainly of a declaration that he would make his own decisions and take neither advice nor direction from Tammany. One reporter spoiled everything by asking, "Mr. Mayor, who is going to be your new police commissioner?" O'Brien scratched his head. "I don't know," he answered. "They haven't told me yet."

Fiorello LaGuardia officiates at the author's wedding

Mayor LaGuardia, the present incumbent, rates a whole book for himself, but as long as he's mayor of the town we all work in, I'd better be careful. Besides, he officiated at my marriage, and I owe him a debt of gratitude. He whipped through the ceremony in three seconds flat, mumbled, "Don't blame me for anything that happens," and was off—probably to attend a fire. Here's one nice story about him. He presides occasionally in Police Court. One bitter cold day they brought a trembling old man before him, charged with stealing a loaf of bread. His family, he said, was starving. "I've got to punish you," declared LaGuardia. "The law makes no exception. I can do nothing but sentence you to a fine of ten dollars."

But the Little Flower was reaching into his pocket as he added, "Well, here's the ten dollars to pay your fine. And now I remit the fine." He tossed a ten-dollar bill into his famous sombrero. "Furthermore," he declared, "I'm going to fine everybody in this courtroom fifty cents for living in a town where a man has to steal bread in order to eat. Mr. Bailiff, collect the fines and give them to this defendant!" The hat was passed and an incredulous old man, with a light of heaven in his eyes, left the courtroom with a stake of forty-seven dollars and fifty cents.

Chapter Eleven

THE TRAIL OF THE TINGLING SPINE

In times of stress there is always a tremendous upsurge of interest in ghost stories and tales that make the heart skip a beat. Several such collections have hit the best-seller lists recently, and Hollywood, which used to produce its so-called "Zombie" pictures at a cost of thirty cents (Confederate money) and regard them as a secret weapon to depopulate theatres, has now turned the attention of some of its fanciest directors and stars to the Trail of the Tingling Spine.

In the following pages I have set down a few of the memorable ghost stories and thrillers that have been told me in the past few years. One of them was narrated in the presence of a man who wears a toupee. He got so excited that in two minutes every hair on the toupee was standing on end.

Probably you have heard about the timid soul who was hurrying down a dark, dark corridor when he suddenly collided with a stout and shadowy personage whom he certainly had not seen approaching him. "Golly," said the timid one, "you gave me a fright! For a second I thought you were a ghost!" "What makes you think I'm not?" answered the other—and promptly vanished.

Try a few of these stories yourself at a dinner party one evening. The results are electrifying. Soon everybody is remembering a macabre story *he's* heard about a haunted house, or an ill-mannered ghost, or a thing that behaved in no fashion that was human. Give the spooks a chance, and they'll pay dividends. I have spooken.

★ ★ ★

Two ladies from the faculty of a famous New England college for women decided to spend one of their vacations in an automobile tour to California and back. They traveled westward by way of the Petrified Forest and the Grand Canyon, and headed for home by the Salt Lake City route. They were two normal, unimaginative women, enjoying to the full a tour of their native country.

Late one evening, they were driving through the flat and monotonous fields of Kansas, intent upon reaching a hostel some thirty miles distant, when their car broke down. They were the kind of drivers who know nothing whatever about motors. They had no choice but to wait for some good Samaritan to come driving along and help them—and it soon became obvious that no other car was likely to come that way until the next morning.

It was then that one of the ladies noticed a two-story, unpainted farmhouse, set back some distance from the road. They approached it gingerly, wary of watch-dogs, and knocked timidly on the front door. Nobody answered. The impression grew on them that the house was uninhabited. When they discovered that the door was unlocked, they entered, calling loudly, and flashing their pocket searchlight in every corner. They found the living room and kitchen in good order, but an undisturbed layer of dust indicated that no human being had been in them for days.

The ladies blessed their luck, and decided to spend the night in the living room. The couch was fairly comfortable, and they bundled themselves up in robes which they fetched from the stalled automobile. There were dry logs in the fireplace; the ladies soon had a roaring fire going, and, in the light of the flickering embers, went peacefully to sleep.

Some hours later, one of the ladies awoke with the distinct feeling that somebody had entered the house. Her friend jumped up at precisely the same moment. A chill seemed to run through the room, followed by the unmistakable scent of the salt sea, although the nearest ocean front was over a thousand miles away. Then a young man walked into the room! Rather he *floated* in, because they heard no footsteps. He was dressed in boots and oilskins; sea-spray glistened on his rough stubble of reddish beard. He moved to the dying fire, shivering violently, and knelt down before it.

One of the women screamed. The figure turned slowly, gave a sort of mournful sigh, and slowly dissolved into nothingness. The terrified women clutched each other desperately, and lay there until the morning sun poured through the dusty window panes. "I saw it; I know I did!" said one of them. "Of course you did; I saw it too," the other reassured her, and then pointed dramatically to the fireplace. Before it was a small puddle of brackish water, and a piece of slimy green weed.

The ladies made for the open air, but the bolder of the two snatched up the piece of weed before they bolted, and held it gingerly at arm's length. When it dried, she placed it carefully in her bag.

Eventually a car rattled along the highway, and the driver cheerfully consented to tow the ladies to the nearest garage. While the mechanic tinkered with the engine, the ladies asked him about the deserted house some miles back on the road. "That must have been the Newton place," he said with no special show of interest. "Been empty nigh on to two years now. When Old Man Newton died, he left it lock, stock and barrel to his son Tom, who said he didn't like farming, and lit out one day for the East. Spoke of taking to the sea, like his great-grandfather did. Ain't none of us seen hide nor hair of him since that day!"

When the ladies returned to their college, they took the green weed, which still seemed clammy and damp, to the head of the botany department. He readily confirmed their suspicions. "It's seaweed, all right," he told them. "Furthermore, it's a kind that's only found on dead bodies!" The ship news reporter of the *Evening Sun* reported that a Thomas Newton had sailed as first-class seaman on a freighter called the *Robert B. Anthony* on April 14, 1937. It had gone down with all hands aboard in a storm off the Greenland coast six weeks thereafter.

★ ★ ★

One summer evening, just before dark, a man was driving his wife along a lonely country road, when she suddenly complained of a violent headache. One look at her agonized expression convinced him that something was radically wrong. He remembered that about ten miles back, he had passed a little cottage with a doctor's shingle on the gate. He turned the car about in a pasture, and drove back to the doctor's house as quickly as he dared.

A gray-haired, white-jacketed little man with sharp, twinkling eyes, answered his summons. He took one look at the ailing wife, and said simply, "Carry her into my office at once." The man waited impatiently while the doctor made a cursory examination, then followed him into his anteroom when bidden. "Something is pressing on your wife's brain," said the doctor. "I'm afraid she must be operated upon immediately. If you wait even until you get her back to town it probably will be too late." The man gasped. "I'm willing to perform the operation," continued the doctor, "but I'm all alone in this house and you will have to help me. I'll do my best but won't answer for the consequences."

There was something in the doctor's manner that inspired confidence. Besides, the woman's condition was obviously desperate. "Go ahead," said the man grimly.

The operation had reached its most delicate stage when the man became aware of an insistent banging on the front door. As soon as he could, he went to throw it open, and found two uniformed men waiting to enter. One of them had a gun under his arm. "The little doctor slipped away from us again," he said. "We usually find him pottering around here." "Who are you?" asked the man. "Guards at the asylum over the hill," was the answer. "Where's the doctor? Got to get him back before he gets violent!"

"Good God!" said the man. "He's in the middle of an operation on my wife's brain. You'll have to let him finish. Get me an ambulance—quick!"

Fifteen minutes later, the doctor came out of the parlor and declared the operation completed. The ambulance from the asylum was already at the door. One attendant helped the man lift his wife gently into the back, while the other led the unprotesting doctor away.

The ride back to New York was a nightmare for the distracted man. His wife had not regained consciousness when he arrived at the home of his own private physician on Park Avenue. "Be quick," he begged. "Something terrible has happened to her. Tell me if anything can be done before it is too late."

It was a sorely puzzled man who came to him a short while

later. "This case baffles me completely," he said. "Your wife will live. She has been saved by an almost miraculous operation. But this is the factor that stops me cold. I know of only one man in this world who has the skill and the knowledge to perform an operation of this character. And that man has been in an insane asylum for the past six years!"

★ ★ ★

A young lady dreamed one night that she was walking along a strange country lane. It led her up a wooded hill whose summit was crowned with the loveliest little white frame house and garden she ever had seen. Unable to conceal her delight, she knocked loudly on the door of the house, and finally it was opened by an old, old man with a long white beard. Just as she started to talk to him, she woke up. Every detail of this dream was so vivid in her memory that she carried it about in her head for days. Then, on three successive nights, she had precisely the same dream again. Always she awakened at the point where her conversation with the old man was about to begin.

A few weeks later, the young lady was motoring to Litchfield for a week-end party, when she suddenly tugged at the driver's sleeve, and begged him to stop. There, at the right of the concrete highway, was the country lane of her dreams! "Wait for me a few moments," she pleaded, and, her heart beating wildly, set out on the lane. She was no longer surprised when it wound to the top of the wooded hill, and the house whose every feature was now so familiar to her. The old man responded to her impatient summons. "Tell me," she began, "is this little house for sale?" "That it is," said the man, "but I would scarcely advise you to buy it. You see, young lady, this house is haunted!" "Haunted," echoed the girl. "For heaven's sake, by whom?" "By you," said the old man, and softly closed the door.

★ ★ ★

John Sullivan was the only son of a doting mother, widowed during the First World War. He was handsome, richly endowed with Irish charm, and a particular favorite of the ladies. They could not resist his fetching smile. In fact, they never tried.

John couldn't explain how he suddenly came to be walking up Euclid Avenue. He had no memory of how he got there, or of what he had been doing previously that morning. "I must be walking in my sleep," he said to himself in some perplexity. Two lovely young girls were approaching him. John stopped them with the confidence born of years of easy conquest. "Could you be telling me the time?" he asked with his easy smile. To his surprise, one of the girls screamed, and both of them careened past him. Several other people, he noticed, seemed terrified by the sight of him. One man flattened himself against a show window of the Halle Store to get out of his way.

Greatly puzzled, John Sullivan started to climb into a taxi. Just as he was giving the address of his home, however, the driver looked at him for the first time, smothered an exclamation, pushed him out of the cab, and drove off with a grinding of gears.

John's head was spinning. He entered a drugstore, and phoned to his mother. A strange voice answered.

"Mrs. Sullivan?" it echoed. "Now who would be expecting to find her in now? Don't you know that her poor son John was caught in a machine at the bindery yesterday and mangled to death? She's out at the cemetery where they're burying him now!"

★ ★ ★

Dick Rodgers, the composer, is also no mean hand at spilling a yarn. He tells of a poker game in which the unfortunate Mr. Jones, with an incurable passion for drawing to inside straights, not only lost his entire bankroll, but had to endure the unmerciful gibes of his companions as well.

"What am I going to use for money until the pay check comes in on Friday?" he wailed. The editor of a weekly magazine fished a five-spot out of his pocket. "Your tears are destroying me," said he. "Take this money and scram." Walking home, the disconsolate Jones was accosted by a bedraggled lady of the streets who burst into tears when he shoved her aside unceremoniously. "I'm starving," she said in a low voice. "If you don't help me, I swear I'm going to kill myself." "Heck," reasoned Jones. "This is my night all right." He handed her the five-dollar bill. "I will never forget you," she assured him. "You've restored some of my faith in humanity!"

The next morning Jones was glancing over the newspaper when he noticed a headline that read "Body of Unknown Woman Taken from River." The description of her dress and hat proved beyond a doubt that the suicide was the woman he had befriended.

He met the editor at lunch. "What did you do after you left us, Jones?" said the editor idly. "Nothing at all. I just walked home," said Jones. "Didn't you spend any money?" "Not a cent. Why?" "Oh," mused the editor, "we were just wondering what would happen to you when you tried to palm off that phony five-dollar bill we gave you."

★ ★ ★

When an intelligent, comely girl of twenty-odd summers was invited for the first time to the Carolina estate of some distant relatives, their lovely plantation fulfilled her fondest expectations. She was given a room in the west wing, and prepared to retire for the night in a glow of satisfaction. Her room was drenched with the light of a full moon.

Just as she was climbing into her bed, she was startled by the sound of horses' hooves on the gravel roadway. Curious, she walked to the window and saw, to her astonishment, a magnificent old coach pull up to an abrupt stop directly below her. The coachman jumped from his perch, looked up and pointed a long, bony finger at her. He was hideous. His face was chalk-white. A deep scar ran the length of his left cheek. His nose was beaked. As he pointed at her, he droned in sepulchral tones, "There is room for one more!" Then, as she recoiled in terror, the coach, the horses and the ominous coachman disappeared completely.

The girl slept little, but the next day she was able to convince herself that she had merely had a nightmare.

The next night, however, the horrible experience was repeated. The same coach drove up the roadway. The same coachman pointed at her and intoned, "There is room for one more!" Then, as before, the entire equipage disappeared.

The girl, now panic-striken, could scarcely wait for morning. She trumped up some excuse to her hosts and left immediately for home.

Upon arrival, she taxied to her doctor from the station and told him her story in tremulous tones. The doctor persuaded her that she had been the victim of a peculiar hallucination, laughed at her terror, and dismissed her in a state of infinite relief. As she rang for the elevator, its door swung open before her.

The elevator was very crowded, but she was about to squeeze her way inside—when a familiar voice rang in her ear. "There is room for one more!" it called. In terror, she stared at the operator. He was the coachman who had pointed at her! She saw his chalk-white face, the livid scar, the beaked nose! She drew back and screamed . . . the elevator door banged shut.

A moment later the building shook with a terrible crash. The elevator that had gone on without her broke loose from its cables and plunged eighteen stories to the ground. Everybody in it, of course, was crushed to a pulp.

★   ★   ★

A macabre story told at a dinner party recently sent everybody scurrying to find its source. Subsequent reports were conflicting, to say the least. One expert claimed it came from the Indian captivity stories. Another said it could be found in Jack London's early tales of the frozen North. The man who had told it at the dinner, however, insisted that the locale was the heart of Africa, and that is where we might as well leave it for the retelling here.

The hero is an intrepid anthropologist who made his way, with one faithful assistant, to the darkest jungle in Africa in the furtherance of his studies. While seeking to record the tribal customs of a band of bloodthirsty savages, the two scientists incurred, first the suspicion, and then the blind hatred, of the tribe. One day they were caught off guard and marched to the tribe's encampment. The doctor's assistant was murdered diabolically, after prolonged and ingenious torture. The chief then strode up to the doctor, spat in his face, and informed him with evident satisfaction that this was just a mild preliminary to what was in store for him, beginning the following morning. It would take them a full week, at least, said the chief, to finish him off. Then he was locked up for the night.

The next morning, when the ordeal was about to begin, the

doctor asked for one last word with the cannibal chief. It was too bad, he said, that they were going to kill him before he could tell them about his discovery of a miraculous herb. A single bite of this herb, he explained, made a man immune to death. Furthermore, it grew in abundance in the immediate vicinity. The chief registered disbelief. This obvious stratagem would get the doctor nowhere. "Very well," proposed the doctor. "Let me gather a few of these herbs and swallow them. Then let your headsman take his sharpest sword and try to kill me with it. You will see that the blow will glance harmlessly off my body."

A hasty powwow ensued, and it was agreed that nothing could be lost by testing the doctor's claim. Heavily guarded, he was allowed to hunt for the magic herb. After some poking about the bushes, he announced that he had found what he was searching for. In front of the entire tribe, he swallowed two of the herbs, and cried, "Now I am immune to death! Strike with your sword. You can never kill me!"

He knelt in the clearing. The tribe watched in breathless silence. The headsman raised his sword and brought it down with all his strength. The doctor's head, severed cleanly at the base of the skull, rolled crazily onto the ground.

★ ★ ★

André Malraux, the author of that brilliant novel, *Man's Hope*, told me this story in a little workmen's rendezvous in Paris, in the shadow of the Sacré Cœur. A flickering candle dripped a widening stain of acrid grease on the checkered tablecloth while he was talking, and an old man with a red beret was plucking the strings of a guitar in the corner in a sad and aimless fashion. We had been talking about World's Fairs, and the discussion drifted back to the Paris Exposition of the last generation. It was at this Fair, said Malraux, that the fastest scenic railway ever constructed was featured. The old fellow with the guitar, in fact, had helped to build it.

"And rode it, too?" I suggested.

"No," was the answer. "He never rode it. That is what I want to tell you about. The man who owned the concession had a mania for speed. He said this ride they were building for him had to be the fastest in the world. For a long time architects and engineers experimented and conferred on plans for a ride that would outspeed the wind.

"Finally, the blueprints were completed, with all the dips and curves and angles calculated to make the cars whiz around the course at a whirlwind pace. When the structure was still in rude state, the new, shiny red cars were sent shooting along the tracks, equipped with instruments and freighted with sandbags approximating the weight of the human cargoes that would be borne when the Fair was opened.

"The last nail in the structure was driven home. In keeping with the custom in such cases, those who had built the racer were entitled to the first ride. There was a scramble for seats. Our friend wasn't agile enough, and had to wait for the next trip. The car started on its dizzy ride, the men in it laughing and cheering.

"He and the others who were left behind heard the car whirl around the curves and roar down the drops as they jostled one another to get near the head of the line for the next ride. Then it pulled into view and rolled to an automatic stop. But there was no answer to the onlookers' yells and eager questions. Not one of the passengers stirred.

"I don't know who rushed forward first. I know that the old fellow over there found himself shaking the shoulders of his closest friend. The others followed suit. One after another the heads of the passengers wobbled loosely on their chests—or back, too far back—or to one side or the other. Every neck had been broken—snapped like a glass stem—on those sharp curves that had been tested only with sandbags!"

The old man sensed that we were talking about him. He smiled at us—a sad, fleeting smile. His fingers never stopped their aimless plucking of the guitar strings.

★ ★ ★

A dozen miles outside of Baltimore, the main road from New York (Route Number One) is crossed by another important highway. It is a dangerous intersection, and there is talk of building an underpass for the east-west road. To date, however, the plans exist only on paper.

Dr. Eckersall was driving home from a country-club dance late one Saturday night. He slowed up for the intersection, and was surprised to see a lovely young girl, dressed in the sheerest of evening gowns, beckoning to him for a lift. He jammed on his brakes, and motioned her to climb into the back seat of his roadster. "All cluttered up with golf clubs and bags up here in front," he explained. "But what on earth is a youngster like you doing out here all alone at this time of night?"

"It's too long a story to tell you now," said the girl. Her voice was sweet and somewhat shrill—like the tinkling of sleigh bells. "Please, please take me home. I'll explain everything there. The address is —— North Charles Street. I do hope it's not too far out of your way."

The doctor grunted, and set the car in motion. He drove rapidly to the address she had given him, and as he pulled up before the shuttered house, he said, "Here we are." Then he turned around. The back seat was empty!

"What the devil?" the doctor muttered to himself. The girl couldn't possibly have fallen from the car. Nor could she simply have vanished. He rang insistently on the house bell, confused as he had never been in his life before. At long last the door opened. A gray-haired, very tired-looking man peered out at him.

"I can't tell you what an amazing thing has happened," began the doctor. "A young girl gave me this address a while back. I drove her here and——"

"Yes, yes, I know," said the man wearily. "This has happened several other Saturday evenings in the past month. That young girl, sir, was my daughter. She was killed in an automobile accident at that intersection where you saw her almost two years ago. . . ."

★ ★ ★

A distinguished English typographer, who will be called Francis Johnson in this story, has an insatiable curiosity that got him into trouble one dreary afternoon in London. A distant relative had died, and the body was dispatched to a suburban crematorium. The funeral services were held in town. When the dreary procession of rented sedans headed for the crematorium, Johnson and his wife decided to drive down in their own roadster, thereby arriving fully thirty minutes ahead of the others.

The period of waiting was not too cheering, and Johnson began fidgeting with the gadgets in view. A black button in the wall engaged his attention, and finally he gave it a push. To his horror, the body slid slowly but inexorably into the cremator!

When the funeral party duly arrived, the body, of course, had disappeared. So had the Johnsons.

★ ★ ★

Saxe Commins remembers a racing meet at a country fair which was interrupted at the close of the fifth race by an official who carried a large megaphone and bellowed an announcement to the milling spectators.

"Ladies and gentlemen," he began (the day of the loud

speaker had not yet dawned). "At exactly four o'clock our patrons are asked to observe two minutes of silence out of respect to the dead President of the United States, Warren Gamaliel Harding. At that hour his body will be lowered into its grave in Marion, Ohio. The audience is requested to bare heads when taps are blown from this stand and remain silent in prayer for two minutes. I thank you."

At the stroke of four a bugler began to blow the mournful dirge for the dead. Hats were removed everywhere. Gradually, however, all eyes were attracted by one giant of a man, near the centre of the crowd, who failed to remove his hat. It was a straw, encircled with a gay ribbon. He stood straight as a poker, with his arms folded across his breast.

Cries of "Take it off! Take it off!" rose to a louder and louder pitch of anger as the man stood oblivious to the clamor. Someone near him hit him in the back. The hat flew off. The man fell. Instantly he was the centre of a milling mob.

By the time the police rescued him he was a bloody mess, his clothes in tatters, his face a pulp. From deep in his throat came guttural noises of pain, tortured but wordless. Then the crowd learned that, of all the thousands there, it was he alone who had faithfully observed the ritual of the two minutes of silence, for he was deaf and dumb.

There was an incident of the same description in New York about a year after Pearl Harbor. A parade was proceeding down Fifth Avenue. When the flag went by, everybody saluted except a frail young man who stood motionless at the curbstone. A beefy, red-faced citizen behind him pushed him violently into the gutter. "Damn it," he cried. "What do you mean by not saluting when our flag goes by?" The young man turned. On his chest was the Purple Heart. He had no arms.

★ ★ ★

A favorite story of New York literary circles a few years ago concerned a beautiful young girl in a white satin dress. It was one of those anecdotes which everybody swore had actually happened to his first cousin or next-door neighbor, and several narrators became very testy when they were informed that several other people's cousins had evidently undergone the same experience just a few weeks before.

At any rate, the legend maintained that a very lovely but poverty-stricken damsel was invited to a formal dance. It was her chance to enter a brand-new world. Who knew but that some rich young man would fall in love with her and lift her out of her life in a box factory? The catch in the matter was that she had no suitable dress to wear for such a great occasion.

"Why don't you rent a costume for the evening?" suggested a friend. Not having thought of this before, the girl became hopeful, and that very night went to a pawnshop near her little flat, where for a surprisingly reasonable sum she rented a beautiful white satin evening gown with all the accessories to match. Miraculously, it fit her like a glove and gave her such radiance that upon her arrival at the party she created a minor sensation. She was cut in on again and again, and as she whirled happily around the floor she felt that her luck indeed had changed for the better.

Soon, however, she began to feel faint and nauseated. She fought against a growing discomfort as long as possible, but finally stole out of the house with barely sufficient strength to stagger into a cab and creep up the stairs to her room. She threw herself onto her bed, broken-hearted, and it was then—possibly in her delirium—that she heard a woman's voice whispering in her ear. It was harsh and bitter. "Give me back my dress," it said. "Give me back my dress! It belongs to . . . the dead . . ."

The next morning the lifeless body of the young girl was found stretched out on her bed. The unusual circumstances led the coroner to order an autopsy. It was found the girl had been poisoned by embalming fluid which had entered her pores when she became overheated from dancing. The pawnbroker was reluctant to admit that he knew where the dress had come from, but spoke out when he heard that the district attorney's office was involved. It had been sold him by an undertaker's assistant who had taken it from the body of a dead girl just before the casket was nailed down for the last time.

★ ★ ★

Carter generally minded his own business on the train, but it was impossible to concentrate on his evening paper after the young man had slumped into the seat beside him. In all his years of commuting between New York and Stamford, Carter had never seen anybody so obviously demoralized and on the verge of collapse. The fellow's hands trembled violently, his body twitched, he gave the air of seeing nothing around him and neither knowing nor caring exactly where he was. He mumbled to himself occasionally too, but when Carter pointedly sighed and folded up his newspaper, he pulled himself together sufficiently to apologize for fidgeting and making a nuisance of himself. Carter did not encourage him in any way, and was rather surprised to find himself suddenly plunged into the middle of the young man's story.

"Nine years ago," the young man said, "I was elected head of my college fraternity. We had a strict rule that only three members of every new freshman class be admitted to membership. That kept our active list to an even dozen. Nobody ever refused our bids. Everyone recognized that we were the kingpins of the campus. In what was probably a subconscious effort to prove to ourselves what superior beings we were, our initiations became more and more elaborate and fantastic as the years went by.

"At initiation time it was my idea to take the three neophytes we had selected and bundle them out to a deserted house about fifteen miles from the campus. It had been unoccupied for years, was windowless, sagging and ugly, and was said by the villagers to be haunted. We picked a black, starless night for the initiation, and all the way out to the place poured tales of horror and the supernatural into the ears of our three apprehensive freshmen.

"I picked the frailest of the kids to go into the house first. He was the son of a famous novelist who had won the Pulitzer Prize the year before, and was by way of being a boy prodigy himself. His eyes betrayed his fear when we shipped him off, but he compressed his lips and set out bravely enough. The rest of us built a bonfire, and relaxed around it.

"I watched him enter the deserted house. It was about two hundred yards from where we were gathered. His instructions were to stay inside for a half-hour, and then come back to us. When forty-five long minutes went by without any sign of him, I experienced my first uneasiness, and dispatched the second freshman to fetch him. Ten minutes more went by. Nothing happened. There wasn't a sound anywhere. The fire was burning low—we just sat there, quietly watching.

" 'These kids are a little too smart for their own good,' I said at last. 'Davis, get in there and bring them back fast.' Davis was our prize conquest—a handsome, two-hundred-pound boy whose scholastic records foreshadowed an almost certain place on the next year's All-American squad. He had already been elected president of the freshman class.

" 'I'll get 'em,' he grinned, and loped toward the house.

"And then we just sat there. I guess it was only ten minutes, but it seemed like hours. 'It looks like my move, fellows,' I said finally. 'We'll have to teach these brats that they can't play tricks on their elders this way.' I got up and walked slowly over to the deserted house.

"The first thing that struck me when I entered was a musty smell like the smell of an attic full of old books and newspapers. I yelled for the boys, and poked my flashlight into every corner but there wasn't a sign of them. Only a faint, steady tap that seemed to come from the roof. Filled with dread, I climbed the creaking stairway to the second floor, and the ladder leading to the roof. I stuck my head through the open skylight. There was Davis, stretched out on his stomach! His hair had turned snow-white. His eyes rolled in his head. He was mad as a hatter. In his hand he held a hammer covered with blood. He was rapping weakly with it on the tin parapet, in a senseless rhythm. I screamed to him, but he paid no attention to me. He just went on tapping with that bloody hammer. I somehow or other got back to the fellows waiting for me and we managed to carry Davis down from the roof. He died in the college hospital the next morning without uttering a single syllable. We never found any trace of the other two boys. . . ."

Carter fidgeted in his seat, not quite certain whether or not he was being gulled. The young man certainly was in a desperate

condition. A drunkard, perhaps, or dope fiend? All this had happened nine years ago, according to the young man's story; surely he had not been in such a state all that time! The fellow turned burning eyes upon him.

"On the anniversary of that night every year," he explained, "one of the nine men who were on that hazing party has gone stark, raving mad. Each has been found gibbering nonsense, and tapping the floor with a blood-soaked hammer. Each has died within twenty-four hours' time.

"Tomorrow," he said, in low and precise tones, "is the ninth anniversary of that night. And I'm the only one left. . . ."

★ ★ ★

This is a story of a hospital ward and three helplessly crippled and broken men who occupied it. The oldest occupant naturally had the bed by the window; the one who arrived last was next to the door. The man in the middle helped make life bearable for the others by his unfailing liveliness and optimism, although heaven knows he had nothing to be happy about.

One cold winter night the man by the window died, and the other two were moved up a peg. Soon the unquenchable optimist was amusing his equally helpless companion with accounts of the things he could see out of the window—automobiles, flower carts, mysterious strangers, pretty girls with their skirts blowing in the wind. Gradually the people who passed every day were given names, and the man in the second bed heard so many anecdotes of their doings from the lips of the other that he began to feel that he knew them well. It helped pass the dreary hours and he was grateful.

Then, suddenly, a new thought entered his head. If something happened to this man next to him, *he* would get the bed by the window! Lying there helplessly day after day, this idea became an obsession. Within his reach was a spoon and a bottle of medicine. His friend sometimes was seized with heart spasms in the middle of the night when no nurse was at hand; he could barely manage to get a spoonful to his lips and swallow it on such occasions in the nick of time. Gradually the spasm would pass. . . .

The man in the second bed brooded and bided his time. One night the attack came. The stricken man reached for his medicine, but the other, by a superhuman effort, lifted his twisted body from the bed and dashed the bottle to the floor. . . .

The next morning they gave him the bed by the window. "I'll wait to look out of it," he gloated to himself, "until the nurse goes out of the room. Then I can see all these things for myself." Finally he was alone, and trembling with excitement, he turned his head toward the window. A dozen feet from it, he discovered, stretching as far as his eye could follow, was a blank gray wall.

★ ★ ★

It never even occurred to Duval that he was breaking a twenty-year-old precedent by accepting the Englishman Rodney's invitation to luncheon on the terrace of the Café de Paris. The impeccably polite, coldly impersonal assistant manager of the Monte Carlo Casino knew intimate details about every guest and every employee, but his own private life was a closed book. He was a lone wolf with no friends and seemingly no avocations.

Rodney, however, had attracted him at sight. He was big, blonde, and handsome, and what was so rare among the grim gamblers who laboriously played their "systems," until inevitably they were cleaned out, he seemed really to enjoy his bouts at the roulette and chemin-de-fer tables. He played in moderation, obviously could afford the trifling losses he had experienced. Every morning, Duval knew, he received a letter in a precise, girlish hand, which pleased him inordinately.

"Those battered old wrecks who haunt the tables in there bother me," said Rodney, over the cocktails. "What happens to them when they lose their last sou? What happens to the big plungers, for that matter, who go broke at Monte Carlo? Don't some of them commit suicide? Why don't I ever read about the penniless victims who kill themselves in your beautiful gardens?"

"We have no penniless suicides in Monte Carlo," said Duval quietly. "If anybody is foolish enough to lose all his money at our tables and then do away with himself on the grounds of the Casino, there are always ten thousand francs in fresh, crisp bank notes on the body when it is found. The coroner often discovers, too, that death came from natural causes. I do not have to tell you that suicides of penniless victims would be a bad advertisement indeed for the interests I represent."

Several days later, Duval was informed that Rodney had received a letter that upset him. It was written in the usual hand, but upon reading it, Rodney, instead of assuming his usual boyish grin, had turned white and swayed on his heels for an instant. Then he had jammed the letter into his pocket and stormed out of the hotel. That night there was a change in Rodney's behavior in the Casino. He shunned the roulette tables entirely and concentrated on chemin-de-fer, where he lost steadily and heavily. His eyes were bloodshot when he rose to go; he barely acknowledged the concerned Duval's salutation. The following two evenings he went from bad to worse. Finally he lost two hundred thousand francs on the turn of a single card, muttered, "Thank

you, gentlemen," and left the room. Duval, who had been watching him closely, was busy elsewhere for the moment.

Ten minutes later, one of the doormen whose business it was to listen for such noises, heard the all-too-familiar sound of a pistol shot, ran and summoned Monsieur Duval. They found Rodney crumpled up under a tree, his face a ghastly white, a spreading red stain on his evening shirt. In his clenched hand was a letter.

Duval was very sad when he locked the drawer of his desk an hour later. Why did things like this have to happen to him all the time? Why did it have to be one of the few people in twenty years whom he had liked instinctively? He looked more sombre even than usual as he took a final turn through the gaming rooms. Suddenly he stopped in his tracks. That voice! That figure! It was Rodney, smiling in a peculiar way at him, with a sizable stock of ten-thousand-franc markers in his hand! Duval passed his hand over his eyes, muttered "Sacré Dieu!" and fled. "I always knew one of them would come back," he said to himself.

The next morning, in the bright sunshine, Duval knew that it was no ghost who stood before him. It was Rodney, wearing his old grin, with the arm of a very beautiful girl tucked into his. "Duval! Duval, my friend," he cried happily. "Look! She's changed her mind! She arrived this morning out of the blue, and tells me she's going to marry me after all!" He seemed to take it for granted that Duval knew everything that had gone before.

"But the suicide?" faltered Duval.

"Oh, that," laughed Rodney. "I really considered it for a moment. You'll notice I had the gun all right! Then I remembered your story about the ten thousand francs you planted on every body. I fired the shot into the air and decided I'd let your casino stake me to one last fling. What a hunch it was! I won back practically everything I had lost. And now my girl has come back to me!"

"But the ashen countenance?" faltered Duval.

"Face powder," said Rodney.

"And the bloodstain on your shirt front?"

"Catsup," said Rodney. "Ordinary catsup."

Chapter Twelve

"HIGHLIGHTS FROM THE WORLD OF SPORTS"

"THAT'S BASEBALL"

The greatest terror on the base paths in all the history of baseball was Tyrus Raymond Cobb, "The Georgia Peach," who scored from first on singles, and got himself trapped off base on purpose to make fools of his opponents by sliding to safety under their very noses. In one year he stole ninety-six bases. When Cobb slid, it was every man for himself. In the 1909 World Series, Cobb was pitted against another all-time star—"Hans" Wagner. Cobb, on first, hollered, "Hey, Kraut Head, I'm coming down on the next pitch." The easygoing Dutchman didn't say a word, but when Cobb came tearing into him, he blocked the

653

bag like a Giant tank, slapped the ball squarely into Cobb's mouth, and knocked out three teeth.

Wagner was quite a man. Pittsburgh's official scorer was offered ten dollars for a picture of Honus that could be inserted in cigarette packages (the price for that sort of thing has gone up). Wagner wrote, "I don't want my picture in any cigarettes, but I also don't want you to lose the ten dollars, so I'm enclosing my check for that sum."

Baseball was different in those days.

★ ★ ★

One-pitch-that-lost-a-championship Department: In the last game of the season in 1904, Jack Chesbro, of the New York Highlanders, uncorked a wild pitch at a crucial moment that cost his team a chance to win the pennant. When the fans saw that one all-important run come in to dash their hopes, they probably forgot that the same Chesbro had racked up forty-one victories that year. Today a pitcher who wins twenty games in a season is hailed as a superman. The "Highlanders," incidentally, didn't become the "Yankees" until several years later. In those days they played on a field that is now the site of the Columbia Medical Center.

★ ★ ★

Most tragic accidental death of a big-league star: In 1903 Ed Delehanty, the only man who ever captured the batting championships of both the National and American Leagues, left a train for no apparent reason at Niagara Falls, started to walk across the Railroad Bridge in the dead of night, evidently never noticed that the draw was open, and disappeared into the swirling waters. Most deeply mourned death: In 1941, in the prime of life, an obscure malady cut down Columbia Lou Gehrig, the so-called "Iron Horse" who only a few years before had completed the incredible record of appearing in 2130 consecutive games for the Yankees. The motion picture based on Gehrig's career was a great tribute to the man and the game he enriched, produced in Hollywood by the Samuel Goldwyn who is featured on another page of this compendium.

★ ★ ★

In 1908, the New York Giants paid the then-fantastic price of $11,000 for a kid pitcher in the bushes at Indianapolis. His name was Richard Marquard, and because he was a tall, wry-necked southpaw, was nicknamed "Rube." He tried so hard to live up to his fancy press notices that he went to pieces, and for two seasons was referred to scathingly as the "$11,000 lemon." In 1911, however, "Rube" Marquard hit his stride, and in 1912 hung up his record of nineteen consecutive wins that has never since been threatened.

★ ★ ★

This is the story of the day "Merkle didn't touch second." The day was September 23, 1908. The Giants, Cubs, and Pirates, who used to dominate the National League completely, were practically tied for first; every game was vital. The Cubs and Giants went into the ninth inning of a humdinger deadlocked at 1–1. In the home ninth, McCormick was on third with two out, Merkle was on first. Bridwell singled. McCormick crossed the plate with the winning run, but Merkle, instead of running down to touch second, dashed for the clubhouse. This was really no "bonehead" play; it was quite customary at the time. But the shrewd, heads-up second-sacker of the Cubs, Johnny Evers, called for the ball, touched second base, and jawed Umpire Hank O'Day into calling Merkle out on a force play. The crowd was all over the field by this time, and resumption of play was out of the question. As luck would have it, the Giants and Cubs finished the season in a dead tie, and the championship was decided by the play-off of this one game. The Cubs won it, 4–2. A freak play gave a smart first-rate player a reputation as a "sap" that he could never live down. Fred Merkle will always be remembered as "the guy who didn't touch second."

Incidentally, Roger Bresnahan, the Giant catcher in that

655

game, swears to this day that Evers never did get hold of the ball that was in play. "Joe McGinnity picked it up on his way to the clubhouse," asserts the Rajah, "and tossed it into the left field bleachers. In my book, Merkle hasn't been forced out yet." Unfortunately, Bresnahan's book was unofficial.

★ ★ ★

Merkle figured unfortunately again in a Giant tragedy in 1912, and as in the 1908 episode, the great Matty was again the mound victim—which increased the public's resentment. The Giants and the Red Sox met in the World Series that year; it was a grueling set of games with the title resting finally on the eighth game in Boston. The Giants broke a 1–1 tie with a run in their half of the tenth; Matty had to retire only three more men to give the Giants their first World's Championship in seven years. The happenings of the next ten minutes are still too painful to be dwelt upon by an old Giant rooter. First Fred Snodgrass muffed a dinky little fly in centre field, putting a runner on second. The next man flied out. Steve Yerkes walked, and the Boston crowd let out a roar as their idol, "Tris" Speaker, strode to the plate. The roar died when Speaker popped a measly foul outside the first base line. "Chief" Meyers, the Giant catcher, and Merkle, on first, however, went into a trance. The ball fell between them. Speaker wasn't the sort of gent who needed more than one reprieve. He lined out the next pitch for a long single, and Gardner's following sacrifice fly sent in the winning run. Matty strode silently to the clubhouse.

But succor for the heart-broken Giants was on its way from an unexpected source. In the town of Gretna, Louisiana, that dismal afternoon, a three-year-old tot was playing in the lazy October sun. His name was Melvin Ott. In another thirteen years, this boy wonder was to hit the Polo Grounds and lead the Giants back to Glory Road.

★ ★ ★

The 1909 series between Detroit and Pittsburgh was played in weather so cold that Umpire Bill Klem wore a heavy winter overcoat. "Doc Cook, the guy who was supposed to have discovered the North Pole," reminisces Klem, "was guest of honor at the first game, and it got so cold that he left in the second inning! I knew then," adds Klem, "that he was a phony bologna!"

★ ★ ★

Cy Young won 511 major league games in twenty-two years, a record that has never been approached, and under present playing conditions probably never will. The last game he pitched, he lost 1 to 0. (It was in 1911.) The box score reveals that a raw recruit beat him. The name was Grover Cleveland Alexander. Later, he compiled quite a record too.

Alexander won an amazing number of games for some amazingly bad baseball clubs, but his greatest triumph was scored in the twilight of his career in the 1926 World Series. "Alex" couldn't keep away from the giggle water; frantic coaches would pick him up anywhere from the morgue to a flea circus on 42nd Street. This day, however, he shuffled out of the bull pen with the bases full in the deciding game of the series, and fanned Tony Lazzeri of the Yankees, on four pitched balls, giving the title to the St. Louis Cards.

They're still talking about it.

★ ★ ★

On July 8, 1914, the Boston Braves wallowed in last place in the National League standings. Then, while the big guns of the Boches were wiping Belgian fortresses off the map in Europe, while Charlie Chaplin and Mabel Normand were beginning to be noticed by movie fans, while a drama called *On Trial* by an unknown youngster named Elmer Rice electrified Broadway, this Boston team, under the inspiring leadership of "Miracle Man" George Stallings, began to click. Three pitchers spearheaded the drive: Dick Rudolph, Bill James, and George Tyler. Among them they won forty-nine games while losing ten; they galloped through the league like wildfire, ending no fewer than ten and a half games ahead of the second-place Giants! To complete the miracle, this one-year wonder team tore through the heavily favored Athletics in the World Series for four straight victories. Fans remember Catcher Hank Gowdy and Second Baseman Rabbit Maranville from that team. Ever since 1914, managers have tried to rouse lagging aggregations by pointing to the exploits of the Boston Braves. The players know, however, that in baseball miracles like that happen once in a hundred years.

★ ★ ★

The story of the 1919 "Black Sox" sell-out, which nearly destroyed organized baseball, is something straight out of gangster movies. Scott Fitzgerald used it in his unsurpassed study of a bootlegger, *The Great Gatsby*. John Lardner's *Satevepost* story on it six years ago is still talked about in sporting circles.

Baseball enjoyed a big season the year after World War One. The Chicago White Sox, one of the great teams of all time, romped through the American League for an easy pennant. Eddie Collins, "Shoeless Joe" Jackson, Ray Schalk, Buck Weaver, Eddie Cicotte, Chick Gandil, and their pals packed too much power for their opposition, even though the club was riddled with dissensions and cliques that the manager, Kid Gleason, could scarcely control. The National League winner, the Cincinnati Reds, on the other hand, was completely lacking in class. It had a star in centre field in Eddie Roush, and a smart hombre in right named "Greasy" Neale (later he became a famous football coach). For the rest, the squad consisted of a bunch of guys named Joe who had managed to nose out some other mediocre teams in a typical National League dog-fight. On paper, the White Sox figured to slaughter the Reds; the first odds in the betting were 5 to 1. It was an ideal set-up for a double-cross, and a gang of smart hoodlums moved in for the kill.

It is generally believed that the evil genius behind the big fix was the notorious gambler, Arnold Rothstein, but there is no evidence to support such a notion. He admitted that he had heard of the goings-on, and won a tidy sum by betting on the Reds, but it was easy to believe that he had no actual part in the plot when the full details were revealed. The affair was man-handled from start to finish. Most of the players involved never got a cent of pay-off money; that's why they were so ready to "sing" when the heat was turned on. The "secret" was so badly kept that on the morning of the first game, the odds had slipped from 5 to 1, where they belonged, to even money—a crystal-clear indication to the gambling fraternity that there was some-thing extremely rotten in the state of Denmark.

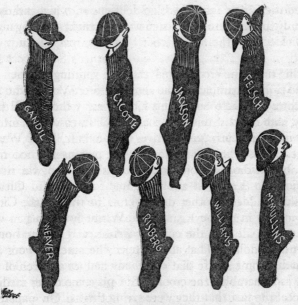

Eight members of the Chicago club were involved in the deal: Gandil, Cicotte, Jackson, Felsch, Weaver, Risberg, Williams and McMullins. They were slated to receive $100,000 for throwing the series; actually they collected a quarter of that sum. The other members of the team knew nothing of the crooked set-up; Collins, Schalk, Kerr, and others played their hearts out in the series; the manager, Gleason, literally cried on the bench while his charges kicked games away with bush-league boners that were incomprehensible at the time.

The Reds won the first game, 9 to 1. Cicotte, a great pitcher, hit batsmen in the back, had his offerings hammered to all corners of the park by third-rate nonentities. In the second game, the Sox pitcher, Claude Williams, noted for his perfect control, passed three men in one vital inning, and literally handed the contest to the Reds by a 4–2 score. The "dope" had been crossed so thoroughly in these games that the public was confounded. Not so the professional gamblers, however. They watched the Cincinnati crowds go delirious with joy, and chuckled grimly to themselves. Chicago won the third game by a shutout. Dickie Kerr, the Sox pitcher that day, was not in on the sell-out.

By this time, the crooked players were whining for their payoff. The tinhorn gamblers came across with ten thousand dollars for Cicotte in time to assure his kicking away the fourth game, 2–0, by such flagrant misplays that the Chicago owner, Charles A. Comiskey, put private detectives on the trail. The White Sox managed to lose the next game too, 5–0, making the count four to one, but in those days it took five victories to bag the world's championship. Kerr won another game for Chicago, and then the insiders added another double-cross to the record. Cicotte really pitched in the next game, the White Sox won in a walk, and gamblers all over the country were neatly euchred out of thousands of dollars. That about ended the party, however. Rumors had become so rife that everybody had the jitters. The last game was a shambles; the crooked Sox players scarcely bothered to conceal the fact that they were giving their all for Cincinnati; the Reds won the series, five games to three.

The crooked players were exposed publicly some months later. Their names were expunged from league records; they were barred from organized baseball for life. Cicotte won jeers with his dogged assertion that he had "done it for the wife and kiddies." Joe Jackson, most pathetic of the disgraced players, had gotten at the most a thousand dollars for his pains; was such a magnificent natural hitter that he hit .375 in the series when he was trying to strike out. "Say it ain't true, Joe," pleaded one of his teen-age fans when the news of the sell-out became public. "Shoeless Joe" hung his head.

That scandal of twenty-five years ago will probably never be repeated in organized baseball. In the first place, controls have been tightened, with doughty old Judge Kenesaw Mountain Landis reading the riot act to any mavericks who stray one step from the fold. In the second place, the 1919 series proved that too many cooks had to be involved in a deal of this sort, with the broth suffering the traditional results. Under the complicated conditions of present-day life, there are a thousand crooked set-ups open to petty chiselers and racketeers; all of them are easier than "fixing" baseball games.

* * *

The speediest pitcher in baseball was Walter Johnson, "The Big Train." Bob Feller was probably the runner-up. When Johnson was right, the batter sometimes never even saw the ball whiz by. Once Chapman of Cleveland watched two strikes zoom by, dropped his bat, and headed for the bench. "You have another strike coming," the umpire reminded him. "Never mind," grunted Chapman. "I don't want it."

* * *

Al Schacht, the inimitable baseball clown, once had a partner named Nick Altrock, but the act broke up because both players suspected each other of deliberately making the rough-and-tumble stuff too realistic. Schacht explained that it was like a pair of old vaudeville comics who did a wooden-shoe number that wound up by their kicking one another in the pants. They began to accuse one another of putting entirely too much behind the kicks, and fought about it so loudly in the dressing room that the acts who followed them complained about the racket.

They were warned that if they created one more disturbance,

their act would be canceled. "That very night," says Schacht, "it happened again." They kicked the daylights out of each other, took their bows, and raced to their dressing room. There they carefully closed the door, took off their wooden shoes, and began to beat each other over the head with them. After every wallop, however, each would put a finger to his lips and whisper "sh-sh-sh."

★ ★ ★

In a World Series game in Chicago in 1932, the crowd, fretful because the home team was taking a shellacking from the Yankees, began to take it out on "Babe" Ruth. The inimitable Bambino strode to the plate, pointed to the flagpole in deepest centre field, and belted the ball out of the lot to the exact spot he had indicated. It was a magnificent performance—the sort of thing only the "Babe" Ruths can ever do—and as he lumbered around the path, the formerly hostile crowd rose and roared out the homage that was due him.

★ ★ ★

One day Ruth heard about a twelve-year-old kid who lay dying in a local hospital. Babe Ruth was his idol. Maybe an autographed baseball would revive him? The Babe pulled a cap off the rack, and taxied over to the hospital. The kid's eyes popped when his god walked into the room and sat on his bed. "Ya know what I'm going to do this afternoon?" said the Babe. "I'm gonna hit a home run just for you. You watch. It's gonna be your home run. Now you hurry up and get well so you can come out and see me play."

Ruth hit the home run that afternoon, just as he had promised. What's more, the kid got well. Stories like that explain why Babe Ruth was the most popular figure in the history of baseball.

★ ★ ★

Bill Dickey's enlistment in the Navy ends the major league career, in all probability, of one of the greatest catchers in baseball history. He wasn't a bad actor either. Remember him in the Lou Gehrig movie?

The Baseball Writers presented Dickey with a plaque as the Player of the Year last winter; Dickey responded with his longest speech on record: "It shore is purty. Much obliged." The night the last World Series ended, the victorious Yankees, including Bill Dickey, went off the wagon with a bang. At the height of the festivities a man he hadn't seen in twenty years, now a beribboned officer, slapped Dickey on the back and chortled, "Remember me, Bill?" "I don't recall the name," mused Dickey. "But you shore were a sucker for a high curve inside!"

★ ★ ★

One big-league ball club that always had a playing system—and a band of followers—unique unto itself was the Brooklyn

663

Dodgers—"dem bums" to its loyal but critical supporters on either side of the Gowanus Canal. Brooklyn outfielders caught flies on their beans instead of in their gloves; Brooklyn runners stole second with a man already on the bag; Brooklyn pitchers heaved balls into the grandstand; the crowd roared its disapproval but never stopped coming.

Once Casey Stengel managed the Dodgers. Ejected by the umpires for the steenth time that season, Casey doffed his cap in mock reverence, and a little bird flew out. The ump, his dignity ruffled, fined Casey fifty bucks. In another game, Stengel lifted his pitcher in the fourth in favor of a pinch-hitter, Babe Phelps, with the sacks full of Dodgers. Phelps came through with a juicy home run: four tallies for the Dodgers. In the eighth the Dodgers needed a pinch-hitter again. "Yah bum, yah," cried a typical Dodger strategist to Stengel. "Whyja waste Phelps before? This is when ya need him!"

The last man who tried to figure out the mentality of a typical Brooklyn fan is cutting out paper dolls in Matteawan this very minute.

★ ★ ★

Dizzy Dean, famous pitcher of the St. Louis Cardinals, and the game's most distinguished modest violet, has delivered himself of an autobiography. Ol' Diz, as he likes to call himself, is considerably more of a humorist than a lot of tired old gag men who make a living that way. He pops off in print and plays the buffoon for the same reason that led him to act that way on the ball field; he knows exactly what the public wants.

He divides his autobiography into four parts. Part One is entitled "Who's the Greatest Pitcher in the World?" Part Two is devoted to "Who's Got the Greatest Throwin' Arm in the World?" ("Not Countin' Days It Was Sore and How It Got That Way.") Part Three discusses "Who's the Greatest Hitter in the World?" ("When He Wants to Be.") The wind-up is the answer to "Who's the Greatest Pitcher-Runner in the World?" ("Not Countin' Days I Was Tired.") Diz demolishes "house dicks" (players who spend most of their time showing off in hotel lobbies) and "pebble pickers" (infielders who alibi fielding bobbles by picking up imaginary pebbles which, they indicate by pantomime, have caused the ball to take a crazy hop); he lingers lovingly (and who can blame him?) on the season when he and his brother Paul won forty-nine games between them for the Cards, and then went on to mow down the Detroit Tigers single- or double-handed in the World Series.

The Dean Dictionary should never have omitted the classic repartee that featured a tense spot in the first Series game at Detroit. The fans were riding him hard that day, and didn't like it at all when he struck out the entire side in one inning, and came swaggering to the bench. "If I was your wife," hollered one lady enthusiast, "I'd give you poison." "If I wuz your husband," snapped back Mr. Dean, "I'd take it!"

★ ★ ★

William Faulkner recalls a ball game once played in Mississippi. It was played in a cow pasture and ended abruptly when a runner slid into what he thought was third base.

★ ★ ★

The wonderful saga of Two-Top Gruskin, the two-headed pitcher, is the brain child of Ed Gardner, the incomparable Archie of Duffy's Tavern radio program. It goes something like this:

Duffy's Irish Yankees have mechanical perfection, but no color. "This guy, Athos and Porthos McGinnes, may be your dish," says Dugan, the shortstop, to the disconsolate Duffy. "They call him Two-Top Gruskin for short, I guess, on account of him having two heads."

"A pitcher with two heads?" says Duffy dubiously. "You think it'd be a novelty?"

"What if it ain't?" points out Dugan. "Who else could watch first and third base at the same time? Besides, he's a great guy to pitch double-headers."

So Two-Top is summoned from his home (Walla Walla, of course) and arrives to sign his contract in a dress suit. "What are all you guys staring at?" he asks sourly. "Ain't none of you seen a tuxedo before?"

"Two-Top," says Duffy, "I'm a man of few words. Report tomorrow. There's a uniform and two caps waiting for you. Waiter, bring my new pitcher two beers."

Two-Top wins a masquerade that very night by disguising himself as a pair of bookends with a copy of *My Son, My Son* between the two heads. The next afternoon Duffy introduces him to his catcher, Gorilla Hogan, who measures 6 foot 14 inches and squats standing up. "Most people," says Duffy proudly, "calls Gorilla a monstrosity, and I agree with them—a swell guy." Gorilla soon gets into trouble with Two-Top, however. He signals for a high fast one. Two-Top nods "yes" with one head, but shakes the other one "no." Confused and mortified, Gorilla hurls off his mask and yells to Duffy, "Duffy, you such-and-such, I am sick and tired of two-headed pitchers around this place."

"Take it easy," soothes Duffy. "Talk it over with the guy. After all, three heads is better than one."

But the Gorilla says, "It's no use, Duffy. I got a feeling that the guy ain't normal. Besides, you notice how he's always got those two heads together? Maybe he's cooking up a strike around here. No, sir, one of us will have to go, Duffy—and don't forget who owns the baseball."

Well, that's the end of Two-Top Gruskin's baseball career. For a while he watches tennis matches for the News of the Day. Then the Army gets him. The doctor takes his chart to the colonel. "Lemme see," says the colonel. "Eyes—blue and brown. Hair, blond and brunette. Mustache: yes and no. This guy sounds as if he's got two heads." "He has," says the doc. "Oh," says the colonel.

Two-Top will be a big success in the Army as soon as he can make up his mind which head to salute.

666

...AND "THAT'S FOOTBALL"

The old Carlisle Indians were a tricky and colorful outfit, especially when they had Jim Thorpe in the backfield. They invaded Cambridge one fall to tussle with a fine Harvard team, and had leather patches sewed on their jerseys that looked exactly like footballs. In the first few scrimmages, the Harvard team thought all eleven opponents had pigskins tucked under their arms, and didn't know whom to tackle. One Carlisle back added to the confusion by slipping the real football under the back of his jersey and galloping unmolested over the goal line. Officials had to change the rules the following season.

★ ★ ★

Knute Rockne had a brief whirl at professional football in its early days. In one of his first games, he faced Jim Thorpe and his Canton Bulldogs at the Polo Grounds. The great Indian athlete was long past his prime, growing fat and sluggish, but he was still a great drawing card. Rockne was desperately anxious to make good. On one of the opening plays, Thorpe came lumbering around his end. Rockne spilled him. As he rose, Thorpe whispered, "Listen, Rock. Don't do that no more. People paid to see Old Jim run. Next time, let him go." On the next play, Rockne spilled him again. Thorpe said nothing this time, but on the very next play, he summoned some reserve force, and for a moment was the flailing, irresistible runner of old. Rockne was knocked cold, and Thorpe galloped for a touchdown while the crowd cheered. Then the Indian returned to where Rockne was coming to, helped to pick him up, and grinned. "That's a good boy, Rock. You let old Jim run!"

★ ★ ★

Dick Hanley, now a Colonel in the Marines, once coached a subnormal Northwestern team, that gave him many a gray

667

hair. On a certain Saturday the boys surpassed themselves, and fumbled so often that Hanley literally fell off the bench with rage. He signaled his last substitute backfield man to warm up, then promptly forgot about him. A substitute centre kept passing the ball faithfully to the lad on the sidelines, but Hanley never signaled him to enter the game. Finally the boy missed a practice pass. From the silence of the dejected Northwestern rooting section came a raucous voice: "Put him in now, Hanley; he's ready!"

★ ★ ★

The most lopsided football game in the record books took place in 1916. Georgia Tech defeated Cumberland College, 220–0. There lives a man who admits he quarterbacked that Cumberland team: George Allen, former commissioner of the District of Columbia. Allen treasures a yellowed clipping which reads, "Allen spearheaded the Cumberland offensive with a brilliant run around left end that resulted in only an eight-yard loss." He tackled one Tech man on the thirty-yard line and hung around his neck all the way to the goal line. "Once I fumbled," he remembers, "and as three Tech ogres bore down, another Cumberland stalwart shied away from the loose ball. 'Pick it up,' I yelled to the guy, but what do you think he answered? 'Pick it up, hell,' he said. 'I didn't drop it!' "

★ ★ ★

In a Rose Bowl game at Pasadena some years ago, a California star emerged in something of a daze from a scrimmage with the football cradled in his arms, lowered his head, and went charging gallantly down the field—toward his own goal line! One of his own teammates managed to nail him on the five-yard stripe, temporarily saving the game and averting one of the prize boners in football history.

★ ★ ★

Harvard and Princeton once broke off football relations for years because their games were getting too rough and bad feeling was rife. The last game before the split wasn't made any gentler by a joke that appeared in the Harvard *Lampoon,* published the morning of the match. "Are you a Princeton man?" queried a sweet young thing. "No," was the answer, "a horse stepped on my face." The Princeton team didn't forget *that* when the whistle blew.

★ ★ ★

The 1935 game between Dartmouth and Princeton was played in a blinding snowstorm. A Dartmouth man was on his way to a touchdown, with no Tiger player within ten feet of him, when from the sidelines a spectator, who had found adequate means of keeping himself warm, suddenly scampered onto the field and made a perfect tackle. The touchdown was allowed, of course, and the doughty tackler was rewarded for his pains by being bounced out of the Palmer Stadium on his ear.

★ ★ ★

The mighty football teams of Notre Dame are supported and rooted for by more fans probably than any other five squads put together. Pat O'Brien, the film star, who thinks nothing himself of flying five thousand miles to see a Notre Dame game, explains that "every American college graduate has two alma maters: his own and Notre Dame." Coach Knute Rockne built the first great team for "The Fighting Irish"; his eleven that included "The Four Horsemen" is considered by many the greatest college football aggregation of all time.

A few days before an Army-Notre Dame encounter, the Green's star fullback, who will remain nameless on this page, flunked a chemistry exam and was declared ineligible. The entire student body, not to mention certain influential graduates, bore down on the professor, who relented to the point of offering the player a second examination the night before the squad entrained for the East. His classmates crammed him for the test, and a sizable cheering section waited outside the professor's house when the ordeal began.

"Now, Joe," the professor reassured him. "All I expect is a

fifty percent grade for passing, and I'm only going to ask you two questions. All set?"

"Yeah," grunted Joe.

"First, what does the chemical formula H_2O stand for?"

"Sulphuric acid," wavered Joe.

"Now, take your time with the second question, Joe. What is the chemical formula for water?"

"I dunno," was Joe's candid reply.

The professor beamed. "That passes you, Joe. You answered the second question correctly."

Another time (aside to Pat O'Brien: I'm only kidding, mister!) the captain of a great Notre Dame team suddenly burst into tears on the bench before the last game of the season began. The coach was aghast. "What on earth have you got to cry about?" he marveled. "You're the captain of the best team we've had in years. You're handsome, rich, and have just been voted the most popular guy in the senior class. What's wrong, man?" "Oh, Coach," sobbed the player, "if I could only read and write!"

Even Notre Dame teams occasionally experience let-downs and form reversals. One Saturday a supposed push-over played inspired football for two quarters and led a highly favored Notre Dame squad, 7–0, at half time. The Fighting Irish took it for granted that Knute Rockne would flay their hides off in the dressing room, but the great coach never even turned up. The players were nervously awaiting the time to reappear on the field when Rockne finally stuck his head inside the door. "Let's go, girls," he said. Notre Dame scored four touchdowns in the next ten minutes.

Bob Considine tells the story of a Notre Dame star who went to a sterling but absent-minded priest every week for confession. The priest had the habit of marking the number of sins on his sleeve with a piece of chalk in order to mete out the proper penance.

"Father," said the player one day, "I ran clear across the field to clip a player in our last game."

"That was very wrong, my son," said the priest, making a chalk mark.

"When he fell, I kicked him in the teeth."

"How terrible, my son! Will you never learn true Christianity?" (Four more chalk marks.)

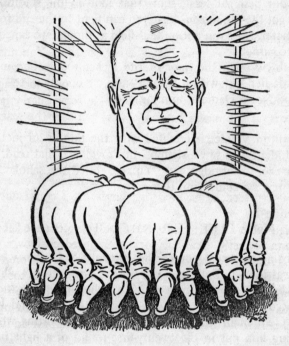

"And then when the referee wasn't looking, I chewed off a piece of his ear."

"Saints preserve us! You're a disgrace to your fine teachers and the college!" By this time the chalk marks were clear up to the priest's elbow. "What was the team you were playing, my son?"

"Southern Methodist," said the player.

"Oh," beamed the priest, rubbing off every mark on his sleeve. "I guess boys will be boys."

A few years ago a forlorn little football squad from a jerkwater college came down to open the season against one of Notre Dame's most powerful elevens. The coach was trying to instil some spirit into his justifiably terrified protégés. "Sure you'll get trimmed," he assured them. "Nobody expects you to do more than your best. At least, show that mob in the stadium that you've got the old moxie—that you can fight to the end for your alma mater. Let's run out on that field as though we expected to win the game!"

He threw open the door of the locker room. The inspired squad dashed out with a whoop—and, as one man, fell smack into the Notre Dame swimming pool.

★ ★ ★

Thornton Wilder is credited with the tale of an inebriated Yale student who saw a signpost in Providence that read, "New Haven 126, Cambridge 54." "Yippee," cried the scholar, "I always knew we could trim those guys!"

A FEW OTHER SPORTS STORIES

Probably the most popular heavyweight champion who ever lived was John L. Sullivan, "the Boston Strong Boy," who won the title from Paddy Ryan in 1882, when bare knuckles and unlimited rounds were still the order of the day, and kept it until "Gentleman Jim" Corbett stunned the sporting world by knocking him out in the twenty-first round of a fight in New Orleans ten years later. Liquor and women played a big part in Sullivan's downfall. He drank bourbon by the stein. Whenever he heard there was a good-looking girl on the premises, he would roar, "Rise her up!" He toured the country offering anybody in the audience a hundred dollars who could stand up to him for three rounds. One punch, of course, generally concluded his evening's work. "My name is John L. Sullivan," was his exit line, "and I can lick any . . . . in the house!" The crowds loved it.

★ ★ ★

He was a blacksmith in Australia, and he owned a single race-horse whose dismal record was a series of unvaried lasts. One day he accidentally broke a bottle of whiskey in the horse's stall. The horse lapped some of it up, and then proceeded to confound the form-players by going out and winning a race hands down.

The blacksmith felt that he had made an important discovery. He was sure of it when his horse, after another nip of Scotch, went out and won a second race. Inside of six months, the steed had captured three of the most important races on the Australian calendar, and the blacksmith was in the chips.

Then the story broke that the horse had been given whiskey before each race. There was nothing illegal about it, but the public reacted unfavorably. The owner was booed the next time he appeared at a track. Disconsolate, he sold the horse, and embarked for America, where he began an entirely new career.

You see, in addition to his other accomplishments, this one-time blacksmith was a handy man with his fists. In fact, he was so good that he developed into one of the greatest heavyweight champions in American ring history. His name was Bob Fitzsimmons.

Years after his retirement from the ring, Fitzsimmons became, for reasons of his own, an ardent prohibitionist. He preached fervid sermons on the subject, vowed that he would die a happy man the day prohibition became a law of the land. When the prohibition act was passed, a friend rushed over to Fitzsimmons' house to tell him the news, but there was no answer to his knocks. Bob Fitzsimmons had died peacefully in his sleep during the previous night.

This is a story told by Bill Stern, the well-known radio sports reporter.

★ ★ ★

The old adage, "All the world loves a winner," does not always apply in the prize ring. Jack Dempsey, for example, was extremely unpopular in the years from 1919 to 1926, when he was the heavyweight champion. But on September 3, 1926, Gene Tunney licked him at Philadelphia, and from that moment on, the fickle public idolized him.

Dempsey was married to Estelle Taylor in 1926. He wasn't a very pretty picture when he left his dressing room after that Tunney fight. "What happened?" exclaimed his wife. "Honey," said Dempsey, "I forgot to duck." That story got around. People liked it. By the time the same fighters climbed into the ring in Chicago the following summer for a return bout, ninety percent of the audience of 135,000—the greatest crowd in ring history— was for Dempsey heart and soul. He almost won back his crown;

674

in the seventh round, after trailing from the start, he suddenly launched a terrific attack, and Tunney went down. In the excitement, Dempsey neglected to go to a neutral corner, thus giving Tunney a "long count." It enabled him to weather the round and eventually win the fight; Dempsey had shot his last bolt.

In all the history of prize-fighting there have been just five gates that ran to over a million dollars; Dempsey was one of the principals in all of them. There were the two bouts with Tunney, one with Carpentier, one with Sharkey, and the fifth, tops of all for sheer drama, with Luis Angel Firpo of the Argentine. Firpo was known as "The Wild Bull of the Pampas." Later it developed that he had been a drugstore clerk in Buenos Aires. But while he lasted, he put up a spectacular battle against the champion. Dempsey knocked him down no fewer than six times in the first round, but suddenly, Firpo connected with a haymaker that knocked the champion clear out of the ring. The crowd was so excited that nobody seems to know how long it took Dempsey to climb back into the arena. He had landed squarely in the laps of a couple of very surprised newspapermen. The referee was so pop-eyed he never even started to count. Dempsey got back in there in time to land one terrific right-hander before the bell sounded. In the second round he knocked Firpo halfway back to the Argentine—but fight fans will never forget that wild first round.

★ ★ ★

When Dempsey was training for his first fight with Tunney, he sent a scout named Mike Trent over to his rival's training camp, to pick up some pointers on Tunney's style of hitting power.

Trent returned in high glee. "It's a set-up," he reported. "I seen the lug reading a book!"

★ ★ ★

Eleanor Holm, who can swim faster on her back than most readers of this book can navigate on their faces, was the heroine of the 1936 Olympic Games, although she never competed in them.

Besides her aquatic accomplishments, the beautiful Eleanor was a night-club star, and for two years preceding the 1936 Olympic Games expedition had toured the country with a big-name band. In a life of this sort a lady learns how to hold her liquor, also how to stay fresh as a daisy until the wee hours of the morning.

The American team crossed on the *Manhattan* in 1936. Miss Holm, as was her custom, drank plenty of champagne, and danced until four. Other contestants undoubtedly would not have thrived on such a routine, but Miss Holm was something else again. The bluenoses in charge of the American delegation, however, very righteous, very pontifical, bounced her off the squad for "breaking training." Miss Holm got about ten times as much publicity as all the rest of the team put together, the

676

United States lost a certain "first"—and virtue, I suppose, triumphed.

Later Eleanor Holm married Billy Rose, and starred in the Aquacade at the World's Fair. Today she's as popular as ever. The master mind who banned her from the Olympics was forgotten years ago. I hope there's a moral in this story.

★ ★ ★

When Quentin Reynolds was an undergraduate at Brown, he became the unexpected hero of an intercollegiate championship swimming meet.

Brown had a renowned plunger on the squad that year who was counted on to bring the first-place trophy home to Providence, but he came down with flu the morning of the meet. The coach was tearing his hair when he spied the two-hundred-pound Quent lumbering across the campus. "Hey, you," he cried, "you look like a guy who can plunge! You gotta plunge your damn head off for Brown tonight."

Reynolds protested weakly that he had never plunged in his life, and then proceeded into town to get most royally plastered. At nine-thirty, sharp, a pistol barked, and five young giants, including Reynolds, took off from the side of the tank. Reynolds went to the bottom like a plummet, and passed out cold. By the time they fished him out of the tank, however—check the records if you don't believe me—he had negotiated the entire length of the pool and broken the intercollegiate record. He had also turned blue. When he came to, they gave him a gold medal and put him on probation for thirty days. He has never plunged since.

★ ★ ★

There is a little Italian priest who frequents Mr. Grecco's de luxe barber shop on 59th Street, and likes to lecture the customers and attendants there on the folly of betting on horse races. "Take my own case," he points out. "When I go out to the track, the owners, the trainers, and the jockeys all know me. They tell me just what horses to bet on. The bookies won't take my bets if they know I'm betting on the wrong horse. On the rare occasions when I lose, they refuse to accept my money. And, gentlemen, so far this year, *even I am three hundred dollars behind.*"

★ ★ ★

Eddie Mead made a classic remark on his way to the track one day: "I hope I break even. I need the money."

★ ★ ★

An inveterate race-track gambler went to Saratoga with Tom Cleland, the artist, a few summers ago. Aware of his own weakness, he took the precaution of buying a return ticket for New York before he left. This was one day on which he enjoyed an extraordinary run of luck, and with only one race left to be run, his pockets were bulging with over a thousand dollars in profits. "Let well enough alone," counseled Cleland, but the gambler waved him aside. "This is my lucky day," he exulted—and bet every cent he had on a nag who promptly proceeded to limp home in last place.

The gambler sadly tore his stubs into shreds. Then he came across the return ticket in his pocket. He looked at it a moment —and tore that up too. "Walk home, you dumb idiot!" he mumbled to himself.

★ ★ ★

Another yarn of Saratoga concerns a young honeymoon couple who shared a passionate love of gambling. For five hectic days they were dogged by persistent bad luck; on the morning of the final day of the meet, they had only two dollars left between them.

"Let me go out to the track alone today, honey," pleaded the boy. "Wait for me at the hotel. I've got a hunch."

A friend drove him out to the track. He picked a 40-to-1 shot on the first race, and won. Every succeeding race was captured by a rank outsider. He was backing it every time. At the end of the afternoon he had over ten thousand dollars.

On the way back to the hotel, he decided to cash in further on his lucky streak, and stopped at one of the clubs that ran gaming rooms in rather open defiance of the state laws. His luck held. He ran his stake up to forty thousand. He was on the point of leaving when the wheel began spinning once more. Suddenly he put the entire forty thousand on "black."

The ball bounced, and settled. "Number fourteen," called the croupier. "Red."

The boy walked back to the hotel. The girl was waiting for him on the verandah.

"How did you make out?" she called eagerly.

The boy lit a cigarette. "I lost the two dollars," he said.

★ ★ ★

José Capablanca, the late Cuban chess wizard, once played sixty-four simultaneous games, vanquished sixty-two opponents, and drew with the other two.

It was he who told me the story of the mighty potentate who was so bored that he offered half of his kingdom to anybody who could find a new way of diverting him. An ancient appeared from nowhere and taught him the game of chess. The potentate was in the seventh heaven.

"You have saved my life," he declared. "Now you must claim your reward."

The ancient's request sounded simple. He asked but a single grain of wheat for the first square on the chess board, double that for the second, double that for the third, and so on down to the sixty-fourth square. The potentate protested. "But I have promised you half my kingdom. Why do you name this paltry reward?" The ancient was adamant, and the potentate ordered the keeper of his granaries to pay off this seemingly modest petitioner. Of course it turned out that there wasn't enough grain in the entire world to pay him off before the fortieth square had been accounted for. If you don't believe it, figure it out for yourself.

There was a time when Charles MacArthur fancied himself

as a chess expert. He had run roughshod over the feeble opposition offered by fellow members of the West Side Tennis Club in Hollywood, and was growing pretty insufferable about it. He took to speaking in what he fondly believed was a Spanish accent, and telling newcomers that he was the champion, José Capablanca.

Eventually Capablanca himself visited Los Angeles and MacArthur's lacerated companions sensed the opportunity for a beautiful revenge. They brought him to the West Side Tennis Club, and introduced him to MacArthur as Mr. Spelvin. "Spelvin plays a pretty good game of chess," they said. "Indeed," beamed MacArthur. "I, señor, am Capablanca. We play a game or two, eh?" And so, while the entire membership watched in unalloyed delight, the real Capablanca and the bogus one sat down to play.

Of course, MacArthur was in the soup by the sixth move. To make matters more embarrassing, the champion, by prearrangement, would make his move in one second flat, and then dart off to the swimming pool, leaving MacArthur to sweat over *his* next move for twenty minutes or so. Then he'd saunter back, make another lightning move, and disappear again. MacArthur, perspiring freely, demanded a second game. There is no telling where the gruesome scene would have ended, had not Helen Hayes, MacArthur's wife, arrived, and learned what was afoot. She dashed to an outside telephone and called her husband. "That's the *real* Capablanca you're playing against, you loon!" she cried. "The whole club is laughing at you."

MacArthur claimed feebly that he had known all the time whom he was playing against. "Anything to give you fatheads a laugh," was his attitude. But he never impersonated Capablanca again.

★ ★ ★

Frank Crowninshield once played a round of golf with Bobby Jones. It was 1930, the year that Jones won all four major golf titles in America and England. Golf had never known such a popular hero before. Crowninshield was so nervous that he flubbed almost every shot. On the twelfth hole he finally said to Jones: "I hate to bother you, but there must be some dreadful mistake I'm making that you have spotted and possibly can correct. Won't you tell me?"

Bobby Jones gravely replied: "Mr. Crowninshield, I wouldn't change your style of golf for anything in the world. Why, man, you're unique! You make eight errors on your upstroke—and correct four of them coming down!"

When he is golfing with his regular companions, Crowninshield cannot be bothered with any such nonsense as waiting for his turn to play. He plows steadily down the course, ignoring the other players, and often thinks of the cleverest things to say just as somebody else—preferably an opponent—is about to take a shot. Grantland Rice calls him a "floating hazard." "One day," relates Rice, "I was just addressing my ball when Crownie, humming brightly, cut in right ahead of me. I reminded him gently of the lady who asked the station master where she would get the Twentieth Century Limited. The answer was that if she didn't get off the track, she'd get it square in the behind. Crownie got the point and promised to be more careful in the future. On the green of that very hole I had to sink a long putt to stay in the match. I had just lined up the cup when a ball hit my foot. Crownie was essaying a few practice putts while he waited."

Speaking of golf, did you ever hear the story of the man who came back from the practice tee so visibly unnerved that his friend rushed out of the locker room to ask what was wrong? "What's wrong?" was the bitter retort. "I just killed my wife. That's what's wrong!" "Holy smoke, how did you do that?" "I was out there practising, and didn't see my wife come up behind me. I took a back swing, hit her on the head—and she dropped dead." "Gee, that's bad! What club were you using?" "A niblick," mourned the golfer. "That's the club," said his friend happily.

Chapter Thirteen

FIRESIDE BOOK OF
SHAGGY-DOG STORIES

Shaggy-dog stories, as almost everybody must know by this time, are the kind of tales in which animals talk, humans do inexplicable things, and the punch lines make no sense at all. They are generally anathema to literal-minded females. There is nothing like a string of shaggy-dog stories to make your wife's Aunt Minnie cut short a visit and go back where she came from. They receive their name from the following legend.

A Kansas City barfly picked up a year-old copy of the London *Times* one day—don't ask me how it got there—and found therein a personal ad offering a ten-pound reward for the return of a very shaggy dog to its bereft owner in Bishop's Bowes, Essex. Ten minutes later he stumbled over the shaggiest darn pup you ever saw. Being a man of decision, he promptly bundled the canine under his arm, took the Twentieth Century to New York, the *Queen Mary* to Southampton, and a limousine to

Bishop's Bowes. In keen anticipation, he sought out the lady who had advertised, and rang her bell. She answered herself. "You lost a shaggy dog, Madam," he reminded her, holding up the pooch. "Would this be it?" "Good heavens, no," she snapped. "It wasn't *that* shaggy"—and slammed the door in his face.

Well, now that we've settled that, we propose to give you thirty-two examples of the species. We figure that fewer than that would not do the subject full justice; more might set the most avid addicts to baying at the moon. Note that we have numbered the entries. You can't tell the bayers without a number.

1. Two race horses fretted impatiently in adjoining stalls the night before a Kentucky Derby. "You might as well save yourself the effort of competing tomorrow," spoke one, "I've got the Derby sewed up." "Says you," scoffed the other. "What makes you so sure of yourself?" "Didn't you see my owner whispering in my ear just now?" said the first horse. "He was telling me that if I won tomorrow, he'd give me two extra bales of hay. And, brother, that ain't money!"

2. "A quarter's worth of rat poison," ordered the man at the delicatessen store. "Yes, sir," the clerk answered. "Shall I wrap it up for you?" "Oh, you needn't bother," the man said pleasantly. "I'll eat it here."

3. A bat family was flying home from a picnic—Papa Bat, Mama Bat, and Sonny Bat. "Thank heaven that picnic's over," said Sonny Bat. "Now the four of us can have some peace." "Four?" queried Papa. "I only see three." Sonny Bat flared up. "You know very well I can't count," he grumbled.

4. "This dog," Mr. Weber once said to Mr. Fields, "is worth five hundred dollars." To which Mr. Fields replied, "How could a dog save that much money?"

5. A customer entered a saloon and ordered a dozen martinis.

He poured the liquor onto the floor, and began munching contentedly on the glasses themselves. The stems, however, he would have no traffic with. A barfly watched the performance with absorbed interest, but pointed to the twelve stems. "You darn fool," he said. "You're leaving the best part."

6. The oysters found a fine new bed several miles up the Sound, and were happily packing their belongings—all except little Mary Oyster, who sat sobbing bitterly in a corner. "What's the matter?" asked her father anxiously. "We'll have a wonderful new home. There's nothing to cry about." "Oh, yes, there is," wailed Mary. "Johnny Bass will never be able to find me now, and I love him with all my heart." "But does Johnny Bass reciprocate your devotion?" inquired the parent. "Indeed he does," Mary assured him. "Last night he took me in his arms at the end of the pier out there. First he kissed me here on the forehead. Then he kissed me here on the lips. And then—my God, my *pearl!*"

7. A very shy young man sat next to a glamorous debutante at a dinner party. In the middle of the main course he seized a bowl of succotash and poured it over the debutante's chic coiffure. The young lady rose indignantly. "How dare you?" she blazed, plucking corn and peas out of her hair. "How dare you throw succotash at me?" The young man blanched. "Good heavens," he stammered. "Was that succotash? I thought it was spinach!"

8. A man's ear was bleeding like a stuck pig. "I bit myself," he explained. "That's impossible," said the doctor. "How can a man bite himself in the ear?" The man said, "I was standing on a chair."

9. Two herrings stopped at a neighborhood café for a couple of snifters. One of them disappeared for a moment, and a puzzled onlooker accosted the one who was left alone at the bar. "Where is your brother?" he challenged. "How in heck should I know," replied the indignant herring. "Am I my brother's kipper?"

10. A man staggered from a railroad car, his complexion a sickly green. "Riding backwards for six hours," he explained. "I never *could* stand that." "Why," his wife inquired, "didn't you ask the party sitting opposite to change seats with you?" "I couldn't do that," said the man. "There wasn't anybody there."

11. A crotchety old bachelor saw a gaily plumed parrot go under the hammer at a country auction, and suddenly decided that the bird might be good company for him on lonely evenings. The bidding grew unexpectedly stiff, but the bachelor was carried away by the spirit of the occasion and before he quite realized what he had done, he bought the Poll for forty-nine dollars. He carried it home, and stood it on the table before him. "Now," he commanded, "talk to me!" The parrot simply drew in its head and glared at him. "I said talk to me," repeated the man. "After all, I bought you to keep me company." Again the parrot glared but said nothing. "Good heavens," cried the exasperated gentleman. "Do you mean to say that after what I paid for you, you can't even *talk?*" "Can't even talk?" echoed the parrot. "Who in hell do you think it was that bid you up to forty-nine dollars?"

12. A cotton-tail rabbit, nibbling thoughtfully at his evening carrot, noticed that his son was in a particularly jovial mood. "What makes Junior so happy?" he asked. Mamma rabbit explained, "He had a wonderful time in school today. He learned how to multiply."

13. At a gala ship concert aboard a liner, a trained parrot did his act, and then teetered excitedly on his perch in the wings while an extraordinary magician performed feats of legerdemain. First he made a goldfish disappear, then a buxom blonde assistant, finally a chest containing three husky sailors. At that moment the liner was struck by a torpedo. The parrot found himself all alone on the Atlantic Ocean, bobbing up and down on a piece of driftwood, with nothing else in sight. "Amazing," marveled the Poll. "What will he think of next?"

14. (Very, very old.) "Give me a soda," commanded the young

sprout, "without flavor." "Without what flavor?" asked the soda jerk. "Without vanilla." "Ain't got no vanilla." "All right, gimme one without strawberry."

15. Two brothers, identical twins, often went fishing together. One twin was always lucky. The other could never catch a thing. They could stand right next to each other and one brother would haul in fish after fish while the other's line dangled idly in the water. One day the unlucky twin decided on a desperate course. He woke in the middle of the night and put on his brother's clothes. He took his brother's rod and went to the very spot where his brother had caught thirty-four trout the day before. For three hours he stood there without getting a nibble. Finally his hopes rose when he saw a magnificent trout swimming his way. The fish ignored the bait and, leaping out of the water, called, "Hey, bud, where's your brother?"

16. Sitting opposite Miss Haas on a northbound subway train one evening sat a man calmly reading his paper with three pigeons resting on top of him—one on his head, the others on his shoulders. Miss Haas contemplated the situation until she could stand it no longer. She tapped his paper, and said, "Pardon me,

but what on earth are you doing with those pigeons in the subway?" "Them?" said the man. "I really don't know, lady. They musta got on at 59th Street."

17. A man dropped in to pay a friend an unexpected visit, and was amazed to find him playing chess with his dog. The man watched in silence for a few minutes, then burst out with "That's the most incredible dog I ever saw in my life!" "Oh, he isn't so smart," was the answer. "I've beaten him three games out of four!"

18. One day a man said to Billy Rose, "Would you like to see me dive into a barrel of water from a thousand feet?" Billy Rose said he certainly would, and next day he called his workmen and had them set up a thousand-foot ladder. Mr. Rose held his breath while the man climbed to the top, and stared fascinated as he took a flying leap and landed, splash, in the barrel of water.

"Magnificent," said Billy Rose. "I'll hire you for $100 a week."

"No," said the man.

"$250 a week," said Billy Rose.

"No," said the man.

"You drive a hard bargain," said Billy Rose, "but your act is worth it. Let's not count pennies. I'll hire you for a thousand a week."

"No," said the man.

"Say, fellow," said Billy Rose, "how much do you want to jump into that barrel?"

"Nothing," said the man. "This is the first time I ever did it, and I don't like it."

19. A worm met another worm coming up from the ground and declared, "You're very beautiful and I'd like to marry you." "Don't be a dope," was the reply. "I'm your other end."

20. (One of the very first.) An elephant looked down at a mouse and exclaimed, "You're about the puniest, most insignificant object I ever laid eyes on." "I'm not always this little," the mouse squeaked angrily. "I've been sick."

21. A dignified old clergyman owned a parrot of whom he was exceedingly fond, but the bird had picked up an appalling vocabulary of cuss words from a previous owner and, after a series of embarrassing episodes, the clergyman decided he would have to kill his pet. A lady in his parish suggested a last-ditch remedy. "I have a female parrot," she said, "who is an absolute saint. She sits quietly on her perch and does nothing but pray from morning until night. Why don't you bring your parrot over and see if my own bird's good influence doesn't reform him?" The clergyman said it was worth a trial, and the next night arrived with his pet tucked under his arm. The bird took one look at the lady parrot and chirped, "Hi, toots. How about a little loving?" "Come to mama," cried the lady parrot gleefully. "What do you think I've been praying for all these years?"

22. A doctor saved a baby elephant's life in the jungle, then returned to America. Years later he was down on his luck, and had to borrow a quarter to see the circus when it came to town. Out came the elephants. One of them saw the doctor, and trumpeted recognition. He wrapped his trunk around the doctor, lifted him out of the twenty-five-cent seat—and planked him down in a box seat worth three dollars.

23. A kangaroo yanked her young one out of her pouch and gave it a healthy smack on the backside. "I'll teach you," she declared, "to eat crackers in bed!"

24. When the manager of the Brooklyn ball club lost his star centre fielder on the eve of a crucial swing through the West, he sent out a frantic call for a replacement. Almost a week went by and there were no applications. The manager sat dejectedly on the bench with his head in his hands. He heard an apologetic whinny behind him, and looking around, saw a horse standing there.

"Go away," he said to the horse. "Can't you see I've got a headache?"

"But I'm applying for that spot in centre field," said the horse.

"That's ridiculous," snapped the manager. "Horses don't play baseball—not even in Brooklyn!"

The horse insisted, however, and finally the manager allowed him to exhibit his wares. It developed that he could field like Tris Speaker and hit like Joe DiMaggio. The delighted manager promptly inserted him into the lineup.

In the ninth inning of that day's game, with the score 0–0, the horse strode to the plate and lashed a wicked liner against the right-field fence.

Then—to everyone's amazement—he stood stock still at the plate, twirling his bat.

"Run, you idiot, run!" beseeched the frantic manager. "This means the game!"

"Don't be silly," said the horse. "Who ever heard of a horse running bases?"

25. A colony of ostriches—ninety-nine birds in all—had their heads buried neatly in the sand when ostrich number one hundred came galumping onto the scene. He looked about in a puzzled way and inquired, "Where on earth *is* everybody?"

26. A reporter was assigned, a long time ago, to interview Mr. Barnum's favorite midget, Tom Thumb. The hotel clerk directed the reporter to Room 308, but when he knocked on that door, it was opened by a giant fully nine feet tall. "I must have the wrong room," apologized the newsman. "Who were you looking for?" countered the giant. "Tom Thumb, the dwarf," laughed the reporter. "Well, come in," said the giant. "I'm Tom Thumb." "You Tom Thumb!" the reporter scoffed. "Why, you're nine feet tall!" "I know," said the giant. "But, you see, this is my day off."

27. Mr. Nussbaum was a regular patron of Finkelstein's Shangri-La Bar and Grille. One evening he declared, "I feel like some fried flounder tonight." The waiter brought a generous portion, but just as Nussbaum was about to dive in, the flounder shook his head and threw a warning glance. Nussbaum ran for the sidewalk. A month later he tried again. "We got fresh flounder for you," said the waiter. "Just came in today." But at the last moment it turned out to be the same old flounder, who shook his head even more vigorously than the first time. "This does it," cried Nussbaum. "Never do I come to this joint again!" Some weeks later his wife took him to a swanky Park Avenue hotel. "Here I will get flounder what is flounder," exulted Nussbaum. The waiter brought a steaming platter, beautifully garnished with parsley and lemon. Just as Nussbaum was reaching for his fork the flounder lifted his head from the plate. "Ah ha!" he sneered. "So Finkelstein's ain't good enough for you no more!"

28. "Do you realize," said a man in a cafeteria to a stranger across the table, "that you are reading your newspaper upside down?"

"Of course I realize it," snapped the stranger. "Do you think it's easy?"

29. A pigeon came home very late for dinner one evening, with his feathers bedraggled, and his eyes bloodshot. "I was out

minding my own business," he explained, "when bingo! I get caught in a badminton game!"

30. The bartender noticed that his customer had a big carrot behind his ear, but he decided not to mention it. "Probably just waiting for people to ask him what it's for. I'll fool him." For twenty-seven consecutive days the customer appeared, with a carrot always tucked behind his ear. Then, on the twenty-eighth day, the routine was varied: a banana had replaced the carrot! The bartender could stand it no longer. "What's the idea of that banana behind your ear, fellah?" he demanded, leaning over the counter. "Couldn't find no carrot today," explained the customer.

31. A couple of frogs were dining at the Ritz one evening. "You're angry at me," accused Abdul Amnal (he was a Turkish frog). "You haven't spoken to me all evening." "It isn't that at

all," explained the other with some difficulty. "I just can't talk tonight. I've got a man in my throat."

32. A brown horse, hitched to a milk wagon, looked up one morning to see a poster staring her in the face. The Ringling Circus was in town! She calmly trotted over to the stage door of Madison Square Garden, and entered. "Hi, girls!" she neighed, to be greeted with noisy expressions of surprise and delight. "But, Beulah," protested one nag, "what are you doing with that cheesy milk wagon you're hitched to? A year ago you were the star of the show here, with blue plumes over your ears, and beautiful performers somersaulting on your back!" "Aw," answered Beulah, "what can you expect from that darn Hollywood agent of mine?"

Chapter Fourteen

GRAB BAG

The organization of this book is as loose as the Nevada divorce laws. My purpose was to include as many good anecdotes as I could remember, not to construct a logical and orderly treatise. When I finished pasting the manuscript together, there were some stories left over that simply couldn't be fitted into any definite category. You will find them here, in no logical sequence whatever.

★ ★ ★

Frank Case, amiable Boniface of the Algonquin Hotel, tells the story of the day the late DeWolf Hopper protested to him that nowhere in New York could he find his favorite dessert, brown betty, on the menu. "I'd have it here for you," Case said, "if I thought there would be a reasonable demand for it." "You put it on your menu tomorrow night," proposed Hopper, "and I'll see to it personally that the demand develops." The next night brown betty was duly added to the Algonquin bill of fare, and Hopper, much gratified, made a personal tour of every table in the dining room. "I am DeWolf Hopper," he announced to the surprised patrons, "and I personally urge you to sample the brown betty this evening. It's delicious!" Hopper then repaired to his own table, toyed with a beefsteak, and summoned his waiter. "Now," he said, rubbing his hands in anticipation, "I'll have a double order of brown betty." "I'm very sorry, sir," said the waiter. "It's all gone."

★ ★ ★

Do you remember the New England hurricane of 1938?

A commuter who lived in Stamford had always wanted to own a barometer. Two days before the big blow he finally bought one at Abercrombie and Fitch. He tacked it up on his wall, read it, and exploded with anger. There was no phone in his house, so he walked a mile to the nearest drugstore and called up Abercrombie. "Fine barometer you sold me," he snorted. "I put it up in my Stamford house and what do you think it registers? *Hurricane!*"

"Return it," soothed the clerk. "We'll replace it with a perfect one."

He went back to fetch the barometer, but by the time he got there, his house had been blown away.

★ ★ ★

Two old friends who had not seen each other in twenty years rediscovered each other recently. "Great to see you, Joe," boomed one of them. "I suppose you are a married man with children by this time." "No," said the other, "I am afraid I never took the plunge." "Joe, you must be crazy," said the first one. "I guess you just don't realize what it means to be married. Take me, for instance. I come home every night from a hard day at the office to a beautiful, warm, comfortable apartment. My wife is waiting to hand me my slippers and the evening paper. Then she runs out to the kitchen, cooks me a luscious dinner. She tops that with my favorite liqueur, plants me in my easy chair by the fire, and hands me my pipe. Then she washes the dishes. Finally, she comes and snuggles down by my side and starts to talk. She talks, and talks, and talks, and talks. *I wish she'd drop dead.*"

★ ★ ★

Newman Levy, author of *Opera Guyed,* has a thirteen-year-old daughter who spends endless blissful hours at the movies. "How did you enjoy the picture this afternoon?" he asked her one Saturday. "It was simply awful," she replied. "I could hardly sit through it the second time."

★ ★ ★

Deaf people have a little publication called *The Volta Review.* One story that this little magazine made famous concerned three deaf gentlemen aboard a train bound for London. "What station is this?" inquired the first gent at a stop. "Wembley," answered the guard. "Heavens," said the second gent, "I thought it was Thursday!" "So am I," exclaimed the third. "Let's all have a drink!"

★ ★ ★

The urbane and witty Frank Crowninshield really surpassed himself on the day that he introduced Amelia Earhart to the members of the Dutch Treat Club.

"Gentlemen," he began, "I mean to tell you a little story about Eliza, a God-fearing and worthy colored girl who died and ascended straight to the Pearly Gates. 'You're in Heaven now, Eliza,' Saint Peter told her, 'and you're an angel in good standing. Just go over to that lot next door and pick yourself out a becoming pair of wings.' 'Wings,' echoed Eliza. 'Lordy me, Mr. Peter, I don't know nothin' 'bout flyin'!' 'You'll learn, you'll learn,' Saint Peter assured her.

"So Eliza picked out a beautiful pair of gossamer wings and made a few tentative flights. She was pretty bad at first, and had a nasty tumble or two, but gradually she caught the knack of the thing, and finally was doing side-slips, Immelmann turns, and the most complicated maneuvers with scarcely any effort whatever. She was so pleased with her progress that she decided to show off a little bit before God.

"God and His Son were on Their thrones, enjoying an after-luncheon nap, when Eliza came zooming into view. God awakened and watched her with mounting astonishment. Finally He shook His sleeping Son. 'Jesus Christ,' He exclaimed, 'can that girl fly!' . . . Gentlemen, Amelia Earhart!"

Another memorable incident at the Dutch Treat Club centred in the appearance of Gertrude Lawrence, who was starring at the time in the very successful *Susan and God*.

Miss Lawrence expressed girlish embarrassment at finding herself the only female in a gathering of some three hundred handsome gentlemen. "Instead of making a silly speech," she suggested, "how would you like it if I raffled off two seats in the fourth row centre for Saturday night's performance of *Susan and God?*" The crowd roared its approval. "O.K.," said Miss Lawrence. "Every one of you has a green hat-check. I'll call out a number at random. The man whose hat-check number corresponds with it gets the ducats." Followed the business of three hundred gentlemen fishing in their jeans for their hat-checks.

"Ready?" asked Miss Lawrence. "The number I pick is 171."

"That's mine," said a happy voice from the back of the room. It belonged to Mr. John Golden, owner and producer of *Susan and God*. Miss Lawrence and Mr. Golden escaped from the room before the stunned audience could translate its mute rage into positive action.

★ ★ ★

Clarence Budington Kelland presided the day that Nicholas Murray Butler, Columbia University prexy, was the guest of the Dutch Treat. "For years," said Kelland, gazing fondly at Dr. Butler, "organizations have been besieging this retiring gentleman to address them—with remarkable success."

★ ★ ★

Harry Hansen climbed into a taxicab, told the driver where he wanted to go, and added, "Please don't go down Third Avenue. I don't like those El pillars."

"Yessir," said the driver—and went right down Third Avenue.

"Didn't you hear me?" screamed Hansen. "I said not to go weaving in and out around those El pillars. It drives me crazy."

The driver stopped his cab and looked at Hansen reproachfully. "Listen, Buddy," he remarked. "What do you suppose it does to *me?*"

★ ★ ★

The twelve-year-old daughter of a publisher of the *New York Times* volunteered to help her mother pass cocktails at an informal reception whipped up for a visiting General. Everything progressed beautifully until the horrified mother heard her daughter say to the General's wife, "May I serve you your eighth martini?"

* * *

Kid Stuff: A famous composer was questioning his ten-year-old son about his history lesson in school that day. "Was it interesting?" he asked. "I'll say!" declared the boy. "We heard all about Nebacadenza!"

* * *

And Leonard Lyons' young hopeful watched his mother try on a new dress. "You sure are beautiful," he assured her. "You look just like Abraham Lincoln!"

* * *

A Navy J.G., home on leave, took his little daughter on a shopping tour. In a crowded department-store elevator, a stout party gave the J.G. an outraged look, and smacked him squarely in the face. The J.G. compressed his lips, and said nothing. As they emerged on the ground floor, his daughter said, "I hated that woman too, papa. She stepped on my foot, so I pinched her right on the heinie!"

* * *

Paul Whiteman, the famous band leader, never could see why some people thought he was fat—even when he tipped the scales at something in the neighborhood of 250. He likes to tell the story of the *really* stout party who made a million dollars without budging from his comfortable couch. A visitor found him one day wearing a bathrobe with enormous checks, and a number sewed on to each check. "What's the idea of those numbers?" he inquired. "Watch me," said the Croesus. He summoned his butler, yawned, and ordered, "Jeeves, scratch Number 23!"

* * *

In my book, Fredric March's kid story still is tops. He found himself alone with a little seven-year-old one evening and, to pass the time before its parents entered the room, inquired,

"What do you want to be when you grow up, sonny?" The boy looked him straight in the eye and replied firmly, "A sex pervert."

★ ★ ★

Olin Clark reports the story of a mother who lost her young daughter in the week-end confusion at Penn Station. After a frantic search, she finally located her in the midst of a group of nuns. Both the little girl and the nuns seemed to be having a very good time. "I hope my daughter hasn't been giving you too much trouble," exclaimed the relieved parent. "On the contrary," chuckled the Mother Superior. "Your little girl seems to have the notion that we are penguins."

★ ★ ★

When Bob Gilham, Paramount's publicity chief, vacationed in the Blue Ridge country a few summers ago, he noticed one old native who sat rocking on his porch day after day, a shotgun across his knees, staring intently into the hills. Uncle Eph was his name, they told Bob. One day he asked the old man what he was gunning for. "Sly old fox in them hills sneaks down ter steal my chickens, an' I'm aimin' ter dispose of him," said Uncle Eph grimly.

A week later Bob went by the cabin, and noticed that Uncle Eph had put away his gun, and was rocking happily with a look on his face that indicated he was at peace with the entire world. "I'll bet you got the fox!" said Bob. "Yep," said Uncle Eph. "Are you absolutely sure you bagged him?" said Bob. "'Course I'm sure," said Uncle Eph. "I been lookin' for him steady from the minute I killed him up there, and by cracky, I only seen him once since!"

Later, Bob remarked to Uncle Eph, "I bet you've seen plenty of changes here in your day." "Sure have," agreed the old man, "and I bin against every single one of them!"

★ ★ ★

Dialogue overheard on a cannibal island: "Who is that lady I seen you with last night?" "That wasn't no lady. That was my dinner."

★ ★ ★

When one famous explorer went on his Antarctic expeditions, report had it that the personnel invariably included the ugliest old crone he could sign up. "She's my yardstick," he explained. "When she starts looking good to me—I know it's time to start for home."

Willie Howard once appeared in a sketch which showed him and a few companions freezing and starving on an Antarctic ice floe. He turned on the radio just in time to hear an announcer describing a Thanksgiving dinner back home. "We'll start with a plate of hot, luscious soup," said the announcer. "With noodles?" groaned Howard. "Yes," said the voice on the radio— "with noodles."

★ ★ ★

"Jimmie" Walker, once mayor of New York, tells the story of the drunk who climbed into a taxi and demanded, "Drive me eighteen times around Central Park." The cab had gotten about as far as 86th Street when he banged on the window and cried, "Fashter, you idiot! I'm in a hurry!"

He probably was a brother of the gent who boarded a cab on 42nd Street, and pointing to the revolving electrical news sign on the Times Building, commanded, "Just follow that sign."

★ ★ ★

Hamish Hamilton, prominent English publisher, overheard two young ladies who were dining together at Lyons (the English equivalent of Child's). One of the ladies asked, "Is your boy friend a freethinker?" The other replied, "Bless me, 'e 'ardly ever thinks of hanything else."

★ ★ ★

There is a bone-dry town in Oklahoma where an honest-to-goodness rattlesnake bite is the only way to get a shot of whiskey. One native came home angry and thirsty and told his wife, "It's about time this burg had more'n one rattler. I stood in line for three hours today and by the time it was my turn the rattler was so tired he wouldn't bite nobody any more."

★ ★ ★

You have read a lot about the knights of King Arthur who fared forth on coal-black chargers to rescue beautiful maidens from dragons' clutches, but did you ever know that one of them was mounted on a St. Bernard dog? His name was Sir Marmaduke, and he and the St. Bernard performed many a deed of derring-do. One evening, however, they were caught in a torrential thunderstorm, and sought shelter at a nearby tavern. "Reservation?" asked the room clerk. "No," admitted Sir Marmaduke. "Sorry," said the clerk, "no room without a reservation." It was at this moment that he discovered that Marmaduke was sitting

astride his faithful St. Bernard. "Hold on," said the clerk. "We'll have to find *something* for you. I wouldn't put out a knight on a dog like this."

★ ★ ★

Barney Greengrass, who sells sturgeon to the White House, is reported to have waited on a customer who ordered a single raisin and one pinch of sugar. "What are you making, Mrs. Geddes?" he inquired. "A cookie?"

★ ★ ★

Earl Wilson tells about a well-known Broadway comedian, in his cups as usual, who careened into the 46th Street Automat, changed two dollar bills into nickels, and began inserting them in the pie slots. He had made a neat pile of four slices of apple pie, three of lemon, and five of peach, and was slipping a nickel into his first coconut pie slot when the manager collared him. "What the hell are you doing with our pies?" he cried. "Cut it out!" "Whaaat?" exclaimed the Broadwayite. "Quit now when my luck's running so good?"

Maybe that's how George Price got the notion for his cartoon of the flabbergasted Automat customer who had deposited a single nickel, and found an assortment of sandwiches, cakes, hard-boiled eggs, and crullers flying into his face. "Congratulations, sir," beamed an attendant. "You've hit the jackpot."

★ ★ ★

The *American Weekly* reports two strange accidents that occurred in New Jersey last year. Nine elephants were plodding peacefully toward the Newark fair grounds when a small boy urged his insignificant puppy to "sic 'em." The pup yapped shrilly at the heels of the leading elephant, and all nine pachyderms thereupon stampeded, scattering traffic and destruction until they were finally rounded up by six radio cops, two emergency squads, and a flock of motorcycle police.

A few blocks away a Mrs. Fitzgerald refused admission to a

bedraggled and bleeding figure at the door, then discovered it was her husband Michael who had fallen off the third-floor sleeping porch.

That brings to mind the story of the battered figure at the Hotel Astor who demanded the key to Room 614.

"Room 614 is occupied by a Mr. James Collins," said the clerk at the desk.

"I know it," rasped the applicant. "I'm James Collins. I just fell out of the window."

★ ★ ★

Mabel Jullup, relates Dorothy Sims, was a lady with taste. She bought a lovely vase at an auction and put it on her table. It was Ming, and it made the Grand Rapids furniture look very cheap. She was sad, so she sold the Grand Rapids and bought "period." That made her whole house look cheap. So she sold the house and took an exclusive apartment in town. But the apartment was so exclusive it made Mr. Jullup look cheap. Naturally she got a divorce, and married a Mr. Preston Potter. But here she was stymied. Mr. Preston Potter made her look cheap.

★ ★ ★

The Prize for Paralyzing Puns this year falls into the lap of the perpetrator of the following horror:

Waitress: Hawaii, mister? You must be Hungary?

Gent: Yes, Siam. And I can't Rumania long either. Venice lunch ready?

Waitress: I'll Russia table. What'll you Havre? Aix?

Gent: Whatever's ready. But can't Jamaica cook step on the gas?

Waitress: Odessa laugh! But Alaska.

Gent: Don't do me favors. Just put a Cuba sugar in my Java.

Waitress: Don't you be Sicily, big boy. Sweden it yourself. I'm only here to Serbia.

Gent: Denmark my check and call the Bosphorus. I hope he'll Kenya. I don't Bolivia know who I am!

Waitress: Canada noise! I don't Caribbean. You sure Ararat!

Gent: Samoa your wisecracks? What's got India? D'you think this arguing Alps business? Be Nice! Matter of fact, I gotta Smolensk for ya!

Waitress: Attu! Don't Kiev me that Boulogne! Alamein do! Spain in the neck. Pay your check and scram, Abyssinia!

FINNISH

★　★　★

An old drunkard from the Panhandle saw so many pink elephants and purple snakes that he hired a hall and put up a sign. "25¢ to See the Zoo." A couple of customers resented the fact that they saw nothing but four bare walls, and swore out a complaint. The sheriff took the warrant and set out to make the arrest. The old boy hauled his jug out from under his counter, the sheriff took three snifters—and paid him $600 for a half interest in his show.

★　★　★

Meyer Levin tells this story about a little eight-year-old girl in a Pennsylvania orphan asylum. She was a gangly, painfully unattractive child, with annoying mannerisms and secretive ways that set her apart from the others. She was shunned by the children and actively disliked by the teachers. The head of the institution longed only for a legitimate excuse to pack her off to a reform school, or get her out of the place some other way.

One afternoon it looked as though her opportunity had arrived. The girl who was the child's very unwilling roommate reported that she was conducting a clandestine correspondence with somebody outside the grounds. "I've seen her write these notes every day for a week now," she reported. "Just a little while ago she took one of them and hid it in a tree near the brick wall."

The head of the asylum and her assistant could scarcely conceal their elation. "We'll soon get to the bottom of this," they agreed. "Show us where she left the note."

Sure enough, they found the note in the branches of the tree. The headmistress pounced on it. Then she hung her head and passed it silently to her assistant.

It read: "To whoever finds this: I love you."

Chapter Fifteen

"*THERE'S A WAR GOING ON*"

A New York sports expert covered a series of Army bouts at a nearby training center. The highlight of the evening was a furious and bloody combat between a young giant and a gray-haired gladiator who looked twenty years older than his opponent. The writer wondered what had happened to the Army's sense of fair play when the entire audience sided with the younger man and cheered wildly when he knocked the daylights out of his adversary. He was even more surprised when the loser was the one who came to the loud speaker. Then he understood.

"Top Sergeant Graham speaking," panted the bruised fighter, grinning broadly. "When my son enlisted in this army four months ago, I never knew the day would come when he could lick the hell out of his old man."

★ ★ ★

A wedding limousine rolled up Fifth Avenue a few weeks ago with a large placard tied to the rear bumper. It read, "Careless talk caused this."

★ ★ ★

College courses are being abbreviated daily to cope with the emergency. A Princeton instructor reports a serious incident on the Nassau campus as a result thereof last week. It appears that a student left the room to go to the washroom, and missed his entire sophomore year.

★ ★ ★

Major Donald S. Klopfer, stationed in England with the Eighth Air Force, tells of a determined London bookseller who trundled down Charing Cross Road despite the warning blasts of an air-raid alert and a red-faced bobby's command that he seek shelter. "My radio is installed in the bookshop, my dear fellow," he explained, "and alert or no alert, I've simply got to get there to tune in on the eight o'clock news." He had his way. A few moments later the Nazi bombers were over the city, giving it what for. When the raid was over, a taxi driver who had overheard the argument said to the bobby, "I wonder if that there bloke heard his eight o'clock news?" " 'Eard it?" echoed the bobby. " 'E *was* it!"

★ ★ ★

An officer on leave from a post in Panama tells a whaling story that's very different from anything in *Moby Dick*.

A mammoth whale was washed up by the tide on the Pacific beach, and a company of coast artillerymen set out to capture it. They discovered, however, that the floundering whale was anticipating a blessed event. Instead of killing it, they waited for high tide and by dint of a prodigious effort, relaunched it. The officer adds that as the grateful whale headed out to sea, it sent out three short spouts and a long one for victory. His pals insinuate that he saw Walt Disney's *Pinocchio* too often and had whales on his mind, but the newspapers printed the yarn, and I pass it on to you for what it's worth.

★ ★ ★

Knut Hamsun, author of *Growth of the Soil* and *Hunger*, Nobel Prize winner and erstwhile literary head man of Norway, shocked his countrymen and disgraced himself eternally by throwing in his lot with the Quislingites when the Nazis invaded Norway. Word has reached these shores of how his countrymen have chosen to register their contempt for him. They have piled up every copy of his books that they could in their homes, their shops, and their libraries, and mailed them back to him without a word of explanation. The little postoffice in his native town was so swamped that it had to take on several extra helpers to

handle the flood of books that poured in day after day. At a public auction recently, a complete set of Hamsun's works, autographed, and bound in full morocco, came under the hammer. The auctioneer knocked down the set to the first and only bidder for a sum equivalent to twenty-five cents in American money. The books were added promptly to the pile that was headed back to Hamsun. He must have quite a few thousand of his books by this time.

★ ★ ★

The infantry regiment assigned to patrol the Makin atoll in the Gilbert Islands has discovered that there was some truth, after all, in those legends about the beauteous South Sea belles. A sergeant of the 165th conveyed to a Makin glamour girl that he wanted a grass skirt for a souvenir. She politely whipped her own off and handed it to him. The red-faced soldier hastily handed her a large bandana handkerchief. She thanked him prettily—and wrapped it around her head.

★ ★ ★

The Teheran Conference brought little solace to Lord Louis Mountbatten, anxious to start a big Allied push against the Japs in Burma. "You'll have to wait," Churchill told him. "Supplies intended for you originally have been diverted elsewhere for something more pressing." Mountbatten returned to Delhi, summoned his staff, and told them gloomily, "I've heard all of you say that you wish you had been here six months ago. Gentlemen, you've got your wish!"

★ ★ ★

An unprecedented rush of business has made it practically impossible to get a table in a New York restaurant during the dinner hour, and Mr. Garfinkle became increasingly aware of this fact while he tried vainly to fight his way past the lobby of a half-dozen high-class eateries. Finally he staggered into a tiny delicatessen, and planted himself at the solitary marble-topped table in the rear.

To his surprise, a waiter appeared instantly, and said, "What'll you have?"

"A couple of soft-boiled eggs," begged Mr. Garfinkle, "and a few kind words."

Five minutes later the eggs were planked down in front of

710

him. "So here are the eggs," he murmured plaintively. "Now how about the few kind words?"

The waiter leaned over and whispered into Mr. Garfinkle's ear, "Don't eat them eggs!"

★　★　★

A prominent author up from Washington to attend a session of the Writers' War Board explained his tardy arrival: "I came by bus and the darn thing stopped at every post on the route. It turned out to be a Greyhound."

★　★　★

A cerain number of crooked gamblers are bound to turn up at every army post, and John Scarne, an expert on the subject, has recently toured camps from one end of the country to the other to expose the methods by which card and dice games can be "fixed" in advance. A private at one of his lectures lingered behind to thank him, and tell of his own initiation to the "galloping dominoes." "I had never shot craps before I joined this outfit," he declared. "They told me I could learn in no time. The first time I rolled the dice I got an 'eleven'—a six and a five. 'That's an easy point,' a sergeant assured me. 'Go ahead and try to make it.' I could tell by the looks on the faces of the other fellows that something was being put over on me, but of course I had no idea what it was. Well, sir, I shot fourteen 'elevens' in a row. It's a lucky thing for me I learned how to throw 'em when I was a kid playing parcheesi."

★　★　★

Clark Lee, author of *Call It Pacific*, tells of an officer, very religious, who insisted on reading a burial service over a hundred Jap soldiers who fell in a pitched battle in New Britain. Fellow officers didn't relish the notion, but he persisted. "They may be Japs," he said, "but they're dead, and I'm going to give them a decent burial." In the middle of the service, one of the "corpses" suddenly rose with a grenade in his hand. The officer dropped his Bible, whipped out a gun, shot the Jap through the temple, calmly reholstered his weapon, and resumed the sermon. "Lord," he declared, "I said I'd give these Japs a funeral, and that goes for every last one of them. Amen!"

★ ★ ★

A collector's item from a Lewis Gannett book review: "But the Fortress flew on with her chin up, like Marie Antoinette walking to the scaffold, even when red flames from her pitted gasoline tanks were spreading from her cockpit to her tail."

★ ★ ★

When André Maurois went to North Africa late in 1943 on a special mission for the Fighting French, he had heard no word of his son for over two years. This son had been an officer in the French Army. Maurois could only hope that he had been taken prisoner somewhere, unharmed. In Casablanca, he heard that Frenchmen who lived only to lick the Nazis were being smuggled across the Mediterranean by the hundreds each week. "Come with me and watch them when they arrive," suggested a friend. Maurois went with his notebook in hand. The first boy who came in that night was his son!

★ ★ ★

A regiment resting up at an undisclosed spot on foreign soil fell to debating noisily over which smelled worse: a goat or a local peasant. Considerable sums were wagered on this vital question, and an agreeable colonel was made judge and stakeholder. First they brought the goat into the tent. The colonel fainted. The men who had bet on the goat reached for the money. Their triumph was short-lived, however. Somebody brought in the peasant—and the goat fainted.

★ ★ ★

A reporter who was doing a feature story on Madame Tussaud's Wax Works in London sought out the laundress who had washed for the exhibition for twenty-five years.

"Tell me," said the journalist. "Do the queens and the duchesses in the wax works wear anything under those gorgeous velvet robes?"

"As a matter of fact, they don't," the laundress admitted. "But I'd rather you didn't make it public. As it is, nobody knows but me and a few Australian soldiers!"

★ ★ ★

Royal Gunnison was broadcasting from Manila for Mutual when the Japs caught up with him and interned him at Shanghai until he returned to this country on the exchange liner *Gripsholm*. One of his anecdotes concerned what must have been the most unusual soft-ball game ever played. The inmates of the Shanghai concentration camp were lucky enough to dig up some soft-ball equipment, and took the game up avidly to kill time and keep fairly fit. The Jap captain of the guard turned out to be a ball fan. He watched the games for days without comment, then suddenly sent a formal challenge to the internees' committee for a game against his own picked team.

The internees sensed trouble, and tried to duck the game. The captain thought they feared a trouncing, and became more and more insistent. Finally a date was set. A big crowd of internees and Japs turned out for the game. The atmosphere was tense as the Americans prepared to take their first turn at bat.

It was a slaughter. Before the Japs had retired three men, the internees had scored 27 runs, were trying desperately to be put out deliberately for fear of reprisals. The umpires were Japs. At the end of three innings the score was 28–1, and the Jap captain had enough. "It more better we do not play for score," he announced, sucking through his teeth. "After this we play for sportsmanship."

★ ★ ★

Eddie Cantor avers that in his bed in an overcrowded Washington hotel he suddenly heard snores emanating from the adjoining bathroom. He investigated, and rushed to the telephone. "Good heavens," he cried, "there's a midget up here snoring in my bathtub!" "A midget?" echoed the room clerk calmly. "He must have pulled the plug out. There's supposed to be two of them!"

★　★　★

From David Niven in London comes the story of the RAF pilot who made a forced landing in Belgium and was rescued by a nun. She shepherded him into her convent, handed him a complete set of nun's habiliments, and counseled: "Lie low. Say nothing. Be as inconspicuous as possible. Sooner or later we will find a way to spirit you back to England." For eight weeks the pilot spoke to no one, shaved eight times a day, was a model convent habitant. One evening, however, he spied a beautiful young sister alone in the pantry, and on a sudden but irresistible impulse, swept her into his arms. A moment later he was reeling from a terrific sock on the jaw. "'Ere, 'ere, you rum bloke," spoke a deep masculine voice. "'Old yer 'orses, carn't yer? I been 'ere since Dunkerque."

★　★　★

Two K.P.'s were staggering under the weight of a steaming kettle they were hauling from the kitchen in Fort Dix, New Jersey. A colonel stopped them. "Get me a ladle," he commanded. One of the K.P.'s rushed for a ladle. The colonel dipped it into the kettle, swallowed a mouthful, gulped, and roared, "Do you call that soup?" "No, sir," came the meek reply. "That's the water we've been washing the dishes in!"

★　★　★

John Hersey, author of *Into the Valley* and *A Bell for Adano*, writes about a friendly encounter between an American Navy officer and a cannibal chief. The officer visited the chief's village, and, in the course of the ensuing powwow, pleaded, "If you see American soldiers come down from sky in parachutes, you must

714

not eat them. They are here to protect you from Japs." The chief replied, "No eat white men—too bitter."

★ ★ ★

The boys in the South Pacific retain their sense of humor. One writes, "I am raising quite a beard on the instalment plan: a little down at a time." Another explained his plight in a note of exactly four words: "Long time no she."

★ ★ ★

If the armed forces ever took a vote for their favorite comedian, Bob Hope would undoubtedly win by something like the 85,000 miles he figures he has traveled to spread sunshine—and Hope—wherever American boys are fighting. Hope does not rely on one or two corny routines. He has fresh and timely gags for every stop on his lightning tours, special quips that only the audience he is playing to can appreciate. That's why most of the beachheads, foxholes, camps, and hospitals have GI's for Hope alone.

Bob Hope was born in England in 1904, but moved to Cleveland while he was still a choir boy. (He says that his voice changed right in the middle of a beautiful solo.) He was a vaudeville performer for years, crashed Broadway in *Roberta* and *Red, Hot, and Blue*, and then discovered pictures and radio, in both of which he was so riotously successful that producers didn't dare to peep when he treated sacred scripts as something to be ignored. When he and Bing Crosby were making *Road to Singapore*, he told the author, "If you hear any of your own dialogue, yell 'Bingo!'"

In Africa, he reported, "The boys were so happy to see me they actually got down on their knees. What a crap game!" In Edinburgh he told his audience, "This blackout isn't all wasted; I just bumped into eight Scotchmen on Princes Street developing films." In Palermo, the Nazis bombed his hotel. "We did a show," said Hope, "and then ran for our lives. But then, I've never done anything else!" In London, he reported, "I just saw Winston Churchill. Best newsreel I've caught in months!" At a base hospital he was introduced to a soldier who was suffering from anemia and sundry other ailments. "I remember giving a pint of blood last year," cracked Hope. "I've got an idea that I'm shaking hands with the guy who got it!"

★ ★ ★

"A Fascist country," opines Robert St. John, "is where they name a street for you one day and chase you down it the next."

★ ★ ★

Milton Sperling, one of the best-known writers and producers in Hollywood, now a captain in the U. S. Marines, brings back this story from an island in the South Pacific.

A complete set of motion-picture equipment and fresh prints of a dozen new features were dispatched for the amusement of the five thousand boys on the island. The equipment was landed in fine style, but unfortunately every film but one was lost in the process of unloading. That film was *Action in the North Atlantic*, a rousing action story that starred Humphrey Bogart.

An outdoor theatre of sorts was set up on a hillside and *Action in the North Atlantic* was run over and over again. Some of the boys saw it twenty times. One tough young marine came in from a little sortie, stripped to the waist, with a belt of ammunition still strapped over his shoulder, and watched the picture with evident satisfaction. The point just had been reached where a Nazi wolf pack attacked the convoy when the air-raid alarm sounded. Almost immediately thereafter the first bomb landed less than two hundred yards from the theatre. The Japs had smashed in over hills which had thrown off the radar system.

The picture stopped abruptly and everybody dove madly for shelter. The marine flung down his cigarette in disgust. "The bastards!" he cried. *"Right at the most exciting part!"*

★ ★ ★

Some Belgian patriots recently blew up a Nazi vessel docked at Antwerp. Only clue was a guard's statement that he had seen a woman lurking in the shadows just before the explosion. The Gestapo began a search for the woman, felt they were on the right track when an anonymous Belgian mailed in the photo of a curvaceous girl, minus name, or address. The photo was reprinted in all Belgian papers, with a hefty reward offered for her identification. Two thousand delighted Belgians promptly claimed the reward. The girl in the photo was Paulette Goddard.

★ ★ ★

St. John was dining in Chicago's Palmer House after his return from the front. A lady at an adjoining table recognized him and said, "Why, there's St. John! I didn't know he was in Chicago." Her companion was impressed. "St. John, eh?" she hazarded. "He's probably here for the Baptist Convention."

★ ★ ★

An accountant now serving in the Air Corps came home on leave last week and brought his young son an airedale puppy. The delighted youngster named it "Hurricane." Two days later, by common consent of the entire family, it was rechristened "P-47."

Austin Stevens, of *The Times*, reports that at his Denver base they're trying to cross a carrier pigeon with a woodpecker. The idea is to develop a bird that will not only carry messages but knock on the door when it arrives.

The rarest tale of poetic justice comes from dusty Texas, where an erstwhile *New Yorker* cartoonist is laboring in a camouflage unit. A loud-mouthed and overbearing officer drove up one day last week, and bawled the daylights out of the entire company. Their efforts, he informed them, wouldn't befuddle a Jap with one eye missing entirely and the other closed by a cataract. "Take down this claptrap," he bellowed, "and start all over again." The officer then climbed into his jeep and drove smack into the camouflaged headquarters hut.

★ ★ ★

717

Frank Gervasi brought this story home from the front, but, under pressure, admitted he didn't exactly see it happen.

A comely young WAC was walking alone on a dusty road when she espied a shimmery lake in a grove of beautiful green trees. Not a soul was in sight. On an impulse, she took off all her clothes, and had a fine swim and sun bath in the altogether. Suddenly she saw an officer heading purposefully in her direction. She made a dive for her clothes, and sighed with relief when she got the last button closed before he entered the glade.

The officer paid no attention to her whatever. He walked to the edge of the lake, wheeled about, and barked, "Camouflage battalion, 'tenshun! Forward march!"

Every tree around the lake marched off!

★ ★ ★

The Canadian correspondent, Matt Halton, tells a tale of the days when the British Eighth Army, not yet molded into a magnificent fighting machine, was playing hide-and-seek with Rommel in North Africa. An English patrol ventured deep into the Libyan desert, where it encountered a Nazi patrol of comparative strength. In the bloody fight that followed, everybody was killed except two English officers and one Nazi lieutenant. The Nazi was promptly made a prisoner, whereupon it developed that he not only spoke perfect English, but was a graduate (he declared) of Cambridge University. That put a different complexion on the situation, and the two Englishmen, very sportin', very school-tie, forthwith declared him one of themselves, sharing their meagre rations with him on an equal basis. The Nazi waited his chance, and, suddenly catching both of the Englishmen off guard, seized one of their pistols, and turned the tables on them. "Now, you —— English," he grunted, "you are *my* prisoners! Get over there!" The English officers, dumbfounded, hastened to obey, but one of them was heard to mutter, "I'll bet the blighter never went to Cambridge after all."

Eventually, the Englishmen outsmarted the Nazi anyhow, and brought him back alive. "A couple of months later," concluded

Halton grimly, "those same English officers had learned what war against the Nazis meant. If you ever think England will be the same after the war, talk to the men or the officers of the British Eighth Army."

★ ★ ★

Liddell Hart, the British military expert, has always declared that a strong defense can hold an offensive three times its size. In support of this theory, he likes to tell the story of the young man who spent one entire week going from store to store in New York changing a dollar bill into two half-dollars, the half-dollars into four quarters, the quarters into ten dimes, the dimes into twenty nickels, and the nickels into one hundred pennies. Directly he had the one hundred pennies, he began reversing the process, until he again had a dollar bill. After he had gone through this strange procedure three times, Hart ventured to inquire what on earth his purpose was.

The young man lifted an index finger and smiled craftily. "One of these days," he explained, "somebody is going to make a mistake—and it isn't going to be me."

★ ★ ★

An Australian infantry division, recalls George Johnston in *Pacific Partner*, was stationed in England during the blitz in 1940. The boys were invited by the city corporation to visit Manchester, and were given a wonderful time.

At the end of their stay, a huge-muscled sergeant respectfully asked the Mayor to attend a little gathering in the City Hall. The Australians, he explained, would like to make a little presentation as a gesture of thanks to the people of Manchester.

The Mayor, touched by the request, attended the function. The sergeant, speaking on behalf of the assembled Australians, made the usual remarks of appreciation and then handed the Mayor a most magnificent collection of Australian curios and native weapons.

The Mayor, stuttering with emotion, pride and gratitude,

mumbled his thanks. The Australians marched out of the hall and filed solemnly to the train that would take them back to camp.

It was not until the next day that the Police Department reported the great burglary of the Manchester Museum, a burglary notable for the fact that the theft was confined to the entire Australian aboriginal art collection.

DR. CHRISTIAN'S RING

The best-known bibliophile in the Hollywood colony is Jean Hersholt, well-loved Danish actor who created the role of Dr. Christian on the screen and radio. Hersholt's collection of "firsts" ranks with the country's finest. When the late Dr. Dafoe (the man who took care of the Dionne quintuplets) visited Hersholt last winter, he picked out five or six of the rarest items in the library (they were worth, conservatively, $20,000) and horrified the collector with the casual, "Jean, I have lots of time for reading during those long nights in Canada. Do you mind if I cart these worn-out-looking books home with me? They are too shabby for a fine library like yours, anyhow."

Every year Jean Hersholt's radio program offers a prize for the best original script involving a new adventure of Dr. Christian. Last year's winner was submitted by Nelson Bond, of Roanoke, Virginia. Dr. Christian, according to Mr. Bond's story, was an ineffectual, namby-pamby young man when he was graduated from Berlin's finest medical college years ago. His sister kept house for him, but was out of patience with his lack of initiative. The roof of their flat leaked, the plaster was cracked, the paper was flaking from the walls, but the landlord pooh-poohed Dr. Christian's pleas for renovation on the grounds that labor was unobtainable, and that the inflation had ruined his business, anyway. As a matter of fact, this was the very height of the German Republic's disastrous inflation spiral. One American dollar was worth a million marks.

One afternoon the young doctor dropped in at a public auction in Wilhelmstrasse, and his eye was caught by an ornate, curiously fashioned ring that came under the hammer. He found himself bidding heatedly for it, in competition with an old priest, who was very agitated. The priest shook his head helplessly when Dr. Christian bid thirty million marks. The doctor slipped the ring onto his finger and walked toward his home. Unusual things began to happen immediately.

First, a pair of bandits, brandishing guns and running pell-mell to escape pursuing police, catapulted into Dr. Christian's arms. Strangely unafraid, the doctor seized and disarmed them, and turned them over to the policeman, who complimented him on his bravery and presence of mind. Then, when he arrived at his home, he read of the arrival in Berlin of the head of a famous American research institute. Dr. Christian, formerly so lacking in initiative, called the great specialist, and talked his way into a job at five times the salary he had envisioned in his wildest dreams. "You sound mighty cocky and sure of yourself," the American said on the phone. "I like young men of your stripe around me." Dr. Christian next collared his landlord, and cowed that individual so completely that he promised to have a crew redecorating the apartment the very next day. "Suddenly I feel able to make everybody do what I want," said the doctor in a somewhat surprised tone.

Two days later there came a knock at the front door, and Dr. Christian discovered that his visitor was the selfsame priest who had bid against him for the old ring. "Doctor," began the priest, "let us not beat about the bush. I've got to have that ring! I couldn't meet your bid of thirty million marks at the auction, but now I'm prepared to give you a hundred million for it!"

"I cannot understand your insistence on possessing that trifling bauble," wondered Dr. Christian.

"Ah, but it's the farthest thing possible from a trifling bauble," the priest said gravely. "That ring is a terrible force for evil. It must be destroyed at all costs, before it does further injury to the entire human race. It belonged originally to Judas Iscariot.

Centuries later it fell into the hands of Genghis Khan, and then Napoleon. The last man who owned it was the Kaiser. It gives everyone who owns it overwhelming delusions of grandeur, and the ability to make whole peoples do his bidding."

"I've noticed myself," said the doctor, "that ever since I've worn the ring I've been imbued with a strange power over people."

"Get rid of it before it is too late," pleaded the priest. "Soon you will find it making you do terrible things. Not only you, but the whole world will suffer."

The doctor could not help being impressed by the priest's passionate plea. "The ring is on the bureau in my bedroom," he said. "I've got some men putting new paper on the walls there,

but, if I can get past the scaffolding, I'll fetch the cursed ring for you."

But the ring was nowhere to be found. Dr. Christian searched high and low for it. Finally he summoned the foreman, who clapped his hand to his head when he heard that the ring had disappeared. "Ach," he exclaimed, "it's that schweinhund I threw off the job this morning! I'll bet he stole it! He was worth-less from the day he started to work for me!"

"It is vitally important that I get that ring back at once!" cried Dr. Christian. "What was your workman's name? Where does he live?"

The foreman opened his record book. "I never did get his address," he said, "but I remember that he had a queer sort of name. I don't think he even was a German. Ah, yes, here it is, sir . . . *Adolf Schicklgruber!*"

★ ★ ★

When the Americans cleaned the Nips out of Attu, they found all sorts of booty which was divided up by avid souvenir hunters. One corporal found what looked like the Japanese equivalent of a ten-cent candy bar. "This stuff doesn't taste bad," he said to a buddy who could read Japanese. "What does the wrapper say?" The translator read it. "Brother," he reported, "you are eating a stick of dynamite."

★ ★ ★

Colonel Rex Smith, first editor of *The Chicago Sun*, relays the latest sergeant-rookie variation. The sergeant spoke his piece on the shoes the rookie wore to assembly. The rookie explained that he had worn them in private life. "So what?" snapped the sarge. "Did you have a high silk hat when you were a civilian, too?" "Why, yes, Sergeant, I did," was the reply. "Then why don't you wear that here, too?" "Don't be silly," snapped the private. "Who ever heard of wearing a top hat with brown shoes?"

★ ★ ★

The engineering department of a defense plant at Newburgh, New York, has been experimenting with steel wire, drawing it out very fine. They finally produced a piece of 120-gauge wire—practically invisible. The boys were proud—so proud, in fact, that they cut off a strand and sent it to a rival defense plant farther upstate. "This is just to show you what we are doing in Newburgh," they wrote.

Weeks went by. Recently, a package arrived at the Newburgh plant. The boys opened it with great care. Inside was a steel block; mounted on the block were two steel standards, and strung between the standards was the same piece of 120-gauge wire. At one end of the block was mounted a small microscope delicately focused on a certain spot on the wire. One by one the engineers placed an eye to the microscope and examined in silence the work of their rivals, who had bored, in the wire, a rather handsome little hole!

★ ★ ★

A correspondent who is writing a book about the Flying Tigers tells of a speech made to a group of Army fliers in Burma by their briefing officer on the eve of a bombing raid on distant Jap installations. "Men," said the officer, "tomorrow's stint is one of the toughest we've ever tackled. The enemy has received reinforcements. Our planes are falling apart. There is a hell of a storm brewing. We'll be lucky if one out of four of us ever gets back alive. We take off at seven sharp. And if any one of you is thirty seconds late, damn it—he can't go with us."

★ ★ ★

"In Southern Italy," reports Vincent Sheean, "an American flier won a coveted Free French decoration, but he was so ugly they couldn't find a French General who was willing to kiss him."

★ ★ ★

From London comes the story of the two Yanks who wanted to see the War Office, but didn't know on what side of the street it was located. They hailed a passing Tommy, and asked, "Which side is the War Office on?" The Tommy thought hard for a moment, then replied, "Gorblimey! Ours—I think!"

★ ★ ★

724

A marine sergeant led his men to the crest of a ridge, and spotted a whole company of Japs peacefully eating chow in the clearing below. "Jack," he called in a stage whisper to a corporal behind him, "bring up the guns on the left flank."

"No! Better on the right flank," a voice answered.

"I said the *left* flank—and on the double," rasped the sergeant.

"And I said the *right*," came the voice.

The infuriated sergeant plunged into the bush behind him with murder in his heart, but instead of the expected corporal, he came face to face with a smiling, English-speaking Jap.

The sergeant shook a finger in his face and hollered, "Damn it, Mac, you run *your* outfit and I'll run *mine!*"

REYNOLDS, THE FUN-LOVING ROVER

One of the most popular figures in the war book industry, which must be about the third biggest in the country by this time, is Quentin Reynolds. This towering, six-foot-something, burly 220-pound hunk of all-round good guy has a way of making you feel you are sharing every one of his adventures. He loves practically everybody and vice versa. When Quent Reynolds starts waving that American flag, it is like standing on the summit of a mountain at sunrise, with a ten-thousand-voice chorus of *The Star-Spangled Banner* ringing in your ears.

Reynolds began his literary career as a baseball writer. What is there about working on a sports page that makes men learn to write so well? Look at Lardner, Broun, Pegler, Runyon, Rice and Considine. Quent had a tougher job than any of them, though, because the team he was assigned to cover was the Brooklyn Dodgers. In those days the Dodgers played a brand of ball that was positively unique. Quent himself tells about the day he was sitting in the last row of the grandstand at Ebbets Field and, glancing into the street behind him, saw a rabid rooter running lickety-split for the entrance gate. "Hurry up," yelled

Quent, "you're missing something big. The Dodgers have three men on base." "Holy mackerel," panted the rooter. "Which base?" Two years with the Dodgers provided ideal training for a career of hair-raising and death-defying experiences.

In 1930, the International News Service sent Reynolds to Berlin, where he saw the Nazis take over. He left Germany by their special request—but fast. "It was those babies," he says, "that made everybody else seem so attractive by comparison." *Collier's* signed him as a sort of reporter-at-large, and his list of "intimate friends" and pals began to stretch into the thousands—from diplomats to taxi drivers, from society queens to broken-down pugilists. The late Charlie Colebaugh, editor of *Collier's*, said that Quent came back from an interview with a steel magnate and declared, "He's a great guy! A wonderful man!" After

a day at Hyde Park with the President, he reported, "He's a great guy! A wonderful man!" Then he visited the Tombs to build a story around a confessed killer. "He's really a great guy," he told the staff later. "A wonderful man! Can that boy cut throats!"

At a recent testimonial banquet to Reynolds in New York, one of the speakers referred to the guest of honor as "Quent, the fun-loving Rover." The Rover was too busy lining up the shortest route to Myrna Loy to pay heed; when the speeches were ended, Wendell Willkie, Deems Taylor, and Quent broke from the barrier as one. "Darling!" cried Myrna, and threw her arms about Mr. Reynolds' rotund bay. "Hell," Mr. Willkie was heard to mutter, "who can buck competition like that?"

No foreign correspondent has the right to have a wife as beautiful as Quent's "Ginny." It makes leaving for the front just that much harder. The day that Virginia Peine became Mrs. Reynolds, the President happened to be in New York. The police cleared Park Avenue for him just as the Reynolds nuptials were about to begin. Quent's father observed the host of motorcycle cops and the suspended traffic and said quite seriously, "I never realized how important my boy has become."

Quent Reynolds' description of the American landing in Salerno, Italy, and the establishment of the beachheads there will, I think, be reprinted in anthologies for years to come. At dawn of D-Day at Salerno he found himself on a boat with Vincent Sheean, now a Lieutenant Colonel. Sheean looked at the gray hills just beginning to be visible behind the town, and said, "Just around that promontory, the road dips sharply and goes by a tiny inn that serves the best damn fettucini in the entire world." Reynolds was deeply impressed. "I didn't know," he said, "that our Intelligence sent back reports in such incredible detail." "Intelligence, my eye," answered Sheean. "Salerno is where Dina and I spent our honeymoon."

Just before Reynolds returned to America, he interviewed General Montgomery. The first thing the General asked him was, "Is it true that back in the States the girls are wearing a beret they've named after me?" He ate one of his last meals in Italy in a little spaghetti joint that had a big sign over the door reading "GUERRA CONTRA LA MOSCA" ("War Against Flies"). When the waiter brought him his "spaghet," the plate was rimmed with flies. A few of them were even struggling in the spaghetti. "Hey," said Quent, "how about that sign, 'War Against Flies'?" "It's true," sighed the waiter. "We had the war here once—but the flies won."

A "welcome home" dinner—one of an endless series—was tossed for Quent at Toots Shor's elegant chop-house. Quent gave Toots an advance copy of *The Curtain Rises*, and wrote on the fly-leaf, "Too bad you are iliterate, otherwise you would enjoy this book." It was Toots who informed the scholar Reynolds (with two honorary degrees) that he had misspelled "illiterate."

★ ★ ★

Clark Gable brought back from abroad the story of a radio dialogue between a Swiss anti-aircraft battery and a U. S. bomber that was flying over forbidden Swiss territory, overheard by an enraged but impotent German radio station. "You are over neutral Swiss territory," said the officer on the ground. "We know," said the radio man in the bomber. "If you don't turn back, we'll have to shoot!" "We know. Go ahead!" The German station heard the sound of intermittent ack-ack, and then the voice of the man in the plane came back on the air. "Your fire is a thousand feet too low," he said. The Swiss answered, "We know!"

★ ★ ★

Washington is laughing over the malicious proposal that directly the war is concluded, a plaque be affixed to the Pentagon Building, reading "Washington slept here."

A new cocktail bar on Pennsylvania Avenue is named "Chez When."

A play opened at the National Theatre. One critic pronounced it a phony. "Act two," he explained, "takes place three weeks after Act One—and the heroine *has the same servants!*"

★ ★ ★

Are you going in for chicken-raising this year? If so, here are a few anecdotes that may amuse you.

A rooster was reading the morning paper aloud to a group of hens. "It says here," he reported, "that Mayor LaGuardia laid a cornerstone yesterday." "My, my," clucked a hen. "I didn't know he had it in him!"

In the next county, an arrogant red rooster was giving chase to a fluttery little hen. She scrambled into the highway to escape him, and was run down by a truck. Two old maids on a nearby porch witnessed the tragedy. "You see," one of them said with an approving nod, "she'd rather die!"

George Price drew a cartoon of a chicken farmer who fell for a box of feed that carried a caption, "Lay or Bust," on the carton. He scattered the feed on the ground; the picture shows the hens exploding all over the place.

★ ★ ★

Before she returned to Russia, Mrs. Maxim Litvinoff lunched with a publisher to discuss the possibility of bringing out her autobiography. "I need a notebook," said Mrs. Litvinoff, "in which to jot down little bits of my life as they come to mind." The publisher took her to a stationery shop around the corner, where she found just the notebook she wanted. When the clerk informed her that the price was a dollar, however, Mrs. Litvinoff protested. "That's outrageous," she said. "I will do without it." "Let me buy it for you," suggested the publisher. "We'll call it part of the luncheon." "Really," beamed Mrs. Litvinoff. "In that case, I will take two."

★ ★ ★

Leonard Lyons reports that one die-hard professor at Oxford still chooses to ignore the fact that, because of the war, female students at the university far outnumber the males. He began all lectures to mixed classes, "Gentlemen." Even when there were forty girls and ten men, he stubbornly addressed them as "Gentlemen." This spring he found that his class consisted of forty-six girls and one lone man. He gritted his teeth, sighed, and began his lecture, "Sir."

★ ★ ★

Ed Wynn, "the Perfect Fool," has proven to be just what the doctors ordered for wounded soldiers at U. S. Army hospitals. They roared at his pole eleven feet four inches long, to be used for people you wouldn't touch with a ten-foot pole. They loved his cigarette lighter: when he pushed down on a little wheel an arrow jumped up and pointed to the nearest man with matches. But the biggest laugh of all came when he demanded of a colonel, "Say, have you seen the morning papers?"; the obliging colonel answered, "No, what's in them?" Wynn cracked, "My lunch, and I'm getting mighty hungry."

Old Wynn enthusiasts believe that he reached his greatest height in a show called *Manhattan Mary*. Wynn was a waiter in one scene. "I don't like all the flies in here," complained one patron. "Show me the ones you don't like," suggested Wynn, "and I'll throw 'em out." When the patron said, "I'm so hungry I could eat a horse," Wynn led a live nag on to the stage. Then he sold it to the customer. "This horse has only one peculiarity," he told the befuddled buyer. "He loves to sit on potatoes. Remember that!" The man made off with his horse, but was back a moment later. "You fraud," he screamed. "I no sooner got that horse to the bridge down the road, when he bolted out of my control, and jumped over the bridge into the river." "Oh, I forgot to tell you," said the contrite Wynn. "That horse loves to sit on fish, too!"

In another scene, Wynn was busy painting a ship. An old dowager entered and asserted, "Mr. Wynn, I have decided to commission you to paint my ancestors." "Oh, I couldn't do that," he protested. "I'm just a ship painter." "Nevertheless," insisted the dowager, "you are the man I want for the job." "But I tell you," he wailed, "I only paint ships." "The question is closed," she announced. "You, and you alone, are going to paint my ancestors." "All right," agreed Wynn finally. "I'll paint your darn ancestors. But I want to warn you now: they're going to look like ships!"

★ ★ ★

One of the heads of the European propaganda division of the British Broadcasting Corporation submitted a letter of resignation recently. "Doing foreign propaganda for the BBC," he

averred, "is like making love to a female elephant. There is no
pleasure in it, you run the risk of being crushed to death, and it
is years before you see any results!"

★ ★ ★

An English bomber flushed a flock of FW-190's over the
Channel on the way home from a raid on Berlin, and the crew
had to parachute to safety. The pilot, a chap named Donald, had
long been prepared for this, and had always worried about freezing, so he never went up without tucking a bottle of brandy in
his Mae West. After an hour or so in the water, he was picked
up by a destroyer—but not until he had consumed the entire
bottle of brandy.

As he climbed aboard the destroyer, the captain said jokingly,
"Sir, you're dripping water all over my clean deck."

Donald haughtily answered, "I never stay where I'm not
wanted," and promptly walked overboard. It took them fifteen
minutes to fish him up again.

★ ★ ★

Lt. Col. Rogers writes from the Pacific area that the most
striking personality in those parts is a cannibal chief with nine

Jap flags tattooed on his stomach. And a hand-lettered sign tacked to the officers' bulletin board reads, "Hats altered to fit any promotion."

A biologist was taken into the Army as a captain, and then proceeded to go right on doing the things he always had done before. They let him use his own laboratory, and he didn't even wear an officer's uniform. "Has your life changed in any way?" a reporter asked him. "Well," he answered, "I work the same. I live the same, and I even think the same; but now if a guinea pig bites me, I get the Purple Heart."

★ ★ ★

A nervous lieutenant had been informed that General Eisenhower was due on an inspection tour. Three times he popped out of his tent to ask Private Nussbaum, "Has General Eisenhower arrived yet?" "No, sir," said Nussbaum each time. Finally he looked at his watch, barked, "When the General comes, let me know at once. It's important," and re-entered his tent. A few minutes later the General drove up. "Are you General Eisenhower?" asked Nussbaum. "Yes, I am," said the General. "Oy," sighed the private. "Are you going to get it from the lieutenant!"

★ ★ ★

A Waco major who had co-piloted a B-26 allowed that the war would last another five years: "One to lick the Nazis, another to take the Nips, and three more to get the Yankees out of Texas!" A fellow officer declared, "The only things these boys are interested in are Death and Texas. Whenever a juke box plays 'There's a Bit of Texas in my Walk' they stand at attention."

★ ★ ★

One of the prize tidbits of the year concerns the Boston author who was scheduled to lecture in Louisville, but was bounced off his plane in Washington to make room for a colonel with a priority. The author couldn't make Louisville in time by train, so he returned in disgust to Boston. The colonel, it developed, had flown to Louisville for the sole purpose of hearing his lecture.

* * *

Ernie Pyle tells about a sergeant who had been a three-striper for over a year and had passed up numerous chances to enter an officers' candidate school. A pal asked him why. "Remember Sergeant York in the last war?" queried the sarge. "Sure do," was the answer. "Chum," said the sergeant, "name me just one of the second lieutenants in that war!"

* * *

An officer, home from strenuous service overseas, was assigned to a desk job in the Pentagon Building. Each day for a week he shifted the location of his desk—next to the window, away from the window, into a corridor, and finally into the men's wash room. "He must be shell-shocked," the authorities figured, but the officer had a different explanation. "It's the only place around here," he said grimly, "where people seem to know what they're doing."